Robert Ford · Tim Bale ·
Will Jennings · Paula Surridge

The British General
Election of 2019

palgrave
macmillan

Robert Ford
University of Manchester
Manchester, UK

Will Jennings
School of Economic, Social and
Political Science
University of Southampton
Southampton, Hampshire, UK

Tim Bale
School of Politics
and International Relations
Queen Mary University of London
London, UK

Paula Surridge
University of Bristol
Bristol, Avon, UK

ISBN 978-3-030-74253-9   ISBN 978-3-030-74254-6   (eBook)
https://doi.org/10.1007/978-3-030-74254-6

This Palgrave Macmillan imprint is published by the registered company Springer Nature
Switzerland AG
The registered company address is: Gewerbestrasse 11, 6330 Cham, Switzerland

FOREWORD

Rob Ford and his team have produced the twenty-first volume in a series of British general election studies that started with the 1945 election. The series has continued without interruption and has no counterpart anywhere else. The 2019 election is remarkable for being the third general election in four years, a unique event in modern British politics.

R. S. McCallum, the originator of the series, envisaged his book on the 1945 general election as an exercise in contemporary history. In a delightful phrase, he said the election 'must be photographed in flight, studied and analysed' and should be of service to future historians. He also enlisted a young numerate undergraduate to provide 'some statistics for my book'. Nobody could anticipate that over 75 years later, the book would be the first in such a long-running series and that the undergraduate David Butler would become inseparable from it; the last one he co-authored was on the 2005 election.

There has been some debate about the predictability in the contents of the books, as befits a series. Michael Howard, then Conservative leader, commented that the 2005 book was 'formulaic'. It might be countered that the series provides the material to plot the changes and continuities in, for example, candidate backgrounds, opinion polling, media coverage, election strategies and so on. But the authors, themselves a changing cast, have had to take account of so many changes in context, notably the fragmentation of the party system, the blanket media coverage and the big shifts in the forces shaping voting behaviour. *The British General Election of 2019* balances these changes and

continuities admirably, making use of so many interviews with key decision makers in the parties and providing detailed and sophisticated analysis of the results. An understanding of contemporary British politics
serious can start in no better place than the present Nuffield study.

The first general early election studies were sponsored by Nuffield
College. David Butler was a Fellow of the College and his co-authors
until 1970 were based at Oxford. Although still called Nuffield election studies, the authorial connection has been steadily extinguished
since then. Ford is based at Manchester, Bale at Queen Mary College,
Jennings at Southampton and Surridge at Bristol.

As the co-author with David of 12 of the election studies, I was always
grateful for the professionalism and adaptability of our publisher Palgrave
Macmillan. The books are feats of teamwork—this one perhaps more
than any of the earlier ones—and the publishing team has been a crucial
player.

Altrincham, UK   Dennis Kavanagh

PREFACE

This volume is the twenty-first in a series which originated in 1945 in Nuffield College, Oxford. The author of that first volume, Ronald McCallum, was irritated by constant misinterpretations of the 1918 election and hoped his book would provide an objective record of events to combat such myths. This is the first volume since 1951 not to feature at least one of David Butler, Dennis Kavanagh and Philip Cowley on the authors list. While the team is new, the aim of this latest entry in the world's longest-running series of elections studies remains the same: to provide an accurate and, as far as possible, impartial account and explanation of the general election.

This book, like its predecessors, would not be possible without the generous support and cooperation of many others. Those who worked on the election for the various different parties were immensely generous with their time and thoughts, usually via Zoom video call as the restrictions of the global COVID-19 pandemic rendered face-to-face interviews impossible. They are not named or listed here as many spoke on condition of strict confidentiality, but we hope that the story we tell is one they recognise, even if they do not agree with all the conclusions we draw. Unsourced quotes used in the book are taken from these interviews, unless otherwise indicated. Many of our sources also reviewed draft chapters, suggesting improvements and challenging us to improve our thinking, for which we are again grateful. All remaining errors belong to the authors alone.

The argument over Brexit dominated this Parliament from start to finish, as Theresa May sought to work to the two-year deadline she herself had triggered by invoking Article 50 of the Lisbon Treaty in March 2017. Unpicking over 40 years of political and economic integration in such a timeframe would be an impossible task for any Prime Minister, and was made more challenging still by May's failure to secure a parliamentary majority at the 2017 election. Both parties, and Parliament itself, began to buckle under the pressures of contradictory demands and impossible deadlines. Every vote became a knife-edge drama, briefly turning Commons debates into an unlikely spectator sport—one of the authors even noticed that his local pub began switching its TVs from Sky Sports to the Parliament Channel so that punters could cheer on their preferred outcome during crunch votes. The pressures proved too much for May, a leader distrusted from the outset by her party's Brexiteer wing, and who lacked the flexibility or powers of persuasion necessary to overcome this distrust or build bridges with opposition MPs. Brexit defined her and defeated her.

May was succeeded by Boris Johnson, once the most prominent Conservative in the 2016 Leave campaign, who had resigned from May's Cabinet in the summer of 2018 in protest against compromises with the EU he claimed were unacceptable, and then, a year later, successfully bid for the top job by promising a more hard-line approach on Brexit. Johnson delivered on his promise from the outset, with several dramatic and deeply controversial gestures designed to underscore his determination to resolve Brexit without delay. He also confounded critics by securing alterations to May's Brexit deal which proved sufficient to win over both his party's Eurosceptics and pro-Brexit Labour MPs. However, unable to force it through Parliament by his self-imposed deadline, he then took the matter to the electorate, urging voters to give him the majority needed to implement his supposedly 'oven-ready' Brexit deal and finally 'get Brexit done'.

British voters were thus, for the second time, invited to the polls early by a Conservative Prime Minister seeking a Brexit mandate. This time, however, the Labour opposition proved unable to shift the focus of the campaign away from Brexit, where their own position was an unappealing compromise, and towards domestic policy. There was no repeat of the 2017 campaign drama. This was a more conventional British election, where the party that started with a poll lead, a better-regarded leader and a more popular policy on the most important issue of the day retained all three from start to finish, then won by a margin largely predictable from the final polling. Several recent elections have been marked by high levels of campaign volatility. This was not one of them. The result, though, was historic—a first large Conservative majority for more than 30 years, capping over two decades of recovery for the party since its collapse in 1997. While authors of this series have long been justly sceptical about naming elections, this was in many key ways the 'Brexit election'. It was called over Brexit by a party which campaigned relentlessly on the issue, voters' Brexit preferences were critical in determining the result, and the conclusion of Britain's fraught exit process from the EU was the most significant immediate consequence of the result. The choice voters made in 2019 will resonate for a long time.

We are grateful to all of our contributors, whose names are listed in the table of contents, and all of whom met tough deadlines in demanding conditions and dealt with our many editorial requests with graceful dispatch. We are also grateful to the authors of the preceding three volumes, Dennis Kavanagh and Philip Cowley, who have provided generous support to the new team, including the contribution of a foreword (Kavanagh) and a chapter (Cowley) to this latest volume. In addition to contributing a chapter and the analysis in Appendix 1, John Curtice, Stephen Fisher and Patrick English also supplied the data from which Appendix 2 has been compiled.

The structure of this book once again follows the broad template of previous volumes in the series, with some variations to accommodate the context of this election. A separate chapter on Brexit is once again necessary, given the issue's dominance of the campaign and the preceding Parliament. We once again open with a chapter on the decision to call an early election. Recent volumes have acknowledged the diverging political context of Scotland with a separate chapter; we expand this into a chapter covering politics in all three of the devolved nations. We have also expanded the remit of the broadcasting chapter to reflect the growing blurring together of broadcast and online campaign coverage. This volume also introduces a chapter analysing the election result at the individual level and promotes the traditional appendix analysis of geographical voting patterns into the main text. Our story ends, like most of its predecessors, with the announcement of the election result, with only brief attention to its aftermath.

None of the authors could possibly have completed this book in the middle of a global pandemic without the amazing forbearance and support of their respective families and especially their respective partners/spouses. Rob would like to thank Maria, Zofia and Adam for putting up with far too many conversations about the BBC—Brexit, Boris and Corbyn. Tim would like to thank Jackie. Paula would like to thank Neil, Thomas and Daniel who have had to forgo far too many family game afternoons. Will would like to thank Natalie and Arthur for their support and patience.

We are also grateful to colleagues who have supported this project in various ways. We owe a special debt of gratitude once again to Wes Ball, who provided invaluable background research and support for Chapters 4, 6 and 7; to Chris Butler for his vital research and support for Chapter 5; and to Ruth Puddefoot for her research contributing to Chapter 9. Thanks also to Siddharth Singh Ahlawat, Nick Allen, Jack Bailey, Matthew Bailey, Martha Bearne, Daniel Braby, Hannah Bunting, David Cowling, Daniel Devine, Alhussein Elrayah, Ed Fieldhouse, Louisa Gabriel, Jennifer Gaskell, Isla Glaister, Matthew Goodwin, Jane Green, Robert Hutton, Laurence Janta-Lipinski, Ian Jones, John Kenny, Beth Mann, Siobhan McAndrew, Lawrence McKay, Jon Mellon, Neil Moss, Tim Oliver, Nick Or, Chris Prosser, Colin Rallings, Andra Roescu, Georgia Shepherd, Maria Sobolewska, Gerry Stoker, Patrick Sturgis, Michael Thrasher, Joe Twyman, Viktor Orri Valgarðsson, Julia Walker, Ian Warren, Paul Webb, Stuart Wilks-Heeg, Christopher Wlezien and Negus Woldegiorgis.

The writing of this book was aided by other excellent accounts of the election, the Parliament and the political parties which came out as it was being produced. These included Gabriel Pogrund and Patrick Maguire's Left Out, David Kogan's Protest and Power, Anthony Seldon and Raymond Newell's May at 10, and Jonathan Tonge, Stuart Wilks-Heeg and Louise Thompson's Britain Votes 2019. We also owe a great debt of gratitude to the UK in a Changing Europe initiative, whose 'Brexit Witness Archive' project was a treasure trove of insights, and will be a vital resource for future historians seeking to understand the domestic and international politics of the UK's departure from the EU. We are indebted to all of these sources and many others for helping to inform our analysis. We do not agree with these authors and sources on every point, but their insights have enriched our own work.

We are also indebted to all of those who have allowed us to reproduce material. This includes the political parties, who all generously allowed us to reproduce campaign materials. We are also once again grateful to Britain's extraordinary talented political cartoonists. Christian Adams, Dave Brown, Ben Jennings, Nicola Jennings, Graham Keyes, Morten Morland, Martin Rowson, Chris Riddell and Martyn Turner all granted us permission to use their outstanding images, and the book is all the better for it. We are also grateful to News UK for granting permissions to use Morten Morland's cartoons. The majority of photos in the plates section at the front, and in the main chapters, come courtesy of either Alamy or Getty. We are also grateful to the anonymous source who provided the cameraphone photo from inside Southside on election night (p. 261).

Rob Ford would like to acknowledge the funding provided by the Economic and Social Research Council (ESRC) and the UK in a Changing Europe initiative Rapid Reaction Funding Scheme for funding research on the Labour Party and Brexit, which has contributed to this volume. Tim Bale would like to acknowledge the funding provided by the Economic and Social Research Council (ESRC) for his research (conducted with Paul Webb and Monica Poletti) on party members (grant numbers ES/M007537/1 and ES/T015632/1). Will Jennings would like to acknowledge funding from the University of Southampton to support research interviews and the ESRC for his research on political trust and UK polling (ES/S009809/1 and ES/S000380/1). Paula Surridge would like to acknowledge a University Research Fellowship from the University of Bristol, which allowed her to have a period of study leave covering the period including the election and its aftermath.

Finally, the author team would like to thank our editors Ambra Finotello and Rebecca Roberts, copy-editor Jon Lloyd and the whole team at Palgrave Macmillan for helping us to tell the story of an extraordinary election.

Manchester, UK   Robert Ford
London, UK   Tim Bale
Southampton, UK   Will Jennings
Bristol, UK   Paula Surridge
May 2021

PRAISE FOR *THE BRITISH GENERAL ELECTION OF 2019*

"If we journalists write the first draft of history, we rely on academia to produce the definitive version when it comes to General Elections. The authors of *The British General Election of 2019* are the experts we—and the nation—need to tell us what really happened and to explain why. Never has this been more important. This was a truly transformative election, as Boris Johnson assembled a new winning Conservative coalition of voters and a record number of inexperienced MPs ended up in Parliament. Painstakingly and perceptively, this essential book exposes the sources of what is going on in British politics today."

—Adam Boulton, Editor at Large, *Sky News*

"An exhaustive, well-researched, informative and highly readable account. A must for anyone who wants to understand British politics."

—Stephen Bush, Political Editor, *New Statesman*

"An invaluable account, superbly researched, of one of the most significant periods of modern British political history. Historians will look back one day in wonder that the UK of all places came to be so infected by the virus of populism that Boris Johnson became Prime Minister. This will be an important part of that story. A must-read for anyone wanting to understand how Brexit, a changed Labour Party and a changed Tory Party combined to give the Tories a majority they are now exploiting to the full, and Labour a disastrous defeat from which they are struggling to recover."

—Alastair Campbell, Editor at Large, *New European*

"A comprehensive romp through the dramatic run-up to the 2019 general election, the culmination of several electrifying years which transformed British politics. From Getting Brexit Done, through Jeremy Corbyn's leadership to the state of the Union, the authors tell the compelling story of an election that fundamentally redrew the political map. Packed with anecdotes, data and analysis, this is a must read for anybody who wants to understands what comes next."

—Pippa Crerar, Political Editor of the *Daily Mirror*

"To be able to identify every tree but never lose sight of the wood is a very difficult skill, but one these authors possess. The result is an adornment to the important series to which this book belongs. A consequential account of a consequential election."

—Daniel Finkelstein, *Times* Columnist, Conservative Member of the House of Lords and Chair of Onward think tank

"This is such a fascinating, detailed and well-sourced account that anyone wanting to go near another election should not only read it but keep it as a talisman against making the same mistakes again. It's a rare mix of authoritative and funny."

—Isabel Hardman, Assistant Editor, *The Spectator* and Author of *Why We Get The Wrong Politicians*

"A riveting read, explaining the deep currents running through the 2019 "Brexit election" and the way the country's political map was changed beyond recognition. Fresh insights from the people in the room bring this remarkable story to life."

—George Parker, Political Editor of the *Financial Times*

"This is more than the definitive study of the last general election: it is a map and compass for anyone trying to navigate the politics that that event has bequeathed us, including the remaking of the Conservative coalition and Labour's steady decline. Existing evidence, new interviews and analysis are bound together tightly but with flair and verve. The book, justly, will serve as a resource for any student of politics for years to come."

—Gabriel Pogrund, Whitehall Correspondent, *The Sunday Times* and Author of *Left Out*

"The *British General Election* series has charted the ebbs and flows of electoral politics for three-quarters of a century. The new team maintain the standard of their predecessors with a mix of shrewd judgement, pertinent comment, and robust statistical analysis."

—Colin Rallings, Emeritus Professor of Politics,
University of Plymouth

"The authoritative account by an alpha team of political scientists. Lucid explanation of complex events and forces is combined with penetrating analysis of the causes and effects of a highly consequential election."

—Andrew Rawnsley, Chief Political Commentator of *The Observer*
and Author of *The End of the Party*

"This is the definitive guide to one of the most important elections in British history. It is full of the best insights, inside accounts of the thinking of the different parties, and what is now established as the best statistical analysis led by Professor Sir John Curtice. The new authors have managed to maintain and even enhance the authority of the long-running series, which is now as essential a part of the British election tradition as the motorcade to Buckingham Palace for the winner to be invited to form a government."

—John Rentoul, Chief Political Commentator, *The Independent*

"This book provides the definitive study of the 2019 UK General Election. It is brilliantly written in easy accessible language, and yet it simultaneously offers a sophisticated statistical analysis of the increasingly fractured and complex landscape of British electoral politics. It should be compulsory reading for anyone who wishes to understand both the electoral result in 2019 and the likely prospects of the major parties in the future."

—David Sanders FBA, Professor of Government, University of Essex

"From the role of Brexit, to perceptions of the party leaders, to the election's consequences: this is the authoritative account of the 2019 general election campaign and is required reading for anyone with an interest in contemporary British politics."

—Sonia Sodha, Columnist and Leader Writer, *The Observer*

"The essential guide to the Get Brexit Done campaign of 2019, from the UK's foremost elections experts. How Boris Johnson was able to bull-doze his way to a majority; what went wrong for Jeremy Corbyn, and much else besides. A must-read."

—Heather Stewart, Political Editor, *The Guardian*

"This book is essential reading for anyone wanting to get under the skin of the most consequential election for decades. The authors marshal a wide range of essential sources with political nous to provide key insights into the Brexit maelstrom out of which the election sprang, and the dra-matic realignment which voters then delivered. This is a foundational text for understanding a political revolution which will continue to play out for years to come."

—Mark Wallace, CEO, *ConservativeHome*

"The decade just passed had no fewer than four extraordinary elec-tions. For those who want to understand what each of them meant, the Palgrave Macmillan guides are nothing of seminal- allowing us to under-stand what really mattered, what really happened amid the ever amplify-ing noise. The 2019 edition is no exception and given it coüvers perhaps the most significant election of the four, it's the most important. Perhaps the most frequent question I'm asked by exasperated viewers and readers is 'what the hell has happened in politics?'- from now on I'll simply refer them to this book."

—Lewis Goodall, *BBC's Newsnight* and Author of *Left for Dead? The Strange Death and Rebirth of the Labour Party*

"An unmissable retelling of one of the most complex and politically bru-tal periods we may ever know, and how it shaped the political landscape we have today."

—Kate McCann, Political Correspondent at *Sky*

CONTENTS

LIST OF FIGURES

List of Tables

LIST OF ILLUSTRATIONS

Photographs

Social Media Posts

Party Advertisements

Cartoons

Theresa May announces the formation of a government with support from the DUP at 10 Downing Street, 9 June 2017 © Finbarr Webster/Alamy Stock Photo

Labour leader Jeremy Corbyn addresses the crowd at Glastonbury, 24 June 2017 © Guy Bell/Alamy Stock Photo

London, 23 July 2019. Boris Johnson arrives at the headquarters of the Conservative Party following the announcement that he had been elected as the party leader and would the following day replace Theresa May as Prime Minister © Mark Kerrison/Alamy Stock Photo

London, 27 May 2019. Vince Cable is joined by activists and the three new MEPs for London to celebrate the best ever European elections result in the party's history. Pictured: Vince Cable with SODEM's Steve Bray in the background. Lambeth Palace Road, London © Michael Melia/Alamy Stock Photo

15 September 2019. Jo Swinson, leader of the Liberal Democrats, answers questions from the floor during the Liberal Democrat Autumn Conference © Mark Kerrison/Alamy Stock Photo

SNP leader Nicola Sturgeon launches the SNP's general election manifesto at the SWG3 Studio Warehouse in Glasgow © PA Image/Alamy Stock Photo

Newcastle upon Tyne, 20 May 2019. Nigel Farage meeting fellow Brexit
Party members © Islandstock/Alamy Stock Photo

MPs from Change UK/The Independent Group Launches Its European
Election Campaign © Finnbarr Webster/Getty Images

London, November 19, 2019. Britain's Green Party co-leaders Jonathan Bartley and Sian Berry, and deputy leader Amelia Womack wave during the launch of the party manifesto at the Observatory at the London Wetland Centre © Reuters/Alamy Stock Photo

London, 21 November, 2017. DUP leader Arlene Foster and deputy leader Nigel Dodds leave 10 Downing Street after meeting Prime Minister Theresa May © Mark Kerrison/Alamy Stock Photo

New leader of Plaid Cymru, Adam Price, on stage after winning the leadership contest election result at the Novotel, Cardiff © PA Images/Alamy Stock Photo

Brussels, 25 September 2017. The EU's chief Brexit negotiator Michel Barnier (left) welcomes British Brexit Secretary David Davis prior to the fourth round of negotiation on Brexit talks at the EU Commission © Xinhua/Alamy Stock Photo

European Commission President Jean-Claude Juncker, EU Council President Donald Tusk, Britain's Prime Minister Theresa May and Germany's Chancellor Angela Merkel arrive for a family photo at the G7 Summit in the Charlevoix city of La Malbaie, Quebec, Canada, 8 June 2018

London, 9 September 2019. John Bercow, Speaker of the House of Commons, announces his intention to step down © Xinhau/Alamy Stock Photo

Taoiseach Leo Varadkar meeting Prime Minister Boris Johnson in Government Buildings during his visit to Dublin © PA Images/Alamy Stock Photo

London, 7 May 2019. Labour's Brexit negotiating team on their way into the Cabinet Office. Front (left to right): Keir Starmer, Rebecca Long-Bailey, Sue Hayman and John McDonnell. Back: Seumas Milne and Andrew Fisher © Imageplotter/Alamy Stock Photo

Leader of the Opposition office chief of staff Karie Murphy (right) arrives for NEC meeting to prepare Labour's European Parliament manifesto, along with (from left) Shadow Cabinet Office Minister Jon Trickett, and Labour Party co-chairs Ian Lavery and Andrew Gwynne © PA Images/Alamy Stock Photo

London, 4 September 2019. Dominic Cummings, special advisor to Boris Johnson, leaves No 10 to attend weekly Prime Minister's Questions in Parliament

19 November 2019. Labour leader Jeremy Corbyn and Prime Minister Boris Johnson debate live on ITV tonight as part of the 2019 general election campaign.

CHAPTER 1

The Calling of the Election

Philip Cowley

Theresa May's departure may have been a long time coming, but its eventual timing was fitting. Her resignation statement, delivered in front of 10 Downing Street, the Prime Minister's voice cracking with emotion at its peroration ('… to serve the country I love'), came the day after Britain voted in elections for the European Parliament.[1] Had the UK left the EU in March, as May had originally promised, it would not have been taking part in an election for an institution it was leaving. The UK's participation, or at least that of the four in ten voters who could be bothered, was the direct consequence of the government's failure to deliver on its central promise, and that failure was in turn the key factor driving May from office. 'It is, and will always remain, a matter of deep regret to me that I have not been able to deliver Brexit', she said.

The European elections also provided powerful evidence of just how deep an electoral hole the Conservatives now found themselves in. When the votes were counted, they had polled under 9%, coming fifth, having haemorrhaged support to Nigel Farage's newly formed Brexit Party. It was the worst result for the Conservative Party in its history and the first time in over a century that either of the main parties had polled below 10% in a nationwide contest.[2]

© The Author(s), under exclusive license to Springer Nature
Switzerland AG 2021
R. Ford et al., *The British General Election of 2019*,
https://doi.org/10.1007/978-3-030-74254-6_1

It was at this point not obvious that before the year was out, the Conservatives would go on to win their largest Commons majority for over 30 years.

* * *

Conservative Party leadership contests have long been marked by the failure of frontrunners to win. The 2019 race was different. The former Foreign Secretary Boris Johnson began as the favourite (with bookies' odds of less than 2/1 at the start of the contest); he led from the beginning; he increased his support in each of the parliamentary rounds; he never had less than double the support among MPs of his nearest rival; and he went on to triumph easily in the final vote of the party's grassroots members.

The contest was also noteworthy for its size. Thirteen Conservative MPs formally declared their intention to succeed May. Plenty of others were known to be considering standing, only for discretion to prove the better part of valour. Three of the 13 failed to achieve the requisite number of eight nominations from MPs. This still left ten, more than any previous contest in a major British political party.[3] All ten were serving or former Cabinet ministers, although one study of the contest refers to them as having 'varying degrees of public recognition', which is a polite way of putting it.[4] When in 1974, Richard Wood, the MP for Bridlington, was approached about running for the Conservative leadership, he replied that 'some of my friends have ideas above my station'. Several of 2019's candidates could have done with a dose of Wood's modesty. Given the number of candidates, the Conservative backbench 1922 Committee inserted additional hurdles to expedite the Commons stage of the contest. Survival after the first round required the support of at least 5% of Conservative MPs; survival after the second required 10%.[5] It still took five rounds of voting, held between 13 and 20 June, to narrow down the race to a final two.

The 2019 contest was the first time that any party's membership had directly chosen a Prime Minister. In 2007, when something similar could have occurred under Labour, Gordon Brown's leadership bid had been unopposed.[6] In 2016, there had been an initial contest among Conservative MPs, only for the second-placed candidate, Andrea

Leadsom, to pull out before the membership could vote. The demographics of the Conservative grassroots—average age around 57, mostly middle class, disproportionately white and southern—triggered some fuss about how the new Prime Minister was being chosen by an unaccountable, elderly, right-wing cabal.[7] Perhaps the most surprising thing about this debate is that it had taken so long for it to become an issue. Labour widened the franchise for its leadership elections to include party members in the early 1980s; the Conservatives did the same in the late 1990s. Yet both changes took place at the beginning of long periods of opposition; that, and the two unopposed contests, meant that it took almost 40 years for this to come to a head.

Johnson led the first ballot of MPs with 114 votes, clearly ahead of Jeremy Hunt, his successor as Foreign Secretary, in second place with 43. The first round of voting saw four candidates eliminated or withdraw. Johnson's vote went up with each subsequent round—one further candidate leaving the contest each time—and it was soon clear he would easily top the poll.[8] Focus shifted to the race for second and inclusion in the run-off postal ballot of the party membership. Hunt led Michael Gove, the Secretary of State for Environment, Food and Rural Affairs, in the first three rounds of voting, but in the fourth ballot Gove edged ahead of him by 61 to 59. When the votes for the fifth round were counted, however, Hunt had narrowly retaken second place by 77 to 75.

Like all successful candidates, Johnson drew support from across the party, but divisions over Brexit were evident. MPs backing Johnson came disproportionately from the Leave wing of the parliamentary party, those who rejected May's Withdrawal Agreement, or were members of the European Research Group (these groups not being mutually exclusive). Support for Hunt—who had voted Remain and backed May's Withdrawal Agreement—was also predictable based on MPs' Brexit position.[9]

The Conservative grassroots were known to be overwhelmingly Leave supporters. Based on their voting in the 2016 referendum, a Gove versus Johnson fight would have been a Leave-on-Leave contest; Gove was also seen by many as a sharper, more combative debater. There were various claims that Hunt reaching the final ballot was therefore the preferred outcome of the Johnson team, or even that they had engineered the outcome by 'lending' support to Hunt in order to block Gove.[10]

The obvious and longstanding vulnerability of May's position meant there had been a considerable amount of polling on possible successors, beginning almost immediately after the 2017 election. This had variously involved dozens of potential candidates, asking a huge variety of questions and polling different audiences—Conservative members or voters. Johnson was not always ahead, and the polling occasionally demonstrated some vulnerabilities, but he always had a strong position and high public recognition. By the time the contest actually began, he was clearly ahead among both party members and Conservative voters. YouGov polls of the party membership, after the final two candidates were known, had Johnson leading Hunt by almost 3:1.

Conservative leadership debates (Morten Morland, *Sunday Times*, 16 June 2019 © Morten Morland)

The Johnson camp had played the parliamentary stages of the contest deliberately low-key, keeping their candidate largely away from public or media scrutiny.[11] Once the contest reached the party membership, there were a string of party hustings and one televised debate.[12] Johnson's performances were not especially impressive; it would have been difficult for any outside observer watching to have identified him as a great communicator. But then Hunt's performances were not without their gaffes and flaws either, and none of it seemed to make much difference anyway. As Patrick Kidd noted in *The Times* after one of the debates:

> Mr Hunt began to swing at him. 'Answer the questions', he demanded again and again as Mr Johnson fluffed and flannelled on various topics. But his rival kept getting the applause. It was as if the audience didn't care whether they had answers as long as they felt cheered up.[13]

Johnson's substantial poll lead even survived the police being called in the early hours of 21 June after a reported altercation between him and his girlfriend Carrie Symonds. As he routinely did when questioned about his private life, Johnson simply refused to comment, and there is no evidence the incident affected his standing with the Conservative membership.

The result was declared on 23 July. On an 87% turnout, Johnson won by 2:1, with 66.4% of the vote to Hunt's 33.6%. The next day Theresa May resigned, and Alexander Boris de Pfeffel Johnson became the 55th person to hold the office of Prime Minister. He joined a long line of British politicians not known by their first name, including at least seven other Prime Ministers.[14]

It was a remarkable turnaround for someone who had withdrawn from the race just three years earlier when his support collapsed and whose hopes had been repeatedly written off. Johnson's critics—both outside and within the party—believed they could recite a lengthy charge sheet. He was variously described as lazy, posh and entitled; he was said to be terrible at detail and to have a problematic relationship with the truth. His prolific journalism included dozens of hostages to fortune, including a series of phrases that were either borderline or in some cases straightforwardly racist or homophobic. He had a private life that could at best be described as colourful, and which some saw as deplorable; he was at this point estranged from his second wife and living with his girlfriend; he had an unknown number of children. His record in office, either as Mayor of London or Foreign Secretary, did not feature a lengthy list of achievements. The bumbling amiable persona was said to mask an unpleasant selfishness and there was considerable debate about what, if anything, he really believed in, aside from the advancement of Boris Johnson.[15]

Johnson supporters saw much of this as carping or prurient censoriousness. To them, he was bright, clever, ambitious, positive, upbeat—a ray of sunshine after what the sketch-writer Quentin Letts called the 'glumbucket' of Theresa May. A big-picture politician, for sure, but one who didn't get bogged down with trivia and who was good at delegating. Yes, he sometimes used colourful language—'occasionally some plaster comes off the ceiling as a result of a phrase I may have used', as he put it—but this helped give him a public appeal that transcended party and a profile that most politicians would kill for.[16] In any case, the over-the-top phrasing and performance was often deployed as part of an iron message discipline, the baroque style helping to mask dull substance or sometimes no substance at all. He was one of the few politicians well enough known to be referred to solely by his (adoptive) first name—'Boris', a nomenclature that infuriated opponents who saw it as lending him an undeserved aura of familiarity.[17] He had fought the good fight on Brexit and had been prepared to resign from Theresa May's Cabinet over her Withdrawal Agreement, albeit only once it became clear that his Cabinet colleague David Davis was also heading for the exit. Perhaps above all, though, his supporters saw Johnson as a winner. He had won the London Mayoralty twice and had helped win the EU referendum as the most prominent politician attached to the Leave campaign. When your party has just crashed to 9% of the vote, a winner becomes more attractive, whatever their other flaws. And while his performance in the leadership contest may not have been particularly impressive, he had won convincingly, yet again.

'Made it Ma! King of the World!' (Dave Brown, *The Independent*, 25 July 2019 © Dave Brown)

* * *

There was little surprise that the most significant policy divide in the leadership contest came over Brexit, the issue that had dominated British politics since 2016. The multiple twists and turns in that story are discussed in more detail in Chapter 2, but it is impossible to understand the calling of the 2019 general election without some discussion of the subject. The candidates in the leadership contest all agreed that Brexit had to be delivered, but differed on how and when, and on whether leaving without a withdrawal agreement with the EU in place—a 'no deal' Brexit—would be acceptable. Launching his campaign, Johnson said that he wanted to 'get Brexit done', a phrase that would be heard repeatedly over the coming months.[18] He claimed to want a different deal—the nature of which was unclear—but would not rule out leaving without one if need be. He also pledged that Britain would leave the EU by October, 'do or die', a phrase that became associated with his candidacy. Like many good political quotations, the origins of the phrase are not quite as straightforward as it seems. It came from an interview for talkRADIO with the journalist Ross Kempsell, who asked Johnson about his priorities for office:

> Boris Johnson: ... And getting ready to come out on October the, the...?
> Ross Kempsell: 31st.
> BJ: Correct.
> RK: Come what may?
> BJ: Come what may.
> RK: Do or Die?
> BJ: Do or Die. Come what may.[19]

The phrase was therefore originally Kempsell's, not Johnson's. On the steps of Downing Street, having accepted the Queen's invitation to form a government, the new Prime Minister used a different formulation to make the same point: 'The doubters, the doomsters, the gloomsters— they are going to get it wrong again. The people who bet against Britain are going to lose their shirts because we are going to restore trust in our democracy and we are going to fulfil the repeated promises of Parliament to the people and come out of the EU on October 31, no ifs or buts.'

A dramatic reshuffle saw more than half of Theresa May's Cabinet return to the backbenches. The press variously described it a 'massacre', 'bloodletting', a 'cull', a 'clear-out', 'brutal' and 'carnage'. In a headline that only really made sense if you understood both the events of 1934 and 1962, *The Sun* referred to it as the 'Night of the Blond Knives'.[20] *The Guardian* said the new Cabinet was 'an ethnically diverse but ideologically homogeneous statement of intent'.[21] Priti Patel became Home Secretary. Sajid Javid moved from the Home Office to the Exchequer. Dominic Raab became Foreign Secretary and First Secretary of State. Overall, there were a record number of ethnic minority Cabinet members, albeit with a smaller proportion of women than in the outgoing Cabinet.[22] Johnson's new team was noticeably more hardline on Brexit, with Brexiters—and would-be no deal Brexiters at that—in almost all the key positions. While Theresa May used to claim that 'no deal is better than a bad deal', few really believed she meant it or that all her Cabinet colleagues believed it. With the Johnson Cabinet, they did. This view was reinforced by his Downing Street appointments—most obviously and controversially the appointment of Dominic Cummings, the former head of the Vote Leave campaign, as one of his two key aides. Supposedly once described by David Cameron as a 'career psychopath', the *Sunday Times* observed that Cummings was 'renowned for playing politics with the studs raised'.[23] Within days of his appointment,

Cummings was reported as saying that it was important to get Brexit done 'by any means necessary'.[24]

The problem, left unresolved during the leadership contest, was *how* the UK would leave the EU in October. The time available to negotiate any new deal was limited; it was not obvious that Parliament would vote through a new deal even if one could be produced, but it was even less likely that Parliament would agree to leave without a deal. The May government had tried three times to secure even outline parliamentary support for its Brexit deal, failing by massive majorities each time. In the same talkRADIO interview, Johnson argued that it was his choice, 'up to the prime minister of the day', not that of Parliament. Yet, as would rapidly become clear, this was not a view Parliament shared. Even with support from the DUP, the government only enjoyed a wafer-thin majority and there were plenty of Conservative MPs on either side of the issue who had already shown they were prepared to defy their whips. May's problems had come, predominantly, from the pro-Brexit wing of the Conservative parliamentary party, who disliked the nature of the deal she had negotiated; Johnson's were to come from the Remain wing, which aimed to avoid a no deal Brexit at all costs. This group was smaller, but still large enough to wipe out his Commons majority.

There was at this point no Brexit masterplan within the new government. A series of meetings at Chequers and Chevening, held in July and August, tried to game out what might happen in the coming months. Some of those involved—and especially those with experience of these issues within the May administration, like Nikki da Costa, the Director of Legislative Affairs—argued that their approach needed to be tough and uncompromising, both when it came to the EU and to critics within their own party. 'We have to play the hardest game', one of the members of the Johnson team said. 'We don't have a majority, and these people are not going to come with you.' Above all, it was important to buy time and to try to stop Parliament taking control of the process. This would require gambles, to take the fight to opponents, along with a recognition that their opponents were going to be unrelenting in turn. Sitting back and allowing opponents to take the initiative would not work. 'They are going to come for us', one said in August. Not everyone on the team bought into this approach, including initially the Prime Minister.

The Commons had risen for its summer recess the day after the new Prime Minister took office. The recess lasted almost six weeks out of 14 remaining until the Brexit deadline. Even before Parliament had returned, and as part of its attempt to try to show some control—and that this was a distinctly different administration from its predecessor—the government announced that after less than a fortnight's business there would also then be an extended prorogation lasting for over a month.

Boris walks into the bear trap (Christian Adams, *Evening Standard*, 19 July 2019 © Christian Adams)

* * *

When Parliament resumed in early September, the government's opponents did—just as predicted—come for them. On 3 September, amid considerable controversy, the Speaker allowed former Conservative Cabinet Minister Oliver Letwin to move a motion under Standing Order No 24 to take control of parliamentary business away from the government.[25] The government lost that vote by 328 to 301, with 21 Conservative MPs joining forces with the opposition parties. The government whips had made it clear that anyone voting in favour of Letwin's motion would have the whip removed, since they would be 'destroying the government's negotiating position and handing control of parliament to Jeremy Corbyn'. All 21 duly lost the whip. They included nine former Cabinet ministers, among them two former Chancellors of the Exchequer. Two had stood for the leadership of the party just months before.[26] The exiles included Winston Churchill's grandson, Sir Nicholas Soames.[27] The government's majority was now gone.[28]

The next day, Letwin's victory facilitated the introduction of the European Union (Withdrawal) (No 6) Bill—that '(No 6)' emblematic of just how much Brexit had dominated the Parliament—by the former Labour Cabinet Minister Hilary Benn. It required the government to seek an extension to Brexit negotiations from the EU, unless the House had approved a deal or given its assent to a no deal outcome by 19 October. The government labelled it 'the surrender bill', arguing that by removing the threat of no deal, the Bill undercut its negotiating position. Against the government's wishes, the Bill cleared all its Commons stages in one day.[29]

The Times journalist Matt Chorley had earlier in the Parliament coined the phrase 'This is not normal' as a recognition of how political business as usual was falling apart under the pressure of Brexit and a divided Parliament. Little of what happened in the autumn of 2019—the government losing control of the legislative agenda, going down repeatedly to defeat on key legislation, the mass expulsion of senior MPs—was normal. By this stage of the Parliament, though, even these abnormal events seemed almost par for the course. The Parliament as a whole saw a total of 89 changes of allegiance by MPs (involving some 52 different MPs), easily a post-war record. There were also record levels of ministerial resignations, more than any government for over a century, as well as Commons defeats for the government on an unprecedented scale.[30]

At various points in the events outlined below, MPs appeared to do things that make little sense—voting against an early election one day only to vote for it the next day, or not agreeing to a Brexit deal on a Saturday, but backing legislation on it the following Tuesday. There are often explanations for these different outcomes, even if they are not always immediately obvious.[31] These explanations almost always reflect the lack of trust that existed, on both sides of the debate, as well as the extraordinarily frenetic nature of politics at the time. 'Seeking for consistency in MPs' thinking is not necessarily fruitful', as one government source put it. 'MPs were thinking in the same way the government was governing: whack a mole, all hour to hour, day to day.' There is a danger in outlining the steps that led to the election (or indeed the events of the election itself) of seeing what happened as inevitable, of imposing a sense of clarity and structure that was not there. Almost none of what happened was obvious at the time.

* * *

Also not normal—at least when compared to most modern precedent—was that these defeats did not bring about the resignation of the government or a general election. On the eve of the Letwin motion vote, the Prime Minister claimed to have no desire for an early election ('I don't want an election, you don't want an election'), but he made it clear that he would call for one if the Benn Bill passed. And indeed within 30 minutes of the Bill receiving its Third Reading, the Prime Minister was at the despatch box, moving an early election motion.

MPs knew they could call his bluff. The Fixed-term Parliaments Act (FTPA), introduced by the Coalition government after 2010, removed the link between defeats on policy issues, even ones previously treated as votes of confidence, and the triggering of an election.[32] This had two consequences that were significant throughout the Parliament. First, it removed the Prime Minister's ability to deem any vote to be an issue of confidence, threatening a general election in the event that the government did not win. Previous governments had on occasion used this to push through legislation with which their own MPs were unhappy; under both May and Johnson, the Conservative whips office were well aware that they lacked levers that had been available to their predecessors.[33] Second, rather than allowing the Prime Minister to call an election whenever he or she desired, the FTPA required the Commons actively to vote for any early election—something it turned out the Commons had no desire to do.

With Labour abstaining, the Prime Minister could muster only 298 votes in favour of an early election, well short of the two-thirds required by the legislation.[34] Johnson described Jeremy Corbyn as 'the first opposition leader in the democratic history of this country to refuse the invitation of an election'. The claim was a bit disingenuous; past opposition leaders could not refuse invitations not offered. Yet Corbyn had accepted a similar invitation from Theresa May in 2017, and Labour were now divided about what to do.[35] Officially Labour favoured an election as the best route to resolving Brexit and some Corbyn allies were bullish, believing a return to the campaign trail would play to the Labour leader's strengths and revive their party's fortunes. But many in the party worried that a dissolution could be used to secure a no deal Brexit by stealth, with the Prime Minister moving polling day past the Article 50 deadline once Parliament was no longer sitting. Others were nervous about the political context—with the Conservatives ahead in the polls, an election with Brexit in the balance might help Johnson unify Leave voters. Somewhere in between were those resigned to an election as risky but politically unavoidable, given Labour's own repeated insistence that it was the best means to resolve Brexit.[36] Counsels of caution prevailed initially. Corbyn denounced Johnson's offer as a sham: 'The offer of an election today is a bit like the offer of an apple to Snow White from the Wicked Queen. What he is offering is not an apple of the election but the poison of no deal.' Like an electoral St Augustine, Labour were eager to go to the polls, just not yet.

At the same time, the Prime Minister was not being entirely truthful in his claim not to want an early election. His team had calculated very early on after taking office that the chances of getting Brexit through the current Parliament—either with a deal or without—were minimal. Therefore, to get Brexit done, they almost certainly needed an election and had started to work out how to get one, ideally before 31 October. The problem was that the polling the party was conducting indicated that the public were noticeably less keen. 'They were not ready for it', said one of those involved. Isaac Levido, the Australian campaign strategist brought in by the Johnson team in early August, was especially concerned that the public might think the election was unnecessary. It was therefore crucial to make any election look as if it was a last resort. In the words of one of Johnson's team: 'You have to show the electorate you have been stymied at every stage.'

The Prime Minister tried for an election again on 9 September, this time with the threat of the extended prorogation of Parliament hanging over MPs. With Labour still abstaining, the result was essentially the same.[37] Parliament prorogued just before 2 a.m. the following morning, supposedly until October, only for the Supreme Court, in a unanimous judgment on 24 September, to rule prorogation unlawful and of no effect. Parliament therefore resumed on 25 September. This episode reinforced the views of many of the Prime Minister's opponents that he was not to be trusted and would do anything to get Brexit through.

The announcement of a fresh Brexit deal on 17 October changed the parliamentary arithmetic. The nature of the deal—discussed in more detail in the next chapter—meant that the government lost the support of the DUP, but this was more than compensated for by bringing back onside pro-Brexit Conservative MPs, while the mere existence of a deal satisfied many of those Tory MPs who most feared a no deal outcome. The possibility of majority support for a deal suddenly looked real. In turn, this demoralised some of the MPs who had been holding out for a fresh referendum as a way to prevent Brexit, while also encouraging those Labour MPs who were willing to vote for a deal, but only if one looked credible and possible. The Prime Minister initially attempted a fourth meaningful vote, the Commons sitting on a Saturday for the first time since the invasion of the Falklands in 1982, only to have Oliver Letwin successfully move an amendment withholding approval until the implementing legislation had been passed.

The government therefore tried legislation, and on 22 October the Commons voted for the Second Reading of the European Union (Withdrawal Agreement) Bill by 329 to 299. The vote saw government MPs joined in the aye lobby by most of their whipless former colleagues, along with 19 Labour MPs. It was the first time the Commons had backed any Brexit deal. Yet this coalition did not hold together when it came to the vote on the Bill's programme motion, which proposed an extremely compressed timetable to implement the legislation ahead of the 31 October deadline. In response, Johnson announced that he would 'pause' the legislation and once again seek an election as soon as the EU responded to his extension request.

Labour attempted private discussions with the government over a revised, longer timetable, but soon concluded that the Conservatives were not negotiating in good faith. At one point, as Labour's Chief Whip Nick Brown attempted to explain to the Prime Minister how a deal could be done, Dominic Cummings interrupted to say that he wasn't interested and wanted an early election. Even if they had somehow managed to agree a revised timetable, several of Johnson's advisers thought there was no guarantee that the temporary coalition of MPs they had pulled together for its Second Reading would necessarily hold for long enough to get the Bill through all its Commons stages. As one government source put it: 'This was a delay tactic. It would have been used to undermine the bill. I doubt we'd have had it in a state the government could have supported by the end. It would have been shredded.' They saw any extended timetable as a trap.

However, Labour was now in a bind. Most Labour MPs still opposed an early election, yet with the EU set to agree the UK's request for an

Article 50 extension, the main argument the party had used to justify opposition was about to disappear. Corbyn convened a Shadow Cabinet to decide how to respond. Again, views were divided into three camps. With no strong steer from the leader, the voices for delay prevailed, and the Shadow Cabinet agreed to oppose Johnson's call.

Yet within days, a shift in stance from the Liberal Democrats and the SNP changed the landscape again. On Sunday 27 October, *The Observer* broke a story that the two parties were planning an early election bill which could be passed by a simple majority.[38] Such a bill would override the FTPA. Some senior Lib Dem figures were upbeat about an early election fought with Brexit undecided, citing the party's success in the European Parliament elections and internal polling analysis which suggested major gains were possible.[39] The SNP had their own reasons to favour an election: they were riding high in Scottish polling and were anxious about the political risks from the looming trial of former party leader Alex Salmond on charges of sexual offences, which was due to begin early in 2020. For both parties, an early election was also a last roll of the dice, the only means to stop Johnson's Withdrawal Agreement completing its passage through Parliament now it had secured a Commons majority. For the government's opponents, a bill also had the advantage that it would set the date of the election in legislation. This nullified one of the fears they had with agreeing to an election under the FTPA, especially after the prorogation episode, that Johnson could simply delay polling day until after the revised no deal deadline has passed. This was described by Number 10 insiders as 'tin-foil hat stuff', but it was again a sign of how little trust existed on either side.[40]

In 2017, the Conservatives had contemplated over-riding the FTPA if Labour had not agreed to an early election.[41] This option was also considered by the Johnson camp initially, but it presented three difficulties. First, whereas a motion under the FTPA could be discussed briefly (the debate triggering the 2017 election lasted a mere 90 minutes), legislation had the potential to eat up time, an especial problem when trying to move quickly for a pre-31 October contest. Second, any bill was amendable. 'Given what they've done to other legislation', said one of those involved, 'what will they do to this?' And third, the government could not be certain even of the simple majority necessary to pass it. But things had now changed. The imminent passing of the 31 October deadline meant that time was less important and with the two smaller opposition parties seemingly onside, there was now a viable route to get the legislation through.

The party leaders had previously been meeting weekly to coordinate their strategies over Brexit and an early election, but the Lib Dem/SNP initiative broke the united opposition front. The Labour Party now faced finding itself in the worst of all worlds, dragged into an early election many privately opposed, but which the party officially claimed to favour. Initially, Labour stuck to their previous line. On Monday 28 October, the party whipped its MPs to abstain on Boris Johnson's third early election motion under the FTPA, which again was easily blocked. However, the same day, the EU announced an extension to the Article 50 deadline through to 31 January. 'No deal' was now effectively off the table. The government immediately introduced an early election bill of its own, setting the date of the election for 12 December. Like the Liberal Democrat/SNP proposal, this required a simple majority to pass.

The Shadow Cabinet reconvened to consider the new situation. The mood was now different. It was now not obvious that Labour could block an election. This time Corbyn took the lead, arguing that Labour could no longer be seen to be going against an early election. 'There wasn't any dissent at that Shadow Cabinet meeting from anybody who had urged caution a week earlier', noted one of those present. 'We agreed to vote for a general election very quickly'.

There was—and still is—a view, held within parts of the PLP that the election was not inevitable, that had the Labour leadership held firm in its opposition, it would have led to some of the smaller parties changing their stance, as well as drawing support from some of the independent Conservatives. The Labour leadership's shift in position to backing an early poll was therefore described by one of the whips' office as a case of 'suicide by electorate'. It is true that the *Observer* story had come as a surprise to many SNP MPs and that the party was divided over the wisdom of an early election; 'It's difficult to say what the settled view was', said one SNP MP, 'because there wasn't one'. Some blamed the Liberal Democrats for leaking the story or saw the move purely as positioning—allowing the SNP to argue they were not frightened of an election—but unlikely to lead anywhere. The SNP Westminster group met at almost the same time as Labour's Shadow Cabinet, with plenty of SNP MPs—one account says a majority—against backing the government's election motion. But by the time that meeting had finished, Labour had already come out for an election and the SNP discussion was redundant.[42]

There was still one final twist. Just as Johnson's team had feared, Labour proposed two amendments to the bill calling for the franchise to be extended to 16 and 17-year-olds and to EU citizens settled in the UK. These proposals had the potential to drive a wedge between the government, who vehemently opposed both, and the smaller opposition parties, who supported both. The Labour whips felt at least one amendment would be passed; the government said it would pull the bill in the event that either did.[43] Yet Deputy Speaker Sir Lindsay Hoyle ruled both out of order, meaning neither amendment would be debated or voted on.[44] He did accept an amendment to change the date of the election to 9 December—which would have been the first not to be held on a Thursday since 1924—but this fell by 315 to 295.[45]

The bill received its Third Reading by 438 to 20 on 29 October. The aye lobby comprised just over two-thirds of the Commons, ironically enough to have passed a motion under the FTPA, exactly the outcome the Commons had rejected just a day before.

Although the bill still had to pass the Lords, the election effectively began. While the bill was being debated, it was announced that the whip had been restored to ten of the 21 rebel MPs expelled earlier in the month. Retiring Tory veterans such as Ken Clarke and Oliver Letwin ended their long Commons careers as exiles, while others, like Dominic Grieve and David Gauke, looked to fight on by contesting their seats as independents.

John Bercow's ten years in the Speaker's chair ended on 31 October, triggering a succession contest with a field of seven senior MPs, including all three of his deputies. Hoyle prevailed after promising (as did all his competitors) a calmer and more hands-off approach to proceedings. With the end of Parliament coming just weeks after a Queen's Speech, there was relatively little incomplete legislation to address during the 'wash-up' period before the formal dissolution of Parliament at 12.01 a.m. on 6 November.[46]

* * *

All general elections have their own distinguishing features, while also being comfortably familiar. They bring to mind the line often attributed to Margaret Mead about how everyone is absolutely unique 'just like everyone else'.[47] Yet when the campaign began, the British general election of December 2019 did look as if it might be more than usually distinctive and significant.

It was the fourth general election in a decade and came in an increasingly crowded electoral cycle. In those ten years there had also been two UK-wide referendums in 2011 (on electoral reform) and 2016 (on EU membership), along with those in Scotland (on independence) and Wales (further devolution). There were also two European elections as well as separate elections in London (in 2012 and 2016), Wales (2011 and 2016), Scotland (ditto) and Northern Ireland (2011, 2016 and 2017). Plus, there were those for Police and Crime Commissioners throughout England and Wales (2012 and 2016), as well as elections for local councils and various mayoralties.[48]

It was the first December election since 1923. As well as some pearl-clutching from those looking for excuses to avoid a contest, there was also genuine concern about the extent to which the short days and inclement weather could affect the campaign—some stressed the safety issues involved, especially given the febrile nature of contemporary politics—and who, if anyone, might benefit as a result. A winter election also raised the possibility of external events—such as a NHS winter crisis or travel chaos—disrupting a party's plans. The terrorist attacks during the 2017 election had demonstrated the potential for events to derail any campaign, and it was not implausible that something of a similar magnitude could happen again.

'December election' (Ben Jennings *The i* paper, 25 October 2019 © Ben Jennings)

It was also unusual for a government to want to fight an election on the back of what was, ostensibly, a high-profile policy failure. Britain had not left the EU by 31 October 'come what may', 'no ifs or buts', let alone 'do or die'. It was not clear when the election was called whether the Conservatives would be blamed for this, as Levido and some other Conservative strategists still feared, or whether—as the Prime Minister clearly hoped—he would be able to use it to his advantage, blaming Parliament and the opposition parties.

The Conservatives went into the election comfortably ahead in the polls. Theresa May's defenestration had led to a clear improvement in Tory polling, and by October 2019, when the election was called, the average Conservative poll lead was a full 11 percentage points. While not quite large enough to guarantee a landslide, a lead of this scale at the opening of a campaign would, at pretty much any point in the preceding 50 or more years, have been enough to make observers fairly certain they knew what the outcome would be. Instead, much of the discussion as the campaign began was of how the election was a gamble for the Prime Minister and of the various risks he was said to be taking. Had he lost, his would have been the third shortest-lived premiership in history.[49] Coverage of the calling of the election in the right-wing press had none of the vainglorious certainty of Conservative victory that had been so common when the 2017 contest had begun.[50]

In part, this was precisely because of events in 2017, an election which had seemed to challenge so much conventional wisdom about British elections—and especially assumptions about the limited effects of the short campaign itself. The 2017 campaign had similarly begun with the Conservatives comfortably ahead, yet had ended with the party losing seats and Jeremy Corbyn closing in on Downing Street. It had provided clear evidence of just how volatile the modern British voter could be and how much party support can change during a campaign. But the doubts and anxieties—shared by many in the parties as well as those whose job it was to write about elections—were more than just acts of compensation for having misread the previous contest. They were also a reflection of the extent to which British politics by 2019 appeared to be in a state of flux, with many old assumptions and norms either breaking down or at least coming under serious strain.

All elections are important, but some are more important than others. David Butler—who was involved with every one of this series of books between 1945 and 2005—once noted how most of the more significant events in British politics were in fact not associated with elections. 'It may sound cynical', he wrote, 'after a lifetime devoted to the study of elections, to argue that elections seldom set the fate of the nation.' Listing a series of key events, beginning with the convertibility crisis of 1947 and ending (when he was writing in the late 1980s) with the Falklands War of 1982, he noted that 'not one of these phenomena was actually associated with an election or a change in government. In almost all cases there must be a strong suspicion that if the other party had been in power at the time, events could have taken much the same course'.[51] Even those elections seen at the time as particularly important can—with a greater historical perspective—sometimes seem less significant. Yet with the parties ideologically so far apart and with the key constitutional question of the day still unresolved, the election of 2019 at least felt as if it could be important, more so than normally, and perhaps on a par with 1979 or even 1945. It felt consequential.

NOTES

1. Her statement was delivered on Friday 24 May 2019. She announced that she would stand down as Conservative Party leader early the following month, on 7 June, staying in place as Prime Minister thereafter only until a replacement had been chosen by her party.

2. Labour also did catastrophically badly, coming a poor third with 13.6% of the vote, a result which had important consequences for the party's approach to Brexit (see Chapter 4, p. 139).

3. It was precisely double the largest number of candidates participating in any Conservative contest at any one time, although in 1975 a total of seven MPs contested the leadership, albeit spread across two rounds with never move than five running at any one time.

4. D. Jeffery et al., 'The Conservative Party Leadership Election of 2019: An Analysis of the Voting Motivations of Conservative Parliamentarians', *Parliamentary Affairs* (2020), https://academic.oup.com/pa/advance-article-abstract/doi/10.1093/pa/gsaa046/5924394?redirectedFrom=fulltext.

5. It is not obvious that the new rules made much difference. In their absence, there would still have been pressure on candidates performing poorly to drop out even if not required to do so, as variously happened in 1990, 1997, 2001 and 2016, and indeed as Matt Hancock did in 2019, withdrawing after the first round, despite his 20 votes being sufficient under the rules for him to have continued in the contest.

6. John McDonnell had attempted a challenge in 2007, but did not secure enough nominations from MPs to get on to the ballot. Brown would go on to complain that more people would be voting for Ed Balls on the TV show *Strictly Come Dancing* than would vote for Johnson to be Prime Minister, which, given the nature of his own selection, did seem to demonstrate a lack of self-awareness.

7. When (or if) Labour eventually gets to do the same, the Prime Minister will be chosen by an unaccountable, elderly, left-wing cabal. For the data, see, for example, Tim Bale's 'Tory Leadership: Who Gets to Choose the UK's Next Prime Minister?', *BBC News*, 23 June 2019, https://www.bbc.com/news/uk-politics-48395211. Occasionally the process was referred to as a 'coup', although it was merely the inevitable consequence of the democratisation of party processes. For a more sensible criticism, stressing the lack of accountability involved, see, for example, Robert Saunders 'Why Party Members Should Never Be Allowed to Elect Prime Ministers', *New Statesman*, 20 June 2019.

8. The first round saw Esther McVey, Mark Harper and Andrea Leadsom fail to achieve the necessary quota, with Matt Hancock withdrawing voluntarily from the contest; the second round knocked out Dominic Raab; the third round did for Rory Stewart; and the fourth took out Sajid Javid. That left Gove, Hunt and Johnson.

9. Johnson's support was also stronger amongst younger MPs, even when controlling for cohort of entry. See Jeffery et al., 'The Conservative Party Leadership Election'.

10. See, for example, 'Tory Leadership: Boris Johnson Supporters Hatch Plot to Knock out Michael Gove', *Daily Telegraph*, 19 June 2019.

11. This is discussed in Philip Cowley, 'Boris Johnson: Conservatives Could Be Making a Major Error in Letting Him Avoid the Press and Public', *The Conversation*, 19 June 2019, https://theconversation.com/boris-johnson-conservatives-could-be-making-a-major-error-in-letting-him-avoid-the-press-and-public-119108. It wasn't the only thing the author got wrong about the contest.

12. Foreshadowing what was to occur during the general election, it is noticeable that the Johnson team ducked several other potential media battles.

13. 'Tory Leadership Debate: BoJo the Mojo Mumbler Versus Wild Eyed Tele-evangelist', *The Times*, 10 July 2019.

14. For example: James Ramsay MacDonald, Arthur Neville Chamberlain, Robert Anthony Eden, Maurice Harold Macmillan, James Harold Wilson, Leonard James Callaghan and James Gordon Brown.

15. His rival for the leadership, Rory Stewart, was later to describe him as 'the most accomplished liar in public life – perhaps the best liar ever to serve as prime minister'. In case there was any doubt about what he was

getting at, Stewart went on: 'He has mastered the use of error, omission, exaggeration, diminution, equivocation and flat denial. He has perfected casuistry, circumlocution, false equivalence and false analogy. He is equally adept at the ironic jest, the fib and the grand lie; the weasel word and the half-truth; the hyperbolic lie, the obvious lie, and the bullshit lie – which may inadvertently be true' ('Lord of Misrule', *Times Literary Supplement*, 6 November 2020). Stewart's article was a review of Tom Bower's biography, *Boris Johnson: The Gambler* (WH Allen, 2020). There is plenty more on the complex character of the Prime Minister in the two earlier biographies: Sonia Purnell's *Just Boris* (Aurum, 2011) and Andrew Gimson's *Boris* (Simon & Schuster, 2016).

16. This phrase came from his campaign launch event, where he also defended his choice of words, arguing that the public were fed up with politicians because they 'feel we are muffling and veiling our language, not speaking as we find, covering everything up in bureaucratic platitudes, when what they want to hear is what we genuinely think'.

17. These concerns dated back to at least 2008, when Labour strategists had tried to stop their own politicians referring him as 'Boris'.

18. The phrase was later to become a general election campaign mantra, after exceptionally positive reactions in a Conservative focus group (see Chapter 6, pp. 195–196). But the Prime Minister had used the phrase before, as indeed had his predecessor.

19. 'Boris Johnson: The talkRADIO Interview', 25 June 2019, https://talkradio.co.uk/news/boris-johnson-talkradio-interview-19062531433. It was the same interview in which Johnson claimed that to relax, he made model London buses: 'I get, I get old, um, wooden crates, right? And I paint them and they have two, it's a box that's been used to contain two wine bottles right? And it will have a dividing thing. And I turn it into a bus and I put passengers … you really want to know this?'

20. The same events were also alluded to when Theresa May's botched post-election Cabinet reshuffle was referred to by *Channel 4 News'* Gary Gibbon as 'night of the plastic forks' (see Chapter 3, pp. 70–72).

21. 'How Representative Is Boris Johnson's New Cabinet?', *The Guardian*, 25 July 2019.

22. There were actually more women as full Cabinet members than in the outgoing May Cabinet, but including those ministers who attended Cabinet shifted the gender balance towards men. The Institute for Government also noted that there were more ethnic minority ministers attending Cabinet 'than in the rest of British political history combined' ('New Government: Live Blog', 23 July 2019, https://www.instituteforgovernment.org.uk/blog/new-government-july-2019-live-blog).

23. Tim Shipman, 'The Fearsome Fixer Dominic Cummings Is Now the Second Most Powerful Person in No 10', *Sunday Times*, 28 July 2019.
24. This prompted at least one of the incoming team to check that he meant any *legal* means; Cummings assured them that he did, although events were to prove otherwise. Curiously, the article by Tim Shipman referred to in fn 23 reported that the phrase—which Cummings used repeatedly—was used by the Prime Minister to Cummings when trying to persuade him to join the team. In 2021, after Cummings had left Downing Street, we got his on-the-record version of events in which he says that before agreeing to work in Number 10, he made Johnson confirm that he was 'deadly serious' about Brexit. As one sketch-writer noted: 'It's revealing that Cummings felt he needed to check this in summer 2019, but then, he'd dealt with Johnson before' (Robert Hutton, 'Classic Dom', *The Critic*, 17 March 2021).
25. As explained in Chapter 2, this was not the first time the Speaker had allowed this manoeuvre, much to the fury of the government.
26. Rory Stewart, who made it to the last five, and Sam Gyimah, who failed to reach the nomination threshold.
27. Much of the media coverage fixated on Soames losing the whip, given the Churchill link. There was some symbolism there—especially as the new Prime Minister had written a (pretty poor) biography of his grandfather—but the Soames expulsion was less significant than the removal of, say, Philip Hammond, who had been Chancellor just months before.
28. Formally, the majority went earlier that day when the Conservative MP Phillip Lee crossed the floor of the Commons chamber to join the Liberal Democrats while the Prime Minister was speaking (see Chapter 5, p. 178). But the further loss of 21 MPs meant the government was now deep under water. It reminded me of when my Dad took me to the cinema in 1978 to see a remake of *The Thirty-Nine Steps*. The denouement took place in the clock tower of the Palace of Westminster, where after some gun play, the baddie was shot. 'Is he dead?', I asked, as the villain staggered around, clutching his chest, at which point he crashed through one of the clock faces and fell to earth. 'He is now', said Dad.
29. It passed its Second Reading by 329 to 300 and its Third Reading by 327 to 299.
30. This was well summarised in https://www.instituteforgovernment.org.uk/publication/whitehall-monitor-2020/ministers. Elsewhere, Gavin Freeguard, then of the Institute for Government, estimated that the number of changes of allegiance was a record dating back to 1886. See https://twitter.com/GavinFreeguard/status/1229789021024505857.
31. As explained in the text, an MP might oppose a FTPA election motion but go on to support an early election bill, because while the latter sets

the date on the election in stone, the former does not. They might similarly back legislation on a Brexit deal—legislation being checkable, amendable and ultimately still rejectable—while not backing a vaguer motion. But to the outsider, this sort of behaviour could look demented.

32. Philip Norton, 'The Fixed-Term Parliaments Act and Votes of Confidence', *Parliamentary Affairs*, 69(1) (2016): 3–18. The requirement for a two-thirds vote was one of the two methods by which the FTPA allowed for an early election; the other was for a vote of no confidence, followed by a two-week period to see if an alternate government could be formed—if not, an election followed. The Johnson camp considered going down this route, although not only did it involve a fortnight's delay, but it was also even more high risk as, rather than automatically leading to an election, it could end in a government led by someone other than the incumbent Prime Minister. Johnson's advisors thought this was a relatively small risk—their view being that the opponents of the government were much better at saying what they were against rather than what they were for—but it was still a risk.

33. Given the scale of the defeats inflicted on the May government (discussed in Chapter 2), it is not obvious that even this nuclear option would have worked had it been available. The May team had variously discussed ways of creating de facto motions of confidence, that would simultaneously fulfil the requirements for the meaningful vote and act as triggers for the FTPA, but they were never pursued.

34. On this, and the two subsequent occasions, the Labour position was to abstain. Because the law required the support of two-thirds of all MPs to result in an early election, an abstention had the same effect as a 'no' vote—although in each case there were between 20 and 40 Labour MPs rebelling against their whip and formally voting no, in addition to Liberal Democrat MPs and various others. The aye lobby was made up almost entirely of Conservative and DUP MPs.

35. One of the more puzzling aspects of this is that the party was divided over this in 2019 when it had not been in 2017, when it had, on paper, been facing a much more severe electoral test. Some of the differences between 2017 and 2019 are discussed further in Philip Cowley, 'Why Labour MPs aren't Turkeys Afraid of a Christmas Election', *The Spectator*, 29 October 2019, https://www.spectator.co.uk/article/why-labour-mps-aren-t-turkeys-afraid-of-a-christmas-election.

36. The various divisions within Labour over this are well summarised in Gabriel Pogrund and Patrick Maguire's *Left Out*. Vintage, 2020, Chapter 14.

37. This time the vote was 293 to 43.

38. This was variously referred to in the press as a 'one-line bill', sometimes even in stories which included the text of the bill and which clearly showed it was in fact longer than one line.

39. Not all Lib Dem MPs, many of whom represented marginal seats, shared their party's enthusiasm for an early election. While sympathetic to the leadership's motives for backing an early poll, they were well aware of the risks it posed. For more discussion on this, see Chapter 5.

40. See, for example, 'Claims Boris Johnson Will Change Election Date to Force No-Deal Brexit Dismissed as "Tin-Foil Hat Stuff"', *Politics Home*, 3 September 2019, https://www.politicshome.com/news/article/claims-boris-johnson-will-change-election-date-to-force-nodeal-brexit-dismissed-as-tinfoil-hat-stuff.

41. Philip Cowley and Dennis Kavanagh, *The British General Election of 2017*. Palgrave Macmillan, 2018, pp. 12–13.

42. The great what if in all of this is what might have happened had Labour remained opposed to an early election. As with most of the great what ifs, it is not possible to answer definitively.

   Many Labour accounts of these events stress the role played by the Liberal Democrats. But even if they had voted with Labour against the bill, this would still not have been enough to secure an opposition majority. This is also, as so often with the Labour Party, evidence of a blind spot when it comes to discussing the Liberal Democrats—an inability to take the party seriously, or understand it, or even to *attempt* to understand it. While there was certainly scepticism in the ranks of the Liberal Democrats, there were also some advantages to an early election, as well as considerable doubt that things were going to get any better for the party if they delayed. Much more important was the position of the SNP, who were, in numerical terms, enough to deliver a majority with the Conservatives. We know that there were plenty of SNP MPs with doubts about the election, and, as noted in the text, on one account the party group had decided to vote against the government only then to find Labour had agreed to an election. According to one SNP MP, the party could not be seen to act alone; it needed other parties, including Labour, to give it cover. It especially could not be seen to back a Conservative government alone, given what had happened in 1979 when the SNP had helped bring down Labour and usher in almost two decades of Conservative dominance. (It has similarly been suggested that the Liberal Democrats too would not have wanted to be seen to be acting with the Conservatives alone.)

   So perhaps, if Labour held their ground, the other parties would have voted with them. If true, this would have meant them voting against a bill which, the election date aside, was effectively identical to the one they had supposedly been promoting just the weekend before; even by the standards of the Brexit era this would have been impressive parliamentary gymnastics, but it might have happened. Yet if the SNP did not want an election, they certainly helped get one. The effect of their initiative with the Lib Dems the preceding weekend was to undercut Labour's position against the election entirely. Once Labour believed it had lost support from the SNP and Lib Dems, it became much harder to hold out against an election. It was one thing to vote against an election and to block it; it was enough to vote against an election only to fail to block it. If, as some SNP MPs believe, their proposed bill was merely positioning, they were wrong. And regardless, why did no one try to communicate with Labour, to make their position clear?

Yet in turn, this debate should prompt two further questions, both probably more significant: *if* it had been possible to delay the election, for how long would such a delay have been feasible? And would this in fact have been better or worse for the Conservatives? At the time, many of those urging delay believed it would make the government's position weaker but given what we know about how the election played out, this is at least moot.

43. The amendments would have been backed both by those who believed in them in principle and by others hoping to derail the election. On the other side, despite being desperate for an election, the Conservatives were genuine in their claim that they would have pulled the bill, seeing the amendments as wrecking amendments designed to derail the election.

44. The reasons for Hoyle's decision are disputed. He came under immense pressure from Labour to accept at least one of these amendments. His defenders argue that he was advised by the clerks that the amendments were unacceptable because they came with resource implications—money would have to be allocated to pay for registering all the new voters. His critics contend that this objection does not make sense, as voter registration is a task handled by local councils, not central government.

45. Various arguments were advanced for this earlier date, including that it would allow students to vote at their term-time address. This was a curious claim. For one thing, most universities were still in term time on 12 December, albeit coming to the end of term (for many on 13 December) and at the point when students begin drifting off home. But more generally, it seemed a novel constitutional development that elections could only be held when students are on campus.

46. The one major piece of legislation to be fast-tracked through was the Historical Institutional Abuse (Northern Ireland) Bill, which provided compensation to the victims of abuse, a victory for Northern Irish campaigners after similar legislation was stalled by the collapse of the Stormont Assembly in 2017. Parliament also passed a Northern Ireland

Budget Act, which was also required by the lack of functioning institutions to pass a devolved budget at Stormont.

47. Like many of the best quotations, I cannot find any evidence that she actually said this.

48. One estimate put the administrative cost of the elections alone at more than £1 billion: see 'Decade of Going to the Polls Has Cost UK More Than £1 Billion', https://www.itv.com/news/2019-11-06/decade-of-going-to-the-polls-has-cost-uk-more-than-1-billion.

49. That is, ahead of just Goderich and Canning (and excluding, as most accounts of the premiership do, Bath and Waldegrave).

50. Cowley and Kavanagh, *The British General Election of 2017*, p. 14.

51. From his essay 'The 1987 General Election in Historical Perspective' in Robert Skidelsky (ed.), *Thatcherism*. Chatto & Windus, 1988, p. 78. In a later work (*British General Elections since 1945* [Blackwell, 1995], p. 123), Butler added the Single European Act, the Maastricht Treaty and the Exchange Rate Mechanism. We could perhaps also add the Gulf War, along with the wars in Afghanistan and Iraq.

CHAPTER 2

The Long Goodbye: Brexit

Anand Menon and Alan Wager

In April 2017, three weeks after Parliament had voted to trigger the Article 50 countdown on Brexit negotiations, Theresa May gambled—and lost—on the willingness of the British people to provide her with a majority to deliver Brexit. She called a general election, she claimed, because 'the country is coming together, but Westminster is not'.[1] The implication was that building on the Conservatives' slim majority was necessary to provide the political space to achieve the best possible deal for the UK in Brexit negotiations. Instead of waiting until 2020, and a general election which would coincide with the end of the Article 50 negotiation window, May sought a decisive mandate for her form of Brexit.[2]

Mrs May got the public mood wrong. The country did not come together as the Prime Minister had hoped in 2017, and divisions over Brexit further deepened as negotiations played out thereafter.[3] In June 2019, three years after the referendum and weeks before May's resignation, the British Election Study found that only 6% of the public did not identify with either the Leave or Remain sides. The outgoing Prime Minister was proved right on one point: without a strong majority, it did indeed prove impossible to persuade a divided Parliament—a microcosm of a divided country—to agree any outcome to Brexit.

May's premiership was defined by Brexit. Little wonder then that early post-mortems in the summer of 2019 judged her term in office a failure.

© The Author(s), under exclusive license to Springer Nature Switzerland AG 2021
R. Ford et al., *The British General Election of 2019*,
https://doi.org/10.1007/978-3-030-74254-6_2

The myriad, overlapping causes of disappointment that critics identified demonstrated the complexity of extricating the UK from the EU within the absurdly short timescale laid down by Article 50.[4] Some argued that May had not succeeded because she treated Brexit as an issue of party management rather than statecraft, while others claimed that it was her failure to build trust and relationships with her backbenchers that cost her in the end. For others still, the root cause was her ultimate unwillingness to countenance a 'no deal' exit from the EU, compounded by a reluctance to confront those within her party who advocated such an outcome. May's detractors argued that the Brexit deal she achieved was a failure of diplomacy. The defenders of her deal would say that her premiership provides a case study in the importance of political communication and salesmanship.[5] What united these critiques was the broad consensus that she had been guilty of 'playing a bad hand really badly'.[6]

Yet all these attempts to attribute the Brexit gridlock to May's character flaws have to reckon with the fact that the Leave campaign had (deliberately) failed to bequeath a clear blueprint for future relations with the EU. The ultimate success of Boris Johnson in 2019 underlined that a different political skillset (not least a willingness to go back on promises about the UK's own union) and a different political profile (as unofficial head of the 2016 Leave campaign) were helpful in breaking the parliamentary gridlock. Yet Boris Johnson also benefited from the fact that his predecessor had tried all available paths to the point of exhaustion and bequeathed him a Parliament willing at last to support a Brexit deal. May's defence, publicly stated three days before she announced her resignation, was that she had 'tried everything I possibly can to find a way through'.[7] Johnson was then perfectly positioned to reap the rewards of this perseverance.

In any case, not all the personal criticisms of Mrs May were necessarily fair or well grounded. She was frequently accused, for instance, of failing to craft a genuinely cross-party approach to Brexit following the 2017 general election. Her political opponents suggested they were waiting by the phone throughout the Parliament, but the call never came.[8] Critics have argued that her apparent reluctance to even try to reach out to the Labour Party was a failure of political imagination and that 'a greater stateswoman than May might have found a way through the morass'.[9] Polls conducted in this period showed majority support for a cross-party approach to Brexit negotiations.[10] Yet—as Chapters 3 and 4 will explain—the notion that the Conservative Prime Minister could have opened inter-party Brexit negotiations with a Labour Party in the summer of 2017 and carried her party is difficult to sustain, given the level of internal Conservative opposition and the Labour leadership's belief in the vulnerability of May's minority government.

Rather than attempting to work with Labour, the Prime Minister signed a deal with the DUP. This turned out to be a fateful decision, as the status of Northern Ireland became one of the main stumbling blocks in negotiations. Yet it is worth noting that while the confidence and supply agreement bound the Northern Irish party to support the Conservative Party on Brexit, the agreement included no demands from the DUP on the direction of Brexit in relation to the province. Critics pounced on May's announcement that she would form a government with DUP support for being tin-eared, given the perceived lack of contrition shown in particular to Conservative MPs who had lost their seats on her watch. However, the tone of the statement was crafted with at least one eye on Brussels, with a view to stressing 'business as usual'. After all, formal negotiations with the EU were due to begin only 11 days after the general election.

The first day of those negotiations was viewed by some as one of the most significant moments of the Brexit process. Prior to the general election, Brexit Secretary David Davis had promised 'the row of the summer' over the sequencing of talks. The EU had insisted that outstanding issues relating to the end of the UK's 45-year engagement with the European project should be resolved prior to any negotiations about a future UK–EU relationship. The UK—or at least David Davis—believed that remaining contributions to the EU budget offered significant negotiating leverage to help secure a beneficial free trade agreement with the EU, and therefore sought to ensure negotiations over departure and future relations were conducted concurrently.

On the evening of 19 June 2017, EU chief negotiator Michel Barnier announced matter-of-factly in a joint press conference with David Davis that the UK had signed up to the EU's preferred timetable.[11] The assumption was that Theresa May was too weak to allow the negotiations to fail at such an early stage and had therefore accepted the EU's timetable in full.[12] However, those inside Number 10 say the decision to acquiesce to the EU's timetable, against the Brexit Secretary's advice, had already been taken by the Prime Minister during the 2017 general election campaign.[13] Whatever the cause, the consequence was that three issues—the money the UK owed to the EU due to its remaining obligations (the 'divorce payment'), citizens' rights and 'other separation issues'—would have to be resolved before trade talks could begin.[14] As the legal commentator David Allen Green put it, the row of the summer had become 'the row-back of the summer'.[15]

The rhythm of negotiations was quickly established, with monthly meetings in four-day cycles. In the early period, a number of potentially thorny issues were resolved with relative ease. Many observers had assumed that money would be an early sticking point. This was hardly an unreasonable assumption, given the bombastic language adopted by the UK and the symbolic importance of the UK's financial contribution to the EU. Yet an agreement on remaining UK payments—principally commitments to the EU's pension scheme and contributions into EU budgets until the UK had fully left the bloc—was accepted with little fuss. The principle that these were liabilities the UK had accrued and should hence pay was publicly accepted in a speech by Theresa May in Florence in September, then a trickle of leaks designed to deflate the issue followed. Agreement on a figure of between £35–39 billion was announced in December 2017.

While the talks in Brussels were proceeding better than expected, strains at home were already beginning to show. Significant tensions emerged between David Davis and Oliver Robbins, Permanent Secretary at the Department for Exiting the European Union (DExEU) and the top official involved in negotiations. Robbins was acting both as the Prime Minister's Europe Advisor and running the department overseeing Brexit. In September 2017, he was moved to a new Europe Unit in the Cabinet Office in Downing Street.[16] This reorganisation increased the isolation of Davis. A new centre of power was created away from his department, which was no longer the hub for Brexit negotiations. Given the importance of Davis to May's survival in the summer of 2017, the speed at which he was then side-lined was surprising.

It was not long before domestic tensions were supplemented by problems in the negotiations themselves. The UK had three mutually incompatible objectives: an exit from the Single Market and the customs union; no hard border on the island of Ireland; and an all-UK approach to Brexit. The difficulty in resolving the tension between these objectives came to be known as the 'Irish trilemma' (Fig. 2.1).[17]

When the talks began in June, the Irish border had been a low salience issue, bracketed along with other miscellaneous issues. Yet it rapidly turned into a key stumbling block that would go on to define the next two years of negotiations. Without guarantees that a physical border

Fig. 2.1 The Irish Trilemma

would not be put in place across the 500 km dividing line, which cut across villages, roads and even houses, and featured 208 border crossing points, the Irish government would not sign off on any deal. The Irish border problem sat uneasily with the other divorce issues. It broke the EU's rule on resolving the past before talking about the future. After all, any resolution was dependent on the nature of the future trade relationship. The UK had in fact pushed for the inclusion of Ireland in phase one of the negotiations. There was an expectation that the border issue could act as a 'Trojan horse', forcing the EU to engage in talks about the future trade relationship within which UK–Irish relations would operate.[18]

Instead, as the autumn of 2017 dragged on, there was little sign of a resolution to the border issue, and there was therefore no possibility of movement to the next stage of negotiations. The European Council's guidelines for the Brexit negotiations, agreed by EU leaders in April 2017, stated that 'sufficient progress' had to be made in phase one before discussions over the future began.[19] With a key European Council meeting approaching in December, the UK was desperate to clear this hurdle.

The UK and EU negotiating teams—led by Oliver Robbins and Sabine Weyand (Michel Barnier's deputy) respectively—agreed that a hard border between Ireland and Northern Ireland must be avoided. If this could not be achieved through the trade agreement between the UK and the EU, the UK would either propose 'specific solutions to address the unique circumstances of the island of Ireland' or remain in 'full alignment' with the EU's Single Market and customs union. This was implicit recognition that, for the Prime Minister, finding a solution that avoided an Irish hard border trumped the UK's other Brexit ambitions. This in turn had implications for two groups. First, strongly Eurosceptic backbenchers in the Conservative Party were concerned about a potential slide towards a softer form of Brexit. Second, there was the DUP, whose raison d'être—the maintenance of Northern Ireland as an equal partner in the UK—appeared threatened. These two groups would go on to form a cohesive and formidable alliance throughout the rest of Theresa May's time as Prime Minister.

When the DUP eventually found out about a leaked draft of the agreement on Monday 4 December 2017—at the very moment when May was en route to Brussels for a lunch with Jean-Claude Juncker to sign off on the deal—the party threatened to pull the plug on its confidence and supply agreement with the Conservatives. This led to a week of whirlwind diplomacy. Negotiations were conducted on two fronts: with the EU Commission in the hope of further concessions and with the DUP's MPs in Westminster, headed by Nigel Dodds and reporting back to their leader Arlene Foster in Belfast. The talks yielded little of substance. The essential problem—that the UK faced a choice between watering down the kind of Brexit it wanted or negotiating different terms for Northern Ireland—remained. In the end, Theresa May simply phoned Arlene Foster at 11 p.m. on Thursday and informed her that she would sign the agreement. The DUP—having said this was 'battle of who blinks first, and we've cut off our eyelids'—buckled, unwilling to pull down the government.[20] That same evening, the Prime Minister slipped out of the Downing Street Christmas Party to board a flight to Brussels from RAF Northolt at 4.30 am on the Friday morning to sign the joint report.

The deal was lauded as a triumph in the House of Commons. The stalwart Conservative Eurosceptic Bill Cash commented on 'the outbreak of unity on the Government Benches'. Anna Soubry, May's most vocal opponent on the opposite wing of the Conservative Party, hailed 'a major step forward'.[21] However, just days later, May's first defeat in the House of Commons demonstrated the fragility of her position (see Chapter 3 pp. 80–81). The rebels were a ragtag group of Conservative Europhiles, who had first begun to meet in September 2016—some determined to rebel, others happy to offer support in private but remain loyal (and, in some cases, remain in government).[22] This group, all careful to note they respected the referendum result, had become more cohesive and assertive after being labelled the 'Brexit Mutineers' on the front page of the *Daily Telegraph* in November 2017. Their amendment to the EU (Withdrawal) Bill, passed by four votes, was designed to force the government to give Parliament a 'Meaningful Vote' over any eventual Brexit deal. These were not anti-government MPs: 7 of the 11 rebels would go on to support Theresa May in the first Meaningful Vote on her deal a year later.[23] Instead, it was the Eurosceptic MPs most vocally opposed to the introduction of the 'Meaningful Vote' who went on to be the group that was most thankful for it.

Meanwhile in Brussels, the European Council greeted the British Prime Minister's short address over dinner with a round of applause before announcing that negotiations could now move on to stage two. For all the warm words, however, a fundamental problem remained. The decision to agree on 'sufficient progress' was based on a fudge, as the 'Irish trilemma' had not been resolved. Rather, the joint report merely confirmed the problem confronting the Prime Minister. Both a 'soft' Brexit, with the UK continuing to align wholesale with the EU's regulations, and a 'hard' Brexit solution that applied to Great Britain but not wholly to Northern Ireland remained live possibilities. May's search for a deal which applied equally to all parts of the UK, gave the UK control over its 'borders, money and laws' and did not create an Irish land border was not over. After all, she told Parliament, 'no UK prime minister could ever agree' to a deal which treated Great Britain and Northern Ireland differently.[24]

Some Eurosceptic Cabinet members were becoming concerned that the joint report had boxed the government in. David Davis, interviewed two days after the deal was signed, described the commitments made on Northern Ireland as merely a 'statement of intent'.[25] The alternative view—which both Dublin and Brussels were keen to stress—was that the UK had made a commitment in good faith which was, in any case, principally a reiteration of the UK's pre-existing obligations under the Good Friday Agreement.

The EU moved quickly to set the terms of the future relationship negotiations. Before the talks began, Michel Barnier unveiled what became an infamous PowerPoint slide displaying the options for a UK–EU trade deal. 'Barnier's staircase'—which descended from the EU flag on the top left to the Canadian flag on the bottom right—was designed to demonstrate the logical implications of the UK's 'red lines'. The

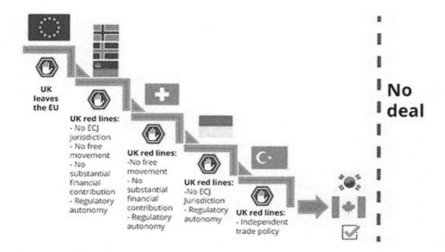

Fig. 2.2   Barnier's staircase

bottom line, which was also the key principle underpinning the EU's negotiating mandate, was that the UK could not 'cherry-pick' which areas of the EU it wanted to engage with. As a result, Theresa May's red lines severely limited the scope of any trade agreement. UK insistence on rejecting any role for the European Court of Justice, commitment to the end of free movement, demands for an end to financial contributions to the EU and emphasis on regaining regulatory autonomy meant that outcomes ranging from the Norwegian arrangement through to Ukraine's association agreement were off the table. The desire for an independent trade policy meant leaving the EU's customs territory, so something akin to Turkey's customs arrangement with the EU was equally off-limits. The power dynamics behind the slide were clear: the EU is a rules-based organisation, unwilling to show flexibility to accommodate the demands of a departing Member State. Beneath this cloak of legal language was naked politics (Fig. 2.2).

The UK, for its part, railed against what one government insider called 'a staircase for rights but an escalator for obligations'.[26] The fact the UK was a large, close competitor to the EU meant each potential model for a deal would come laced with disadvantageous conditions. The EU hoped to ensure that the negotiations were defined by what the UK could not have rather than innovating to accommodate UK demands. Even the bottom rung of the staircase—an agreement like the Comprehensive Economic and Trade Agreement (CETA), which Canada and the EU signed in 2017—was not really on offer. In exchange for a similar comprehensive trade agreement, the UK would have to commit to a regulatory 'level playing field' with the EU in a way that Canada had not.

Theresa May unsuccessfully set out in the first few months of 2018 to change the terms of this discussion. In a speech in March at Mansion House in the City of London, she railed against the EU's approach. She pointed out, not unfairly, that every trade agreement had unique aspects and 'if this is cherry-picking, then every trade arrangement is cherry-picking'.[27] She then set out her desire for a deal that allowed for the free flow of trade in goods but not services, permitted continued membership in select EU agencies and meant that the UK could diverge from EU rules in some areas, while opting in to others. It set out the fundamental principle that the UK must have political freedom, while making the economic case for some convergence with the EU. The speech appeared to have relatively broad support across her party—both Jacob Rees-Mogg, Chair of the Eurosceptic backbench European Research Group (ERG), and Nicky Morgan, then de facto head of the Europhile group of Conservative MPs, took to the *Daily Telegraph* to praise it. Needless to say, in Brussels the speech flopped. One EU diplomat noted acidly that 'she shows she hasn't understood the principles'.[28]

May's Mansion House speech also contained the kernel of a technical idea that was to play a prominent part in the debates to come. The plan for a Facilitated Customs Arrangement (FCA) between the UK and the EU had been cooked up in Whitehall and worked on for over nearly a year. It was conceived as a means of squaring the circle of the UK's key aims—creating a mechanism for the UK to have independent customs rules, while avoiding customs checks on its border with the EU in Ireland. The UK would mirror EU rules and standards on goods coming from the rest of the world, but could then set lower tariffs. These tariff differences could be enforced by tracking, which would involve the UK collecting tariffs on behalf of the EU and vice versa. It was hoped the scheme could unlock the negotiations. Yet while it was supported by May and her inner team, the practical workings of the idea were fiendishly complex.

Perhaps more important than any practical problems was the vehement opposition that the scheme attracted from both the EU and Conservative Eurosceptics. For the former, the scheme was impractical and unworkable. In evidence to the House of Lords EU Select Committee in July 2018, Michel Barnier argued that the FCA would be technically difficult to implement and would create additional red tape.[29] At a press conference a week later, he added that the EU 'cannot – and will not – delegate the application of its customs policy and rules, VAT and excise duty collection to a non-member, who would not be subject to the EU's governance structures'.[30]

Conservative Eurosceptics, meanwhile, felt the customs plan was a customs union by another name and instead preferred an idea that came to be known as 'Maximum Facilitation'—a framework in which technology would be deployed to avoid the need for physical border checks and infrastructure. A proposal reliant on yet to be created 'technological solutions' was even more disliked by the EU than May's customs plan. Yet the broad principle that the border problem could and should be circumvented through technical innovation had influential supporters at the top of government, including David Davis, Boris Johnson, Michael Gove and Sajid Javid. In early May 2018, a crunch meeting of the Brexit Strategy and Negotiations Cabinet Sub-committee was lined up to decide which approach should be government policy. It was split down the middle and no decision was made.

As spring turned to summer, negotiations within the UK government continued. The EU Council in June, seen as a moment of truth for the 'Irish question', came and went with talks on the border issue stalled. Yet the hope remained that by October 2018, a deal could be finalised. The theory was that this would give some time for the process of ratification to be completed by March 2019. In short, time was ticking away and these domestic disagreements needed to come to a head. This was the logic behind the Cabinet showdown at Chequers on Saturday 6 July 2018. May had three main objectives in calling the meeting: to move her colleagues towards explicitly recognising the trade-offs between the economy and political control; to secure collective Cabinet support for a route forward on Brexit; and to gain the explicit approval of the EU for the direction being taken.

What was perhaps most striking about the discussions at Chequers is that they focused on a Brexit solution that was far from ideal for the UK economy. The government's proposal centred on the UK signing up to a 'common rulebook', which meant effectively staying in the EU's Single

Market for goods. This did nothing to protect the UK's much larger services sector, protecting UK–EU trade in the areas where the UK had a trade deficit while damaging the largest sectors of the UK economy.[31] It was not the explicit customs union that both the small Europhile wing of May's party and the Labour Party were now noisily demanding. Yet it also envisaged a continued role for the European courts, enraging those animated by the UK regaining its sovereignty. The core of the plan was the Facilitated Customs Arrangement, which was seen as hugely problematic within the Conservative Party and hard for the EU to swallow. It did a remarkably effective job of pleasing nobody.

The key benefit of the package—and the reason May would stake what remained of her political capital on it—was it offered a route to an all-UK Brexit that did not necessitate a border in Ireland. Boris Johnson criticised it on exactly these grounds in June, arguing in a private discussion subsequently leaked to the press that by putting the Irish question before everything else, May was 'allowing the tail to wag the dog'.[32] For a Foreign Secretary, it seemed remarkably undiplomatic language on the Anglo-Irish relationship. It was also the approach made explicit in the joint report, which had been signed up to and supported six months earlier by the entire Cabinet. However, the Foreign Secretary had a point: the entire Brexit process now hinged on Northern Ireland.

The drama and spectacle of the day at Chequers was designed to engineer the semblance of consensus among a fragmented Cabinet. Ministers were greeted in the foyer that morning with business cards for local taxi firms, so they could make the 40-mile journey back to London if they resigned and lost access to ministerial cars. In the run-up, May's political team spent weeks courting each Cabinet member individually.[33] Junior pro-Brexit ministers who did not attend were offered ministerial promotions as they were lined up to back the proposals.[34] The morning saw presentations from Oliver Robbins on the plan's feasibility, the Business Secretary Greg Clark outlining why dynamic alignment with the EU was vital for UK manufacturing, and Julian Smith, the Chief Whip, describing an increasingly restless House of Commons. May was finally attempting to turn the screw.

That afternoon, a five-hour meeting saw each Cabinet minister express their view. Seven out of the 27 present spoke out against the plans: David Davis, Boris Johnson, Andrea Leadsom, Penny Mordaunt, Liam Fox, Esther McVey and Sajid Javid.[35] May's team were braced for, and unsurprised by, the intervention of Davis. Johnson said that attempts to talk up the proposal were 'polishing a turd'. Some textual changes were fought for and won by Johnson—including one that would prevent British citizens appealing directly to the European Court of Justice and a second that spelt out how Parliament could scrutinise or reject future EU regulations. Yet apparently the pivotal intervention was from Michael Gove, who delivered a speech that, in the words of one minister present, 'pulled the rug from under Boris and David Davis's feet'. Gove said he was convinced of the unknowable risks to the Brexit project of not pushing through this plan.

In a sense, the choreography of Chequers was effective. Most ministers caveated their concern with messages of loyalty. During the evening meal, Boris Johnson made a speech toasting the return of Cabinet unity. David Davis gave indications to May's inner circle throughout the day that he was not happy, telling one during the lunchtime break 'if you think I'm just going to accept this and we're fine, you've got another thing coming'. His body language throughout the day showed he was unhappy.[36] However, he later gave a speech indicating he would continue in government, and Johnson spoke of his relief that the whole Cabinet was now 'singing from the same hymn sheet'.[37] Gavin Barwell, May's Chief of Staff, said that 'the meeting itself went better than we could ever have hoped ... the mood at the end of the day was almost euphoric'.[38] The *Sunday Times* ran the next day with: 'Chequers Mate: Theresa May Ambush Routs Cabinet Brexiteers'.

This apparent return of Cabinet unity proved short-lived. Within 48 hours, May had lost her Foreign and Brexit Secretaries. The latter, David Davis, resolved to resign in the car on the way back from Chequers. The former, Boris Johnson, followed—his resignation widely viewed, including within Downing Street, as a direct result of Davis' departure and an act of political positioning. May promoted another Brexiter to the Cabinet, with Dominic Raab replacing Davis (having rung him to secure permission) as Brexit Secretary.[39] Yet the damage from these resignations would reverberate in the months to come, with the departed rallying opposition to the Prime Minister at every turn. The failure of Chequers also did damage to already weak public support for May's approach to Brexit (see Chapter 8, pp. 284–285). Approval ratings of the government's performance on Brexit from YouGov fell a little from −63 to −72 among Remain supporters after Chequers, but among Leave voters there was a much larger fall from −27 to −60.[40]

'Cabinet discipline in tatters' (Nicola Jennings, *The Guardian*, 1 July 2018 © Nicola Jennings)

Chequers also failed to gain clear support from the EU. May had spent the days in the lead-up to Chequers meeting with both the Prime Minister of the Netherlands Mark Rutte and the German Chancellor Angela Merkel. Both had indicated support for the UK's direction of travel, and the aftermath of these meetings was the moment some in May's team felt most optimistic that they could see the Brexit process through to completion.[41] Michel Barnier and his team of negotiators privately saw Chequers as a positive step and were encouraged that the UK was beginning to flesh out a plan on the basis of a free trade area partnership. Yet the EU's public reaction was muted. The EU's negotiators quietly banked May's idea of a common rulebook before opposing it as 'cherry-picking'. And they flatly rejected the notion that the UK might collect some customs duties on behalf of the EU on the grounds that it would damage the territorial integrity of the Single Market. It was no small irony that May's successor would eventually find a route through stage one of Brexit by using a very similar customs plan and applying it to Northern Ireland alone.

The aftermath of Chequers was not the first time May was left isolated by the EU's negotiators and would not be the last. The EU's leaders had long taken the view that any alternative Conservative Prime Minister was likely to be even more difficult to deal with. Yet this did not lead them to offer much support to the embattled incumbent. As it was, it took a special summit of EU leaders in Salzburg in September—and a further humiliation of the Prime Minister—for the unravelling of Chequers to be complete. Domestic support had collapsed and neither wing of May's party was in the mood to compromise. However, May went to Salzburg—supported in part by civil service briefings—hoping that the EU would welcome Chequers as a sign of a new realism, breathing live into her plan and reinforcing her position at home.

Tone-deaf diplomacy from the UK and Instagram diplomacy from the EU soon put paid to that. An article from the Prime Minister published in the German newspaper *Die Welt* overnight called for an evolution in the EU position.[42] On Wednesday evening, after dinner, May was given the floor to make her case. Yet she merely treated her colleagues to a recap of her op-ed: the UK had shown flexibility, the EU should reciprocate. To the EU, it sounded like more of the same. Chequers was meant to signal a shift to a more flexible UK approach. However, once again, the UK was appealing to EU leaders, over the head of the Commission, for special treatment. The next day, after a leaders' lunch with May outside the room, it was agreed that the Chequers proposals should be rejected wholesale. Donald Tusk, the President of the European Council, delivered a damning press conference, before posting a photo on Instagram with Theresa May, hovering over a tray of cakes in Salzburg, with the caption 'A piece of cake, perhaps? Sorry, no cherries'.[43] The Prime Minister, believing she had shown flexibility, was visibly angry and shaken. In response, she sought solace in a favourite line, telling the press conference that 'no deal is better than a bad deal'. Heading into the final few months of talks, UK–EU relations had never been more strained.

The thrust of the Chief Whip's presentation at Chequers was that, unless the Cabinet started making decisions, Parliament would begin to force the government's hand. By July 2018, just 3 of the 12 pieces of legislation necessary to prepare for Brexit had made it into law. Key legislation on trade and customs, required for the UK to operate its own trade policy, had been on hold for months. Other issues requiring legislation, such as fisheries policy, had only just seen a White Paper published. On immigration, there was radio silence. The reason for this delay was that legislation would provide a vehicle for dissent, demonstrating support in the House of Commons for varieties of Brexit that May did not want to deliver.

Prior to Chequers, the main concern for May's management of her parliamentary party was a small, vocal rump of Europhile MPs. In February 2018, following the second reading of the Trade Bill, Jeremy Corbyn had shifted Labour policy towards a 'comprehensive UK-EU customs union' (see Chapter 4, pp. 119–120). The latent cross-party opposition to the government's approach now had a tangible alternative policy proposal with which to attract the potentially critical votes of 'soft' Brexit Conservative rebels. Opposition parties, including the SNP and Liberal Democrats, were willing to tactically back a customs union as a means of prising apart the government's majority. As a result, the government's Brexit legislation programme stalled.

By July, the government decided it could wait no longer. In the penultimate week before the summer recess, the Customs and Trade Bills had their Third Reading in the House of Commons. Their fate underlined the dilemma confronting the government. Emboldened by the resignations at Chequers, Eurosceptics used the Customs Bill to launch a campaign of guerrilla warfare against the Chequers proposals. They introduced amendments designed to make a nonsense of the core tenets of the Chequers package: making it illegal for the UK to collect customs on behalf of the EU, as well as binding the government to oppose any type of customs border in the Irish sea. The Trade Bill, on the other hand, came with the long-anticipated prospect of soft Brexit backbench amendments calling for the negotiation of a customs union. Having chosen a middle path, Theresa May found herself squeezed from both sides.

The government's response underlined where Number 10 thought the power lay within the Conservative Party: the ERG were appeased, while the Europhiles were taken on and defeated. The government accepted the Eurosceptic amendments, arguing (implausibly) that they did not contradict the core tenets of the Chequers plan. The next day, pro-EU

MPs tabled an amendment calling for membership of a customs union. A dozen Tory MPs rebelled, but a group of five pro-Brexit Labour MPs rebelled in support of the government and the amendment was seen off by six votes. In desperation, Chief Whip Julian Smith broke pairing arrangements with MPs on maternity leave. A leaked WhatsApp message from government whips suggested that 'if Labour rebels hadn't stepped in tonight, we'd have pulled third reading, confidence vote tomorrow, GE in 2 weeks' time. That's what our 12 Remain MPs did tonight'.[44] The whips' narrow and hard-fought victory on the Trade and Customs Bills helped the government live to fight another day, but was to prove one of its final Brexit victories in the House of Commons.

In truth, the Labour and Conservative frontbench positions on Brexit were not a million miles apart. Both parties wanted to leave the Single Market, neither was calling for a second referendum, and the distance between a UK–EU 'common rulebook' for goods and a 'customs union' with the EU was not huge. Yet on the backbenches and at the grassroots level, the Brexit debate was beginning to shift opinion in both parties towards more extreme outcomes. The public, too, were becoming more polarised. While there had been no decisive shift in overall perceptions of whether Brexit was a good or bad idea, Remainers had become more emotionally attached to their view on Brexit.[45] In the referendum, the enthusiasm gap had worked in the opposite direction. Yet Leave voters were also increasingly bullish about the most extreme resolution to the Brexit process: leaving the EU with no deal in place at all. Three-quarters of Leave voters felt the disruptions of no deal would be brief and relatively minor, with many thinking there would be no costs at all.[46] By the time party conference season kicked off in September and October 2018, a further referendum on EU membership and a 'no deal' Brexit had both entered the political mainstream as mechanisms to resolve the Brexit impasse.

'Second Referendum' (Martin Rowson, *The Guardian*, 12 November 2018 © Martin Rowson)

The People's Vote campaign, launched in April 2018, was a coalition of nine disparate pro-EU campaign groups. Its name—first mooted by the Green MP Caroline Lucas—was an attempt to project an anti-estab-lishment image. Yet far and away the largest group within the People's Vote network was Open Europe, a renamed version of the official 2016 Remain campaign. It brought with it vital data from that referendum campaign, but also political baggage. The Chair of the People's Vote campaign, Roland Rudd, a PR director and brother of Cabinet Minister Amber Rudd, gave interviews to the *Today* programme live from Davos. People's Vote senior staff were a mix of New Labour veterans such as Peter Mandelson and Alistair Campbell, Labour Corbynsceptics such as Chuka Umunna and Patrick Heneghan, and Liberal Democrats. All of which did little to dampen the idea that this was a centrist 'Remainia redux'. Yet the campaign quickly became effective as a lobbying force within the Labour Party, which was from the outset its main target (see Chapter 4, pp. 120–122).[47] For pro-referendum campaigners, fears of a no deal Brexit—an outcome Leave campaigners had repeatedly disavowed in 2016—helped mobilise support for another vote. Perhaps more importantly, framing a second referendum against a no deal Brexit set up a fight the People's Vote campaign felt it could win.

The 'People's Vote' swiftly became part of the lexicon of British politics. It quickly gained the official support of all the smaller pro-Remain parties in the Commons.[48] Key to the campaign's messaging was the idea that a referendum could be used as a method of last resort to avoid a no deal Brexit. This framing was essential to win support from Labour MPs either nervous of being seen trying to overturn the previous referendum or suspicious of a campaign staffed by so many opponents of the Corbyn project. The campaign won its first success at the 2018 Labour conference, when the principle of a second referendum was accepted by the party for the first time, albeit only as one of several options to be considered if Labour could not secure a general election (see Chapter 4, pp. 123–124). Corbyn's allies had hoped concession on the referendum principle would resolve the issue, but the People's Vote team banked the win and continued agitating for a stronger Labour commitment within and outside Parliament.

While the People's Vote campaign focused on Labour, the campaign to normalise no deal was primarily a fight within the Conservative Party. Official preparations for a no deal were ramped up over the summer, a concession made by May to Eurosceptics to keep them onside at Chequers. In August, the government went public with a series of no deal notices setting out the impact of trading with the EU without an agreement. Prior to the Conservative Party conference, David Davis shared a platform with Nigel Farage supporting a 'clean Brexit'. For highly Eurosceptic Conservative members, the stars of the conference were Davis and Boris Johnson. Johnson did not explicitly call in his speech for no deal, but attacked May's plans as a 'constitutional outrage' and called for the party to 'Chuck Chequers'.[49] Yet while May repeated in her speech that the UK would leave with no deal if necessary, she clearly had little intention of doing so. She survived the conference, but the appeal of no deal had risen and little had been done to lay the groundwork for the necessary compromises to come.

While party politics played out at the conference centres, in Brussels the negotiations were reaching their endgame. The day after May's conference speech, Michel Barnier signalled that negotiations were close to completion. A host of issues, ranging from warm words on a security partnership to guarantees on the rights of UK and EU citizens, had been resolved. The two parts of the Brexit withdrawal process, a legal withdrawal agreement on the 'divorce' issues and a political declaration on ambitions for future trade talks, were nearly ready to sign.

The outstanding issue remained the Irish border and what had come to be known as the 'backstop'. Both sides agreed that a central aim of any future trade deal should be to avoid a border. The question was how best to avoid it if a trade deal was not achievable. May's proposal was that if it came to it, the UK would effectively stay in the customs union with the EU for a limited period. The EU instead favoured Northern Ireland staying in the EU customs union, large parts of the Single Market and the EU VAT system, thus diverging from the rest of the UK. Michel Barnier continually emphasised that any insurance policy could only apply to Northern Ireland rather than the UK as a whole. An all-UK customs agreement was seen as something to be negotiated in the next stage of the process, hence not something that could be included in the withdrawal agreement. As ever, there were political interests lurking behind this legalistic rhetoric. There were fears among the Member States that an all-UK customs arrangement would allow the UK tariff-free access without the full obligations of customs union membership, providing British firms with a comparative advantage. With no agreement in sight, the October EU Council summit, pencilled in as the moment of truth, came and went.

It was at this point, in the final weeks of the negotiation, that the UK secured its hardest-won concession. Due in part to pressure from the Irish government, Barnier relented: if a solution to the Irish border issue could not be found, the whole of the UK would remain a de facto member of the EU's customs union until an arrangement to avoid a hard border was mutually agreed. For May, this ensured, come what may, an all-UK approach to Brexit. The aim remained a looser relationship with the EU and an imaginative solution to border issues. But, failing that, the agreement ensured that Northern Ireland and the UK would be treated the same. A draft deal had been agreed in principle. On Wednesday 14 November, a marathon five-hour Cabinet session backed the deal and, that evening, the draft text was published. An emergency summit was scheduled for the last Sunday of November, bringing together all EU leaders to sign off on the deal. Both sides had four and a half months to ratify the agreement.

The only problem was that Eurosceptic Conservative MPs saw the backstop differently from the outset—not as a temporary fix, but as a back door to indefinite customs union membership. Why, they asked, would the EU negotiate a solution to the Irish border issue when it had locked the UK in to being a rule taker (on goods) and a permanent part of the EU's economic orbit? Worse still, they saw the political declaration as providing evidence—given its promise to 'build on' the plans set out in the backstop—that the direction of travel was towards such a closer relationship. With no time limit on the backstop and no way for the UK to leave it unilaterally, the UK could be stuck with the supposedly temporary arrangement indefinitely. For the EU and UK negotiators, the backstop was a sub-optimal compromise solution to cut the Gordian knot of the Irish border. To most of the key advocates of Brexit in the Conservative Party, it was not a compromise; it was a trap.[50]

The morning of 15 November 2018 is one Theresa May will want to forget. Her Brexit deal—sweated over for months—fell apart within hours. Just before 9 am, Dominic Raab took to Twitter to announce his resignation. Number 10's Director of Legislative Affairs Nikki da Costa, employed to smooth the passage of the treaty through Parliament, also handed in her resignation. At 10.30 am, the Prime Minister took to the House of Commons to defend the published agreement. For the first time, she made explicit the Hobson's choice she wished to force upon MPs, telling the Commons 'the choice is clear: we can choose to leave with no deal; we can risk no Brexit at all; or we can choose to unite and support the best deal that can be negotiated – this deal'.

'Support my deal or else!' (Ben Jennings, *The i* paper, 24 November 2018 © Ben Jennings)

The Prime Minister did not get the response she wanted. Eight of the first ten Conservative MPs to stand spoke against the agreement. Sir Bill Cash described the 585-page document as 'a testament to broken promises, failed negotiations and abject capitulation to the EU'.[51] The only support for the deal came from the Europhile wing of her party, which, if anything, emboldened the larger Eurosceptic wing—confirming that this was not a deal they could, or should, support.

The launch of May's deal provides a case study in failed political strategy, communications and tactics. The strategic problem for May was that she had spent the previous two years telling her MPs that 'no deal was better than a bad deal'. It was therefore hard for her to credibly claim now that what to her Eurosceptic MPs looked like a bad deal was in fact better than no deal. A majority of Conservative MPs not only believed by this point that no deal was viable, but also that the obstacles to an acceptable alternative deal were being exaggerated.[52] Meanwhile, those Labour MPs opposed to a second referendum and apparently willing to vote for a deal did not believe the Prime Minister when she said she would carry through no deal if necessary. May's hope was for a domino effect: first the DUP and some Conservative Eurosceptics would back the deal, then deal-curious Labour MPs would get the government over the line. But rather than playing one side off against the other, May's strategy merely emboldened both. Everyone expected someone else to budge first and take the political hit from backing the deal.

The communications problem reflected a failure by the government and the Prime Minister to articulate the benefits of their proposed Brexit deal. Rory Stewart—until then a largely unknown Prisons Minister—rose to prominence in large part because he was one of the few frontbenchers willing to publicly defend the government's agreement with any conviction. After the EU formally approved the deal, the decision was made to conduct an intense two-week campaign appealing directly to the electorate over the heads of MPs. This in itself was a curious strategy, as it was Parliament that would ultimately decide on its fate. Moreover, this approach backfired even on its own terms. Polls showed around a quarter of the electorate supported the deal, while half opposed it—and opposition increased as people heard more about the deal.[53]

The tactical difficulties centred around what the government should do next, as it became obvious that the Commons vote on the deal would be heavily lost. In normal times, a process of attrition and bargaining would take place as government whips picked off dissenters. But times were not normal. A tipping point had been reached, and a large number of Conservative MPs simply could not be negotiated with. While the whips had known for some time there was trouble, by early December, enough Tory MPs had made public their opposition that even a close result was impossible. As a result, after three and a half days of debate, May decided on 11 December to delay the vote until after Christmas, conceding her deal would be 'rejected by a considerable margin'. The next day, she faced a challenge to her leadership (see Chapter 3, pp. 89–90).

The Prime Minister went into the Christmas break boxed in and without a plan. Meanwhile, Tory MPs went back to their constituencies to be lobbied by Conservative members now strongly against the deal. The one virtue of delay lay in the fact that it pressed MPs closer against the Brexit deadline of 31 March, potentially focusing minds on the potential for the UK to 'fall out' with no deal.

All this changed the week Parliament returned from recess, thanks to an amendment tabled by the pro-referendum Tory MP Dominic Grieve. Speaker John Bercow—in his most controversial and probably most significant act in the Brexit story—allowed the vote on Grieve's proposal as an amendment to a business motion, in apparent contravention of precedent and, according to some, against the advice of the Commons Clerk, Sir David Natzler.[54] The Grieve amendment specified that, in the event the Prime Minister lost the 'Meaningful Vote', the House of Commons would be able to vote on an alternative. May, in other words, would have to quickly come up with an alternative plan to avoid Parliament taking matters into its own hands. The government had under-estimated the willingness of its parliamentary opponents to do whatever it took. The Prime Minister responded by imploring MPs to consider the gravity of the political moment, telling the House of Commons that this was 'the most significant vote that any of us will ever be part of in our political careers'.

When the defeat came, it was even more shattering than expected. A total of 202 voted in favour of the agreement, while a massive 432 voted against. May suffered the largest defeat experienced by any government for at least a century. In all, 118 Tory MPs rebelled—the largest mutiny in post-war history for the Conservative Party. Less than a third of Conservative MPs who did not hold a government job voted for the Brexit deal. Just three Labour MPs did so.

'Nothing has changed!' (Morten Morland, *Sunday Times*, 20 January 2019 © Morten Morland)

With hindsight, the emphatic parliamentary rejection brought with it a certain clarity. There was no route to a deal via the parliamentary Conservative Party. The EU—which had (once again) refused to offer the Prime Minister any help in December—would again be faced with its own Hobson's choice: resume the negotiations in order to provide the Prime Minister with something to take to her restive party or face the possibility of her replacement. The state of opinion in the Conservative Party, as well as the processes by which it selects its leaders, suggested any alternative would be even more hardline on Brexit.

Yet, remarkably, between the first and second votes—on 15 January and 12 March 2019 respectively—nothing at all changed. The two negotiations May was conducting—in Westminster with parliamentarians and in Brussels with the EU—may as well have been taking place on different planets. At home, Conservative MPs came up with two schemes notionally intended to reunify their party. The 'Malthouse Compromise', named after MP Kit Malthouse, was sold as an attempt to bridge the divide between Conservative Brexit factions. In truth, it was little more than a jargon-laden rehash of the 'technical solutions' approach to the Irish border issue as well as a wilful misinterpretation of what was permissible under international law. The 'Brady Amendment' was more successful at achieving its limited core objective—signalling to the EU that the Conservative Party would only support backstop arrangements with an 'exit clause' or time limit. The amendment passed the Commons with a majority and near-universal support from Conservative MPs. The message was clear: remove the backstop and a deal could be passed by the UK Parliament.

It was up to the UK's negotiators, led by Oliver Robbins, to parse this signal into something the EU could accept. This proved an impossible ask. The negotiations produced no new compromises and instead merely reprised some of the greatest hits of the previous two years. Donald Tusk made an incendiary public intervention, speaking of a 'special place in hell' for those who had campaigned for Brexit. May personally appealed to EU capitals, to little effect. A second vote on the deal, pencilled in for Valentine's Day, was delayed.

In what came to be her penultimate throw of the dice, May turned to her Attorney General, Geoffrey Cox. The Eurosceptic wing of her party were looking for legally binding guarantees that the UK could not be stranded in the backstop in perpetuity. May despatched Cox to Brussels to seek such a guarantee. The political narrative almost wrote itself: Cox—whose previous legal advice that the UK could not unilaterally exit the backstop had been made public—performed a volte face, thus providing the cover Eurosceptics needed to back the Prime Minister's deal. Cox's style—he sunnily proclaimed to Michel Barnier on his arrival that 'I haven't been here in 40 years'—was reported to have been a problem in negotiations.[55] But more fundamentally, there was an acute difference when it came to substance. At the margins of the EU-Arab summit on 24–25 February, in informal talks with Jean-Claude Juncker and Donald Tusk, May had got a hint of what was available from the EU: a commitment that the EU would not act in bad faith to keep the UK in the backstop against its will.

This, however, was never going to be enough for Cox. On 12 March, the day of the second Meaningful Vote, he presented his advice that the legal principles behind the backstop remained unchanged. The vote which followed was the second-largest defeat for any government for at least a century. A handful of backbench MPs, including David Davis, switched to support May. Yet she still lost by 149 votes. She could only cling on in the hope that other Brexit options would fail, leaving her deal as the only route forward. The following day, a non-binding but highly symbolic vote was held on the principle of ruling out a no deal exit. As the government was still notionally committed to no deal as an option, May whipped against. However, pro-deal Conservative MPs—among them 13 ministers, including four Cabinet ministers—voted against no deal and the government suffered yet another defeat, by 321 to 278. The next day, the House of Commons voted in favour of an extension of Article 50 if a deal could not be agreed.

Throughout February and March, May had argued the only alterna-tive to her deal was a no deal Brexit on 31 March.[56] Asking her troops to march through the lobby in favour of an extension put an end to that pretence. It was almost of secondary importance that only 112 of the Prime Minister's 320 MPs followed her. May took to a public broadcast, appealing to the public over the heads of her restive MPs: 'you are tired of the infighting. You are tired of the political games and the arcane pro-cedural rows … it is now time for MPs to decide'.[57]

It was certainly true that, having voted against both the deal on offer and against no deal, MPs had given no indication what, if anything, they would support instead. Disparate cross-party groups proliferated in the House of Commons: the People's Vote campaign, its momentum bol-stered by the largest public demonstration in London since the Iraq war; advocates of the UK remaining members of the Single Market and a cus-toms union (the 'Common Market 2.0' approach); proponents of a cus-toms union only; and the hard Eurosceptic no deal-sympathetic ERG. Members of May's Cabinet and inner team had been pressing for a series of 'indicative votes'—unwhipped, with MPs able to demonstrate unhin-dered where opinion lay in the House of Commons. For some, the hope was that this might clear a path towards a softer Brexit. Others hoped it would underline to MPs that the Prime Minister's deal was the only form of Brexit available.

Rather than providing a novel means of achieving consensus, the indicative votes turned into a circular firing squad. The failure of both rounds of indicative votes to produce a majority for any route forward served merely to reinforce impressions of a deadlocked Parliament. There were some near-misses. A customs union received the support of 276 MPs, failing to gain a majority by an agonising three votes. Advocates of Single Market membership reluctantly lent their support to a second referendum on the assumption that the favour would be reciprocated. Yet the People's Vote campaign adopted a scorched earth strategy, pressing MPs to reject any form of Brexit to ensure that none could muster a majority unless tied to a second referendum (see also Chapter 4, pp. 124–126). Partly as a result, the referendum proposal received the most votes—280—and if the eight Conservative MPs who had voted in favour of both a Single Market and a customs union had backed it, it would have garnered a majority. Yet even if one of the narrowly defeated proposals had won a majority, it would have faced substantial obstacles to becoming policy. Within Number 10, there was no working assumption that any option under consideration in the process—even the customs union option that May was most sympathetic towards—would be taken up as government policy regardless of the votes it received.[58]

'Zen-like calm' (Martin Rowson, *The Guardian*, 12 April 2019 © Martin Rowson)

Between these two rounds of indicative votes, on 29 March (the original Article 50 deadline) May had one final go at passing her Brexit deal. Speaker John Bercow ruled out another 'meaningful vote' on the deal, but this did not prevent the government from bringing forward the legislation—the Withdrawal Agreement Bill. Options, particularly leaving without a deal, appeared to be slipping off the table. May sensed an opportunity and played what felt like her final card, promising the 1922 Committee she would resign once her withdrawal agreement has been secured. As a result, the numbers began to move. Staunchly pro-Brexit MPs, including Boris Johnson and Jacob Rees-Mogg, indicated that they would vote for the deal. If pro-Brexit Labour MPs and the DUP could be brought onside, the numbers were looking close.

Yet if Brexiters saw an opportunity in May's downfall, the 20 or so Labour MPs who were 'deal-curious' saw a problem. Few were willing to back the deal without changes, but with May's political authority shot, the concessions they sought in exchange for their support were undeliverable. Guarantees from May on elements like workers' rights and parliamentary powers would not bind her successor. In the end, May fell to a 57-vote defeat—closer, but nowhere near close enough.

With all other options now exhausted, May turned her mind to two sets of negotiations she had long promised to avoid: cross-party talks with the Labour Party and discussions over a lengthy extension of the Article 50 deadline with the EU. The former were doomed to failure and the latter were only a negotiation in the loosest sense. The cross-party talks were taken seriously by all involved (see Chapter 4, pp. 126–127). Yet the divide between Labour, led by Keir Starmer, and the Conservative Party, led by David Lidington, was unbridgeable. No matter what substantive policy changes the government was willing to make—and it was ready to agree to near-enough anything—it was unable to deliver the referendum now demanded by a growing cohort of Labour MPs. Labour's negotiators, like the 'deal-curious' MPs who were flirting with supporting the government, also doubted May had the authority to push through any concessions, describing the process as 'like trying to negotiate with a company going into liquidation'.[59] The Conservative negotiators did, in fact, offers provisions to allow a vote on a referendum at the Second Reading and Report Stage. But neither side could magic away the parliamentary arithmetic, which favoured neither the deal nor a second referendum.

There was significant disagreement within the EU on how much extra time the UK should be given. Following a brief technical extension of a fortnight, a special European Council meeting was convened on 10 April. This turned out to be fraught. While an extension could mean the UK's continued membership, complicating discussions around the next EU budget, a long extension of 9 or 12 months was supported by the vast majority. Yet French President Emmanuel Macron set himself up against any lengthy extension—ostensibly to force the UK into a decision, but primarily due to his desire to be seen as a defender of the European project against the Brexit threat, something he saw as playing well against the populist opponents he faced at home. At one point, Jean-Claude Juncker was said to have interrupted the discussion to say that 'we are now only solving French domestic problems'.

The eventual outcome—an extension to 31 October, with a review at the June European Council summit—was arguably the worst of all worlds: long enough to enrage Brexiteers, but too short to change the political fundamentals. Donald Tusk warned the UK not to 'waste' the additional time, but in truth the five months—much of it over summer— gave time for little else than the Conservative leadership contest that followed soon after. May, outside the room, had to accept whatever she was offered, the UK's immediate future being out of its own hands.

A tortuous set of elections for the European Parliament, an inevitable side-effect of this extension, were hardly the best use of political energy. The UK government was legally obligated to hold a contest that had, for two decades, provided a platform for Nigel Farage. While May attempted to wish these elections away—hoping they would not have to take place and then, when they did, holding no launch event and producing no Conservative manifesto—Farage had been preparing for this event for months. Farage's new vehicle, the Brexit Party, was formally launched in April 2019. Within five weeks, the party had 100,000 members and millions in donations. Discontent within the Conservative Party had been given an outlet and a figurehead (see Chapter 5, pp. 166–168).

That Farage proved adept at political insurgency surprised no one who had followed his long political career. Perhaps more surprising was the surge in support for the Liberal Democrats. Invigorated by a successful performance in local elections and the salience of the Brexit question, the party topped the poll in London—including in Jeremy Corbyn's home turf of Islington—with a straightforward pro-referendum message:

'Bollocks to Brexit' (see Chapter 5, pp. 169–171). The results for the Conservative Party were diabolical: the party polled just 9%, dropping from 19 seats to 4 under the list-based system. Less than one in five of the Conservative Party's own members voted for the party. Nor did Labour fare much better, winning 14% with fewer than half of the party's members voting for it.[60]

Both major parties emerged with difficult lessons to learn. For Labour, the result underscored a deepening dilemma: in attempting to please both sides, they had pleased neither, losing votes in both Remain and Leave areas. The biggest problem for the Conservative Party was the new Brexit Party insurgency. But the resurgence of the Liberal Democrats also opened up a new defensive front for the Conservatives in affluent, older areas in the south. Opinion polling in the summer of 2019 suggested an unprecedented four-party contest (see Chapter 8, pp. 282–284). Some polls had the Brexit Party and the Liberal Democrats tied with Labour and the Tories.[61] May announced her resignation the day after polling day.

When Donald Tusk told the UK not to waste the Brexit extension, a Conservative leadership contest was not necessarily what he had in mind. Yet given the time provided by the compromise at the EU Council, an internal party contest was probably one of the few routes to breaking the deadlock. The contest certainly shed light on the consensus within the governing party: four of the five candidates, including frontrunner Boris Johnson, made clear they were willing to countenance a no deal Brexit (see Chapter 1, pp. 1–9).

Elected as leader and Prime Minister at the end of July, Johnson had two options: he could seek to kill off the Brexit Party by embracing a no deal Brexit or he could attempt to renegotiate the existing Brexit deal. He was open to either path, but, regardless of which route he eventually chose, he was determined to make the threat of a no deal departure credible to the EU. Senior figures in the European Commission are clear that, under May, they never saw no deal as a serious threat. Under Johnson, who had won the leadership campaign on a pledge that he would rather 'die in a ditch' than have the UK remain an EU member after 31 October, the EU never laboured under this illusion. In truth, contingency planning for a no deal Brexit had been taking place for some time, and £4.2 billion of Treasury resources had already been allocated to preparations. Yet the Johnson government committed a further £2.1

billion, as well as to a 'Get Ready for Brexit' publicity blitz informing the UK public to prepare, come what may, for the implications for leaving the EU on 31 October. While this activity reinforced the perception that Johnson was pursuing a no deal strategy, it was the leaked contingency planning for no deal—known as 'Operation Yellowhammer' —that underlined what was at stake, with warnings of a rise in public disorder, higher food prices and reduced medical supplies.

Boris Johnson's opponents inside and outside his party were concerned that the new Prime Minister would choose a no deal Brexit as the path of least political resistance. As a result, when Parliament returned after the summer recess, the anti-no deal Commons majority looked to flex its muscles. The opponents of no deal Brexit were now reinforced by a tranche of Conservative ex-ministers who came to be known as the 'Gaukeward Squad', after their ringleader, former Justice Secretary David Gauke. The removal of this group of MPs from government meant that there was unity around the Cabinet table, but their presence on the backbenches strengthened Europhile Tory rebels. The new Prime Minister lost six votes in six days, forcing the government to release its no deal planning, putting through legislation to stop a no deal Brexit and rejecting Johnson's attempt to force a snap election. When the rebels voted to change House of Commons standing orders to allow the passage of legislation enabling a further extension of the Article 50 deadline, Johnson withdrew the whip from 21 of them, including the Father of the House, two former Chancellors (one of whom headed the Treasury just 40 days previously), a candidate in the recently concluded leadership contest, a further seven former Cabinet ministers and Nicholas Soames, the grandson of Winston Churchill.

Johnson's next move, proroguing Parliament, backfired when the Supreme Court ruled unanimously that the government had acted unlawfully in doing so. Yet while Johnson lost the legal case, this dramatic move helped him to win the political argument, demonstrating to Leave voters that he would do whatever it took to 'get Brexit done'. Polls showed voters who had flirted with the Brexit Party over the summer were beginning to coalesce around Johnson's Conservatives. These debates also demonstrated the limitations of Johnson's opponents, who could still agree on nothing beyond stopping a no deal scenario. Johnson's success in convincing his opponents that he intended to leave without a deal helped him with his next manoeuvre: selling a flawed renegotiation of May's deal. Opponents of Brexit had put their chips on opposing no deal. When Johnson returned with a renegotiated agreement, they were gazumped.

While the domestic politics of no deal took centre stage, in the background Johnson's EU sherpa David Frost was laying the groundwork for a renegotiated deal. It was reported that Johnson's inner team fractured during the repeated defeats of early September, opening up a divide between those who leaned towards continuing the campaign against MPs blocking no deal, led by senior aide Dominic Cummings, and others who felt there was an opening for a deal.[62] Johnson was persuaded to opt for a deal after attending security briefings on the sobering prospect of a return to terrorist violence in Northern Ireland. He subsequently appealed to German Chancellor Angela Merkel, who told him that going over the head of the EU's negotiators would be fruitless: a deal needed the support of Dublin and Brussels, who were both working in close cooperation. To drive this home, Merkel told Johnson that it would always be easier for Germany to leave the EU than the UK, given the UK's commitments to retaining peace in Northern Ireland.

The key moment in talks came on 10 October at Thornton Manor in Liverpool, following bilateral discussions between Irish Taoiseach Leo Varadkar and Johnson. For three hours, the two leaders met alone. The key to a solution was that Northern Ireland would leave the EU customs union with the rest of the UK. However, it would be treated for administrative purposes as if it had not in order to ensure no hard border. Akin to Theresa May's proposed customs partnership, a system of rebates would ensure that Northern Ireland residents would pay the UK tariff only on goods that were not destined for the European Single Market. The deal entrenched a permanent relationship between Northern Ireland and the EU that was different from that between Great Britain and the EU. The UK could not then be 'trapped in the backstop' because it had become the 'frontstop'—applied from the outset, but only to Northern Ireland.

'Nearly...within...reach...' (Dave Brown, *The Independent*, 15 October 2019 © Dave Brown)

As a result, the Prime Minister secured something old: repackaging the customs plan mooted by May. He also secured something new: a consent mechanism which meant that, in theory at least, Northern Ireland could leave these arrangements if a cross-community majority supported doing so. However, the numbers to get this deal through Parliament were extremely tight. The DUP—now facing a deal which explicitly treated Northern Ireland differently from the rest of the UK—felt betrayed. As a result, the Prime Minister now also needed something borrowed—a significant number of Labour MPs keen on a deal—and something blue: united Conservative benches.

Parliament was still not pliant. Many MPs—mostly from the group of ex-Conservatives expelled by Johnson in September—were concerned about two things, both of which would require a further extension of Article 50: allowing time for scrutiny and amendment of the legislation and ensuring that the UK would not fall out of the EU with no deal while this took place. As a result, the former Conservative frontbencher Oliver Letwin successfully pressed amendments ensuring that Johnson's deal would only be approved when legislation implementing Brexit had been passed. Johnson would therefore have to request a further extension of Article 50. Despite this setback, the Second Reading of the EU Withdrawal Bill demonstrated that Johnson had successfully changed the Commons arithmetic. The legislation was voted through by 329 votes to 299, with every Conservative MP, and 19 Labour MPs, backing the government. However, Johnson had only secured the passage of his deal with the votes of Labour and Conservative MPs intent on, as one put it, 'bending the legislation out of shape'. These could plausibly include mandating the aim of a customs union.

However, what these MPs could not do was change the content of the legally binding treaty that Johnson and the EU had agreed. In effect, if Eurosceptics were willing to suck up the demands of Labour MPs and Europhile Conservatives written into domestic legislation, they could get the Brexit they wanted. The key was that, without the legal commitment to continued alignment of the sort that had been in Theresa May's backstop, Great Britain would have the freedom to pursue as hard a Brexit as it wanted in the future. As no Parliament can bind its successor through domestic legislation, these guarantees written into domestic law could later be ripped up. Eurosceptics in the ERG trusted the Prime Minister—who they saw as both 'one of them' and a political winner—to do just that. Once Brexit had happened, all bets were off.[63]

The pro-referendum forces in the House of Commons could see the writing on the wall. In this hung parliament, the myriad smaller parties, determined to do all they could to stop Brexit, had increased influence, but by failing to unite with Labour around an alternative approach, they had squandered it. With a majority of MPs now backing Johnson's Brexit deal, the only option available to its opponents was to gamble on an election fought on Johnson's turf: asking the British public whether or not, now the UK had agreed a deal, they wanted to 'get Brexit done'. The public, whose 2016 votes had begun the Brexit process, now got the final say on how to end it.

NOTES

1. 'Theresa May's General Election Statement in Full', *BBC News*, 18 April 2017, https://www.bbc.co.uk/news/uk-politics-39630009.
2. Chris Wilkins, *Brexit Witness Archive, UK in a Changing Europe*, 22 June 2020, https://ukandeu.ac.uk/brexit-witness-archive/chris-wilkins; Philip Hammond, *Brexit Witness Archive, UK in a Changing Europe*, 13

and 20 November 2020, https://ukandeu.ac.uk/brexit-witness-archive/philip-hammond.

3. See, for example, S.B. Hobolt et al.'s work on affective polarisation 'Divided by the Vote: Affective Polarisation in the Wake of the Brexit Referendum' (2020) *British Journal of Political Science*, https://doi.org/10.1017/S0007123420000125, supported by J. Curtice, 'The Emotional Legacy of Brexit: How Britain Has Become a Country of Remainers and Leavers', *NatCen/UK in a Changing Europe*, 22 October 2018, https://whatukthinks.org/eu/a-nation-of-remainers-and-leavers-how-brexit-has-forged-a-new-sense-of-identity.

4. Indeed, Lord Kerr, who drafted the Article 50 text, says this short time-frame was a deliberate deterrent against its use by Member States.

5. For the argument that May prioritised party management over state-craft, see Bagehot, 'The End of Theresa May', *The Economist*, 29 March 2019, https://www.economist.com/britain/2019/03/28/the-end-of-theresa-may. For the view that her leadership was primarily about a failure of parliamentary management, see C. Tominey, 'Theresa May Is in Last Chance Saloon Where Support Has Gone Dry after Latest Brexit Panic', *Daily Telegraph*, 21 May 2019, https://www.telegraph.co.uk/politics/2019/05/21/prime-minister-last-chance-saloon-support-has-run-dry. On May's unwillingness to reject no deal, see R. Behr, 'Brexit Is a Sham, But Theresa May Just Won't Admit It', *The Guardian*, 21 May 2019, https://www.theguardian.com/commentisfree/2019/may/21/brexit-theresa-may-no-deal. For the view that her unwillingness to embrace no deal was fatal, see C. Moore, 'There Is an Inner Reason Why Theresa May Still Shies Away from a Full Brexit', *Daily Telegraph*, 2 February 2019, https://www.telegraph.co.uk/politics/2019/02/02/inner-reason-theresa-may-still-shies-away-full-brexit.

6. T. McTague and C. Cooper, 'Inside Theresa May's Great British Failure', *Politico*, 21 June, 2019, https://www.politico.com/story/2019/06/21/theresa-may-brexit-1376417.

7. T. May, 'May Speech on New Brexit deal', 21 May 2019, https://www.gov.uk/government/speeches/pms-speech-on-new-brexit-deal-21-may-2019.

8. 'Political Party Show 103—Keir Starmer', https://soundcloud.com/thepoliticalparty/show-103-keir-starmer-live.

9. A. Seldon, *May at 10*. Biteback, 2019, p. 301; interview with Rt. Hon. John Bercow.

10. M. Smith, 'Two Thirds Want Other Parties Included in Brexit Negotiations', *YouGov*, 13 July, https://yougov.co.uk/topics/politics/articles-reports/2017/07/13/more-two-thirds-brits-want-other-parties-included.

11. M. Barnier, 'Speech by Michel Barnier, the European Commission's Chief Negotiator', 19 June, 2017, https://ec.europa.eu/commission/presscorner/detail/en/SPEECH_17_1704.
12. C. Cook, 'Part IV: May's Indecision', *Tortoise*, 19 May 2019, https://members.tortoisemedia.com/2019/05/19/brexit-part-4/content.html?sig=SPBq0YgFcqzw0uaL4pA1_AUO5KUnGdF2IvZYp1_aYn4.
13. Gavin Barwell, *Brexit Witness Archive, UK in a Changing Europe*, 1 and 25 September 2020, https://ukandeu.ac.uk/brexit-witness-archive/gavin-barwell; Denzil Davidson, *Brexit Witness Archive, UK in a Changing Europe*, 14 September 2020, https://ukandeu.ac.uk/brexit-witness-archive/denzil-davidson.
14. This was formally confirmed by the Terms of Reference for the Article 50 negotiations, published on 19 June. See https://ec.europa.eu/commission/sites/beta-political/files/eu-uk-art-50-terms-reference_agreed_amends_en.pdf.
15. D. Allen-Green, 'The Significance of the Brexit Sequencing U-Turn', *Financial Times*, 20 June 2017, https://www.ft.com/content/c7923fba-1d31-39fd-82f0-ba1822ef20d2.
16. The best overview of the mechanics of that decision is J. Rutter, 'Reshuffling Brexit: What to Make of Olly Robbins' Move', *Institute for Government*, 19 September, https://www.instituteforgovernment.org.uk/blog/brexit-olly-robbins-reshuffle-civil-service.
17. The progenitor of the 'Irish Trilemma' was the Deputy Director of the Centre for European Reform, John Springford, in March 2018: see https://www.cer.eu/insights/theresa-mays-irish-trilemma.
18. Raoul Ruparel, *Brexit Witness Archive, UK in a Changing Europe*, 11 August 2020, https://ukandeu.ac.uk/brexit-witness-archive/raoul-ruparel.
19. 'European Council (Art. 50) Guidelines for Brexit Negotiations', https://www.consilium.europa.eu/en/press/press-releases/2017/04/29/euco-brexit-guidelines.
20. T. Newton Dunn, 'May's Bid to Save Bill', *The Sun*, 6 December, https://www.thesun.co.uk/news/5082912/prime-minister-theresa-mays-belfast-brexit-divorce-bill.
21. Hansard HC debate, 'Brexit Negotiations', 11 December 2017, vol. 633, col. 35.
22. T. Shipman, *Fall Out*. William Collins, 2018, Chapter 4.
23. Three of the four who did not—Heidi Allen, Anna Soubry and Sarah Wollaston—would go on to help form Change UK in February 2019, and two (Allen and Wollaston) would then later join the Liberal Democrats (see Chapter 5, pp. 162–164).

24. Hansard HC debate, 'Prime Minister's Questions', 28 February 2018, vol. 636, col. 824.

25. *The Andrew Marr Show*, 10 December 2017, https://www.bbc.co.uk/programmes/p05qnhmh.

26. Private conversation with UK negotiator.

27. T. May, 'PM Speech on Our Future Economic Partnership with the European Union', 2 March, https://www.gov.uk/government/speeches/pm-speech-on-our-future-economic-partnership-with-the-european-union.

28. T. McTague et al., 'Theresa May's 3 Brexit Audiences', *Politico*, 5 March 2018, https://www.politico.eu/article/theresa-mays-3-brexit-audiences.

29. 'Oral Evidence: Scrutiny of Brexit Negotiations', House of Lords Select Committee on the European Union, 17 July 2018.

30. M. Barnier, 'Statement at the Press Conference Following His Meeting with Dominic Raab, UK Secretary of State for Exiting the EU', 26 July 2018, http://europa.eu/rapid/press-release_SPEECH-18-4704_en.htm.

31. In 2017, services accounted for 45% of total UK exports, or £277 billion. Unlike goods, where it runs a deficit, the UK ran a total trade surplus in services of £112 billion.

32. A. Spence, 'Let Trump Handle Brexit: An Explosive Leaked Recording Reveals Boris Johnson's Private Views about Britain's Foreign Policy', *Buzzfeed*, 7 June 2018, https://www.buzzfeed.com/alexspence/boris-johnson-trump-brexit-leaked-recording?utm_term=.bfoXzn6M#.wfm6Bl1L.

33. Interview with Gavin Barwell, 1 and 25 September 2020.

34. Seldon, *May at 10*, p. 432.

35. Notably, Javid, the only one of these seven Cabinet ministers who campaigned for Remain, was also the only one of this number who subsequently made his way into Boris Johnson's first Cabinet, though he did not survive long after the 2019 election.

36. Julian Smith, *Brexit Witness Archive, UK in a Changing Europe*, 20 July 2020, https://ukandeu.ac.uk/brexit-witness-archive/julian-smith; Gavin Barwell, *Brexit Witness Archive, UK in a Changing Europe*, 1 and 25 September 2020, https://ukandeu.ac.uk/brexit-witness-archive/gavin-barwell.

37. David Lidington, *Brexit Witness Archive, UK in a Changing Europe*, 3 June 2020, https://ukandeu.ac.uk/brexit-witness-archive/rt-hon-sir-david-lidington; Philip Hammond, *Brexit Witness Archive*.

38. Gavin Barwell, *Brexit Witness Archive, UK in a Changing Europe*, 1 and 25 September 2020, https://ukandeu.ac.uk/brexit-witness-archive/gavin-barwell.

39. Interview with one of the chapters authors and David Davis at the 2019 Conservative Party conference: https://ukandeu.ac.uk/video-audio/conservative-party-conference-rt-hon-david-davis-mp-in-conversation-with-professor-anand-menon.

40. J. Curtice, 'Why Chequers Has Gone Wrong for Theresa May', *NatCen*, 17 July 2018, https://whatukthinks.org/eu/why-chequers-has-gone-wrong-for-theresa-may.

41. Gavin Barwell, 1 and 25 September 2020, *Brexit Witness Archive*.

42. T. May, 'May Warns EU Not to Treat UK Unfairly in Brexit Talks', *Die Welt*, 19 September 2018, https://www.welt.de/debatte/kommentare/article181579426/Theresa-May-May-warns-EU-not-to-treat-UK-unfairly-in-Brexit-talks.html.

43. https://www.instagram.com/p/Bn8Luwbjzf9/?hl=en.

44. https://twitter.com/Peston/status/1019291556157804547.Punishment, however, was reserved for the Labour rebels: both Frank Field and Kate Hoey immediately lost votes of confidence within their local Labour associations.

45. Over half of those who identified as a 'Remainer' said they feel that way 'very strongly', compared to four in nine Leavers: Curtice, 'The Emotional Legacy of Brexit'.

46. R. Ford and A. Wager, 'What Voters Actually Think about a No Deal', *New Statesman*, 13 September 2018, https://www.newstatesman.com/politics/staggers/2018/09/what-voters-actually-think-about-no-deal-brexit.

47. For the best pieces so far on the People's Vote campaign, see H. Mance, 'How the People's Vote Fell Apart', *Financial Times*, 7 August 2020, https://www.ft.com/content/e02992f6-cf9e-46b3-8d45-325fb183302f; and D. Sabbagh, '"There's No Chance Now": How the People's Vote Movement Died', *The Guardian*, 18 December 2019, https://www.theguardian.com/politics/2019/dec/18/theres-no-chance-now-how-the-peoples-vote-movement-died.

48. The SNP (35 MPs), the Liberal Democrats (initially 12 MPs, rising to 20 by the dissolution), Plaid Cymru (four MPs) and the Greens (one MP). They were later joined by the newly established ChangeUK-The Independent Group (12 MPs initially, falling to seven across two parties). At their peak, between them these parties commanded 67 votes in the Commons.

49. 'Full text: Boris Johnson's Tory Fringe Speech', *The Spectator*, 2 October 2018, https://www.spectator.co.uk/article/full-text-boris-johnson-s-tory-fringe-speech.

50. One might legitimately ask at this point why, if Conservative Brexiters were so confident that technological solutions could be devised to deal with the issue of the Irish border, they were so convinced the backstop was never going to be superseded.

51. 'EU Exit Negotiations', Hansard, 15 November 2018, vol. 649, col. 431–81.

52. A survey of Conservative MPs in the winter of 2018 found that 55% of them thought that difficulties on the Irish border question have been exaggerated as an EU negotiating tactic: see https://ukandeu.ac.uk/new-survey-finds-70-of-mps-think-theresa-may-has-done-a-poor-job-of-negotiating-brexit.

53. S. Fisher, 'The Opposite of Enthusiasm: Why Do People Support or Oppose the Brexit Deal?', *UK in a Changing Europe*, 15 January 2019, https://ukandeu.ac.uk/the-opposite-of-enthusiasm-why-do-people-support-or-oppose-the-brexit-deal.

54. M. D'Arcy, 'Brexit: Second Commons Defeat for Theresa May in 24 hours', *BBC News*, 9 January 2019, https://www.bbc.co.uk/news/uk-politics-46805269.

55. T. Connelly 'How the Backstop Deal Was Done—And Why Cox Blew It Apart', *RTE*, 16 March 2019, https://www.rte.ie/news/analysis-and-comment/2019/0315/1036688-backstop-deal-cox.

56. P. Waugh, 'Why a No-Deal Brexit Is Now Theresa May's Fallback Plan to Save Her Party—And Herself', *Huffington Post*, 11 February 2019, Available At: https://www.huffingtonpost.co.uk/entry/theresa-may-no-deal-brexit-fallback-plan_uk_5c617348e4b0910c63f30fc8

57. C. Barr, 'How Populist Was Theresa May's Brexit Address?', *The Guardian*, 21 March 2019, https://www.theguardian.com/world/ng-interactive/2019/mar/21/how-populist-was-theresa-mays-brexit-address.

58. David Lidington, *Brexit Witness Archive*; Gavin Barwell, *Brexit Witness Archive*.

59. John McDonnell, *Brexit Witness Archive, UK in a Changing Europe*, 19 February 2021, https://ukandeu.ac.uk/brexit-witness-archive/john-mcdonnell; James Schneider, *Brexit Witness Archive, UK in a Changing Europe*, 11 January 2021, https://ukandeu.ac.uk/brexit-witness-archive/james-schneider.

60. C. Curtis, 'If Everyone Revealed How They Voted Last Week Labour Would Have to Kick out Four in Ten Members', *YouGov*, 30 May, https://yougov.co.uk/topics/politics/articles-reports/2019/05/30/if-everyone-revealed-how-they-voted-last-week-labo.

61. D. Cutts et al., 'Resurgent Remain and a Rebooted Revolt on the Right: Exploring the 2019 European Parliament Elections in the United Kingdom', *Parliamentary Affairs*, 90(3) (2019): 496–514.

62. A. Wickham, 'Boris Johnson's Top Team Is at War over Whether to Call an Election', *BuzzFeed*, 23 October 2019, https://www.buzzfeed.com/alexwickham/boris-johnson-top-team-war-election.

63. Indeed, by the autumn of 2020, the Johnson government's threat to break international law showed they had correctly judged the Prime Minister's willingness to adopt a disruptive approach to talks on the future UK–EU relationship.

CHAPTER 3

Rebuilding the Ship at Sea: The Conservatives

While argument raged over precisely who was to blame, all Conservatives agreed that the 2017 election campaign was a disaster not to be repeated. Although the party had increased its vote share for the fifth election in a row, from 37 to 42%, Theresa May had blown a 20-point poll lead and lost her parliamentary majority. But before anyone could think too seriously about the next election, there was the urgent matter of forming a government. With no majority in the Commons, how did the Conservatives propose to continue running the country and so deliver on the government's commitment to seeing the UK leave the EU?

That question was answered pretty rapidly. The Conservatives formed a minority administration with the backing of the pro-Brexit Democratic Unionist Party (DUP), whose support was enshrined in a written agreement signed within weeks of the election. In return for an estimated £1 billion of additional state funding for Northern Ireland, the DUP pledged to grant the Conservatives 'confidence and supply'.[1]

To the surprise of some, given her prominent role in the botched 2017 campaign, there was never any determined effort to persuade May to stand down. For a start, in the words of one of her advisors: 'There was a tacit understanding all round that she wasn't going to lead the party into another general election. But there was also an understanding that most of the party … wanted to get Brexit done and changing leaders and having more uncertainty put that at risk.' It also helped that none of her Cabinet colleagues was remotely prepared for a challenge or even appeared to want the job.[2]

© The Author(s), under exclusive license to Springer Nature Switzerland AG 2021
R. Ford et al., *The British General Election of 2019*,
https://doi.org/10.1007/978-3-030-74254-6_3

A pivot towards a softer Brexit that might have been achievable by 'reaching across the aisle' to a Labour Party then still officially committed to leaving the EU was never seriously considered either. May remained convinced that the referendum not only had to be meaningfully honoured, but that Leave had won in large part because of public concern about immigration, therefore making continued membership of the Single Market—which many Labour MPs favoured but which allowed uncontrolled entry by EU citizens—impossible. As one of her frustrated Cabinet colleagues, Chancellor Philip Hammond, observed, 'the Prime Minister was obsessed by migration, as were a sizeable chunk of the Tory Party. Even people who weren't in the extreme wing of the party were very nervous about delivering something on migration'.[3]

There were narrower partisan factors at play too—seeking support from Jeremy Corbyn's Labour Party was anathema to a lifelong, deeply tribal Conservative like May, and would have prompted an immediate revolt from hardline Tory backbenchers, particularly those in the Eurosceptic European Research Group (ERG) who were already worried they might 'lose Brexit' altogether. Just as crucial, there was a genuine fear (from the Cabinet all the way down to the backbenches) that the instability triggered by any such backbench uprising might spin out of control and somehow end up with Corbyn moving into Downing Street. The priority therefore was on rebuilding the Prime Minister's authority within her party. May managed to recover from her poorly received 9 June apology to defeated Conservative candidates and former colleagues when, on Monday 12 June, she addressed her MPs at a packed meeting at the 1922 Committee with just the right combination of contrition, humility and determination.[4]

May's internal position was already more secure by this point. She had ensured the rapid reappointment of 'big beasts' like Boris Johnson, David Davis, Amber Rudd and (ironically, because he had expected to be axed had May won a majority) Philip Hammond, while agreeing the equally rapid departure of her much-criticised chief advisors Nick Timothy and Fiona Hill.[5] May appointed as her new Chief of Staff the highly astute and well-liked Gavin Barwell, who had lost his Croydon seat the week before.[6] Barwell's performance was widely praised across the political spectrum, including even those Labour Party figures who worked with him during later cross-party Brexit talks. According to one senior Cabinet Minister:

Gavin became a tremendous confidante of the Prime Minister, and she trusted him. He never let her down, but he absolutely, I think, developed the most productive relationship with her, in that he knew exactly where his boundaries were ... He just knew when her wish was that something got resolved, and he knew instinctively how far he had permission to go. He almost never got it wrong ... He was a, sort of, Medici-esque, Machiavellian negotiator between the various factions.

Barwell remained in post until May resigned in the summer of 2019, becoming heavily involved in her increasingly desperate attempts to negotiate a deal with the EU-27 that could simultaneously command the support of frontbench and backbench MPs, as well as that of the party in the media (the editors and columnists who exert so much influence on MPs) and the party in the country (the grassroots members in local associations throughout the land).[7]

Barwell's first task was to steady the ship, telling special advisers, according to one of those in Number 10: 'At the moment it's one hour at a time. In a week, it'll be one day at a time.' His task, however, was not made any easier when, just a few days after the general election, the Prime Minister was widely criticised for failing to appear at the scene of the terrible fire that destroyed the Grenfell tower block in North Kensington, an error she compounded by choosing (in marked contrast with Jeremy Corbyn) only to meet emergency services staff rather than the survivors and the families of the 72 people who had perished. It was, as May herself later admitted, a bad mistake, and one that the Prime Minister did a lot (albeit more in private than in public) to atone for later.[8] It reinforced the impression formed during the election campaign of a leader who lacked the common touch and the emotional intelligence that most politicians need if they are to rise to the top. It was hoped that the promotion of more fluent media performers like Damian Green (Cabinet Office), David Lidington (Justice) and David Gauke (Chief Secretary) would help, although, as Remainers, their appointments had to be balanced by the Cabinet return of high-profile Leave campaigner and former leadership candidate Michael Gove, and the promotion of prominent ERG members like Steve Baker into junior frontbench roles.

Meanwhile, Barwell continued to work hard to improve the atmosphere within Number 10 and repair relations with ministers who had been bruised by trying encounters with May's former advisors. There was also a concerted attempt to rebuild relations between Number 10 and the parliamentary party through weekly lunches with assorted groups of backbenchers. Barwell was also instrumental in refreshing the Number 10 operation after the election. JoJo Penn stayed on as May's Deputy Chief of Staff, as did Stephen Parkinson as her Political Secretary. But the Downing Street Policy Unit's John Godfrey and Will Tanner both resigned, reasoning (correctly) that the small majority and the focus on Brexit would leave little room for other policy ambitions.[9] Godfrey was replaced as Policy Unit Director by James Marshall. Chris Wilkins, May's Director of Strategy and Chief Speechwriter, also decided to go after apparently being passed over for the post of Director of Communications, which had been vacant since Katie Perrior's departure in April. The new Director of Communications was Robbie Gibb, a BBC news and current affairs producer, an avowed Brexiteer and brother of Conservative MP Nick Gibb. The reorganisation also saw an enhanced role given to James Johnson, who had been doing public opinion research (paid for by CCHQ) for May from early on in her leadership.

Johnson led the internal post-mortem on the election and would advise the Prime Minister on possible ways forward. But his review would inevitably take months and some essential changes were needed immediately to prepare for the next election. Chief amongst the advocates of reform was the Party's Treasurer, Sir Mick Davies. A successful businessman and generous party donor, Davies composed a no-punches-pulled memo to May outlining what had to be done—and done urgently. It recommended a radical restructuring of CCHQ. The party needed not just a Chairman, but a full-time, permanent, professional (as opposed to political) CEO. It had to expand its donor base to reduce reliance on a few high net-worth individuals. It needed to plan for a major expansion of organisational capacity and to present a better proposition to potential donors—one that should include a pledge to revamp field campaigning, digital comms, data capture, membership recruitment and retention, fundraising, business engagement, and support for incumbents in marginal seats. Never again should the Conservative Party do what it had done after the general election in 2015, namely bank the win and wind down the organisation on the assumption that the machine could simply be fired up for an election in five years' time.

If Party Chairman Patrick McLoughlin had concerns about some of the suggestions, in particular the creation of the CEO role which might cut across his own role, he apparently did not try to talk Theresa May out of them or, indeed, out of accepting Sir Mick Davies' offer to take on the new CEO role himself. As a result, internal changes came thick and fast. The most immediate was the decision to move forward with an existing plan, implemented by the Director of Campaigning, CCHQ stalwart (and future CEO) Darren Mott, to hire at least 70 (rising to 100) campaign managers. They would be placed in marginal and target seats, funded mainly by CCHQ, but also, where possible, from local associations, very few of which nowadays contribute much money to CCHQ itself, despite often possessing substantial financial resources.

In contrast to the agents of old (nearly 300 of whom, for example, were employed by the party in the early 1970s), many of these campaign managers were young, politically passionate recent graduates whose largely untested skills and suitability would be measured by assessing their performance at the 2018 local elections—one reason why a fair few were posted to London in the first instance, particularly in vulnerable boroughs like Barnet, which the Tories were desperate to hold and in which lay highly marginal parliamentary seats such as Chipping Barnet (2017 majority 353), Finchley & Golders Green (2017 majority 1,657), and Hendon (2017 majority 1,072). But whether the new hires were placed in seats the Conservatives were defending or intending to target, the hope was that, especially once they gained experience and were given proper training, they might be able to offset the advantage a larger and more active membership supposedly gave Labour—particularly if a combination of canvassing and data purchased by CCHQ allowed them to better identify potential Tory voters.

This contrast between the Tory and Labour grassroots may not have bothered everyone at the top of the Conservative Party, but CCHQ had clearly begun to take it seriously.[10] It was not just the difference in raw numbers; the massive expansion of Labour's dues-paying membership meant that, for the first time in years, there was a realistic prospect of the Conservatives being outspent by their main rival. Labour's revival also played into wider Conservative concerns about a support base that was increasingly 'pale, male and stale', with relatively few women, people from ethnic minorities and employees in the public sector. Such an unrepresentative activist base might find it increasingly difficult to engage directly with potential voters, both during and outside election campaigns, and digitally as well as 'on the doorstep'. The 2017 election had only served to confirm that, in the words of one CCHQ insider, the

Tories had fallen 'light years behind Labour' on social media since 2015. Accordingly, CCHQ strengthened its marketing and its membership sections, and accelerated progress towards a single, centrally administered membership system in order to improve recruitment and retention by providing an improved membership experience. It also set itself an ambitious goal of boosting membership to between 275,000 and 300,000 by October 2019, although this target was later scaled back to 200,000.

The 2017 election had also revealed major problems with the Conservative Party's data collection and analytics—problems had seen canvassing teams all over the country sent to households they were told were Tory prospects, but turned out to be either immune to the party's charms or actively hostile. Lack of good-quality information on and analysis of potential and actual Conservative voters was also hamstringing the party's attempts to improve communications and targeting. The proposed solution was not only to spend more on all this but also to bring more of it back in-house, ramping up the capacity to interpret data gathered on the doorstep and through the purchase of commercially available databases, and then to put it to use improving voter communication. After all, as CCHQ noted: 'Data is a valuable asset, but without it converted into actionable insight, and then acted upon, it is merely an expensive one.' Internally, 2019 was declared to be 'the year of data' (2018 having been 'the year of the campaign manager') and CCHQ also wanted a year-round increase in resources going to Tory MPs in marginal seats to assist them in developing localised business and media campaigns to help them better leverage the electoral benefits that often accrue to incumbents.[11]

The party also looked to beef up the Conservative Research Department (CRD) to improve not only its rebuttal and attack operation but also its policy capacity—something which always tends to suffer when the party goes into government. A start was made on this by hiring Adam Memon, the 26-year-old Economic Adviser to the Chief Secretary to the Treasury, to be the new CRD Director—the youngest person, and first British Asian, to occupy the post. More important, though, was his grip on financial matters, since it was widely felt that the party had been unable to effectively land its attack on Labour's economic policies in the 2017 campaign. Under Memon, the CRD's staffing compliment, in single figures when he arrived, doubled—and included people with more real-world economics experience, as well as (a result of a conscious effort) more women. By the time Memon moved on in the summer of 2019 to become a special adviser to the new Chancellor, Sajid Javid, CRD had gone from being, in the words of one involved in revamping it, 'a bit of a shell to being a machine that could fight an election'—a task made easier by the occasional leaks it received of Labour's economic policies.

None of CCHQ's changes came cheap, notwithstanding the fact that political commitment often enables parties to hire staff on lower salaries than they could command elsewhere. The Party's annual conference was now netting around £2 million every year, substantial but nowhere near enough to finance the rebuilding and retooling envisaged. Nor was there much scope for savings, even if some staff were let go. Hence the ambition to achieve a 50% increase in revenue, in part by expanding membership of the tiered 'donor clubs' for well-heeled supporters, but also by trying to increase smaller donations (solicited, for example, through direct mailshots) in order to decrease the party's reliance on a few very dedicated and very rich supporters. Initially, there was some reluctance on the part of both newly approached and established donors unimpressed by the 2017 campaign to part with their money. That reluctance, interestingly, continued longer among some strong advocates of Brexit (who refused to give until the latter was delivered or on the grounds that the government wasn't Leave enough) than among former Remainers, who had accepted the result of the referendum and whose main goal now was preventing Jeremy Corbyn from getting into Downing Street. Conversations with potential donors now featured a fully costed, detailed business plan which stressed, in the words of Sir Mick Davies (still a significant donor himself), that they were being presented with 'an investment proposition rather than a donation proposition'. This more business-like approach, combined with greater fear of a Corbyn-led Labour Party in Downing Street, helped ensure that the ambitious fundraising target was met. This achievement was all the more impressive given donors' concerns about the Tories' increasingly obvious internal divisions in the Cabinet and Parliament.

Party donors weren't the only supporters to have expressed dismay at the Conservatives' performance at the 2017 general election. Many MPs and candidates felt angry and let down by the leadership and CCHQ—and so did their grassroots activists. Diagnosing the problems and prescribing solutions was important, but it would not be enough. The rank and file—'the party in the country'—needed an opportunity to express their frustrations lest they fester over the summer, only to burst out when politics proper returned in the autumn. The review into the election defeat that Theresa May and Patrick McLoughlin commissioned from the veteran former Cabinet Minister (and former Party Chairman) Sir Eric Pickles provided the vehicle for catharsis.

Pickles, who had stood down from Parliament in 2017 after over three decades as an MP and council leader, was pretty much the perfect choice: as one of those involved put it, not only was he 'masterful in the way he handled everything and everybody', but he 'was seen to be an honest broker—not particularly a Theresa May ally, not particularly associated with people who were against her. He allowed that process to take place and facilitated it in a way that people felt they were venting and it was being heard. That was clearly important. Had that not happened we would have imploded'. Just as importantly, they stressed, Pickles agreed that there was no point in trying to 'find victims to nail to the cross'. After all:

> We were in crisis at that stage ... We'd had a couple of sacrifices – Theresa's two chiefs of staff had fallen on their swords and gone – [but] ultimately if you were going to hold anybody accountable it would have been the Prime Minister. She called the election and ... she lost the election ... At the time we were not ready for a leadership contest and the party had to try and pick up the pieces.

By inviting submissions and testimony from right across the country, Pickles—assisted by Graham Brady, Chairman of the 1922 Committee, Patrick McLoughlin, the party Chairman, Sir Mick Davis, the party's new CEO, Rob Semple, the Chairman of the voluntary party's National Convention, and MP Nus Ghani—was able to put together his review in time for the 2017 party conference in Manchester.[12] By that time, as one of those involved in its production confirmed, the review had:

> allowed for a whole range of people to vent, for people engaged in the process to do a little bit of penance, and for Pickles to get up and present a report which laid no blame anywhere other than to say that, going forward, these are the sort of things that we should be concentrating on. And it did the trick because we moved on quite smartly after the report was presented at the Conference in October 2017.

Many of its 126 recommendations were already seen as common sense and as part and parcel of the rebuilding process already underway at CCHQ. But more than that, its underlying message reinforced the rationale for the CCHQ reforms—namely, as one of those involved put it:

> you can't go into a general election without proper preparation. And that means that you have to have a proper campaign machine, effective activists on the ground, people [who] have to be trained and know what to do … The underlying current of the review was that we were grotesquely unprepared to fight a general election even though the polling suggested it would be a romp in the park.

However, for all that it allowed the grassroots and candidates to safely let off steam, as well as helping to get buy-in for reforms already underway, the Pickles Review could do nothing to prevent the 2017 Tory conference ending in farcical fashion. Theresa May, making a closing speech intended to highlight pledges on housing, health and student finance, was handed a P45 by a prankster ('Boris asked me to give you this'), then fought a losing battle with a sore throat and a persistent cough while assorted letters began to disappear one by one from the slogan 'Building a country that works for everyone' glued to the backdrop behind her.

It is worth noting, as Stephen Parkinson, the Prime Minister's Political Secretary, recalled, that May's struggles on and offstage were not viewed unsympathetically by all:

> She got thousands of letters – including lots from people who hadn't voted Conservative in the general election – saying 'I feel terribly sorry for you,' or 'I was so impressed: in my job I don't have to make a speech, let alone a speech lasting an hour to the whole nation, I don't know how you do it' … The country outside was quite sympathetic and I think that was quite a good shorthand for how they saw her premiership. There were a lot of people thinking, 'This poor woman, she's got a difficult task and good on her for sticking at it.'[13]

But for many Conservative MPs, any such sympathy had its limits. The more Eurosceptic among them were already losing faith in May's ability to deliver the uncompromising Brexit that, ominously, her Foreign Secretary

Boris Johnson was once again pushing in the media.[14] As for the rest, they were still left wondering whether she had truly worked out what had gone wrong in the election and how she was going to fix it.

'Hour Glass' (Nicola Jennings, *The Guardian*, 3 October 2017 © Nicola Jennings)

Behind the scenes, Number 10 was trying to get a more precise answer to that second question through an analysis conducted over the summer by James Johnson, working with Tom Lubbock at CCHQ. That analysis, which primarily used British Election Study (BES) surveys conducted before and immediately after the election, was presented to a Political Cabinet just after Conference.

The analysis began by putting across some hard truths about just how old the Tory electorate had become and, most importantly, about how much of the surprise result was actually down to 'perceptions of Conservative performance on domestic issues like public services – the NHS … tuition fees, schools, public spending, austerity … and the real influence that had on voters' views of the Conservative Party'.[15] The furore over the manifesto was important, Johnson noted, but only in the context of voters' deeper concerns about successive Conservative governments since 2010 presiding over declining public services. Conservative attacks on Corbyn in 2017 hadn't cut through for all sorts of reasons: they seemed too shrill; people didn't trust the media that was carrying the attack message; they cared less about personality than promises on public services and Brexit; and Labour didn't look like winning anyway—which (interestingly in hindsight) while 'it wasn't important for swing voters … *was* important for those longer-term Labour voters who didn't like Corbyn [and] who felt they could vote for him without it costing anything'. The Tories' commitment to Brexit, he argued (to the chagrin of less Eurosceptic ministers), had, overall, turned out to be a net benefit: it encouraged Leave voters to plump for the Tories, while those who did not vote Conservative were discouraged less by their dislike of Brexit than their fear that a Conservative government would revert to type on austerity—a finding which one leading minister described as the most depressing thing he'd heard in the Cabinet Room.

Johnson's team segmented voters into groups that the government could use to produce electorally attractive policies over the next few years. One group, the Traditional Conservatives, would carry on supporting the party regardless. Conversely, the Labour Left—relatively young, university educated and Remain voting—were pretty much unreachable. Labour's Working Class—inner city, low-paid or unwaged Leave voters—would be hard to reach, but weren't altogether a lost cause because of Brexit. Then there were Urban Middle-Class Defectors—not yet middle aged, often living in southern England, Remain-supporting, but needing reassuring on public services. New Conservative Supporters were older, working-class Leave voters for whom Brexit really mattered. And finally there were Conservative Considerers—a volatile group who tended to be working class, to live in the North and the Midlands, a little bit more female and somewhat Leave—voters the party hadn't quite persuaded in 2017, in the main because they were more concerned with domestic issues and had doubts as to whether the Tories were really interested in looking out for them. This was the group that should be uppermost in ministers' minds when making policy, although this was not necessarily a message some of the more socially liberal, sometimes Remain-supporting, fiscally conservative ministers around the Cabinet table wanted to hear: to them, it felt like doubling down on the failed 2017 strategy. That said, their reluctance had relatively little impact on policy choices, since it was already pretty clear from the June Queen's Speech that Brexit was going to leave room for little else.

The post-conference political cycle began relatively well, with the government moving quickly towards agreement on how much the UK would pay into Brussels' coffers upon leaving the EU with few of the feared fireworks from backbench Brexiteers. But it wasn't long before some of the problems that were going to give the Prime Minister and her party recurring headaches over the next two years became apparent. May's decision to move top civil servant Oliver Robbins out of his job as Permanent Secretary at the Department for Exiting the European Union (DExEU) and into the Cabinet Office—a move intended to resolve the apparent tension between him and the Brexit Secretary, David Davis—backfired since it effectively drained the latter of authority. Over time, Davis, who had loyally backed the Prime Minister in the immediate aftermath of the election, became increasingly detached from Downing Street, likely hastening his resignation from the government in the summer of 2018. Key to his eventual departure was another of May's decisions—namely that in order to prevent a hard border on the island of Ireland but at the same time not treat Northern Ireland any differently from Great Britain, the whole of the UK would have to remain in a close economic relationship with the EU until more permanent arrangements could be forged.

By the time the EU-27 agreed at the end of 2017 to see its talks with the UK proceed to the second phase, none of this was yet set in stone. However, Brexiteers on the Tory backbenches (who now included Priti Patel, sacked from the Cabinet in late November for being less than forthcoming about meetings she'd held on a trip to Israel) were already beginning to worry; after all, wasn't the whole point of Brexit to 'take back control' of immigration and trade deals? And they were not the only ones who were anxious. In another development with long-term implications, 11 'Europhile' Tory MPs voted with the opposition to secure an amendment to the EU (Withdrawal) Bill tabled by Conservative backbencher and former Attorney-General Dominic Grieve, which obliged the government to provide a 'meaningful vote' in the Commons on any Withdrawal Agreement with the EU in the form of an amendable bill.

'Snowball' (Ben Jennings, *The i* paper, 2 March 2018 © Ben Jennings)

That rebellion might arguably have been prevented had May's first (and, in that job at least, highly rated) Chief Whip, Gavin Williamson, not been promoted to Secretary of State for Defence to replace Michael Fallon, who had resigned amidst allegations of sexual harassment, as #MeToo finally caught up with Westminster. But Williamson may well have been promoted anyway soon after in the Cabinet reshuffle undertaken by May in January 2018—one mischievously dubbed 'night of the long plastic forks' by Channel 4's Gary Gibbon after it emerged that Jeremy Hunt had kept his job after refusing to move, while Justine Greening resigned rather than leave the Department for Education.[16] More worrying for Tory Brexiteers, since Greening was seen as a 'Remainer' while Williamson had embraced Brexit with the zeal of a convert, was the promotion of the emollient former Minister for Europe, David Lidington, to de facto Deputy Prime Minister. Otherwise, there were no big moves, although one or two of the smaller ones were later to create cause for concern, most obviously the appointment of Karen Bradley as Secretary of State for Northern Ireland. Bradley, who was later to confess to a journalist that before her promotion, she 'didn't understand things like when elections are fought, for example, in Northern Ireland—people who are nationalists don't vote for unionist parties and vice versa', was perhaps not the ideal choice to manage relations with a divided region at the centre of growing Brexit disputes.[17] Meanwhile, closer to home, Patrick McLoughlin was finally granted his wish to stand down as Party Chairman and was succeeded by the former Immigration Minister, Brandon Lewis, with James Cleverly becoming Deputy Chairman.

Lewis was a reliable media performer and, as an Essex boy, very much not an identikit, plummy-voiced Tory. He had an impressive record as a campaigner, having wrested control of Brentwood Council from the Liberal Democrats in the early 2000s before going on to take the parliamentary seat of Great Yarmouth from Labour in 2010 on a swing of nearly 9% and holding it (against both Labour and UKIP) with an increasing majority ever since. Just as importantly, Lewis and Sir Mick Davis immediately struck up a good personal relationship. The party's new Chairman agreed with its CEO that, while CCHQ would still want to bring in hired guns like Lynton Crosby at election time, it nevertheless needed to create in-house capacity:

> My logic was that we should be getting to a position where, to use a really bad analogy from *Bake Off*, we bake the cake ... and then get whoever the expert's going to be at the end to check that it's firm and put the dressing on top, maybe. We should be able to bake the cake ourselves – build up our data, our online, digital work. Having campaign managers was about professionalising how we campaigned and where we campaigned but also about driving up membership. Because one of the things members find very frustrating is when you turn up on Saturday morning to deliver leaflets you spend an hour arguing about 'Who's got the map? Is it the right map?' With a professional there that should be done already. Around the country and around the weeks, that builds up a lot of extra hours of campaigning. People get there, they enjoy it – it's one of the things that the Lib Dems often used to do better than us: they *used* their volunteers and their volunteers *wanted* to be used. So getting that structure and organisation focused was really key – and that would drive up membership.[18]

All this would take time to bear fruit, but CCHQ took some early encouragement from the party's performance at the May 2018 local elections. True, local Tories could do little to prevent the loss of Trafford in Greater Manchester or to stop the Lib Dems taking the heavily Remain-voting London borough of Richmond. But they held on to their 'flagship' London boroughs of Kensington and Chelsea, Wandsworth and Westminster, and regained control of Barnet while also winning control in places like Basildon and Peterborough. There were early signs too that, with the collapse of UKIP, some of the Leave voters who had held back from voting Conservative at the general election the year before were now coming on board. The potential for Tory gains in Leave England was underscored by Labour's losses in Nuneaton, Derby and Bedworth, and its failure to win councils like North East Lincolnshire (which contains Grimsby) and Walsall in the West Midlands, as well as a swing to the Tories in Sunderland.

In fact, the local election results were particularly encouraging given that voters had gone to the polls just days after the Home Secretary, Amber Rudd, had been forced to resign. What became known as the 'Windrush Scandal' was the revelation that the UK had, as a result of the 'hostile environment' regime established by Theresa May in her previous role as Home Secretary, tried to deport (and in a few cases *had* actually deported) a number of elderly people of Afro-Caribbean and Asian origin who, in reality, had every right to remain in the country, having lived there perfectly legally since childhood.[19] May replaced Rudd with Sajid Javid, the UK's first Home Secretary from an ethnic minority, who pledged to put things right. The Prime Minister also had to put up with a series of defeats in the House of Lords on her European Union (Withdrawal) Bill. That said, her decision, earlier in April 2018 to allow the UK to take part in an allied operation to bomb bases in Syria in response to the Assad regime's continued use of chemical weapons had not triggered much parliamentary or public protest, while her firm handling of the nerve-agent attack in Salisbury in March had actually received widespread praise—not least because it contrasted so markedly with Jeremy Corbyn's initial reluctance to join with the government and the country's allies in laying the blame squarely on the Putin regime in Moscow (see Chapter 4, pp. 107–157).[20]

As the spring of 2018 turned into summer, then, the government could argue that things were looking up. It had managed—just— to reverse all the amendments made in the Lords to what on 26 June became the European Union (Withdrawal) Act. And in the middle of the month it had announced a new five-year funding settlement for the NHS involving a 3.4% average real-terms annual increase in NHS England's budget between 2019/20 and 2023/24—still not really sufficient, many argued, but nevertheless a significant improvement on the average 1% real terms increase seen since 2009/10. All this was very much in keeping with what James Johnson's opinion research had suggested the government needed to do to build a potentially election-winning coalition of voters. Yet moments like this—where the government talked about and acted on something other than Brexit—were becoming rare.

Throughout the first half of 2018, May and her inner circle, having conceded that they would need to secure an agreement on citizens' rights, UK payments and Ireland before going on to negotiate a future relationship with the EU, had been trying to come up with a way forward on Brexit (see Chapter 2, pp. 29–67). What was needed was something that would allow the UK to trade as freely as possible with the EU, not least so as to avoid a hard border in Ireland (something the PM became increasingly convinced must be avoided at all costs if peace and the union were to be preserved), yet also enable the British government to pursue its own trade deals with other countries (a *sine qua non* for Brexiteers).

May's speech at the Mansion House in the City of London at the beginning of March had attempted, on the one hand, to signal to her own Eurosceptic ultras that she was committed to their cause, while, on the other hand, signalling to the EU that it could not simply dismiss her demands for a bespoke deal as 'cherry-picking'. It soon became apparent that she had convinced neither audience. Her 'Facilitated Customs Arrangement' was dismissed as unworkable by Brussels, while Tory Brexiteers were soon talking up their even less realistic solutions. The Cabinet needed to hammer out a deal that it could unite behind and persuade Parliament to pass before time ran out.

This would not be easy since, behind the scenes, the government was becoming increasingly dysfunctional. In the words of one of one SpAd: 'Instead of being like a castle with strong external walls bringing the keeps together, it was just lots of individual towers and ministers with SpAds in each tower throwing things at the other towers and building their walls against them. It was chaos and everything was leaked.'[21] Negotiations with the EU were never, of course, going to be conducted in the open, but when trust within Whitehall had broken down as much as it had, the secrecy surrounding those talks was even more paramount than usual. Consequently, it was always going to be difficult to provide those ministers not directly involved in negotiations with, as one of May's closest aides put it, a 'sense of authorship or ownership'.[22] Talk of a 'common rule book', a 'joint institutional framework' and 'continued harmonisation' could only go so far—so much so that even numerous committees, bilateral meetings and confidential briefings (and there were plenty of them in an effort to convince ministers that they weren't being bounced)[23] still proved insufficient to properly 'roll the pitch' and pre-pare the Cabinet (and by extension the parliamentary party) for what was to come. Yet the time had arrived to bite the bullet and decide.

It was, then, no particular surprise when the elaborately constructed compromise that the Prime Minister and her team believed they had managed to achieve at the end of an all-day Cabinet meeting at Chequers on 6 July fell apart almost immediately.[24] David Davis, who had been communicating growing concerns about the direction of travel to Number 10, resigned—a move he had been contemplating for some time and went through with in spite of reportedly being offered the Foreign Office.[25] He was swiftly followed by Boris Johnson—because, in the opinion of most of his colleagues (including some who were there that day and saw him come round, by the evening, to support the deal), he feared that staying in post would lose him the backing of Leave-supporting MPs and grassroots members he needed for any future lead-ership bid. The reaction over the weekend from the parliamentary party, widely reported in the press, was also worryingly negative.

As a result, any hope that the EU would acquiesce to the 'Chequers plan' rapidly evaporated—something brutally confirmed by the President of the European Council after it met informally in Salzburg in late September (see Chapter 2, p. 29). The EU would not make signif-icant concessions for a deal which lacked convincing support at home. Chequers was also the moment when support for the Prime Minister from Tory MPs—particularly hardline Leavers—began to bleed away. Back in January 2017, more convinced than ever that only a hard Brexit (leaving the Single Market and the customs union) would honour the result of the referendum, and persuaded by Leave-supporting ministers like David Davis that the UK had to be able to threaten to walk away if it wanted to get what it needed from the EU, May had declared in her Lancaster House speech that 'no deal for Britain is better than a bad deal for Britain'. Yet now, to Brexiteers, who were growing keener on a no deal Brexit that they believed represented the 'clean break' they were looking for, she seemed to believe *any* deal was better than no deal.

Had Davis (replaced by another arch-Brexiteer, Dominic Raab) and Johnson (replaced by the moderate Remainer, Jeremy Hunt) stayed on, some Brexiteers might have given the proposals the benefit of the doubt. But their departure from the frontbench, along with that of the ERG's best organiser, Steve Baker, was proof positive that the empress had no clothes—a conclusion reinforced when Donald Trump, on an ill-timed state visit to Britain just a few days later, told *The Sun* newspaper that May had nixed the chances of doing a trade deal with the US, throwing in for good measure that Boris Johnson 'would be a great prime minister. I think he's got what it takes'. Chequers was also the moment when many voters began to doubt whether May was ever going to be able to get Brexit over the line.[26] For some Remainers, this encouraged hopes of stopping Brexit altogether with the help of a second referendum (see Chapters 2, pp. 29–67 and 4, pp. 107–157). For many Leavers, Chequers provided confirmation that they weren't going to get the hard Brexit they wanted out of this particular Prime Minister—something of which Boris Johnson, having returned to penning his weekly column in the *Daily Telegraph*, was more than happy to remind them.

May's angry reaction to her humiliation at Salzburg—in a Downing Street statement on 21 September, she reminded the EU that 'I have always said no deal is better than a bad deal'—may have bought her one or two cheers from government loyalists.[27] But it did not prevent her now-former Brexit Secretary David Davis from making an extraordinary appearance alongside Nigel Farage at a rally in Bolton the next evening organised by 'Leave means Leave', the cross-party pressure group which was already raising large amounts of money and was eventually to help give birth to the Brexit Party (see Chapter 5, pp. 159–192).[28] Nor did it cut much ice with backbenchers on both sides of the Brexit debate who were looking to use Parliament to force the Prime Minister's hand. In mid-July, the government felt obliged to accept hostile amendments to its Customs Bill tabled by the increasingly well-organised and uncompromising ERG. The next day it was forced to pull out all the stops to defeat an amendment calling for a customs union tabled by 'Europhile' backbenchers (see Chapter 2, pp. 29–67). A few weeks into August, the government had also issued guidelines on how the UK would handle a no-deal departure, although to many observers, this was more an effort to placate the ERG than a serious attempt to prepare for an outcome which May's Chancellor, Philip Hammond, was known to be determined to prevent. Indeed, Hammond made it pretty obvious in any case that he was loath to spend even more public money than the millions (possibly billions) the government had already spent on what he thought were 'ludicrous gestures' designed to pretend to the EU-27 and to Brexiteers that departure without a deal was an serious option for the government as opposed to something forced on it by failure.[29]

As Conservatives from around the country gathered in Birmingham for the party's 2018 conference—hundreds of them sporting lapel badges calling on the government to 'Chuck Chequers' and queuing for hours to listen to Boris Johnson doing his king over the water routine at a *ConservativeHome* rally—things were not looking good for May.[30] Indeed, the only bright spots on the horizon were, first, the fact that the veteran, intensely Eurosceptic *Daily Mail* editor Paul Dacre was going to be replaced by the relatively moderate Geordie Greig, and, second, the fact that in a few weeks' time, her Chancellor would be announcing in his Budget that the age of austerity really was over. But, for once, May outperformed expectations—prancing on stage to make her closing speech to the tune of ABBA's 'Dancing Queen' where she painted an uplifting picture of a post-austerity Britain that would finally build the houses it needed and the health service it deserved.[31] Brexit naturally got a mention, but with less stress on the details and more on the need for party unity on the issue. And in a thinly veiled rebuke to Johnson and the 'Chuck Chequers' crowd, she noted that while it was 'no surprise that we have had a range of different views expressed this week … it is my job as prime minister to do what I believe to be in the national interest'.

The speech was widely judged a success—especially when compared with her disastrous effort the year before. But it did not put Johnson and the ERG back in their respective boxes for long; indeed, the hostile language used about her by critics remained as intense (and, to some, deeply unpleasant) as ever, with one anonymous MP telling the *Sunday Times'* Tim Shipman: 'The moment is coming when the knife gets heated, stuck in her front and twisted. She'll be dead soon.'[32] But the speech, along with Philip Hammond's austerity-busting Budget in October, did buy May some time to look for a new way forward. The UK and the EU-27 were by that stage not so far apart: the future relationship would be signalled in a Political Declaration, while a legally binding treaty—a Withdrawal Agreement—would set out the financial settlement, arrangements for citizens, and arrangements to avoid a hard border in Ireland. And while the latter proved too tricky to resolve by the time the European Council met again in mid-October, a compromise on it was eventually reached a month later—one facilitated by the EU-27 conceding (thanks to lobbying by the Irish government) to May's demand that rather than Northern Ireland being treated differently from the rest of the UK, the whole of the UK would effectively remain in the customs union until a permanent solution could be found (see Chapter 2, pp. 29–67).

Sadly for the Prime Minister, however, it turned out to be a case of déjà vu (or at least Chequers) all over again. The morning after the Cabinet (in many cases reluctantly) had signed off on the draft agreement, complete with the 'Northern Ireland backstop', Brexit Secretary Dominic Raab, doubtless with one eye on the next leadership contest, took to Twitter to tender his resignation. Raab was followed by Number 10's Director of Legislative Affairs Nikki da Costa, along with the Work and Pensions Minister Esther McVey, and the junior minister at DExEU (and prominent ERG member) Suella Braverman. Michael Gove was persuaded to stay: had that not been the case, his departure might well have brought the house of cards crashing down there and then.

While the departures reflected real differences in principle over Brexit, they were also symptomatic of accelerating decline in deference among Tory MPs—one exacerbated by social media. As one of May's closest advisors recalled ruefully:

Everybody now is a star on Twitter. Being a Member of Parliament is really quite bleak. You don't get invited on TV programmes. You get a mailbag that tells you you're doing a terrible job and you're letting people down. And you don't even get called that often in the Chamber. Twitter is a brilliant outlet: 'I'll say something and I'll get a hundred retweets and lots of likes and I'll feel good about myself.' And it connects people up: whatever your opinion there's somebody else out there who's pleased. And that erodes all the nuance. And if you get all those retweets then you might get invited on telly. So being a minister just doesn't hold the same attraction for lots of people – as you saw with the large number of people who very happily resigned their ministerial posts and wrote a resignation letter for Twitter. They often put it on Twitter before they sent it to the Prime Minister, which is just bad manners. But that's how they conceive of the job now: 'Now I'm taking a stand and I'm going to tell everyone.' That's just a general trend now.[33]

The departures served to undermine attempts by Number 10 to sell May's package to Tory MPs, although, by then, in the words of one of her advisors, Brexit had gone 'beyond logic' and become 'near-religious' for many of them. Suitably emboldened, and convinced that the Withdrawal Agreement was 'Brexit in name only' because the backstop could see the UK trapped in the customs union forever, the hardcore Eurosceptics of the ERG piled in. True, in the words of her Political Secretary, Stephen Parkinson, May was always 'much more comfortable in the Chamber of the House of Commons being held to account, even [under] quite hostile questioning, than in a TV studio answering more frivolous questions'.[34] But even she must have found the parliamentary monstering she received that day at the hands of some of her own backbenchers pretty difficult to take.

Once they were done savaging the Prime Minister's deal in the chamber, the ERG's leading figures like Jacob Rees-Mogg, Steve Baker and Mark Francois, moved on to discuss how best to force May out of Number 10 via a vote of no confidence in her as Conservative Party leader—a process that required only 15% of Tory MPs to write to Graham Brady, Chairman of the 1922 Committee. Brady announced that the letters needed to trigger the vote had been delivered soon after the government, knowing it was facing a heavy defeat, announced it was pulling the 'Meaningful Vote' on the Withdrawal Agreement until after Christmas. Yet despite a comprehensive whipping operation on their part (run, ironically, out of the office of Iain Duncan Smith, who had been removed as Tory leader by the same procedure in 2003), too few of the ERG's less hardline colleagues were at that point willing to pull the trigger, possibly because opinion research suggested getting rid of the Prime Minister would not be a silver bullet, especially when it was far from obvious, at that stage anyway, that a successor who could unite the party could be crowned in short order. May beat off the challenge by 200 votes to (a nonetheless wounding) 117—although not before formally conceding with voting already underway that (as most of her parliamentary colleagues had long hoped—or even assumed—would be the case) she would not lead the party into the next general election.

However, Downing Street's hopes that May's victory in the confidence vote would provide a boost to her authority were swiftly dashed. A survey of party members and voters released just after the New Year bank holiday suggested that the overwhelming majority of the Tory rank and file continued to be consumed by Brexit, hadn't changed their mind about it and were opposed to her deal by a 60:40 margin, preferring instead a no deal outcome, believing as they did that talk of the disruption it would cause was overblown and that it would be positive for the economy in the long term.[35] True, many Tory rank-and-file members doubted there was anyone else who could have done better than May: leaving aside the 15% who thought 'She's got a good Brexit deal', some 43% agreed that 'She's got a poor Brexit deal, but any other leader would have done just as badly'. Nevertheless, that left 37% who thought that 'She's got a poor Brexit deal, and an alternative leader would have got a better deal'. Moreover, that substantial minority probably contributed to the equally substantial minority of members (44%) who thought that, should Parliament vote to reject her deal, May should resign as leader and Prime Minister. And if May took any comfort from the fact that exactly half of the Conservative rank and file thought she should stay in the job regardless, she would have been alarmed at the fact that only 51% of her party's members thought she was doing well as Prime Minister, while 48% thought she was doing badly.

May, then, had failed not only to convince voters that her Brexit deal was a good one, but she had also failed to persuade her party faithful. As 2019 began and MPs returned to Westminster, the ERG now knew for sure that they, and not she, had the grassroots with them. Just as importantly, it was now obvious that they cared far more about getting the Brexit they wanted than they did about party unity—or, indeed, about the broader constitutional stability of the UK. Since both the Cabinet and the EU-27 had signed off on the deal, the chances of May being able to deliver further last-minute concessions that might have secured extra votes were vanishingly small. As a result, the government's Chief Whip, Julian Smith, and his team were effectively powerless. Indeed, like Dickens' Mr Micawber, they were reduced simply to hoping something would turn up.

The government nevertheless tried to begin the New Year on an optimistic note and remind target voters that politics wasn't all about Brexit, announcing on 7 January the new (and by recent standards generous) ten-year funding plan for the NHS. But it was fooling no one. On 9 January, the government was unable to prevent the Commons supporting an amendment tabled by the pro-European Conservative backbencher (and former Attorney-General) Dominic Grieve which obliged the government to table its alternative approach swiftly should May's Withdrawal Agreement be rejected in the upcoming Meaningful Vote.

But if that first defeat was wounding, the defeat which followed in the Meaningful Vote itself was brutal both in terms of the historic overall margin involved (432 to 202) and the sheer number of Tory MPs (118) who rebelled against their own Prime Minister; the whips, it turned out, had been unable to persuade more than two-thirds of their backbench colleagues to support the government.

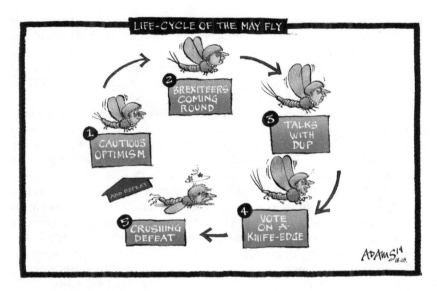

'Life Cycle of the May Fly' (Christian Adams, *Evening Standard*, 18 March 2019 © Christian Adams)

This stark result strongly suggested that no amount of confronting the Brexiteer backbench ultras with the reality of the situation was going to convince them to back May's deal. Indeed, the response of the ultras to the Meaningful Vote was to propose two fantasy Brexit solutions– the so-called Malthouse compromise and the Brady amendment—neither of which stood the slightest chance of being accepted by the EU.[36] The Prime Minister's rejoinder, having refused even to contemplate the suggestion by some ministers that she offer to run her deal against Remain in a second referendum, was threefold. First, she finally gave in into some of her advisors' pleas that she at least agree to exploratory talks with Labour. Second, she agreed, purely on the grounds that it might at least offer a way of bringing the ERG on board, to throw the government's weight behind the Brady amendment—a mistake in the view of some in the Cabinet, since it was so obviously a 'unicorn', yet encouraged the hardliners to continue thinking that they could get what they wanted. Third, she tried again somehow to persuade the EU-27 to agree to a Northern Ireland backstop that was time-limited and contained some kind of escape clause. This took her up to Leave-voting Grimsby to make a speech practically begging the EU to do so.[37] Following this speech, she dispatched Attorney-General Geoffrey Cox to Brussels to see if he could do any better (see Chapter 2, pp. 52–53). Predictably enough, both initiatives failed and the government lost the second Meaningful Vote by another huge, albeit slightly smaller, margin (391 to 242).

Humiliation was immediately piled on humiliation when the government was not only defeated (321 to 278) on a motion to block a no deal departure from the EU, but felt unable—to the private fury of some of its members—to take any disciplinary action against the dozen or so frontbenchers (including four Cabinet ministers) who refused to toe the party line. Nor was it possible the day after to take action against the eight Cabinet ministers who opposed the government's motion to extend Article 50 and delay the UK's departure (the motion passed by 412 to 202). Behind the scenes, and without May's knowledge, discussions had already begun at CCHQ about how it could fight an early election, albeit one nobody there or in Number 10 really wanted. Meanwhile, ministers—even relative loyalists like Michael Gove, Chris Grayling and Liam Fox– were feeling cut off as May withdrew into her inner circle.[38]

Denied, for the moment, a third Meaningful Vote by Speaker John Bercow (who thereby cemented his position as a hate figure on the Conservative benches), May had run out of options and, on 20 March, requested a three-month extension to Article 50 from the EU-27. Furious and frustrated in equal measure, she made what many in her team would later concede was an unwise decision to deliver a Downing Street address to the nation in which she attempted, in populist language largely drafted by Robbie Gibb, to put herself on the side of the public. Voters, she claimed, were 'tired of the infighting, tired of the political games and the arcane procedural rows, tired of MPs talking about nothing else but Brexit when [people] have real concerns about our children's schools, our National Health Service, and knife crime'.

Parliament, she claimed, had done 'everything possible to avoid making a choice'.[39]

The speech, conceived in frustration and delivered in the heat of the moment, went down badly on all sides, but especially among Conservative MPs. It may well also have contributed to the Commons voting through, just a few days after hundreds of thousands marched through central London to demand a 'People's Vote', a plan to stage a series of 'indicative votes' in Parliament at the end of March—the first of two such unsuccessful attempts to break the logjam (see Chapters 2, pp. 54–55 and 4, pp. 126–127). May and her advisors had little or no expectations that those votes would produce an option capable of demanding sufficient support on the Tory benches for it to be politically viable. But she did hope that the frustration which followed the votes' failure might at last persuade the House to approve her deal, which she now put to what was effectively a third Meaningful Vote. In a further last-ditch effort to drum up support, she promised to resign once her deal was passed—a move sufficient to bring leadership hopefuls like Boris Johnson back on board, but, partly because she refused to name a precise resignation date, insufficient to persuade the ERG hardliners. However, May would not promise either the soft Brexit concessions or the second referendum promise that might have attracted significant support from the Labour benches. Without either the DUP or the so-called 'Spartans' (the least malleable members of the ERG who were now convinced that they would soon be able to replace May with a 'real' Brexiteer), May was nowhere near the critical mass needed to convince the minority of pro-Brexit Labour MPs that their support could be decisive.[40] As a result, her deal was rejected for a third and final time by a 344 to 286 margin.

Knowing the game was up, and with little hope that renewed talks with Labour could offer a way out, May could do nothing but accept the EU-27's insistence that the extension she requested should run until 31 October. This second extension also obliged the UK to hold elections to the European Parliament on 23 May. May and her team were under no illusions: the Conservative Party was bound to suffer a humiliating defeat (although quite how humiliating, perhaps nobody could have guessed). Yet May remained convinced that the no deal Brexit favoured by her hardline backbenchers and party members would have been even worse: breaking the government and blowing apart the union between Great Britain and Northern Ireland.

The Brexit Party, now led by veteran UKIP leader Nigel Farage, formally launched soon after, on 12 April (see Chapter 5, pp. 166–167). Focus groups conducted for Number 10 on the Thursday before and the Monday after suggested it had made an immediate impact.[41] Ten days later, some 70 Conservative association chairmen signed a motion of no confidence in Theresa May, prompting the 1922 Committee to ask her to clarify her position. She refused to commit, occupied as she was dealing with a leak from the National Security Council that led her to sack Defence Secretary Gavin Williamson, as well as the last-gasp attempt to construct a cross-party Brexit deal with Labour. Those talks began in early April and limped on until mid-May, though it quickly became obvious that there little real prospect that they would succeed. Labour wanted a softer Brexit than the Conservative side felt able to deliver, while the Conservative side wanted a harder Brexit than the Labour side could support. With May's days clearly numbered, the Conservative team lacked the authority to sell any compromise to their own side, while many on the Labour team feared that enabling a 'Tory Brexit' could split their party (see Chapter 4, pp. 126–127).[42]

May maintained her silence as her party went down to a bad defeat in local elections on 2 May and an even worse one at the European Parliament elections three weeks later. By then, everyone in the higher reaches of the Conservative party knew she was on her way out. Tory leadership hopefuls began to gear up in anticipation of an imminent vacancy. Having suffered the indignity of two colleagues—Rory Stewart and Boris Johnson—announcing they would be standing in the contest to replace her before she had even formally announced her departure, May finally tendered her resignation on 24 May, effective 7 June, after which she would stay on in a caretaker capacity until her successor was chosen. This would leave her a few weeks to try and deliver on some of her domestic agenda, in particular moves towards net zero carbon emissions and the introduction of a Domestic Abuse Bill. However, hopes that she could persuade the Chancellor Philip Hammond to approve significant new funding for schools—something that Number 10's opinion research showed was a top priority for 'Conservative considerers'—quickly foundered on his understandable reluctance to approve a multi-year, multi-million-pound package at the behest of a Prime Minister who had already announced her resignation.[43]

'May resignation' (Ben Jennings, *The i* paper, 25 May 2019 © Ben Jennings)

May was leaving behind a party on the edge of a nervous breakdown. The local elections were always going to be difficult because the Tories had done particularly well when those seats were last contested in 2015. But with 44 councils lost and more than 1,300 Conservative councillors defeated, it was the party's worst local election performance since 1995. The fact that Labour also did poorly was little consolation. But it was the results of the European Parliament elections—elections which the party, reasoning that its activists would refuse to get involved and not wishing to waste any money, made little or no effort to actually contest—that were genuinely frightening. The Conservatives notched up their worst performance in a nationwide election since the advent of full franchise democracy in 1928, taking just 8.8% and finishing fifth, behind the Green Party. Like Labour, they were routed by uncompromising parties on opposite poles of the Brexit divide—Nigel Farage's new Brexit Party topped the poll on 30.5% while the Liberal Democrats rode the wave of Remainer rejection, scoring nearly 20% and second place by urging voters to say 'Bollocks to Brexit' (see Chapter 5, pp. 170–172). According to the pollsters Lord Ashcroft and YouGov, around two-thirds of those who had voted Tory in 2017 had deserted the party, with the vast majority switching to the Brexit Party, which also picked up nearly 70% of 2017 UKIP voters.[44] Number 10's own research, conducted on polling day, suggested that the shift from the Conservatives to the Brexit Party had little to do with the *details* of May's Brexit deal and everything to do with the repeated *delays* in implementing Brexit.[45]

The mood of the grassroots was also growing toxic. According to one veteran agent—a Brexit supporter like most members—his charges had been growing increasingly disillusioned with May's leadership:

> She started with great goodwill ... That turned into mild irritation ... and then very quickly to despair ... The nadir for us was when we announced we would be holding European elections. That was the point where everyone on my wing of the party just gave up and thought: 'This can't go on.'

Membership had been slipping for a year or so: 'There was no rush of angry emails, more an atrophy of people not renewing or stopping being active.' As a result, 'it was a case of trying to hold the ship steady ... and dealing with wave after wave of anger and disappointment as various deadlines to Leave just came and went', while the few domestic policy achievements the government managed to chalk up were 'just marginalised in the cacophony of Brexit'. Unsurprisingly, therefore, at the Europeans:

> There was no activism. There was no campaign apart from the mailshot. The message from our members was: 'If you ask us to do anything, you'll be told where to go.' I turned a blind eye to many, many members campaigning for the Brexit Party.

Clearly something had to change—and change fast. And, fortunately for all concerned, it did. One of the arguments that had persuaded Conservative MPs not to dump May when she had faced a vote of no confidence back in December was that it would trigger a long and divisive contest to replace her as leader. However, although it was quickly apparent that there was no chance of the parliamentary party coalescing around one candidate and so avoiding the need for a full ballot of grassroots members (as happened in 2003 and 2016), the process, as shown in Chapter 1, took only around six weeks and was as good as over before it began, with Boris Johnson the clear frontrunner from start to finish. Moreover, as also shown in Chapter 1, Johnson signalled straight away, both in his rhetoric and his choice of colleagues and advisors, that he was determined, as Dominic Cummings put it at the first meeting of the government's SpAds, to achieve Brexit 'by any means necessary'.[46]

'Doing the Maths' (Brian Adcock, *The Independent*, 27 May 2019 © Brian Adcock)

By the time of that meeting on 27 July, Cummings had already recruited the man he and Johnson had agreed should run the next general election for them, the Australian Isaac Levido. Not long afterwards they had also secured the services of the polling expert, Michael Brooks. Both had worked on Conservative campaigns before as colleagues of Lynton Crosby, but, just as importantly, both had earlier that year been crucial components in the team that had pulled off a surprise third term for the Australian Liberal Party.

To those who remembered the difficulties of the disastrous 2017 Tory campaign—one ostensibly managed by Crosby—the choice of two Crosby protégés to run things in 2019 may have looked somewhat perverse. But that, in the view of the two men themselves, was to overlook a couple of the main reasons why things had gone wrong two years previously—namely, the failure to establish who was actually in charge from

the outset and to persuade voters that a general election was actually necessary. The new campaign chiefs were determined to ensure neither mistake would be repeated.

On the first point, things were clarified from the get-go. As Levido
himself puts it, they 'came to a very clear mutual agreement' that he
would be 'in charge of the campaign—building it and executing it ...
all the way through ... hiring and firing ... At the end of the day the
only one who could overrule my decisions would be the Prime Minister.
So effectively, I answered to the PM.'[47] Brooks, who was hired just after
him, made it equally clear that, in his words, 'there had to be a clear
decision making structure and it had to be very clear who was calling
the shots', and that direct access to the Prime Minister was crucial.[48]
Just as importantly, and to an extent that may surprise those convinced
that Cummings must somehow have run the show, Johnson's supposed Svengali 'was not', to quote one of those involved, 'a daily, min-
ute-by-minute participant'. As another of those involved put it:

> Dom didn't get involved in the day-to-day running of it. He devolved all
> of those decisions at the beginning and was happy to do so and completely
> stuck to his word ... So, no, he was not in the campaign, he was sort of off
> to the side. He'd contribute occasionally here and there on a phone call ...
> He was much more interested in the manifesto process. You know, what
> the government plans were post the election. But in terms of the actual
> running of the campaign, he stayed pretty clear.

None of this, of course, prevented other members of the Vote Leave
team coming on board in the run-up to the campaign itself. However,
people like Hanbury's Paul Stephenson, as well as some of the consul-
tancy's data analytics team, were brought in not because they were
'friends of Dom', but because they had valuable expertise and experience
(in Stephenson's case, for example, attack and rebuttal). This applied,
in spades, to the need to augment the party's in-house digital capacity,
particularly on the creative side. The Conservatives therefore brought in
New Zealand firm Topham Guerin, which had delivered a widely praised
online campaign for the Australian Liberal Party six months previously.

Convincing voters of the need for an election was an even more vital
goal. As Levido put it: 'The fundamental thing was voters in 2017 did
not see a burning need for an election and so we had to firmly establish that in in voters' minds.'[49] For all the talk of no deal and/or of the

Conservatives being desperate for an election now that Johnson had taken over, the hope was always that the Prime Minister would be able to negotiate an agreement with the EU. However, whether he was able to or not, Levido was adamant that it was vital that in any election that did take place, the Tories were able to tell voters that:

> This was a last resort. There was no other choice ... We are having this election because Parliament is broken. The only way we're going to be able to get this issue, whether you voted Leave or Remain, off the table so we can move on as a country is with a strong majority government that is going to be able to deliver that.[50]

Achieving the UK's withdrawal from the EU (ideally with a deal, but, if necessary, without one) may have been important in and of itself to the Conservatives, yet, for many of those whose support they were hoping to win, Brexit was more a means to an end. The party's campaign managers were convinced that this would mean that the coming campaign would need to focus not just on getting Brexit done, but also on what the government would deliver on health, education and policing once the whole thing was finally over.

Notes

1. 'Confidence and supply' essentially entails a support party (i.e. a party which is not actually in government, but which is enabling that government to form and to continue in office) promising the party or parties in government, first, that it will support the government in the event of a confidence motion being tabled in Parliament and, second, that it will vote for legislation enacting the government's Budget and other finance bills, money bills and appropriation legislation. In this particular case, the DUP also promised to support legislation pertaining to the UK's exit from the EU and to national security. It also agreed to work towards the formation of a new Northern Ireland Executive, which at the time was in abeyance. See Anthony Seldon with Raymond Newell, *May at Ten*. Biteback, 2019, pp. 269–79 for more detail on the negotiation and signing of the agreement.
2. See Seldon with Newell, *May at Ten*, pp. 246–48.
3. Philip Hammond, *Brexit Witness Archive, UK in a Changing Europe*, 13 and 20 November 2020, https://ukandeu.ac.uk/interview-pdf/?personid=42190.

4. For details of the meeting, see Seldon with Newell, *May at Ten*, pp. 284–87.
5. For details on their departure, see Seldon with Newell, *May at Ten*, pp. 235–37. On Hammond, see Philip Hammond, *Brexit Witness Archive, UK in a Changing Europe*, 13 and 20 November 2020, https://ukandeu.ac.uk/interview-pdf/?personid=42190.
6. For a portrait of Gavin Barwell, see Annabelle Dixon, 'Theresa May's Mr Nice Guy', *Politico*, 19 July 2017, https://www.politico.eu/article/theresa-mays-mr-nice-guy.
7. Barwell's own reflections can be found by going to Gavin Barwell, *Brexit Witness Archive, UK in a Changing Europe*, 1 and 25 September 2020, https://ukandeu.ac.uk/interview-pdf/?personid=42484.
8. See Theresa May, 'I Made Mistakes But One Year on I'm Going Green for Grenfell, Writes Theresa May', *Evening Standard*, 11 June 2018, https://www.standard.co.uk/comment/comment/i-made-mistakes-but-one-year-on-i-m-going-green-for-grenfell-writes-theresa-may-a3860046.html.
9. Will Tanner, interview, 17 July 2020.
10. For more on the differences between attitudes to membership in the Conservative Party and other parties, see Tim Bale, Paul Webb and Monica Poletti, *Footsoldiers: Political Party Membership in the 21st Century*. Routledge, Chapter 9.
11. Timothy Smith, 'Incumbency Advantage of UK Members of Parliament 1959–2010', PhD thesis, University of Nottingham, 2019, http://eprints.nottingham.ac.uk/56179.
12. The Conservative Party tends to remove even quite important documents from its website fairly swiftly, but there is a copy stored (for the moment) here: https://esrcpartymembersprojectorg.files.wordpress.com/2016/07/tory2017_ge-review-document.pdf.
13. Stephen Parkinson, interview, 19 June 2020.
14. See, for example, Boris Johnson, 'My Vision for a Bold, Thriving Britain Enabled by Brexit', *Daily Telegraph*, 15 September 2017, https://www.telegraph.co.uk/politics/0/boris-johnson-vision-for-brexit-bold-thriving-britain.
15. James Johnson, interview, 2 July 2020.
16. Gibbon was drawing a contrast with a clinical but brutal reshuffle that really did make an impact—albeit not as positive an impact as its author, Harold Macmillan, hoped it would when, on 13 July 1962, in a move that quickly became known as 'The Night of the Long Knives' after Adolf Hitler's purge in 1934, he sacked a third of his Cabinet. The same allusion was then later applied in a more direct way to Boris Johnson's first Cabinet reshuffle in 2019, dubbed the 'Night of the Blond Knives' by *The Sun* (see Chapter 1).

17. See Sebastian Whale, 'Karen Bradley: "I'm Not Here for the Headlines. I'm Here to Get the Best Thing for the Country"', *PoliticsHome*, 6 September 2018, https://www.politicshome.com/thehouse/article/karen-bradley-im-not-here-for-the-headlines-im-here-to-get-the-best-thing-for-the-country.
18. Brandon Lewis, interview, 29 June 2020.
19. For a detailed and harrowing account of the Windrush Scandal by the journalist who broke the story, see Amelia Gentleman, *The Windrush Betrayal: Exposing the Hostile Environment*. Guardian Faber Publishing.
20. See Seldon with Newell, *May at Ten*, pp. 386–92.
21. Sam Coates (SpAd to Sajid Javid), interview, 15 June 2020.
22. Stephen Parkinson, interview, 19 June 2020.
23. See Joanna Penn, *Brexit Witness Archive, UK in a Changing Europe*, 16 October and 17 November 2020, https://ukandeu.ac.uk/interview-pdf/?personid=43200.
24. For blow-by-blow accounts of the run-up, the meeting itself and the immediate aftermath, see Seldon with Newell, *May at Ten*, pp. 426–47. According to one Cabinet Minister, May could perhaps have handled it better: '[T]he Prime Minister was less robust than she needed to be at Chequers. She allowed a head of steam to gather in the room. I went into that room confident in my own mind that she was going to nail it, and she didn't. She allowed it to go on, and on, and on. Just when you think you've got to the point where you can bring this to a conclusion now, she tried to get more people to contribute ... We knew what the outcome was going to be, so the question was "Could we keep everybody on board?" because the outcome was, in a sense, predefined. The trick was to try and to do it while keeping everybody on board. And I thought she could. At one stage during the discussion, I thought we were there, but then it went on too long. Obviously, at the end of the session, nobody spoke out. Nobody said "Up with this I cannot put." Everybody toddled off. Then, of course, the gremlins got to them afterwards.'
25. Chris Smyth, 'Theresa May Offered Boris Johnson's Job to David Davis', *The Times*, 29 October 2019, https://www.thetimes.co.uk/article/theresa-may-offered-boris-johnsons-job-to-david-davis-nmt2tbx6z.
26. John Curtice, 'Why Chequers Has Gone Wrong for Theresa May', *What UK Thinks: EU*, 17 July 2018, https://whatukthinks.org/eu/why-chequers-has-gone-wrong-for-theresa-may.
27. See Theresa May, 'PM Brexit Negotiations Statement: 21 September 2018', https://www.gov.uk/government/news/pm-brexit-negotiations-statement-21-september-2018.

28. Pat Hurst, 'Nigel Farage Slams EU "Gangsters" at Brexit Rally in Bolton', *Manchester Evening News*, 22 September 2018, https://www.manchestereveningnews.co.uk/news/greater-manchester-news/nigel-farage-slams-eu-gangsters-15188212.

29. Philip Hammond, *Brexit Witness Archive, UK in a Changing Europe*, 13 and 20 November 2020, https://ukandeu.ac.uk/interview-pdf/?personid=42190.

30. Boris Johnson, 'Speech to Conservative Party Conference', *Brexit Central*, 2 October 2018, https://brexitcentral.com/boris-johnson-speech-conservative-party-conference.

31. This unusual but disarmingly effective piece of self-mockery sprang from earlier, cruelly amusing footage of the Prime Minister dancing awkwardly on an overseas trip that had gone viral on social media: 'Theresa May Dances on the Stage at the Tory Party Conference: Video', *Reuters/The Guardian*, 3 October 2018, https://www.theguardian.com/politics/video/2018/oct/03/theresa-may-dances-on-to-the-stage-at-the-tory-party-conference-video.

32. Tim Shipman and Caroline Wheeler, 'Four Meetings and a Political Funeral', *Sunday Times*, 21 October 2018, https://www.thetimes.co.uk/article/four-meetings-and-a-political-funeral-n2079bn3v.

33. Stephen Parkinson, interview, 19 June 2020.

34. Ibid.

35. For full details, see ESRC Party Members Project, 'No Deal Is Better Than May's Deal', 4 January 2019, https://esrcpartymembersproject.org/2019/01/04/no-deal-is-better-than-mays-deal. Some 72% of grass-roots Tory members, and 68% of current Tory voters, had voted Leave in 2016. And those members were preoccupied by Brexit: while 60% of voters as a whole ranked Brexit as the most important issue facing the country, that figure rose to 68% among Tory voters and a whopping 75% among Tory members. Nor had the latter changed their minds on the merits of leaving the EU: some 79% of Conservative Party members thought voters made the right decision in the 2016 referendum, including 97% of those who voted Leave two years previously.

But what was really striking in the findings was how little support there was at the Tory grassroots for May's deal. Conservative Party members, like most voters, thought that the government had made a mess of negotiating Brexit: 68% of the Tory rank and file (and 78% of Leave-voting members) gave their government a poor grade. And their dissatisfaction extended to the Withdrawal Agreement itself. Some 49% of voters overall said they opposed May's deal, with only 23% saying they supported it. Among those intending to vote Conservative, things looked a little more optimistic: 46% in favour and 38% against. However, among card-carrying members of the Conservative Party, opposition to the deal outweighed support by a margin of 59 to 38%. Furthermore, a majority of them (53%) thought May's deal did not respect the result of the referendum, rising to a super-majority of 67% among members who had voted Leave in 2016.

Even more worrying for the government, the Tory rank and file were convinced that no deal—a prospect that May herself had helped to legitimise after all—was better than the deal the Prime Minister was offering. Respondents were asked what their first preference would be in a three-way referendum where the options were (a) remaining in the EU, (b) leaving with the proposed deal, or (c) leaving without a deal. Among voters as a whole, some 42% of them plumped for Remain, with 13% going for the Prime Minister's deal and 25% for no deal. The respective figures for Tory voters, however, were very different: 23% Remain, 27% deal and 43% no deal. Among Tory members, support for no deal was even higher: 57% said leaving without a deal would be their first preference, compared to just 23% whose first preference was the current deal and only 15% saying Remain. Members' strong dislike of the Prime Minister's deal also emerged when asked about binary choices. Asked to choose between May's deal or no deal, only 29% of Tory members said they would vote for the Prime Minister's deal, compared to 64% who would vote to leave without a deal.

An overwhelming majority of the Conservative rank and file—presumably following the lead of celebrity Eurosceptics like Jacob-Rees Mogg and, of course, Boris Johnson—were convinced that the Irish backstop was a bad idea: only 11% thought it made sense and should be part of the deal; some 23% thought it was a price worth paying to get a deal; but 40% thought it was a reason in itself to reject a deal—and, added to that, 21% considered it irrelevant because May's deal was a bad one anyway. Tory members—like Tory voters—were also utterly unconvinced, despite their own government's best recent efforts, that a no deal Brexit would cause serious disruption: some 72% of voters who were intending to support the Conservatives thought the warnings were 'exaggerated or invented'—a figure that rose to 76% among Tory members. Meanwhile, members were convinced by a margin of 64 to 19% that leaving without a deal would have a positive effect on Britain's economy in the medium to long term. And asked how they would feel if the UK were to leave on the basis of May's deal, some 23% said they would feel betrayed and 10% angry, with a further 22% confessing they would be 'disappointed'.

36. It is clear that (in Number 10 at least) Brady and Malthouse were both seen as attempting to be helpful rather than wanting to create mischief. See Philip Hammond, *Brexit Witness Archive, UK in a Changing Europe,*

13 and 20 November 2020, https://ukandeu.ac.uk/interview-pdf/?personid=42190; Gavin Barwell, *Brexit Witness Archive*, *UK in a Changing Europe*, 1 and 25 September 2020, https://ukandeu.ac.uk/interview-pdf/?personid=42484; and Joanna Penn, *Brexit Witness Archive*, *UK in a Changing Europe*, 16 October and 17 November 2020, https://ukandeu.ac.uk/interview-pdf/?personid=43200.

37. Theresa May, 'PM Speech in Grimsby', 8 March 2019, https://www.gov.uk/government/speeches/pm-speech-in-grimsby-8-march-2019.

38. Seldon with Newell, *May at Ten*, p. 561.

39. 'PM Statement on Brexit: 20 March 2019', https://www.gov.uk/government/speeches/pm-statement-on-brexit-20-march-2019. See also Gavin Barwell, *Brexit Witness Archive*, *UK in a Changing Europe*, 1 and 25 September 2020, https://ukandeu.ac.uk/interview-pdf/?personid=42484; and Joanna Penn, *Brexit Witness Archive*, *UK in a Changing Europe*, 16 October and 17 November 2020, https://ukandeu.ac.uk/interview-pdf/?personid=43200.

40. The ERG hardcore took their nickname from the film *300*—a comic-book version of the battle of Thermopylae in 480 BCE when a few hundred Spartan soldiers attempted to hold out against a Persian army that massively outnumbered them. Some pointed out that the Brexiteers' choice of moniker might be a little ironic since all the Spartans had died, although, to be fair, Sparta, together with other Greek city-states, eventually won the war of which the battle was just one part.

41. James Johnson, interview, 2 July 2020.

42. On the Conservative side, see Gavin Barwell, *Brexit Witness Archive*, *UK in a Changing Europe*, 1 and 25 September 2020, https://ukandeu.ac.uk/interview-pdf/?personid=42484; Philip Hammond, *Brexit Witness Archive*, *UK in a Changing Europe*, 13 and 20 November 2020, https://ukandeu.ac.uk/interview-pdf/?personid=42190; and Joanna Penn, *Brexit Witness Archive*, *UK in a Changing Europe*, 16 October and 17 November 2020, https://ukandeu.ac.uk/interview-pdf/?personid=43200.

43. James Johnson, interview, 2 July 2020. For a sense of the frosty relations between the two at this stage, see Seldon with Newell, *May at Ten*, pp. 635–36. See also Philip Hammond, *Brexit Witness Archive*, *UK in a Changing Europe*, 13 and 20 November 2020, https://ukandeu.ac.uk/interview-pdf/?personid=42190.

44. See https://lordashcroftpolls.com/2019/05/my-euro-election-post-vote-poll-most-tory-switchers-say-they-will-stay-with-their-new-party and https://yougov.co.uk/topics/politics/articles-reports/2019/05/30/if-everyone-revealed-how-they-voted-last-week-labo.

45. James Johnson, interview, 2 July 2020.

46. Katy Balls, 'Inside Dominic Cummings' First Meeting with Government Aides', *The Spectator*, 27 July 2019, https://www.spectator.co.uk/article/inside-dominic-cummings-first-meeting-with-government-aides.
47. Isaac Levido, interview, 13 July 2020.
48. Michael Brooks, interview, 24 July 2020.
49. Isaac Levido, interview, 13 July 2020.
50. Ibid.

CHAPTER 4

The Man Who Wasn't There:
Labour Under Corbyn

In 2017 Jeremy Corbyn became the first Leader of the Opposition to survive election defeat since Neil Kinnock 30 years earlier. Corbyn's position was secure despite presiding over his party's third successive loss, thanks to a historically unprecedented campaign surge in support. Labour achieved the largest increase in its share of the vote since 1945 and the largest rise in support during an election campaign since polling records began. Corbyn himself saw a sharp rise in his previously dismal personal poll ratings, confounding claims he would be an electoral liability. By polling day in 2017, Corbyn was, for the first time, as popular with voters as the Prime Minister he opposed. Labour's loss was not perceived as such, at least internally.

At Glastonbury on 23 June 2017, Corbyn quoted Shelley to an ecstatic, sun-drenched crowd: 'Rise like lions after slumber, in unvanquishable number ... ye are many, they are few.'[1] Both he and the activists who had propelled him into the leadership believed they were turning the political tide. After all, Labour had come within a whisker of victory while campaigning on the most radical manifesto since 1983, and now opposed a demoralised and unstable Conservative minority government, one that some of Corbyn's advisors thought unlikely to survive long.[2] Corbyn's advisors did not, however, have many ideas about how to engineer the government's collapse, an event that many seemed to assume would simply occur without their intervention. Relatively little time was spent in the summer of 2017 reflecting on some of the

R. Ford et al., *The British General Election of 2019*, https://doi.org/10.1007/978-3-030-74254-6_4

weaknesses the campaign had not resolved: a chaotic Leader's Office, a dysfunctional party organisation, deep and unresolved factional divisions over Brexit and much else besides, and a leader who some felt struggled to exert authority over his own aides, let alone his party. While some efforts were made to plan for a future contest, mapping out broad areas of weakness to be addressed, the status of the 2017 campaign as a blueprint for future success went largely unquestioned.[3] As some involved later came to realise, an opportunity for more fundamental reorganisation was missed that summer.

'Corbyn at Glastonbury' (Ben Jennings, *The i* paper, 30 June 2017 © Ben Jennings)

The Leader of the Opposition's Office (known to all as 'LOTO') was more stable after the 2017 election than in the initial years of Corbyn's leadership, the success of the campaign conferring new authority on the team who presided over it. Seumas Milne, Corbyn's Executive Director of Strategy and Communications, and Andrew Fisher, Executive Director for Policy, had both worked with the leader since the autumn of 2015, while Karie Murphy, Corbyn's Chief of Staff, first joined LOTO in February 2016.[4] James Schneider, a co-founder of the pro-Corbyn activist group Momentum, had joined as Director of Strategic

Communications in October 2016. Corbyn's most senior aides had navigated a referendum and mass ministerial resignations, had seen off a leadership challenge and had run a general election campaign in just under a year.[5] Corbyn's LOTO also maintained close links to the leadership of the Unite trade union, Labour's largest donor, with regular input from Unite General Secretary Len McCluskey, and Unite chief of staff Andrew Murray working part-time with a leadership team which featured several Unite veterans.[6] There were two senior appointments in the spring of 2018, both hired as deputies to Seumas Milne: Anjula Singh, a former BBC manager, was brought in as Director of Communications, and Carl Shoben, a former NHS communications manager, was hired to take charge of LOTO's polling and focus group operations as Director of Strategy.

Stability at the top had its benefits, but meant that a number of concerns about LOTO performance went unaddressed. Some had concerns that Milne's dual role as Executive Director of Strategy and Communications led him to neglect the longer-term thinking required for strategic planning, focusing instead on the day-to-day cut and thrust of communications, which was in any event more comfortable terrain for a former journalist. Milne's unorthodox working habits, privileged access to Corbyn's ear and sometimes poor communication with colleagues were reportedly also a source of internal frustration.[7] Karie Murphy was widely praised for bringing order to Corbyn's chaotic LOTO early in her time as Chief of Staff, but as time went on, concerns grew about her expansive interpretation of the role and the control she exercised over access to Corbyn.[8] As one aide reflected:

> She was right for the time … But after we had a very good result in the 2017 election we needed to build on that. We had unified internally and improved, but now we needed to professionalise the operation to get to the next level. It's like in football, the manager who gets you promoted isn't necessarily the one to get you into Europe.

A failure to reorganise senior staff contributed to broader structural problems in LOTO, where inexperienced juniors worked in poorly defined roles, with messy decision-making processes and inconsistent communication and execution. 'There was absolutely no process', one LOTO staffer complained 'It was just a battle of wills, and a big factor is that Jeremy couldn't make decisions and would agree with the last person he met.' However, any LOTO restructuring would inevitably require letting loyalists go, and Corbyn was unwilling to move against staff who had stood by him through a difficult year. The opportunity for renewal slipped away.

Corbyn also resisted calls from some aides for a major Shadow Cabinet reshuffle to broaden his base and refresh an inexperienced top team, again because doing so would require firing loyalists: 'Who would you take out?' he asked aides. 'I don't want to take anyone out.'[9] Much of the Shadow Cabinet line-up cobbled together at the height of the 2016 leadership crisis now became permanent.[10] Longstanding Corbyn allies held two of the biggest portfolios for the whole Parliament—John McDonnell as Shadow Chancellor and Diane Abbott as Shadow Home Secretary. Emily Thornberry, a fellow veteran of Islington Labour politics and an early backer of Corbyn's 2015 leadership bid, served as Shadow Foreign Secretary throughout. Keir Starmer, another North London MP, but one without close links to Corbyn, served as Shadow Brexit Secretary, leading policy development on the defining issue of the day throughout the Parliament, even as his evolving position put him increasingly at odds with some LOTO advisors.[11] Jonathan Ashworth at Health, Angela Rayner at Education, Rebecca Long-Bailey at Business, Richard Burgon at Justice and Barry Gardiner at International Trade were others who served through the whole Parliament, becoming familiar Labour voices in the media. Veteran Chief Whip Nick Brown was retained throughout in the same role he once performed for Prime Ministers Tony Blair and Gordon Brown. Corbyn made one post-election gesture of reconciliation by bringing back Owen Smith, the rival he defeated in the 2016 leadership contest, as Northern Ireland Secretary.[12] He also rewarded the co-chairs of Labour's 2017 election campaign: Andrew Gwynne was promoted to the Communities and Local Government brief and Ian Lavery to Chair of the Labour Party—a post stripped from Deputy Leader (and outspoken Corbyn critic) Tom Watson. Meanwhile, a number of recent entrants to Parliament were handed ministerial portfolios, including Anneliese Dodds, Nick Thomas-Symonds and Marsha de Cordova.

Elsewhere, however, there were changes. The left's control of Labour's internal levers of power was precarious despite Corbyn's two leadership election successes and the 2017 general election advance. Most Labour MPs were, at best, reluctant supporters of the Corbyn project.[13] Though many new pledges of fealty arrived in the summer of 2017,[14] the Parliamentary Labour Party (PLP) remained restive and swift to criticise the leadership, while LOTO in turn was seen as reluctant to engage with MPs they distrusted. LOTO also still lacked a reliable majority on Labour's ruling National Executive Committee (NEC), and distrusted the career bureaucracy at Labour's Southside HQ, believing both staff and management there to be ideologically hostile to Corbyn and unhelpful in the 2017 election campaign.[15] Corbyn's aides were determined to put the political capital earned in 2017 to work by exerting a stronger grip on the party machine. Reforms offered LOTO an opportunity to entrench Corbyn's authority, while giving Corbyn's allies in Momentum a chance to advance the longstanding Bennite ideological goal of a more democratised, member-focused party.[16] Yet enthusiasm for empowering the party membership was not universal in LOTO or the Shadow Cabinet, and many of Corbyn's strongest allies in the trade union movement were opposed.

Corbyn's more vocal PLP critics expected to be the one of the targets of the reform agenda, with rumours of rule changes to facilitate the deselection of incumbent MPs circulating throughout the summer of 2017, often encouraged by more outspoken LOTO allies. In July, Ian Lavery, Labour's new Chairman, warned that Labour had become 'too broad a church' and that some MPs would have to 'work very hard' to avoid deselection, though he later backtracked.[17] Another Corbynite MP, Chris Williamson, spent the whole summer agitating for selection reforms, saying 'no MP should be guaranteed a job for life'.[18] Corbynsceptic MPs reported warnings from local activists and Momentum groups that their behaviour was being watched closely, with one Momentum group publishing a 'deselection hit list' of 49 MPs.[19] The launch of a wide-ranging 'democracy review' led by Corbyn's former political secretary Katy Clarke at the 2017 party conference gave notice of the leadership's plans, but the reforms that Corbyn's LOTO eventually brokered with their union allies at subsequent party conferences were modest and incremental.[20] The threshold for leadership nominations in the Commons was cut, making it easier for future left candidates to get on the ballot,[21] and three new membership elected representatives were added to the NEC (along with one trade union member). New rules to facilitate reselection contests against sitting MPs were indeed introduced, but these fell far short of what Jon Lansman and other party democracy activists had hoped Corbyn would deliver.[22]

Objections from the trade unions prevented more radical reforms, and while the new trigger ballot rules provoked some anxiety among MPs, they proved to be a paper tiger.[23] Only six MPs faced a renomination vote under the new rules and none was deselected. The threat of deselection may, however, have hastened the departure of some outspoken Corbyn critics who resigned the whip or defected to other parties over the course of 2019 (see Chapter 5), and encouraged some MPs worried about 'triggers' to spend more time courting local members. While democracy reformers regarded this greater attention to member concerns as a partial victory, some MPs felt that the time and energy focused inwards would have been better directed outwards.

***

Senior Southside managers had clashed repeatedly with LOTO during the 2017 campaign, and relations between the two organisations were strained for much of Corbyn's first two years in office. Veteran Executive Director of Elections, Campaigns and Organisation Patrick Heneghan believed from the moment the 2017 exit poll appeared that he and his colleagues would be held responsible by LOTO aides for Labour's failure to win the election outright and enter government. While Heneghan vigorously disputed this analysis, contending his team helped save threatened Labour incumbents in Leave-leaning marginals, he felt that LOTO hostility would soon render his position untenable.[24] Heneghan resigned in September 2017 and was initially replaced on an interim basis by Anna Hutchinson, the party's North West regional director. Niall Sookoo, a longstanding Corbyn ally who had served as LOTO's Director of Campaigns in 2017, took over as Southside's elections Executive Director in August 2018.

Further changes followed in the spring of 2018, triggered by the departure of longstanding Miliband-era appointee Iain McNicol as General Secretary. McNicol was replaced by Jennie Formby, a close ally of Corbyn Chief of Staff Karie Murphy and Unite leader Len McCluskey. Aside from a brief flirtation with the role from Momentum founder Jon Lansman, Formby faced no credible opposition and was confirmed as the new General Secretary by the NEC on 20 March 2018.[25] Her appointment was the tipping point for several senior Southsiders, who apparently felt unable to work under a Corbynite General Secretary, and departed ahead of Formby's appointment. 'They had worked with her on the NEC, she was seen as Karie [Murphy]'s and Len [McCluskey]'s tool', one former Southsider observed. Whether or not that was fair, LOTO found recruiting replacements with sufficient experience in management or political organisation difficult, reflecting the limited pool of appropriate candidates with loyalties to the left.[26]

Murphy, McDonnell and others moved swiftly in the summer of 2017 to enact another reform initiative: a 'community organisers' programme aiming to embed paid Labour activists as a presence in the everyday life of local communities. This idea had a long heritage, reflecting growing concerns that the decline of institutions such as blue-collar trade unions and working men's clubs had eroded Labour's presence in the communities the party aimed to serve. David Miliband (hardly a Corbynite figure) made this case in 2010 when he called for a 'movement for change'.[27] Ed Miliband had employed American veteran activist Arnie Graf to develop a community organiser network early in his term as Labour leader, though his enthusiasm for the idea was not shared by some aides, and the project ran into the sand.[28] Community organisers had much stronger support across the Corbyn leadership, with many Corbynites seeing the initiative as one which could give greater substance to their vision of Labour as a social movement. Community organisers also provided LOTO with a network of paid activists who some believed could be used to bypass a still-distrusted party bureaucracy.

An earlier LOTO push to roll out community organiser schemes ahead of the 2017 campaign had been rebuffed by Southside managers, who saw it as a distraction and likely to cause problems with the declaration of electoral expenses. The plan was revived after the election, and a new community organising unit was set up under Dan Firth, with resourcing substantially expanded after Jennie Formby's arrival as General Secretary in 2018, and additional funding shifted from a proposed large social media training project to develop a 'digital community organiser' programme.[29] While theoretically under the authority of Southside and party regional offices, in practice the dozens of paid organisers recruited by the unit apparently had little contact with the traditional party management, and often had strained relations with regional Labour offices. While some looked to make the best of a new resource, other regional managers resented the undercutting of their authority and their lack of control over Labour employees formally within their responsibility. Managers at Southside and the regions expressed concern that the young activists brought in on the programme, while full of zeal and energy, were not well trained or directed, engaged in divisive or ineffective campaigns and, owing to their inexperience, risked inadvertently breaking laws regulating their activity as paid employees of a political party.

The community organisers themselves were recruited primarily from the pool of young, strongly Corbynite activists mobilised by Momentum. Although by the summer of 2018 they were operating in a range of seats, legal and organisational constraints limited their deployment in key marginals: regional parties often already had local organisers in place in the most competitive seats and were not keen to change these. The community organisers were therefore mainly placed in stretch targets, a choice which dovetailed with LOTO's desire to rebuild Labour's presence in places where the party had struggled in recent elections. As the tide turned against Labour in 2019, this left many community organisers high and dry, operating in seats which Labour had little chance of winning.

While the community organising unit proved a disappointment, Labour under Corbyn nonetheless remained one of the most imposing political organisations in Western Europe. Membership had more than doubled in the first two years of his leadership, prompting boasts that Corbyn had created the largest mass movement in European politics. Though numbers fell back a little after 2017, they remained above half a million, providing Labour with a £16 million annual income stream. Corbyn's party was also effective at securing donations, receiving £18 million in the election years of 2017 and 2019, and a still healthy £6 million in 2018. Labour could also rely on substantial resource provision from its affiliated trade unions, the largest being the £1.5 million a year provided by Unite.[30] Despite these impressive organisational and financial resources, Labour found itself under strain through the 2017–19 Parliament. The party normally spends heavily during an election, then cuts back to rebuild reserves and clear debts in the aftermath. But the widespread belief that Theresa May's government was unstable led Labour to maintain itself on a 'war footing', keeping many extra staff on the payroll in readiness for a snap election. This drained resources as the months wore on and the government obstinately refused to collapse, eroding the advantages Labour might otherwise have enjoyed from a relatively strong financial and organisational position.

The dramatic expansion of Labour's membership under Corbyn had not made it more representative of the broader electorate. Older, white, middle-class professionals dominated the party's activist base, and its political views reflected these skews.[31] Liberal left views were dominant— pro-immigration, anti-austerity and overwhelmingly pro-Remain. Over 80% of Labour members surveyed in 2017, before the launch of the People's Vote campaign, favoured a second referendum, while over 90% wanted Britain to stay in the Single Market and the customs union.[32] This intense and vocal pro-Europeanism caused repeated headaches for instinctively Eurosceptic LOTO aides, as Corbyn resisted stances which would put him at odds with the party membership. This apparent reluctance to oppose the will of members bolstered the position of more pro-EU and later pro People's Vote members of his Shadow Cabinet, in particular Shadow Brexit Secretary Starmer, who could press for more pro-Remain positions safe in the knowledge that these were favoured by the party rank and file.

***

Momentum, the grassroots activist movement founded soon after Corbyn's election as leader, remained active in the new Parliament. With over 40,000 active members, Momentum had organisational and fundraising capacities equivalent to a substantial political party. Its members were younger, more vocal and more politically radical than the broader Labour membership, and its campaigning priorities reflected this. Momentum argued strongly for democratisation reforms to facilitate deselection of sitting MPs and to open up selection processes more broadly. Momentum also organised high-profile 'Unseat!' campaigns against prominent Conservative MPs representing relatively marginal seats, including Amber Rudd, Iain Duncan Smith and Boris Johnson. The returns to this campaigning were disappointing. Proposals for internal reform were watered down in the face of union opposition, changes to reselection procedures for sitting MPs had relatively little effect, and the impact of Momentum's constituency campaigning was debatable.[33]

Yet Momentum's impressive organisation on the ground and on social media ensured they remained an influential voice. Momentum activists successfully campaigned to increase the number of Constituency Labour Party representatives on the NEC, mobilised to support pro-Corbyn candidates for internal elections and in parliamentary selections, and provided many of the activists recruited into the community organising unit. Momentum also acted as outriders for radical new policy directions on issues such as the environment, housing and education, something which John McDonnell in particular was said to have encouraged as the Parliament wore on, as one Momentum leader recalled:

> LOTO weren't that interested in us supporting policy, but I think the more nuanced people within the Left like John McDonnell started to understand that we could help. We could outride for policy positions helpful to the leadership. Which clearly we did on the Green New Deal in 2019. We also made an impact on both education and housing, where Jeremy and John had two of their least helpful Shadow Ministers … Angie Rayner wasn't going to propose abolishing private schools. John Healey wasn't going to propose rent caps. And Jeremy probably didn't want to have that fight [with them]. But both of those policy ideas came through Momentum and we supported them through campaign groups.

This growing policy activism combined with deepening divisions over Brexit to increase the tensions within the Momentum leadership, between a radical policy-focused 'avant garde' and a Corbyn loyalist 'praetorian guard'. Many of the 'avant garde' were ardently pro-Remain, as was much of the Momentum membership, while the 'praetorian guard'— including the majority of Momentum's National Coordinating Group— opposed Brexit stances which would cause problems for Corbyn.[34] In Momentum, as in the broader Labour Party, the compromise which best satisfied both factions was to talk about something else, but this became ever harder to sustain as the Brexit debate polarised and Remain sentiment intensified in the rank and file. While Momentum never became openly critical of Labour's stance, they became more reluctant to reflexively back the leadership. Even the activist movement brought into being by Corbyn's rise could not escape the Brexit divisions which strained all parts of the Labour coalition as the Parliament wore on.

***

Labour began the Parliament with a manifesto commitment to accept the EU referendum result but implement Brexit differently, a compromise reflecting designed to help focus the 2017 campaign on domestic policy. This vague compromise was not sustainable in a Parliament dominated by Brexit wrangling from the start. Labour constantly needed to respond to the government's long struggle to negotiate and implement the specifics of the UK's withdrawal from the EU (see Chapter 2). Hanging over this constant tactical manoeuvring were bigger strategic questions. Should Labour agree to Brexit in principle, but attack the government's approach to achieving it? Or should they instead reject the whole idea of Brexit and campaign to keep Britain in the EU? If the referendum mandate was accepted, then Labour's parliamentary and electoral strategy could be focused on building support for a Labour vision of Brexit. If Labour committed to Remain, then their strategic goal would be mobilising voters inside and outside Parliament to reverse the entire Brexit process, most likely through a second referendum.

A halfway house strategy risked undermining both goals. Campaigns for a 'Labour Brexit' would lack credibility if the party leading them looked like it would rather not implement Brexit at all, while demands to reverse Brexit would be similarly unconvincing coming from a party still promising to negotiate a departure deal. The polarising logic of the situation seemed to require a clear choice. Yet avoiding such a choice remained the primary goal of the leadership, for whom the need to keep a fractious party united overrode all other considerations. The resulting muddled compromises left Corbyn's LOTO unable to grasp the political opportunities presented by the May government's troubles over Brexit, as the opposition's Brexit proposals were no more appealing than the baroque mess being offered by the government. In the words of one senior advisor, observing LOTO's Brexit strategy was like watching the director of a play rewriting the script on the fly to keep the cast happy while the audience headed for the exits.

Labour's Brexit dilemma would have taxed any leader's resources, but it posed unique problems for Corbyn. After 2017, Labour had a strongly Remain membership and an increasingly Remain electorate,[35] but the party's path to a parliamentary majority ran through strongly Leave-voting constituencies where the Conservative vote had grown sharply in 2017.[36] The voters and seats Labour held leaned Remain, but the voters and seats Labour needed to win leaned Leave. Layered on top of this electoral problem was a deeper ideological tension. Brexit was a clash of two electoral mandates: the national voter mandate from the 2016 EU referendum and the internal party mandate from party members in two Labour leadership contests. Leave voices in Labour regarded the referendum mandate as inviolate—Labour had to 'respect the result'. Yet the Bennite wing of Labour from which Corbyn hailed regarded the will of the strongly Remain party membership as similarly sacrosanct. Many believe Corbyn, who had no strong religion on Europe, was genuinely torn. Leavers in LOTO, the Shadow Cabinet and the unions—who regarded some Labour Remain agitation with suspicion as opposition to Corbyn by proxy—warned of a looming electoral apocalypse in Leave seats if Labour opposed Brexit.[37] Yet equally influential Remain voices insisted that a Labour backed Brexit would be just as electorally costly, provoking a revolt among Labour's Remain majority and harming the broader Corbyn project by putting the leader at odds with overwhelmingly pro-EU party members.[38]

The remorseless Article 50 countdown pushed Brexit to the top of the agenda from the moment Parliament reconvened. At the start of the Parliament, the Labour discussion was still focused on what form departure from the EU should take rather than whether it should happen at all. Most Labour Remain MPs were resigned to Brexit, but wanted to limit the harm by keeping Britain within the EU's main economic institutions—the Single Market and the customs union.[39] More Brexit sympathetic voices, including senior LOTO advisors, opposed these institutions as a constraint on economic radicalism and a source of avoidable electoral headaches over immigration. Yet rather than setting out a clear Labour approach to Brexit, Corbyn and LOTO let this debate drift, using procedural and policy devices to defuse internal fights as they arose, while delaying firm decisions whenever possible.[40] Refrains such as 'we are not ruling anything out' and 'all options are on the table' became wearily familiar from Labour politicians. These were messages designed to convey flexibility and openness, but they also seemed to underline the leadership's reluctance to choose, as one advisor recalled:

> LOTO were averse to taking bold initiatives to change the political weather. It always seemed more easy to just do what oppositions do in British politics, which is just oppose and don't take any initiatives until you absolutely have to … Corbyn preferred a more passive approach.

The first flashpoint came on 29 June 2017, when more than 50 Labour MPs rebelled to back an amendment to the Queen's Speech tabled by Chuka Umunna calling for the UK to remain in the Single Market. Three Shadow Ministers were sacked for defying the whip.[41] The amendment frustrated some in the leadership, who saw it as troublemaking by PLP Corbynsceptics. As one aide recalled: 'Regardless of the politics around the issue, this was meant to be the first big test of whether Theresa May had a majority and we turned it into "Labour's had a rebellion of 45-odd people".' While distrust of Corbyn was doubtless a motive for some rebels, many sincerely wanted to press the case for Single Market membership with a leader who showed little enthusiasm for the idea but also never ruled it out. A compromise proposal by Keir Starmer sought to win over pro-EU MPs with an offer to keep Britain in the Single Market for a lengthy transition period. This defused the row without resolving it, and Remain MPs and members sought to make their case again at Labour's annual conference, putting in pro-Single Market resolutions and briefing that a major Brexit policy debate was coming. Yet rather than seize the opportunity to hash out internal differences, Corbyn and LOTO moved to keep the issue off the conference agenda entirely, mobilising Momentum loyalists behind a slate of conference proposals which did not mention Brexit. Railway nationalisation was up for debate at the 2017 Labour conference, but Britain's EU membership was not. LOTO succeeded in averting a fight at conference, but at a heavy price. The organised suppression of debate on the defining issue of the day seemed at odds with Corbyn's longstanding advocacy of internal democracy, and infuriated many Remainers in the party.

Labour's ducking and weaving continued through the autumn as the raft of legislation needed to enact Brexit wended its way through a fractious Parliament (see Chapter 2, pp. 31–36). Officially, the party would support any Conservative approach to Brexit which passed six 'tests' formulated by Shadow Brexit Secretary Keir Starmer.[42] These tests were vague enough to be interpreted however Labour wanted, yet clear enough in their crossing of Theresa May's 'red lines' that the government was sure to reject them.[43] Starmer's gambit furnished Labour with the political cover needed to whip MPs repeatedly against government Brexit legislation without setting out a clear alternative. By the end of the autumn session, Labour MPs, working with Conservative soft Brexit rebels, had succeeded in extracting from the government pledges for further 'meaningful votes' on any deal agreed with the EU. But in the absence of any Labour alternative, it was not clear what the test of a 'meaningful vote' could achieve. If May's deal failed the test, there was no 'Plan B' to offer.

Corbyn sought to flesh out Labour's 'jobs first Brexit' in a speech in Coventry in February 2018.[44] He announced that Labour would seek a bespoke customs union with the EU.[45] A Corbyn government would take Britain out of the Single Market and would end free movement within the EU, but would keep Britain within various other EU institutions and would use the negotiation of a bespoke customs union agreement to ensure that no border arrangements were imposed on Northern

Ireland. The Coventry speech laid out a clearer vision of how Labour would approach future Brexit negotiations, but it was soon overtaken by events inside and outside of Parliament.

Corbyn's Coventry proposals were also not sufficient to settle the Brexit debate within his party. Three broad factions had emerged in the PLP, which might be termed 'swift Brexit'; 'soft Brexit' and 'stop Brexit'. The most pro-Leave Labour MPs increasingly favoured ending the Brexit impasse as quickly as possible by backing any viable Brexit deal capable of securing a parliamentary majority, even if this required terms close to those negotiated by the Conservatives. These 'swift Brexit' MPs mostly represented heavily Leave-voting seats, and were motivated by a mix of sincere belief in respecting the 2016 result and fear that failing to do so would be electorally fatal. The 'soft Brexit' faction also supported Brexit in theory, but its members had more defined views about the kind of Brexit they wanted to see. Labour soft Brexiteers saw amendment and delay tactics as a valuable mechanism to force their preferred options on to the agenda, putting them at odds with their 'swift Brexit' colleagues who regarded parliamentary gridlock as electorally toxic. The third Labour faction was not interested in debating the terms of departure, because their goal was to prevent Brexit happening at all. There were relatively few 'stop Brexit' Labour MPs early on, but internal Conservative divisions and parliamentary deadlock were already raising questions about whether the May government could implement any Brexit plan (see Chapters 2, pp. 37–46 and 3, pp. 84–88) when the 'People's Vote' (PV) campaign emerged. This changed the terms of Labour's factional debate by providing 'stop Brexit' MPs with what they regarded as a credible means to prevent Brexit altogether.

The PV campaign, launched early in 2018, was a well-resourced organisation built on the remains of the official 2016 Remain campaign. Labour campaign veterans including Alastair Campbell, Tom Baldwin and Patrick Heneghan were a prominent presence on and offstage in PV activities.[46] Their main goal from the outset was to pressure Labour into backing a second public vote, as one of those involved recalled:

> There was only one big party whose stance was in question and that was the Labour Party. And our goal was to change their frontbench position. Because to get to a majority for a People's Vote in the House of Commons, you needed virtually the entire Labour party cohort.

The PV campaign pursued a three-pronged strategy to persuade Labour: pushing motions and amendments at conference; building an organised

faction (complete with whips) within the PLP; and lobbying local
Labour party groups to pressure their MPs. PV campaigners also sought
to shift the public narrative about the electoral calculus Labour faced
over Brexit. The campaign sponsored regular polling research, splashed
on the front pages of Remain-leaning newspapers, which claimed voters
were shifting towards Remain and towards a second referendum, and
warning that Labour faced greater electoral risks from backing Brexit
than opposing it. The polling research included sophisticated constituency-level 'MRP' analysis, which delighted newspaper editors and equipped
campaign activists with figures claiming to show shifts towards Remain in
Labour-held seats.

People's Vote protesters march on Parliament, 23 June 2018 (© Simon
Dawson/Getty Images)

The PV bandwagon offered a tempting outlet for a broad coalition
of pro-European Labour MPs who found it easier to unite on stopping
Brexit than to agree an approach to softening Brexit. Remain-leaning
Labour backbenchers were the low-hanging fruit for PV campaigners.
The bigger prizes lay in LOTO and the Shadow Cabinet. But an organ-
isation led by a mix of Conservatives and Corbynsceptic Labour veterans

had little purchase in the upper echelons of the Corbyn leadership. Such lobbying was therefore often left to Labour members and other grass-roots campaigners who LOTO would find it harder to ignore. Prominent left wingers organised a 'Labour for a People's Vote' group and a 'Left against Brexit' tour in the summer of 2018 to press the Corbynite case for a second referendum. The Momentum grassroots also supported a second referendum, as polling of the group's membership confirmed in the summer of 2018, obliging the Momentum leadership to signal in September that it would not block a conference debate on Brexit as it had the previous autumn. While many of Corbyn's closest aides remained firmly opposed to a second referendum and reportedly sought to limit the leader's exposure to pro-referendum arguments,[47] the growing enthusiasm of party members was becoming difficult for Corbyn to ignore.

The Brexit dividing lines were also shifting in LOTO and the Shadow Cabinet. Despite the passions it aroused elsewhere, few of the most senior figures in the Labour Brexit debate had strong feelings about the issue in either direction (Emily Thornberry and Seumas Milne were perhaps the two most notable exceptions). One belief which therefore united nearly all involved was frustration that Labour was obliged to spend so much time on the issue. The Shadow Cabinet was divided, with Remainers such as Shadow Foreign Secretary Thornberry and leader of the European Parliamentary Labour Party Richard Corbett balanced by supporters of a Labour Brexit such as Jon Trickett and Ian Lavery. Over the course of 2018, the evolving positions of three pivotal figures—Keir Starmer, John McDonnell and Diane Abbott—helped to tip this balance towards (caveated) endorsement of a second referendum, despite continued resistance from some senior LOTO aides.[48] Neither Starmer nor McDonnell were seen as passionate about Europe, and both were believed to see the issue primarily through the lens of party unity and election strategy, while Abbott, a longstanding Eurosceptic, came to regard Brexit as an expression of intolerant nationalism. The growing appeal of a second referendum among the membership and Labour voters suggested to all three that Labour had to show greater willingness to consider the idea. Abbott warned the Labour leader he would be remembered as 'Ramsay MacCorbyn' if he broke with Labour members to impose a 'Tory Brexit'.[49] McDonnell, who had cut his political teeth in the early 1980s, worried that ruling out a second referendum could split the parliamentary party, with dozens of the most pro-EU MPs defecting or resigning the whip to form an SDP-style breakaway.

Things came to a head in September at Labour's annual conference in Liverpool. Keir Starmer convened a marathon meeting with union and CLP delegates to try and broker a unified stance on Brexit. A new compromise was hammered out in five hours of gruelling discussion. Labour would continue to prioritise a general election as their preferred means to break the Brexit deadlock, but would now explicitly endorse the option of a second referendum as one of several alternatives to consider if a general election proved impossible. LOTO Eurosceptics remained opposed to a second referendum, but accepted this compromise to avert a damaging fight on the conference floor. The concession was, in theory, only symbolic: while Labour were now naming a second referendum as one way to resolve Brexit, Corbyn retained the power to decide when (or if) to exercise that option. The policy gave no clear trigger, so Corbyn could always argue the time was not right. In practice, the change was more consequential. The main debate within Labour from now on was no longer what kind of Brexit to back, but whether to back Brexit at all.

Labour conference 2018 (Ben Jennings, *The Guardian*, 23 September 2018 © Ben Jennings)

The implications became clear from the moment the policy was announced. John McDonnell sought to downplay its significance in his morning broadcast round, emphasising the need to 'respect the result of the last referendum' and hinting that a second vote need not include an option to Remain. The futility of this framing became evident within hours, when Keir Starmer drew a standing ovation by declaring—apparently without warning colleagues in advance—that not only was a second referendum one option to break the impasse, but that 'nobody is ruling out Remain as an option'.[50] Wide sharing of this clip provoked a counterblast from Leave-leaning Shadow Cabinet members, who criticised Starmer for upsetting the balance of the new policy.[51] In reality, Starmer didn't need to play anything up—Labour members cheered the idea of a second referendum with a Remain option because it was the policy most of them now wanted. Corbyn himself sought to restore balance the next day, emphasising in his leader's speech that he would vote through a Brexit deal on Labour's terms if Theresa May brought one back from Brussels. This was not so enthusiastically received in the conference hall and was criticised by second referendum advocates, who saw it as an effort to row back from Starmer's commitment. The laboriously negotiated 2018 conference compromise was supposed to restore party unity on Brexit. Instead, it accelerated the process of disintegration.

The extent of this Balkanisation became clear when the debate moved back to the Commons, where Labour MPs unhappy for different reasons with the conference compromise forged ahead with their own parliamentary initiatives. The resulting procedural acrobatics won senior Labour backbenchers several notable victories over the government (see Chapter 2), but did not secure any substantive concessions. This risked emboldening the soft Brexit and stop Brexit factions by creating the illusion of progress, as one senior aide recalled:

> When you defeat the government, time and again, with these massive votes it all looks very exciting, and you look like you're going somewhere. Actually it didn't seem to me that it was really going anywhere because it didn't lead on to anything. We had no mechanism to get to the point we wanted to.

By the spring of 2019, the focus of both soft Brexit and stop Brexit Labour MPs became forcing an extension of the rapidly approaching Article 50 deadline. Fear of a 'no deal Brexit' united them, as each group hoped that winning extra time would enable their preferred outcome to prevail. This hope proved to be forlorn. A broad coalition of Labour,

Conservative and smaller party opponents of May's Brexit deal could unite to block the government's proposals, but could not agree on what to do instead.[52] The division between soft Brexit and stop Brexit proved just as hard for Labour to bridge on the Commons benches as it had been in the conference hall. Second referendum supporters argued that the only route to a Commons majority for any Brexit deal was by making it subject to final approval from the public. This did not persuade soft Brexit Labour MPs, who countered that many in their camp would never countenance a second referendum that was seen (not unreasonably) as a stalking horse for stopping Brexit altogether. Yet the soft Brexiteers in turn could not win a majority for any alternative Brexit deal unless they signed up most of their pro-second referendum colleagues. And a substantial cohort of these—dubbed by one frustrated soft Brexit Labour MP 'the People's Vote Taliban'—refused to soil their hands with support for any form of Brexit on any terms.

A strong stance from the Labour leadership might have helped coalesce parliamentary support, but Corbyn was perceived to be missing in action once again. Pro-Brexit LOTO aides saw merit in the parliamentary soft Brexit initiatives, and Corbyn himself sounded supportive in private meetings with their organisers. But LOTO never offered clear public backing to any single initiative, instead sticking to the letter of Labour's ambiguous conference proposal by keeping all options open.[53] Without a clear stance from Corbyn, it was not clear how opponents of the government's approach could overcome their own internal divisions and coalesce around an alternative. The need to decide was becoming ever more urgent, yet Corbyn still prevaricated. The leadership vacuum combined with growing polarisation at all levels of the party to produce an escalating briefing war, as LOTO aides, Shadow Cabinet members and backbenchers all sought to influence Labour's position in an increasingly public and ill-tempered tug of war. Conflict was the only constant in Labour's messaging, an aspect the media were happy to magnify, as one aide recalled:

> It was a huge challenge because you could not rely on anyone to hold a line … clarity of messaging wasn't really possible.…Certain people couldn't be relied upon on broadcast, and their own teams are briefing anyway … And the media loves that juicy story of Diane Abbott has got a different view on what Brexit means to Ian Lavery.

The government's Withdrawal Agreement was in deep trouble with Tory backbenchers, but as long as the Labour Brexit factions remained at odds with each other, there was little danger of a majority emerging for anything else. With the Labour leader himself planting no flag to rally around, the cross-party group of backbenchers who had waged effective guerrilla war against May's deal now sought to develop new parliamentary mechanisms to force the government's opponents to coalesce behind a single alternative. They twice secured parliamentary time for 'indicative votes' designed to gauge the relative popularity of alternative Brexit policies. Yet hopes among the Labour whips that the process would bring unity were soon dashed:

> Previously, we had always tried to have these overlapping coalitions. But as soon as it got to MPs picking your favourite options, it worked from the government side as a means of dividing your enemies rather better than it did at bringing people together.[54]

A Brexit sympathetic LOTO aide agreed, citing the lack of compulsion in the voting process as a critical factor:

> It failed because there was no compulsion. It ended up basically being a system where people only voted for their preference and voted against everything else, or just didn't vote at all … Basically any scenario that involved some compulsion to vote in some way, something which involved good faith engagement by the overwhelming majority of MPs, then basically May plus customs union just wins.

Despite three huge Commons defeats for Theresa May's Withdrawal Agreement, this repeated failure to build a majority for anything else dashed the opposition's credibility and handed the initiative back to the government. With no other cards left to play, May finally agreed to an approach she had spent two years avoiding—offering Labour's leaders direct talks to seek a bipartisan agreement. The cross-party Brexit negotiations of April 2019 were, from Labour's perspective, earnest, cordial and largely pointless. There was much praise for Gavin Barwell, who led negotiations on the Conservative side and worked hard to seek a viable compromise, as did the Labour negotiators. Yet the elephant in the room was obvious to all. As John McDonnell reflected, negotiating with a Prime Minister who had lost the confidence of her own MPs was like 'trying to enter into a contract with a company that's going into administration'.[55]

Even if a compromise was struck, it was moot: 'the people who are going to take over are not willing to fulfil that contract'. This problem infiltrated all aspects of the negotiation. Labour negotiators would agree a set of concessions with their Conservative counterparts only to find, as one of those involved recalled, 'when the text came through that had been signed off by the Ministers, it never had the proper compromises in it that we had been promised'. Although all involved thought the grounds for compromise were there, the political situation made it impossible. Even if May's team had managed to deliver on promised policy concessions, Labour could not take the huge risk inherent in backing a bipartisan deal—as one aide noted, 'we could have ended up with half the frontbench resigning and then people defecting'—when they could not trust a lame duck Prime Minister to deliver the votes of her own MPs. The talks collapsed in mid-May and the PM announced her departure soon after.

'Cross-party talks continue' (Dave Brown, *The Independent*, 9 May 2019 © Dave Brown)

Labour's approach to Brexit once Boris Johnson took office was a series of variations on now well-worn themes. The party had another impassioned conference debate in September, with another round of ill-tempered briefing wars, culminating in a floor vote on two options, with delegates strongly backing LOTO's preferred proposal, then narrowly voting down a stronger commitment to Remain, thanks in part to a strong intervention from Unite leader Len McCluskey calling for loyalty to the leader.[56] Labour would therefore go into the 2019 election committed to negotiate a new Brexit deal within six months, which would then be put to the public in another referendum, but without saying how the party or its leader would campaign in such a referendum. This position enabled Labour once again to duck the question of Leave or Remain by saying the outcome of negotiations couldn't be pre-judged. While this just about satisfied opinion internally, it seemed unlikely to appeal to either side of an increasingly polarised electorate. There was then another round of parliamentary drama, where the government's opponents again came together to delay Brexit, then again failed to unite behind any alternative. 'Swift Brexit' Labour MPs, many of whom had privately expressed a willingness to vote for May's deal in the spring but pulled back when it became clear that she could not unite her own MPs, now began to lose patience with their more pro-EU colleagues. Frustration in Labour Leave constituencies was boiling over: 'We had pissed off a lot of people. I was spat at in my own constituency, where I've lived all my life. It was dreadful', said one MP. Many of those in Leave seats, regardless of their own views about the EU, began to feel that any Brexit resolution was better than fruitless delay and mounting frustration. Once Boris Johnson was able to demonstrate he had unified his own benches behind a Withdrawal Agreement, a group of Labour Leave MPs finally jumped on board, more than enough to provide him with a majority. The party whose main divide was over whether to soften Brexit or stop it altogether ended up providing the decisive votes for Johnson's renegotiated Withdrawal Agreement, enabling him to go into the subsequent general election touting an 'oven-ready' hard Brexit deal. As one LOTO aide ruefully reflected:

> Everybody should look back on that – May's side, our side, the hard remain side, the Lib Dems and some of our own side – and just think 'we all fucked up'. Your number one 'don't end up with this' is a hard Brexit, and that is what we got. It was an utter failure.

'Our position is perfectly clear...' (Chris Riddell, *The Observer*, 21 September 2019 © Chris Riddell)

***

Domestic policy was always of greater interest than Brexit to Corbyn's LOTO and particularly to John McDonnell's Shadow Treasury. Corbyn had won two leadership elections as a principled radical with plans to remake Britain. Two policy teams based in LOTO and Shadow Treasury worked closely together under the direction of Andrew Fisher throughout the Parliament to turn those ambitions into reality. Over time, a sweeping agenda was constructed, focused on increased state investment and regulation, nationalisation of key industries and radical cuts to greenhouse gas emissions was developed, with major tranches of policy announced at each of the three party conferences of the Parliament.[57] In 2017 came pledges to tax online gambling firms, cap credit card interest payments, make rental housing contracts more secure, and provide more cash for the NHS and Sure Start centres. The headline announcement was a pledge by John McDonnell to end Private Finance Initiative contracts, a symbolic (and expensive) break with a flagship Gordon Brown policy initiative. While internal battles over Brexit and party democracy dominated coverage of Labour's 2018 conference, the party also pressed ahead with another major raft of policies, including proposals to extend green jobs, green energy and free childcare, to give workers a stake in their companies and seats on their boards, to nationalise water provision and to rewrite Treasury investment rules to 'end the bias against investing in the regions and nations'.[58] The 2019 conference was also overshadowed by Brexit and internal feuding, but once again Labour rolled out plenty of radical policies, including proposals for a National Education Service (paid for in part through taxes on private schools), free personal care services, a four-day working week, rent caps, a big minimum wage hike, a million afforda-ble homes and pledges to end in work poverty during their first term in office and to decarbonise the economy by 2030.

Labour's biggest domestic policy initiative of the Parliament—its plan to decarbonise the UK economy—illustrate the scale of radical pol-icy ambitions under Corbyn. Branded the 'Green New Deal' or 'Green Industrial Revolution' (GIR), the plan was designed to address the threat of climate change while also generating millions of 'green jobs' in sectors such as renewable energy and electric vehicles.[59] The GIR agenda served political ends as well, with regular policy announcements used to raise the profile of younger Corbynites such as Rebecca Long-Bailey, seen as a potential future leadership candidate for the left, who promoted the agenda as Shadow Business Secretary. Labour policy advisors had high hopes for a plan which made an ambitious case for state-led economic transformation, and worked to flesh it out in minute detail, spelling out where each factory would be located and how many green jobs would be created in every constituency. As one advisor recalled, the GIR was seen as an agenda which could unite both the Leave and Remain parts of Labour's electoral coalition:

This is the one thing that can unite Leavers and Remainers. Urban areas who care about it are more likely to care about environment, left behind areas more likely to care about good jobs. This is a way of using radical action on climate change to create good jobs and bring investment back to areas that have been starved of it.

While there was an underlying economic strategy underpinning much of Labour's policy development, cutting across this was a growing tendency to use policy announcements as a communications strategy. This began in the spring of 2017, when Labour had launched a 'policy blitz' during the Easter recess, as one policy advisor recalled: 'this was the first time,

I think, from when Jeremy became leader that we got quite rolling positive news coverage ... I think we started to take the lesson from that that we did best when we talked about policy'. From that point onwards, some in the leader's office came to see policy announcements as a way to generate positive headlines, at least with sympathetic newspapers, and treated Labour's policy teams as a cookie jar to be raided whenever a quick hit of good news was needed. Advisors were told to quickly generate new policies to accompany speeches by Corbyn or to combat negative coverage of Labour's internal disputes. As one advisor recalled:

> Our response to any damaging crisis was 'oh, quick, think of a policy announcement, that's the only way to get on the front pages of the papers'. Policy announcements were seen in practical terms and political terms as the way out of a hole.

Leaning on policy to generate positive coverage worked well initially, but generated increasing problems over time. As one policy advisor put it: 'It started to seem like we were doing things backwards. We should do a speech when we've got something to announce rather than come up with something to announce because we've got a speech to do.' The stream of expensive announcements undermined the coherence of Labour's policy offer and opened the party up to traditional charges of profligacy and waste. The communications strategy itself also yielded diminishing returns because, as one advisor reflected, 'it stopped being newsy to hear "Labour announces radical new policy"'.

John McDonnell was keenly aware of the need for clearer links between policy development and strategic communications, and sought to build a more effective Shadow Treasury team to help make the case for Labour's agenda. Early in the Parliament, he brought back an old ally, Madeleine Williams, to reorganise a fractious Shadow Treasury team. McDonnell, a radical left veteran with a divisive image, sought to rebrand himself as a reassuring managerial figure, as one of his aides explained: 'we had a strategy for presenting John in a different way ... Tea and toast in the local café ... lots of visits and meetings in the City with hedge fund managers and banks. People would see that you've got a personable, perfectly reasonable human being who's really on top of the brief, and change their views'. But if the team enjoyed some success in promoting a more moderate, avuncular image for their chief, communicating Labour's broader policy agenda proved more difficult.

No effective coordination process emerged to balance McDonnell and Fisher's desire for building a coherent long-term policy framework with the regular LOTO demands for headline-grabbing initiatives. Communication of policy across the broader Labour machine was often seen as poor, hampered by persistent LOTO and Shadow Treasury distrust of the Southside policy team charged with handling much of the routine policy briefing and communications work, as one aide recalled:

> We really needed an operation that was making politicians feel confident that 'this is what we're trying to get across. This is why their criticisms are ridiculous. Here are lines that are going to help you do that' ... But that work never really happened, because the Southside briefing team shared the scepticism of the journalists that were asking questions ... When we moved over to Southside in 2019 I got to see first hand how the briefing team actually worked. They would take the politician into a side room and read through the policy briefing we had provided, and kind of shrug their shoulders when the politician asks 'well what do I say if they say this?'. Then they would come back to their desks bitching about what a stupid policy it was.

Growing Brexit fault lines also disrupted the policy process, with the two most senior figures managing domestic policy development—Andrew Fisher and John McDonnell—increasingly aligned with more pro-second referendum and Remain-friendly stances, while the two most senior figures in charge of communications strategy—Seumas Milne and James Schneider—were more opposed to a people's vote. Broader factional battles between Corbynistas and Corbynsceptics across the party also disrupted policy development, with frequent leaks discouraging those working on policy from communicating ideas under development, as one advisor recalled: 'Policy couldn't be talked about anywhere because it all leaked. There was a lot of stuff that wasn't done properly because people didn't trust each other not to leak it.' The constant need to firefight internal crises over Brexit, relations with the PLP and anti-semitism also distracted LOTO attention from policy, preventing sustained or coherent development of the agenda: 'You need engagement from senior politicians and from the executive directors and from the press team. And if everyone there is on their phones 12 hours a day, dealing with anti-semitism crises, they're just not looking at our stuff.'

In the end, the radical domestic policy agenda which was the source of Corbynism's distinctiveness and was seen by many in the project as the driver of the party's unexpected electoral success in 2017 fell victim to the same factional feuding which undermined all of Labour's activity during the Parliament. A disciplined and organised LOTO organisation might have helped offset some of these weaknesses, but Corbyn and his most senior advisors never managed to build one. Instead, they presided over an organisation widely seen as chaotic and dysfunctional, with inexperienced staff, high turnover and toxic office politics. Internally and externally, there were repeated complaints that those appointed to lead were failing to offer direction and focus. One crisis, more than anything else, came to epitomise these problems and push strained relations at the top past breaking point.

***

Relations with Jewish communities had been a recurring issue from the outset of Corbyn's leadership, but escalated as an issue in the 2017–2019 Parliament, crippling Labour internally and dominating media coverage of the party for weeks at a time.[60] Anti-semitism disputes involved several overlapping issues: controversial statements and behaviour by Corbyn supporters, including Labour members, candidates and representatives; allegations that party officials—particularly allies of the leadership—were failing to act swiftly or effectively to sanction intolerance; perceptions that senior aides in LOTO were resisting calls for decisive action; and controversial past actions and statements by Corbyn himself. The overlap between these conflicts and broader factional disputes within the Labour Party made them particularly hard to resolve. Some Corbyn allies—and many Labour members—believed the issue was being trumped up (or at least ramped up) by political and media opponents trying to damage Corbyn personally.[61] This attitude further incensed campaigners, whose outrage over anti-semitism in the Labour Party was intensified by the sceptical responses of some Corbyn allies who questioned their sincerity. The passions aroused by the issue were intense and drove a total breakdown of trust, which then made constructive resolution almost impossible. As battles over the issue raged on and on, the need for strong intervention from the leader himself became increasingly obvious. Yet Corbyn allegedly refused to respond to allegations he found personally distressing and was reported to have disengaged from his leadership team entirely for extended periods at the height of the crisis.[62] While stronger action by Corbyn might not have satisfied all of his critics, his reluctance to take proactive steps, and resistance to the proposals his advisors suggested, worsened the crisis and increased the damage it did to his leadership.

'The Constant Gardner' (Brian Adcock, *The Independent*, 1 April 2018 © Brian Adcock)

The first major controversy over anti-semitism in the 2017–2019 Parliament unfolded in the spring of 2018, following a series of media reports of bigotry posted on Corbyn-allied social media pages.[63] These escalated when Christine Shawcroft, a former Momentum director and Corbyn ally serving as chair of Labour's disputes panel, was accused of intervening on behalf of a Labour member suspended for alleged anti-semitism. Shawcroft said that she had been unaware of the nature of the allegations and agreed to step down from the disputes panel, but then stated in a social media post (which she subsequently removed) that although she abhorred anti-semitism, the row was being 'stirred up to attack Jeremy'.[64] Soon after Shawcroft's departure, the *Sunday Times* published a report of undercover investigations into anti-semitic messages posted on Corbyn-supporting Facebook groups, and leaked minutes from disciplinary proceedings which suggested that Corbyn allies were blocking or watering down action against Labour members charged with making anti-semitic statements. The pressure grew for a stronger and clearer Labour response to the problem. The leadership

of Momentum, Corbyn's praetorian guard, issued a collective statement in April 2018 describing anti-semitism as 'more widespread in
the Labour Party than many of us had understood even a few months
ago' and announcing Momentum would work with outside groups to
develop awareness training for its activists.[65] The LOTO response was
more limited, with statements reiterating Corbyn's personal opposition
to anti-semitism and promises of stronger action to stamp out anti-semitism in future. Even the statements Corbyn was persuaded to give were
often undermined by the manner in which the leader made his case, as
one aide recalled:

> Jeremy had a funny irritating tic on this. Nearly every time he condemned
> anti-semitism, he would also say, 'and all other forms of racism'. You don't
> need to do that. Just condemn anti-semitism if that's what you're talking
> about. There are other places to condemn Islamophobia, which is at least
> as big a problem in British society, and other forms of racism. Just let the
> Jewish community know that you hear them.

The crisis intensified in the summer of 2018, as new scandals emerged
and efforts to address the issue backfired, enraging the very groups
they were supposed to mollify.[66] LOTO proposed a new set of guidelines on anti-semitism incorporating most, but crucially not all, of the
International Holocaust Remembrance Alliance (IHRA) definition of
anti-semitism. Corbyn allies defended the new guidelines as the most
rigorous the party had ever produced and claimed that the omissions
were necessary to prevent legitimate political criticism of the Israeli government being sanctioned as anti-semitism.[67] This triggered an immediate backlash amongst Jewish groups, who saw LOTO's reluctance to
adopt in full a guideline document used by numerous public bodies as
evidence of a continued inability to take the problem of anti-semitism
seriously. Angry accusations flew back and forth in meetings, on the airwaves and the front pages for the rest of the summer. LOTO launched
disciplinary proceedings against MPs Margaret Hodge and Ian Austin—
both from Jewish backgrounds[68]—after altercations with Corbyn and his
allies.[69] This in turn triggered a strong response from John McDonnell,
who regarded the decision as indefensible, criticised it on the airwaves
and lobbied LOTO to drop the disciplinary action and change its
approach.[70] As the summer of 2018 wore on, the stream of negative stories about Corbyn's past became a flood, including clips from an event
in 2013 where Corbyn claimed that 'some Zionists don't understand

English irony despite living here all of their lives', a 2012 appearance on the Iranian government-sponsored channel 'Press TV' in which he claimed to see the 'hidden hand of Israel' in an Egyptian massacre during the Arab Spring, and a photograph of Corbyn attending a 2014 wreath-laying ceremony in Tunisia at a cemetery containing the graves of terrorists involved in the 1972 Munich massacre of Israeli Olympic athletes.

The row became ever more toxic as longstanding Corbyn allies became frustrated at the leader's obstinate refusal to bow to political reality or recognise the sincerely held concerns of his critics in the IHRA dispute. The credibility of LOTO's stance was eroded when leaked recordings of Corbynite veteran NEC member Pete Willsman were published, in which Willsman dismissed anti-semitism allegations as 'made up' by 'Jewish Trump fanatics'.[71] LOTO was eventually forced to back down, but only after a long list of senior Labour movement figures, including the party's three previous leaders, the chiefs of the largest Labour allied unions, the Deputy Leader and most of the Shadow Cabinet had publicly called for the adoption of the full IHRA definition. If any doubts remained about Corbyn's resistance to the change, he dispelled them with a last, futile effort to append a 'clarification statement' to the IHRA definition at the NEC meeting where it was adopted.[72] The self-defeating foot-dragging and inflexibility shown over the IHRA definition was symptomatic of Corbyn's approach to anti-semitism, which repeatedly threw a spotlight on some of the worst dysfunctions of his leadership. Corbyn failed to comprehend the depth of feeling about anti-semitism and repeatedly resisted his aides' proposals for bold gestures to restore trust. While reluctant to listen to close allies who urged decisive action, he was reportedly also too eager to heed instead the siren call of old campaigning allies who dismissed the entire issue as ginned up by ideological and factional opponents, and unworthy of a response.[73]

Only clear and decisive interventions from Corbyn himself could have resolved a crisis in which he was so personally embroiled. But Corbyn seemingly would not or could not provide such leadership, for reasons which were unclear even to his closest allies. He refused to get out in front of the escalating crisis. He would go silent when criticised on the issue in person and became prickly when questioned on it in media interviews. When matters were at their worst in the summer of 2018, he would sometimes drop off the radar altogether, apparently refusing to respond to calls or emails from aides. Corbyn had described himself as 'present, but not involved' at one of the controversial events emerged that summer. Yet too often when the Labour Party most needed leadership on anti-semitism, it seemed the leader wasn't even present.

The Labour anti-semitism crisis caused anguish for many in a party which saw anti-racism as one its core values. Jewish Labour MPs gave emotional testimony in Parliament and in interviews about their personal experiences of hatred and abuse, their fears for their safety and that of their families, and the heartache caused by their own party's failure to stand up effectively to the hostility they faced.[74] Some resigned the whip over the matter, including widely respected figures not regarded as factional troublemakers, who found themselves unwilling to remain within a party which had failed them on such a bedrock issue. The repugnance felt at the behaviour and attitudes uncovered in the anti-semitism disputes was so intense that even longstanding allies and true believers in the Corbyn project became reluctant to represent Labour publicly when they knew that doing so would oblige them to defend the indefensible on anti-semitism. The lengthy controversy culminated in an unprecedented referral of the Labour Party to the Equalities and Human Rights Commission (EHRC), the anti-discrimination public body itself created (like its predecessor the Commission for Racial Equality) by a Labour government.[75] The anti-semitism crisis, and Corbyn's failure to resolve it effectively, was one for which he and his party paid a heavy price.

Anti-semitism was not the only trigger for conflicts between Corbyn and his party. Another argument boiled up in the spring of 2018, when Sergei Skripal, a former Russian intelligence agent, and his daughter Yulia were (along with a police officer investigating the case) hospitalised in Salisbury after being poisoned with a nerve agent. The evidence pointed to an assassination attempt by Russian agents on British soil, exposing British citizens to a deadly poison. LOTO, however, resisted this conclusion, instead highlighting previous failings in order to call into question the credibility of British security intelligence.[76] Corbyn and Milne's reluctance to criticise Russia reopened divides over foreign policy, an area where Corbyn's LOTO had found itself isolated and at odds with its MPs before.[77] A series of senior Labour MPs lined up to support Theresa May's strong condemnation of Russia, siding with her over their own leadership. Corbyn and LOTO eventually backed down as evidence of Russian involvement continued to mount, but by then the damage had been done. Corbyn seemed to voters more concerned with giving the Putin regime a fair hearing than with defending the security of British citizens. LOTO's position looked at best obtuse and at worst sympathetic to hostile regimes abroad—a charge the Conservatives had long looked to pin on Corbyn. Unlike earlier foreign policy spats involving Corbyn, Salisbury had cut through with voters, perhaps due to its persistence in national media, with the laborious decontamination of exposed Salisbury streets, the collapse of the city's tourist industry and the later identification of two Russian security agents who visited Salisbury on the day of the Skripals' poisoning all receiving extensive coverage.[78] Every time the story returned, voters were reminded of Corbyn's reluctance to trust British intelligence services and his apparent sympathy towards the Russian government's protestations of innocence.[79] Voters continued to raise the Skripal poisonings in election campaign focus groups 18 months later as an example of Corbyn's weakness and untrustworthiness on foreign policy.[80]

✱✱✱

LOTO's responses to both anti-semitism and Salisbury helped precipitate another internal disruption—the February 2019 departure of seven Labour MPs to form The Independent Group (see also Chapter 5, pp. 162–164). Most of the defections were not a surprise to LOTO or the whips' office; figures such as Chuka Umunna, Chris Leslie and Mike Gapes had been frequent critics of Corbyn's leadership since the beginning. The biggest shock was Luciana Berger, a young Jewish MP with a weighty Labour family heritage—her great-uncle was Manny Shinwell, a minister in the Ramsay MacDonald and Clement Attlee governments. The heavily pregnant Berger, the parliamentary chair of the Jewish Labour Movement, announced she was too 'embarrassed and ashamed' to continue representing a party riddled with 'bullying, bigotry and intimidation'.

The Labour defectors enjoyed a long moment in the sun with the media, with Berger and Umunna in particular able to attract regular print and broadcast headlines. Deputy Leader Tom Watson, another regular critic of the Corbyn leadership, set up a new 'Future Britain' group in early March, quickly recruiting 80 MPs and 70 peers, with former Labour leader Lord Kinnock and former New Labour strategy guru Lord Mandelson addressing its first meeting. Watson insisted the group was designed to hold the party together, but many in LOTO, in particular John McDonnell, feared it could be the vehicle for a second, larger wave of defections. Rumours circulated of plans to win over a majority of backbench MPs and then seek to deny Labour the status of official opposition. No second wave of defections came in the end, and the Change UK rebellion fizzled out, unable to sustain media or voter interest as the

Brexit drama escalated. The founding group fragmented and none of the original defectors won re-election. Perhaps the most important effect of the short-lived split was to push Labour, and in particular McDonnell, towards greater acceptance of a pro-second referendum stance to help ensure strongly Europhile MPs remained inside the party.

Labour were already preparing for difficult local elections in the spring of 2019 when the extension of the Article 50 Brexit deadline obliged the party also to prepare for a European Parliament contest. Labour's local election showing was poor, though the Conservatives fared even worse in elections where frustrated voters turned against both main parties.[81] This was a harbinger of worse to come in the European elections. Labour bled support on both sides of the Brexit divide, losing Leavers to the Brexit Party and Remainers to the Liberal Democrats, Greens and the SNP. Although this was a low-stakes election where protest voting over the Brexit impasse was to be expected, the scale of the defeat was alarming. Labour lost nearly half of its 2014 support and finished in third place, behind the Lib Dems and only narrowly ahead of the Greens. The beating handed out by the Brexit party in Leave-voting Labour areas was to some extent priced in by the leadership, though it worried MPs representing Leave-voting seats. Defeat in the heavily Remain local authorities of London and other big cities came as more of a shock to the party's frontbench. Corbyn was reported to be personally alarmed by the Lib Dem surge in his home patch of Islington. So were other Shadow Cabinet members representing inner London seats, such as Emily Thornberry and Diane Abbott, who pointed to the results as evidence of the urgent need to communicate Labour support for a second referendum more clearly to Remain voters.

Labour's polling troubles continued through the summer, increasing anxieties that the decline with Remainers was more than a blip. Labour's problems were compounded by Boris Johnson's early success in reuniting Leave support behind the Conservatives following his election as Conservative leader in July. Corbyn's senior aides recognised that Johnson was a very different kind of leader to May, one who was quite happy to break with his predecessors on austerity and spend big on popular policies, and who would pursue the goal of Brexit with reckless determination. Milne and others expected Johnson to precipitate a crisis over Brexit in the early autumn and use it to try and force an early election.

Anxieties grew as the 2019 conference approached with Labour still under 30% in the polls, well behind the resurgent Conservatives, who were now topping 40%. YouGov polling data obtained by Labour's Southside analysis team underlined the huge risks Labour now faced.[82] The modellers projected Labour to fall below 140 seats, with massive losses to the Conservatives in Leave-voting areas, while formerly safe seats in the Remain-heavy big cities were now threatened by the surging Liberal Democrats. Presenting these findings to a Sunday morning meeting convened by John McDonnell at the Labour conference, the Southside elections analysts argued such dire figures underscored the urgency of winning back Remain voters from the Lib Dems, characterising these voters, whose values and ideology were often in sympathy with Corbyn's Labour, as 'low-hanging fruit'.[83] Once Labour had secured its Remain flank, the party could make a big push to win back Leave-leaning voters with a public services focused offer. This analysis was rejected by campaign co-chair Ian Lavery, who claimed the polling data which drove it came from a 'Tory firm' and therefore could not be trusted.[84] Lavery asserted bluntly that working-class heartland seats would 'never vote Tory'.[85] While McDonnell was sympathetic to the analysis, regarding it as rigorous and serious, it was not taken seriously by LOTO. In the words of one senior Southsider: 'It was received like a bucket of cold sick. And then ignored.'

'Brexit Acrobatics' (Dave Brown, *The Independent*, 18 September 2019 © Dave Brown)

This refusal to engage with the polling warning signs was one symptom of the deepening dysfunction in LOTO, where members of the inner circle were at odds with each other and with other parts of the party. Complaints about both Karie Murphy and Seumas Milne, the pair at the apex of the LOTO management structure, had continued. The methods Murphy used to impose order on a chaotic office generated increasing resentment, culminating in an official complaint letter against her sent to Corbyn and Jennie Formby by the local union branch within LOTO.[86] Poor personal relations were not the only issue. LOTO lacked clear reporting structures, and stances agreed with Corbyn in meetings were reportedly watered down later by senior aides with the most access to the leader. These operational problems were exacerbated by the deep divisions opening up over which aspects of Labour's Brexit policy to emphasise to voters in the coming election campaign. John McDonnell, Andrew Fisher and Southside elections director Niall Sookoo favoured an emphasis on Labour's second referendum offer to consolidate Remain voters, fearing disaster if they defected en masse, and arguing that many Leave voters could be won over by Labour's economic policies. Seumas Milne, Karie Murphy and Carl Shoben argued for Labour to instead emphasise its promise of a new Brexit deal to secure its Leave flank, arguing that promoting a second referendum risked alienating a critical mass of Brexiteers in the Leave-leaning battleground where the election would be won and lost. Neither side could make a decisive case and Corbyn was unable to resolve the impasse by committing to one approach, as one senior aide recalled:

> If you disagree about fundamental strategy, you're going to have incoherent decisions and messaging. Unless there is somebody who is cutting through that and saying 'no, we're going to do *that*'. And Jeremy's position was very much focused on holding together the party … So he would make a final decision about particular things but he wasn't doing it in a way that chose between the two arguments. He was doing it to hold together an increasingly fractious operation. He wasn't saying 'actually I'm going to come down on this side of the argument'.

Labour's struggles to agree a strapline for the now widely anticipated early election provided a case study in the disruptive consequences of division at the top.[87] John McDonnell's team had commissioned advertising agencies to offer pitches over the summer. The best-received pitch came from Harry Barlow, who suggested 'It's Time', a slogan which polled well and was seen by some aides as a valuable peg on which to hang policy offers: 'you build up around it. You say "it's time that we got decent social care" "it's time that Amazon paid their taxes", you build it and build it and in the end, you say "it's time for Labour"'. But Milne was not convinced and instead favoured 'real change', a slogan suggested by Paul Hilder, a campaigner with close links to Momentum. Milne's enthusiasm for Hilder's pitch was not widely shared, but he pressed ahead and unilaterally combined the two messages into 'It's time for real change'. The resulting amalgam was rushed out as Labour's strapline without testing in polling or focus groups. It was criticised by others involved as less than the sum of its parts: 'The two together are quite bad. They don't build. How do you build anything called "real change?"'. It's meaningless ... It doesn't work.'

Jeremy Corbyn and John McDonnell at the Labour conference, 23 September 2019 (© Chris Bull/Alamy Stock Photo)

Long-simmering discontent within and about Corbyn's dysfunctional office came to a head at the 2019 conference. A botched effort to remove Tom Watson by abolishing his post as Deputy Leader generated a wave of negative press, and was immediately followed by the leaked resignation letter of Corbyn's policy chief, Andrew Fisher. Fisher, one of Corbyn's longest-serving advisors and most trusted allies, excoriated a 'lack of professionalism, competence, and human decency which I am no longer willing to put up with daily'. Corbyn was aware of the problems in his office, and throughout 2019 he was reported to have regularly discussed the idea of removing Murphy from the LOTO operation with other aides.[88] Fisher's resignation, alongside the disruptive failed move against Watson, finally spurred the leader to action. Corbyn and McDonnell recruited retired senior civil servant Bob Kerslake to conduct a review of the LOTO organisation. As part of this reorganisation, Karie Murphy would move from LOTO to Southside. Ostensibly Murphy was dispatched to help run the coming election campaign in Labour HQ, but in reality Corbyn was offering a face-saving measure to a loyal lieutenant he was unwilling to fire outright. Several of Murphy's allies left LOTO in protest and joined her at Southside.[89]

The decision to shift Murphy to another high-profile role, while taking no action against Seumas Milne, meant that the changes only served to deepen the dysfunction they were supposed to address. With its main organising force removed, Corbyn's LOTO disintegrated further. There was little time for Corbyn's new appointment Helene Reardon-Bond to get a grip on operations or make effective changes before the election campaign began.[90] Murphy and her allies were enraged by what they described as a 'coup' orchestrated by pro-second referendum figures to marginalise those advocating a stronger offer to Leave voters, one which disrupted Labour's election preparations at a critical stage.[91] Murphy reportedly set about building a new power base at Southside, filling a leadership vacuum produced by the frequent absence due to the ill health of General Secretary Jennie Formby.[92]

Labour, then, would go into the election campaign with relations among its senior leadership team at an all-time low. LOTO advisors who had blamed internal opponents for the failure to win in 2017 were now proving just as capable of falling out among themselves. They could not agree a coherent strategy, as those charged with developing policy were not talking to those charged with communicating it. John McDonnell, chair of the campaign, was regularly at odds with both Karie Murphy at Southside and Seumas Milne, in charge of campaign strategy and communications at LOTO. Andrew Fisher, tasked with overseeing Labour's manifesto while working his notice, was reluctant to share its contents with many of those tasked with building a campaign around it. Even the 'grid' used since the Blair era to coordinate activity fell victim to the toxic atmosphere of mutual distrust. Virtually no one could use it for planning purposes because Murphy, who was in charge of developing it, reportedly refused to share its contents with those whose plans it was supposed to coordinate. As one senior aide recalled:

> We didn't have a functional office. Loads of senior people weren't communicating with each other. No one trusted anyone else. It was very hard for Jeremy because his office had broken up … Jeremy completely respects John McDonnell and Karie [Murphy], Seumas [Milne] and Andrew [Fisher] in different ways. And they weren't working together.

Though Corbyn was widely praised by his aides as a consensus builder who 'doesn't do conflict', he entered his second general election campaign presiding over a divided party and a leadership team at war with itself. Elevated to the leadership on the basis of his principled idealism, Corbyn now took his party to the voters with a compromise Brexit policy nobody favoured and a compromise party slogan nobody liked.

Notes

1. A music festival in the Southern English countryside where entry cost upwards of £240 per person (plus booking fees) was perhaps an appropriate venue for Corbyn to celebrate an electoral breakthrough fuelled in part by a surge in Labour membership and voting among better-off, middle-class graduates. Corbyn told festival organiser Michael Eavis he expected to be Prime Minister by Christmas. See Graeme Demianyk, 'Jeremy Corbyn Tells Michael Eavis He'll Be Prime Minister "in Six Months"', *HuffPost*, 25 June 2017, https://www.huffingtonpost. co.uk/entry/jeremy-corbyn-prime-minister-trident-michael-eavis_ uk_59500b88e4b02734df2b25ad.
2. Others were less optimistic, with one aide telling the authors of the previous volume in this series: 'It'll go for the full five years. Why would they just give up?' (Philip Cowley and Dennis Kavanagh, *The British General Election of 2017*. London, Palgrave Macmillan, 2018, p. 443). Some Southside staffers were happy to encourage LOTO belief that the government was unstable, given that the possibility of an election at any time made it look imprudent to embark on sweeping reforms to the Labour bureaucracy in the teams responsible for campaign planning and

organisation, which might otherwise have been a more immediate LOTO priority.

3. Seumas Milne gave a presentation to the party's National Executive Committee soon after the election, laying out the successes of 2017 and broad areas of weakness—Scotland, older people, post-industrial areas—the party would need to address in order to get to Downing Street. Other aides complained that these broad brushstrokes did not amount to an electoral strategy, and there was little attention devoted to building a more detailed plan.

4. Milne's appointment only became permanent in early 2017—before this, he was officially on temporary leave from his post at *The Guardian*. Murphy was initially appointed as LOTO office manager. She was promoted to Executive Director of the Leader's Office in June 2016.

5. There were a couple of changes in personnel: Katy Clarke, Corbyn's Political Secretary, departed in the autumn of 2017 to lead the Labour Party's democracy review and was replaced by Amy Jackson. Laura Parker, Corbyn's Private Secretary, departed around the same time to become national coordinator of Momentum.

6. Karie Murphy and Corbyn's Political Secretary Amy Jackson both had close links with Unite, as did Jennie Formby, who took over as the party's General Secretary in 2018. Both Jackson and Formby had worked for Unite, with the latter serving as a Unite representative on Labour's National Executive Committee, while Murphy was a Unite lay official and close friend of Unite General Secretary Len McCluskey.

7. Such complaints tended to fall into three categories: that Milne was frequently absent from the office; that he did not respond to colleagues' requests, delaying urgent communications which required his sign-off; and that the responses he did give often came at the very last moment, thus cutting off discussion and ensuring that on contentious issues, his preferred outcome was communicated as a fait accompli. See also Gabriel Pogrund and Patrick Maguire, *Left Out*. Vintage, 2020, pp. 15–16; Owen Jones, *This Land*. Penguin, 2020, pp. 101–3. Milne's defenders note that controlling Labour's message was a core part of his job, and one made exceptionally difficult by persistent problems with leaks, problems which worsened as the Parliament wore on and factional divisions deepened.

8. In particular, there were complaints that Murphy prioritised loyalty over effectiveness, as one former aide recalled: 'Karie's approach was "who's going to be loyal to me?" That was always the main driver for her.' Other aides concede that, as the most visible face of LOTO authority and the woman charged with controlling access to the leader, Murphy bore the

brunt of complaints which were really about dysfunctions originating elsewhere.

9. Pogrund and Maguire, *Left Out*, p. 29.

10. Philip Cowley and Dennis Kavanagh, *The British General Election of 2017*. Palgrave Macmillan, 2018, pp. 81–86.

11. Starmer's legal and technical skill, which was vital in a complex and fast-moving Brexit negotiation, helped make his job secure, despite growing tensions with more pro-Brexit LOTO aides, as Corbyn and others saw removing him as too risky.

12. Smith resigned after less than a year to back a second EU referendum and was replaced by the veteran MP Tony Lloyd, who had returned to Parliament in 2017 after his stint in devolved politics—first as Police and Crime Commissioner for Greater Manchester (2012–2015) and then as the appointed interim Mayor of the Greater Manchester Combined Authority (2015–2017)—had come to an end. He was defeated in the selection contest by former Cabinet minister Andy Burnham, who replaced him as Mayor in May 2017. Lloyd returned to Parliament, where he had previously served for 15 years as MP for Manchester Central, the following month as the new MP for Rochdale.

13. A total of 21 members of Corbyn's Shadow Cabinet had resigned on 26 June 2016, and two days later MPs in the PLP had passed a vote of no confidence in Corbyn's leadership by a margin of 172 to 42. For further discussion, see Cowley and Kavanagh, *The British General Election of 2017*, Chapter 4.

14. Deputy Leader Tom Watson, whose separate mandate from the membership had made him a rallying point for internal opponents, made clear in public and private statements that he would no longer stand in the way of Corbyn's proposals for change. Chuka Umunna, hitherto one of the most voluble and media-savvy Corbyn critics, sounded a very different note after the 2017 election: 'unity is our watchword, government is our aim'. Harriet Harman, Mother of the House, interim leader during the first leadership contest Corbyn won and another regular critic of his leadership, paid tribute to Corbyn for 'confounding expectations'. See Peter Walker, Anushka Asthana and Rajeev Syal, 'All Labour MPs Now Keen to Serve Under Corbyn, Says Harriet Harman', *The Guardian*, 13 June 2017, https://www.theguardian.com/politics/2017/jun/13/i-was-wrong-about-jeremy-corbyn-leadership-says-harriet-harman.

15. Aides pointed to the different employment contracts in Southside as a driver of persistent resistance and hostility. The permanent staff of Labour's career bureaucracy could not be removed without compelling cause, obliging the leadership's more radical staffers (typically on insecure temporary contracts) to work with headquarters colleagues whose

ideology and factional loyalties sometimes reflected their appointment under very different Labour leaderships many years before. As one aide, not without sympathy for the situation despite his ideological disagreements with Southside staff, observed: 'At a very senior level there's sometimes a way that you can get rid of the likes of [General Secretary] Iain McNicol ... But for a 400–500 person organization that's not possible. There's people who mortgages to pay, rent to pay, families. Some of them probably enjoy sticking around to try and undermine the project from within, but others just don't want to leave because they need a job. And they're all on permanent contracts, unlike staff in Parliament.'

16. The founder of Momentum, Jon Lansman, had in his youth been a leading figure in the 1970s and 1980s Campaign for Labour Party Democracy, of which Corbyn himself was also an early associate. See David Kogan, *Protest and Power*. Bloomsbury, 2019, Chapters 1–3.

17. Lavery later clarified that he did not 'see deselection as a way forward': Patrick Maguire, 'Corbyn Ally Ian Lavery Rules out Changes on Labour Deselection', *The Times*, 8 July 2017, https://www.thetimes.co.uk/article/corbyn-ally-ian-lavery-rules-out-changes-on-labour-deselection-gsz-6z8w7l.

18. Helen Pidd and Rowenna Mason, 'Labour MPs Critical of Corbyn Fear Deselection after "Get on Board" Warning', *The Guardian*, 6 July 2017, https://www.theguardian.com/politics/2017/jul/06/labour-mps-critical-of-corbyn-fear-deselection-after-get-on-board-warning. Williamson continued to campaign for mandatory deselection throughout 2017 and 2018.

19. Patrick Maguire and Sam Coates, 'May Tells Labour to Confront Members Threatening MPs', *The Times*, 7 July 2017, https://www.the-times.co.uk/article/hard-left-in-plot-to-oust-dozens-of-labour-mps-with-deselection-hitlist-gk70r6z8m.

20. One aide involved with the process and sceptical of the democratisation proposals believes that Unite, and in particular its General Secretary Len McCluskey, were pivotal in brokering this compromise: 'That compromise was completely Unite. It's a dog's dinner, I hate it, but it's as good as we could have got to at that point. But we had to show movement, otherwise open selections would have happened. Len went into meetings with the "big five", to bring the unions on board. We also had to push with the Leader's Office. They really wanted open selections, they were unhappy, but you can't win anything in conference if you don't have Unite and Unison behind you, so it would have been a loss for the Leader's Office. It was basically one of those situations where no one is really happy, so you know you're doing the right thing.'

21. The cut was from 15 to 10% of Labour MPs and MEPs (with Britain's exit from the EU in 2020, this now reverts to just MPs). However, nomination in the Commons was now just the first stage in a complex new system—candidates also needed to secure support from either at least 5% of Constituency Labour Parties or 5% of affiliate members, including at least two trade unions. This compromise approach gave candidates two routes to the ballot paper after winning nominations in the Commons—via the membership or via the trade unions.

22. One senior Momentum figure was philosophical about their failure to secure stronger reforms: 'There is an almost irreconcilable difference of approach [between Momentum and the unions]. The more I have thought about it, the more I have understood the Union position. Of course you have to have bloc votes, and delegates with firm mandates because that's how it functions in unions. Because that's how you get your strike action, which at the end of the day is the only thing you can do if you're in a union. But if you contrast that with some of the Momentum members, who had come from organisations like UK Uncut or climate camp where, if you want to express an opinion in a meeting, you just wave your hands to signal agreement, there's no voting … Absolutely cultural polar opposites. So it's not a surprise that we didn't get everything that we wanted, but it was a disappointment and it's one of the examples of the leadership not having political capital. They had to rely so much upon the Left unions to sustain them, particularly in the second leadership campaign, that they just weren't going to take this one on.'

23. One aide with long experience of selections processes was unsurprised by this: 'I always thought that, because they lived in a bubble, a lot of people around Corbyn completely misjudged the membership. The membership *hate* this sort of stuff [deselection], in the main. You've got your bloody headbangers of course … On the surface it was often all these left-wing people shouting. But in actuality the majority of the membership just want the Labour Party to win, and they like their MPs. If you're a good MP you've got nothing to fear, the membership likes you.'

24. Patrick Heneghan, 'Labour's 2017 Campaign and the Myth of the Stab in the Back', https://patrick91053.wixsite.com/website/post/labour-s-2017-campaign-and-the-myth-of-the-stab-in-the-back.

25. Lansman, who had been seeking to democratise Labour's internal power structures since managing Tony Benn's deputy leadership campaign in 1981, found little support for his ideas among union bosses, who believed increased activist influence would come at the expense of union power. Once it became clear his candidacy was hopeless, he withdrew.

26. Those departing included Director of Policy and Research Simon Jackson, Acting London Regional Director Neil Fleming, Acting PLP Secretary Dan Simpson, and Director of Governance and Legal John Stolliday. Regarding the struggles to find experienced and effective replacements, one LOTO aide observed: 'The left came out of nowhere, wasn't part of a steady build-up of the left becoming more powerful within the party. It won out of nowhere, and we didn't have the people who had the experience of being bureaucrats.'

27. See, for example, David Miliband's Keir Hardie Memorial Lecture in July 2010: https://labourlist.org/2010/07/david-milibands-keir-hardie-lecture-full-speech.

28. Graf's own reflections on his work with Miliband on community organising highlight a failure to understand the task of organising and 'the limited regard too many in the national leadership' had for organisers in the field: Arnie Graf, 'Labour's Failure Had Little to Do with Organisers in the Field', *LabourList*, 4 August 2015, https://labourlist.org/2015/08/labours-failure-had-little-to-do-with-organisers-in-the-field.

29. The Community Organising Unit's budget was reportedly well over £1 million a year. See Sophie Wilson, 'Labour Still Needs Community Organising—But it Has to Change', *Tribune*, 17 May 2020, https://tribunemag.co.uk/2020/05/labour-still-needs-community-organising-but-it-has-to-change.

30. All figures from Labour Party accounts reported to the Electoral Commission.

31. A total of 77% of Labour members in 2017 were from the middle-class ABC1 groups (compared to 60% of the party's voters); 55% of members were over 55 (36% of voters) and 57% of members were graduates (29% of voters). Although Labour receives large majorities of the vote from every ethnic minority community, just 4% of its members in 2017 identified as belonging to a BAME group. See Tim Bale, Paul Webb and Monica Poletti, *Footsoldiers: Political Party Membership in the 21st Century*. Routledge, 2020.

32. Ibid, Chapter 4.

33. None of the incumbent Conservative MPs targeted by Momentum campaigns lost their seats. Labour did capture Justine Greening's seat of Putney, which was the target of both Momentum campaigns and the community organising unit, but Greening herself had already stood down as MP.

34. Some of the 'praetorian guard' were themselves 'Lexiteers' who shared the Eurosceptic stances of more pro-Brexit LOTO aides.

35. Polling by the Party Members Project in the summer of 2017 showed that a majority of Labour members supported remaining in the Single

Market and 70% backed a second referendum. (Anuska Asthana, 'Big Majority of Labour Members "Want UK to Stay in the Single Market"', *The Guardian*, 17 July 2017). British Election Study research showed that Labour gained much more ground in 2017 among Remain supporters than Leave supporters (Ed Fieldhouse and Chris Prosser, 'The Brexit Election? The 2017 General Election in Ten Charts', *British Election Study*, 1 August 2017, https://www.britishelectionstudy. com/bes-impact/the-brexit-election-the-2017-general-election-in-ten-charts/#.YO771OhKiUk). More than half of Remainers backed Labour in 2017 compared to around a quarter of Leavers (John Curtice, 'Brexit Reshapes the Basis of Party Support–Again', *What UK Thinks EU*, 19 December 2019, https://whatukthinks.org/eu/ brexit-reshapes-the-basis-of-party-support-again).

36. John Curtice, Stephen Fisher, Robert Ford and Patrick English, 'Appendix 1: The Results Analysed' in Cowley and Kavanagh, *The British General Election of 2017*.

37. The most influential pro-Brexit allies included Karie Murphy, Seumas Milne and James Schneider in LOTO; Andrew Murray and Len McCluskey in Unite; and Ian Lavery, Jon Trickett and Richard Burgon in the Shadow Cabinet.

38. Influential figures who argued for more Remain-friendly stances included Andrew Fisher in LOTO, and Keir Starmer and Emily Thornberry in the Shadow Cabinet. John McDonnell adopted a steadily more pro-second referendum stance over the latter half of the Parliament.

39. The first organisation of pro-Single Market MPs and peers launched on 16 June 2017, less than two weeks after the 2017 election. The prominence of longstanding Corbyn critics from the Labour right such as Chuka Umunna and Alison McGovern in such groups was another source of LOTO scepticism and resistance.

40. LOTO and Starmer had different motives for vagueness in this period. Eurosceptic LOTO aides saw vagueness as a way to deflect pro-EU MPs and activists lobbying for Labour to commit to a 'soft Brexit' retaining UK institutions such as the European Economic Area (EEA) or the customs union, which they opposed as 'Brexit in name only'. Starmer favoured commitments to some of these institutions from early on in the process, but seems to have accepted vagueness as a way to buy time and keep options open, while waiting to see how the debate evolved.

41. Andy Slaughter, Catherine West and Ruth Cadbury. A fourth minister, Daniel Zeichner, stepped down ahead of the vote in order to back the amendment.

42. The six tests, first set out by Starmer in July 2017, were as follows: (1) MPs get the 'final say on whether to approve the withdrawal agreement

and how best to implement it'. (2) The transition period requested by the Prime Minister is added into the legislation. (3) A 'completely different approach' to the use of so-called Henry VIII powers which the government argues it needs to make technical changes to regulations repatriated from Brussels, but which Starmer described as 'silencing Parliament and handing sweeping powers' to ministers. (4) A guarantee that workers' and consumer rights, as well as environmental standards, are not watered down after Brexit. (5) A concession to devolved administrations which want repatriated powers that would normally fall under their remit to go straight to Scotland, Wales and Northern Ireland, rather than first being taken over by the Westminster government. (6) Putting the EU Charter of Fundamental Rights into UK law.

43. The strategy of setting a list of tests which sounded substantive and precise, yet were in fact open to interpretation, was reminiscent of the 'five tests' Gordon Brown and his advisors devised regarding British membership of the euro. Like Brown's tests, they succeeded in justifying covert opposition without ever obliging overt opposition.

44. https://labour.org.uk/press/jeremy-corbyn-full-speech-britain-brexit.

45. A lot of ink was spilled over the difference between 'a customs union' and 'the customs union'. The distinction reflected Labour's desire for a bespoke arrangement which removed Britain from obligations required under the EU's general customs union rules.

46. Respectively: Press Secretary for Tony Blair as Leader of the Opposition (1994–1997) and Prime Minister (1997–2003); Campaign Director for Labour in the 1997, 2001 and 2005 general elections; and Head of Communications for Labour and Senior Advisor to Ed Miliband (2010–2015) and Labour Party Executive Director (Elections, Campaigns and Organisation) (2012–2017).

47. One senior aide noted that dissenting views on Brexit became steadily less welcome in LOTO over the course of 2018, stifling proper discussion of the issue: 'We'd have meetings, but certain aides and politicians weren't invited … We had a Brexit Strategy Group that markedly moved from being inclusive of everyone to being wholly Leave.'

48. Seumas Milne, Karie Murphy, James Schneider and Andrew Murray were all in the 'respect the result' camp, arguing that enraging Leave supporters by offering a new EU referendum was a bigger political risk than alienating Remain supporters by negotiating a new Brexit deal. Unite General Secretary Len McCluskey was also in this camp. Andrew Fisher was the most prominent member of the LOTO inner circle to become convinced of the electoral merits of a more pro-Remain stance, though he was by no means an ardent EU enthusiast.

49. Abbott's decades-long friendship with Corbyn, and her regular commutes with him to and from Westminster, made her a particularly persuasive lobbyist of the Labour leader. Her repeated reference to Ramsay MacDonald, the leader much reviled by Labour's left for breaking with his party to cooperate with the Conservatives, was felt by LOTO aides to be a particularly effective line of argument with a leader very proud of his left-wing principles and loyalty to grassroots members.

50. Though broadcast cameras also zoomed in on veteran Eurosceptic MP Dennis Skinner, stony-faced and motionless in his front row chair, as others around him rose to give the line a prolonged standing ovation.

51. One senior aide close to the process felt that both McDonnell and Starmer were both in fact trying in good faith to stick to the agreed line on the new policy, and that the differences in emphasis in their comments were greatly magnified by both activists and a press pack eager to seize on stories of Labour division over the issue: 'John McDonnell's comments reflected what he understood the compromise to be … Keir then tried to redress the balance with John, not thinking he get this huge moment in the conference hall. If you actually watch the video of it, he looks slightly taken aback. Like, oh shit, this is a … Fuck, I didn't mean to cause this moment. So he looks a bit wide eyed and astonished even for Keir who often looks a bit like that anyway, bless him.'

52. The SNP, the Liberal Democrats, Plaid Cymru, the Greens and, from February 2019, The Independent Group were all anti-Brexit, and nearly all of their MPs favoured a second referendum.

53. While this in part reflected Corbyn's indecisiveness and aversion to conflict, it also reflected his need to try and keep together an increasingly divided and fractious leadership team and Shadow Cabinet.

54. The voting process used in the indicative votes process was poorly designed to achieve its goal. There was no mechanism in the process for eliminating options or ranking preferences between them. As a result, the indicative votes did not force the people who needed to choose—proponents of the 'soft Brexit' and 'stop Brexit' approaches—to make a choice. Both sides used the ambiguous vote outcomes to continue lobbying for their preferred policy. The same problem occurred on the other occasion indicative votes were used—when MPs were presented with options for reform of the House of Lords in 2003. Here, too, there was no mechanism to coalesce opinion or rank preferences. And here, too, such freedom produced fragmentation, with no reform option able to win a majority.

55. See, for example, McDonnell's interview with Andrew Marr on 5 May 2019: https://twitter.com/johnmcdonnellMP/status/1125014785563738112?s=20.

56. The praetorian elements in the Momentum leadership also pushed this argument hard, lobbying activists to put loyalty to Corbyn and his broader radical policy agenda before their desire to oppose Brexit.

57. Large parts of the agenda, and some of the slogans, were subsequently copied or adapted by the Johnson Conservative government. In politics, imitation is the sincerest flattery.

58. John McDonnell, speech to Labour conference. This was one of the policies imitated soon after by the Conservatives as part of their 'levelling-up' agenda.

59. Within a year of the 2019 election, a much less ambitious version of the same policy agenda (with the same slogan) had become a central policy tentpole of the Johnson government.

60. For Corbyn's earlier problems with the issue, see Cowley and Kavanagh, *The British General Election of 2017*, pp. 79–80.

61. When asked to express which of three options was closest to their view, 49% of party members polled in 2016 felt 'Labour does not have a problem with anti-semitism and it has been created by the press and Jeremy Corbyn's opponents to attack him'. Another 35% felt 'Labour has a problem with anti-semitism but it is being used by the press and Jeremy Corbyn's opponents to attack him'. Just 10% took the view that 'Labour has a problem with anti-semitism and it is right that the media report on it'. While these figures most likely changed as the issue unfolded over the course of the 2017–19 Parliament, they do at least suggest that scepticism about the magnitude and seriousness of Labour's anti-semitism problem, and the motives of those drawing attention to it, was widespread among Labour's rank-and-file members. See https://esrcpartymembersprojectorg.files.wordpress.com/2015/09/balewebb-polettisubmission4chakrabarti3rdjune2016-1.pdf.

62. Several advisors close to Corbyn emphasised that his disengagement in part reflected the very negative personal impact repeated public anti-semitism allegations, often directed at him personally, had on the Labour leader, who regarded anti-racism as a central personal value.

63. One story implicated Corbyn himself, after a Facebook thread emerged on which he expressed opposition to the removal of a controversial mural which used obviously anti-semitic imagery. Corbyn said his opposition was on free speech grounds and he was not aware that the mural was anti-semitic, having not looked closely at it before expressing a view. Some felt this was not a particularly credible defence, given that the mural featured a large image of a group of men with Jewish features playing a game of monopoly on a table made out of crouching, naked people.

64. Heather Stewart, 'Christine Shawcroft: Antisemitism Row "Stirred up to Attack Jeremy"', *The Guardian*, 30 March 2018, https://www.the-

guardian.com/politics/2018/mar/30/christine-shawcroft-antisemitism-row-stirred-up-to-attack-jeremy-corbyn.

65. Jessica Elgot, 'Labour Antisemitism More Widespread Than Thought, Momentum Says', *The Guardian*, 2 April 2018, https://www.the-guardian.com/politics/2018/apr/02/labour-antisemitism-more-wide-spread-than-thought-momentum-says. Momentum founder and veteran Bennite Jon Lansman, himself Jewish, faced anti-semitic abuse from self-declared Corbyn supporters on social media in March 2018 when he publicly contemplated running against Corbyn's preferred candidate Jennie Formby for the post of General Secretary: Kevin Schofield, 'Jennie Formby Condemns "Anti-semitic" Attacks on Labour Rival Jon Lansman', *PoliticsHome*, 3 March 2018, https://www.politicshome.com/news/article/excl-jennie-formby-condemns-antisemitic-at-tacks-on-labour-rival-jon-lansman.

66. For more detailed accounts of the anti-semitism crisis in the summer of 2018, see Kogan, *Protest and Power* Chapters 32 and 33; Pogrund and Maguire, *Left Out*, Chapter 6.

67. Some aides wondered if the omissions reflected anxiety that past state-ments by Corbyn himself or some of his senior advisors would otherwise fall foul of Labour's own guidelines.

68. Austin is not himself Jewish, but had close family links to the Jewish com-munity. His adopted parents were Jewish refugees from the Holocaust.

69. Hodge was accused of personally accusing Corbyn of being racist in a heated discussion behind the Speaker's chair. Austin was referred for a row with Labour Party Chair Ian Lavery.

70. Pogrund and Maguire, *Left Out*, pp. 115–16.

71. Lee Harpin, 'Bombshell Tape Shows Corbyn Ally Blamed "Jewish Trump Fanatics" for Inventing Labour Antisemitism', *Jewish Chronicle*, 30 July 2018, https://www.thejc.com/news/uk/bombshell-record-ing-proves-corbyn-ally-blamed-jewish-trump-fanatics-for-false-antisemi-tism-clai-1.467802.

72. The most controversial element in Corbyn's page-and-a-half-long draft 'clarification' statement was the claim that: 'It cannot be considered racist to treat Israel like any other state or assess its conduct against the standards of international law. Nor should it be regarded as antisemitic to describe Israel, its policies or the circumstances around its foundation as racist because of their discriminatory impact, or to support another set-tlement of the Israel-Palestine conflict.' Corbyn withdrew the statement once it became clear that a majority of NEC members opposed it. See Dan Sabbagh, 'Labour Adopts IHRA Antisemitism Definition in Full', *The Guardian*, 4 September 2018, https://www.theguardian.com/politics/2018/sep/04/labour-adopts-ihra-antisemitism-definition-in-full.

73. This theory was particularly popular with old friends from Islington politics, who Corbyn consulted regularly over the issue and who urged an intransigent, 'don't give an inch' strategy, much to the frustration of aides: 'Often we would have a sense ... he was engaging with the issue better and then he'd go back and talk to people, mainly old Jewish Trotskyists in his constituency or elsewhere, who'd tell him "There's no problem. This is all capitulating to Zionism"' (Pogrund and Maguire, *Left Out*, p. 109).

74. See, for example, the Commons debate on anti-semitism on 17 April 2018, in which Jewish Labour MPs including Luciana Berger and Margaret Hodge, recounted their personal experiences of anti-semitism, including from self-described Labour supporters: https://hansard.parliament.uk/Commons/2018-04-17/debates/9D70B2B4-39D7-4241-ACF8-13F7DFD8AEB2/Anti-Semitism.

75. The EHRC report would later judge that cases of 'harassment, discrimination and political interference' by and within the Labour Party had breached the Equality Act 2010, a failure which went all the way to the top: 'equally of concern was a lack of leadership within the Labour Party on these issues, which is hard to reconcile with its stated commitment to a zero-tolerance approach to antisemitism'. The only previous political party to be referred to the EHRC was the far-right British National Party in 2010.

76. This statement was so contentious that it led the Press Association to name Seumas Milne directly as the source rather than referring to 'Labour spokesman', in breach of convention. By the autumn, Corbyn had publicly accepted that the evidence pointed to Russian involvement in the attack, saying at the Labour Party conference in September that 'the evidence painstaking assembled by the police now points clearly to the Russian state'. See Oliver Milne, 'Jeremy Corbyn Says He Accepts That the Evidence "Clearly Suggests" Russia Was Behind the Salisbury Attack', *Daily Mirror*, 26 September 2018, https://www.mirror.co.uk/news/politics/jeremy-corbyn-says-accepts-evidence-13312716.

77. In November 2015, Corbyn found himself publicly at odds with his own Shadow Foreign Secretary Hillary Benn over RAF bombing of ISIS in Syria (Cowley and Kavanagh, *The British General Election of 2017*, pp. 75–76) and he repeatedly clashed with Shadow Defence Secretary Nia Griffith over issues such as NATO and Trident.

78. An interview with the two 'fitness instructors' named by Bellingcat.com as the main suspects in the affair, which aired on Kremlin aligned news network *Russia Today*, provided a surreal coda to the affair. Alexander Petrov and Ruslan Borishov claimed they were tourists visiting to see the Cathedral which in Borishov's words (and Wikipedia's) was 'famous

not just in Europe, but in the whole world ... for its 123-m spire [and] for its clock, the first one [of its kind] ever created in the world, which is still working'. The Russians were unable to explain why their jaunt to the Cathedral took them past CCTV cameras near to the Skripals' home, which is on the other side of Salisbury.

79. Corbyn's defenders regarded this perception as driven by persistent media bias in reporting of the Labour leader and issued regular complaints about this on traditional and social media, including one surreal episode when Corbyn allies attacked the flagship BBC *Newsnight* programme for allegedly altering a photograph of Jeremy Corbyn to make the hat he was wearing look 'more Russian'.

80. James Johnson, 'Key Moments That Led to Corbyn's Fall in Popularity', *The Times*, 16 December 2019, https://www.thetimes.co.uk/article/ key-moments-that-led-to-corbyns-fall-in-popularity-r2bs5tdtc.

81. Labour lost just 82 seats, far below the Conservatives' losses of 1,382, but the latter were more exposed having performed well when these seats were last up in 2015. BBC projections put both parties on 28%, just the second time that both parties had been below 30% since such calculations began. Ominously for Labour, the largest falls in its vote came in Leave-leaning areas of longstanding party strength in the Midlands and the North. See John Curtice, 'Local Elections: The Main Parties Have Been Punished', *BBC News*, 4 May 2019, https://www.bbc.co.uk/ news/uk-politics-48132541; https://www.theguardian.com/politics/ 2019/may/04/local-elections-brexit-dithering-and-delay-hurts- the-main-parties.

82. Specifically, the Multiple Regression and Poststratification modelling technique made famous in 2017 by YouGov. For more detail on the methodology, and Labour's particular advantages in applying it, see Chapter 8.

83. The meeting was attended by senior Southside and Shadow Treasury staffers, campaign co-chairs Andrew Gwynne and Ian Lavery, and one LOTO aide. Neither Corbyn nor the rest of the senior LOTO leadership team attended.

84. See also Pogrund and Maguire, *Left Out*, pp. 300–2. Lavery was referring to the argument, frequently expressed on Corbynite social media, that YouGov was a Conservative-run firm because one of its founders, Nadhim Zahawi, went on to become a Conservative MP. There was no foundation for Lavery's claim, as researchers have found no evidence of a pro-Conservative bias in YouGov polling in 2017 or earlier elections. Indeed, it was YouGov's 2017 MRP model which first projected many of Labour's gains in the 2017 campaign; see Will Jennings, 'The Polls in 2017' in Dominic Wring, Roger Mortimore and Simon Atkinson (eds),

Political Communication in Britain: Campaigning, Media and Polling in the 2017 Election. Palgrave Macmillan.

85. This reflected a misunderstanding of the findings. Lavery assumed the grim model predictions were the product of direct Labour-to-Conservative switching in these seats. In fact, many of predicted Northern seat losses were due to fragmentation of the Labour vote as Labour voters defected to the Brexit Party, the Liberal Democrats and the Greens as well. Such fragmentation hurt Labour's chances in many seats, even if very little direct switching to the Conservatives occurred.

86. See Pogrund and Maguire, *Left Out*, pp. 157–61. A number of LOTO staff disavowed the letter publicly and Formby made a formal reply in January, noting that it was impossible to investigate the allegations because they were made anonymously and urging any individual who had specific concerns to follow the formal grievance procedure.

87. See also ibid., pp. 305–6.

88. The possibility of moving Seumas Milne was also mooted by Corbyn, but less frequently. Though many of his allies supported the idea of restructuring LOTO, Corbyn was characteristically reluctant to act against long-serving staffers.

89. See Pogrund and Maguire, *Left Out*, Chapter 13.

90. Reardon-Bond was hired as 'Director of LOTO'. Karie Murphy retained the title of Chief of Staff, but Reardon-Bond was in effect taking over her job of overseeing LOTO operations.

91. Pogrund and Maguire, *Left Out*, pp. 282–86.

92. Formby had been diagnosed with cancer in early 2019, resulting in several extended leaves of absence while she received treatment. LOTO and Southside did not replace her, and she had no official deputy, so instead a rotating system was used to fill her role during absences, with different Executive Directors unofficially acting as the General Secretary on different days. In the words of one senior Southsider: 'It was a bit like the collective Presidency in Yugoslavia after Tito died. It wasn't clear who was in power from day to day, it wasn't clear who said no to things, and it wasn't clear who was going to be in charge if anything went wrong.'

CHAPTER 5

An Unexpected Journey: The Smaller Parties in Parliament and at the Polls

The 2017 election had returned 12 Liberal Democrat MPs to Parliament, with 8 of the 12 either elected for the first time or regaining seats lost in 2015. Although the party had improved marginally on its dismal 2015 result, it had failed to capitalise on being the 'stop Brexit' party and struggled to win over the 'progressive' remain vote from the Labour Party—so much so that immediately after the election, the Lib Dems had been described as a 'party without a purpose'.[1]

It was also clear there was a 'Tim Farron problem'[2]—a question of leadership thrown into sharper relief by the return to Parliament of Liberal Democrat 'big beasts' Vince Cable, Jo Swinson and Ed Davey.[3] Farron had a poor campaign and did not particularly enjoy the role of leader—a senior Lib Dem campaigns staffer said: 'He'd absolutely hated the experience ... he's a constituency MP and being leader almost demands you not to be a constituency MP effectively.' Farron had decided during the campaign to resign after the 2017 election, but wanted to give the new cohort of MPs time to get settled in and to ensure a 'good transition'.[4] However, some Lib Dem peers—unaware of his intention[5]—pushed for a quicker resignation than was planned. On 14 June 2017, just six days after the election, Lord Paddick, who had been the UK's most senior gay police officer and Liberal Democrat

R. Ford et al., *The British General Election of 2019*, https://doi.org/10.1007/978-3-030-74254-6_5

candidate for London Mayor in 2008 and 2012, resigned his position as home affairs spokesman, citing concerns over Farron's views. Later that day, Farron himself resigned unexpectedly, seemingly in reaction to the Lords group moving against him. As a result, there was much less time than expected to prepare the ground internally for a contest.[6] The two candidates most popular with the party at Westminster, Jo Swinson and Ed Davey, both ruled themselves out.[7] Returning veteran Vince Cable put his name forward, and within the party many were content to back him as a caretaker leader until their preferred candidate was ready to step up.[8] Few expected Cable to lead the party into the next general election (at that time expected to be in 2022 when he would be 78 years old). Cable was therefore elected unopposed on 20 July 2017, the irony being that, had the 2017 election been a few months later, he had intended to stand down from his constituency and not seek re-election at all.[9]

From the outset of Cable's leadership there were regular suggestions, including from Cable himself, that he might soon step aside before a general election to allow 'one of my very able younger colleagues to take over'.[10] Despite this caretaker status, Cable nonetheless had an agenda for change within the party and a vision for how to 'pick the party up from two awful elections'.[11] His priorities were to 'capitalise on the fact that we were the only unambiguously Remain party' and to build on the 'one real strength … our continuing local government base'.[12] This was not an easy task: the Liberal Democrats were polling in single digits throughout 2017; it was difficult for the party to generate media interest; the party was allocated just one question at PMQs every four weeks; and it was difficult to maintain donor support after two election disasters in two years. Despite all this, the party grassroots remained healthy, with membership rising from 79,507 at the end of 2016 to 103,300 by the time of the 2017 leadership contest and 106,075 by the time of the 2019 leadership contest (which is discussed in detail below).[13]

'Cableman' (Brian Adcock, *The Independent*, 18 September 2018
© Brian Adcock)

Cable's priorities also highlighted a tension for the party that would continue to play out right up to the 2019 election: there was a growing opportunity to appeal to strongly pro-Remain voters as the campaign for a People's Vote gained momentum, but the base from which the Liberal Democrats usually built was their local councils, many of which were located in more Leave-leaning areas. Though this tension was evident in the demographic profiles of these voter groups, it was less obvious in the polling and electoral fortunes of the party in the first 18 months of the Parliament. And even as growing polarisation over Brexit saw the party's fortunes dramatically improve in 2019, switching between these priorities remained difficult. As one campaigner said,

> We've been taught that the way you win a seat is you work it for years, build up a membership base, build a council group, and it's all very gradual and up it comes. Suddenly … we're ahead in seats where we've done nothing.[14]

The 2018 local elections were at least a small step forwards, against a backdrop of the collapse of UKIP (which lost 123 councillors), a Labour

Party treading water and a Conservative Party demonstrating remarkable resilience after eight years in government. The Liberal Democrats gained 75 councillors and control of four additional councils (Richmond upon Thames, Kingston upon Thames and South Cambridgeshire from the Conservatives, and Three Rivers Council from no overall control). The councils taken from the Conservatives were a source of optimism for the party, suggesting it could win over 'liberal' (or at least pro-Remain) Conservatives, though this advance wasn't entirely on the basis of a 'Remain' pitch to these voters, but often also involved a more locally based anti-Tory message. The Lewisham East by-election in June 2018, where the Liberal Democrats took second place with a 20 percentage point increase in vote share, provided further evidence that they might be able to mobilise Remain supporters to renew their electoral appeal.

From the middle of 2018, however, there was chatter about the potential launch of a new 'centrist' party for MPs who felt they had been made 'politically homeless' by the polarised stances of their parties, particularly on Brexit.[15] One MP told the journalist Isabel Hardman: 'We can't go on like this until the next election. There is a group of voters who feel homeless and detached from the main parties – and it's fair to say that there's a group of us in Parliament who feel that too.'[16] The Liberal Democrats were as aware as everyone else of these rumours and were keenly aware of the danger this could pose to Westminster's existing centrist pro-Remain third party. As one of the parties' peers put it:

> I think there was a lot of nervousness towards the end of 2018 towards a new party, because we were constantly being told that there were people with millions and millions of pounds to put into such a thing and potentially a large breakaway from Labour with a few Tories … That suddenly there was a glitzy new party with lots of resource behind it and that was obviously both an opportunity but a threat.[17]

Accordingly, discussions were held behind the scenes with MPs seen as possible defectors and, in a speech at the National Liberal Club in Westminster in September 2018, Cable publicly reached out to those considering these options saying that 'by opening up our party, I hope to convince those who agitate for a new force that there is already a strong movement for open, centrist and internationalist politics: it is the Liberal Democrats'.[18] In the same speech, he indicated that he wanted to lead the party into the 2019 local elections, but not into a general election.

'First @TheIndGroup meal out before votes tonight at Nando's!', 26 February 2019 (@ChukaUmunna/Twitter, https://twitter.com/ChukaUmunna/status/1100121204093009921?s=20)

Cable's words had little effect. After months of speculation, the new centrist party was finally born on 18 February 2019 when seven Labour MPs (Luciana Berger, Ann Coffey, Mike Gapes, Chris Leslie, Gavin Shuker, Angela Smith and Chuka Umunna) simultaneously announced their resignations from the Labour Party. Their new formation, 'The Independent Group', was not (yet) a formal political party ready to contest elections, but a coalition of MPs in Parliament. They were joined by another Labour MP, Joan Ryan, a day later, and then two days later by three strongly Remain Conservative MPs (Sarah Wollaston, Heidi Allen and Anna Soubry).[19]

The timing of the launch owed little to strategy in relation to potential upcoming elections and more to logistics (Berger was in the late stages of pregnancy and it was important to launch before she went on maternity leave). The plans had long been afoot, with one source indicating that the group were clear they were leaving their parties from the end of 2018, yet they seemed unready for the spotlight and the realities of setting up a party that could stand in elections.

'Taking the plunge...?' (Dave Brown, *The Independent*, 22 February 2019 © Dave Brown)

Given their venture had long been touted across the pages of the Sunday papers, the group had something of a stuttering launch. Recognising the opportunity presented by the necessary upcoming European Parliament elections, the group had to move more swiftly than intended to register as a political party.[20] The name 'The Independent Group' was rejected by the Electoral Commission and 'Change UK—The Independent Group' was registered instead. The Electoral Commission also rejected the initial submission of logos. Both the party's various names and its logo efforts were widely panned on social media and by media sketchwriters.[21]

When the new party launched, journalist Matt Chorley wrote in *The Times* that it was 'a miserable time to be Vince Cable … someone else is having a party at the same time as yours, and theirs sounds much cooler and everyone is talking about it, even though yours is exactly the same'.[22] Cable was in fact very alert to the problem, seeing Change UK as an 'existential threat to the party', and annoying some of his colleagues with attempts to keep MPs from this group on cordial terms.

However, after months of speculation about new 'centrist' parties, it was the launch of a very different breed of new party which had the greatest impact on politics in 2019. Having sat out the 2017 election, erstwhile UKIP leader Nigel Farage was nonetheless quick to respond to the results, suggesting the morning after that the hung parliament result left Britain 'looking down the barrel of a 2nd referendum', a prospect that would leave him 'no choice' but to return to campaigning. Twelve months later he did just that, joining the Leave Means Leave campaign, headed by his colleague from the Leave.EU campaign Richard Tice. Leave Means Leave had grown out of Leave.EU after the EU referendum, as a campaign group aiming to ensure the UK 'makes a swift, clean exit from the EU'.[23] Farage's involvement moved the organisation into a new phase of higher-profile public campaigning characterised by the mass rallies and social media engagement that the Brexit Party later built on. The first Leave Means Leave rally in Bolton in September 2018 was some 1,600 people strong and was explicitly cross-party, bringing on board the pro-Brexit Labour MP Kate Hoey.

Leave supporters on the first leg of the March to Leave from Sunderland to Hartlepool, 16 March 2019 (© Kevin J Frost/Alamy stock photo)

Alongside these rallies, Leave Means Leave were also behind the 'March to Leave', which set out from Sunderland on 16 March 2019 and covered a 270-mile route, arriving in London, 13 days later, on what should have been 'Brexit day'. The march did not attract the crowds seen at the People's Vote marches in London, leading to unfavourable comparisons in the Remain-leaning media.[24] But the march did have symbolism on its side, with echoes of the legendary Jarrow March[25] and passed through several Leave-voting constituencies represented by Remain-leaning MPs. The march ended in London with a rally in Parliament Square, addressed by many of the high-profile Leave campaigners who would later add their support to the Brexit Party.[26]

Although he had alluded to a return to frontline politics throughout the months following the 2017 election, the key motivation for this uptick in campaigning by Farage in the second half of 2018 and early 2019, before the formal launch of the Brexit Party, was the 'betrayal' of Brexit in the Chequers deal, which Farage believed confirmed the fears he had expressed after the 2017 election. Feeling that UKIP had moved into a space defined more by its opposition to Islam than by Brexit, and opposed to the party's flirtation with Tommy Robinson, Farage formally resigned from his former party in December 2018 and had already begun to think about another electoral vehicle to defend the kind of Brexit that he wanted to see. Brexiteers concerned about the Chequers deal, the gathering momentum of the People's Vote campaign (financially and institutionally) and by the growing belief that a second referendum was becoming inevitable, applied to register a limited company called 'The Brexit Party' at Companies House on 23 November 2018. Polling that month had suggested that the situation 'wasn't quite bad enough'[27] to launch a new party at that point. Nevertheless, it was time to get the party 'on the shelf' just in case.

Initially fronted by Catherine Blaiklock, the Brexit Party was first announced on 20 January 2019 and was formally registered by the Electoral Commission on 5 February 2019, with Farage hearing about the approval while at lunch in Devon. It was quickly revealed, to the *Sun on Sunday*, to have the backing of Farage, who said he would stand as a candidate for the party in any forthcoming European Parliament elections (though at this time there was no indication such elections would be held). There was some early controversy when it emerged that Blaiklock had previously shared anti-Islam posts on Twitter. Blaiklock accepted these were her tweets and apologised, then resigned as party leader soon after, on 20 March 2019.[28] This meant Farage taking over the leadership of the party a little sooner than originally anticipated, but also meant he had a well-established link to the party when it was formally launched on 12 April.

The Brexit Party was not a conventional political party. Inspired by movements elsewhere in Europe, notably the Five Star movement in Italy and Geert Wilders 'Party for Freedom' in the Netherlands, it had neither party members nor party machinery to encumber it.[29] This proved important in the run-up to the formal launch as it allowed the leadership (Farage was soon joined by Leave Means Leave boss Richard Tice) to move quickly, making decisions on everything from slogans to logo colours in the space of 10 days in April. But it did generate suspicions as to where the party's funding was coming from, especially because by the time of the European Parliament elections, the party had more than 100,000 registered supporters, each of whom had paid £25, via PayPal, for the privilege. Concern was expressed by, among others, Gordon Brown, suggesting that donations made via PayPal could be from foreign or untraceable sources in breach of British electoral law.[30] The Electoral Commission, after this intervention from the former Prime Minister, attended the offices of the Brexit Party on 21 May, just two days before the European elections.[31] The Electoral Commission later issued a statement which said that, while it had 'very serious concerns' that the Brexit Party was not collecting data on the source of donations systematically, there was no evidence that it had broken the law and there was no further formal investigation.

Nigel Farage speaks at the launch of the Brexit Party at a metal factory in Coventry, 12 April 2019 (© Tommy London/Alamy stock photo)

Neither of the 'new' parties (Change UK and the Brexit Party) contested the 2019 local elections. Both lacked the party machinery to do so and for different reasons neither saw the elections as a priority—Change UK had never intended to contest elections immediately and the opportunity presented by the European Parliament elections appeared to take its MPs by surprise. For the Brexit Party, its raison d'etre was to contest, and convincingly win, the European Parliament elections that it officially hoped would never take place.

The arrival on the political scene of two new parties shook up voting intention polls, with the Brexit Party almost immediately jumping above the Liberal Democrats, and Change UK slotting in just behind them (see Chapter 8). There wasn't initially a huge sense of optimism about the 2019 local elections in the Lib Dem ranks, as fighting for media time against the two new parties was difficult and morale in the party was low. Yet these elections proved in fact to be a watershed moment for the party, which gained 704 councillors and control of an additional 11 councils.[32] The councils won were not all in high Remain areas either, although this was something of a mixed blessing—while it suggested the party was recapturing some of its traditional local and anti-incumbent appeal, it also highlighted the tension between the electoral needs of the Liberal Democrats and those of the wider Remain cause.

'Extinction Rebellion' (Nicola Jennings, *The Guardian*, 22 April 2019 © Nicola Jennings)

Re-energising the Liberal Democrats at a local level was a key part of Vince Cable's strategy as leader, but this was not always an easy priority to advance internally. When asked what in particular had improved the party's local performance, Cable pointed to the hard work needed to 'persuade the people in Head Office that we weren't just a branch of the Remainer movement but actually a political party trying to do things at the grassroots'. His efforts here paid wider dividends as the boost from the local campaign almost certainly helped to see off the challenge from Change UK in the European Parliament elections just three weeks later.

The 2019 local elections also completed the demise in local politics of UKIP, which lost more than four in five of its councillors, the third successive local elections wipeout for the party since the EU referendum.[33] At the other end of the ideological spectrum, 2019 saw a surge in support for the Green Party in England, which gained a record 194 councillors. There was also strong support for all manner of independent candidates and minor (often 'local') parties; as a group, these were in fourth place, only just behind the Liberal Democrats in terms of the total number of councillors elected—a symptom, perhaps, of an electorate increasingly frustrated with the traditional choices on offer. The absence of the two new parties launched months earlier meant that it was even more difficult than usual to read across from the local results to the national picture. Nonetheless, there were already warning signs for the main parties, with the BBC's projected national share for both the Conservatives and Labour falling below 30%.[34]

The local election results were a huge boost for the Liberal Democrats. But the European Parliament elections were a different test and one in which both the new parties (along with the more established Greens) were keen to make breakthroughs in an election where a proportional electoral system offered greater opportunities to smaller parties. An approach from Cable, prior to the local elections, to have a joint platform for the pro-European parties was rejected by both Change UK and the Green Party, with a spokesperson for Change UK highlighting that they wanted 'no alliance and no pacts, but to be a new party standing on its own',[35] though reports suggest this was not a unanimous position within the new party.[36] More widely, the pro-European parties wanted the elections to be seen as a 'soft referendum' on Brexit.[37]

The Brexit Party, too, understood that these elections would be read as an indication of what the British public thought should happen next, and it was much further ahead in the preparation for these elections than Change UK. Building on the model used by Leave Means Leave in the latter part of 2018, the Brexit Party announced a full list of candidates for the European Parliament elections that crossed party lines. Led by Farage, who stood in the South East region, these included former Conservative MP Ann Widdecombe, Annunziata Rees-Mogg (sister of Tory Brexiteer Jacob Rees-Mogg MP), former UKIP Welsh Assembly member Nathan Gill and former member of the Revolutionary Communist Party Clare Fox.[38] The party was clear that it had only one policy area at the European Parliament elections: Brexit. No wider manifesto was issued, though the party did issue a pledge card that included a commitment to push for Brexit on World Trade Organization terms. It had already done some 'road testing' of potential slogans and, after learning that despite the febrile atmosphere in British politics, 'Fighting Back' did not work as a slogan,[39] opted instead for 'Change Politics for Good'—for Change UK, an unfortunate overlap with its newly developing identity.

The Liberal Democrats did have a manifesto for the European Parliament elections and launched it with the memorable slogan 'Bollocks to Brexit'.[40] The slogan's profanity may have offended some, but Cable repeated it live on *The Andrew Marr Show* on 19 May and explained the etymology of a word, which, he claimed, had since the eighteenth century been used to mean 'nonsense'.[41] The Liberal Democrat leader repeatedly stressed that his party offered a 'clear and unambiguous' position on Brexit, which he contrasted with the cloudier position adopted by Labour. Given he had by this stage already announced his intention to stand down as leader of the Lib Dems, Cable had little to lose by gambling on controversial and polarising positions.

The Green Party also went into the European Parliament election in a buoyant mood and under new leadership of sorts. The Green Party of England and Wales is unique in British politics in having a shared leadership, with two 'principal speakers', one male and one female.[42] First elected in 2016, Jonathan Bartley initially shared the leadership role with Caroline Lucas, the party's only MP. When she stepped down from the role in 2018, Bartley stood again on a joint platform with Sian Berry, a member of the London Assembly, and secured more than 75% of the 8,329 votes cast. The local elections of 2019, their first electoral test as co-leaders, had been the best ever for the party, more than doubling their cohort of local councillors and gaining representation on an additional 54 councils. At their launch event for the European Parliament election, Bartley declared they would be 'tough on Brexit and tough on the causes of Brexit', and the Greens had high hopes that they, too, would benefit from polarisation over Brexit and disaffection with the mainstream parties.[43]

While the Liberal Democrats, the Green Party, Change UK and Labour battled for the Remain vote, the Brexit Party was the biggest threat to the Conservative Party and its embattled leader Theresa May, whose failure to deliver Brexit and further extension request had enraged large sections of her party (see Chapter 3, pp. 69–105). Polling for *ConservativeHome*[44] suggested that three out of five Conservative Party members (and two out of five Conservative councillors) intended to vote for the Brexit Party in the European elections. The reasons for this were varied: opposition to ongoing Brexit talks with Labour; the traditional use of European Parliament elections as a risk-free chance protest vote; or the hope that a disastrous result might help pressure the party to replace May with a leader more amendable to members. But while the motives may have been mixed, what was clear was that the Brexit Party was in pole position to benefit from Tory discontent.

'Labour and Tories Isn't Working' (Martin Rowson, *The Guardian*, 28 May 2019 © Martin Rowson)

Foreshadowing developments in the winter general election campaign, the Leave vote in the European Parliament elections coalesced around a single party, which therefore prevailed over fragmented Remain opponents. The Brexit Party, with 30% of the vote, topped the poll in all regions of Great Britain, except for Scotland and London, the only Remain-voting regions, where the SNP and the Liberal Democrats came top respectively. There could be no argument that Farage's new party had pulled off a remarkable feat, winning a national election just three months after first registering its existence with the Electoral Commission. The 'Remain' parties had wanted the election to be a referendum on Brexit, and it was, just not entirely in the way they had intended. While the combined vote share of the Liberal Democrats, the Green Party and Change UK was (marginally) greater than that of the Brexit Party alone, the Brexit party polled more than twice the Labour vote and four times the Conservative vote.

The fears the Liberal Democrats had about the 'new' centrist party in late 2018 were swept away by the results. Change UK polled just 3.3% of the votes, signalling a swift end to their mission to remake British politics. Just three weeks later, their highest-profile ex-Labour MP, Chuka Umunna, joined the Liberal Democrats.

This was an endorsement of the approach Cable had taken to the new party from the outset, maintaining open and cordial relationships with the MPs, despite the reservations of some within his party. It was also one of the strengths identified by Cable at the start of his leadership which enabled the Liberal Democrats to counter the 'existential' threat Change UK posed—namely, its strength in local government and local campaigning. When asked about this period, Cable said:

> When it eventually came to the local elections [in 2019] ... this was our big advantage because we could run local elections but they [Change UK] couldn't ... subsequent to that with the European elections that was in a way the defining moment for us. Had they made a breakthrough at that point I don't think the Lib Dems would have been able to recover ... we came out of the local elections very well because we had prepared hard for it, I had worked hard on it, and we were able to build on it with the European elections. A lot of that was due to being able to outflank the new party, Change UK. There was a point at which they could have done for us.

Had Change UK been ready to fight elections at the outset and had there not been a set of local elections immediately prior to the European

Parliament elections, the story might have been different. Change UK founding member Chuka Umunna admitted he had over-estimated the desire for a new political vehicle: 'I had thought that the millions of politically homeless people in the radical centre ground of British politics ... wanted a new party. And I was wrong about that.'[45]

'TiGs—we don't like Brexit' (Ben Jennings, *The i* paper, 22 February 2019)

The period immediately following the European elections saw polls in the UK that suggested a new period of (at least) four-party politics (see Chapter 8). The Brexit Party, the Liberal Democrats and Labour all topped the headline figures in polls fielded during late May 2019, though the Conservatives did not do so again until 21 June.[46] In this context, a by-election provided an important test of public opinion beyond the unusual context of European Parliament elections. In the event, there were two such elections, in very different seats, during the summer of 2019: one in Peterborough on 6 June and another in Brecon & Radnorshire on 1 August.

The Peterborough by-election arose after a successful recall petition against the sitting Labour MP, Fiona Onasanya, who had been convicted of perverting the course of justice for her role in a false name being given in relation to a driving offence. The Peterborough seat had been won narrowly by Labour in 2017 with a majority of just 607 votes over the Conservatives and, having flipped between Labour and the Conservatives between 1997 and 2017 and with an estimated Leave vote share of 61.3%, it wasn't an obvious target for the rejuvenated Liberal Democrats. There was, though, much more talk about it as a target for the Brexit Party, although it had only seen a moderate UKIP vote in 2015.[47] On the eve of polling, the Brexit Party was widely tipped to take the seat, but in the end Labour managed to hold off the challenge, albeit with just 30.9% of the vote and the Brexit Party snapping at their heels in second place with 28.9%.[48] It was, however, a warning—if one were needed—for both the Conservatives, in the midst of their leadership election, and the Brexit Party of the dangers of a split Leave vote; after all, taken together the two parties had won more than 50% of the votes cast, but neither had emerged victorious.

'I'd better be off!' (Morten Morland, *The Times*, 15 March 2019 © Morten Morland)

As for the Liberal Democrats, Peterborough made little or no difference. They were rapidly gaining new members, new donations and had reached their highest level in the opinion polls since the 2010 election. Now it was time to capitalise on their progress by electing a new leader. Cable had indicated his intention to step back from the leadership of the Lib Dems as early as 2018, but the process was formally begun after the European Parliament elections were held.[49] In the event, just two candidates emerged—Ed Davey and Jo Swinson, the two membership favourites who had sat out the previous contest. Both had served in the coalition government and both had lost their seats in 2015, before regaining them in 2017.[50] Though the campaign featured plenty of public hustings, these were largely dull affairs as there was little to separate the two ideologically. Swinson, however, was seen as being more open to working closely with the MPs who had founded Change UK, six of whom had resigned from the party they helped to found amid widespread rumours that several were contemplating joining the Liberal Democrats.[51] Chuka Umunna became the first to formally join, arriving before the Lib Dem leadership election was completed.[52]

Rather unusually, and in sharp contrast to the divisions in the two main parties, the Liberal Democrat Chief Whip Alistair Carmichael announced that Lib Dem MPs would remain neutral during the campaign in order to indicate to the wider membership that they would work with whoever was chosen.[53] The result was announced on 22 July, with Swinson winning a clear majority, with 62.8% of the 76,429 votes cast.[54] In her acceptance speech, she appealed directly to MPs in other parties:

> This is the time for working together, not the time for tribalism. And my message to MPs in other parties who share our values is this; if you believe our country deserves better, that we can stop Brexit, that we can stop Johnson, Farage and Corbyn, then work with us, join us. My door is always open.[55]

In the first poll after Swinson took over, the Liberal Democrats were still riding high on 23%, though the Conservatives were already beginning to recover ground and would soon recover more in the wake of Boris Johnson's election as their new leader. The optimism among the Lib Dems at this point was intense, but proved illusory: this was a peak in polling they would not see again. Even so, they were arguably in a better place than the Brexit Party: having been in first place in mid-June polls, Farage's new party had been drifting relentlessly downwards as the growing likelihood of a Johnson premiership saw Leave voters drifting back to the Conservatives. By the time Johnson was confirmed as the new

Conservative leader, the Brexit Party had dipped below 20% in the polls (see Chapter 8). This was not, however, particularly good news for the Lib Dems, who needed a split Leave vote to have much hope of making significant seat gains from the Conservatives.

Despite the Conservative poll recovery, the Liberal Democrats had grounds to hope that Johnson's election would further improve their appeal with liberal, Remain-leaning Conservative voters. After all, the Tories had elected a leader who was closely associated with the Leave campaign and had what critics argued was a less than exemplary record on issues of gender, race and equality.[56] The party also had a much bigger war chest to finance appeals to such voters. In a little over 12 months, the Lib Dems had gone from a precarious financial position necessitating redundancies and a bare-bones target list of 20 seats to having record donation pledges to finance their next general election campaign.[57] Figures from the Electoral Commission suggest that the party was able to spend almost £14.5 million in the 2019 election period, almost £1.5 million more than Labour and more than double its spend in 2017. As a result of one donation after the European Parliament elections, the party was able to undertake an MRP poll analysis, received by the party during the leadership election. This analysis, based on fieldwork conducted in June when the party was riding high in the polls, suggested that the Lib Dems were at that point ahead in 73 seats and within a 5% swing in a further 219 seats—an astonishing turnaround for a party targeting at most 32 seats at the start of the year. Yet some within the party were wary, as the analysis was based on an exceptionally strong polling position, and many of the seats that it claimed were now competitive were not places with any traditional Liberal Democrat presence. The projected seat gains also depended heavily on the Brexit Party remaining strong in the polls and thus taking a substantial chunk of the Leave vote from the Conservatives.

A second summer by-election, this time in a seat where the Liberal Democrats had placed second in 2017, offered an opportunity to test the party's new polling strength in a real election contest. The Brecon & Radnorshire by-election on 1 August 2019, as with Peterborough, was triggered by a successful recall petition, in this case after the sitting Conservative MP Chris Davies had been charged with, and pleaded guilty to, falsely claiming expenses in early 2019. The Liberal Democrats, riding the wave of their local and EU election successes, were well placed to contest the seat, with bookmakers making them the favourites to win it. However, the MRP model they had been given in June indicated that it was the Brexit Party that was on course to have the highest vote share—the MRP predicted the Brexit Party on 32%, the Lib Dems on 27% and the Conservatives on 21%.[58] The Brexit Party put forward Des Parkinson, an erstwhile UKIP candidate for the UK Parliament, Welsh Assembly and Police and Crime Commissioner in Wales.

The by-election also provided an early test for what would later become the Unite to Remain electoral pact (see Chapter 6, p. 193) between the Liberal Democrats, the Green Party and Plaid Cymru, with the latter two parties both standing aside and endorsing the Liberal Democrat candidate Jane Dodds. These parties all campaigned strongly for Dodds, and the seat was visited by Jo Swinson four times and by Heidi Allen, who had led Change UK into the European Parliament elections. In contrast, Farage did not visit the constituency to campaign, and there were rumours that an electoral pact between the Brexit Party and the Conservative Party had been discussed.

In the event, the Liberal Democrats won the seat. But the results provided some worrying portents, both for them and the Brexit Party. Where the Lib Dems' MRP had suggested that Farage's party would win one-third of the votes, on polling day it won just one-tenth, while the Conservatives came a close second, just 4.5% behind the winner, well ahead of where the MRP projection had them just a few weeks earlier. In the national polling at the time, the 'Boris bounce' was already beginning. Taken together, this evidence should have been a warning to the Liberal Democrats that their MRP projections were not going to hold up,[59] with Brexit Party voters starting to move en masse to the Conservatives.[60] The by-election was also a warning for the Brexit Party for the same reasons: as the psephologist John Curtice noted the morning after, in Remain-leaning seats the message was 'Vote Farage, Get Swinson', a risk that was later taken seriously within the Brexit Party leadership.[61]

Victory in Brecon & Radnorshire brought the total number of Liberal Democrat MPs to 13,[62] a number which soon rose further with a string of defections in the late summer and early autumn. The first was Sarah Wollaston, MP for Totnes,[63] and coming just two weeks after the by-election victory, this defection gave a continued sense of momentum and highlighted that the Liberal Democrats were able to attract people from both sides of the traditional party divide. This was highlighted again just three weeks later when Luciana Berger (originally elected for Labour) and Philip Lee (elected as a Conservative MP) were also announced as new Lib Dem MPs.[64]

Lee's was certainly the less anticipated of the two defections, and he chose to do so in dramatic style by physically crossing the floor of the house during a statement from Boris Johnson on the G7 summit. The dramatic defection also meant that Johnson lost his working parliamentary majority as it reduced the combined total of Conservative and DUP seats to 319.[65] Lee turned out to be a controversial figure within the Liberal Democrats, having previously run a campaign to prevent people with HIV from coming to the UK and having abstained in the 2013 vote on same-sex marriage—a further illustration of the way in which the politics of Brexit brought otherwise very different views together.[66] Angela Smith, MP for Penistone & Stocksbridge, shortly afterwards became the third MP in a week to join the Liberal Democrats.[67] This brought the total number of MPs to 17 as the party headed to Bournemouth for its annual conference.[68] There was a strong sense of momentum, with the party gaining members, MPs and influence. As the BBC's Chris Mason noted:

> Not long ago at Westminster, if you were on the hunt for a smile, you wouldn't bother with the Lib Dems. There weren't many of them, for a start, and those left were the last survivors of a near apocalypse for the party; shrivelled, ignored and drowned out. Not anymore. They are bouncy, tiggerish and expanding.[69]

There was more to come. Sam Gyimah, who only a few weeks previously had intended to run for leader of the Conservatives, was announced to the delegates at the party conference as the 'newest Liberal Democrat MP'.[70] Pictures from the conference in Bournemouth showed a hopeful, enlarged, group of MPs walking on the beach, highlighting their young, optimistic 'Liberal Democrat candidate for Prime Minister'.[71]

New Liberal Democrat party leader Jo Swinson with her MPs on the beach in Bournemouth during the party's 2019 conference (© PA Images/Alamy stock photo)

A key plank of the Liberal Democrat general election campaign and manifesto was the politically controversial 'revoke' policy—as passed by the conference on 14 September 2019 with the wording 'Conference calls for Liberal Democrats to campaign to Stop Brexit in a General Election, with the election of a Liberal Democrat majority government to be recognised as an unequivocal mandate to revoke Article 50 and for the UK to stay in the EU'.[72] Reporting this after the conference, many outlets specifically identified the policy with Swinson, though it had been a long-running debate within the party and she was clear that it was a difficult balance with the membership: 'Some in the party had been wanting to adopt a revoke policy for, like, three conferences, ... Since the previous conference that petition had got 6 million signatures so it didn't really feel like we could turn round to members and say "Well that's just ridiculous".'[73] The belief that it would inevitably pass as a conference motion was widespread within the party; however, there remains some disagreement about the handling of the motion after the conference. Two interviewees made this clear, a Leader's Office staffer highlighting the inevitability of the position:

A lot of people say incorrectly that this was something that was pushed by the leadership, that it was her choice. None of that's true. I'm not suggesting she was against it, but it's certainly true that the discussion ... among activists in the party wasn't about whether we did Revoke or not, the discussion was about whether we made the policy Revoke right now or whether we make the policy Revoke if we win a general election ... She had a choice – she could get on board with it or she could get run over by it.[74]

However, another senior campaigns source was less convinced this was the right messaging for the party:

The mistake we made was not to keep our line the same and keep saying Stop Brexit rather than Revoke.[75]

In the event, while some sort of 'revoke' commitment was inevitable given the mood of the membership, the policy agreed at the conference was sprung too quickly on campaigns staff for a full assessment of how to present it in an election to be conducted. The speed at which events subsequently unfolded in Parliament during September and October 2019 then left party staff little time to think carefully about messaging:

I don't think we had the capacity to have done all the campaign and messaging work on what our opponents were going to say about this and how do we guard against it. There's always an element to which you can't guard against it ... but I don't think we were as on top of that as we could have been.[76]

The conference motion made clear that 'revoke' was a position only to be adopted in the event of a Liberal Democrat majority government. In all other circumstances, the party would back a second referendum, making this the de facto policy for any realistic election outcome. But the subtleties of a conference motion could not survive the heat and light of the Brexit debate in the autumn of 2019. Despite careful wording and the backing of European Parliament Brexit Coordinator Guy Verhofstadt, who attended the Lib Dem conference, it was simply too easy for the other parties and the media to focus on the revoke pledge and frame it as extreme and even anti-democratic.[77]

The party conference season ended with the Liberal Democrats and Labour still fighting for second place in the polls—the Remain vote was still divided in the public as well as in Parliament. Johnson's election as Conservative party leader had allowed the Tories to regain some of the support lost to the Brexit Party, which had slipped further back to 11–13% in the polls, lagging in fourth place with a level of support similar to that of UKIP in 2015.

August is known as 'silly season' for news stories,[78] a period usually marked by unusual stories filling up the empty columns normally reserved for Westminster gossip and parliamentary business. However, August 2019 saw no let-up in the Brexit wrangling as Johnson sought to find a way through the parliamentary blockages that had done for his predecessor and MPs on all sides of the house sought to prevent a no deal Brexit (see Chapter 1, pp. 1–27). While the Brexit Party was already planning for a possible autumn election, it was not (directly) involved in the parliamentary manoeuvring, watching from outside Parliament (albeit on one occasion via a rally in Westminster).[79] The Liberal Democrats, however, were becoming central to the evolving parliamentary arithmetic. After the wave of summer defections to the party, they numbered 19 MPs, a significant number for Brexit votes that were often balanced on a knife edge.

The idea that Johnson and his team were considering a plan to suspend/prorogue Parliament in the run-up to the Brexit deadline on 31 October emerged even before he was confirmed as leader, sparking outrage among MPs and moves to find ways to ensure that, whatever parliamentary procedures could be used, there was no possibility of a no deal Brexit.[80] This also gave rise to growing calls for the pro-Remain (or perhaps more accurately the anti-no deal) MPs to come together in a government of national unity to oversee a request for an extension to the Brexit deadline and enact legislation for a second Brexit referendum (see Chapter 2, pp. 29–67).

As Liberal Democrat leader, Jo Swinson was in the centre of these discussions, and having persuaded MPs from both main parties to join her party in the previous six weeks, she was in a strong position to promote cross-party working. However, the sticking point was the Labour leader. It was clear to Swinson that the idea was a non-starter unless Jeremy Corbyn was prepared to step aside for another leader: 'I obviously took a lot of stick for saying it can't be led by Corbyn which I did think was a case of stating the obvious ... people like Dominic Grieve and David Gauke were not going to ever let that happen.'[81] Yet Labour were equally adamant that as leader of Her Majesty's Most Loyal Opposition,

Corbyn had to be the head of any interim 'stop no deal' coalition government. There was perhaps greater potential to find a parliamentary majority for a second Brexit referendum, the so-called 'People's Vote', by combining those who were actively in favour of it with those who would do anything to prevent a no deal Brexit. But, as Swinson realised, this prospect collapsed as soon as Johnson returned from Brussels with a new Brexit deal:

> The thing that killed the People's Vote was when Boris got the deal and then he got that through ... Basically nobody trusted the government. So they [the Tory rebels] were with us on the Saturday but by the time that [the Brexit Bill] came on the Tuesday they were back in the fold.[82]

Once the other options to stop Brexit had dried up, there seemed to be only one course of action left to the Liberal Democrat leader—support the SNP in their initiative to secure an early general election:

> So here you have the situation where if you had to either win a vote on a People's Vote in Parliament – and I just didn't see where those votes were coming from when those 20 Tory MPs were back in the fold and 19 Labour MPs just voted for Brexit – so then it felt like if you were going to have a general election when would you do it? ... If you want it done by Christmas ... it basically needed to be called incredibly quickly ... We had been on the record saying we will not allow an election where we could crash out with no deal in the middle of it but once an extension was secured, the logic is different. It was definitely not our preferred option but a final chance to Stop Brexit.[83]

Within the party, this was later perceived as a mistake, and there is some suggestion that it caused internal tensions at the time,[84] though others suggest the parliamentary party was supportive, as it recognised that 'Brexit was going to end up being delivered very soon. A general election was the last chance saloon of trying to stop that happening'.[85] After all, the Liberal Democrats had reason to think the election might work out well for them: they were still polling well, they had secured new donations and were in a stronger position to fund an ambitious target seat list, and had high hopes for securing seats with their new of MPs.

Yet balancing these advantages were a number of challenges. The newly defected MPs had had little time to develop relationships in the constituencies in which they stood, or in some cases even to establish where they would be standing. In some cases, the seats they represented had already selected candidates who were, unsurprisingly, reluctant to step down. Some of the defectors had their own views about the best places to stand. Luciana Berger was seen as a natural fit for Finchley & Golders Green and after initial discussions, Chuka Umunna was happy to stand in Cities of London & Westminster. The summer 2019 MRP had given the party reason to think both of these seats were in play, but they were not traditionally Liberal Democrat areas and the party had little organisation in place on the ground.[86]

While autumn's Brexit drama was focused on Parliament (see Chapter 2, pp. 29–67), the Brexit Party was looking to maintain its profile through further large public rallies. Although the resurgence of the Conservatives under their new leader continued to erode its support, the party was still perceived as a threat to the Conservatives, who would need a united Leave vote. Within the Brexit Party there was a view that the Remain parties would come together into some form of alliance and that would force the Conservatives to the table to forge a Leave alliance. Cue talk of various kinds of electoral pacts between the two pro-Brexit parties. At the start of September, Farage wrote:

> Boris Johnson faces a clear choice. He needs to face down the Remainer establishment inside and outside Parliament … and deliver a clean-break Brexit by the deadline of October 31st. If Boris has the verve and nerve to do that, we are prepared to put country before party, back him and make him a hero. If Boris continues to backslide away from a clean-break Brexit … the Brexit Party will have no choice but to stand against the Conservatives … in every seat up and down the country.[87]

The 'oven-ready' deal that Johnson secured was not quite the 'clean-break' Brexit that Farage and the Brexit Party were demanding, but the threat of a second referendum had become very real during September and October. This gave Farage and his colleagues new strategic headaches, as they recognised that a split Conservative vote could benefit pro-second referendum parties and thus increase the risk of the Brexit mandate being overturned altogether in a new public vote. In the end, the deal was good enough, the risks high enough, and the pressure applied sufficient to persuade Farage to stand down Brexit party candidates in Conservative-held seats (see Chapter 6, p. 193).

The 2017–19 Parliament highlighted the power of 'other' parties, even though the two-party share of the vote and of MPs elected at its start was relatively high. The period saw that two-party share of public support in polling plummet from 87% at the start to a low of 36% in the summer of 2019. The actions of those elected to represent the smaller parties proved central to the parliamentary manoeuvrings in a finely balanced legislature. But perhaps most consequential of all were the actions of the one party that did not have a direct role to play in the parliamentary process at all. Topping the poll in the European Parliament elections that it had been primed and ready for meant that the Brexit Party could exert pressure on the government, possibly hastening the departure of Theresa May,[88] and was a key driver of the enthusiasm with which the Conservative Party then embraced Boris Johnson as leader. The rise of the Brexit Party and the astonishing results of the European Parliament elections helped to move the Conservative Party from 'ABB—anyone but Boris' in January 2019 to seeing Johnson as the only solution to their troubles six months later.

But the Brexit Party was also the architect of its own demise. The party's ratings began to slide as soon as it became apparent that Johnson—the Leave campaign leader Brexiteers had done much to assist over the years—would become Conservative leader. And once Johnson was in office, the pro-Brexit tabloid press, once so favourable to Farage, turned against him. The *Daily Mail* launched a campaign against the party at the start of the official election period, and with hostile media and continuing falls in poll numbers, at no point in the official campaign did it look likely that it would manage to secure representation in a House of Commons elected under the first-past-the-post system.

On election night, Farage said he had 'killed the Liberal Democrats'[89]—perhaps a slight over-statement, given that the 'cockroaches'[90] of British politics returned 12 MPs and his party had none, but it was one that contained a grain of truth. After all, the performance of the Brexit Party at the European Parliament elections had helped lead the Lib Dems to think they had a chance in a whole swathe of seats that, in reality, were beyond their reach without the Brexit Party splitting the Leave vote. Conversely, it was the threat posed by the Lib Dems to Brexit that helped prompt the Brexit Party to stand down in Conservative-held seats.[91] The danger of a Corbyn-led minority government with a mandate to hold a second referendum was simply too great for those who had made achieving Brexit their lifetime political goal.

The Lib Dems had thus risen too far, too fast; paradoxically, had they remained weaker for longer, they might have had a better shot at making gains, since Farage might then have kept his Brexit candidates in the running in Conservative Remain seats. While the Brexit divide played out as an internal conflict for the two main parties, it gave the smaller parties on both sides of the argument a renewed sense of purpose and relevance. For a brief period in the summer of 2019, it looked as though it was about to give rise to a new period of multi-party politics despite the constraints of the electoral system. In the end, the ability of one side of the divide to unite while the other remained fragmented led to a decisive outcome—and one that had seemed quite unlikely only a few months before the election was called.

NOTES

1. 'The Lib Dems Should Have Capitalised on All That Remainer Sentiment', *The Independent*, 10 June 2017.
2. Senior Liberal Democrat source.
3. Edward Malnick, 'Returning Liberal Democrat Big Beasts Urged to Challenge Tim Farron for Party Leadership', *Daily Telegraph*, 9 June 2017, https://www.telegraph.co.uk/news/2017/06/09/returning-liberal-democrat-big-beasts-urged-challenge-tim-farron.
4. Interview with BBC Radio 5 Live, 14 July 2017.
5. In an interview with BBC Radio 5 Live (14 July 2017) after his resignation, Farron said he had decided to resign during the first two weeks of the campaign, but had 'put that into a drawer' and not spoken to anybody else about it.
6. Senior Liberal Democrat source.
7. Both Swinson and Davey had returned to Parliament in 2017 having lost their seats in 2015 and both felt they needed some time to re-establish their parliamentary presence. Both also had family reasons for delay. Swinson had a young child and was keen to have another—her second child was born in 2018—while Davey wanted to spend time with his young daughter and disabled son.
8. Cable was first elected as MP for Twickenham in 1997 and held the seat until 2015. Like Davey and Swinson, he lost his seat in the 2015 wipeout, then returned two years later. He had previously served as Deputy Leader of the party from 2006 to 2010 and as Business Secretary in the Coalition from 2010 to 2015. He had also briefly served as interim leader of the party during the 2007 leadership contest of October–December 2007, during which he made a memorable Commons intervention

noting Prime Minister Gordon Brown's 'remarkable transformation in the last few weeks from Stalin to Mr Bean'.

9. Vince Cable interview, 19 June 2020.

10. Vince Cable interview, BBC Radio 5 Live, 20 June 2017.

11. Vince Cable interview, 19 June 2020.

12. Vince Cable interview, 19 June 2020.

13. Figures taken from https://www.markpack.org.uk/143767/liberal-democrat-membership-figures.

14. Senior Lib Dem campaign source.

15. Though frequently described as 'centrist', this was a reference to being cross-party and therefore not on the left or right of the traditional two-party space, on the Brexit divide that drove much this chatter the disaffected 'centrists' were very definitely at the pro-European end.

16. Isabel Hardman, 'Is Now the Moment for a New Centrist Party?', *Evening Standard Magazine*, 27 September 2018.

17. Dick Newby interview, 5 June 2020.

18. Peter Walker, 'Vince Cable to Step Down "After Brexit Is Resolved or Stopped"', *The Guardian*, 7 September 2018, https://www.theguardian.com/politics/2018/sep/07/vince-cable-step-down-lib-dem-leader-brexit-resolved-stopped.

19. For an in-depth analysis of Change UK, see Louise Thompson, *The End of the Small Party? Change UK and the Challenges of Parliamentary Politics*. Manchester University Press.

20. Initially the group had a longer-term plan of canvassing over a period of six months, talking to experts across policy areas to try to build an alternative policy platform. The European elections offered both an opportunity and a challenge: 'suddenly we had to find and field a full slate of candidates ... we were standing on our own two feet alongside the big parties and it was never going to work' (Change UK source).

21. For example, Phil McDuff, '#Change UK—Really? If You Don't Get the Internet, You Shouldn't Be in Politics', *The Guardian*, 18 April 2019, https://www.theguardian.com/commentisfree/2019/apr/18/change-uk-internet-politics-european-elections-party-logo.

22. Matt Chorley, 'A Rival Party is in Town But Keep the Noise Down, Cable Needs His Sleep', *The Times*, 23 February 2019, https://www.thetimes.co.uk/article/a-rival-partys-in-town-but-keep-the-noise-down-cable-needs-his-sleep-vgpcqnbrh.

23. https://brexitcentral.com/author/leave-means-leave.

24. Though the People's Vote campaign claimed there were an estimated one million people on their march on the 23 March, experts in crowd estimation put the number at between 312,000 and 400,000; see https://fullfact.org/europe/peoples-vote-march-count.

25. A march from Jarrow in North East England to London in October 1936 to protest against unemployment and poverty in Jarrow.

26. As well as Nigel Farage, speakers also included Leave Means Leave Chairman Richard Tice, Claire Fox and Weatherspoons founder Tim Martin.

27. Brexit Party source.

28. Blaiklock's departure was, it seems, strongly encouraged behind the scenes by others involved in the party.

29. According to an email released under a Freedom of Information request to the Electoral Commission, the official reason for this was to 'stop the EDF and BNP members who are banned by our party'; see Alex Spence, 'The Brexit Party Doesn't Accept Members Because it Feared Supporters of Far-Right Groups Would Join', *BuzzFeed News*, 27 September 2019, https://www.buzzfeed.com/alexspence/the-brexit-party-doesnt-accept-members-because-it-feared

30. It was later revealed that Gordon Brown had written to the Electoral Commission suggesting that an investigation into the Brexit Party was 'urgent and essential'; see Brandan Carlin, 'Electoral Commission Is Accused of Anti-Brexit Bias for "Raiding" Nigel Farage's Party HQ Within Hours of Gordon Brown Demanding an Investigation', *Daily Mail*, 11 August 2019, https://www.dailymail.co.uk/news/article-7345281/Electoral-Commission-accused-anti-Brexit-bias-raiding-Farages-party-HQ.html.

31. Severin Carrell, 'Electoral Commission to Visit Brexit Party Offices Over Funding Concerns', *The Guardian*, 20 May 2019, https://www.theguardian.com/politics/2019/may/20/electoral-commission-visit-brexit-party-offices-funding-gordon-brown-paypal.

32. These were 10 existing councils—Bath & North East Somerset, Chelmsford, Cotswold, Hinckley & Bosworth, Mole Valley, North Devon, North Norfolk, Teignbridge, Vale of White Horse, and Winchester—along with the newly formed council of Somerset West & Taunton.

33. UKIP's fall in local politics was as dramatic as its rise. In 2017, UKIP lost 143 of 144 councillors elected in 2013; in 2018, 123 of the 126 councillors elected in 2014 were defeated; in 2019, it lost 145 of the 176 councillors elected in 2015. In total, the party gained 446 council seats in the three years running up to the EU referendum, then lost 411 of these again in the three years after the referendum result was announced.

34. https://www.bbc.co.uk/news/uk-politics-48091592.

35. Rob Merrick, 'Liberal Democrats Attack Other Anti-Brexit Parties for Refusing to Fight on Joint Ticket for European Elections', *The Independent*, 17 April 2019, https://www.independent.co.uk/news/uk/

politics/eu-elections-brexit-lib-dems-greens-change-uk-european-parliament-a8873731.html.

36. Frances Perraudin, 'Heidi Allen Threatened to Quit as Change UK Leader Over Lib Dem Row', *The Guardian*, 22 May 2019, https://www.theguardian.com/politics/2019/may/22/change-uk-leader-heidi-allen-threatened-to-quit-over-lib-dem-row.

37. Jessica Elgot, 'Brexit: Pro-EU Parties to Use European Elections as "Soft Referendum"', *The Guardian*, 13 April 2019, https://www.theguardian.com/politics/2019/apr/13/pro-eu-parties-to-use-european-elections-as-soft-referendum.

38. Since made Baroness Fox of Buckley.

39. Though it was used on some official placards and features in part on the image used for the Brexit Party pledge card at the European Parliament elections.

40. Though widely reported, this was an alternative title, with much campaign material featuring the more sedate slogan 'Stop Brexit'.

41. As 'nonsense to Brexit' doesn't make any sense, it is pretty clear the Liberal Democrat slogan was using the more profane sense of the word.

42. The Green have gone back and forth on this dual leadership model. It was dropped in 2008 following a referendum of Green members. Caroline Lucas served as the Greens sole leader from 2008 to 2012 (and sole MP from 2010 onwards), Natalie Bennett then served as sole leader from 2012 to 2016. The Greens returned to a co-leadership model after Bennett stepped down.

43. *The Independent*, 9 May 2019.

44. Paul Goodman, 'ConHome's Survey. Our Panel and the European Elections. Three in Five Tory Members Will Still Vote Brexit Party', *ConservativeHome*, 7 May 2019, https://www.conservativehome.com/thetorydiary/2019/05/our-panel-and-the-european-elections-three-in-five-will-still-vote-for-the-brexit-party.html.

45. Heather Stewart and Matthew Weaver, 'Chuka Umunna Joins Lib Dems: "No Room for Two in Centre Ground"', *The Guardian*, 14 June 2019, https://www.theguardian.com/politics/2019/jun/13/chuka-umunna-joins-liberal-democrats-after-quitting-change-uk.

46. Polling began to shift back in the Conservatives' favour as soon as it became clear to the public that Johnson would win the leadership contest and become Prime Minister.

47. The UKIP candidate Mary Herdman polled 15.9% in Peterborough in 2015, though the party did not stand a candidate in the seat at the 2017 general election.

48. The Peterborough result was a major moral boost for embattled staff in Labour's Southside elections team, as one aide later recalled: 'We had

absolutely no right to be even in contention for that. And we won ... And I think that is really important because it shows that if you run a campaign professionally, irrespective of where on the spectrum of Labour you come, you actually can win. You can never win organisationally, and you can never really just win from the politics, it's a combination of the two. Peterborough showed that if we had a really decent message locally, and we had a good campaign, we could drive it and win.'.

49. Only serving MPs were eligible to stand for leader. Cable had sought to change the rules to allow non-MPs to stand, but the proposal was rejected by the Spring Conference in 2019. This meant there was a pool of 11 candidates to choose from. In order to stand for leader, nominees were also required to have the backing of 10% of the parliamentary party (in this Parliament that equated to one MP) and be supported by at least 200 members spread across at least 20 local parties. See 'Lib Dems Start Leadership Contest', *BBC News*, 24 May 2019, https://www.bbc.co.uk/news/uk-politics-48403038.

50. Ed Davey was Secretary of State for Energy and Climate Change from 2012 to 2015; Jo Swinson served as Parliamentary Private Secretary to Deputy Prime Minister Nick Clegg, and as a Parliamentary Under Secretary of State for Business, Innovation and Skills.

51. Sebastian Payne, 'Change UK Splits Over Plan to Join with Lib Dems', *Financial Times*, 4 June 2019, https://www.ft.com/content/a408cc38-86dc-11e9-a028-86cea8523dc2.

52. 'Chuka Umunna Joins Lib Dems After Quitting Change UK', *BBC News*, 14 June 2019, https://www.bbc.co.uk/news/uk-politics-48631116.

53. Carmichael explicitly made this contrast and wrote: 'Uniquely in British politics at the moment, for the Liberal Democrats a leadership election is an opportunity and not a threat.' Alastair Carmichael, 'How Lib Dem MPs Will Approach the Leadership Election', *Liberal Democrat Voice*, 31 May 2019, https://www.libdemvoice.org/alistair-carmichael-mp-write-show-lib-dem-mps-will-approach-the-leadership-election-60993.html.

54. Though by that time, it was clear that Johnson would win the Conservative leadership election, and the Lib Dem announcement was somewhat overshadowed by the Conservative one just 24 h later.

55. Peter Walker, 'Jo Swinson Elected New Lib Dem Leader', *The Guardian*, 22 July 2019, https://www.theguardian.com/politics/2019/jul/22/jo-swinson-elected-new-lib-dem-leader.

56. The Liberal Democrat Election Review (https://www.libdems.org.uk/2019-election-review) described this as 'a summer of optimism'.

57. Senior Liberal Democrat campaigns source. The Liberal Democrat Election Review says that at the start of 2019, they were planning 'on a

shoestring budget, with a list of 32 target seats, which many people considered optimistic'.

58. Liberal Democrat Election Review.

59. When the initial MRP model was delivered to the party, there was no election on the horizon. As one senior campaign source said: 'If we had been taking decisions in August about expanding the target list with a view that there was going to be an election in three months' time, then it would have been a shorter list of seats.' Later, target lists were refined and polling during the campaign made it clear that the initial MRP model was overly optimistic as the dynamics of party support changed.

60. By the beginning of August, it was becoming clear that at least some of the Brexit Party support had returned to the Conservatives after Boris Johnson became Prime Minister. The closest national polling to the Brecon by-election had the Brexit party down to 13% of the headline voting intention.

61. John Curtice, 'The Boris Bounce is Real, But the Lesson from Brecon Is: "Vote Farage, Get Swinson"', *Daily Telegraph*, 2 August 2019, https://www.telegraph.co.uk/politics/2019/08/02/boris-bounce-real-lesson-brecon-vote-farage-get-swinson.

62. Twelve were returned to Parliament in 2017, but Stephen Lloyd had resigned the whip in 2018 as he had stood in his constituency on a platform of respecting the referendum result and felt this was incompatible with the Lib Dems' second referendum policy. The arrival of Umunna brought the total back to 12.

63. Elected as a Conservative MP in 2017 and having held Totnes for the Conservatives in 2010 and 2015, Wollaston was one of the group that joined Change UK in February, leaving the party in June to sit as part of the Independents group with other ex-Change UK MPs.

64. Luciana Berger was first returned to the Commons as Labour MP for Liverpool Wavertree in 2010. She had given emotional testimony about the toxic anti-semitism she had faced as a Jewish Labour MP at several points during the Parliament, before becoming one of the founding members of Change UK. She left Change UK to sit as an independent in June 2019, then became a founder member of 'The Independents' in July 2019. Phillip Lee was elected as Conservative MP for Bracknell in 2010 following an open primary. He had resigned as a minister in Theresa May's government in June 2018, citing his opposition to Brexit.

65. Although in theory the line for a majority in a 650-seat Parliament is 326 seats, in reality the line for a 'working majority' is lower. The seven Sinn Fein MPs elected in 2017 did not take their seats (in keeping with a long-standing party policy), while the Speaker and his three deputies do not usually vote. Excluding these 11 MPs brings the effective Commons total

to 639 seats, and hence 320 is the line for a working majority. See Kate Proctor, Peter Walker and Heather Stewart, 'Phillip Lee Quits Tories, Leaving Government without a Majority', *The Guardian*, 3 September 2019, https://www.theguardian.com/politics/2019/sep/03/phillip-lee-quits-tories-leaving-government-without-a-majority.

66. Some party members spoke out publicly against his acceptance as a Liberal Democrat MP, with Jennie Rigg, who had chaired the Liberal Democrat LGBT caucus, quitting the party; see Jon Stone, 'Phillip Lee: Lib Dem LGBT + Members Revolt over Decision to Let Tory MP Join the Party', *The Independent*, 3 September 2019, https://www.independent.co.uk/news/uk/politics/liberal-democrats-lgbt-phillip-lee-brexit-boris-johnson-gay-rights-a9090831.html.

67. Smith was first elected as a Labour MP in 2005 and was a founding Labour member of Change UK (in February 2019) and then of 'The Independents' (in July 2019).

68. In a tweet the day before the announcement, Jo Swinson had posted an image of music notation for the song 'Sixteen Going on Seventeen', sparking speculation over who the seventeenth would be.

69. 'Former Conservative MP Sam Gymiah Joins Lib Dems', *BBC News*, 15 September 2019, https://www.bbc.co.uk/news/uk-politics-49703214.

70. On 2 June 2019, Gyimah, who had been Conservative MP for Surrey East since 2010, became the thirteenth candidate for the Conservative leadership, but the only one pledging a second Brexit referendum. He withdrew from the race before the final list of candidates was formalised on 10 June.

71. Later to become a problem for Swinson, this line was initially used as a harmless crowd pleaser for the conference floor.

72. *Liberal Democrat Voice*, 12 September 2019, https://www.libdemvoice.org/to-revoke-or-not-to-revoke-that-is-the-question-62014.html.

73. Jo Swinson interview, 16 July 2020.

74. Leaders Press Office interview, 12 June 2020.

75. Campaign team interview, 12 June 2020.

76. Swinson interview, 16 July 2020.

77. Leader of the Alliance of Liberals and Democrats for Europe in the European Parliament, European Parliament Brexit Coordinator and Chair of the Brexit Steering Group. Verhofstadt had also campaigned for the Liberal Democrats during the European elections. See Jon Stone, 'Brexit: Guy Verhofstadt to Knock on Doors for Lib Dems in European Parliament Elections', *The Independent*, 2 May 2019, https://www.independent.co.uk/news/uk/politics/brexit-european-elections-lib-dems-guy-verhofstadt-change-uk-a8896661.html.

78. Mark Easton, 'Why August's "Silly Season" Is Good for the Soul', *BBC News*, 18 August 2019, https://www.bbc.co.uk/news/uk-45212334.
79. A Brexit Party source claimed that the party's leadership believed a general election in September or October was a greater than 50% chance.
80. Sam Coates, 'Boris Johnson Team Considering Plan to Suspend Parliament in Run up to Brexit', *Sky News*, 16 July 2019, https://news.sky.com/story/boris-johnson-team-considering-plan-to-suspend-parliament-in-run-up-to-brexit-11764347.
81. Swinson interview.
82. Swinson interview.
83. Swinson interview.
84. The Liberal Democrat Election Review notes the 'absence of consultation among other parts of the Liberal Democrats' in the summer of 2019 when the leader's team were looking at election scenarios.
85. Liberal Democrat source.
86. One source said 'we've got the research for Finchley and Golders Green … it looks good because it's stuffed full of Remainers … [but] we had nothing there zero councillors, zero campaigners … Labour fought us to a standstill'.
87. 'Farage Orders Boris to "Face Down Remainer Rabble and Blackmail from EU" to Deliver Brexit', *Sunday Express*, 1 September 2019.
88. Sources within the Brexit Party firmly believed that Theresa May's departure was due to the European Parliament election results, while those within the Conservative Party indicated that this decision was made prior to these elections.
89. 'General Election 2019: "I Killed the Liberal Democrats and Hurt Labour" Says Farage', *BBC News*, 12 December 2019, https://www.bbc.co.uk/news/av/uk-politics-50765372.
90. 'The Cockroach Party: Britain's Lib Dems Cling on', *The Economist*, 12 May 2018, https://www.economist.com/britain/2018/05/10/the-cockroach-party-britains-lib-dems-cling-on.
91. See Chapter 6 on decisions taken during the campaign.

Get Brexit Done: The National Campaign

One lesson both big parties took from 2017 was the need to be prepared. The scramble to secure candidates, recruit volunteers, pull together policies and develop messages was not an experience either was eager to repeat.[1] With Brexit deadlock making an early election ever more likely, the party leadership teams devoted many hours throughout 2019 to planning for the next contest, whenever it came. Indeed, Labour's leadership team was devoting so much time to election planning from the summer onwards that it risked doing more harm than good, as one senior aide recalled:

> The leadership team, both politicians and staff, was in election mode from July. We were having very regular meetings of the election campaign committee, or other election planning and executive committees, three times a week or more, sometimes every night, for weeks and months. Which actually is probably not a good idea, because it exhausts everybody, and probably didn't help from the point of view of the fractiousness.

By the autumn of 2019, the Conservatives had overhauled their party machine, improved their finances and secured the services of the figures who would run their campaign. Labour's election planners had been just

© The Author(s), under exclusive license to Springer Nature Switzerland AG 2021
R. Ford et al., *The British General Election of 2019*,
https://doi.org/10.1007/978-3-030-74254-6_6

as active, though probably to less effect. Candidates were recruited early for most target seats, but the target list itself was internally disputed, and new reselection processes were a distraction for some incumbent MPs. There were running internal disputes over Brexit policy, target seat lists, community organising and much else besides. The contrast between an anxious but united Conservative team and a divided, chaotic Labour leadership set the tone for the campaign to come.

The Conservatives began the campaign with double-digit polling leads and Boris Johnson being strongly preferred over Jeremy Corbyn in the leadership polling. But memories of the 2017 campaign were fresh in CCHQ and nothing was taken for granted. As one of those involved admitted: 'A huge proportion of how we behaved in this election ... was a direct reaction to 2017. It was just this enormous shadow cast over everything.' Voters were fickle and the first winter election campaign since 1974 was unknown terrain. Discipline and focus were the watchwords in Matthew Parker Street.

The Prime Minister launched the Conservative campaign in Birmingham on 6 November with a speech in the centre of a crowd of activists, criticising a Parliament 'as incapable of digestive function as an anaconda that has swallowed a tapir' and promising to end the deadlock over Brexit, which was 'like a bendy bus jack knifed on a yellow box junction ... blocking traffic in every direction'.[2] In a front-page article in the *Daily Telegraph*, Johnson compared Corbyn's Labour to Stalin's communists: 'they point their fingers at individuals with a relish and a vindictiveness not seen since Stalin persecuted the kulaks'.[3] The Prime Minister laid into his Brexit Party rival Nigel Farage with similar relish, calling him a 'candle seller at the dawn of the electric lightbulb'.[4] The resulting controversy over Johnson's pugilistic rhetoric provided a badly needed distraction, as the Conservative campaign was rocked by a scandal-driven Cabinet resignation the day it launched.[5]

Boris Johnson speaking at the Conservative Party general election campaign launch, Birmingham NEC, 6 November 2019 (© PA Images/Alamy Stock Photo)

The Conservatives' campaign targeted a swathe of Leave-voting seats in the Midlands and the North which had been slowly drifting away from Labour even before the EU referendum, and where Conservative vote shares rose substantially in 2017. These seats were dubbed the 'Red Wall' by Conservative analyst James Kanagasooriam, whose statistical modelling had identified a set of historically Labour-held target seats where the local mix of voters ought to be most open to Conservative appeals. Breaking through this 'Red Wall' was seen as the route to a new majority.[6]

The parliamentary pyrotechnics of the autumn had helped the Conservatives to make the case for an election to break to deadlock. CCHQ sought relentlessly to reinforce this message once the campaign was underway, deploying a slogan which by December was lodged in the brains of every British voter. The election was needed, Conservative politicians, leaflets and Facebook posts insisted, to 'get Brexit done'. This slogan had emerged in focus groups where voters vented their frustration at the parliamentary impasse. One CCHQ pollster recalled the electric reaction when he put the phrase to participants: 'As soon as we said it they were just like "Yes! That's it! That's the one!" because it captured the essence of what they were trying to say.' The slogan was also, crucially, a good fit with Johnson's own personality and approach to Brexit. His short tenure as Prime Minister had already become defined by an intense, even reckless, determination to get the issue resolved as quickly as possible:

> It was what voters wanted but it was also what the PM felt comfortable saying. And this is something that should never be underestimated. Because political campaigns can come up with the perfect slogan for the context, but it has to ring true for the person who is fronting the campaign and saying it. If you get misalignment, then there's a sort of inauthenticity that just doesn't gel with the public.

Other messages were hung on the peg of 'get Brexit done'. The Withdrawal Agreement was promoted as 'oven-ready', with the Prime Minister deploying various culinary props to hammer home the point, and there were a string of campaign trail events featuring Johnson brandishing 'oven-ready' food such as pies, biscuits, bagels and donuts. This was contrasted with Labour's 'dither and delay', a spontaneous 'Borisism', reflecting his ability, as one of CCHQ's team put it, 'to distil an idea into a simple communication that's completely bang-on' and one which the campaign swiftly adopted as an attack line.[7]

'Boris's Brexit Deal—Oven-Ready' (© Conservative Party)

The Labour campaign began strongly, with a slick launch video posted online on the day the General Election Bill passed, which garnered a million views within 24 hours. The campaign team started with high hopes—most of the senior figures involved had happy memories of the 2017 campaign surge and hoped to ride another wave this time. Corbyn set the tone with a punchy launch event in central London's Battersea Arts Centre where he promised 'a once in a generation chance to change our country'. But behind the scenes, the contrast with the overhauled and united Conservative machine was stark.

The Labour Leader's Office was still reorganising in the wake of Karie Murphy's move to Southside just weeks earlier, and the campaign team was deeply divided. All involved recognised the electoral threat posed by Brexit, but there was no agreement on how to respond. One faction, led by John McDonnell and Andrew Fisher, and backed by Southside elections analysts, argued that consolidating Remain support was an essential first priority. A split Remain vote risked precipitating a historic parliamentary wipeout, and even in Leave-leaning seats, most of the votes Labour won in 2017 came from Remainers. Once the Remain 'low-hanging fruit' had been harvested, the party could pivot to a broader pitch for working-class, Leave-leaning voters. This strategy was vehemently opposed by more pro-Brexit aides, including Seumas Milne and Karie Murphy, who believed the only route to a Labour victory ran through Leave-leaning seats where an emphasis on a second referendum would play badly. The focus on consolidating Remain supporters looked to them like a return to the defensive 2017 Southside campaign mindset, one which risked losing the election from the outset by alienating Leave-sympathetic voters in the battlegrounds where the election would be won or lost.[8] These were arguments about methods as well as strategy—those who favoured a focus on Remain voters also tended to favour traditional targeting and communications techniques, while those favouring a focus on Leave voters also preferred a more aggressive 'left populist' communications and organisation strategy. As one Southside campaign strategist observed, LOTO's 'left populists' 'never bought into using tools like Experian, demographic profiles, voter intelligence, voter ID, as a way of winning elections'. While LOTO radicals saw traditional targeted campaigning and messaging as the route to failure, many in Southside still saw such methods as the only means to avert catastrophe.

Arguments about campaign strategy cut across older factional and organisational divides. Corbyn loyalists and LOTO tended to be more radical, and Corbynsceptics and Southside more conservative, but by 2019 there were anti-second referendum 'left populists' in Southside (such as Karie Murphy and Jennie Formby), while the Remain-focused campaign traditionalists included longstanding Corbyn allies such as John McDonnell and Andrew Fisher. With no agreed hierarchy among feuding senior leadership figures, agreeing a common approach proved impossible, and strategic planning was crippled by endless argument. As one LOTO advisor recalled:

> We had these twice daily campaign team strategy group meetings and we would just have the same arguments all day, every day: 'are we trying to appeal to these Remainers or are we trying to appeal to these non-traditional Tory voting leavers?' Which always ended in stalemate.

Labour's traditional campaign infrastructure was also not in great shape. New technology platforms had been installed in Southside months earlier and were not fully road tested. There were early problems with the IT systems for the design of leaflets, internet advertising and telephone canvassing, compounded when the party was hit by disruptive cyber-attacks on 11 and 12 November, just as freepost mailouts to voters were being prepared. 'Every new technology project Labour managed went horribly wrong', one Southside manager observed. 'The lesson of trying to have our own in-house technology is simple: it doesn't work.' Longstanding disagreements over social media strategy meant that Labour's online campaigning was split across two teams—a LOTO team managing Corbyn's personal accounts and a Southside team running Labour Party accounts—who distrusted each other and cooperated only sporadically. This reflected broader fragmentation and duplication, often the product of factional distrust, sometimes the result of poor organisation.[9] The community organisers network Labour had developed since 2018 was reportedly siloed off by the Corbynites running it from Labour's hierarchy of local and regional offices, which they distrusted. LOTO polling director Carl Shoben had signed a retainer agreement with ICM for twice weekly campaign polling weeks before the election was called, while Southside's election team continued to update their separate Multiple Regression and Poststratification (MRP) model using polling data from YouGov. LOTO aides dismissed Southside modelling while Southside analysts rubbished LOTO's polling. Even coordination with the Corbynites' strongest organisational resource—Momentum's huge network of activists—was sporadic at best.[10] Momentum's social media team worked closely with LOTO, and the Momentum leadership were kept appraised of Corbyn's diary, but Momentum were not included in strategy discussions and were given little information about the party's seat targeting. As one leading Momentum figure recalled:

> There was no big sit-down strategic discussion ... But it wasn't that Momentum wasn't part of a strategic discussion, rather I don't think there was much of a strategic discussion. LOTO was chaotic in the 2017 election. 2019 was clearly worse. There was a small cupboard with generals who didn't get on with each other.

One longstanding thorn in LOTO's side was removed on 6 November when Corbyn's deputy Tom Watson announced his resignation as Deputy Leader and retirement as an MP. To the surprise of many, Watson went quietly, calling his decision 'personal not political' and urging support for the Labour leadership.[11] The morale boost from Watson's peaceful departure did not last long. The next day, two other retiring former Labour MPs—Ian Austin and John Woodcock—announced their endorsement of Johnson's Conservatives with a broadside against their former leader: 'Jeremy Corbyn is completely unfit to lead our country ... the Labour Party's been poisoned with anti-Jewish racism under his leadership', Austin told the *Today* programme.[12] On the same day, the *Jewish Chronicle* ran a front-page splash addressed 'to our fellow citizens', laying out their concerns about anti-semitism in Corbyn's Labour and urging voters to reject the party.

To all our fellow British citizens

FULL COVERAGE OF THE GENERAL ELECTION P2-9

8 NOVEMBER 2019 ● WWW.THEJC.COM ● £2.70
ך'דוז 790 ● 10 CHESHVAN 5780 ● 7855 ● SINCE 1841

This front page is addressed not to our usual readers—but to those who would not normally read the Jewish Chronicle. In other words, to non-Jews. This is why:

Jewish Chronicle front cover splash, 8 November 2019 (© Jewish Chronicle)

The Liberal Democrats launched their campaign in Westminster on 5 November with Jo Swinson telling voters 'I never thought I'd stand here and say that I'm a candidate to be prime minister. But when I look at Boris Johnson and Jeremy Corbyn, I am absolutely certain I could do a better job than either of them'. Such apparent confidence put a brave face on an election campaign which, coming just months after Swinson became leader, posed serious problems for her and her party. As one senior aide noted:

> There wasn't enough time to iron everything out and get it running like a well-oiled machine … Campaigns are time, money, ideas and we didn't have any time. We had some money, and some ideas, but we didn't have any time. And especially Jo didn't.

The needs of the moment were not the only reason Swinson drew heavily on a small group of advisors in election preparation, generating some frictions with those outside her inner circle. The new leader also distrusted parts of a party machine which in her campaign for the leadership she had promised to overhaul. As one senior advisor recalled:

> I think historically Jo didn't trust parts of HQ on things like attention to detail, which to be fair parts of HQ had not been brilliant on … She saw

the Lib Dems as a broken party which she wanted to fix. She's the ultimate perfectionist and that's not the worst thing in the world – you should have very high quality control. But because of the small timescales at this election, I think the circle of people that she fully trusted was very, very small.

Swinson's inner circle also reflected the unusual circumstances of 2019, with an influx of MPs defecting from other parties and seen by the campaign leaders as a valuable resource. 'The quality of those defectors was very high', noted one senior campaign staffer, 'almost to a person, frontbench material, they were really fricking good.' Figures such as Chuka Umunna and Sam Gyimah were brought into the leadership team, despite having only joined the party months earlier. The leadership saw this as putting valuable new talent to use, but it ruffled feathers among party veterans who felt they were denied the same kind of access.

Two central planks of Swinson's pitch soon proved contentious and later came to be seen as an albatross around the party's neck: the pledge to unilaterally revoke Article 50 and thus halt Brexit without a second referendum, and the focus on Swinson herself as a Prime Minister in waiting. Both decisions made some sense when they had been taken in the early autumn—the Liberal Democrats had surged in the polls over the summer and had enjoyed a triumphant European Parliament campaign with the provocative slogan 'Bollocks to Brexit' (see Chapter 5, pp. 170–174). But both unravelled in the harsher winter campaign climate. Many in Swinson's team were from the outset uncomfortable with the 'revoke' idea, preferring to stick with the existing 'stop Brexit' messaging that had served the party well—'It's broad, whether you're for revoke or for another referendum, it works for you. We didn't need to divide Remainers'—but a petition calling for revocation of Article 50 had gathered six million signatures over the summer and emboldened the party's ardently pro-European activists. The leadership embraced the idea, reasoning that it could do little harm as revocation could only be enacted in the far-fetched scenario where the Liberal Democrats won a Commons majority.[13] The idea was seen as a useful signal of the party's opposition to Brexit, providing a clear dividing line from the now pro-second referendum Labour Party.[14] Yet the claim that the 'revoke' scenario was too unlikely to matter was at odds with the other central plank of Liberal Democrat messaging—the focus on Swinson as a potential prime minister, a framing also encouraged by the buoyant summer poll numbers:

At that time [late summer] you had three parties polling within a few percentage points and as late as September 30th us and Labour were still neck and neck ... The mistake around the [Swinson for Prime Minister] line is that what you could say credibly in September when you're polling ahead of the Labour Party you can't credibly say in November where we're 10 points behind Labour and clearly not going to win.

Leader-focused campaigning—Jo Swinson speaking in front of the 'Jo Swinson's Liberal Democrats' battle bus, Kirkintilloch, 22 November 2019 (© Colin Fisher/Alamy Stock Photo)

Both messages backfired. The 'revoke' policy divided the Remain voters that the party needed to unify, with many seeing it as undemocratic to reverse the referendum Brexit mandate without holding another public vote. The promotion of Swinson as a potential prime minister was criticised as hubristic and did not prevent endless questions about what the Liberal Democrats would do in the event of a hung parliament. Worse still, the strategy undermined anything else the party wanted to get across. As one senior staffer put it:

You have to sound credible in order to give people permission to listen to everything else you have to say. We didn't sound credible. Anyone who had a basic understanding of politics knew that the Liberal Democrats were not going to win 350 seats and form a majority government, or even the 200 or whatever you would require to be the largest party.

The party also struggled to calibrate its seat targeting in response to the upheaval wrought by Brexit. Swinson and her aides aimed to avoid the chaos of 2017, when the shock early election call caught the party unprepared, through careful planning and earlier targeting. Yet earlier targeting brought problems of its own in a fluid political context. The party's elections team had commissioned regular MRP analysis from YouGov to build a constituency-level model of their new support. The first models, built on polling from the summer, revealed a dramatic shift towards graduate-heavy, strongly Remain areas such as the London sub-urbs, with support stagnating or falling in more Leave-leaning traditional strongholds such as the West Country. This analysis fed into a tiered tar-geting strategy, with most resources focused on the top tier of 40 seats, with another 40 also receiving substantial support.[15] The choice of seats required balancing the traditional Liberal Democrat focus on local pres-ence and profile with the demands of the radically changed political con-text. As one of those involved noted:

Of that top 80 it was a mixture of new seats and old seats. All the new seats massively outperformed the old seats, but the old seats were starting off at a much higher level. When we were drawing this list up we were hav-ing all these arguments 'we have no councillors there! We've never spoken to anyone there'. It really went against a lot of our instincts.

The timing of the election did not help—the Liberal Democrats had no time to organise in their new targets, yet the party's polling position was still too strong to justify cutting back early, particularly with Swinson making her party's high ambitions a keynote of the campaign. As a result, concerns that the party had over-reached itself were present from the outset and grew as the poll numbers declined. Yet two factors kept hope alive—the 'Unite to Remain' initiative to keep smaller parties from splitting the Remain vote, and the potential for Nigel Farage's Brexit Party to divide the Leave vote.

The 'Unite to Remain' pact announced on 7 November emerged from negotiations between the Liberal Democrats, the Greens and Plaid Cymru led by Heidi Allen, who had joined the Lib Dems from the Conservatives via a brief interim leading the breakaway Change UK grouping. While all three parties agreed to endorse the strongest local candidate, the Lib Dems' greater national presence made them the principal beneficiaries: 43 of the 60 Unite to Remain seats had Liberal Democrat candidates, including many of the party's target seats such as Cheltenham, Cheadle and Hazel Grove. Yet while reducing the number of smaller parties fishing in the Remain pond was useful, the main competition for Remain votes was the Labour Party, which rejected any cooperation with the 'pro-austerity' Liberal Democrats. Without Labour backing, gains from 'Unite to Remain' were likely to be minimal.[16]

Former UKIP leader Nigel Farage launched the Brexit Party national campaign in Westminster on 1 November with an attack on Johnson's Withdrawal Agreement—'Boris tells us it's a great new deal. It's not. It's not Brexit. It's kicking the can down the road'—and a pledge to stand candidates in 600 seats unless Johnson dropped his deal. Yet the need for a separate Brexit Party was not obvious in an election where the Conservative leader was a 'Vote Leave' veteran campaigning to 'get Brexit done'. With the Conservatives' election strategy focused on uniting Leave voters, Nigel Farage's new outfit risked acting as a spoiler, helping the opponents of Brexit by dividing the Leave vote.[17] Pressure for Farage to stand down in favour of the Conservatives began even before the Brexit Party campaign launched. A parade of high-profile Eurosceptics including Conservative MPs Steve Baker, Bill Cash and Jacob Rees-Mogg, and former UKIP colleagues Douglas Carswell and Aaron Banks called on their former comrade to stand down. 'It's such a pity Nigel hasn't worked out that he's won', lamented Rees-Mogg.[18] 'What kind of conceited arrogance is this?' Farage shot back.[19] The Eurosceptic press, hitherto friendly to Farage, were also sceptical of his new enterprise. The *Daily Mail* worried it would be 'vote Farage, get Corbyn',[20] while *The Sun* dubbed Farage 'Wrecker Nigel' and warned readers tempted by the Brexit Party to 'face some harsh realities': 'Farage's party … is far more likely to prevent Boris winning the majority which is vital to delivering Brexit.'[21] Private pressure was also allegedly applied, with both Farage and Brexit Party Chairman Richard Tice claiming Conservative sources offered inducements to stand down.[22]

Johnson walks over Farage (Christian Adams, *Evening Standard*, 12 November 2019 © Christian Adams)

Farage initially stood firm, claiming his was the only party which could reach alienated voters in Labour Leave seats. But his Brexit Party foot soldiers were wavering. Within a week of the party's launch, the *Daily Telegraph* was reporting that more than 20 candidates had already stood down, with some endorsing their Conservative rivals.[23] Farage gave way on 11 November, announcing he would stand down all candidates in Conservative-held seats, while continuing in seats held by other parties. There was not much electoral logic to this—a split Leave vote in Labour-held Tory target seats was more likely to help Labour incumbents than Tory challengers—but it enabled Farage to retreat while saving face. The more important effect of Farage's announcement, along with helping the Conservatives focus on offense over defence, was the broader signal it sent to Leave voters, as one senior figure in the Conservative campaign noted:

> Farage stepping back ... was one of the most important moments of the campaign for us. Not running in our seats ... actually didn't help us that much, although it meant fielding far fewer phone calls from Conservative

MPs. It was the message it sent to their voters, to the people that were considering them ... It really hurt the credibility of their message.

This was reflected in the Brexit Party's polling numbers, which fell sharply in the wake of Farage's decision and continued falling through the rest of the campaign. The Brexit Party had polled over 20% in the summer, but was below 5% by election day. Farage's retreat was greeted with dismay in Liberal Democrat HQ, as it dealt a body blow to the party's election strategy, which relied on Brexit Party candidates siphoning off Leave voters in Conservative-held targets.[24] As one staffer recalled:

The Brexit Party standing down against the Tories, when Farage announced that, it was probably one of the most depressing days of my career ... Because there's no way around it. They were taking votes away from the Tories that we couldn't take away. It was simple. That was clear. That screwed us the most.

Torrential downpours lashed large parts of Yorkshire and the Midlands in mid-November, producing criticism of Conservative under-investment in flood defences, and of Boris Johnson for tardiness in visiting the affected regions. Yet Labour's ability to capitalise on footage of Johnson being confronted by angry locals when he finally arrived on the scene was limited by their own leader's reluctance to revisit the flooded regions himself, much to the irritation of campaign staff.[25] Still, as the floodwaters receded, a different kind of winter crisis—one much more up Corbyn's street—rose up the agenda, as NHS statistics published on 14 November revealed the worst Accident & Emergency (A&E) waiting times on record.[26] The resulting 'NHS crisis' headlines were the stuff of Labour dreams and Tory nightmares, coming the day after Labour had promised a £26 billion real terms increase in health spending by 2023/2024. Polling released the same day underscored the stakes, showing that the 'Labour Leave' voters courted by the Conservatives rated Brexit as the most important issue for the country, but the NHS as the most important issue for their own families.[27] Labour's internal polling and focus groups painted a similar picture, giving hope to some in the campaign that anxieties about the public sector and the NHS were gaining traction and could yet offer a means to shift the campaign conversation away from Brexit: 'Voters just didn't trust Johnson on the NHS. That was the strength we could exploit.'[28]

Labour sought to shift attention to domestic issues through a series of dramatic pledges, reflecting LOTO's belief that ambitious policy announcements were Labour's best option for driving the political conversation. These kicked off with a promise of a £55 billion investment in public sector infrastructure from Shadow Chancellor John McDonnell on 8 November, followed by a £3 billion commitment for a 'National Education Service' from Shadow Education Secretary Angela Rayner on 12 November. The £26 billion announced by John McDonnell and Shadow Health Secretary Jonathan Ashworth the same day represented the NHS's slice of the Labour spending cake.

'You'll get a free chocolate!' (Morten Morland, *Sunday Times*, 3 December 2019 © Morten Morland)

While such commitments polled well in isolation, the parade of big spending pledges had no narrative thread to link them together. The process for knitting together policy and messaging into a coherent campaign narrative had broken down. Even the Shadow Cabinet ministers charged with making Labour's case on broadcast media were seldom given much notice of, or briefing on, the policy announcements they were then expected to explain. The teams developing policy under Andrew Fisher and John McDonnell distrusted some of their colleagues and feared leaks, so shared little. The Southside team under Karie Murphy in charge of the 'grids' organising announcements and events thought and behaved likewise, with communications and event planning impeded by severely restricted access to the grids. Mutual distrust was making effective campaign coordination impossible. The result was a policy offer both vaunting in its ambitions and largely incomprehensible to voters, who struggled to make sense of a blizzard of haphazardly announced and poorly explained Labour promises.

Labour's communications on the NHS—their biggest area polling strength throughout the campaign—illustrate the dysfunction. The disastrous A&E statistics had landed the day after the party unveiled its large NHS cash infusion, a piece of lucky timing which put the Conservatives' NHS record under scrutiny. The Shadow Health Secretary arrived at a TV studio expecting to continue the attack on health, only to be asked by the show's producers to comment on Labour's £20 billion proposal for universal state-provided free broadband, a policy he was informed about minutes earlier via text message: 'This just tells you what our campaign was like. We had a good week on the NHS ... and we just darted off in a completely different direction.'

The Conservatives responded to Labour's policy blitz by criticising the credibility of the overall package, but avoiding arguments over specifics. CCHQ researchers did some dubious arithmetic to produce a suitably alarming number of £1.2 trillion in Labour spending pledges for newspapers to splash on the first weekend of the campaign,[29] but in general senior Conservative figures refused to be drawn on the specifics of Labour's announcements, frustrating 'left populist' LOTO aides who had hoped to use spats over policy to draw campaign contrasts:

> In 2017 every day we would put out a policy ... and the Tories would go 'this is evil, terrible, awful, AAARGH!' and amplify it and make themselves look stupid at the same time. In 2019, the Tories only responded to one of our policies [in the whole campaign]. Instead the journalists had to get a boring comment from the IOD or something ... Cummings, Cain, Levido – they all know that it's rows and controversy that drive attention. It's all a kind of dance over who can start rows and who can shut them down.

However, the Conservatives were happy to splash out on policy areas where they felt electorally vulnerable. Spending cuts were seen as a key weakness in 2017 (see Chapter 3, pp. 98–99), and Johnson was keen to distance himself from his predecessors' unpopular austerity legacy. There were pledges of extra cash for policing, green energy, flood protection, free childcare, town high streets and the NHS. The sums offered were generally lower and more tightly targeted than Labour's; nor did they, it was repeatedly stressed, break the Chancellor's much-vaunted fiscal rules.[30] But they nevertheless conveyed the impression that Johnson's Conservatives were willing to spend on the issues voters cared about, continuing a strategy pursued since the start of his premiership, as one senior aide recalled:

> A lot of the voters in Leave seats were overcoming in some cases mul-ti-generational hesitation in voting for the Conservatives … We did a lot of work … on public services to … not win on them, but at least neutral-ise [them].… talking about schools, hospitals and police relentlessly since [Boris] became PM helped negate those hesitations.

Labour's team had anticipated this strategy, and entered the campaign expecting that the Conservatives would look to neutralise the electoral threat of radical policies with big spending pledges of their own. But internal divisions once again hampered the response.[31] With no effec-tive or credible Labour challenge, Johnson's message that austerity would end under his stewardship began to take hold, as one LOTO aide recalled:

> We never found a way to create big dividing lines with the Tories on the NHS in the entire campaign. We were basically saying more money and the Tories were also saying more money. It's hard to tell those apart … When you put 10 billion next to 30 billion, it's not more against less. It's two big numbers next to each other.

* * *

Both the Labour and Conservative teams saw the final fortnight of November as a critical phase for the campaign 'air war', with a series of high-profile events, including speeches at the Confederation of British Industry (CBI) Annual Conference, manifesto launches, the first head-to-head leaders' debate, and a Friday night *Question Time* special with leaders of the four largest parties. Labour saw this phase, dubbed by one strategist as 'bazooka week', as their best opportunity to turn the election their way.[32] The Conservatives, acutely aware that the manifesto launch in particular was the point when the wheels came off their 2017 campaign, planned a safety-first strategy, reassuring voters that getting Brexit done would see money spent (sensibly) on priorities like the NHS and policing. As one of those involved put it bluntly, 'the overwhelming pressure was to avoid fucking it up'.

All three party leaders set out their stalls to Britain's business community at the CBI Annual Conference on Monday 17 November. Jeremy Corbyn sought to reassure delegates that his Labour Party was 'not anti-business', telling attendees 'your businesses have so much to gain from a Labour government'. While Corbyn signalled sympathy, Johnson took a harder line, telling CBI delegates a previously promised corporation tax cut was no longer affordable, as the money was needed for public services. Meanwhile, Jo Swinson won a round of applause by framing Brexit as anti-business: 'if you want to get Brexit done ... then you are not the party for business.' Attendees interviewed afterwards sounded more impressed by Mr Corbyn's pitch than Mr Johnson's, not an outcome many would have expected, but one both parties' strategists were probably happy with.

The first ever head-to-head leaders' debate followed the next day, offering Corbyn a chance to re-introduce himself to the public and to revive his sagging approval ratings in a set-piece event which had once again become a major focus of campaign media attention.[33] The biggest surprise about the event was that it was happening at all. Parties trailing in the polls usually demand debates, in the hope of engineering a reversal, but frontrunners usually decline them for the same reason. In keeping with tradition, Corbyn had laid down the gauntlet the day after the Early Parliamentary General Election Act passed. In a break with tradition, Johnson took it up. CCHQ saw the risks of running from televised duels with his opponent as greater than the risks of embracing them. May's avoidance of debates in 2017 had damaged her campaign, making her look weak and evasive when she was running as 'strong and stable'.[34] Conservative strategists felt Johnson was a good enough TV performer, and Corbyn sufficiently unpopular, that agreeing to debates was the less risky option. The first televised head to head debates between the Conservative and Labour leaders were therefore agreed for 19 November (ITV) and 6 December (BBC) (see Chapter 9, pp. 311–312 for more on the negotiations).

Both parties took the event very seriously, with a senior Labour aide saying 'we thought they were a huge opportunity', a view echoed by a senior Conservative strategist: 'These were extremely dangerous moments for us. Any campaign can be lost in a moment.' The Conservatives brought in Brett O'Donnell, an experienced Republican operative who had coached George W. Bush and Mitt Romney for presidential debates, and staged full dress rehearsals, with Michael Gove cast as Corbyn. The Labour team avoided staging mock debates—'Jeremy didn't like that kind of panto-style, West Wing-esque stuff'—but some involved in the Labour debate preparation were concerned about the more informal approach, and the lack of time in Corbyn's intense and often haphazard schedule for debate rehearsal and preparation:

> Jeremy wouldn't cancel any time on the road to prepare for the debates. So we would have ridiculous situations where he would be at an event like a CLP meeting with 300 people the night before and not have time to rehearse or get prepped for the debate. And the debate would be watched by six and a half or seven million people. However, in his head, he wanted to concentrate on the kind of campaigning which had been successful in 2017.[35]

The first debate failed to live up to the pre-match hype. Both leaders acquitted themselves well, but there were few standout moments. Corbyn's best passage came when he brandished a heavily redacted document which he claimed was from UK–US trade negotiations and accused Johnson: 'You're going to sell our National Health Service out to the United States and big pharma.' Johnson dismissed the claim as an 'absolute invention ... our NHS will never be for sale', then pivoted to Brexit, winning his biggest round of applause by attacking Corbyn for 'trying to conceal the void at the heart of his Brexit policy and refusing to answer the question of which side he would take'. A snap YouGov poll after the debate suggested a bore draw, with 51% declaring Johnson the winner and 49% Corbyn. The Labour leader had more reason to be happy with that result—a draw is practically a win if you enter the event trailing badly—but it did not provide the dramatic breakthrough Labour strategists knew they needed: 'it wasn't the kind of knockout blow we wanted. 2017 was better. Partly it was the comparison with May where she didn't play it well. Johnson did. He stuck to his script'. Perceptions of both leaders' strengths and weaknesses were reinforced, not re-assessed. The stars of the night were the audience, whose mocking laughter—heard when Corbyn claimed he had made Labour's Brexit position clear and when Johnson claimed that truthfulness mattered in this election—provided the most widely shared moments from the event.[36]

The Liberal Democrats launched their manifesto the next day, overshadowed in the morning by coverage of the debate and in the evening by a Buckingham Palace announcement that Prince Andrew was withdrawing from all duties following a disastrous interview with BBC journalist Emily Maitlis. While the party could do little about royal scandals, they may have regretted booking their launch immediately after the biggest political TV event of the campaign. Like the bigger parties, the Lib Dems sought to shower voters with cash, with promises of extended free childcare, frozen rail fares and 20,000 extra teachers, all paid for with the £50 Billion 'Remain bonus' the party claimed Britain would reap from scrapping Brexit. Swinson sold her manifesto as a 'bold plan for a brighter future', but journalists were unconvinced, noting that the 'bold plan' contained little novelty. The party's 'revoke Brexit' pledge and big spending commitments had been heavily trailed, and the new policies— extended free school meals and frozen rail fairs—were small beer. With no big-ticket items to grab attention, Swinson soon found herself instead having to rebut a bizarre viral social media story alleging she liked to shoot stones at squirrels from a homemade catapult.[37]

The 2017 manifesto was one topic which united Labour's fractious leadership team. All of Corbyn's senior aides regarded it as a triumph, demonstrating that a radical Labour programme could also be a vote winner.[38] Andrew Fisher, principal author of the 2017 document, was also charged with orchestrating its successor. LOTO expected Johnson's Conservatives to abandon austerity and promise big spending on voter priorities, so Fisher needed to up the radical ante further, yet without undermining Labour's fiscal credibility. Fisher could draw upon more resources than in 2017, as two tightly knit policy teams in LOTO and the Shadow Treasury had worked on developing detailed and fully costed policy initiatives for much of the 2017–2019 Parliament. The task now was to pull them together into a manifesto package and secure agreement to it from the various interests in the Labour coalition. Each of the four heads of Labour's policy team sought input from Shadow Cabinet members in their areas, and then drafted chapters bringing together ministers' ideas with the policies Labour had already committed to over the Parliament.[39] These drafts were returned to politicians for approval before reverting to Fisher, who knitted them together into a full draft manifesto. This full draft was then taken to the Trade Union Liaison Officers (TULO) meeting, where representatives of Labour's affiliated unions were each given a numbered copy to read through and offer feedback. The TULO meeting went smoothly. Labour's policy team had been consulting the unions throughout the process and had anticipated most of the issues they might raise.

The final stage of the process was the 'Clause V' meeting where Labour's various stakeholders formally approve the manifesto. The debate was 'long-winded, technocratic and focused on minutiae', and few substantial changes were made. A conference pledge to extend free movement rights after Brexit, already the focus of hostile Conservative attention, was watered down to a statement that free movement after Brexit would be 'subject to negotiations'. The main changes came on climate change policy, where the most radical ideas for decarbonisation of the economy by 2030 were diluted in the face of opposition from union leaders.[40] No further changes were made to Labour's Brexit policy, which occupied just ten minutes of the day-long discussion.

The manifesto was launched with a speech by Corbyn at Birmingham City University the Thursday after the Clause V meeting. Corbyn introduced the manifesto with a combative speech penned by Joss Macdonald and Alex Nunns, which channelled Franklin D. Roosevelt and Pablo Neruda in a rallying cry for radical change: 'Ignore the wealthy and powerful who tell you that's not possible. The future is ours to make, together.' The Labour manifesto delivered amply on this rhetoric, with a torrent of spending pledges pouring from its 109 pages: a £400 billion National Investment fund, with £250 billion earmarked for Green Transformation and £150 billion for Social Transformation; a 4.3% real terms increase in spending on the NHS, with major cash infusions for mental health and social care; a National Education Service free to everyone throughout life; more nursery workers, police, council houses, wind turbines and libraries; and nationalised rail, power, water and broadband. This was a manifesto that bet the house in an effort to restore clear red water between Corbyn's Labour and a Conservative party which, under Johnson, was more willing to spend big too.

The risk was that such radicalism would go too far, looking irresponsible to voters worried about who would foot the bill. Labour were aware of the problem, though as ever they could not agree on a single solution. John McDonnell focused on transparency as a route to credibility, and a lengthy costings document—'Funding Real Change'—was published to accompany the manifesto so that, as in 2017, Labour could claim that all of their ambitious manifesto pledges were 'fully costed'.[41] Seumas Milne was more concerned to head off traditional Conservative attack lines about tax rises, and therefore sought to ensure Labour stuck to their previous pledge to limit tax rises to the top 5% of earners, despite the massive increase in Labour's spending commitments. Each approach made sense in isolation, but the combination of very large spending commitments with limited scope for revenue raising risked stretching commentator and voter credulity. Critical reports from the Institute for Fiscal Studies and the Resolution Foundation poured cold water on Labour's claims that its massive expansion of the state solely with tax rises on the richest 5%.[42] Polls and focus groups revealed widespread scepticism that so much 'free stuff' could be provided competently by Labour, as well as worries about who would ultimately foot the bill. Voters liked many of Labour's manifesto proposals in isolation, but the sheer profusion of them also left electors confused about Labour's priorities and unconvinced that so many promises could really be delivered. Labour needed the 2019 manifesto to be, in one senior advisor's words, the '2017 manifesto plus plus'. Yet the party's new proposals arguably added more to the debit than the credit column—few of the big new pledges captured the public imagination, but the price tags attached brought plenty of criticism and eroded Labour's fiscal credibility. Claims that a once-in-a-generation expansion in the state could be paid for entirely by corporations and the richest 5% simply didn't seem plausible.[43]

The spotlight returned to the party leaders on Friday 22 November, with Jo Swinson and Nicola Sturgeon joining Johnson and Corbyn for a BBC *Question Time* special held at the Sheffield Octagon. Jeremy Corbyn was up first and faced hostile questions on anti-semitism, foreign policy and Brexit. He handled these calmly, but was unable to shift the conversation to his party's domestic policy agenda. Instead, it was again a Brexit line which drew headlines, as Corbyn promised to remain personally neutral when his government held a second referendum on the new Brexit deal it had negotiated. The problems that this stance would pose were evident in the televised exchanges—the initial questioner asked 'why would anyone vote Labour without knowing [where Corbyn stood on Brexit]?' and the audience was audibly unconvinced by Corbyn's response.[44] Voters were too polarised, and the issue too urgent, for neutrality to be a viable stance.[45] One senior Conservative strategist admitted he was:

> flabbergasted when Corbyn said that … I thought he was going to come out and take a position, which is what concerned me … This guy's running to be Prime Minister, and he can't even … take a position on the biggest issue facing the country and affecting the lives of every single one of the people in the country? It was the absolute worst of both worlds.

There was no such reticence from Nicola Sturgeon, up after Corbyn, who made clear from the outset her strong support for remaining in one political union while leaving another. Sturgeon repeatedly emphasised that a second Scottish independence referendum would be her price for putting Corbyn in Downing Street, causing headaches for Labour strategists, who remembered the problems this gave Ed Miliband in 2015.[46] Jo Swinson, up third, faced the most audience hostility of all, with both Leave and Remain questioners expressing anger at the party's pledge to unilaterally revoke Article 50. In a gruesome half-hour, Swinson was also criticised for supporting Conservative welfare cuts and tuition fee rises during the Coalition, and for claiming she could be the next Prime Minister. There were few softball questions and precious little applause.

Boris Johnson, up last, was also given a rough ride. Audience members pressed the Prime Minister on his divisive past journalism and strained relationship with the truth. Johnson stuck doggedly to his party's main attack lines, with his efforts to lever 'get Brexit done' into every answer drawing groans by the end. He faced a tricky moment when one questioner criticised the early election as unnecessary—a line of attack Tory strategists had worried about in their election planning[47]—but fended it off by ridiculing Corbyn's Brexit neutrality pledge. The Prime Minister's toughest moment came when he was grilled on 'WASPI women', a cohort of women in their early sixties who faced substantial financial losses due to the rise in the state pension age: 'I cannot promise that I can magic up that money for [the WASPI women] tonight.'[48]

Labour was well placed to pounce on this vulnerability, with John McDonnell launching a major, though long-planned, new commitment for WASPI women the very next morning, promising to 'compensate women who were unfairly hit by the rise in the state pension age and give them the respect they deserve'.[49] Labour aides had been working on this issue for years, though the specific solution McDonnell announced, and the £58 billion needed to pay for it, were not included in the manifesto or Labour's costings.[50] One of those involved defended the surprise announcement of such an expensive pledge as a necessary roll of the dice by a trailing campaign:

> By that time in the campaign I think a lot of minds were made up. I was hoping WASPI would be a game changer. In fact, a lot of people thought it could have been, because there's so many women affected and who would have benefited.

While the proposal was designed to put the spotlight on the Conservatives' poor treatment of older women voters, the WASPI pledge ended up also putting Labour's fiscal credibility under further scrutiny. Labour briefings underlined that the costs of the policy represented a 'special arrangement' designed to address a unique historic injustice, but this did not satisfy sceptical journalists, who continued to raise the high costs of the proposal in broadcast interviews and print coverage. The issue had cut through, though not in the way Labour had hoped, as voters began to raise it on the doorstep alongside free broadband as an example of rash promises and indiscipline. Some aides were not impressed with the timing of the announcement. As one recalled: 'It literally came out four days after we published our costings document, and blew a massive hole in it.' A defeated MP from the Red Wall battleground agreed that the policy was poorly executed:

> You could have made an announcement which cost a lot less money which would have satisfied that constituency and you could have done it in a way that didn't look ridiculous. By the time it came, it looked bonkers. It was something which should have won us votes but it managed to lose us votes because it was done all wrong.

All those involved in the preparation of the 2019 Conservative manifesto had painful memories of 2017, when a policy-heavy manifesto, prepared without sufficient consultation, had unravelled within days, forcing Theresa May into a rapid U-turn over reforms to social care, a humiliation she compounded by obstinately insisting that 'nothing has changed'.[51] The 2019 manifesto team was led by Rachel Wolfe and Munira Mirza, with Robert Colvile brought in later to help produce the final draft. Wolfe negotiated individual sections with Cabinet ministers, while Mirza worked with the Prime Minister and his team. Cabinet ministers were told that only absolutely necessary proposals should be included, as the team were determined to avoid hostages to fortune. While the manifesto would break with austerity, and from the outset the plan was to lead with big spending commitments on the NHS, schools and police, discipline was not being abandoned entirely. The Conservatives wanted a clear fiscal dividing line with Labour, who they anticipated would spend big, and to help enforce that, a member of Sajid Javid's Treasury team was embedded in the process, as one of the team recalled: 'Adam Memon was set next to us, doing the scorecard every second.' Another central goal for the manifesto team was ensuring that any policies they decided to include not only appealed to the voters the party hoped to win, but were actually deliverable once the election was over.

The over-riding desire to avoid the missteps of 2017 also encouraged the team to seek input from a wide range of sources, despite the risk of leaks. The Cabinet all saw drafts, at least of the sections pertaining to their departments, and draft sections were also considered before a large Cabinet committee several times. The authors also wanted to avoid any complex or difficult to explain policies, which could then be misinterpreted, as happened when Theresa May's social care proposals were recast as the 'dementia tax'. The team avoided a detailed proposal on social care itself, partly out of concern that the public still did not understand an issue not widely discussed in politics since the 2017 campaign, but also due to fiscal constraints: 'The view from the Treasury team was we can go into this election with a proper social care proposal – or we can go into this election with a fiscally responsible manifesto. But we can't do both.' Ross Kempsell, a former journalist turned trusted Number 10 advisor who led the due diligence process on the manifesto, went through decades' worth of Tory manifestos, making a spreadsheet of every issue ever mentioned previously that might need to go in again, lest any journalist were to do some digging, notice the absence and then claim that the Tories had dropped this or that commitment.[52] Kempsell also helped ensure that none of the photos in the manifesto could lead to problems later on. And he and others, supported by the Conservative Research Department, also 'red teamed' the document, hunting for statements and issues which political opponents would pick up and attack.[53] Once the document was fully drafted and polished by Colvile, who 'took our document and turned it into a Tory manifesto', the entire Cabinet was brought into the conference room at CCHQ, phones were confiscated and members were invited to read the paper draft. Then after a final round of checks by the Chancellor, the Prime Minister and a 'bomb-proofing' read-through by Oliver Dowden, it was dispatched to the printers.

Johnson launched this heavily stress-tested, safety-first manifesto in a low-key Sunday evening event on 24 November. Out went tax cuts for higher earners and homeowners, which cast the Conservatives as the party of the rich. Out went promises to review fox hunting and the imagery of fusty rural privilege associated with them. And out went the ambitious root-and-branch reform of social care, replaced by watery words about 'building cross-party consensus'. In came headline-grabbing nuggets of generosity whose specificity masked their modesty—nurses hired, hospitals renovated, and more police on streets which (thanks to a new fund) would have their potholes filled in. With roughly £3 billion of new spending pledged in total, it was a manifesto which risked over-correcting from 2017, avoiding controversy but promising very little of substance. As Paul Johnson of the Institute for Fiscal Studies observed: 'If a single Budget had contained all these tax and spending proposals we would [call] it modest. As a blueprint for five years in government the lack of significant policy action is remarkable.'[54] This was a risk the manifesto authors anticipated but accepted:

> The media seeks a narrative and there were really only two narratives: narrative one was 'They've fucked it up again' and narrative two was 'Isn't this [thin and/or] boring'. We preferred to have narrative two rather than narrative one.[55]

After the launch, the manifesto authors waited nervously for the traditional and social media reaction: 'We were anxiously watching Twitter as the manifesto dropped ... and when the tweets were coming in from journalists saying "A very safe manifesto from the Conservatives", we would stand up and cheer.' The first few days were seen as critical, and as the initial 'safety-first' framing took hold over multiple news cycles, the manifesto team began to breathe a little easier. They had avoided a repeat of 2017. On the Wednesday night, with three uneventful campaign days under their belt, the manifesto authors decided that it would no longer be tempting fate to take their whole team out to celebrate: 'We thought, "OK. We've finally done our bit".'

Televised leader interviews with veteran journalist and broadcaster Andrew Neil were a heavily promoted element in the BBC's 2019 campaign coverage. Neil had a longstanding reputation as a pugnacious interviewer, so the BBC saw the interviews as a vital part of its public service remit, while the parties' campaign teams saw them as an ordeal to endure with as little collateral damage as possible. A polished performance by SNP leader Nicola Sturgeon saw off the Neil threat early, while Jo Swinson's more faltering performance came too late in the campaign to do much damage. The main loser from the interviews was Jeremy Corbyn, whose excruciating half-hour with Neil, which aired on 26 November, was described by one journalist as 'not so much a car crash as a multiple lorry pile-up'.[56] There were awkward exchanges on Brexit and domestic policy, but it was the Labour leader's responses on anti-semitism which drew the most criticism. In an interview broadcast on the same day that Britain's Chief Rabbi Ephraim Mirvis had warned that British Jews were 'gripped by anxiety' about the prospect of a Corbyn government, the Labour leader was irritable and evasive when confronted with evidence of his party failing to take action against anti-semitic members and four times refused invitations to apologise to the Jewish community for his party's failings on anti-semitism. According to WhatsApp messages leaked the next day, Labour activists were being urged to take to social media to 'drown out' coverage of the 'truly horrific' interview.[57]

The only consolation for Labour aides was the hope that Neil would be equally brutal in his interrogation of the Prime Minister, whose own political and media career was not short of controversial episodes. Yet that grilling, which Labour aides were assured the Conservatives had agreed to, never came (see Chapter 9, pp. 324–326). Johnson and CCHQ repeatedly rebuffed BBC requests for an interview, resulting in an escalating war of words with the broadcaster which culminated in a monologue to camera from Neil himself:

> There is no law…that can force Mr Johnson to participate in a BBC leader's interview. But the Prime Minister of our nation will, at times, have to stand up to President Trump, President Putin and President Xi of China. So it is surely not expecting too much that he spend half an hour standing up to me.

'Did I say dead in a ditch?' (Chris Riddell, *The Observer*, 1 December 2019 © Chris Riddell)

Voter registration closed on **26 November** and postal votes started landing soon after. Labour remained well behind in the polls, and the party's best hope of a second dramatic turnabout had now passed. The Labour manifesto had foundered on questions of cost and credibility, the surprise WASPI women announcement had flopped, Corbyn's campaign and media appearances lacked spark, and the party was dogged by unresolved questions over Brexit and anti-semitism. The Conservatives had avoided the pratfalls and controversies of **2017** with a safety-first manifesto and a leader whose verbal eccentricity disguised an iron message discipline. Johnson's ability to breathe life into platitudinous soundbites with idiosyncratic rhetoric and personal energy was one of his under-estimated political talents. Evasive, but never dull, he was no 'Maybot', earning grudging admiration even from one of his rivals in the Labour campaign:

> It really was very impressive. The moment I most remember was watching this video of Boris Johnson in a bakery in Golders Green. He's in a Jewish bakery and he's making donuts and he's squishing 'get Brexit done' onto the donuts saying 'Get Brexit Done. Get Brexit Done. Who wants a donut? Here's a donut. Get Brexit Done, on the donut, in your mouth, Get Brexit Done.' The whole video is like a minute of him doing that as more and

more people come to the counter ... Having been in those filming situations myself that's 45 minutes of him just solidly saying 'get Brexit done' in a pantomime way in front of a room full of people. It's an embarrassing thing to have to do, yet that's the Prime Minister and yes, he will do that because they have this ruthless discipline about what they're trying to do.

The second head-to-head clash between the two leaders offered few surprises to voters and left the status quo undisturbed. The polls showed the Conservative lead holding steady overall, as both big parties continued to mop up support from the Leave and Remain fringes at a similar pace (see Chapter 8). The goal in CCHQ for the rest of the campaign was more of the same: 'the strategy in Conservative Campaign Headquarters is for a drama-free two weeks in which the party will double down on its core messages ... If that sounds a bit boring, that's the point. As former Tory election guru Lynton Crosby used to tell colleagues: elections are not about keeping journalists entertained.'[58]

While the Conservatives stuck to their script, Labour's divided leadership changed course in late November. Labour had risen in the polls by recovering Remain support from the Liberal Democrats, but the intelligence from the Leave-voting battleground seats of the Midlands and North was dire.[59] Big spending policy pledges, the leaders' debate and the manifesto launches had all failed to move the dial, and the 'left populists' in LOTO now successfully pressed for a change in approach. The party changed its strapline to 'On Your Side', criticised by one senior aide as 'a hackneyed local government election kind of slogan', and refocused its messaging on retail politics, with John McDonnell fronting an event announcing Labour's policies would save the average family £6,700 a year, a figure immediately disputed by the Institute for Fiscal Studies. Labour also sought belatedly to ramp up its defensive efforts in threatened Northern and Midlands seats, and dispatched pro-Brexit party chair Ian Lavery on a bus tour of the heartlands. Dozens of Labour seats with large Leave majorities were added to the target seats list, but none of the Conservative-held 'offensive' targets were removed, meaning resources were spread thin—as one Southsider observed, 'I suspect the list of seats we weren't supporting was smaller than the list of seats we were by the end'. Yet the shift came too late to make much substantial difference—much of the central support given to target seats had already been scheduled and delivered. As always, the new approach divided Labour's leadership team, with sceptics worrying the new approach wouldn't work with Leave voters whose distrust of Labour and Corbyn were too entrenched, and could put at risk the party's campaign gains with Remainers. But with Labour trailing badly and running out of time, even those unconvinced by the new approach agreed Labour had little option but to roll the dice, as one senior aide recalled:

> It was clear by halfway through the campaign that it wasn't working. Now, people say, well, it's daft to change halfway through a campaign, but it's not daft if you're doing the wrong thing. The sooner you stop doing it and start doing something else, the better.

***

At around 2 pm on Friday 29 November, convicted terrorist Usman Khan, armed with two knives and apparently wearing a suicide bomb vest, threatened to blow up Fishmongers' Hall, the central London venue where he had been attending a conference on prisoner rehabilitation. Khan, who had been released on licence the previous December after a conviction for plotting a previous terror attack in 2012, fatally stabbed two people then fled the scene before being wrestled to the ground on London Bridge. He was shot dead shortly after by armed police.[60] Within minutes, reports of the incident flooded the airwaves and social media. Terror had struck in the midst of an election campaign once again.

'Vote Boris' (Ben Jennings, *The Guardian*, 1 December 2019 © Ben Jennings)

The Conservatives and Labour scrambled to respond. Johnson and Corbyn spoke within hours of the attack, and jointly agreed not to suspend campaigning as they had in the wake of the 2017 Manchester Arena bombings. With the contest continuing, both parties' attention turned to their political responses. Conservative and Labour strategists alike were aware that the Manchester and London terror attacks had been another pivotal moment in 2017. Labour had unexpectedly seized the initiative then by framing the terror threat as a consequence of cuts to policing and security services overseen by Theresa May as Home Secretary. At a seven-party BBC debate hours after the attack, Shadow Business Secretary Rebecca Long-Bailey looked to press the same charge again, supported by leaders of the other opposition parties, attacking the Conservatives, represented by Rishi Sunak, Chief Secretary to the Treasury, for overseeing cuts to police numbers. CCHQ, determined to avoid May's missteps, counter-attacked immediately. Home Secretary Priti Patel blamed the London Bridge incident on early release policies introduced by the previous Labour government in 2008, policies which Boris Johnson pledged to end immediately for those convicted of serious terror offences. This in turn drew criticism from the father of one of those killed, who accused Johnson of politicising his son's death. After this intense round of charge and counter-charge, the terror debate faded from the agenda. The conversation moved on more quickly than in 2017, though whether this was due to a swifter and surer Conservative response, the lack of any campaign suspension or simply because the crisis was less severe and more swiftly resolved is impossible to know.

The London Bridge attacks came at the end of an eventful week also featuring Labour's most memorable campaign stunt. What was billed as a speech on the NHS by Jeremy Corbyn on the morning of Wednesday 27 November soon turned into something rather more theatrical when Corbyn brandished before the cameras a sheaf of papers, which he announced were '451 pages of unredacted documents and information' from US–UK trade talks.[61] As nurses in scrubs handed copies of the leaked dossier to attending journalists, Corbyn claimed the documents proved that 'under Boris Johnson the NHS is on the table and will be up for sale'. What Labour had discovered was 'not only a plot against the NHS, it's a plot against the whole country'. But the document failed to live up to Labour's hype, consisting mainly of dreary technical notes from a trade and investment working group set up by Theresa May in 2017, with some vague language about drugs purchasing as an issue of concern. Preliminary exchanges between trade bureaucrats conducted two years before Boris Johnson became Prime Minister were hardly the smoking gun Labour claimed. As a result, while the stunt briefly shifted the discussion away from Corbyn's car-crash interview with Andrew Neil the night before, the story soon petered out—yet another example of Labour's inability to keep a good story going. As one LOTO aide noted:

> We found it hard to get traction. We should have done more off the back of it. Ideally, you want to build up a story like that over a few days, and then have something that reinforces it the next day. We just had too many announcements. We were always moving on to the next thing.

Jeremy Corbyn holds a redacted copy of the Department for International Trade's UK-US Trade and Investment Working Group readout, Westminster, 27 November 2019 (© PA Images/Alamy Stock Photo)

Consistent polling leads did not entirely settle Conservative nerves as November drew to a close. While Labour had not achieved the kind of campaign breakthrough seen in 2017, their poll numbers had recovered, an advance which the Conservatives had fended off by squeezing the Brexit Party vote. Public and internal polling suggested growing public attention to the NHS, an ominous shift given enduring public scepticism about Conservative health promises. Having squeezed Brexit Party support perhaps as low as it could go, the Conservatives were vulnerable if Labour's recovery continued or if Nigel Farage staged a late rebound and split the Leave vote in 'Red Wall' Labour targets. The campaign therefore looked to lock in socially conservative Leave voters with more red meat on immigration and national security, pledging tougher action against terrorists and illegal immigrants, while also reiterating the promises of cash for the NHS and schools.[62] Johnson and other Cabinet figures avoided personalised attacks on Corbyn, which CCHQ felt had backfired in 2017, instead aiming to reinforce doubts about the Labour leader through under-the-radar local and social media campaigning. Such doubts were already nearer the surface after two years of critical stories about anti-semitism, Labour's response to the Salisbury incident and Corbyn's past associations, as one senior LOTO aide recalled:

> The first time I was in the North with Jeremy during the campaign I was really shocked when someone raised the issue of him being an IRA sympathiser outside an event, and then it got picked up by regional media. But for the past two years, that's what they've been told he was, and we hadn't tackled that at all. We had just written it off as hostile right-wing press. We had misjudged the impact of those messages being laid down in solid layers over serval years.

A comprehensive assessment of the state of play came on 28 November when YouGov published its MRP model estimates of party support in each constituency. This model had accurately predicted the scale and scope of Labour's 2017 surge, and its sequel was therefore eagerly anticipated.[63] YouGov gave the Conservatives a 68-seat majority, a gain of 42 seats on 2017. Labour were projected to lose 51 seats in their worst seat performance since 1935, hurt in part by an SNP surge to 43 of Scotland's 59 seats (up eight). The Liberal Democrats were forecast a net gain of just one seat. The model projected major Conservative gains in Leave-leaning Labour constituencies, with double-digit swings away from Labour in seats such as Bolsover, Don Valley and Leigh that the party had held for generations. 'Labour's "Red Wall" is Crumbling', the analysts concluded.[64] The only scraps of comfort for Labour came from evidence that the Brexit Party was still hurting Conservative prospects in some Labour-held seats, many of which remained too close to call. But without a dramatic turnaround in the final weeks, election night looked set to be a disaster for Corbyn and his party.

Donald Trump and Boris Johnson at the NATO leaders summit in Watford, 4 December 2019 (© Reuters/Alamy Stock Photo)

A visit from President Donald Trump was a nightmare scenario for Conservative campaigners eager to avoid hostages to fortune: Trump's outbursts on broadcast and social media could not be predicted or controlled, and his regular expressions of affection for Boris Johnson were unlikely to be a campaign asset to the Conservatives given his toxicity with British voters. It was therefore with some trepidation that Johnson's advisors prepared for the arrival of the US President on 3 December for a two-day NATO summit. The 'Trump test' for Johnson's team was worthy of the *Mission Impossible* franchise: they needed to guide the volatile and attention-seeking US President through 48 hours in London, including trips to Downing Street and Buckingham Palace, while avoiding any headline-grabbing feuds, spats, ad libs or embarrassing tweets, and minimising footage of Trump with Johnson that political opponents would use against them. All this needed to be done without offending a notoriously vain and short-fused President and while simultaneously managing an international summit attended by many other world leaders. The Conservatives picked their way through this minefield with remarkable aplomb, impressing even their opponents. 'They were so disciplined they managed even to get Donald Trump to be disciplined which is quite extraordinary', said one Labour advisor. 'That is discipline on a special plane.' Trump said nothing contentious in the opening press conference, even emphasising that the US, contra Labour's claims, had no interest in the NHS, declaring 'we wouldn't want it if you handed it to us on a silver platter'.[65] His meetings with Johnson in Downing Street and at the NATO summit in Watford were not caught on camera. Nothing newsworthy happened at the Buckingham Palace leaders' reception, Johnson got through his own press conference without using the US President's name, and Trump even cancelled his end-of-conference press conference to fly home early, to big sighs of relief in CCHQ.

The Conservatives' successful negotiation of the Trump minefield added to mounting Labour worries. Corbyn had proved unable to rekindle the magic of 2017 and his dismal personal leadership ratings stubbornly refused to budge, leaving him well behind Johnson, despite the latter's lukewarm scores from voters (see Chapter 14, pp. 522–524).[66] Labour strategists had one last opportunity to turn this around, with a second head-to-head debate chaired by BBC Political Editor Nick Robinson on the final Friday night of the campaign. Despite the high stakes, Corbyn again refused to bend on his rule not to cancel campaign commitments for debate preparation, much to the frustration of his team. In the end, Corbyn's aides were only able to carve out two hours with him before the debate, much less than they had hoped for: 'it was an amazing, brilliant platform, but we just didn't have enough time to prepare properly ... we could have made more of it with more time to rehearse'.

Johnson's abundance of caution and Corbyn's lack of polish combined to produce another underwhelming contest. Johnson attacked Corbyn as weak on terrorism and national security, and indecisive on Brexit. Corbyn attacked Johnson as untrustworthy and a threat to the NHS. Corbyn turned every question into an opportunity to talk about austerity and the NHS, while Johnson sought to work the phrase 'get Brexit done' into every response while emphasising that his party too would invest heavily in public services. None of this offered anything new to most voters, or indeed to viewers who had watched the first debate on ITV a few weeks before.[67] There were a couple of flashpoints—when Johnson criticised Corbyn's record on anti-semitism as a failure of leadership, the Labour leader shot back: 'A failure of leadership is when you use racist remarks to describe people in different countries or in our society. I will never do that and my party will never do that.' Snap polling by YouGov in the wake of the event suggested few minds were changed—viewers declared the second event a dead heat, just like the first.[68] Johnson was once again seen as more prime ministerial and likeable, and Corbyn as more trustworthy and in touch with ordinary people. It was another hazard negotiated by the frontrunner and another opportunity missed by his opponent.

There were other opportunities for Corbyn to re-introduce himself to voters, with a turn on the *This Morning* sofa and an interview with ITV's Julie Etchingham. Neither went very well. Reporting of the Etchingham interview was dominated by Corbyn's tongue-tied response when asked whether he watched the Queen's Speech on Christmas Day,[69] while coverage of the *This Morning* interview focused on Corbyn belatedly offering the personal apology for anti-semitism he had repeatedly failed to give Andrew Neil. Anti-semitism again returned to the headlines in the final weekend of the campaign, with a widely covered leak of the Jewish Labour Movement submissions to the Equality and Human Rights Commission investigation into Labour on Friday 6 December. The submission, which included sworn testimonies from over 70 politicians and officials, concluded that 'the Labour Party is no longer a safe space for Jewish people'. Two days later, there were further leaks on the same topic, this time a dossier of documents and recordings from Labour's disciplinary process passed to the *Sunday Times*.[70] John McDonnell, touring the broadcast studios to make Labour's final weekend policy pitch, was obliged instead to spend much of his time apologising for the party's past failings on anti-semitism. Meanwhile, Nicola Sturgeon punched another old bruise by again reminding voters that the SNP would demand a second independence referendum as the price for supporting a Corbyn-led government.[71]

Corbyn was not the only leader on the ropes as the campaign drew to a close. Liberal Democrat leader Jo Swinson was under fire after presiding over a campaign in which her party's support had almost halved in a month. While Swinson put on a brave face in public, the mood within the Liberal Democrat campaign by this stage was grim, as one senior campaign figure recalled:

> We started ahead of Labour amongst strong Remainers, then in a two-month period Labour just destroyed us amongst that group … we lost strong Remainers to Labour in droves across a two-month period. If you'd said to anyone in September 'come election day Jo Swinson is going to be less popular than Jeremy Corbyn amongst Remain voters', they'd have responded 'No fucking chance!'

The loss of strong Remainers to Labour, the refusal of weaker Remainers to defect from the Conservatives and the absence of Brexit Party candidates to split the Leave vote left the Liberal Democrats in an impossible bind in their mostly Conservative-held target seats. As one senior figure in the campaign recalled: 'The Tories were getting about 80% of the Leave vote and 20% of the Remain vote. If it's a 50/50 seat, it was over. We can't beat those numbers.'

The Brexit Party was also fading fast as polling day approached. It was polling consistently under 5% in national polls and its claim to be helping deliver Brexit was undermined by the YouGov MRP analysis, which showed the party out of contention practically everywhere and suggested that the presence of Brexit Party candidates generally helped Labour more than the Conservatives.[72] This message was reinforced on 5 December by four of Farage's own MEPs, elected just months earlier, who resigned from the party and in a joint London press conference urged voters to back the Conservatives instead. This was more in sorrow than in anger—Annunziata Rees-Mogg insisted that 'I find it absolutely unbelievable but tragic that the Brexit Party, with so many wonderful people dedicated to a cause, are now the very party risking Brexit'.[73]

When Andrew Neil made the same point to Farage in his interview with the Brexit Party leader, Farage responded by attacking the MEPs he had 24 hours earlier shared a party with: 'One of them is the sister of a Cabinet minister, another one has a boyfriend working for that Cabinet minister. Fact. And another one is a personal friend of Boris Johnson.' Farage insisted that the defectors 'didn't understand' how the Brexit Party posed the most credible challenge to Labour in Labour Leave seats. Farage's traditional supporters in the Eurosceptic press were unconvinced, with both *The Sun* and the *Daily Mail* giving favourable coverage to Ms Rees-Mogg's claims. Farage also faced headaches from those still standing for his party, with repeated controversies over Islamophobic statements by Brexit Party candidates in the final weeks of the campaign.[74]

The final week of the Conservative campaign began with the 5 December announcement of a post-Brexit budget from Chancellor Sajid Javid, pledging a hike in the National Insurance threshold and more money for schools. Rumours of growing Tory optimism began to circulate in the media, despite the best efforts of CCHQ to guard against them. As one aide recalled, 'all these polls out there going "We're going to win by X100 seats", of course it breeds a massive worry about complacency'. There were still nervous moments. Boris Johnson's turn on the *This Morning* sofa risked backfiring as daytime TV presenters Philip Schofield and Holly Willoughby confronted him with the kind of difficult questions he had avoided by refusing an interview with Andrew Neil: 'Does it help that a Prime Minister of this great nation would use the terms "bank robber" and "letter box" to describe Muslim women who wear a burqa?' asked Schofield. 'Many people who will point out I have said things that have caused offence. Well, I'm deeply sorry for the offence that I caused', Johnson (eventually) responded. The Prime Minister enjoyed an easier reception from the nation's most widely read newspaper, *The Sun*, whose political editor published a video diary of his day on the campaign trail with Johnson. In response to the question 'How does the Prime Minister keep going?', Johnson stated: 'I sometimes succumb to flapjacks, which are not medically recommended. And I seem to be able to drink an unlimited amount of coffee without impeding my ability to sleep at the end of the day.'[75]

The campaign moved to 'closing arguments' over the final weekend. The Conservatives' focus returned to Brexit with a 'Vote Leave blitz'. The Liberal Democrats, still falling in the polls, made a big final push for Remain voters on the other pole of the Brexit debate, targeting in particular tactical votes from Remain supporters in the Conservative-held seats where the party was still in contention. The Brexit Party sought to do the same in safe Labour seats, arguing only it could overcome engrained cultural hostility to the Conservatives. Labour, having failed to shift the conversation away from Brexit or to agree on a coherent campaign message, spent the final days campaigning on partisan muscle memory, as one LOTO senior aide recalled:

We needed to end the campaign with *something*. And we haven't been able to make it about something else. We hadn't built. We hadn't hit the same message over and over again … So we ended the campaign in the most traditional territory we could: 'Labour on your side, save the NHS.' The bedrock of every past Labour campaign. The lowest common denominator that everyone sort of agrees with? That's the thing we did.

Even within the Labour campaign, most by now expected a Conservative victory the following Thursday. That belief was widely shared—one poll had 57% of voters expecting a Conservative victory compared to 19% anticipating a Labour win.[76] Bookmakers priced a Conservative win at 4/11 on. The final polls all pointed in the same direction—the Conservative lead had held up and looked to be large enough to ensure a comfortable parliamentary majority. The result looked all but certain, but after 2017, no one could really be sure.

Notes

1. Though the precise timing of the election announcement came as a surprise to many in both parties' organisations, Labour aides in both LOTO and Southside suspected Theresa May would seek an early poll and had begun preparations for a campaign in early 2017. However, these were hampered by deep divides between LOTO and Southside over election strategy. See P. Cowley and D. Kavanagh, *The British General Election of 2017*. Palgrave Macmillan, 2018, pp. 91–95.
2. 'Boris Launches Campaign Pledging to Unleash Britain's Potential', *Conservatives*, 5 November 2019, https://www.conservatives.com/news/boris-campaign-launch.
3. B. Johnson, 'A Deal is Oven-Ready. Let's Get Brexit Done and Take This Country Forward', *Daily Telegraph*, 5 November 2019, https://www.telegraph.co.uk/politics/2019/11/05/deal-oven-ready-get-brexit-done-take-country-forward. Ironically, this kind of combative, polemical rhetoric was exactly what many of Corbyn's closest aides hoped to provoke, believing it played to their benefit, but Johnson seldom indulged in similar personal attacks again, and CCHQ discouraged other Conservative politicians from using them. As one senior strategist noted: 'We were told if you're going to attack Corbyn, you're going to have to have the gloves on, not the gloves off. There was a strong feeling that CCHQ gone way too far in 2017, basically trying to brand him as a terrorist. This time we didn't want to paint him as a bad man.'

4. 'They remind me a bit of candle-sellers at the dawn of the age of the electric light bulb, or the makers of typewriters on beholding their first laptop computer. They have a terrible sense that they are about to lose their market. Because this deal delivers everything that I campaigned for Brexit.' 'Boris Launches Campaign Pledging to Unleash Britain's Potential', *Conservatives*, 5 November 2019, https://www.conservatives.com/news/boris-campaign-launch.

5. Alun Cairns quit as Welsh Secretary after an aide was accused of sabotaging a rape trial, a lurid story which many Conservatives were doubtless relieved did not receive sustained attention (see Chapter 12, pp. 421–459).

6. Similar analysis by Kanagasooriam for the Scottish Conservatives had helped them identify the seats where they had the most potential to advance in 2016 and 2017, seats where the Scottish party did indeed prove able to post major gains.

7. This was perhaps not the spontaneous 'Borisism' aides believed it to be—the same phrase had been used by Jeremy Corbyn to attack Theresa May's approach to Brexit in 2018.

8. This suspicion persisted even though a widely respected Corbyn loyalist, Niall Sookoo, was now in charge of the Southside elections analysis team. At one meeting where he presented his team's analysis to the party's election strategy group, a LOTO aide reportedly told Sookoo 'you sound like Patrick Heneghan'. Heneghan was Sookoo's predecessor as Southside Executive Director for Elections and had repeatedly clashed with LOTO aides over election strategy during the 2017 campaign.

9. Such factionalism and duplication was not a 2019 novelty—the same issues were seen in 2017. It is, however, striking that such internal fractures persisted despite the installation of Jennie Formby and other LOTO loyalists at Southside. Changes at the top of Labour's bureaucracy were not enough to overcome an entrenched culture of mutual distrust.

10. The judgments against Conservative officials for breaking electoral spending rules in South Thanet, issued in 2019, were a key barrier to co-ordination between Labour and Momentum. These judgments, according to Southside sources, removed any doubt that straightforward cooperation with Momentum had serious consequences for campaign spending, making it almost impossible to get Momentum campaign expenditure to be arranged lawfully by Party HQ in Southside. See, for example, R. Syal, 'Tory Official Convicted of Falsifying Expenses in Race Against Farage', *The Guardian*, 9 January 2019, https://www.theguardian.com/politics/2019/jan/09/craig-mackinlay-tory-mp-cleared-breaking-2015-general-election-expenses-rules.

11. Sources in LOTO credit the defusing of the potentially explosive Watson situation to the more diplomatic and consensual approach of new Corbyn Chief of Staff Helene Reardon-Bond. For a more detailed account of his departure, see G. Pogrund and P. Maguire, *Left Out*. Vintage, 2020, pp. 306–309.

12. Both were former Labour MPs as both had resigned the Labour whip in protest against Corbyn's leadership during the 2017–2019 Parliament. John Woodcock had previously had the whip withdrawn pending investigation of a sexual harassment investigation. He denied any wrongdoing, but resigned the whip before the investigation (which he criticised as politically motivated) was completed. The investigation was dissolved without being concluded. Woodcock, now sitting in the Lords as Lord Walney, has pressed for a new investigation process, emphasising that he was 'committed to finding a genuinely independent and impartial route for the matter to be investigated'. See https://twitter.com/LordWalney/status/1289238953275478028?s=20.

13. It is puzzling that the Liberal Democrat leadership were surprised that a pledge unlikely to be enacted could cause them political grief, given how much trouble the party had over the 2010 campaign pledge to end tuition fees, another promise that was unlikely to be enacted without a Liberal Democrat majority government.

14. Pragmatic party management was also a factor here: the new leadership were also reluctant to pick a high-profile fight with activists over the policy at Swinson's first conference as party leader.

15. A third tier of 20–40 stretch targets was dropped early on in the campaign, as polling numbers fell.

16. As indeed analysis of the results suggests they were—see Chapter 13.

17. Analysis by Professors Colin Rallings and Michael Thrasher highlighted the danger to Johnson from Farage: 'In places such as Bassetlaw, Bishop Auckland and Great Grimsby, all of which swung to the Tories in 2017 and which they need to go on and win this time, it could be that Brexit Party contestation means that the balance of any movement will be to Labour's advantage.' Rallings and Thrasher also noted that the Brexit Party could prove beneficial to Liberal Democrat challengers in Conservative-held seats where the Lib Dems were second: C. Rallings and M. Thrasher, 'Nigel Farage's Brexit Party is Unlikely to Win Seats But Can Wound Boris Johnson', *Sunday Times*, 3 November 2019, https://www.thetimes.co.uk/edition/news/nigel-farages-brexit-party-unlikely-to-win-seats-but-can-wound-boris-johnson-nb0bvcl7p.

18. Rees-Mogg was speaking on his podcast for *ConservativeHome*, 'The Moggcast', 5 November 2019, https://www.conservativehome.com/

highlights/2019/11/the-moggcast-its-such-a-pity-that-nigel-hasnt-worked-out-that-hes-won.html.

19. G. Heffer, 'General Election: Farage Attacks Tories for "Conceited Arrogance" over Brexit', *Sky News*, 4 November 2019, https://news.sky.com/story/general-election-farage-attacks-tories-for-conceited-arrogance-over-brexit-11854210.

20. J. Stevens, 'Vote Farage, Get Corbyn?', *Daily Mail*, 1 November 2019, https://www.dailymail.co.uk/news/article-7637239/Vote-Farage-Corbyn-Tories-miss-nearly-90-seats-Brexit-Party-splits-vote.html.

21. '*The Sun* Says: Votes for Nigel Farage's Brexit Party Could Put Corbyn in Downing Street—His Voters Should Think Again', *The Sun*, 2 November 2019, https://www.thesun.co.uk/news/10262792/brexit-party-votes-corbyn-no10.

22. Farage alleges he was offered a peerage, and Tice a safe Conservative seat. The Conservatives strongly denied such allegations, which were referred to the Metropolitan Police to investigate. See 'General Election 2019: Police "Assessing" Call for Peerage Claim Probe', *BBC News*, 16 November 2019, https://www.bbc.co.uk/news/election-2019-50443430.

23. C. Hope, 'Nigel Farage Unveils Candidates to Fight Every Seat at Election as it Emerges 20 Have Already Quit', *Daily Telegraph*, 5 November 2019, https://www.telegraph.co.uk/politics/2019/11/04/nigel-farage-sets-sights-labour-heartlands-despite-claims-candidates.

24. Labour strategists also saw the Brexit Party's retreat as a net negative for them, but Farage's new outfit did not seem to be as central to their discussions as it was for the Liberal Democrats.

25. Pogrund and Maguire, *Left Out*, p. 314.

26. This was slightly less bad than it sounded as statistics on the headline 'maximum four-hour wait' target have only been collected since 2004.

27. 'Labour Leave voters were more likely to see health as the most important issue facing them and their family (45 percent), not Brexit. Less than a third of Labour leavers listed Brexit in their most important issues, the lowest of all political and demographic groups. Crime (27 percent), the economy (21 percent) and pensions (20 percent) were all important for this group.' R. Carter, 'Brexit is Not Labour Leavers' Number One Priority', *Hope Not Hate*, 13 November 2019, https://www.hopenothate.org.uk/2019/11/13/brexit-is-not-labour-leavers-number-one-priority.

28. However, as on every issue of Labour campaign strategy, others took a very different view, expressing scepticism that Labour would ever be able to separate credibility on the NHS from credibility on Brexit with Leave voters. As one of those involved noted: 'There was than a lot of hypothetical polling which asked Labour Leave voters "If you were to

say which issue most concerns you, the NHS, your family's economy, or leaving the EU", and they always ticked the NHS very high up ... I know what those voters were saying because they were telling me exactly the same thing [in focus groups]. It was "we want to get Brexit done" and "we think the Tories are going to destroy the NHS" and "we don't like the Tories but they're going to get Brexit done and you've betrayed us on it so we're not going to vote for you this time". And once that narrative gets set in, and the Tories were extremely good at exploiting that ... suddenly those polls that said they care more about the NHS etc. becomes "this party promised us something and now its betrayed us so we can't trust them. Why should we vote for them when we voted [for Leave] and they didn't take that vote seriously?"'.

29. For example, '£1 Trillion Labour Splurge "to Bankrupt UK"', *Sunday Times*, 10 November 2019, https://www.thetimes.co.uk/article/election-2019-1-trillion-labour-splurge-to-bankrupt-uk-m0dktnw32.   The fact-checking website *Full Fact* criticised the Conservatives dossier, saying 'there are serious problems with the Conservatives' claim'; see 'There are Serious Problems with the Conservatives' Claim That Labour Would Spend £1.2 trillion', *Full Fact*, 11 November 2019, https://fullfact.org/news/conservative-claim-labour-1-trillion.

30. These were that the government would run a balanced budget on its current account by the middle of the next Parliament and that borrowing for infrastructure spending would be kept within 3% (up from 2%) of GDP.

31. In a memo circulated in August 2019, Milne had predicted that Johnson would 'seek a mandate to deliver Brexit' and that the Conservatives 'will try and portray Johnson as fresh, optimistic, decisive, action-oriented: setting out a new agenda of delivering Brexit, ending austerity and cutting taxes.' The diagnosis proved accurate—the prescription 'move off Brexit and on to the main domestic agenda' proved hard to implement. Pogrund and Maguire, *Left Out*, pp. 229–32.

32. S. Bush, 'Labour was Meant to Surge This Week, But it's the Tories Who Think Victory is Theirs for the Taking', *New Statesman*, 20 November 2019, https://www.newstatesman.com/politics/uk/2019/11/labour-was-meant-surge-week-it-s-tories-who-think-victory-theirs-taking.

33. The massive interest in leaders' debates has been a recurring theme in recent British campaigns—see, for example, Cowley and Kavanagh, *The British General Election of 2017*, pp. 212–21; P. Cowley and D. Kavanagh, *The British General Election of 2015*. Palgrave Macmillan, 2015, pp. 161–62; D. Kavanagh and P. Cowley, *The British General Election of 2010*. Palgrave Macmillan, 2010, pp. 164–71. Before 2010, the main campaign story was typically the incumbent's determination to avoid such debates. The mocking of such supposed cowardice by dressing

an unfortunate junior journalist in a chicken suit to pester the offending leader at campaign events became a Westminster media ritual.

34. Cowley and Kavanagh, *The British General Election of 2017*, pp. 212–15.

35. Corbyn's reluctance to focus on broadcast events also reflected growing weariness and suspicion of the media. As one aide noted: 'He was just ground down by years of hostile press and media, often camped outside his front door.'

36. The laughter regarding Johnson's claim to value truthfulness looked particularly apposite when it emerged soon after the debate that CCHQ had controversially changed the Conservatives' Twitter profile to resemble that of 'factcheckUK', a well-known non-partisan fact-checking service, for several hours during and after the debate.

37. A. Gregory, 'Lib Dem Leader Jo Swinson Forced to Deny Shooting Stones at Squirrels After Spoof Story Goes Viral', *The Independent*, 19 November 2019, https://www.independent.co.uk/news/uk/politics/jo-swinson-squirrels-shooting-stones-lib-dems-slingshot-fake-news-a9209196.html.

38. There was not such universal acclaim at the time, with a lot of internal tensions over the credibility of the manifesto policies and costings, and a major LOTO panic when the draft manifesto leaked (see Cowley and Kavanagh, *The British General Election of 2017*, Chapter 8).

39. This process was generally but not always harmonious, and Fisher's team pushed back against proposals which they felt cut against the broader goals of the manifesto.

40. There was more to this row than meets the eye. Union bosses were reportedly angry at what they saw as insufficient consultation on the development of the manifesto Brexit policy, which they felt reneged on previous LOTO promises of full consultation. They therefore engaged in a collective show of strength over the 2030 climate change pledges in order to signal discontent at what they saw as a violation of due process on Brexit policy.

41. Labour Party, 'Funding Real Change', https://labour.org.uk/wp-content/uploads/2019/11/Funding-Real-Change-2019.pdf. Several aides expressed disappointment that the immense effort put into researching and developing the costings document was not reflected in the meagre political and media attention it received.

42. The IFS team argued it was 'unlikely' Labour's tax policies would raise enough to cover their spending plans: 'If you want to transform the scale and scope of the state then you need to be clear that the tax increases required to do that will need to be widely shared rather than pretending that everything can be paid for by companies and the rich.' See 'Labour Manifesto: An Initial Reaction from IFS Researchers', *Institute for Fiscal*

Studies, 21 November 2019, https://www.ifs.org.uk/election/2019/article/labour-manifesto-an-initial-reaction-from-ifs-researchers. The Resolution Foundation described Labour's manifesto as 'simply huge in the scale of the changes it proposes … more radical than anything we have seen in the UK in a generation', but called for 'more honesty about the difficulties involved … the reality is we will all need to pay higher taxes if we want a state the size of Germany's that delivers not just free social care but free broadband'. See T. Bell, 'Doubling Down on a Bigger State: Assessing Labour's Manifesto', *Resolution Foundation*, 22 November 2019, https://www.resolutionfoundation.org/app/uploads/2019/11/Labour-Manifesto-2019-1.pdf.

43. For examples of voter scepticism, see the campaign focus group discussions summarised in Chapter 14.

44. A subsequent audience member came to Corbyn's rescue by claiming that Corbyn's predecessor Harold Wilson had adopted a similar stance in the 1975 EEC referendum. However, while Wilson (like Corbyn) was keen to avoid a strong commitment on principle for or against EEC membership in the 1974 general elections and allowed members of a divided Labour Cabinet members to campaign on either side, the circumstances Wilson faced, and his personal approach as leader, were quite different from Corbyn's situation. In 1974, Wilson proposed to open a renegotiation of Britain's EEC membership and set out a series of seven objectives for these negotiations. As was widely expected, at the end of the negotiations, Wilson declared that Labour's objectives had been met, endorsed the new deal with the EEC and campaigned for it personally in the subsequent referendum. Corbyn was ruling out in advance personally campaigning for or against any deal his government negotiated, regardless of whether it met Labour's objectives, something Wilson never did. For more on this, see R. Saunders, *Yes to Europe! The 1975 Referendum and Seventies Britain*. Cambridge University Press, 2018, Chapter 2.

45. A LOTO advisor knew how Corbyn's stance would dominate media reporting on the event: 'Johnson had a bad day there. Swinson got absolutely annihilated. And Jeremy had a good day … so good that we were able to do a like 15 or 16-minute edit of Jeremy's full 26 minutes and just put that out because more than half of the minutes were good. Which you definitely couldn't say of the other three … But still the takeaway was our line on Brexit. That was still the thing that came out of it.'

46. See Cowley and Kavanagh, *The British General Election of 2015*, Chapter 7.

47. CCHQ campaign strategists were worried that their opponents would challenge the premise the election was necessary. As one senior team member recalled: 'They could have quite credibly said "Boris Johnson is

having you on. He could have got Brexit done without having this election. He's having it only to further his own political interest. He's only ever been it for himself".' They were surprised, and relieved, that this attack never came.

48. In this statement, Johnson strayed perilously close to one of his predecessor's most damaging lines in 2017. May, also responding to a hostile questioner on the 2017 Leader's *Question Time* special, had insisted there was 'no magic money tree'(then Home Secretary Amber Rudd had earlier used the same line when standing in for May at a debate, suggesting it was not a slip of the tongue). Johnson's greater willingness to throw money at any potential electoral threat throughout the campaign may have helped him swiftly to neutralise a vulnerability which proved so damaging for his predecessor.

49. J. Corbyn and J. McDonnell, 'Labour Pledges Compensation Packages for Millions of Women Hit by State Pension Age Rises Imposed by the Tories', *Labour Party*, 23 November 2019, https://labour.org.uk/press/labour-pledges-compensation-packages-for-millions-of-women-hit-by-state-pension-age-rises-imposed-by-the-tories.

50. The manifesto did feature a promise to act on WASPI women, but there was no specific or costed proposal attached to this promise. One reason for this was disagreements between McDonnell and Seumas Milne over how to pay for it. Another reason was political strategy, with the policy held back as a potentially game-changing surprise announcement. McDonnell, a longstanding supporter of the WASPI campaign, helped convince the Labour campaign team that a major intervention on this would help Labour with a key voter group—older women—which made the policy a gamble worth taking, despite its high costs.

51. Cowley and Kavanagh, *The British General Election of 2017*, p. 197.

52. The spreadsheet, which ended up with 600 rows, helped the team identify and avert a number of problematic omissions, including child poverty, grammar schools and Gibraltar. There was then 'an enormous period of horse-trading about what would get a mention and what wouldn't'. Interview with Ross Kempsell, 4 September 2020.

53. The red team adversaries proved more formidable than the Conservatives' real-life political opponents. As one of those involved put it, 'the version we all came up with of "This is how they're going to tear this apart" was *so* much harsher than what we actually got from the Labour Party. Everyone fixated on the 50,000 nurses and that became the lead. But that's an argument that you're happy to have because it reminds people that you're going to hire more new nurses'. The attack line which most worried the team—that Johnson's Brexit deal was so harsh it was essentially a no deal Brexit in disguise—never emerged.

54. 'Conservative Manifesto: An Initial Reaction from IFS Researchers', 24 November 2019, https://www.ifs.org.uk/election/2019/article/ conservative-manifesto-an-initial-reaction-from-ifs-researchers.

55. While the Conservative manifesto proposals were framed as unambitious compared to those floated by Labour during the election campaign itself, when the same policies and the same spending envelope were announced a few months after the election, in the Budget, they were widely seen as more significant.

56. P. Waugh, 'Is Jeremy Corbyn's Anti-semitism Problem a Leadership Problem?' *HuffPost*, 26 November 2019, https://www.huffingtonpost. co.uk/entry/jeremy-corbyn-andrew-neil-bbc-anti-semitism-waugh-zone_uk_5ddd9f8ce4b0913e6f7568f6.

57. The unidentified original messenger also requested that those in the group 'don't share the info I've posted outside of here'. The exchanges were duly leaked within hours. See https://twitter.com/ rowlsmanthorpe/status/1199397923836047363?s=20.

58. K. Balls, 'Boris Johnson Is the Front-Runner So He's Going to Play It Extremely Safe until Election Day to Get His Victory', *The i* paper, 26 November 2019, https://inews.co.uk/opinion/boris-johnson-is-the-front-runner-so-hes-going-to-play-it-extremely-safe-until-election-day-to-get-his-victory-367629.

59. Two focus groups by former Number 10 pollster James Johnson of previous Labour voters in Birmingham Northfield (a seat Labour would go on to lose for the first time in 30 years), which were shown on *Channel 4 News* on 2 December, illustrated just how bleak the situation was. None of the participants intended to vote Labour again in 2019. Their responses when asked why: 'Jeremy Corbyn', 'Jeremy Corbyn', 'Same'. When asked about Labour's spending plans: 'We don't know where they're getting the money from.' 'Where's the money coming from?' 'I don't trust a word he says.' When asked why they no longer trust Labour: 'I don't know what the Labour Party stands for anymore.' 'The working people in the North voted to Leave but Corbyn's gone against that.' 'You don't know what Corbyn is going to do on Brexit. He's sitting on the fence.'

60. The police believed he was about to detonate his explosive vest, which turned out to be fake.

61. The origin of these documents, which Labour had acquired just days earlier, remains unclear.

62. The need to consolidate Leave voters also drove the only significant campaign intervention from senior Johnson advisor (and former Vote Leave campaign impresario) Dominic Cummings. In a blog published on his personal website on 27 November, Cummings sent a 'bat signal'

to alert Leave voters that 'Brexit was in danger', warning that a vote for the Brexit Party 'is effectively a vote for Corbyn-Sturgeon' and that Johnson's opponents 'will do anything to stop YOU, normal voters, taking back control of THEM'.

63. YouGov's MRP analysis gave little new information to the Conservatives, Labour or the Liberal Democrats, who were all conducting their own MRP models throughout the campaign.

64. M. Smith, N. Wildash, T. Abraham, A. McDonnell and C. Curtis, 'The Key Findings from Our MRP', *YouGov*, 27 November 2019, https://yougov.co.uk/topics/politics/articles-reports/2019/11/27/key-findings-our-mrp.

65. E. McCahill, 'Donald Trump Says He "Wouldn't Take the NHS If It Was Offered on a Silver Platter"', *Daily Mirror*, 3 December 2019, https://www.mirror.co.uk/news/politics/breaking-donald-trump-says-wouldnt-21015102.

66. For example, Corbyn's favourability ratings in the first four weeks of the campaign from Ipsos MORI were −39, −38, −35 and −38. The figures for Boris Johnson were −8, −9, −14 and −14. This less than fulsome endorsement from the electorate still put Johnson well ahead of both Corbyn and his rivals from the smaller parties—Nigel Farage's ratings hovered around −30 throughout the first month, while Jo Swinson's fell steadily, from −20 at the start to −31 four weeks in. The only party leader to enjoy net positive approval ratings was SNP leader and Scottish First Minister Nicola Sturgeon.

67. There was less audible laughter at the candidates' responses from the audience in the BBC event, no doubt to the relief of both.

68. YouGov also found that Corbyn did better on the NHS and Johnson on Brexit, confirming that its poll respondents were at least awake during the broadcast. The most popular word chosen to describe the event was 'frustrating'. See M. Smith, 'YouGov Snap Poll Finds Viewers Split on Who Won ITV General Election Debate', *YouGov*, 19 November 2019, https://yougov.co.uk/topics/politics/articles-reports/2019/11/19/who-won-itv-general-election-debate.

69. When asked 'Do you sit down to watch the Queen's speech, Mr Corbyn?', the exchange proceeded as follows: 'It's on in the morning usually, we have it on sometimes.' 'It's not on in the morning, it at three o'clock in the afternoon, that's when everybody watches it.' 'Well … our Christmas is … sometimes…' 'You don't watch it do you Mr Corbyn?' 'There's lots to do. I enjoy the presence of my family and friends around me at Christmas obviously like everybody else does and I also visit the homeless shelter.' This was hardly the appearance of the straight-talking, honest politics Corbyn had once promised.

70. G. Pogrund, J. Calvert and G. Arbuthnott, 'Revealed: The Depth of Labour Anti-semitism', *Sunday Times*, 8 December 2019, https://www.thetimes. co.uk/article/revealed-the-depth-of-labour-anti-semitism-bb57h9pdz.

71. Like Miliband, Corbyn had sought to duck the issue by insisting Labour would not do deals with any other party. Sturgeon was having none of it: 'We will offer our support to a minority Labour government with certain conditions attached to that ... I don't think they're going to turn their backs on that.'

72. A pattern borne out in the final results; see Chapter 13.

73. Her former Brexit Party colleagues did not take this lying down, organising a rival press conference in the same venue, which provoked the following exchange between the Brexit Party spokesman and the former MEPs:

> 'You're all slags', shouted the spokesman.
> 'You're the slag', returned one of the former MEPs.
> 'Who are you calling a slag, slags?', retorted the spokesman.

See J. Crace, 'A Bad Day for Farage as Brexit Party MEPs Realise They've Been Had', *The Guardian*, 5 December 2019, https://www.theguardian.com/politics/2019/dec/05/a-bad-day-for-farage-as-brexit-party-meps-realise-theyve-been-had.

74. Allegedly Islamophobic statements by Brexit Party candidates in Birmingham Ladywood and Edinburgh South West were put to Farage during the Andrew Neil interview. The party also had trouble with candidates in several other seats.

75. Johnson also admitted to relaxing at the end of a long campaign day with 'quadratic equations and a bit of Greek lyric poetry. Nothing complicated. Everybody should do it'. The response of readers of *The Sun* to this invitation was not recorded. See T. Newton-Dunn, 'Keeping up with BoJo: *The Sun* Joins Boris Johnson's Gruelling 16 Hour Day on the Campaign Trail', *The Sun*, 3 December 2019, https://www.thesun.co.uk/news/10477306/boris-johnson-gruelling-camping-trail.

76. 'The Fifth of Our Tracking Studies for the *Mail on Sunday*', *DeltaPoll*, 8 December 2019, http://www.deltapoll.co.uk/polls/general-election-2019-part-6. However, more voters expected a hung parliament (42% total: 29% Conservatives largest party, 13% Labour largest party) than a majority for either party (34%: 28% Conservative majority, 6% Labour majority), suggesting the surprise 2017 outcome still loomed large.

CHAPTER 7

The Red Wall Falls

As the final week of the campaign began, the battle to frame the election was largely over. All the parties could do now was to play their strongest cards one last time. For Britain's two main parties—Labour and the Conservatives—there was little doubt what these were. The Conservatives wanted a Brexit election, while Labour wanted an NHS and public services election. Meanwhile, in Scotland, the SNP wanted an election focused on Scottish opposition to Brexit, and independence as a route to remaining in the EU. Things were less clear, however, for the Liberal Democrats and the Brexit Party. Polling suggested their headline arguments had failed and they were now left without effective closing pitches. All Nigel Farage could do was to cast doubt, yet again, both on the Conservatives' ability to deliver a 'real' Brexit and on Boris Johnson's promise to bring down immigration. Jo Swinson began the final week trying once again to undo the electoral damage done by her party's 'revoke Article 50' pledge. Having spent some of the weekend denying she would resign if the party lost MPs on Thursday, she admitted on the Radio 4 *Today* programme that the Liberal Democrat majority needed to secure revocation was unlikely and instead sought to focus attention on the party's support for a second referendum.

The Conservatives, privately growing more confident that their polling lead would deliver a comfortable majority, began the week determined to hammer home yet again the 'get Brexit done' message which had played so well in the Leave-voting seats they were targeting. At the start of a whirlwind tour of five 'Red Wall' seats on Monday 9 December, Boris Johnson posed with a glistening cod in Grimsby's fish market before returning in his stump speech to Brexit in tones shot through with the populism that had helped win the 2016 Referendum:

> The Labour Party has let you down most of all. Under Jeremy Corbyn, they promised to honour the result of the referendum, before voting against Brexit every chance they had. They won their seats on a false pro-spectus and then stuck two fingers up to the public. Now they are pro-posing another referendum, this time rigging the result by extending the franchise to two million EU citizens. It's been the Great Betrayal, orches-trated from Islington by politicians who sneer at your values and ignore your votes.
>
> You voted to leave the EU because you wanted to stop sending the EU money we could spend at home, to end uncontrolled and unlimited immigration from the EU, to take back control from an unelected elite in Brussels, and to force politicians in Westminster to listen to you, not just London and the southeast.[1]

Boris Johnson holds a fish during a campaign visit to Grimsby fish market, 9 December 2019 (© Reuters/Alamy Stock Photo)

Johnson's aim, as always, was to focus attention on the symbolism of Brexit while avoiding the more controversial substance. The Prime Minister completely ignored, for instance, documents leaked the previous weekend showing that (despite Conservative denials) there would indeed have to be checks on goods going from Great Britain to Northern Ireland. Instead, he highlighted Leave voters' frustration, reminding them that there had been '1,264 days of dither and delay, prevarication and procrastination, obfuscation and obstruction'.

That same day, Home Secretary Priti Patel burnished the Conservatives' law and order credentials in an article for the *Daily Telegraph*, claiming Labour's concerns about stop and search powers would result in fewer seizures of weapons. She then reeled off alarming statistics provided by the Conservative Research Department about the extra violent crimes that would allegedly result—an 'extra killing a week' in the *words* of The *Sun*.[2] Like Johnson, Patel was careful to stress the binary choice facing voters:

> between a functioning Conservative majority which will turbocharge the recruitment of 20,000 additional police officers and increase sentences for serious and violent criminals. Or a Labour-SNP coalition who support automatic release of those convicted of terrorist offences.

Patel then trotted out another CCHQ campaign line that focused on combating any complacency among Conservative-leaning voters:

> Make no mistake, a hung parliament with Corbyn in Downing Street supported by Nicola Sturgeon is a real possibility. I've been to every region of the country in the last few weeks speaking to voters and I can promise you that this election is very close.

She wasn't alone in sounding this warning. The next day's edition of the *Daily Telegraph* miraculously got hold of 'a Tory Party memo, dated 7 December' warning CCHQ's campaign manager, Isaac Levido, that 'Jeremy Corbyn is much closer to becoming prime minister … than many voters realise'. Despite the opening caveat that 'all the evidence suggests that one party has things pretty much sewn up', this was clearly an attractive framing for broadcasters eager to maintain a sense of drama, or who were themselves viewing polls with caution after the 2017 experience. The BBC's Political Editor, Laura Kuenssberg, for example, had already written on the BBC website on Monday morning about 'how unsure, frankly, the Tory headquarters is that they will end up with anything like a safe majority'.[3] Meanwhile, Remain pressure group Best for Britain released another MRP analysis on the final Monday with the message that tactical voting in as few as 36 seats could still deny the Conservatives what they wanted. All this was welcomed by CCHQ staff, who were not worried about tactical voting, but saw the headline message of a close election as another bulwark against voter complacency.

In fact, the start of the campaign's final week hadn't gone entirely to plan for the Conservatives. An early morning interview Johnson did with ITV reporter Joe Pike had gone viral—and not in a good way. What, asked the reporter, did the Prime Minister have to say regarding the four-year-old boy forced to lie on the floor on a pile of coats owing to a shortage of space for patients in Leeds General Infirmary's A&E Department?[4] Johnson made a bumbling effort to trot out the party line that such shortages made it all the more necessary to end dither and delay over Brexit and focus on the NHS. But then, having repeatedly refused to look at the photo the reporter was brandishing on his mobile, Johnson took the phone and slipped it into his own coat pocket, leading to a video clip of this bizarre move that was viewed on social media over 3.5 million times before the day was out. That provided a boost to Labour's struggling campaign, as it played in to their preferred 'NHS in Crisis' closing narrative and gave the party a powerful visual to help frame the Prime Minister as out of touch and uncaring.

This was one real source of concern for otherwise confident Tory strategists. Voter attention in relation to the state of the NHS had been steadily rising as the campaign progressed. Labour's most-viewed campaign video was an emotional tribute to the NHS from actor Rob Delaney, which had received over seven million views. A YouGov poll released in the final week showed health had drawn level with Brexit as the main issue for voters—a marked contrast with the start of the campaign when Brexit had enjoyed a 28-point lead.[5] And although CCHQ had an answer for those voters—that getting Brexit done would allow them to devote more time and money to the NHS—the issue was inevitably one that played better for Labour. Moreover, time spent on the NHS was time not spent on stronger terrain for the Tories, such as immigration, law and order, Jeremy Corbyn or Labour's alleged profligacy. Health Secretary Matt Hancock was therefore dispatched to Leeds to show the government was responding to the A&E crisis that generated the photo, and hopefully put the story to bed. His appearance at the hospital attracted in turn a small but lively group of protesters, some of whom could clearly be seen and heard heckling him. This in turn became a distracting campaign process story when the media was briefed that one of the protesters had thrown a punch at one of Hancock's special advisors—a story duly tweeted out by a number of prominent political journalists to millions of followers, only for video footage to emerge soon after showing that no such assault had occurred (see Chapter 9).[6] The waters were then further muddied over the next few days by conspiracy theories, shared by Conservative media advocates on Facebook and Twitter, incorrectly claiming that the original story about Leeds Infirmary's A&E Department was some sort of set-up.[7]

The start of the week wasn't all bad news for the Conservatives, however, since it marked the release of a widely praised YouTube ad based on the film *Love Actually*.[8] As a predictably impressed *Daily Express* explained to its readers, it featured the Prime Minister 'playing the role of Mark from the famous placard door scene. Rather than a confession of love however, Mr Johnson implores the resident to vote for the Conservative Party to get Brexit done'. How many of the people who watched the ad were Labour Party supporters outraged that the Tories had supposedly ripped off a similar advert by Labour candidate Rosena Allin-Khan, we shall never know. What we do know, however, is that Labour critics were mistaken. In fact, Topham Guerin, continually hoping to create eye-catching election broadcasts and clips, had already test shot the Tory version (using a stand-in for the Prime Minister) a couple of days before Allin-Khan's video came out.[9] After her version appeared, they had decided to go instead with another idea.[10] Then with ten days to go, they got the go-ahead to revive the original idea—one which would turn out to work well not only on its own terms, but also because of the attention boost provided by accusations of plagiarism. Within a few hours of its release on Monday evening, it had over half a million views on Twitter, and getting on for that on Facebook, picking up millions more from its broadcast on television and hundreds of thousands (possibly even millions) of pounds-worth of free advertising when it was picked up by the newspapers and their websites the next day.[11] Moreover, by beginning with a shot of a (mixed-race) couple sitting on their sofa watching another Conservative advert, 'Boris Johnson's Funny *Love Actually* Parody' (to give it its official YouTube title) may also have contributed to the 3.5 million views clocked up by that earlier ad too, although those numbers were also boosted by the small fortune spent to get it onto the top banner of YouTube's homepage. Much the same, incidentally, was done for a shorter ad, with deliberately low production values, that had run on the Sunday, garnering only slightly fewer (three million) views.[12] Yet, impressive as these figures were, they were dwarfed by the figures achieved, largely without expensive promotion, by Labour's social media channels. Nine of the top ten most-viewed political videos of the campaign came from the Jeremy Corbyn, Momentum and Labour Party social media sites.

While Labour had some success in reprising its dominant social media performance of 2017, it was unable to repeat the success of 2017s mass outdoor rallies. Persuading voters to venture out in the early December cold was a tough ask, even for Corbyn's committed fanbase. Labour pressed ahead with such events regardless, although journalists who attended the one he held (and characteristically turned up late for) in Bristol city centre on the Monday before polling day couldn't help but notice both how small and listless the audience was compared to the raucous crowds Corbyn drew in 2017.[13] Nor, incidentally, could they see any obvious logic to a late whistlestop tour of the West Country that took Corbyn out of the Labour-held seats that, polls suggested, his party was now struggling to defend. Analysis released by the Press Association later in the day suggested that lack of defensive focus was of a piece with Corbyn's schedule throughout the campaign: 31 out of his 68 campaign visits were to Tory-held marginals and 13 to Labour-held marginals, while another 16 were to Labour strongholds. Of course, some of the latter (as was the case in Bristol West) were bordered by target seats, where potential Labour voters might have been geed up by footage of Corbyn addressing large (or large-ish) crowds. But by the last week, it was becoming painfully obvious that Labour's priority ought to be defending as many incumbents as possible rather than pretending to itself and its supporters that it was still in the business of making gains.

The contrast between the two parties in this respect was also reflected in the way they advertised on social media. As the fact-checking organisation Full Fact noted on the eve of polling day in the course of a piece analysing widespread claims that the Tories' content was far more misleading than Labour's:

> The Conservatives have focused on adverts that include their key election pledges and attack lines (many of which include fact checkable claims) and have released a larger number of adverts, many [with] relatively low sums of money spent on them.

Labour, by contrast, have focused more heavily on messages to activate their supporters—general sentiments or calls to action, rather than fact checkable claims. They have also put out fewer adverts overall, but have spent more heavily on some individual adverts than the Conservatives.[14]

The Tories 'little and often' ad strategy seemed to be borne out by figures coming from Google's ad library, which showed they had added some 201 ads compared to Labour's 68.[15] However, the same report noted that on:

Saturday, Sunday and Monday, the Conservatives splashed out on the masthead advert on YouTube's UK site. One message sent right across the country - the equivalent of buying a commercial slot in ITV's News at Ten 25 years ago. Those of you who wrote in certainly noticed. A clutch sent in screenshots, with a couple saying it was the first election ad they had seen. 'An ad for the Conservatives popped up as I looked for Bob the Builder videos for my son', wrote one.[16]

Shadow Chancellor John McDonnell fronted Labour's Monday media event, with a policy-heavy speech highlighting Labour's plans to renationalise utilities, set up a national investment bank and introduce a post-election budget to 'end austerity'. When asked by a journalist at the event whether he believed the Prime Minister was a liar, he replied: 'Of course ... I don't believe Boris Johnson has any moral compass whatsoever.' McDonnell further muddied the waters of Labour's Brexit messaging by indicating he would probably vote against any putative Labour Brexit deal, since he couldn't conceive of any Labour deal being a better option than Remain. Labour were now campaigning on a promise to negotiate a deal which all the most senior Shadow Cabinet ministers – John McDonnell, Emily Thornberry, Diane Abbott and Keir Starmer – had already indicated they would most likely oppose and on which their leader would remain neutral. As one advisor noted:

You end up in this absurd situation where any deal negotiated by Labour would be presented to the British public as an unwanted orphan, with the people who negotiated it campaigning against it and Jeremy himself saying nothing ... No one was going to campaign for it apart from Ian Lavery and Barry Gardiner.

Tuesday was a better day for the Tories. Johnson's afternoon visit to a JCB factory in Uttoxeter owned by the Conservative peer and arch Brexiteer Anthony Bamford produced one of the iconic images of the campaign when the PM drove one of the firm's machines, its bull-dozer bucket bearing the slogan 'Get Brexit Done', through a wall of Styrofoam bricks on which was stamped one word—'Gridlock'.[17] The stunt may have been crude, but it was nevertheless a novel and arresting way to convey an otherwise repetitive final message, as one advisor recalled:

> Good political campaigning does push on the boundaries ... because you're trying get your message out and, to keep on repeating stuff like Get Brexit Done, you need to come up with imaginative ways to do it. The reason we had the PM driving a digger through the wall was because that was on every single paper the next day and across all the bulletins ... We were accused of being macho and juvenile. But that is part of what you're trying to do, right? Come up with ways to get people's attention.

Delayed only by some Extinction Rebellion activists dressed as bees, who had glued themselves to his campaign bus, Johnson then set off across the country for more constituency visits, ending with shelf stacking with workers on the night shift in Warrington.

Johnson on a JCB (© Ben Stansall/Getty Images)

Tuesday did not go so well for Labour. It began well enough, with news that the party's video 'Mean Tweets with Jeremy Corbyn', featuring the Labour leader reading out critical tweets about himself, picking up around 1.5 million views on Twitter and 700,000 since its Monday evening release. There was also some media pick-up of Labour's dossier claiming patients in over 100 NHS trusts faced increased risks due to chronic underfunding.[18] Meanwhile, the party was determined to keep the Leeds Infirmary story going, spending tens of thousands promoting it with content that gained over two million impressions, attracting attention in particular from women 45 and under.[19]

However, thanks to right-wing website *Guido Fawkes*, things took a turn for the worse for Labour just before 10 am that morning.[20] Shadow Health Secretary Jonathan Ashworth was, to use his own words, 'stitched up like a kipper, played like a fiddle—whatever the right metaphor is' by a Tory friend who had recorded a phone conversation about the campaign. During it, Ashworth had told him (he claimed in jest, even when he talked about Corbyn being a security risk) that:

it's dire for Labour ... it's dire ... it's awful for them, and it's the combination of Corbyn and Brexit ... outside of the city seats ... it's abysmal out there... they can't stand Corbyn and they think Labour's blocked Brexit. I think middle-class graduates – Remainy people – Labour's doing well among ... but not in big enough numbers to deny the Tories a majority.

As a result, and much to the delight of Tory managers who feared another day dominated by photos of children waiting on A&E floors, Ashworth's planned tour of the studios instead turned into a series of embarrassing inquisitions. This was yet more proof that, as Norman Smith, the BBC's veteran Assistant Political Editor, put it, 'despite all the attempts by the parties to have a carefully choreographed campaign, events [come] in, wham, bam, at the last minute to knock them off course'.[21] All Jeremy Corbyn, campaigning in the afternoon in (Conservative-held) Carlisle and (Conservative-held) Morecambe, could do was assure reporters he was 'cool' with the whole thing and, as was his wont, continue to regale his adoring audiences of Labour activists with an inspirational quote about the NHS 'lasting as long as there's folk with faith left to fight for it' by Labour icon Nye Bevan—a quote fact-checking sites had already exposed as fake in the previous election campaign.[22]

Consolation for Labour came with the release of a slick social media video entitled 'Hope' early in the evening, then, later on in the evening, the release of YouGov's final MRP poll showing a tightening race.[23] YouGov's projection now had the Conservatives heading for a majority of 28, down 40 seats on the previous estimate, and with many seats too close to call. The impression that the election wasn't yet a done deal, conveyed, for instance, by the *Daily Mail*'s Wednesday morning headline 'Britain's Future Down to the Wire', was in many ways music to ears of Tory strategists, still privately confident of their own polling, but keen to avoid any complacency among Conservative voters.

As dawn broke (in fact, well before dawn broke) on the final day of campaigning, Boris Johnson was delivering milk to a house in Guiseley, West Yorkshire (albeit not before two bottles of milk already on the doorstep were hastily removed). But the Tories' early morning plans soon went awry again. Johnson's minders were unable to prevent him being approached as he loaded crates on to the van by *Good Morning Britain*'s Jonathan Swain, who was filming live as hosts Piers Morgan and Susanna Reid looked on back in the studio.[24] Johnson's bizarre response this time was to take refuge in a walk-in fridge with his staff, one of whom (the Conservatives' Head of Press Rob Oxley) uttered an expletive in front of the millions watching at home.[25] Cue myriad reports of the Prime Minister 'hiding in a fridge' to escape media scrutiny, the inevitable hashtag #fridgegate and a viral video clip which rapidly racked up hundreds of thousands of views. The incident dominated the morning campaign coverage, marginalising other party leaders including Nigel Farage, who, at his last appearance of the campaign, laid into the Tories' compromise deal with the EU, insisting (not wholly inaccurately, it turned out) that it would lead to further 'years of agonising negotiations'.

Jeremy Corbyn's morning hadn't begun quite so badly, with focus group discussions in Peterborough suggesting the NHS stories of the last few days were cutting through.[26] However, this was soon followed by news that 15 former Labour MPs had written an open letter urging voters not to back the party, citing its leader's record on anti-semitism, extremism and national security—a letter they planned to run as full-page ads in marginal seats across the North of England.[27] Corbyn began his last day of campaigning with a rally in Scotland alongside Labour's beleaguered Scottish leader Richard Leonard. Speaking in Glasgow, he majored once again on Labour's pledge to end austerity and save the

NHS, as well as (along with John McDonnell, who did the morning broadcast round) criticising the Tory campaign for serial obfuscation and deceits. Inevitably, however, the bigger draw north of the border was Nicola Sturgeon, making a photogenic trip to a greengrocer's and a florist's in Edinburgh, while pushing the message that 'The SNP is the main challenger to the Tories and voting for other parties risks helping the Tories' and seeing Scotland 'dragged out of Europe against our will'. It was a message she also hammered home in the evening during a televised debate with the other Scottish party leaders. It was unclear if this would be sufficient to power a repeat of the SNP's 2015 landslide—at least according to the former leader of the Scottish Conservatives, Ruth Davidson, who declared in that morning's *Daily Telegraph*: 'I will happily wager to strip naked on the banks of Loch Ness and subject myself to a Hogmanay wild swimming session should such a result occur, safe in the knowledge that my modesty (and others' eyeballs) will remain unmolested.'[28] Meanwhile, from Wales, Plaid Cymru's Adam Price managed to get a little media pick-up for his party's draft law which would make lying by politicians a criminal offence.

Jo Swinson, appearing (like Price) on the BBC's *Today* programme, did her best to again play down her party's unpopular revoke policy by talking about legislation for a second referendum, which she emphasised was now 'the most likely way to stop Brexit'. Stopping Brexit was also the theme of her first campaign stop with her deputy, Ed Davey, in his Kingston & Surbiton constituency. From there, she moved on to nearby strong pro-Remain targets Esher & Walton (held by Foreign Secretary Dominic Raab), Guildford and Wimbledon (where she appeared alongside drag queen Rose Zinfandel)—all seats the Lib Dems were hoping to capture from the Conservatives. Yet, while Swinson continued to campaign hard in target seats, the collapse in the party's polling numbers and her personal approval ratings had long ago dispelled the buoyant early campaign mood in Lib Dem HQ. Indeed, by that stage, the main goal was not to make gains, but to avert disaster. As one advisor recalled: 'In the final days it was like "if we hold seats, this is great". The writing was on the wall. There was a very clear trend.'

As for the Prime Minister, his photo-op caravan had moved on to a catering company in Derby where he was snapped putting the finishing touches to a beef and ale pie, which he then put into the oven before (in true *Blue Peter* style) removing an already cooked one: 'a perfect metaphor', he said, 'for what we're going to do in the run-up to Christmas if we can get a working majority. We have a deal. It's ready to go. You saw how easy it is, we put it in, slam it in the oven, take it out and there it is – get Brexit done'. From there it was a short plane hop to South Wales for a suitably festive photo-op at the factory said to supply wrapping paper and Christmas crackers to the Queen, and then on to a spot of doorstep campaigning in Essex and yet another photo-op—this time literally hammering home a 'get Brexit done' placard in a front garden in Benfleet.[29] Johnson then joined warm-up man Michael Gove in London for the Tories' final campaign rally at the 7,000-seat Copper Box arena in Hackney Wick.

Johnson hammers home the message in South Benfleet, 11 December 2019 (© Reuters/Alamy Stock Photo)

Corbyn, too, ended the day in the East End after trips to Middlesbrough South (which the Conservatives held the next day with a majority of over 12,000), Rother Valley (Conservative gain), Ashfield (Conservative gain) and Bedford (Labour hold). Returning to inner London to speak to a predictably adoring crowd in trendy Hoxton, he urged voters to 'shock the establishment, by voting for hope' and laid into Britain's billionaires. But while campaign organisers boasted that 'On Facebook Jeremy Corbyn and Labour achieved 86.2 million views on campaign videos, compared with only 24.5 million views for Boris Johnson and the Conservatives', Corbyn himself was enough of a traditional campaigner to realise that, on polling day at least, the ground war was what mattered most, declaring: 'Tomorrow we're out knocking on doors like our life depends on it'.[30]

The polling day weather in Britain's first winter election for a generation was wet and windy for most, with snow and ice in parts of rural Scotland and December downpours hitting much of the rest of the country. The usual reporting restrictions resulted in the usual stilted coverage, with broadcasters rotating through familiar sequences of polling stations setting up and party leaders casting their voters. Boris Johnson got in first, arriving at 8.30 am with his Jack Russell cross Dilyn to cast a ballot and pose for photos. Jeremy Corbyn was greeted at his polling station by a man dressed as the Sesame Street puppet Elmo when he arrived to vote shortly before 10 am. Jo Swinson and Nicola Sturgeon cast ballots without incident, and posed in front of frosty Scottish polling stations soon after. Reports of long morning queues in parts of London triggered familiar speculation about a possible turnout surge—speculation which, as in the past, proved largely unfounded.

All the parties privately expected a Conservative majority with internal speculations focused on how large this was going to be. Internal Conservative analysis pointed to a national swing of around 2.5 points from Labour to the Conservatives, and a firming up in the Conservative vote in target seats sufficient according to their MRP model to deliver upwards of 360 seats, a substantial majority. One Labour MP campaigning in the Red Wall concurred that the swing to the Conservatives came right at the end, reflecting the long hesitancy of voters who were, in many cases, breaking the habit of a lifetime:

> I had people in the last three days saying to me 'unfortunately, I'm going to have to vote Conservative for the first time in my life' ... They had to convince themselves first before they told you. And they weren't prepared to do that until the 11th hour. It was something they didn't really want to do.

'The Red Wall' (Morten Morland, *Sunday Times*, 10 December 2019 © Morten Morland)

The mood in CCHQ on election day was one of 'relief' according to one senior advisor, though relief tempered with continued caution: 'We could see the numbers broadly solidifying … we were broadly comfortable, but you still suspend belief.' These final day nerves reflected the scars of 2017, but also the stakes of the contest against a Labour leader whose politics many of them rejected utterly, as one aide recalled:

> It was so existential. It's not even just about delivering Brexit. [It's about] Jeremy Corbyn becoming Prime Minister. The Tory Party exists to stop people like Jeremy Corbyn becoming Prime Minister!

As the polls closed at 10 pm, the exit poll jointly commissioned by the BBC, ITV and Sky was published simultaneously by all three broadcasters. The results pointed to the largest Conservative majority in a generation, falling just short of the 100-seat majority threshold the broadcasters had set for calling their projection a 'landslide' victory. The figures broke down as follows:

Conservatives 368
Labour 191
SNP 55
SNP 55
Liberal Democrats 13
Plaid Cymru 3
Greens 1
Brexit Party 0
Others 18

The Prime Minister watched the announcement with senior advisors in the first floor study of 10 Downing Street. The initial reaction was one of disbelief at the scale of the win, which exceeded even the most optimistic predictions team members had made earlier in the evening: 'There was a stunned silence. Everyone was looking at the Labour numbers trying to work out what it meant.'[31] Then as the scale of the victory sank in, there was 'jubilation', with the Prime Minister 'pumping his fists like a footballer when they score a last-minute goal'. The reaction in CCHQ was similarly ecstatic 'an explosion of relief', one advisor recalls: 'I don't remember much about election night but I do remember singing "Things Can Only Get Better".'

The exit poll was also initially met with silence in Finsbury Park, where Jeremy Corbyn had gathered his most senior aides to watch the results in the offices of a non-governmental organisation (NGO) near his Islington home.[32] The mood was funereal. Many present already expected an awful night, but the exit poll still came as a shock, projecting Labour's worst seat total since 1935, a result at the bottom end of already pessimistic expectations. As one senior advisor recalled: 'It was like watching a slow-motion train crash ... nobody says anything in those circumstances. What was there to say?'[33]

Labour Party staffers had gathered at the party's Southside HQ that evening to monitor the results as they came in, using an automatic system the team had programmed to aggregate and analyse the intelligence emails they were receiving from counts all over the country. The results were projected on a big screen in one of the Southside offices and made for grim reading from the outset. As one Southsider recalled: 'It's hard to communicate how upset everyone was. It was just utterly grim ... Seeing that outcome it's just "Oh, God" ... It was a horrible miasma of doom.'

The exit poll projected a Conservative majority of 86, which if accurate would be their best performance since Margaret Thatcher's landslide of 1987. Labour's projected fall below 200 seats would be the worst showing since 1935, below even the post-war low ebb of 1983. Dozens of traditional Labour strongholds in the 'Red Wall' regions of the post-industrial Midlands and North were projected to fall, while the SNP were projected to surge again, taking seats from all of their competitors in a landslide rivalling 2015. On ITV, former Shadow Chancellor Ed Balls called the result a 'hammer blow for the Labour Party', while former Chancellor George Osborne declared the dawn of 'the Boris Johnson era of British politics'. On Sky, Conservative Vice Chairman James Cleverly attributed the result to 'fury in longstanding Labour seats in the Midlands and the North at both the Labour Party and Jeremy Corbyn. There was a feeling that the Labour Party had stopped talking to these communities', while Shadow Cabinet member Barry Gardiner bemoaned 'a devastating result for all the people who really needed a Labour victory to improve their lives'.

While the exit poll had a strong track record, its projection was still uncertain. In 2015, the exit poll's initial projection pointed to a hung parliament, yet by dawn on Friday the Conservatives had a majority as the toss-up seats all broke Cameron's way.[34] Many of the projected Conservative gains were narrow and uncertain at the time of publication, so there was again much potential for the picture to change as the night wore on. Meanwhile in Scotland, the projection of another SNP landslide was even more uncertain, reflecting the volatility of Scottish four-party politics and the limited number of sampling points available for the exit poll to capture it. Exit poll impresario Sir John Curtice urged Scottish voters to be cautious and patient: 'Scotland is the bit of the exit poll about which we are least confident.' All eyes therefore turned to the early counts for signs of the story to come.

Newcastle Central was the first seat to declare at 11.26 pm, 25 minutes later than in 2017, and again narrowly ahead of local rivals Houghton & Sunderland South, which declared two minutes later. Both seats were held by their Labour incumbents, but with large swings to the Conservatives. Bridget Phillipson's majority in Houghton & Sunderland South was slashed from 12,000 to just over 3,000.[35] The real hammer blow for Labour came minutes later, when Blyth Valley declared. A Northumberland mining seat where Ronnie Campbell, a former miner and National Union of Mineworkers (NUM) official himself, was standing down after over three decades in the Commons, Blyth Valley and its predecessor seats had returned Labour MPs in every election since 1931.

At 11.31 pm, the returning officer declared Ian Levy, a former Newcastle healthcare assistant, to be Blyth Valley's first Conservative MP in three generations (and only its third in 250 years) with a 712 vote majority. The Conservative vote rose 5.8 points, but Labour's plunged by 15 points, producing an overall ten-point swing. On ITV, George Osborne called Blyth Valley 'a spectacular win' and Professor Colin Rallings observed that if the large early swings against Labour were repeated, it 'could take us all the way off the end of the battle board and into some very safe Labour seats'.

Broadcasters and party spokespeople had a long interval to digest the stunning Blyth Valley result, with just two additional declarations following in the next hour.[36] On the BBC, Sir Nicholas Soames, the scion of the Churchill dynasty briefly evicted from the Conservative Party by Boris Johnson for his rebellions on Brexit, called the result a 'watershed' and admitted 'this is a different Conservative Party'. Labour MP Gareth Snell, speaking from the count in the Stoke constituency he expected to lose, blamed 'a toxic combination of the Labour Party trying to stop Brexit and … Jeremy Corbyn'. On ITV, George Osborne called Corbyn 'the handmaiden to a Boris Johnson landslide … Every Tory I know was cheering when he got elected as leader of the Labour Party and they have been cheering ever since'. There was also a heated factional dispute between veterans of the Labour left (Jon Lansman) and right (Alan Johnson):

> *Lansman*: Jeremy Corbyn has achieved a great deal. He has changed the narrative on austerity.
>
> *Johnson*: The working classes have always been a big disappointment for Jon and his cult. Corbyn was a disaster on the doorstep. Everyone knew he couldn't lead the working class out of a paper bag.

A familiar refrain was already emerging from allies of the Labour leadership as the early results rolled out—the defeat was about Brexit, not Labour's policies or voters' views of Corbyn. Variations on this theme were offered by John McDonnell on the BBC, Owen Jones, Ash Sarkar and Jon Lansman on ITV, and Dawn Butler and Richard Burgon on Sky. Similar claims were made in a LOTO briefing, allegedly authored by Seumas Milne, which leaked shortly before declarations began, urging Labour spokespeople to frame the result as 'overwhelmingly down to … Brexit' while defending Labour's 'highly popular' manifesto. Corbyn critics and New Labour veterans in the broadcast studios were not buying it. Ed Balls observed on ITV that 'the idea that this is only about Brexit … is not going to wash at all'. Ian Murray, Corbynsceptic Labour MP for Edinburgh South, tweeted: 'Every door I knocked on …mentioned Corbyn. Not Brexit but Corbyn … We've let the country down and we must change course and fast.'[37] With only a few seats declared, Labour's factional battle over the meaning of the defeat was already beginning.

The first result from the South of England came at 12.29 am from Swindon North, a Labour-held marginal in the New Labour years but now a safe Conservative seat.[38] There was another substantial swing to the Conservatives in this wealthier, more suburban and Remain-leaning seat, with the party increasing its vote by 5.5 points and nearly doubling its majority to 16,000 as the Labour vote slumped. The pattern was replicated soon after in Nuneaton, where the Conservative majority in the one-time West Midlands battleground seat shot up to over 10,000. The road back for Labour in seats which had returned Labour MPs in the Blair years was looking long indeed.

Rutherglen & Hamilton West, which Labour had recaptured from the SNP in 2017, was the first Scottish seat to declare at 1.24 am. Margaret Ferrier, the defeated SNP candidate from 2017, took the seat on a five-point swing. The seven-point rise in the SNP vote was a little below the exit poll's initial predictions, suggesting it would a long night for all the parties in Scotland's many marginal seats.

Things went from bad to worse for Labour in the Midlands and North as the night unfolded. Workington, held by Labour in general elections since 1918 and a seat which acquired totemic status in the campaign thanks to Conservative think-tank Onward's creation of 'Workington Man', fell to the Conservatives on a swing of nearly ten points. Soon after, Labour Party chair Ian Lavery barely held on in Wansbeck, where a swing of over 11 points slashed his majority slashed from 10,000 to just 800. Leigh, former seat of Greater Manchester Mayor Andy Burnham and Labour since 1922, fell to the Conservatives at 2 am on a 12-point swing. Seat after seat in the historically Labour, heavily Leave-voting 'Red Wall' fell with massive swings. Others, such as Ed Miliband in Doncaster North and Yvette Cooper in Normanton, Pontefract & Castleford, held on despite collapsing support as Leave votes divided between the Conservatives and the Brexit Party.[39]

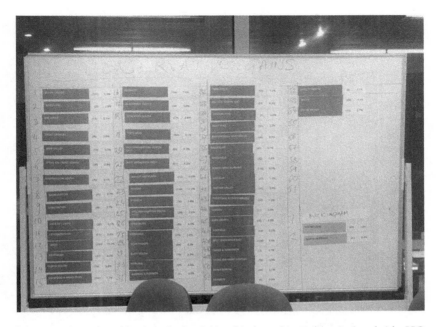

'The morning after the night before' (A whiteboard in Labour's Southside HQ, where the party kept track of seats about to change hands using real-time sampling data from across the country, showing the scale of the defeat)

The first declarations from Wales arrived just before 2 am, with the Conservatives capturing both Vale of Clwyd and Wrexham. The result in Wrexham, which had been held by Labour since 1935, in particular confirmed that the Conservatives' appeal to Leave voters was also working in traditionally Labour parts of Wales. However, the swing in both seats was under six points, considerably below the equivalent swing recorded in more Leave-leaning English seats, suggesting 2019 would not end the long Conservative run of weaker performances in Wales.[40]

The first London declaration in Putney at 1.54 am was Labour's only gain of the night, as Fleur Anderson took a seat held since 2005 by former frontbencher Justine Greening, who was retiring from the Commons, on a swing of 6.4 points. Putney epitomised the divergence of prosperous, diverse and heavily Remain-voting big-city seats from the rest of the country[41]: 23 of the 25 seats in England and Wales with 2019 swings to

Labour were Remain-voting, while 16 of 25 were in big cities or university towns. As Professor Colin Rallings observed on ITV after the result came in from Putney: 'London really is another country now, electorally.'

Jeremy Corbyn speaks after the results are announced for the Islington North constituency (© PA Images/Alamy Stock Photo)

Jeremy Corbyn was elected for a tenth term as Labour MP for Islington North at 3.17 am. By this point, it was clear that Labour's defeat would be nearly as heavy as the exit poll had indicated, with the party's Commons cohort falling to its lowest level in generations. Earlier in the night, Corbyn had discussed how he should personally respond to the defeat with his most senior aides. They agreed Corbyn had to resign, but that standing down immediately, as his predecessor Ed Miliband had done in 2015, would be a mistake. Therefore, Corbyn would remain in post during the leadership election process. While they correctly anticipated some critics would attack this as a refusal to take personal responsibility for defeat, Corbyn and his aides strongly believed that Ed Miliband's immediate resignation at the 2015 count had been a mistake, leaving the party rudderless and chaotic at the start of a new Parliament. Corbyn, the chief internal beneficiary of the 2015 chaos, now sought to engineer a smoother transition of power for his successor.[42] Speaking at his count, he was defiant to the end, criticising the media for 'disgusting attacks' and insisting that the policies in Labour's 'manifesto of hope' were 'extremely popular', but 'Brexit has so polarised and divided debate in this country that it has overridden … normal political debate.' He then officially confirmed he would not lead the party in any future general election, but would not resign immediately, instead proposing to lead the party for an unspecified further period to facilitate a 'process of reflection'.

'Period of reflection' (Christian Adams, *Evening Standard*, 13 December 2019 © Christian Adams)

Half an hour later, the broadcasters cut to Uxbridge & South Ruislip, where Boris Johnson, flanked by Lord Buckethead, Count Binface, Yace 'Interplanetary Time Lord' Yogenstein and a fathers' rights activist dressed as Elmo from Sesame Street, was re-elected as Conservative MP. Johnson told those attending the count that his 'one nation Conservative government' had been given:

a powerful new mandate. To get Brexit done! And not just to get Brexit done but to unite this country and to take it forward and to focus on the priorities of the British people, above all on the NHS ... Above all, I want to thank the people of this country for turning out to vote in a December election that we didn't want to call, but that I think will turn out to be a historic election. That gives us now in this new government the chance to respect the democratic will of the people, to change this country for the better, and to unleash the potential of the entire people of this country. And that is what we will now do ... That work will begin today.

Boris Johnson speaks from the count at Uxbridge, with vanquished competitors including Lord Buckethead and Count Binface looking on (© Alamy/Stock Photo)

Johnson's campaign had gambled that a united Leave vote would prevail over a fragmented Remain vote. Declarations in two Remain-leaning seats immediately before and after his own result underscored both the risks and the payoffs from that gamble. Minutes before Johnson's result was announced, his Foreign Secretary Dominic Raab narrowly held off a massive Liberal Democrat surge in his 60% Remain seat of Esher & Walton. Then just after the Uxbridge announcement, Liberal Democrat leader Jo Swinson, who had staked everything on a radical Remain stance, lost her own seat to the SNP by fewer than 150 votes, on an 80% turnout. At both ends of the country, unified support for the nationalist causes of Leave and Scottish independence was triumphing over the fragmented support of their opponents. Speaking at her count, Swinson warned that the 'wave of nationalism that is sweeping both sides of the border' would bring 'dread and dismay' for 'millions of people in our country'.

With a thumping Conservative majority no longer in doubt, broadcasters' attention turned to the challenges that now faced the Prime Minister as he returned to Downing Street with a new mandate, and the massive rebuilding task ahead for Labour. Michael Gove, speaking to the BBC at 4 am, set a high bar for the new government by promising it would act 'not only to honour the Brexit mandate but also to heal the divisions in our society'. The prospects for such healing looked dim to SNP leader Nicola Sturgeon, speaking minutes later: 'Scotland has sent a very clear message. We don't want a Boris Johnson-led Conservative government. We don't want to leave the European Union. And we want Scotland's future to be in Scotland's hands.' Johnson had labelled his a 'One Nation' Conservative government. Whether he would be able hold that nation together was clearly now an open question.

Down in London, Johnson gave the first of two victory speeches to staff in CCHQ early on Friday morning. Not only had they, the Prime Minister told them, 'routed the doubters and confounded the gloomsters' by securing 'a huge great stonking mandate' to get Brexit done and fulfil 'the will of the British people', they had also helped ensure that the Conservative Party now represented every part of the country. As such, it was in a great position to deliver its 'one nation agenda' of 'fantastic public services' and 'unleashing Britain's potential'.[43] The one-nation theme ('We're going to unite and level up') was also prominent in the later, rather more sober, address to the nation delivered on the steps of Number 10. Johnson promised his government would 'repay the trust' of those voters who had switched to the Conservatives and would seek to build a friendly relationship with the EU, with London and Brussels treating each other as 'sovereign equals'. 'Let the healing', he declared, 'begin.'[44]

'The Lying King' (Martin Rowson, *The Guardian*, 13 December 2019 © Martin Rowson)

After that, Johnson wasted no time in rubbing salt in Labour's wounds by travelling up to Tony Blair's old seat of Sedgefield, now held by the Conservatives for the first time since 1931, as well as by having his spinners brief the media that he had 'called in senior civil servants ... and announced that the whole government had to shift its focus to improving the lives of the working-class voters in the north of England who backed Brexit and switched to the Tories'.[45]

Jeremy Corbyn confirmed at his Islington count that he would not lead Labour into the next election, but the 'process of reflection' he had called for was not getting off to the best of starts. The wounds of defeat were raw, and internal critics unhappy at Corbyn's failure to resign there and then were further enraged by more repetition of the claims that Labour's 'manifesto for hope' and 'extremely popular' policies had 'won the argument', and that Labour's defeat was 'mainly about Brexit'. In a short statement issued on Saturday morning, Corbyn showed little contrition about the dreadful result and offered no apology to the many Labour MPs who had lost their seats. This in turn triggered a wave of calls, led by London Mayor Sadiq Khan, for the Labour leader to go as soon as possible.

An op-ed under Corbyn's byline in Sunday's *The Observer* went down similarly poorly. While at least mentioning, albeit briefly and in passing, his own responsibility for defeat, Corbyn doubled down on Brexit as the primary explanation for the election result, amplified, he claimed, by 'billionaire-owned and influenced hostility' from the media.[46] Factional opponents within Labour saw Corbyn's arguments as designed to make the case that left radical politics was still Labour's best electoral option, thus preparing the ground for a Corbynite successor in the leadership contest to come. Labour's most successful election-winner Tony Blair took a very different view, perhaps also with the succession in mind, when he declared a few days later that Labour under Corbyn had become 'a glorified protest movement with cult trimmings' and a 'combination of ideology and terminal ineptitude'.[47] While past and present Labour leaders argued, the contest to come was already heating up, with Keir Starmer, Rebecca Long-Bailey, Lisa Nandy and Emily Thornberry in the frame as potential candidates—a list to which Jess Phillips and Clive Lewis were soon added.[48] In the meantime, 'Labour Together'—a new grouping bringing together MPs and activists from across the ideological spectrum, with one eye to the post-Corbyn succession—announced an inquiry into what had gone wrong in the 2019 election that would seek to draw on evidence and reflections from all Labour's factions.[49] While a thorough post-mortem seemed unlikely to unite a fractured party, the prospect of one at least addressed one of the errors of 2017—the failure to systematically analyse the election result and properly interrogate simplistic narratives about what had happened. However, enlightened analysis was not the only motive in play. The review offered a platform for politicians and advisors looking for influence in the coming post-Corbyn era, while also providing an outlet for longstanding Southside Corbyn critics silenced by the relative success of 2017 to air long-running grievances about Corbyn's LOTO, not least because of the threat of job losses now hanging over them.[50]

Disappointment among Liberal Democrat staffers and activists at a poor result was also widely shared, though the internal atmosphere was less toxic. Jo Swinson, who had stepped down immediately on learning that she had lost her seat (and would be replaced in the interim jointly by Ed Davey, her Deputy, and Sal Brinton, the party's President), made an emotional speech in which, while she defended trying to stop Brexit by standing on a revoke platform, she took responsibility (and apologised) for the poor result.[51]

The other big winner of the night was the SNP's leader Nicola Sturgeon.[52] Although the SNP's 48-seat haul was a little below the initial exit poll projection of 55 seats, this was still a remarkable result, giving the party an overwhelming majority of Scotland's 59 seats. Sturgeon moved quickly to frame this resurgence as a renewed and strengthened mandate for a second Scottish independence referendum—a claim soon countered by Downing Street briefings that the Prime Minister had 'reiterated his unwavering commitment' to the union in a phone call with the First Minister.[53] The arguments on both sides soon spilled over into the tabloids and looked set to run and run through the next Parliament.[54]

Further constitutional wrangling and upheaval also looked likely in Northern Ireland. Though she was betrayed by Boris Johnson effectively agreeing a border in the Irish Sea with the EU and although the DUP lost seats at the election, Arlene Foster looked to be in no danger (or at least imminent danger) of losing her job as the party's leader.[55] The need to shore up her position may have been one of the factors that delayed the conclusion of long-running negotiations—facilitated by the UK and Irish governments—to get the Northern Ireland Executive back up and running.[56] Although talks ran through into the new year, the Executive did at last return in January 2020 after a three-year hiatus (see Chapter 12, pp. 450–451).

That deal, while important, was not the first priority of the new government. Johnson wasted no time bringing back to Parliament the Withdrawal Agreement Bill that his majority would now allow him to pass comfortably. He retracted the concessions offered to ease its passage in the previous session and added a new clause making it difficult for ministers, let alone Parliament, to extend the transition period due to end on 31 December 2021—a wise move, given reports that new MPs were swiftly swelling the ranks of the Brexit ultras' brotherhood, the European Research Group(ERG). Whether new Conservative MPs approved of the government's decision to boycott particular news and current affairs shows such as BBC Radio 4's flagship *Today* programme— allegedly to bring them to heel after what the Prime Minister's advisors saw as its anti-Tory bias during the election—is less clear.[57] The same could be said for MPs' attitudes to the many pre-Christmas briefings of plans being dreamed up by Johnson's supposedly all-powerful Chief Advisor, Dominic Cummings, first, to shake up Whitehall and reduce the size of Cabinet and, second, to involve himself in the upcoming Defence Review.[58]

However, there did seem to be widespread support among Tory MPs, old and new, for the Queen's Speech laying out the government's programme, delivered to a packed House of Commons a week after the election. Johnson's commitment to the NHS was symbolised by a bill enshrining in law his government's planned spending increase, while his one-nation credentials were burnished with a bill aimed at outlawing no-fault evictions by landlords. Tougher sentencing and release provisions for terrorists were promised, as well as new legislation to beef up the powers of the security and intelligence services. Meanwhile, trade unions were to be prevented from causing chaos on the country's train network. The speech also flagged up a Constitution, Democracy and Rights Commission, which opponents feared would weaken checks and balances, and a plan to repeal the Fixed-term Parliaments Act, restoring to the government the automatic power to call elections when it believed the time was right rather than every five years.[59] Parliament adjourned for the Christmas recess the next day, and MPs returned home to recover from a gruelling winter campaign. As they recuperated over the New Year, reports began to emerge of a mysterious new virus striking down citizens in the Chinese city of Wuhan.

NOTES

1. Steven Swinford and Kate Devlin, 'Election 2019: Johnson to Blitz Seats in Labour Heartlands', *The Times*, 9 December 2019, https://www. thetimes.co.uk/article/election-2019-johnson-to-blitz-seats-in-labour-heartlands-c86vmzslk.
2. See Priti Patel, 'The Tories Will Do What It Takes to Keep Britain Safe', *Daily Telegraph*, 8 December 2019, https://www.telegraph.co.uk/ politics/2019/12/08/tories-will-do-takes-keep-britain-safe; and Kate Ferguson, Murder Danger: Labour's Soft Stance on Stop and Search Could Lead to Extra Killing a Week, Tories Warn', *The Sun*, 8 December 2019, https://www.thesun.co.uk/news/10510284/labours-soft-stance-on-stop-and-search-could-lead-to-extra-killing-a-week-tories-warn.
3. Laura Kuenssberg, 'DUP Could Matter in a Big Way', *BBC News* election live blog, 8.38 am, 9 December 2019, https://www.bbc.co.uk/news/ live/election-2019-50707285/page/10.
4. See Paul Byrne, 'Little Boy with Suspected Pneumonia Forced to Sleep on Hospital Floor Due to Lack of Beds', *Daily Mirror*, 9 December

2019, https://www.mirror.co.uk/news/politics/little-boy-pneumonia-forced-sleep-21053225; and 'Boris Johnson Takes ITV Reporter's Phone After Refusing to Look at Photo of Boy on Hospital Floor', *ITV News*, 9 December 2019, https://www.itv.com/news/calendar/2019-12-09/boris-johnson-takes-itv-reporter-s-phone-after-refusing-to-look-at-photo-of-boy-on-hospital-floor.

5. See Chris Smyth and Oliver Wright, 'Voters Lose Interest in "Get Brexit Done" Pledge', *The Times*, 11 December 2019, https://www.thetimes.co.uk/edition/news/voters-lose-interest-in-get-brexit-done-pledge-dtzc9m78x.

6. See Ross McGuinness, 'Top BBC Journalist Says Sorry for Wrongly Tweeting That Labour Activist Punched Tory Adviser at Leeds Hospital', *Yahoo! News*, 10 December 2019, https://uk.news.yahoo.com/laura-kuenssberg-says-sorry-for-wrongly-tweeting-that-labour-activist-punched-tory-adviser-110952226.html.

7. See https://twitter.com/marcowenjones/status/1204183081009262592?s=20.

8. Conservatives, 'Boris Johnson's Funny *Love Actually* Parody', *YouTube*, 9 December 2019, https://youtu.be/nj-YK3JJCIU.

9. 'Creative, Actually: "Digi Kiwis" Lift the Lid on Boris Johnson's Video Masterstroke', *Sydney Morning Herald*, 18 December 2019, https://www.smh.com.au/world/europe/creative-actually-digi-kiwis-lift-the-lid-on-boris-johnson-s-video-masterstroke-20191216-p53kk6.html.

10. Conservatives, 'Boris and Stanley Johnson Made Some Mince Pies and It Was Brilliant', *YouTube*, 24 December 2019, https://www.youtube.com/watch?v=OuaQDxEWRlA.

11. This was, however, the only Conservative video to feature in the top 10 most-viewed campaign videos on social media. The other nine were all Labour or Momentum videos, led by a montage of inequality footage from Jeremy Corbyn's personal page entitled 'If you're not sure who to vote for, watch this', which was viewed 11.6 million times, more than four times the views achieved by the 'Boris, Actually' video.

12. Conservatives, 'Stop the Chaos. Get Brexit Done. Vote Conservative', *YouTube*, 9 December 2019, https://youtu.be/izCQOp6HS6k.

13. John Crace, 'Corbyn Plays All the Old Favourites in Bristol But No One's Dancing', *The Guardian*, 9 December 2019, https://www.theguardian.com/politics/2019/dec/09/corbyn-plays-all-the-old-favourites-in-bristol-but-no-ones-dancing.

14. 'The Facts Behind Labour and Conservative Facebook Ads in This Election', *Full Fact*, 11 December 2019, https://fullfact.org/election-2019/ads. For more on misleading ads, see also Joe Tidy and Rachel Schraer, 'General Election 2019: Ads Are "Indecent, Dishonest and

Untruthful"', *BBC News*, 17 December 2019, https://www.bbc.co.uk/news/technology-50726500.

15. Rory Cellan-Jones, 'Do Social Media Ads Work, Are They Fair?' *BBC News*, 11 December 2019, https://www.bbc.co.uk/news/technology-50734805.

16. For 'masthead takeover', see https://twitter.com/WhoTargetsMe/status/1204006527838904322?s=20. It usually means the ad buyer gets a big banner ad and an autoplaying video (with the sound off). It also means the same video often shows up as pre-roll on other videos elsewhere. It's not very targeted (although a lot of people, of course, visit the YouTube homepage), but you do get millions of impressions for your money—not bad for a spend of under £100,000 per day. See also 'Party Spending Race during #GE2019', https://whotargets.me/en/party-spending-race.

17. https://twitter.com/BorisJohnson/status/1204454731193688065?s=20.

18. Researchers in Southside had done a lot of work developing this story, and some campaign staff were frustrated that more was not done to promote it.

19. https://twitter.com/WhoTargetsMe/status/1204432032505442306?s=20.

20. 'Ashworth: Civil Service Machine Will Have to Move Quickly to Safeguard National Security from Corbyn', *Guido Fawkes*, 10 December 2019, https://order-order.com/2019/12/10/ashworth-civil-service-machine-will-move-quickly-safeguard-national-security-corbyn.

21. Norman Smith, 'Analysis: Parties Knocked Off Course Despite Choreographed Campaign', *BBC News* election liveblog, 10 December 2019, https://www.bbc.co.uk/news/live/election-2019-50722828/page/5.

22. Martin Belam, 'Jeremy Corbyn's Nye Bevan Quote is Pure Fiction', *The Guardian*, 17 May 2017, https://www.theguardian.com/politics/2017/may/17/jeremy-corbyn-tweets-fake-nye-bevan-quote-on-fighting-for-the-nhs.

23. https://twitter.com/jeremycorbyn/status/1204460519278563328?s=20.

24. Note that Johnson wasn't the only leader who refused appearances—unlike Johnson, for instance, Corbyn refused an invitation to appear on BBC Radio 5 Live's *Election Call* programme. It is also worth noting that Johnson consented to being interviewed on other shows and channels—including an appearance on talkRADIO which went out on the last day of the campaign.

25. Talia Shadwell, 'Boris Johnson Hides in Fridge to Avoid Questions as Aide Swears at GMB Reporter', *Daily Mirror*, 11 December 2019, https://www.mirror.co.uk/news/politics/breaking-boris-johnson-hides-fridge-21070803.

26. Rachel Wearmouth, '"Dear Boris, Please Don't Privatise the NHS": Undecided Voters in Key Marginal Back Corbyn', *HuffPost*, 10 December 2019, https://www.huffingtonpost.co.uk/entry/boris-privatise-nhs-corbyn-peterborough-general-election_uk_5deed5ade4b-05d1e8a56b2ef. See also Matt Chorley and Anna Lombardi, 'NHS Is Key Issue of the General Election, According to Google', *The Times*, 11 December 2019, https://www.thetimes.co.uk/article/nhs-is-key-issue-of-the-general-election-according-to-google-bl2qtxbbc.

27. The open letter was actually one of two that Corbyn had to cope with on the last day of the campaign. The other came from over 100 families of victims of IRA violence demanding a meeting with him to discuss his 'affinity with terrorist groups'. See Joe Murphy, 'IRA Victims Ask to Meet Labour Leader Jeremy Corbyn over His "Affinity with Terrorist Groups"', *Evening Standard*, 11 December 2019, https://www.standard.co.uk/news/politics/ira-labour-jeremy-corbyn-a4310711.html.

28. Ruth Davidson, 'I'll Go Skinny-Dipping in Loch Ness if the SNP Win Big on Thursday', *Daily Telegraph*, 11 December 2020.

29. 'Johnson Urges Tories to Do "National Duty' as General Election Race Tightens', *Express & Star*, 11 December 2019, https://www.expressand-star.com/news/uk-news/2019/12/11/johnson-urges-tories-to-do-national-duty-as-general-election-race-tightens.

30. Ian Lavery, 'Labour Runs Most Successful Election Social Media Campaign Ever Seen', 11 December 2019, https://labour.org.uk/press/labour-runs-most-successful-election-social-media-campaign-ever-seen.

31. Communications Director Lee Cain predicted a majority of 30, while Johnson himself announced he 'had a dream the night before' where the Conservatives won a majority of 45. Dominic Cummings was, characteristically, most bullish, predicting a majority of 68. Tim Shipman, 'Sedgefield Fell—Then They Erupted into Song: Things Can Only Get Better!' *The Times*, 15 December 2019, https://www.thetimes.co.uk/article/sedgefield-fell-and-they-erupted-into-song-things-can-only-get-better-9cjfz9hj8.

32. In 2017, Corbyn and his inner circle had watched the exit poll announcement from his Islington home. His house was small and easily accessible from a public road, making access difficult and privacy impossible. A larger and more private venue was chosen for 2019, enabling more aides to join together with Corbyn and watch the results.

33. The 'slow-motion train crash' referred as much to the weeks and months preceding election night as to the night itself, with Labour advisors aware of the disastrous trajectory the party was on, yet unable to agree a way to change course.

34. However, the exit poll model did suggest all along that a Conservative majority was a real possibility, which is why the prediction made at 10 pm was not of a 'hung parliament', but instead that the Conservatives would be the largest party.

35. This result was the point when the magnitude of the defeat to come became clear to Southside staff. As one recalled: 'Once we got Bridget [Phillipson]'s result we knew we were fucked.'

36. Sunderland Central declared at 12.10 am and showed the same pattern as the other North East seats, with a big fall in Labour vote share (−13.3%), a modest rise in Conservative vote share (+2.1%) and a substantial vote for the Brexit Party candidate (11.6%). Labour also slumped by 15% in Middlesbrough, though Labour MP Andy McDonald comfortably held the very safe seat.

37. https://twitter.com/IanMurrayMP/status/1205271817839095810?s=20.

38. Swindon North had provided the first indications in 2015 that the Conservatives might do rather better than the exit poll had indicated (Philip Cowley and Dennis Kavanagh, *The British General Election of 2015*, Palgrave Macmillan, 2015, p. 218). This time the dismal result for Labour and the strong Tory showing was broadly in line with exit poll expectations.

39. For analysis of how the Brexit Party may have saved many Labour MPs, see Chapter 13.

40. See Roger Awan-Scully, '1859 and All That: The Enduring Failure of Welsh Conservatism', in Philip Cowley and Robert Ford (eds), *Sex, Lies and the Ballot Box*. Biteback, 2015.

41. Organisation as well as demographics may have helped Labour in the big-city seats. Momentum were a much larger and more active presence in such seats, and Labour sources believe the stronger party presence on the ground made a difference.

42. Some aides also held out hope that a longer and more orderly transition process would improve the chances of a Corbyn loyalist emerging as a frontrunner for the succession, and consolidating support from the membership.

43. For an audio recording, complete with chanting and cheering, see 'Listen: "A Huge Great Stonking Mandate". The Prime Minister's Victory Speech

at CCHQ', *ConservativeHome*, 13 December 2019, https://www.conservativehome.com/video/2019/12/listen-a-huge-great-stonking-mandate-the-prime-ministers-victory-speech-at-cchq.html.

44. A video of the speech is available at *ConservativeHome*: 'Watch: "I Urge Everyone to Find Closure and Let the Healing Begin"—Johnson's Downing Street Speech in Full', 13 December 2019, https://www. conservativehome.com/video/2019/12/watch-i-urge-everyone-to-find-closure-and-to-let-the-healing-begin-johnsons-downing-street-speech-in-full.html.

45. Tim Shipman, 'Now for the Boris Johnson Revolution: PM to Wield Axe in Radical Cabinet Reshuffle', *Sunday Times*, 15 December 2019, https://www.thetimes.co.uk/edition/news/now-for-the-boris-johnson-revolution-pm-to-wield-axe-on-cabinet-0cpdldlk6.

46. Jeremy Corbyn, 'We Won the Argument, But I Regret We Didn't Convert That into a Majority for Change', *The Guardian*, 14 December 2019, https://www.theguardian.com/politics/2019/dec/14/we-won-the-argument-but-i-regret-we-didnt-convert-that-into-a-majority-for-change.

47. Archie Mitchell, 'Tony Blair: Labour Must Be Rescued from the Far Left', *CityAM*, 18 December 2019, https://www.cityam.com/tony-blair-labour-must-be-rescued-from-the-far-left.

48. See Rowena Mason and Peter Walker, 'Jeremy Corbyn "Very Sad" at Election Defeat But Feels Proud of Manifesto', *The Guardian*, 13 December 2019, https://www.theguardian.com/politics/2019/dec/13/jeremy-corbyn-very-sad-at-election-defeat-but-feels-proud-of-manifesto.

49. The commission heading the review was a broad church including Ed Miliband, Corbyn's predecessor as Labour leader; Lucy Powell, one of Miliband's closest allies; James Meadway, a former economic advisor to John McDonnell; Ellie Mae O'Hagen, a prominent Corbynite journalist; Jo Platt, the Labour MP defeated in Leigh; and Mary Wimbury, the defeated Labour candidate in Wrexham. See Kate Proctor, 'Labour Election Inquiry Will Not Recommend Leadership Candidate', *The Guardian*, 23 December 2019, https://www.theguardian.com/politics/2019/dec/23/labour-election-inquiry-will-not-recommend-leadership-candidate.

50. Francis Elliott and Henry Zeffman, 'Election 2019: Chaos and Dejection Inside Labour Campaign HQ', *The Times*, 14 December 2019, https://www.thetimes.co.uk/edition/news/election-2019-chaos-and-dejection-inside-london-campaign-hq-s22dhlzb0.

51. See Peter Walker, '"Devastated" Jo Swinson Apologises to Lib Dems for Election Failure', *The Guardian*, 13 December 2019, https://www.theguardian.com/politics/2019/dec/13/devastated-jo-swinson-apologises-lib-dems-election-failure.

52. For Sturgeon's live reaction, see https://www.youtube.com/watch?v=AS4kaxRJYqU.

53. 'General Election 2019: PM Johnson "Remains Opposed" to Holding Indyref2', *BBC News*, 14 December 2019, https://www.bbc.co.uk/news/election-2019-50789771.

54. Alex Matthews, '"Absolutely Not": Michael Gove Rules Out Second Scottish Independence Referendum as SNP Accuse Tories of Raging against Reality', *The Sun*, 15 December 2019, https://www.thesun.co.uk/news/politics/10556212/michael-gove-rules-out-second-scottish-independence-vote-as-snp-accuse-tories-of-raging-against-reality. See also Carly Read, 'Britons Furious as SNP Claim Westminster "Not Needed" for Independence Vote—"Wrong!"', *Daily Express*, 18 December 2019, https://www.express.co.uk/news/politics/1218506/Nicola-Sturgeon-news-Scotland-independence-indyref2-general-election-Boris-Johnson.

55. Suzanne Breen, 'DUP Insists No Plans to Ditch Arlene Foster as MP Sir Jeffrey Donaldson Fails to Back Her', *Belfast Telegraph*, 13 December 2019, https://www.belfasttelegraph.co.uk/news/politics/general-election-2019/dup-insists-no-plans-to-ditch-arlene-foster-as-mp-sir-jeffrey-donaldson-fails-to-back-her-38783875.html.

56. Arthur Beesley, 'Northern Ireland Talks on Resuming Stormont Put on Pause', *Financial Times*, 20 December 2019, https://www.ft.com/content/5494fd7a-236c-11ea-b8a1-584213ee7b2b.

57. Matthew Taylor and Jim Waterson, 'Boris Johnson Threatens BBC with Two-Pronged Attack', *The Guardian*, 15 December 2019, https://www.theguardian.com/media/2019/dec/15/boris-johnson-threatens-bbc-with-two-pronged-attack.

58. See, for example, Steven Swinford, 'Dominic Cummings: Whitehall in Fear of "Valentine's massacre"', *The Times*, 21 December 2019, https://www.thetimes.co.uk/edition/news/dominic-cummings-whitehall-in-fear-of-valentines-massacre-wb27gdwsj; and Helen Warrell, 'UK's Military Seeks New Place in World After Brexit', *Financial Times*, 23 December 2019, https://www.ft.com/content/ee18fbdc-2343-11ea-92da-f0c92e957a96.

59. The need for this power was not obvious given that only one of the three elections held since the passage of the 2011 Fixed-term Parliament's Act had followed its intended timetable, while the most recent 2019 election had underlined how easy it was to bypass the Act's restrictions with a simple majority election bill.

CHAPTER 8

The Polls: Redemption?

Just six months before the general election, the polls had got it badly wrong in May's European Parliament elections, over-estimating support for the Conservatives, Labour and the Brexit Party, and understating late surges for the Liberal Democrats and the Greens. With memories of recent polling misses still remembered, this prompted renewed concerns that British polling had finally had its day, unable any longer to accurately capture the rapidly shifting sands of the public mood. Yet on the morning of 13 December 2019, Britain's pollsters were vindicated, accurately anticipating a big Conservative win, and banishing memories of the disaster of 2015 and the mixed performance in 2017.

This triumph came in an exceptionally difficult context. The period between the 2017 and 2019 elections saw a strange combination of at first relative stability of the polls and later on, in the second half of the Parliament, unprecedented polling volatility. In the year and a half following the 2017 election, support for the government remained relatively stable, while Labour's support exhibited a very gradual decline. As Brexit wrangling dragged on in Westminster, support for the Conservatives and Labour collapsed to such an extent that several polls had the traditional parties of government trailing both the Liberal Democrats and the Brexit Party at points during the summer of 2019. The Conservatives hit a low of 17% and Labour bottomed out just a point higher, while the Brexit Party peaked at 26% and the Liberal

© The Author(s), under exclusive license to Springer Nature Switzerland AG 2021
R. Ford et al., *The British General Election of 2019*,
https://doi.org/10.1007/978-3-030-74254-6_8

Democrats at 24%. For a brief period, it seemed that a chaotic four-party system might be on the cards, or perhaps that one or both of the parties that had dominated British politics for most of the last century could finally be overtaken in a general election. But the moment did not last. By late summer, the Conservatives were rebuilding their support, with the tide turning even *before* Boris Johnson took over as party leader. Labour's support slipped further and took longer to recover, leaving the party well behind Johnson's resurgent Tories, but by the time the campaign began, it was already clear they were not going to be overtaken by either the rapidly fading Liberal Democrats or the flash-in-the-pan Brexit Party newcomers.

The campaign polling itself proved remarkably uneventful. Commentators regularly alluded to the experience of 2017, when Labour support had surged unexpectedly, to underline the potential for campaign drama. But the polls moved sluggishly this time—while both large parties steadily gained support at the expense of the smaller parties, continuing the pre-campaign trend, the Conservatives' lead over Labour was quite stable throughout. Those hoping Corbyn might spark a repeat of the 2017 fireworks were left disappointed. However, nagging doubts about polling accuracy meant this predictable polling was treated with more scepticism than in past campaigns. For those who believed them, the polls told a clear and consistent story throughout: the Conservatives had a commanding lead, built on support from Leave voters, while Labour's electoral coalition had been weakened by the cross-pressures of Brexit and the unpopularity of the party's leader. No close follower of the polls would have been surprised by the headlines on Friday 13 December. In many ways, this was the election many anticipated in 2017 before that campaign confounded expectations: a dominant Conservative Party crushed its divided opponents and won a mandate to 'get Brexit done'.

The volume of political polling rose in 2019, having fallen in 2017 following the polling disaster of 2015. Some 455 national polls were conducted in the 2017–2019 Parliament, an average of one every two days, up from 258 polls between 2015 and 2017 (a poll every three days), but still well below the high-water mark of 1,965 polls fielded between 2010 and 2015 (over a poll a day).[1] There were a total of 81 polls during the campaign, an average of nearly two per day.[2] This reflected continued demand for polling from the media and the public, and a gradual recovery of confidence in the industry following its improved performance at the 2017 election.

During the campaign, there were also three national polls of Wales, five of Scotland and two of Northern Ireland. A number of constituency polls were also conducted by Survation and Deltapoll. The constituencies selected fell into three groups: first, highly marginal seats such as Kensington, won by 20 votes by Emma Dent Coad for Labour in 2017; second, seats held by high-profile incumbents targeted by opposing parties on the basis of their Brexit position, such as Esher & Walton, a Remain-leaning seat held by Foreign Secretary Dominic Raab; third, seats held by parliamentary Brexit rebels and defectors of various stripes, such as South West Hertfordshire, where former Justice Secretary David Gauke was running as an independent. Constituency polling is notoriously difficult, but most polls fielded during the campaign came within a few points of the result for the leading candidates, with the odd poorly performing outlier, such as Wrexham and Kensington, where in both cases the Labour vote was under-estimated by around 10 points. As both main parties in England and Wales gained support during the campaign, constituency polls fielded earlier on understandably tended to be less accurate predictors of party performance than those closer to election day.

The dominance of the SNP in Scotland has posed new problems for Westminster polling since 2015. Nationally representative Britain-wide samples tend to reveal little about shifts in voting intentions north of the border, as the sub-samples of Scottish respondents are usually too small[3] to act as a reliable guide to public opinion in Scotland. The rise of the SNP has also meant it is not possible to extrapolate shifts in Scottish voting from changes in Labour and Conservative support in England and Wales, i.e. based on 'uniform swing'. This has made polls of Scotland (and to a lesser extent Wales) more important than ever as patterns of voting have fractured across the UK.[4]

In 2017, multilevel regression post-stratification (MRP) models, which estimated the state of public opinion in every constituency, took the campaign by storm, with YouGov publishing a widely reported set of projections daily in the eight days leading up to the election. YouGov's modelling successfully identified the closeness of the race and called some of the most surprising results early, such as Canterbury—a seat held by the Conservatives for over a century which YouGov's models correctly projected Labour to win. For this election, YouGov again undertook MRP modelling, but updated it less frequently, publishing just two projections over the six-week campaign. These were again widely reported and again correctly identified some of the most important constituency trends. The final YouGov MRP correctly called 18 of the 25 'Red Wall' seats picked up by the Conservatives, but failed to predict gains in Birmingham Northfield, Burnley, Gedling, Heywood & Middleton, Hyndburn, North West Durham, and Stoke-on-Trent Central.[5] While subsequent commentary has tended to broaden the concept to cover any Conservative gain north of the M25, the original 'Red Wall' category was developed to capture a set of constituencies where the Labour vote share was higher, and the Conservative vote share lower, than would be predicted by statistical modelling of local demographics— in other words, seats with concentrations of habitually Labour-voting residents who national polling suggested would be most receptive to Conservative messaging (see Table A8.1 at the end of the chapter).

The 2017 success of YouGov's MRP models encouraged other firms to experiment with the technique: FocalData released two MRP projections, and DataPraxis and Savanta ComRes one each. MRP projections did not, however, replace traditional national polls despite their success in 2017—the huge samples required make them very costly and time-consuming. The statistical modelling techniques used to process these samples and generate constituency estimates are computationally intensive and required highly skilled staff to undertake correctly.[6] They are useful for providing a granular picture of political geography, but are of much less use for tracking day-to-day campaign trends. The long fieldwork period, slow and uncertain production processes, and in particular the high expense make MRP estimates less attractive for the media clients who commission most polling. Political editors work to tight deadlines and are in any event often more interested in tracking the day-to-day ebb and flow of the campaign than painting a granular picture of political geography.

Two new firms joined the UK polling scene in 2019. Joe Twyman and Martin Boon, industry veterans formerly of YouGov and ICM respectively, founded a new pollster, Deltapoll, in 2018. After briefly appearing in the *Sun on Sunday* in 2018, their polls took up regular residence on the pages of the *Mail on Sunday*. Matt Singh, who gained prominence for anticipating the polling miss of 2015, entered the polling business with Number Cruncher Politics, releasing five polls during the Parliament and publishing its final poll of the campaign with *Bloomberg*.

The other pollsters in this Parliament had all operated in previous elections and had regular media outlets for their public polling of voting intentions in 2019. As in 2017, Opinium published their polls in

The Observer and Ipsos MORI in the *Evening Standard*. YouGov published with *Sky News* and *The Times* and the *Sunday Times*, Survation with ITV's *Good Morning Britain* and the *Daily Mail*, BMG Research in *The Independent*, and Savanta ComRes in the *Daily Telegraph* and the *Sunday Telegraph*. Previously the pollster for *The Guardian*, ICM Research, released their final poll of the campaign with *Reuters*. Kantar, Panelbase, Qriously and FocalData all published final polls of the campaign independently of news organisations, with self-publishing by pollsters now an increasingly common occurrence in the age of the internet and social media. Hanbury Strategy, which had been publishing in *Politico*, released their final public poll of election year in September 2019—they ceased public polling to take up an in-house role with CCHQ as the party geared up for the general election.

The growth of social media has seen a parallel increase in the online release of poll results, especially on Twitter, where the UK's biggest poll aggregator @BritainElects had an audience of over 200,000 followers. During the campaign, its tweets of poll numbers would regularly yield thousands of engagements (i.e. 'retweets' and 'likes') and between 450,000 and 600,000 impressions (i.e. the total number of times a tweet was seen by Twitter users).[7] Pollsters were also active in sharing their poll results on social media, via corporate and individual accounts. While forming something of a Westminster bubble for the most politically attentive and poll-obsessed, this small world is nevertheless significant as the place where first impressions are often formed— by politicians, journalists and commentators—regarding the narrative of the campaign, even when those impressions are sometimes distinctly off-beam.

There were some changes in the methodologies of pollsters in 2019. Following a recommendation of the inquiry into the 2015 polling miss,[8] in 2018 the British Polling Council (BPC) introduced a requirement for its members to publish a statement on the level of uncertainty that has historically been associated with voting intention polls, which was intended to discourage the interpretation of small changes in the polls as signifying meaningful evidence of shifts in popularity.[9]

A number of pollsters (Ipsos MORI, ICM Research and Savanta ComRes) abandoned turnout models adopted at the 2017 election to correct for the over-statement of Labour support in 2015.[10] These over-corrected for the original problem, leading to under-estimation of the 2017 Labour vote by an unprecedented five percentage points.[11]

As such, it was somewhat back to basics for the polling industry, as over-complicated models were stripped back and there was a renewed focus on calibrating the demographic balance of their samples and improving sample quality—the fundamental issues identified by the 2015 inquiry. Ipsos MORI and Survation remained the only firms conducting their surveys by telephone, with the rest of the industry carrying out polling fieldwork online. Methods differ substantially within this broad group of online pollsters. Some firms, such as YouGov, maintain an in-house panel of respondents, to whom surveys are distributed. Most other firms purchase samples of respondents from larger market research platforms. A few firms, notably Qriously and Number Cruncher Politics, use a method called 'river sampling'. This is where samples are gathered via click-through ads on websites or mobile apps—with respondents screened and assigned to a survey, and then weighted by key demographics to make the sample representative. While online panels are potentially vulnerable to bias via attrition (i.e. through higher rates of dropout from the panel among supporters of a particular party), river samples come with greater uncertainty regarding the stability of the sources (the websites or apps) that samples are drawn from.

In 2019, local electoral pacts between the Remain-supporting parties (the Liberal Democrats, the Green Party and Plaid Cymru) and the decision of the Brexit Party not to stand in Conservative-held seats presented another methodological challenge for pollsters. If these local variations weren't addressed, then respondents could have expressed a voting intention for a party that was not standing in their constituency. Most firms therefore asked respondents to state a voting intention drawn *only from parties standing in their constituency*. Ipsos MORI and Kantar instead asked respondents who they would vote for *if their preferred party was not standing locally* and allocated them to that party if their favoured party was not standing.[12] In the final reckoning, it does not appear this choice mattered much to the accuracy of the polls, but it certainly was a concern for the pollsters ahead of election day.

Much of the day-to-day fluctuation of the polls is simply noise—a mixture of the random error from sampling processes, differences in the composition of pollsters' samples (with the panels used varying from firm to firm) and variations in 'non-response bias' among partisans, whereby party supporters become more or less likely to respond to surveys based on how their side is doing when the poll is in the field. For this reason,

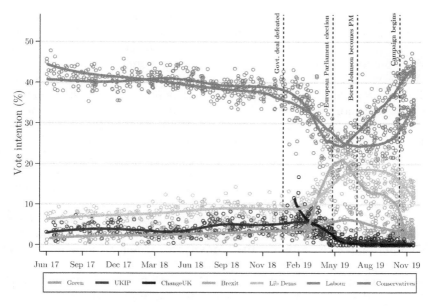

Fig. 8.1 Voting intentions for Westminster elections, 2017–2019 (*Note* LOWESS, bandwidth = 0.2)

changes in the polls are best viewed through a long-distance lens—patiently waiting for systematic trends and key turning points to come into focus.

The polling story of the 2017–2019 parliament is a play in three acts (Fig. 8.1). The first was a period of stability, with the Conservatives and Labour locked in a statistical dead heat, but with support for both slowly declining. Between the 2017 election and the first defeat of the government's Brexit Withdrawal Agreement on 19 January 2019, the poll lead changed hands regularly: Labour were in front 87 times, the Conservatives 88 times, and 35 polls produced ties. Both parties varied in a narrow band from around 35% to around 45%. In the second act, as the Brexit process descended into chaos, the party system also seemed on the verge of breakdown. The traditional parties collapsed as support surged behind new challengers—first there was a brief flurry of voter interest in Change UK/The Independent Group, launched in February 2019. Then there were larger and longer surges in support for two parties on opposite poles of the Brexit divide—the Brexit Party and the longer-established, but now firmly Remain-associated Liberal Democrats in the run-up to the 2019 European Parliament elections. Support for the Conservatives went into freefall, dropping around 20 points between the defeat of Theresa May's deal and its low ebb around the time of the European Parliament elections. Labour's popularity entered a slightly slower but more sustained tailspin. By the time voters went to the polls for the European Parliament elections, Nigel Farage's Brexit Party was topping both European and Westminster polls, peaking in the mid-20s and eviscerating Conservative support among Leave voters, while also precipitating the final collapse of Farage's previous insurgent party UKIP.

The third act in the polling drama was the revival in the traditional governing parties' fortunes in the second half of 2019. The turnaround in Conservative polling had already begun during Theresa May's final weeks, but accelerated after Boris Johnson took over. During the summer and early autumn, the Conservatives under Johnson steadily regained the confidence of voters—and Leave voters in particular—to build a substantial lead over Labour, whose poll numbers remained stuck in the mid-20s. As the Conservatives rose, the Brexit Party fell in lockstep. Labour did belatedly begin to rebuild support in the autumn, as Remain voters began to return to the party from the Liberal Democrats, but they began the election campaign still more than ten points adrift of their opponents. Labour gained further ground through the short campaign, but could only ever manage to at best maintain parity with the Conservatives, who were still recovering support from the imploding Brexit Party. A 2017-style surge never materialised for Labour.

Much of this unprecedented voter volatility was driven by the Conservative government's failure to resolve Brexit. The government's ratings on the issue had declined steadily from 2017, and by April 2019, only 5% of people said the government was handling the issue well, while 87% thought it was handling it badly (see Fig. 8.2). The replacement of May with Boris Johnson, a figure relatively better liked and trusted by Leave voters, brought a slight uptick in perceptions of government performance, but the number saying it was doing badly was still 74% in November 2019 (versus 18% saying it was doing well)—hardly a resounding vote of confidence in the Johnson approach to Brexit.

Labour's decline over the Parliament was inextricably linked with the growing unpopularity of its leader Jeremy Corbyn. James Johnson, former pollster to Theresa May, reported that his focus groups had revealed

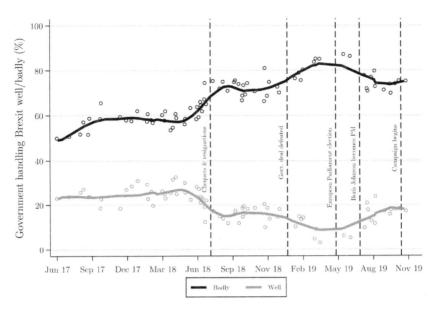

Fig. 8.2 Government handling of Brexit (YouGov), 2017–2019 (*Note* LOWESS, bandwidth = 0.2)

three key moments that crystallised voters' views that Corbyn could not be trusted.[13] The first was the Labour leader's equivocal response to the Salisbury attacks in April 2018. The second was the controversy in August 2018 following the disclosure by the *Daily Mail* that Corbyn had been present at a wreath-laying ceremony in Tunisia near to the graves of Palestinian activists with links to the Black September group responsible for the 1972 Munich massacre.[14] The third was the February 2019 defection of seven Labour MPs, forming The Independent Group (later Change UK), due to disaffection of the party leadership's handling of Brexit and anti-semitism. This split, according to Johnson, further underlined to voters Corbyn's inability to address anti-semitism in his party as well as reminding them of his prevarication over Brexit. The sustained decline in Corbyn's ratings across the Parliament completely wiped out the gains achieved in the 2017 election campaign (see Fig. 8.3). They were not due to negative contrasts with the new Conservative leader, as the majority of the decline occurred well before Johnson took over as Conservative leader in July 2019.

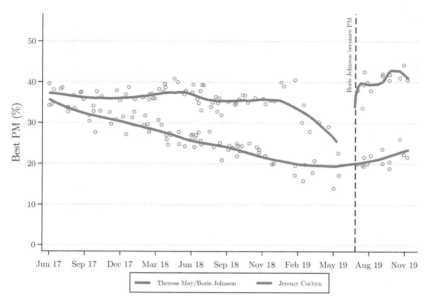

Fig. 8.3 Best Prime Minister (YouGov), 2017–2019 (*Note* LOWESS, bandwidth = 0.2)

There was much less volatility in the issues voters paid attention to during the Parliament. Brexit dominated the issue agenda from start to finish, usually being named by over 60% of poll respondents as one of the 'most important issues' facing the country. Interestingly, the economy and immigration declined in their importance to voters over this same time period, while the environment and crime gained in salience. Towards the end of the campaign, there was a sharp increase in voters' attention to health, suggesting that the Labour campaign's efforts to focus attention on the issue had some cut through, while some of the final polls suggested that the salience of Brexit might have fallen right at the end as voters were making their final decisions (Fig. 8.4).

In 2017 the manifestos were widely perceived as having had an impact on the campaign. Labour's proposals leaked early and despite an initial panic, this proved a lucky break for the party, boosting coverage for a radical package which proved popular with voters. In contrast, the Conservative manifesto launch was overshadowed by its complex proposals on social care, which were swiftly branded a 'dementia tax' by

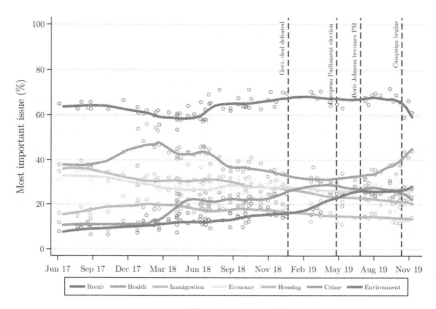

Fig. 8.4 Most important issue facing the nation (YouGov), 2017–2019 (*Note* LOWESS, bandwidth = 0.2)

opponents and soon became toxic for the party and its leader. By the time the party dropped the idea, significant damage had been done.[15]

The Conservatives—burned by the painful experience of the previous election—took a much more low-key, safety-first approach to the 2019 manifesto (see Chapter 6, pp. 216–218). There were substantial spending packages on offer, but these promises were kept simple, popular and tightly limited, with nothing that risked distracting voters from the relentlessly repeated pledge to 'get Brexit done'. Labour, forced to up the ante in response to a bigger spending Conservative campaign, offered a huge suite of policy offers and expensive pledges in its ambitious manifesto. Many of these were popular when polled in isolation: 60% supported increasing income tax for those earning over £80,000 a year, 56% supported nationalising the railways, 54% supported requiring companies to put workers on boards and 50% backed nationalising water companies.[16] The problem was that policies that were seen as good ideas individually were not considered affordable collectively. Voters did not trust Labour's reassurances that the pledges were fully costed and worried that the bill would come due through higher taxes for them. Some 53% of people believed that Labour's spending promises were not affordable and a whopping 67% thought those promises would require tax rises (the figures for the Conservatives were 33% and 46% respectively). Crucially, Corbyn and Labour were not trusted to run the economy: 57% of voters thought the country would go into recession if Labour took power, while Johnson was trusted over Corbyn to manage the economy by a margin of two to one (34% Johnson versus 16% Corbyn).

Overall public reactions to the manifestos were captured by a YouGov poll late in the campaign. More of Labour's manifesto commitments were recalled by voters compared to the Conservatives, for whom Brexit dominated. But policy cut-through did not translate into electoral advantage, as 45% said of Labour 'they have a lot of policies, but they don't seem very well thought through', compared to 23% for the Conservatives.[17] (Table 8.1).

Table 8.1   Public recall of manifesto pledges by the conservatives and labour

Conservative party		*Labour party*	
Policy	*%*	*Policy*	*%*
Brexit	43	NHS/health	22
NHS/more nurses	22	More spending/money for services	19
'Lies/rubbish'	9	Nationalisation	17
No tax increase/increases in NI allowance	6	Brexit negotiations	15
More spending/money for services	5	Free broadband	12
Immigration/Australian point-style system	5	Second referendum	11
Education	3	Tax increases	9
Selling NHS/privatisation	2	Green Deal/environment/planting trees	5
Lower/same spending	1	'Lies/rubbish'	5
		WASPIs/pension reform	4
		Increasing the minimum wage	3
		Scrapping tuition fees/Universities related spending	3
		Housing	1
		Scrapping universal credit	1
		Four-day week	1
Other	5	Other	8
Don't know	33	Don't know	31

Note YouGov asked respondents 'From what you've seen or heard, what were the MAIN policies that the Conservative/Labour Party put forward in their manifesto?' Survey fieldwork was undertaken 1–2 December, with open-ended question categorised by YouGov

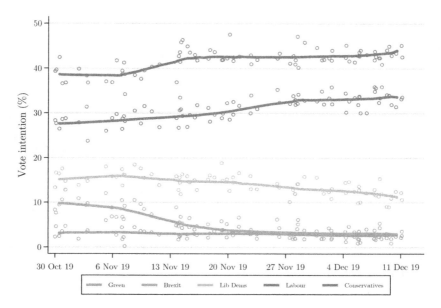

Fig. 8.5 Voting intentions in public polls, 30 October–11 December 2019 (*Note* LOWESS, bandwidth = 0.4)

As in every general election, fluctuations in the electoral horse race were a source of considerable interest for all and anxiety for some. But in 2019 there was not so much fluctuation to report (see Fig. 8.5). The average poll lead of the Conservatives over Labour throughout the campaign was just under 11 points, not far off the lead recorded on polling day. Campaign polls reported leads as low as five points (Savanta ComRes, 9–10 December) and as high as 15 points (Opinium, 4–6 December) within just a few days of one another. This occasionally gave the illusion, aided by excited coverage of outliers, that the race was narrowing when it was not. While random fluctuations of a few points in either direction could imply a landslide was on the cards or that a hung parliament was still an outside possibility, the general trend seen in the poll averages was one of stability, particularly in the later weeks of the campaign (Fig. 8.6).

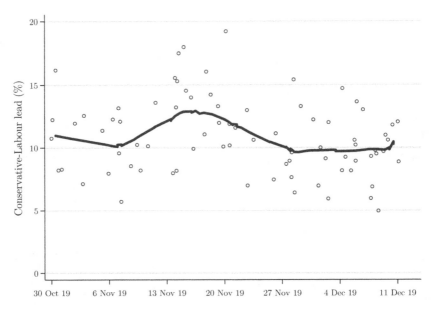

Fig. 8.6 Conservative-Labour lead in the polls, 30 October–11 December 2019 (*Note* LOWESS, bandwidth = 0.4)

The European election polling miss earlier in the year—where the Conservative vote had been over-estimated by over three points and Labour's vote over-estimated by nearly six points (see Table A8.2 at the end of the chapter)—generated a good deal of nervousness about whether polling would prove be a reliable guide to the outcome of December's general election. Those concerns proved to be misplaced; the final polls for the general election proved very accurate. Table 8.2 reports the final poll released by each polling firm signed up to the British Polling Council ahead of the election. As a group, these marginally under-stated Conservative support and over-stated Labour support, but the average error in absolute terms for the two main parties (1.4 points) was the lowest since 1979 (see the Appendix Table A8.3 at the end of this chapter for a historical summary of poll accuracy)—offering a clear riposte to the industry's critics. More broadly, the polls told a clear story about the election that was borne out in the results, consistently pointing to a large Conservative lead that was likely to translate into a

Table 8.2 Final polls for the December 2019 general election

Pollster	Fieldwork	Sample	Con	Lab	Lib Dem	Brexit party	Green
Survation	10–11 Dec	2,395	44.5	33.7	9.3	3.1	3.2
Panelbase	10–11 Dec	3,174	43	34	11	4	3
Opinium	10–11 Dec	3,005	45	33	12	2	2
Ipsos MORI	9–11 Dec	2,213	44	33	12	2	3
Deltapoll	9–11 Dec	1,818	45	35	10	4	3
Kantar	9–11 Dec	2,815	44	32	13	3	3
BMG	6–11 Dec	1,660	41	32	14	4	3
SavantaComRes	9–10 Dec	2,051	41	36	12	3	2
Number Cruncher Politics	8–10 Dec	1,009	43	33	12	3	3
YouGov (MRP)	4–10 Dec	105,612	43	34	12	3	3
FocalData (MRP)	27 Nov–10 Dec	21,213	42	34	14	3	3
ICM Research	6–9 Dec	2,011	42	36	12	3	2
Poll average			*43.1*	*33.8*	*11.9*	*3.1*	*2.8*
Result (GB)			44.7	33	11.8	2.1	2.8
Qriously	5–8 Dec	2,222	43	30	12	3	4
Result (UK)			43.6	32.1	11.6	2	2.7
Mean absolute error			*1.6*	*1.2*	*0.9*	*1.0*	*0.4*
Mean net error			*−1.5*	*+0.6*	*+0.2*	*+1.0*	*+0.1*

sizeable parliamentary majority. Of the individual firms, Ipsos MORI secured the lowest error (measured in absolute terms) across all the parties,[18] just 0.2 points, while Opinium did best for the two main parties—the Conservatives and Labour (a 0.15-point error).

Full constituency-level projections built from MRP models were also released by a number of firms: YouGov, FocalData, Savanta ComRes and Datapraxis (though both FocalData and Datapraxis relied on the YouGov panel for their respondents). The range of seats predicted for the Conservative Party was small (from a low of 337 to a high of 344) and not that much larger for Labour (from 221 to 235). As a result, the MRP polls collectively under-estimated the Conservative majority by on average 50 seats. The final update to YouGov's by now famous MRP model was released two days before the election and caused a stir by suggesting a narrow majority of just 28 seats (40 below its MRP projection from just over a fortnight earlier). Such a scenario looked rather close for comfort

Table 8.3 Final MRP seat projections for the December 2019 general election (GB)

Pollster	Fieldwork	Con	Lab	SNP	Lib Dem	Plaid Cymru	Green	Brexit party	Majority
FocalData	27 Nov–10 Dec 2019	337	235	41	14	3	1	0	24
YouGov	4–10 Dec 2019	339	231	41	15	4	1	0	28
Savanta ComRes	6–8 Dec 2019	340	233	45	11	2	1	0	30
Datapraxis	7 Dec 2019	344	221	47	14	4	1	–	38
Seat average		340	230	43.5	13.5	3.3	1	0	30
Result (GB)		365	202	48	11	4	1	0	80
Mean absolute error		25.0	28.0	4.5	2.5	0.8	0.0	0.0	50.0
Mean net error		25.0	−28.0	4.5	−2.5	0.8	0.0	0.0	50.0

for the Conservatives and was at odds with national polling. However, YouGov had been unlucky with their sample for the final poll, which had been in the field between Wednesday 4 and Tuesday 10 December. In particular, the data from the Sunday night into Monday had shown unusually good numbers for Labour, and while the data for the Tuesday, the final day of planned fieldwork, showed an uptick in Conservative support, it was not enough to offset the seeming outlier sample from the day before. YouGov's unpublished fieldwork for the final day of the campaign had seen that increase in Conservative support continuing, which would have pushed its projection back towards the eventual result. The firm had, however, devised a release plan a long time in advance of the election and stuck to it, not wishing to change its design on the hoof. CCHQ had seen a small drop in their own internal polling over the same period, but the bounce back reassured them that that the nasty surprise of the 2017 MRP was unlikely to be repeated (Table 8.3).

MRP projections are now also widely used by the parties to inform targeting strategies and the allocation of campaign resources. The modelling side of MRP projections is important in producing a reliable estimate of local variations in voter behaviour, but an accurate reading of the national political climate is also crucial. If that snapshot of current opinion is wrong or if voters' intentions subsequently shift, then parties may commit strategic blunders which leave their pieces on the wrong part of the battlefield. This was a problem faced by the Liberal Democrats, who had commissioned MRP modelling over the course of the summer which soon looked over-optimistic as the party's poll numbers began to flag in the autumn. At the time that the first MRP model was commissioned, the party was polling in the low 20s, not far behind Labour and the Conservatives, and the MRP put it ahead in 73 seats and within a five-point swing in 219 others. The party's internal review of the election campaign described the projection as being 'like all our Christmases come at once'. As a result, targeting plans were 'developed at the height of optimism and unconnected from the reality of what the party could achieve on the ground'[19] and weren't subsequently adapted sufficiently when polling revealed the party's support to be shrinking later in the year.[20] Selective attention to the evidence seems to have driven this misjudgement:

> What happened instead was the party paid very great attention to the MRPs it commissioned, both of which were taken while the party was still on an upward trend in June and September 2019, but paid rather less attention to the publicly available MRPs that came out subsequently, which indicated catastrophically bad outcomes for the party.[21](p. 45)

While MRP polling clearly played a role in driving inflated expectations, particularly among those less familiar with the limitations of the method, sources in the campaign suggest the limitations of the polling were made clear to senior Liberal Democrat decision makers and were not the only driver of internal optimism. The party's experience nonetheless provides a cautionary tale regarding the risks to campaigns of getting carried away by exciting findings from novel statistical modelling.[22]

The Conservatives were more judicious in their use of polling, MRPs and focus groups during the campaign—with the team headed by Isaac Levido, who had recently served as deputy director of the Australian Liberal Party's surprise federal election victory in May 2019, and Michael Brooks of C|T Group, with Hanbury Strategy working on data collection that fed into CCHQ's in-house MRP model. MRP projections informed the targeting of marginals, but were used alongside institutional knowledge within CCHQ. Polling and targeting was another area where the party looked to correct the errors of 2017, when it had over-extended when the polls looked good, wasting resources on more aggressive targets which soon moved out of reach when the tide turned. The amount of data required for MRP modelling had meant that the shift in the electoral mood took too long to feed through, leaving the party unable to correct course quickly. This time, the approach was more calculating and less vulnerable to short-term fluctuations in the models. Tory pollster Michael Brooks notes that the mindset informing targeting was 'We're going to make sure that we win 350 and anything over and above that is a bonus', with the clear rationale that 'the difference between gaining a seat between 330 and 340 seats is massive. The difference in gaining a seat between 360 and 370 seats is marginal'. This led to decisions to lock in target seats rather than go for possible gains at the outer limits. The party's final MRP projection had it on about 364 seats, just one off the actual result. Campaign chief Isaac Levido observed: 'You could see the numbers really solidifying the final 72 hours.'

The Conservatives also ran a nightly tracker poll of 500 respondents in marginal seats from which they produced a three-day rolling average, allowing their team to identify changes in the mood of the electorate that didn't come through quickly in the MRP estimates, such as the drop-off in the party's lead after Labour's manifesto launch. Polling didn't decide policies, but was used to identify the best way to communicate them and to spot any that weren't going down well with voters—Stamp Duty being one such issue. Focus groups in particular, Brooks suggests, were particularly useful in testing messaging and gauging the emotional reaction of voters. This included the defining slogan of the election:

> Everyone goes on about 'Get Brexit Done'. That came out of a focus group in Bury. We were going through a load of different ideas and catchphrases ... We'd written them down and we were testing them. They were talking about it in the group and I remember I just passed a note to the moderator that said 'Just ask them what they think of this' and as soon as we said it they were just like 'Yes, that's it! That's the one!' because it captured the essence of what they were trying to say.

The CCHQ polling operation was a tight ship, with a clear organisational division of responsibilities—and directly linked to the party leadership. Labour's polling activities, in contrast, were characterised by the same internal divisions that affected the rest of the party's campaign. The targeting team in Southside HQ were producing their own MRP projections using a sample of 25,000 respondents from the YouGov panel, as well as detailed analysis of demographic trends. However, this analysis became caught up in the factional conflict dividing the senior leadership team—it was promoted by those such as John McDonnell who were pressing for a focus on consolidating Remain support, but was dismissed by those such as Seumas Milne who favoured a greater focus on Leave voters and seats. The target seats lists produced by the Leader's Office were not informed by MRP modelling, but instead by relatively basic swing calculations, with a focus on the offensive targets Labour needed to win to secure a majority. During the campaign, LOTO disregarded Southside MRP modelling in favour of regular polling commissioned from ICM by Seumas Milne's deputy Carl Shoben, which was used to test campaign messaging and reactions to policy proposals. However, as with many aspects of the LOTO operation, the use of this evidence was inconsistent and the process for feeding it into a divided decision-making team was unclear. It was only a few weeks into the campaign that adjustments in the targeting strategy were made, after the first YouGov MRP had been published in *The Times*, and by then it was too late.

Even though the general election had been called at short notice, the broadcasters and the exit poll team—made up of academics representing the BBC, Sky News and ITV, with Ipsos MORI responsible for the fieldwork—had been planning for the eventuality of a snap election since earlier in the year. The 2019 election did present new challenges that meant there was some trepidation that the exit poll could come unstuck, despite its impressive record since 2005.

The first major point of concern was uncertainty concerning the impact of a winter election—the first since 1974—on voting behaviour. The exit poll methodology relies on comparing change in on-the-day voting at a given polling station from voting at the previous election. With sunset in mid-winter occurring before 4pm, five hours earlier than for a May or June election, and with voters being put off going out by lower temperatures and worse weather, it was possible that rates of postal voting might increase, depressing on-the-day turnout. If the sort of person who switched from in-person to postal voting was also more likely to vote for one party, then this could skew the exit poll sample and impact on its accuracy. There were also more practical concerns regarding the fieldwork, specifically the response rate and potential bias in the participation of voters in the exit poll. Would voters be willing to stand around in cold, wet weather to complete a mock ballot? How would people feel about a stranger approaching them to interview in the dark outside the polling station? Would the rate of participation differ between the supporters of different parties? While these unknowns made the task more unpredictable than usual, the exit poll operation went smoothly on the day, producing yet another accurate projection of the overall result based on 22,790 interviews as people exited 144 polling stations across Great Britain. The 368 seats projected for the Conservatives was just three more than the result, while the 191 projected for Labour was 11 fewer than its final seat tally. As a result, the projected majority of 86 seats was slightly higher than the final outcome of the election, an 80-seat majority for Boris Johnson's Conservatives. This put the accuracy of the exit poll slightly behind 2010 and 2017, but ahead of 2015.

How to communicate the exit poll projection is usually a matter of substantial discussion between psephologists and broadcasters. From early in the day, it had been apparent that the Conservatives were on course for a thumping win. As the day wore on, discussion turned to how to communicate the expected result. A parliamentary majority of 86 seats was substantial, but was it enough to be described as a 'landslide'? A Labour win clearly was not on the cards and a hung parliament seemed extremely improbable too. So the Conservatives would be projected to win with an overall majority. After much debate, it was determined that the yardstick for a landslide would be a projected majority of 100. While this was an outside possibility (more likely indeed than a hung parliament), it was not possible to be confident that this threshold would be cleared. So as headlines rolled at 10pm, the exit poll was announced as predicting that the Conservatives were set to win a majority and their best result since the 1987 election.[23]

The exit poll accurately told the story of the election and set the narrative for the broadcasters on the night. This was the Brexit election: the exit poll found that the stronger the Leave vote in a constituency, the greater the swing from Labour to the Conservatives. Labour was set to lose heavily in its 'Red Wall'—heavily working-class and Leave-voting seats in the North and the Midlands that had traditionally voted for the party. But the Labour vote also fell back in Remain-voting areas, which suggested that it was not just Leave voters abandoning the party. The exit poll made clear the divide in voting across the union: in England and Wales, the Conservatives dominated, winning two-thirds of the seats, but in Scotland, the SNP won 48 out of 59 seats (Table 8.4).

Table 8.4 National exit poll for the December 2019 general election (GB)

Pollster	Con	Lab	SNP	Lib Dem	Plaid Cymru	Green	Brexit party	UKIP	Other	Majority
2019										
BBC/ITV/Sky News exit poll	368	191	55	13	3	1	0		19	86
Result	365	202	48	11	4	1	0		19	80
Seat error	+3	−11	+7	+2	−1	0	0		0	6
2017										
BBC/ITV/Sky News exit poll	314	266	34	14	3	1		0	18	
Result	317	262	35	12	4	1		0	19	
Seat error	−3	+4	−1	+2	−1	0		0	−1	
2015										
BBC/ITV/Sky News exit poll	316	239	58	10		2		2	23	
Result	330	232	56	8		1		1	22	
Seat error	−14	+7	+2	+2		+1		+1	+1	
2010										
BBC/ITV/Sky News exit poll	307	255		59					29	
Result	307	258		57					28	
Seat error	0	−3		+2					+1	

After a rough few years, Britain's pollsters returned a fine performance in 2019, which suggested that reports of the demise of political polling had been premature. Crucially, the polls accurately told the story of the election—in terms of the overall national vote, the distribution of support across regions and social groups, and of the constituencies likely to change hands. Expectations of a dramatic shift in voters' sentiments during the campaign did not materialise. Pollsters' MRP models did not fare quite as well as in 2017, but the absence of any big surprises on election night meant these shortcomings received little attention. The polling performances of the political parties were distinctly mixed. CCHQ ran the smoothest polling operation of all the parties by far, making effective use of the data analysis to craft its message and targeting, but not allowing polling to dictate its strategy. The Liberal Democrats fell victim to over-optimism, in part due to MRP projections produced at the height of the party's popularity, but also due to a lack of alternative sources of intelligence on their fortunes in some of the heavily Remain areas where the party had no historical strength, but MRP models projected them to surge. Just like Theresa May's Conservatives in 2017, the party found out too late that it had over-reached, leaving many campaign resources stranded in the wrong places. Labour's polling activities exemplified the deep splits between the leadership and party HQ, and within the leadership team itself, with data analysis produced by Southside, and even that produced by LOTO itself, often ignored in a campaigning and targeting strategy shaped more by efforts to bridge factional divisions than a coherent approach to maximising Labour seats. The simple lesson of the 2019 election is that, done well, polling and related data analysis can be a considerable asset to a party, but badly done or badly used polling can equally do considerable harm.

Appendix

Table A8.1   The 40 'Red Wall' seats

North West
Blackpool South
Bolton North East
Burnley
Bury South
Chorley
Heywood & Middleton
Hyndburn
Oldham East & Saddleworth
Wirral South

Yorkshire & Humberside
Batley & Spen
Bradford South
Don Valley
Great Grimsby
Halifax
Hemsworth
Penistone & Stocksbridge
Rother Valley
Scunthorpe
Wakefield

North East
Bishop Auckland
Darlington
Newcastle upon Tyne North
North West Durham
Sedgefield
Tynemouth

West Midlands
Birmingham, Northfield
Coventry North West
Coventry South
Dudley North
Newcastle-under-Lyme
Stoke-on-Trent Central
Stoke-on-Trent North
West Bromwich
Wolverhampton North East

East Midlands
Ashfield
Bassetlaw
Bolsover
Chesterfield
Gedling

Source James Kanagasooriam, Hanbury Strategy

Table A8.2   Final polls for the May 2019 European parliament election

Pollster	Fieldwork	Sample	Con	Lab	UKIP	Lib dem	Green	Brexit party	SNP	Plaid Cymru	Change UK	Other
BMG	20–22 May	1,601	12	18	2	17	8	35	3	1	4	1
Ipsos MORI	20–22 May	1,527	9	15	3	20	10	35	3	0	3	3
YouGov	19–21 May	3,864	7	13	3	19	12	37	3	1	4	2
Number Cruncher Politics	18–21 May	1,005	15	19	2	16	7	33	4	1	4	1
Kantar	14–21 May	2,316	13	24	4	15	8	27	3	0	5	1
Panelbase	14–21 May	2,033	12	25	3	15	7	30	4		3	1
ComRes	13–17 May	4,161	12	22	3	14	7	32	3	1	5	1
Poll average			11.4	19.4	2.9	16.6	8.4	32.7	3.3	0.7	4.0	1.4
Result (GB)			9.1	14.1	3.3	20.3	12.1	31.6	3.6	1	3.4	1.6
Survation	22 May	2,029	14	23	3	12	7	31	3		4	4
Opinium	17–20 May	2,005	12	17	2	15	7	38	3	1	3	2
Poll average			13.0	20.0	2.5	13.5	7.0	34.5	3.0	1.0	3.5	3.0
Result (UK)			8.8	13.6	3.2	19.6	11.8	30.5	3.5	1	3.3	4.7
Mean absolute error			3.2	5.8	0.7	4.3	3.9	3.1	0.5	0.4	0.8	0.9
Mean net error			2.7	5.6	−0.5	−4.3	−3.9	1.8	−0.4	−0.4	0.5	−0.5

Table A8.3 Poll error by general election (conservative and labour parties), Great Britain 1945–2019

Election	Vote share		Final polls		Net error		Mean absolute error			Con-Lab margin
	Con	Lab	Con	Lab	Con	Lab	Con	Lab	Avg.	
1945	39.3	48.8	41.0	47.0	1.7	-1.8	1.7	1.8	1.8	3.5
1950	42.9	46.8	44.5	43.8	1.6	-3.0	1.6	3.0	2.3	4.6
1951	47.8	49.4	49.8	45.3	2.0	-4.1	2.0	4.1	3.1	6.1
1955	49.2	47.4	50.6	47.4	1.4	-0.1	1.4	0.2	0.8	1.5
1959	48.8	44.6	48.6	45.5	-0.2	0.9	0.4	1.2	0.8	1.1
1964	42.9	44.8	44.3	45.8	1.4	1.0	1.4	1.5	1.5	1.4
1966	41.4	48.7	40.1	51.3	-1.3	2.6	1.5	2.6	2.1	3.9
1970	46.2	43.8	44.0	48.2	-2.2	4.4	2.3	4.4	3.3	6.5
1974 (Feb)	38.6	38.0	38.6	36.0	0.0	-2.0	1.3	2.0	1.7	2.6
1974 (Oct)	36.6	40.2	34.1	43.3	-2.5	3.1	2.5	3.1	2.8	5.6
1979	44.9	37.7	44.7	38.8	-0.2	1.1	0.7	1.3	1.0	1.6
1983	43.5	28.3	45.9	25.6	2.4	-2.7	2.4	2.7	2.6	5.1
1987	43.2	31.5	42.4	34.3	-0.8	2.8	1.0	2.8	1.9	3.6
1992	42.8	35.2	37.6	39.1	-5.2	3.9	5.2	3.9	4.6	9.2
1997	31.5	44.3	30.2	47.7	-1.3	3.4	2.3	3.8	3.1	5.6
2001	32.7	42.0	30.9	45.1	-1.8	3.1	1.9	3.1	2.5	5.0
2005	33.2	36.1	31.8	38.0	-1.4	1.9	1.4	1.9	1.7	3.3
2010	36.9	29.7	35.4	27.5	-1.5	-2.2	1.5	2.2	1.9	1.3
2015	37.8	31.2	33.6	33.5	-4.2	2.3	4.2	2.4	3.3	6.5
2017	43.5	41.0	43.5	36.0	0.0	-5.0	1.3	5.0	3.2	5.3
2019	44.7	33.8	43.1	33.0	-1.6	+0.8	1.7	1.1	1.4	2.5

NOTES

1. 2010–2015: 1,965 polls over 1,827 days; 2015–2017: 258 polls over 763 days; 2017–2019: 455 polls over 917 days.
2. From the date that Parliament voted for an early election (30 October).
3. Typically around 100 respondents for a Great Britain-wide poll of around 1,000 people.
4. Northern Ireland, which has had a different party system since at least the 1970s, has long been excluded from British polls (which are therefore British, not UK-wide). Specialist polls of Northern Ireland itself are infrequent.
5. The 'Red Wall' refers to 40 Labour-held seats identified as Conservative targets by James Kanagasooriam of Hanbury Strategy (see Appendix, Table A8.1). The seats that the YouGov MRP correctly predicted changing hands were: Ashfield, Bassetlaw, Bishop Auckland, Blackpool South, Bolsover, Bury South, Darlington, Don Valley, Dudley North, Great Grimsby, Newcastle-under-Lyme, Penistone & Stocksbridge, Rother Valley, Scunthorpe, Sedgefield, Stoke-on-Trent North, Wakefield and West Bromwich West.
6. The long lead times for processing the MRP models are also the likely reason that the final MRP polls were released on 10 December, two days before the end of the campaign.
7. Source: correspondence with Ben Walker, Britain Elects, 9 February 2021.
8. Patrick Sturgis et al., 'Report of the Inquiry into the 2015 General Election Opinion Polls' (2016), http://eprints.ncrm.ac.uk/3789/1/Report_final_revised.pdf.
9. British Polling Council, 'British Polling Council Introduces New Rule on Uncertainty Attached to Polls', 1 May 2018, https://www.britishpolling-council.org/british-polling-council-introduces-new-rule-on-uncertainty-attached-to-polls.
10. See Philip Cowley and Dennis Kavanagh, *The British General Election of 2015*. Palgrave Macmillan, 2015, Chapter 9 for discussion of the 2015 polling miss and its repercussions.
11. Will Jennings, 'The Polls in 2017' in Dominic Wring, Roger Mortimore and Simon Atkinson (eds), *Political Communications: The General Election of 2017*. Palgrave Macmillan, 2017.
12. British Polling Council, 'Principal Changes in the Conduct and Reporting of Polls in the 2019 General Election', 29 November 2019, https://www.britishpollingcouncil.org/principal-changes-in-the-conduct-and-reporting-of-polls-in-the-2019-general-election.

13. James Johnson, 'Key Moments That Led to Corbyn's Fall in Popularity', *The Times*, 16 December 2019, https://www.thetimes.co.uk/article/key-moments-that-led-to-corbyns-fall-in-popularity-r2bs5tdtc.

14. 'Definitive Proof Jeremy Corbyn WAS Standing at the Graves of Munich Terrorists for Wreath-Laying—Yards from the Victims He Claimed to Be Honouring', *Daily Mail*, 15 August 2018, https://www.dailymail.co.uk/news/article-6061281/Definitive-proof-Jeremy-Corbyn-standing-graves-Munich-terrorists-wreath-laying.html.

15. See Philip Cowley and Dennis Kavanagh, *The British General Election of 2017*. Palgrave Macmillan, 2017, Chapter 8.

16. Matthew Smith, 'Labour Economic Policies are Popular, So Why aren't Labour?', *YouGov*, 12 November 2019, https://yougov.co.uk/topics/politics/articles-reports/2019/11/12/labour-economic-policies-are-popular-so-why-arent.

17. Sarah Prescott-Smith, 'The Public Recall More Labour Commitments Than Conservative', *YouGov*, 9 December 2019, https://yougov.co.uk/topics/politics/articles-reports/2019/12/09/2019-election-manifestos-which-policies-have-publi.

18. Scotland is not included for purposes of comparison as some firms combine voting intentions for the SNP and Plaid Cymru.

19. Liberal Democrats, *2019 Election Review* (2020), p. 9, https://d3n8a8pro7vhmx.cloudfront.net/libdems/pages/58994/attachments/original/1589548753/embedpdf_The_2019_Liberal_Democrat_Election_Review.pdf?1589548753.

20. Ibid., p. 7.

21. Ibid., p. 45.

22. The Liberal Democrats faced some further hurdles to capitalising on the MRP findings because the dramatic Brexit-driven shifts in their support base meant they had to make targeting decisions regarding seats where the MRP showed they were strong, but the party was hitherto extremely weak. They had no local intelligence or institutional knowledge from councillors or strong local parties to draw on in assessing the credibility of the MRP projections in some of these seats.

23. Greg Heffer. 2019. 'General Election: Conservatives Predicted to Win with Commanding Majority—Exit Poll.' *Sky News*, 12 December 2019. https://news.sky.com/story/general-election-conservatives-predicted-to-win-with-commanding-majority-exit-poll-11885003.

CHAPTER 9

Fragmented and Polarised: Broadcasting and Social Media

During the 2001 election, the Deputy Prime Minister John Prescott punched a voter on the campaign trail in Rhyl. News filtered out slowly, with broadcasters rushing footage of the incident back to the studios for the evening bulletins and stories running in the next morning's newspapers.[1] Despite the potential damage, Labour were able to brush off the story, with Tony Blair saying it was just 'John being John'. It had little lasting impact on the campaign, though it remains an iconic moment in British political folklore.[2]

In 2019, the tale of *the punch that never was* revealed how much campaign coverage had changed over two decades. False claims that an aide to Health Secretary Matt Hancock had been 'punched in the face' by a Labour protestor were briefed by Conservative aides to leading journalists who shared them with millions on Twitter before the truth of the allegations had been fully checked out. After a few hours, the claims were rolled back as footage revealed that the advisor had walked into a protestor's arm, but by then the claims had been picked up by many other journalists and seen by huge numbers of voters on PCs, tablets and smartphones. The incident highlighted both the downsides of the off-the-record briefings so often relied on by high-profile (and intensely competitive) journalists and the way in which social media has vastly accelerated the campaign news cycle. Contemporary political journalists

© The Author(s), under exclusive license to Springer Nature Switzerland AG 2021
R. Ford et al., *The British General Election of 2019*,
https://doi.org/10.1007/978-3-030-74254-6_9

can reach mass audiences via informal social media channels often subject to weaker editorial controls, and parties can seek to use their influence with those journalists to impact the campaign conversation at critical points. The development of social media has leapt ahead of reporting norms and regulation, so such stories fall into a grey area, with the right balance to strike between speed and veracity often left for journalists 'in the field' to judge for themselves.

At the same time, the polarised and febrile context of British politics in the post-Brexit era has raised the stakes for broadcasters, who now face near-constant complaints of bias from all sides, from grassroots partisans replying on their social media accounts to party campaigns issuing formal complaints. The 2019 campaign also witnessed an escalation in tensions between the political campaigns and the broadcasters tasked with reporting them, with the Conservative campaign in particular unilaterally disengaging from outlets and withdrawing from broadcast commitments. News organisations like the BBC, ITV, Channel 4 and Sky News found themselves navigating a turbulent political environment both online and offline, and faced regular populist attacks from citizens and politicians alike.

A Divisive and Bad-Tempered Media Environment

The polarised political climate and electoral volatility of 2019 added to the challenges UK broadcasters faced in meeting their regulatory obligation to provide impartial coverage of politics and public affairs—an obligation always closely scrutinised during election campaigns, not least by the parties themselves. As in previous election cycles, the media regulator Ofcom published guidance for broadcasters, but as in 2017 the regulator did not issue judgements about which parties should be deemed 'major' or 'minor' during the campaign, providing more discretion to the broadcasters themselves to interpret their obligations to provide fair coverage to the parties in proportion to their strength.[3] In its guidance for 2019, Ofcom emphasised that greater weight that should be given to past election performance (both votes won and candidates elected, over two election cycles) over current opinion polling. This advice had potentially important consequences for the Liberal Democrats and the Brexit Party, who had both surged in the polls in 2019—the former had performed poorly in the previous two general elections and the latter had no electoral track record at all prior to the 2019 European Parliament elections.

The broadcasters once again took their impartiality obligations seriously, but faced growing difficulties in meeting them in a fast-changing media environment. Many prominent broadcast journalists now also 'broadcast' news and opinions individually via their social media channels, and as yet that social media output is in some respects a regulatory and normative grey area,[4] which, as the 'punch that wasn't' incident illustrated, can pose serious problems, given the speed and scope of contemporary social media reporting. The apparent behaviour of the governing Conservative Party also risked upsetting the balance in a different way, with the party reported to have unilaterally withdrawn its leader Boris Johnson from set-piece interviews, including one which was explicitly part of a BBC package designed to meet Ofcom balance requirements. The broadcasters' attempts to punish such behaviour by 'empty chairing' uncooperative parties at set-piece events then provoked complaints from the parties in turn that such retaliation itself breached impartiality requirements. In an often ill-tempered campaign where all of the political parties were apparently more distrustful than ever of the broadcast media and more willing to air their complaints to large audiences via social media, broadcast editors faced attacks from all sides, criticised for being both too robust and not robust enough. At the same time, they were having to cope with a campaign news cycle which thanks to social media has become more rapid and relentless than ever before.

Broadcast Coverage
in a Fragmented Media Environment

The broadcasters' campaign choices matter, because they remain one of the main sources of political information for many voters—and despite talk of a loss of trust, television remains considerably more trusted than the news print media.[5] As Fig. 9.1 illustrates, roughly half of voters reported getting election news via the television, just behind the 56% who reported consuming political news online. However, online coverage is often itself driven by broadcasters' output—the broadcast websites themselves, particularly the BBC's online pages, are a primary news source for many voters, while much of the election-focused news media or social media output is driven by TV news or campaign coverage clips.[6] For example, Andrew Neil's challenge to Boris Johnson to face questioning was viewed online 7.9 million times, while Joe Pike's interview on *ITV News* where the Prime Minister pocketed the journalist's phone was viewed 12.2 million times. With smartphones now in the hands of most

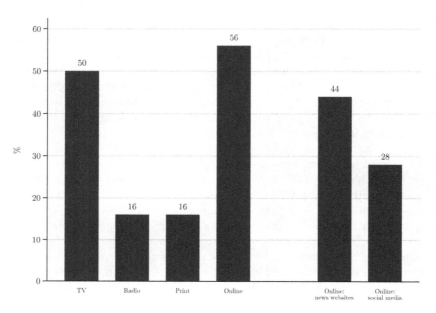

Fig. 9.1 News media usage during the election campaign (*Source* Reuters Institute[7]: 'Which of these have you used to get news about the 2019 UK general election in the last week?' [Sample = 752 respondents, 4 November–15 December])

voters, dedicated news smartphone apps are another growing source of campaign information. Here, again, the traditional broadcasters dominate—10% of voters reported using the BBC news app during the election campaign, while 3% used the Sky News app. No other media outlet received more than 1% usage (Fig. 9.2).

It is also notable that, while Twitter is the app of choice for many politicians, journalists and pundits in Westminster, it lags well behind other platforms as far as the general public is concerned. During the campaign, voters were far more likely to access YouTube, Facebook, WhatsApp or Instagram. Tracking data collected by the Reuters Institute suggested that on average people spent five times as much time on Facebook as Twitter during the campaign, though of course much of the time spent on either site will not have been spent consuming political news.

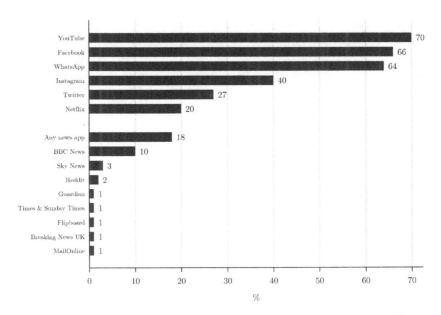

Fig. 9.2 News app usage during the campaign (*Source* Reuters Institute[8]: percentage of users who accessed each app [Sample = 758 respondents who accessed the internet using a mobile app, 4 November–15 December])

THE CAMPAIGN ON BROADCAST NEWS

The topics focused on by broadcasters helped to frame the election contest, not only in the issues covered by their main news bulletins but also in the issues raised in interviews and debates. The definitive Loughborough study of issues analysed the issues covered in all main news bulletins to provide a detailed breakdown of the issues covered in broadcast campaign coverage (see Table 9.1). Unsurprisingly, Brexit dominated—being covered by nearly one in five news items. Indeed, discounting stories about the electoral process— 'horse race'-type stories about who was up or down in the election campaign, political gaffes, internal party divisions, where parties were standing, issues of tactical voting and electoral pacts, the role of social media and traditional media,

Table 9.1   Issues covered in major television news bulletins (BBC, ITV, Sky News, Channel 4 and Channel 5)

Topic	Percentage of news items 2019
Electoral process	31
Brexit/EU	18
Health/healthcare	7
Business/economy/trade	6
Scotland/Wales/Northern Ireland	5
Standards/scandals	6
Taxation	4
Minorities/religion	4
Public services	4
Environment	4
Defence/military/security/terrorism	3
Immigration/border controls	2
Social security	1
Crime/law and order	1
Education	1
All other issues	3

Source Deacon et al., *General Election 2019*[9]

toxicity and incivility of political debate—which now routinely take the biggest share of election coverage, Brexit was by far the most covered substantive topic in the campaign. Stories on the issue took up 18% of all coverage and more than a quarter of the coverage devoted to all substantive policy topics. The time given to Brexit was up substantially on 2017, suggesting the Conservatives had greater success in their second attempt at framing a 'Brexit election'.

But this was not a single-issue campaign. Broadcast media also paid plenty of attention to Labour's preferred topics, with the share of time devoted cumulatively to health, public services, the environment or education very close to that given to Brexit (17% of all coverage and 25% of all substantive coverage). Brexit may have been the lead story, but other issues did not get shut out. Security issues received much less attention in 2019 than in the previous campaign, as although the late campaign was disrupted by the Fishmongers' Hall terror incident, this was a much less severe terror crisis than the two attacks which occurred in 2017, resulting in less attention to an issue which had surprisingly played to Labour's benefit in the previous election. Another surprising absence from the broadcast conversation was immigration, an issue near the top of the agenda in every campaign since 2005, but barely getting a mention in this campaign, with just 2% of broadcaster attention.

Negotiating the Debates

Set-piece events involving party leaders, particularly debates between them, were once again a major campaign preoccupation in 2019 and the subject of intensive negotiations between the broadcasters and the campaigns. One big focus was the prospect of head-to-head debates between the Conservative Prime Minister and his Labour opponent. These would be the first in history, owing to the traditional reluctance of frontrunners to take an unnecessary risk by participating in such events.[10] Two broadcasters, ITV and the BBC, sought commitments from the two largest parties for 'Johnson vs Corbyn' debates, though the packages proposed were very different. Discussions between ITV and the parties were reported to focus on the details of the head-to-head debate: which topics would be covered and in what order, with the placement and prominence of Brexit a particular sticking point, and on ensuring a balanced audience. The focus on a single headline event of mutual interest to the campaigns and the broadcasters smoothed negotiations, and on 2 November, ITV announced that Julie Etchingham would moderate 'Johnson vs Corbyn' on 19 November. To balance out the focus on the 'big two', ITV offered live interviews with the leaders of the Liberal Democrats, the Brexit Party, the SNP and the Green Party to air immediately after the head-to-head event.

The BBC negotiations were more complex, as the public service broadcaster put together a broad package designed to ensure that all parties were ensured proportionate airtime in set-piece televised events. Alongside a proposed second two-way debate, there would be seven-way debates, a *Question Time* event involving the leaders of the three largest Britain-wide parties plus the SNP leader, and a series of one-to-one interviews between party leaders and veteran journalist Andrew Neil. Labour aides had concerns about aspects of the package, in particular the interview with Neil, whose aggressive style was seen as posing a lot of downside but little upside, but the package was reportedly presented as something which had to be accepted or rejected in full. There were also negotiations over the content of the events, again with the role of Brexit looming large, and over venue and audience, to ensure not just partisan balance but also Leave/Remain balance. The BBC announced its pro-gramme of election events, to which all parties had apparently signed up in full, on 9 November. The 'Prime Ministerial debate', moderated by Nick Robinson, was announced for 6 December, the final Friday night before polling day. Proposals for a further head-to-head debate on Sky News, and a three-way debate featuring Jo Swinson on Channel 4 News, both slated for late November, came to nothing allegedly due to the refusal of the Conservatives to participate.

The smaller parties were understandably unhappy with the focus on events which excluded them, with the Liberal Democrats particularly aggrieved. The 2010 campaign had been transformed when their leader Nick Clegg stole the show in three-way debates with David Cameron and Gordon Brown, and the party argued that its polling position in 2019 was stronger than it had been in 2010 when Clegg had been given a top spot. The party launched a legal challenge (joined by the SNP) to its exclusion from the ITV debate on 11 November, with party leader Jo Swinson arguing that the format choice marginalised Remain voters: 'People know more about where they stand on Brexit than for which party they will vote for. So it is vital for our democracy to have both sides of the Brexit debate represented at the top table of the leaders' debates.'[11] The courts rejected the case a week later, saying that as a private broadcaster, ITV's decisions were not subject to judicial review, and suggesting the parties lodge a complaint with Ofcom instead after the broadcast. This in effect killed efforts by the smaller parties to change the format and ensured the ITV debate would go ahead as planned (Table 9.2).

THE HEAD-TO-HEAD DEBATES AND THE BBC QUESTION TIME LEADERS' SPECIAL

'Johnson vs Corbyn: The ITV Debate' went out live at 8 pm on Tuesday 19 November, hosted by Julie Etchingham, who had also anchored ITV's debate programmes in the previous two elections. The show's ratings of 6.7 million, while the highest for any of the broadcast events with published ratings, were perhaps disappointing given the novelty of the format and the attention given to it in the broader campaign coverage.[12] Though more people tuned in to watch Johnson and Corbyn verbally joust than had engaged with any of the various set-piece events in 2017,

Table 9.2   Chronology of set-piece televised events in the 2019 campaign

Date	Venue/Organisers	Ratings (millions of viewers)	Participants (bold indicates party leaders)
17 November	Cardiff, ITV Cymru Wales	0.28	David Davies (Con), Nick Thomas-Symonds (Lab), Jane Dodds (LibDem), Liz Saville Roberts (Plaid), Nathan Gill (Brexit)
19 November	Salford, ITV	6.7	**Boris Johnson (Cons)** **Jeremy Corbyn (Lab)**
22 November	Sheffield Octagon, BBC Queston Time	4.2	**Boris Johnson (Con),** **Jeremy Corbyn (Lab),** **Jo Swinson (Lib Dem),** **Nicola Sturgeon (SNP)**
26 November	Pembrokeshire, BBC Wales	*	David Davies (Con), Nia Griffith (Lab), Jane Dodds (Lib Dem), Liz Saville-Roberts (Plaid), James Wells (Brexit)
28 November	Channel 4 (Climate change)	*	**Jeremy Corbyn (Lab),** **Nicola Sturgeon (SNP),** **Jo Swinson (Lib Dem),** **Sian Berry (Green),** **Adam Price (Plaid Cymru)** *Boris Johnson (Con) and Nigel Farage (Brexit) declined invitations and were replaced with ice sculptures*
29 November	Senedd, Cardiff BBC Wales	*	Rishi Sunak (Con), Rebecca Long-Bailey (Lab), **Nicola Sturgeon (SNP),** **Jo Swinson (LibDem),** **Adam Price (Plaid),** Caroline Lucas (Green), Richard Tice (Brexit)
1 December	Salford, ITV	*	Rishi Sunak (Con), Richard Burgon (Lab), **Nicola Sturgeon (SNP),** **Jo Swinson (LibDem),** **Adam Price (Plaid Cymru),** **Siân Berry (Green),** **Nigel Farage (Brexit)**

(continued)

Table 9.2   (continued)

Date	Venue/Organisers	Ratings (millions of viewers)	Participants (bold indicates party leaders)
3 December	Wrexham, BBC Wales	*	Fay Jones (Con), David Hanson (Lab), Steffan John (Lib Dem), Rhun ap Lorwerth (Plaid), Nathan Gill (Brexit)
3 December	Glasgow, STV	*	**Jackson Carlaw (Con), Richard Leonard (Lab), Nicola Sturgeon (SNP), Willie Rennie (Lib Dem)**
6 December	Maidstone, BBC	4.4	**Boris Johnson (Con), Jeremy Corbyn (Lab)**
8 December	Leeds, Channel 4 (Everything but Brexit)	*	Angela Rayner (Lab), Philippa Whitford (SNP), **Jo Swinson (Lib Dem), Jonathan Bartley (Green), Adam Price (Plaid)**
8 December	Belfast, UTV	*	Emma Little-Pengelly (DUP), **Michelle O'Neill (SF), Colum Eastwood (SDLP), Steve Aiken (UUP), Naomi Long (Alliance)**
9 December	York, BBC (*Question Time* under 30s special)	*	Robert Jenrick (Con), Angela Rayner (Lab), Humza Yousaf (SNP), **Jo Swinson (Lib Dem), Jonathan Bartley (Green), Adam Price (Plaid), Nigel Farage (Brexit)**
10 December	BBC Scotland	*	**Jackson Carlaw (Con), Richard Leonard (Lab), Nicola Sturgeon (SNP), Willie Rennie (Lib Dem)**
10 December	Belfast, BBC Northern Ireland	*	Jeffrey Donaldson (DUP), **Michelle O'Neill (SF), Colum Eastwood (SDLP), Steve Aiken (UUP), Naomi Long (Alliance)**

the figure was well below the 9.4 million attracted by the first ever leaders' debate in 2010 or the 8 million who watched the first seven-way ITV debate in 2015.[13] Growing media fragmentation and waning viewer engagement with political output may mean that, less than a decade after their first introduction, televised debates are already losing their ability to dominate the campaign conversation.

The debate itself was a disappointing affair, with both leaders disciplined but dull. Each made an opening statement (with Boris Johnson drawing the first of several rebukes from Etchingham for running over his allotted time) after which they took questions from members of the Salford studio audience. Both leaders delivered solid performances in the opening discussion on Brexit, with Corbyn attacking the credibility of Johnson's deal, and Johnson repeatedly criticising Corbyn's refusal to say whether he would campaign for his own proposed Brexit deal. Corbyn's dramatic flourish ten minutes into the discussion, brandishing documents he claimed showed that the NHS would be up for sale in trade negotiations, did not faze his Conservative opponent, who continued to press the Labour leader on his Brexit ambivalence. Questions of trust and personal integrity were trickier terrain for the Prime Minister, and the audience were audibly contemptuous of Johnson's claim that the truth mattered to him, though this potential weakness was balanced out by criticism of Corbyn's record on tackling anti-semitism within Labour. The second half of the event opened with questions on Labour's comfort zone, the NHS, and continued in a similar vein with questions on the impact of austerity, then a final section with a grab-bag of topics including the monarchy, climate change and Christmas presents. Corbyn reeled out Labour's policy ambitions, while Johnson sought to sound reassuring while repeating his Brexit soundbites wherever possible. Though Corbyn gave clear and persuasive answers on many questions, neither he nor moderator Etchingham ('Mr Johnson, *Mr Johnson*, *ENOUGH*, Mr Johnson!') found an effective way to deal with the debating technique political sketchwriter Michael Deacon had earlier characterised as the 'Johnson juggernaut':

> Boris Johnson is unstoppable. Literally. His interviewers can't get a word in edgeways. Because the man will not stop talking. Quite plainly, it's a deliberate and well-honed technique. Call it the juggernaut, because that's what it's like: the helpless interviewer is utterly drowned out by a vast onrushing juggernaut of bluster, 10 solid tons of thundering waffle. BLAM! At maximum speed the juggernaut roars straight through all obstacles, traffic cones scattered, crash barriers crushed, its driver hell-bent on just blasting on through, zooming away from whatever question he's been asked by babbling out buzzwords and unrelated policy announcements for whole minutes on end, louder and faster, louder and faster, the interviewer now no more than a frantic dot in his rear-view mirror.[14]

The Prime Minister and the Labour leader were joined by the Liberal Democrat leader Jo Swinson and the SNP leader Nicola Sturgeon in Sheffield for the *Question Time Leaders' Special* on Friday 22 November. The show received an average audience of 4.2 million, a similar figure to the *Question Time* special featuring Corbyn and Theresa May in 2017, though less than the 2015 edition featuring David Cameron and Ed Miliband (4.7 million). Each leader took the stage alone to field questions from the audience and host Fiona Bruce for half an hour. The studio audience seemed impartial in the sense that it was visibly and audibly hostile to all of the participants, perhaps with the partial exception of Sturgeon. Corbyn received the opening slot and was given a hard time from the off: 'Should business be frightened of a Labour government?' 'I don't think its businesses who should be scared, I think it's everyone.' 'I don't buy this nice old grandpa act ... I'm terrified for my daughters.' Corbyn dealt with this initial barrage with good humour and cogent, positively received replies. However, he was once again obliged to spend a substantial portion of his airtime defending his past associations with controversial figures such as Bolivian President Evo Morales and his party's track record on anti-semitism rather than setting out Labour's policy agenda. Even when he was able to focus the conversation on Labour's reforming ambitions, he faced an audience clearly incredulous about ideas such as free nationalised broadband. The audience were similarly unimpressed by his defence of Labour's Brexit policy, which drew repeated questions, and (more surprisingly) he faced a late barrage of questions regarding the party's policy on Scottish independence.[15] In this regard, the event was a disappointment for Labour, with Corbyn neither able to effectively address his or Labour's weaknesses nor consistently focus the discussion on his party's strengths.

Audience questions for Nicola Sturgeon were also dominated by the issue of Scottish independence, and the SNP's relations with other parties, reflecting perhaps the predominantly English audience's lack of familiarity with domestic Scottish politics. Sturgeon ruled out ever putting Johnson into Downing Street in her very first answer, then, despite having apparently undercut her own negotiating leverage, spent much of the following answers repeatedly trying to justify why a second independence referendum would be a reasonable demand to make of the Corbyn minority government she had already seemingly committed herself to supporting.

Liberal Democrat leader Jo Swinson took to the stage third and faced perhaps the most hostile reception of all. The first question set the tone: 'Do you regret starting the campaign by saying you will be PM and do you now agree how ridiculous that sounded?' The audience continued in a similar vein, with hostile questions on Liberal Democrat support for 'harsh and uncaring benefit cuts', tuition fees and fracking during the Coalition, and repeated audience criticism of Liberal Democrat behaviour towards the Conservatives (too supportive) and Labour (too critical). The low point, however, came as both Leave and Remain audience members attacked the Liberal Democrats' 'revoke Article 50' Brexit policy. A Leave-supporting questioner asked 'Is revoking Article 50 confirming to 17.4 million people that you think they are stupid and didn't know what they were voting for?' and was immediately followed by a 'passionate Remainer' angry that: 'The Liberal Democrats [are] standing on a manifesto to unilaterally cancel Brexit. It has absolutely cost you my vote … It is undemocratic.' Swinson's attempts to respond were repeatedly interrupted by angry audience interjections, and the barrage of Brexit criticism continued in follow-up questions. The *Question Time* special was the Liberal Democrats' best opportunity to introduce their lesser-known young leader to the public. An excruciating half an hour focused almost exclusively on unpopular Coalition-era choices and criticism of their current Brexit policy was not what the party's strategists would have hoped for.

Boris Johnson took to the stage last and it was clear from the opening question—'How important do you think it is to always tell the truth?'—that the feisty Sheffield audience had no intention of giving him an easy time either. Johnson sought to pivot immediately to Brexit, but was pressed by the questioner, who turned out to be a 'WASPI'—an older woman from the group who had lost out financially from changes to the state retirement age. Johnson came perilously close to repeating his predecessor's 'there is no magic money tree' gaffe, saying 'I cannot promise that I can magic up that money'. These opening exchanges were followed by questions on food banks, austerity and the NHS. Johnson was also put under sustained pressure regarding provocative and intolerant statements in his past journalism. He faced audible hostility to his efforts to defend, evade and change track to his preferred talking points on Brexit and his record as London Mayor. This was a tough half-hour for the Prime Minister, but his opponents had not fared much better.

The 'BBC Prime Ministerial Debate' was hosted by the BBC's Nick Robinson in Maidstone on 6 December, the final Friday evening of the campaign. Average viewing figures were 4.4 million, well down on the audience for the ITV clash. The format again involved audience members (selected by pollsters Savanata ComRes) asking questions on selected topics, with Robinson often adding his own thoughts and follow-up questions. Both Johnson and Corbyn repeatedly returned to their preferred talking points in an event which represented their highest-profile opportunity to make closing arguments to the electorate. Johnson sought to work the phrases 'one nation Conservative government' and 'get Brexit done' into every response, regardless of the topic. He also successfully punched Labour's Brexit bruise: 'This deal that he thinks he can get in three months' time—who is going to negotiate it? Because as far as I can see everybody on the frontbench is campaigning to Remain, apart from Mr Corbyn who is neutral. How can you get a deal from Brussels if you don't actually believe in it?' Corbyn sought to return the focus to Labour's closing pitch on the NHS and public services. The Labour leader repeatedly attacked the Conservative government's austerity policies and public services cuts, and sought to reframe Brexit along similar lines by claiming Johnson's Brexit deal and trade policy opened the door to NHS privatisation. Both candidates were disciplined, but again there were few standout moments. The second head-to-head debate, like its predecessor, was an anti-climax: a forgettable hour with two familiar figures exchanging well-worn lines.

THE OTHER DEBATES: TOO MUCH OF A GOOD THING?

Viewers keen to see politicians argue in front of podiums were well served in 2019, particularly if they lived outside of England. There were two seven-way debates on 29 November (BBC) and 1 December (ITV) featuring Labour, the Conservatives, the Liberal Democrats and the SNP, alongside Plaid Cymru, the Greens and the Brexit Party. Labour and the Conservatives sent deputies to both events, correctly anticipating that the absence of their leaders would depress viewer interest. The relatively junior figures sent by the biggest parties—Richard Burgon and Rebecca Long-Bailey for Labour, and Rishi Sunak for the Conservatives—gave creditable but bland performances, while the leaders of the smaller parties made few memorable interventions.[16] Even

Brexit Party leader Nigel Farage was uncharacteristically subdued. Both events were overshadowed by the Fishmongers' Hall terror attack, which occurred the afternoon before the BBC event, and was still dominating media coverage when the ITV event aired two days later.

There were also debates focused on particular issues: a climate change debate (Channel 4, 28 November), an everything but Brexit debate (Channel 4, 8 December) and an under-30s *Question Time* special (BBC, 9 December). The most controversial of these ended up being Channel 4's climate change debate. Johnson, along with Brexit Party leader Nigel Farage, had declined to participate, and the debate's producers responded by installing slowly melting ice sculptures behind the two leaders' allotted podiums. A row erupted when Michael Gove, flanked by Johnson's father Stanley, belatedly turned up at the TV studio and asked to represent the Conservatives in place of Johnson. The Channel 4 producers refused to let Gove on stage, provoking a strong response from Johnson's communications chief Lee Cain, who had begun his journalistic career ridiculing David Cameron for evading difficult press events in the 2010 general election by chasing after him dressed as a chicken on behalf of the *Daily Mirror*.[17] Cain lodged an official complaint against Channel 4 with Ofcom, calling the channel's refusal to allow Gove to participate 'part of a wider pattern of bias by Channel 4 in recent months'.[18] The most memorable moments in the other two events were Plaid Cymru's Adam Price giving a moving account of his personal struggles with depression at the 'everything but Brexit' debate, and Labour's Angela Rayner accusing Brexit Party leader Nigel Farage of 'peddling hate' at the under-30s debate.

Devolution meant extra debates for Scottish, Welsh and Northern Irish viewers. Scotland held two leaders' debates on 3 December (STV) and 10 December (BBC Scotland) featuring the Scottish leaders of the four largest parties—the SNP, the Conservatives, Labour and the Liberal Democrats. Northern Ireland held two leaders' debates on 8 December (UTV) and 10 December (BBC Northern Ireland) featuring the leaders of Sinn Féin, the SDLP, the UUP and the Alliance (the DUP sent MPs in place of its leader). There were three Welsh debates on 17 November (ITV), 26 November (BBC) and 3 December (BBC) featuring an assortment of Welsh politicians from five parties—the Conservatives, Labour, the Liberal Democrats, Plaid Cymru and the Brexit Party—but no party leaders.

Table 9.3   Issues covered by the main Britain-wide televised debates

Date	Channel	Participants	Electoral process	Brexit/EU	Business/ economy/ trade	Health/ healthcare
19 November 2019	ITV	Johnson, Corbyn		✓	✓	✓
29 November 2019	BBC	Sunak, Long-Bailey, Sturgeon, Swinson, Price, Lucas, Tice		✓		✓
1 December 2019	ITV	Sunak, Burgon, Sturgeon, Swinson, Price, Berry, Farage	✓	✓	✓	✓
6 December 2019	BBC	Johnson, Corbyn		✓	✓	✓

			Standards/ scandals	Taxation	Minorities/ religion	Defence/mil- itarysecurity/ terrorism
19 November 2019	ITV	Johnson, Corbyn	✓	✓	✓	
29 November 2019	BBC	Sunak, Long-Bailey, Sturgeon, Swinson, Price, Lucas, Tice				✓
1 December 2019	ITV	Sunak, Burgon, Sturgeon, Swinson, Price, Berry, Farage		✓	✓	
6 December 2019	BBC	Johnson, Corbyn	✓	✓	✓	✓

(continued)

Table 9.3   (continued)

			Public services	Environment	Immigration/ border controls	Scotland/ Wales/ Northern Ireland
19 November 2019	ITV	Johnson, Corbyn		✓	✓	
29 November 2019	BBC	Sunak, Long-Bailey, Sturgeon, Swinson, Price, Lucas, Tice		✓	✓	
1 December 2019	ITV	Sunak, Burgon, Sturgeon, Swinson, Price, Berry, Farage	✓	✓		✓
6 December 2019	BBC	Johnson, Corbyn	✓		✓	

			Social security	Crime/law and order	Education	Politician trust
19 November 2019	ITV	Johnson, Corbyn				✓
29 November 2019	BBC	Sunak, Long-Bailey, Sturgeon, Swinson, Price, Lucas, Tice			✓	✓
1 December 2019	ITV	Sunak, Burgon, Sturgeon, Swinson, Price, Berry, Farage				✓
6 December 2019	BBC	Johnson, Corbyn			✓	✓

The profusion of broadcast set-piece events in 2019 may have been too much of a good thing. Repetition did not increase the charm of watching politicians rattling off campaign talking points, and both viewing figures and follow-on media coverage declined. The big head-to-head debates retained the power to dominate the next day's headlines, but there was nothing akin to the agenda-setting power of Nick Clegg's debate performances in 2010 or even of Theresa May's debate missteps in 2017. The main parties' leaders were sufficiently disciplined to avoid any major gaffes, but also sufficiently well known to make a debate-driven reassessment unlikely. The big tent events with five or seven leaders were too fragmented for participants to make much of an impact, and the second-tier politicians dispatched to many of them by Labour and the Conservatives generally failed to make much of an impression. Even the participants struggled to maintain interest across so many evenings of repetitive argument—'I was bored of it, to be honest', one LOTO aide heavily involved in the debates reflected. 'I knew what all the answers were going to be'.

TELEVISED INTERVIEWS WITH THE PARTY LEADERS

The BBC's election broadcast package scheduled interviews with the leaders of all the largest parties hosted by veteran journalist and broadcaster Andrew Neil. Neil had a longstanding reputation as a robust interviewer and in a hybrid media era, the parties' campaign teams reportedly worried that the shows would be mined by opponents for damaging clips to share on social media. All therefore saw their principal objective as to get through the encounter with as little negative footage as possible, though they had varying degrees of success. SNP leader and Scottish First Minister Nicola Sturgeon was grilled first on Monday 25 November. There were tough exchanges on her devolved government's failure to hit multiple healthcare targets—'You've called for legislation to protect the NHS from Donald Trump. Maybe the NHS needs legislation to protect it from Nicola Sturgeon'—and on the details of her plans for returning an independent Scotland to the EU, but Sturgeon was seen to have emerged with her reputation as a polished and combative media performer intact.

While the Neil interviews were difficult for all involved, it was the Labour leader Jeremy Corbyn who was widely regarded to have had

Table 9.4 Major TV leader interviews with political journalists during the 2019 campaign

Leader	Date	Presenter	Channel
Adam Price (Plaid)	24 November	Sophie Ridge	Sky News
	24 November	Andrew Marr	BBC
Boris Johnson (Con)	3 November	Sophie Ridge	Sky News
	1 December	Andrew Marr	BBC
	8 December	Sophie Ridge	Sky News
Jeremy Corbyn (Lab)	17 November	Andrew Marr	BBC
	26 November	Andrew Neil	BBC
	1 December	Sophie Ridge	Sky News
	5 December	Julie Etchingham	ITV
Jo Swinson (Lib Dem)	19 November	Nina Hosain	ITV
	3 November	Sophie Ridge	Sky News
	24 November	Andrew Marr	BBC
	4 December	Andrew Neil	BBC
	8 December	Sophie Ridge	Sky News
Nicola Sturgeon (SNP)	3 November	Sophie Ridge	Sky News
	19 November	Nina Hosain	ITV
	24 November	Sophie Ridge	Sky News
	25 November	Andrew Neil	BBC
	8 December	Andrew Marr	BBC
Nigel Farage (Brexit)	3 November	Andrew Marr	BBC
	19 November	Nina Hosain	ITV
	5 December	Andrew Neil	BBC
	8 December	Sophie Ridge	Sky News
Sian Berry (Green)	17 November	Sophie Ridge	Sky News
	19 November	Nina Hosain	ITV

the most torrid time—his interview, which aired on 26 November, was described as 'so brutal, the BBC should have shown it after the watershed'[19] and 'a bloodbath' by commentators.[20] There were awkward exchanges on his Brexit stance, the cost of Labour's WASPI women pledge, and the prospect of tax increases. But it was Corbyn's apparently irritable and evasive responses when confronted with evidence of his party failing to take action against anti-semitic members, and his repeated rejection of Neil's requests that he apologise to the Jewish community for his party's failings on anti-semitism which dominated responses in traditional news and social media. In another illustration of the blurring together of traditional and social media campaigning, leaked

WhatsApp messages revealed that Labour activists were apparently being encouraged to take to social media with positive messages about Corbyn and Labour in order to 'drown out' social media sharing and coverage of the Neil interview.[21]

Labour aides could at least hope their leader's torrid Andrew Neil interview would be balanced by an equally difficult interrogation of Johnson, which was initially due to air the same week as Corbyn's appearance. But the Conservatives, claiming the public were 'fed up' with interviews, refused to make Johnson available. Furious Labour aides bombarded the BBC with complaints, but the broadcaster lacked any mechanism to force Johnson to attend. The row was also soon over-taken by events—the terror incident at Fishmongers' Hall occurred at its height, making it hard for the BBC to then refuse requests for the Prime Minister to communicate with the nation during a security crisis. Thus it was that Johnson found himself on the sofa with Andrew Marr, days after postponing his head-to-head with Andrew Neil. Marr seemed keen to demonstrate he was not a softer touch than Neil, leading to some robust exchanges, with the host interrupting and talking across the Prime Minister repeatedly, interjecting that the government had 'been in power for ten years' and at one point cutting Johnson off: 'I'm sorry but you just keep going on and on and on. You're chuntering.' While it was an ugly and unseemly affair (the BBC received over 12,000 complaints that Marr had been biased against Johnson), it was difficult not to conclude that the Marr interview was an easier ride for Johnson and that avoiding dodging the grilling by Andrew Neil had been a politically savvy move.

The Andrew Neil interviews resumed on 4 December with Liberal Democrat leader Jo Swinson. Swinson was once again repeatedly pressed hard over her support for austerity policies during the Coalition govern-ment, something which had also featured heavily in the BBC *Question Time Leaders' Special*. With the Lib Dems by this point falling fast in the polls, Swinson also had to fend off questions about her future if her party were to end up losing seats on election day:

> I'm taking a very clear position on Brexit, I want to Remain in the EU. And I recognise some people are not going to like that. Some people don't like what I have to say on Scotland staying in the UK. Some people don't like the way I talk or what my shoes look like or whatever else … But I am still going to stand up for what I believe in because I want to change things.

Nigel Farage's interview with Andrew Neil the following day was at times a heated affair. The Brexit Party leader had just seen three of his MEPs (Annunziata Rees-Mogg, Lance Forman and Lucy Harris) resign from the party and endorse the Conservatives, with another (John Longworth) having had the whip removed earlier in the week over disagreements with the party leadership. Neil brought this up in typically diplomatic style: 'Four of your MEPs, a week before polling day, have resigned and said "vote Tory".' Farage countered that each of the defectors had links to the Conservative Party: 'One of them [Annunziata Rees-Mogg] is the sister of a Cabinet Minister', to which Neil replied 'What's that got to do with it? Smear', repeating the retort a further couple of times. Farage also argued that his party standing in places like Great Grimsby would hand extra seats to the Conservatives, due to the Brexit Party picking up the Labour vote.

Neil used the end to the interview with Farage to call out the Prime Minister for his continued refusal to subject himself to the same interrogation as the other party leaders. 'It is not too late. We have an interview prepared. Oven-ready, as Mr Johnson likes to say', Neil quipped in his closing monologue. 'The theme running through our questions is trust – and why at so many times in his career, in politics and journalism, critics and sometimes even those close to him have deemed him to be untrustworthy. It is, of course, relevant to what he is promising us all now.' Neil solemnly told viewers:

> We do them [leader interviews], on your behalf, to scrutinise and hold to account those who would govern us. That is democracy. We have always proceeded in good faith that the leaders would participate. And in every election they have. All of them. Until this one.

Neil then listed the questions he wanted to ask the Prime Minister: about delivering on his promises for the NHS, whether he had always been an opponent of austerity, about his promise that there would never be a border down the Irish Sea. Neil's broadside against Johnson was insufficient for Labour, who continued to press the BBC with an open letter of complaint, accusing the Corporation of bias and suggesting that it had given the party a 'clear understanding that Boris Johnson had agreed the same terms … including a Neil interview' and had been 'complicit in giving the Conservative Party an unfair electoral advantage'.[22] There was, however, little the BBC could do to force Johnson to participate, and Labour's efforts to exact a political cost on Johnson for his evasion had little impact.

The Andrew Neil interview was not the only broadcast commitment the Conservatives declined. Johnson also ducked a scheduled interview with ITV debate moderator Julie Etchingham, and two other proposed debates were cancelled, apparently due to his refusal to participate. And then, as we have seen, the Conservatives did not participate in two of the Channel 4 debates which did air. Yet none of this disengagement seemed to do any political damage either to Johnson or his party. The 2019 campaign thus set a worrying precedent that frontrunners could apparently withdraw from agreed broadcast commitments without consequence—something which will doubtless make future negotiations between broadcasters and parties over election coverage even more fraught.

The Campaign on Social Media

A big part of the campaign conversation now takes place online, with the political parties using social media to persuade voters, while most journalists are also active in reporting the campaign from their Twitter accounts.[23] This provides an additional layer of often personal commentary to the reports provided in print and on broadcast, and also tends to erode the traditional structures of political journalism—as broadcast and news-print journalists operate in real time, chasing the breaking daily stories minute by minute rather than waiting to deliver their version of the news at the allotted time of day (the 10pm news bulletin, the front pages of the morning newspapers, etc.). The days of a structured news environment are long gone and a lot of reporting is now done on the hoof, with journalists tapping instant reactions from the field into their smartphones.

As Table 9.5 shows, many of Britain's leading broadcast journalists now have hundreds of thousands of followers on Twitter and received tens and hundreds of thousands of 'engagements' ('likes' and 'retweets') on the platform during the campaign. Some broadcast journalists

Table 9.5 Twitter follower count of selected politics broadcast journalists and presenters

Name	Position	Broadcaster	Followers	Number of tweets during the campaign (30 October–11 December)	'Engagements' (Likes + RTs)	Replies
Political Editors						
Laura Kuenssberg	Political Editor	BBC	1,125,000	434	291,818	167,162
Robert Peston	Political Editor and presenter, *Peston*	ITV	1,038,000	359	269,282	88,841
Beth Rigby	Political Editor	Sky News	167,000	327	193,847	31,604
Adam Boulton	Editor-at-Large and presenter, *All Out Politics*	Sky News	165,000	252	48,106	7,824
Deputy Political Editors						
Sam Coates	Deputy Political Editor	Sky News	128,000	230	52,009	7,055
John Pienaar	Deputy Political Editor	BBC	81,000	18	600	231
News Anchors						
Jon Snow	News anchor	Channel 4	1,386,000	32	71,263	3,730
Huw Edwards	News anchor	BBC	78,000	38	37,939	5,886
Krishnan Guru-Murthy	News anchor	Channel 4	580,000	287	508,332	27,434
Julie Etchingham	News anchor	ITV	46,000	76	2,931	245

(continued)

Table 9.5 (continued)

Name	Position	Broadcaster	Followers	Number of tweets during the campaign (30 October–11 December)	'Engagements' (Likes+RTs)	Replies
Kay Burley	Presenter, *Kay Burley @ Breakfast*	Sky News	450,000	421	149,562	19,625
Interviewers						
Andrew Neil	Presenter, *The Daily Politics*	BBC	985,000	203	591,012	57,812
Sophy Ridge	Presenter, *Ridge on Sunday*	Sky News	135,000	78	6,070	1,187
Emily Maitlis	Presenter, *Newsnight*	BBC	208,000	70	50,923	4,906
Andrew Marr	Presenter, *The Andrew Marr Show*	BBC	147,000	39	10,167	1,248
Nick Robinson	Presenter, *Today* programme	BBC Radio 4	960,000	123	68,531	20,428

are very frequent users of the platform—BBC Political Editor Laura Kuenssberg tweeted over 400 times during the campaign, and ITV and Sky News Political Editors Robert Peston and Beth Rigby over 300 times each. These posts attract a lot of attention, much of it hostile, with senior female broadcasters (like senior female politicians) often the target of sexist abuse on social media.[24] The political editors of the BBC, ITV and Sky News all received hundreds of thousands of engagements, and tens of thousands of replies, well ahead of their colleagues, with the exception of Andrew Neil, who was (as discussed above) himself at the heart of a major campaign dispute.

The growing agenda-setting power of political journalists' Twitter output is illustrated by Fig. 9.3, which lists the news accounts most followed by MPs in January 2020, soon after the campaign ended. The tweets of an elite group of journalists from a small number of

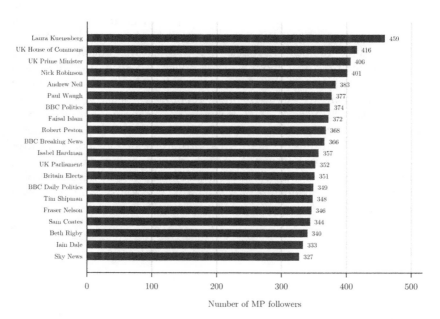

Fig. 9.3 Top political accounts followed by MPs on Twitter (*Source Politico,* January 2020[26])

outlets—including ITV, *The Spectator*, the *Sunday Times* and Sky News—
are followed daily by a majority of MPs in Westminster. The enduring
power of the BBC is also evident in this new online news environment—
three of the top 20 accounts are BBC News or BBC Politics news feeds,
and the three most-followed journalists all work for the Corporation.[25]
The BBC Political Editor Laura Kuenssberg has the most-followed
account of all, with more MPs reading her daily thoughts than following
the accounts of the Prime Minister or the House of Commons.

The explosive rise of social media output and consumption means
many broadcast events now also simultaneously unfold as social media
events, with journalists and parties producing, and audiences consuming,
social media commentary in parallel to political interviews or debates.
Growing numbers of voters experience campaign events wholly or mainly
via the clips and comments which circulate on social media.[27] The inter-
section of social media and broadcasting gave rise to several spats during the campaign. A first row erupted early in the campaign when the
Conservatives released on social media a clip of an interview between
Labour Brexit Secretary Keir Starmer and ITV presenter Piers Morgan
carefully edited to make it appear that Starmer was unable to answer
Morgan's question on Labour's Brexit policy.[28] A second erupted during the first debate between Boris Johnson and Jeremy Corbyn on 19
November when the Conservatives rebranded their official Twitter
account (@CCHQPress) as 'factcheckUK'—changing the logo and
header for the account to post anti-Labour posts. This created a storm
on social media during the debate and prompted a complaint to Twitter
from the non-partisan charity Full Fact. Twitter indicated in response
that: 'Any further attempts to mislead people by editing verified profile
information—in a manner seen during the UK Election Debate—will
result in decisive corrective action'.[29]

@CCHQPress Twitter account rebranded as 'FactCheckUK'

In 2017, Labour was considered to have resoundingly won the social media battle.[30] Labour's social media performance was again impressive on many metrics in 2019, creating innovative and engaging content that achieved substantially higher levels of sharing and engagement than their opponents. Facebook posts by the Labour Party and Jeremy Corbyn accounts were shared almost four times more than posts by the Conservatives and Boris Johnson (3.9 million vs 1.1 million) during the campaign (see Table 9.6). While the number of Facebook video views had fallen from 59 to 29 million for official Labour accounts, this was more than offset by an increase from 66 to 98 million for views on Corbyn's Facebook page. The Conservatives and Johnson between them

Table 9.6 Performance of the Labour and Conservative Party and leaders' Facebook and Twitter accounts, 2017 and 2019

	Labour			Jeremy Corbyn			Conservatives			Johnson/May		
	2019	2017	±	2019	2017	±	2019	2017	±	2019	2017	±
Facebook shares	1.0m	1.1m	−9%	2.9m	1.3m	+123%	0.7m	0.3m	+133%	0.4m	0.1m	+300%
Facebook video views	29.4m	59.0m	−50%	97.9m	66.2m	+48%	17.8m	22.4m	−21%	16.5m	13.9m	+18%
Twitter retweets	538k	381k	+41%	3.3m	1.4m	+136%	235k	159k	+48%	470k	96k	+390%

Source: Post-election report on social media performance to the Labour Party National Executive Committee

had just under 35 million video views compared to Labour/Corbyn's 127 million. Of the top 10 videos shared and viewed on Facebook, nine were posted on the Corbyn, Labour or Momentum channels—with a number 'going negative' using damaging clips of their opponents, such as interviews with Nicky Morgan and Liz Truss, and a feature on 'Boris Johnson's Lies' (see Table 9.7). Just one, the infamous 'Brexit, Actually' sketch, was posted on Boris Johnson's page. But was Labour simply preaching to the converted? Commentators often like to declare that 'Twitter is not Britain', and in the 2019 campaign Labour's big advantage on social media clearly did not translate into competitiveness at the ballot box. The population consuming political content on Facebook and Twitter is in general younger and more left-leaning, with such biases likely to be greatly magnified amongst those signing up to follow output from the Labour Party, Jeremy Corbyn or Momentum.[31] Much of the voluminous Labour traffic in views and shares on social media may thus have been material bouncing around 'echo chambers' of committed Labour supporters, but without reaching the wider electorate, who were less receptive to Corbyn-branded social media content as views of the Labour leader had soured considerably in 2019 (see Chapter 14).[32]

The Conservatives were also not much concerned by apparently daunting Labour performance on some social media metrics. They devoted more of their attention and spend to Google and YouTube ads,

Table 9.7   Top 10 videos on Facebook across Labour, Jeremy Corbyn, the Conservatives, Boris Johnson and Momentum

Video	Channel	Shares	Video views	Minutes viewed
Montage of Inequality	Jeremy Corbyn	241,000	11.6m	10.9m
Nicky Morgan Car Crash	Momentum	118,000	8.4m	11.1m
Rob Delaney on our NHS	Jeremy Corbyn	137,000	7.1m	6.1m
60 Seconds Challenge	Jeremy Corbyn	74,000	4.3m	2.5m
Boris Johnson's Lies	Labour Party	46,000	4.0m	3.8m
Liz Truss housing interview	Momentum	56,000	3.9m	4.0m
Tories making stuff up	Momentum	56,000	3.4m	1.8m
Brexit, Actually	Boris Johnson	33,000	2.7m	N/A
Gogglebox Reacts	Jeremy Corbyn	31,000	2.7m	2.7m
Nurses challenge Johnson	Momentum	25,000	2.7m	1.5m

Source Post-election report on social media to the Labour National Executive Committee

which they deemed a better means to reach less engaged swing voters, something which is reflected in much higher Conservative expenditure on Google channels (see Table 9.8). Conservative sources were very happy with a social media campaign which they felt had delivered plenty of impactful and influential content, and closed the creative gap with Labour, who they believed had not built on their 2017 advantages.[33] While each party will tend to emphasise the stronger aspects of its performance, and in a field as dispersed and technical such as social media it is often hard to adjudicate rival claims, it does seem clear that the Conservative performance in 2019 was a major improvement on the previous election and at the very least reduced the party's disadvantage in this new and rapidly changing media environment (Table 9.8).

However, general voter distrust of social media content may limit the impact of even the most effective online campaign materials. Research by the Electoral Commissions, suggests that more than half (58%) of voters saw online campaigning as 'untrue or misleading', and few regarded online media as a trustworthy source of political information. Nearly half of voters raised concerns about campaigning based on incorrect

Table 9.8 Parties' political advertising and expenditure on Google and Facebook during the 2019 campaign

Platform	Party	Number of advertisers	Number of adverts	Average impression (million)	Average spend (£m)
Facebook	Labour	367	9,018	144.2	2.1
	Conservatives	300	13,759	89.8	1.5
	Liberal Democrats	243	14,204	92.6	1.4
	Brexit Party	77	4,824	26.8	0.7
	Other	232	4,164	30.0	0.4
	Total	1,219	45,969	383.4	6.0
Google	Conservatives	2	298	107.3	1.8
	Labour	2	114	60.9	0.7
	Liberal Democrats	3	185	16.7	0.2
	Brexit Party	1	7	8.3	0.2
	Other	3	50	4.2	0.02
	Total	11	654	197.4	3.0

Source Dommett and Bakir, 'A Transparent Digital Election Campaign?'[35]

information or untrue claims, with an even higher share citing inadequate control of political activity on social media as a major concern they had about the election. Social media may be a new creative frontier for parties, but voters are under no illusions about the quality or regulation of information on the online 'Wild West'.[34]

The Punch that Wasn't: Media Hybridisation and Its Effects

The blurring of lines between traditional and social media not only impacts the way that voters experience the campaign, but can also shape how events themselves unfold. On 9 December, with just three days to go until polling day, the BBC and ITV became embroiled in a campaign reporting controversy which put the growing hybridisation of broadcast and online reporting under the spotlight. The story began with a picture of a four-year-old boy with suspected pneumonia forced to lie on a pile of coats on the floor of Leeds General Hospital due to a shortage of beds that had been published in the *Yorkshire Post* the previous day. It escalated when ITN political correspondent Joe Pike had repeatedly attempted to get Boris Johnson to respond to the photo, only for the Prime Minister to grab the reporter's phone midway through his interview and put it in his pocket. Clips of the incident, which epitomised concerns about Johnson's evasiveness and awkward relationship with the truth, went viral on social media, forcing the Conservatives to make a stronger response. Health Secretary Matt Hancock was sent to Leeds General to offer a mollifying response, where he was met by a small crowd of angry local medical staff and protesters attacking Conservative cuts. Based on briefings from 'senior Conservatives', at 4.37 pm BBC Political Editor Laura Kuenssberg tweeted 'So Matt Hancock was despatched to Leeds General (sorry not just Leeds Hospital), to try to sort out mess, hearing Labour activists scrambled to go+protest, and it turned nasty when they arrived—one of them punched Hancock's adviser'. ITV's Political Editor Robert Peston similarly tweeted that the adviser had been 'whacked in the face by a protestor' (with ITV political correspondent Paul Brand similarly reporting the claim that 'a Conservative political advisor was assaulted outside the hospital'). Kuenssberg's and Peston's tweets were both sent instantly to audiences of over one million followers, and breaking news alerts and push notifications quickly amplified the claims further and propelled them into other news reports. The false reports prompted a response from West Yorkshire Police at 5.31 pm: 'We are aware of information circulating on social media in relation to an alleged incident involving election campaigners at Leeds General Infirmary this afternoon. We are currently unaware of any reports of this nature but are seeking to verify.'[36] The story had spiralled out of control.

Robert Peston ✓
@Peston

It was @MattHancock's adviser @jnjokugoodwin who was whacked in the face by a protestor as he tried to help Hancock into his car outside Leeds General Hospital. Police on scene. All sounds very unpleasant

12:00 PM · Dec 9, 2019 · Twitter Web App

@Peston tweet on 'punch that wasn't'

Paul Brand ✓
@PaulBrandITV

Conservatives say Labour paid for taxis to transport around 100 activists to Leeds General Infirmary, to protest against the Health Secretary's visit. They say a Conservative political advisor was assaulted outside the hospital.

4:38 PM · Dec 9, 2019 · Twitter for iPhone

@PaulBrandITV tweet on 'punch that wasn't'

Laura Kuenssberg ✓
@bbclaurak

So Matt Hancock was despatched to Leeds General
(sorry not just Leeds Hospital), to try to sort out mess,
hearing Labour activists scrambled to go + protest, and
it turned nasty when they arrived - one of them
punched Hancock's adviser

4:37 PM · Dec 9, 2019 · Twitter Web App

559 Retweets   **776** Likes

Laura Kuenssberg ✓ @bbclaurak · 55m
Replying to @bbclaurak
Not entirely clear what happened, but Tories suggesting Labour campaigners
offered to pay cabs for activists to go and heckle Hancock - fair to say today
not panning out as anyone had expected in what has been a relatively flat
campaign

♡ 1.3K   ♺ 216   ♡ 408

Deleted @BBCLauraK tweet on 'punch that wasn't'

As video footage of the incident from multiple angles emerged soon
after, it became apparent that there had been no punch or assault—
the advisor hadn't been looking where they were going and walked
into the flailing arm of a cyclist without any link to Labour. Peston
and Kuenssberg were forced into swift retractions, deleting their original tweets and apologising for their errors.[37] Labour campaigners were
understandably furious that senior political journalists' decisions to
tweet out unchecked and unsourced Conservative campaign briefings
had for several hours turned a true story about pressures on the NHS
into a false story about violence by Labour activists. Labour supporters
took to Twitter to express their annoyance—there were 14,000 replies
to Kuenssberg's apology and 12,000 to Peston's correction. Many
interpreted the incident as further evidence of media bias against the
Labour campaign. Jeremy Corbyn's Twitter account shared a screen-
grab of the original tweets by Peston, Kuenssberg, *The Sun* politics editor
Tom Newton-Dunn and ITV political correspondent Paul Brand, and

declared: 'This never happened ... This is what media bias looks like.'[38] Whether or not the briefing of the assault by senior Conservative sources was an intentional attempt to redirect a negative news cycle or simply a result of 'a routine cock-up' in the words of Peston—as two eyewitnesses had claimed the advisor had been 'lamped'[39]—may never be known. But the incident highlights the new challenges faced by broadcast journalists who are, on the TV screen, bound by strong rules and norms, but on the phone screen face relentless pressure to break the stories of the campaign in real time, pressures which can make it hard to fully check the stories' veracity before commenting on them. As the once distinct worlds of broadcast and online media become ever more blurred together, there is a growing need to address relative lack of formal and informal guidelines on campaign reporting conducted via personal social media accounts. Confused and misleading accounts risk leaving voters confused, fuel distrust and could jeopardise broadcasters' commitments to fair and impartial coverage.

Laura Kuenssberg ✓
@bbclaurak

Happy to apologiSe for earlier confusion about the punch that wasn't a punch outside Leeds General - 2 sources suggested it had happened but clear from video that was wrong

6:48 PM · Dec 9, 2019 · Twitter for iPhone

@BBCLauraK apology tweet regarding 'punch that wasn't'

Robert Peston ✓
@Peston

It is completely clear from video footage that @MattHancock's adviser was not whacked by a protestor, as I was told by senior Tories, but that he inadvertently walked into a protestor's hand. I apologise for getting this wrong.

6:06 PM · Dec 9, 2019 · Twitter Web App

@Peston apology tweet regarding 'punch that wasn't'

IMPARTIALITY IN A POPULIST AGE

While past elections have often seen claims and counterclaims of broadcaster bias, the 2019 general election featured perhaps the most febrile atmosphere yet. Brexit had polarised voters, stoking distrust of a supposedly 'liberal, London-based media' among Leavers and of a media insufficiently willing to highlight the costs of the UK's impending exit from the EU among Remainers. The broadcasters found themselves subject to intense scrutiny and criticism from all sides. This was not helped by occasional missteps in coverage and the widespread use of anonymous briefings, which encouraged suspicions that journalists were laundering unreliable information, especially via social media.

Sky News' adoption of 'the Brexit election' as its slogan for campaign coverage was the subject of a complaint to Ofcom from the Labour Party, accusing the broadcaster of giving 'undue and unfair weight to the Conservative Party's political agenda'. The complaint was rejected by the regulator, finding there were no grounds to pursue it—describing Brexit as 'an important background contextual factor' to the election. In the final reckoning, the broadcasters' decision was vindicated, with Brexit unmistakably shaping the outcome of the election. Sky News was also on the receiving end of criticisms from Brexit supporters about its coverage. The choice of former Speaker John Bercow as one of the main guests for the election night show threw Leavers into a rage online—the announcement by @SkyNews on Twitter received over 2,000 replies, many of them not entirely complementary.

In much the same way, the BBC got it in the neck from all sides over its coverage of the election campaign. It received complaints from the public that it was biased in favour of Labour (in coverage of the party's campaign launch on 31 October), biased against Conservative Party Chair James Cleverly (in an interview on 6 November), biased against the Prime Minister (in an interview on 15 November), biased in favour of the Prime Minister (editing out audience laughter at Johnson's response in a clip from the *Question Time Leaders' Special* on 22 November), that the audience for the *Question Time Leaders' Special* had been biased generally (22 November), biased against the Prime Minister in an interview on Radio 5 Live (15 November), biased against Michael Gove in an interview on the *Today* programme (13 November), biased against the Prime Minister's father Stanley Johnson in an interview about his attendance of the Channel 4 Climate Debate (29 November), biased against Jeremy Corbyn in his interview with Andrew Neil (26 November) and biased against Boris Johnson in Andrew Neil's closing monologue, at the end of his interview with Nigel Farage (5 December).[40] Complaints were received *both* that the BBC had interviewed Boris Johnson on *The Andrew Marr Show* despite his no-show for an interview with Andrew Neil *and* that Andrew Marr had been biased against Boris Johnson in his aggressive questioning (1 December). Everyone felt that *their side* was being treated unfairly. The public service broadcaster seemingly could do no right in a deeply divided political environment.

While the broadcasters did not always help themselves, they were operating in an intense, fast-moving and often toxic environment, facing criticism from all sides that was not always made in good faith. The populist politics unleashed by Brexit, combined with the increasingly blurred boundary between broadcast news and social media—and the hyper-engagement of the most politically interested voters and activists—meant that every misstep was pounced upon and every editorial decision was subjected to intense scrutiny, often through a partisan lens.

NOTES

1. Colin Brown, 'The Truth about Prescott and That Punch', *The Independent*, 20 July 2013, https://www.independent.co.uk/news/uk/politics/the-truth-about-prescott-and-that-punch-8722563.html.
2. The incident received extensive coverage in the 2001 edition of this series—see David Butler and Dennis Kavanagh, *The British General Election of 2001*. Palgrave Macmillan, 2001, pp. 95–96, 142.
3. In part this reflects a general trend towards lighter-touch regulation of public service broadcasters, but may also be a response to the more volatile and fragmented context of contemporary British politics, which has made such judgements more difficult and controversial. For example, in 2015 (the final election when such guidance was issued), there was intense debate over the decision to award UKIP (but not the Green Party) 'major' party status on the basis of their strength in opinion polling—UKIP were polling well ahead of the Greens at the time, but unlike UKIP, the Greens had returned an MP to the Commons in the previous general election. See Ofcom 'Review of Ofcom List of Major Political Parties for Elections Taking Place on 7th May 2015', https://www.ofcom.org.uk/__data/assets/pdf_file/0016/72142/major_parties_statement.pdf.
4. Six months after the election, Sky News introduced guidelines for its journalists emphasising the importance of adhering to the broadcaster's obligations and values, and of avoiding giving impressions of bias through the expression of opinions or liking/retweeting tweets; see 'Sky Presenters' Tweeting Wings Clipped', *Guido Fawkes*, 16 June 2020, https://order-order.com/2020/06/16/sky-presenters-tweeting-wings-clipped. The BBC issued its staff with new guidance on social media usage aimed at maintaining impartiality a few months later; see 'BBC Issues Staff with New Social Media Guidance', *BBC News*, 29 October 2020, https://www.bbc.co.uk/news/entertainment-arts-54723282.
5. Polling by Ipsos in early 2019 (29 January–8 February) found a net score of +32% trust in television and radio as a reliable source of news and information compared to just +1% for newspapers and magazines (see Ipsos, 'Trust in the Media', 2019, https://www.ipsos.com/sites/default/files/ct/news/documents/2019-06/global-advisor-trust-in-media-2019.pdf).
6. The *BBC News* website is well ahead of every other media outlet in terms of its 'reach' online, with some 44% of people who accessed a news website during the campaign visiting it. This was followed by the MailOnline (32%), *The Sun* (30%), *The Mirror* (30%) and *The Guardian* (29%). See Richard Fletcher, Nic Newman and Anne Schulz, *A Mile Wide, an Inch*

Deep: Online News and Media Use in the 2019 UK General Election. Reuters Institute for the Study of Journalism, 2020, https://reutersinstitute.politics.ox.ac.uk/sites/default/files/2020-02/Fletcher_News_Use_During_the_Election_FINAL.pdf.

7. Ibid.
8. Ibid.
9. Deacon et al. sampled election-related news items in major news programmes—*Channel 4 News* (7 pm), *Channel 5 News* (6.30 pm), *BBC News at 10, ITV News at 10, Sky News* (10 pm)—on Mondays to Fridays between 7 November and 4 December. See David Deacon, Jackie Goode, David Smith, Dominic Wring, John Downey and Cristian Vaccari, *General Election 2019: Report 5, 7 November–11 December 2019.* Centre for Research in Communication and Culture, 2019.
10. Since their introduction, leader debates had followed a multi-party format in the 2010, 2015 and 2017 elections. Various efforts to stage televised debates in elections before 2010 came to nothing, typically due to the frontrunner's refusal to participate in them.
11. 'General Election 2019: Lib Dems Launch Legal Action over ITV Debate', *BBC News*, 11 November 2019, https://www.bbc.co.uk/news/uk-50380116.
12. Though the format was seen as novel by the broadcasters and the two parties involved, it was perhaps less of a novelty to less politically engaged voters, who may have regarded it as a minor variation on a now well-established campaign theme.
13. For discussion of earlier events and their audiences, see Martin Harrison, 'The X-Factor Election: On the Air' in Dennis Kavanagh and Philip Cowley, *The British General Election of 2010.* Palgrave Macmillan, 2010; Charlie Beckett, 'The Battle for the Stage: Broadcasting', in Philip Cowley and Dennis Kavanagh, *The British General Election of 2015.* Palgrave Macmillan, 2015; and Stephen Cushion and Charlie Beckett, 'Campaign Coverage and Editorial Judgements: Broadcasting', in Philip Cowley and Dennis Kavanagh, *The British General Election of 2017.* Palgrave Macmillan, 2018.
14. Michael Deacon, 'Boris Johnson is a BBC Interviewer's Nightmare ... for This Very Simple Reason', *Daily Telegraph*, 1 October 2019, https://www.telegraph.co.uk/politics/2019/10/01/boris-johnson-bbc-interviewers-nightmare-simple-reason.
15. Given that the event was held in Sheffield, the number of audience members with strong Scottish accents asking Corbyn questions on Scottish independence was a little unusual. Six of the last eight audience members to quiz Corbyn were audibly Scottish, and all asked hostile questions on Labour's Scottish independence policy, obliging Bruce to intervene and

reject further questions from yet more Scots in the audience seeking to continue grilling Corbyn on the issue.

16. Sunak did not remain a junior figure for long—within three months, he would be leading Britain's response to the COVID-19 pandemic as Johnson's Chancellor.

17. See, for example, Kevin Rawlinson, 'Boris Johnson's Spin Doctor "Used to Dress up as Tory-Ridiculing *Mirror* Chicken"', *The Guardian*, 30 July 2019, https://www.theguardian.com/politics/2019/jul/30/boris-johnson-spin-doctors-life-as-mirror-chicken-revealed.

18. Ofcom ruled against the Conservatives, arguing that the Conservative viewpoint on climate change was adequately reflected in the debate, while also noting 'the globe ice sculpture was not a representation of the Prime Minister personally'.

19. Michael Deacon., 'Andrew Neil Interviewed Jeremy Corbyn on Antisemitism … and Utterly Dismantled Him', *Daily Telegraph*, 26 November 2019, https://www.telegraph.co.uk/politics/2019/11/26/andrew-neil-interviewed-jeremy-corbyn-antisemitism-utterly-dismantled.

20. John Crace, Tweet, 26 November 2019, 7.30 pm, https://twitter.com/JohnJCrace/status/1199410022079500288?s=20.

21. Richard Hartley-Parkinson, 'Secret Messages from Labour Backers Trying to "Drown out" Reaction to "Truly Horrific, Awful" Jeremy Corbyn Interview', *The Metro*, 27 November, 2019, https://metro.co.uk/2019/11/27/secret-messages-labour-backers-trying-drown-reaction-truly-horrific-awful-jeremy-corbyn-interview-11224506.

22. 'Labour Complains to BBC Director General over "Slanted and Biased" Election Coverage', 5 December 2019, https://labour.org.uk/press/labour-complains-to-bbc-director-general-over-slanted-and-biased-election-coverage.

23. Though many journalists use multiple social media platforms, and the political parties focus their social media campaigning on Facebook, Twitter has become the medium of choice for communication within the political elite and a growing obsession for politicians themselves (see Chapter 3, p. 88).

24. 'Why Do People Hate Laura Kuenssberg So Much?', *New Statesman*, 10 May 2016, https://www.newstatesman.com/politics/media/2016/05/why-do-people-hate-laura-kuenssberg-so-much. Regarding sexist abuse directed at female politicians in 2019, see Genevieve Gorrell et al., 'Which Politicians Receive Abuse? Four Factors Illuminated in the UK General Election 2019', *EPJ Data Science* (2020), https://epjdatascience.springeropen.com/articles/10.1140/epjds/s13688-020-00236-9.

25. Though one of these three, Andrew Neil, also has strong links to *The Spectator*, and left the BBC in 2020 to become Chairman of *GB News*, a news channel that launched in 2021.

26. James O'Malley, 'New UK Parliament's Twitterati, Mapped', *Politico*, 23 January 2020, https://www.politico.eu/article/new-uk-parliaments-twitterarti-mapped.

27. A collaboration between *The Guardian* and the research agency 'Revealing Reality' which tracked political media consumption on six volunteers' smartphones provided some startling insights into the ways in which traditional and social media consumption is blurred together by smartphone users—their consumption of broadcast output often came via social media posts or in response to the social media posts of friends or political opponents. See Jim Waterson, 'Secrets of Their Smartphones: See How Voters Follow the News in Memes', *The Guardian*, 5 December 2019, https://www.theguardian.com/politics/2019/dec/05/memes-shares-and-arguments-how-do-people-consume-election-news-on-their-phones.

28. The edited clip, viewed more than a million times, made it look like Starmer responded to a question with silence, when he had in fact given an immediate and detailed response. Conservative Party Chairman James Cleverly initially defended the clip as 'light-hearted and satirical'; see John Johnston, 'Tory Chairman James Cleverly Defends Party Video amid "Fake News" Claims', *PoliticsHome*, 6 November 2019, https://www.politicshome.com/news/article/tory-chairman-james-cleverly-defends-party-video-amid-fake-news-claims. Following criticism from the Labour campaign, Conservative MPs and Morgan himself, CCHQ eventually dispatched Rishi Sunak to apologise to Morgan and his viewers: 'It was done in the spirit of humour, but I appreciate it didn't land properly and it probably went a bit too far.' See Nicholas Mairs, 'Conservative Minister Apologises for "Doctored" Keir Starmer Video", *PoliticsHome*, 12 November 2019, https://www.politicshome.com/news/article/watch-conservative-minister-apologises-for-doctored-keir-starmer-video.

29. 'Twitter Says UK PM Johnson's Party Misled Public with "Factcheck" Account', *Reuters*, 20 November 2019, https://www.reuters.com/article/britain-election-twitter-idUKL9N27700V.

30. Cowley and Kavanagh, *The British General Election of 2017*, p. 311.

31. Jonathan Mellon and Christopher Prosser, 'Twitter and Facebook are Not Representative of the General Population: Political Attitudes and Demographics of British Social Media Users', *Research & Politics* (2017), https://doi.org/10.1177/2053168017720008.

32. The 'echo chamber' problem with Labour's approach to social media was extensively discussed in the Labour Together report on the 2019 election: https://electionreview.labourtogether.uk/chapters/the-online-war.

33. One striking example was the 'Lo fi boris wave beats to relax and get Brexit done to' video posted on YouTube—an hour-long loop of Johnson clips set to a relaxing 'chillout' soundtrack, with a rolling video graphic of Boris reading on a train. The video was viewed over a million times on YouTube, though it must have been rather mystifying to older Conservative voters: https://www.youtube.com/watch?v=cre0in5n-1E.

34. Electoral Commission, *In Depth: Campaigning at the 2019 UK Parliamentary General Election* (2020), https://www.electoralcommission.org.uk/who-we-are-and-what-we-do/elections-and-referendums/past-elections-and-referendums/uk-general-elections/report-2019-uk-parliamentary-general-election-was-well-run/depth-campaigning-2019-uk-parliamentary-general-elec.

35. Katharine Dommett and Mehmet Emin Bakir, 'A Transparent Digital Election Campaign? The Insights and Significance of Political Advertising Archives for Debates on Electoral Regulation', *Parliamentary Affairs*, 73(S1) (2020): 208–24, https://doi.org/10.1093/pa/gsaa029.

36. West Yorkshire Police, Tweet, 9 December 2019, 5.31 pm, https://twitter.com/WestYorksPolice/status/1204091196806696967?s=20.

37. Laura Kuenssberg, Tweet, 9 December 2019, 6.48 pm, https://twitter.com/bbclaurak/status/1204110491242643457; Robert Peston, Tweet, 9 December 2019, 6.06 pm, https://twitter.com/Peston/status/1204100056762265600.

38. Jeremy Corbyn, Tweet, 9 December 2019, 10.37 pm, https://twitter.com/jeremycorbyn/status/1204168230346067968?s=20.

39. Freddy Mayhew, 'Robert Peston Says He was "Not Spun" over Hospital "Punch" Error and Interviewing May was "Nightmare"', *Press Gazette*, 9 March 2020, https://www.pressgazette.co.uk/robert-peston-says-he-was-not-spun-over-hospital-punch-error-and-interviewing-may-was-nightmare.

40. BBC, 'Archived BBC Public Response to Complaints: 2019', https://www.bbc.co.uk/contact/sites/default/files/2020-03/BBC%20public%20complaints%20responses%202019.pdf.

CHAPTER 10

Enduring Brands: The Press

David Deacon, David Smith, and Dominic Wring

INTRODUCTION: 'JINGLE POLLS'

In marked contrast to 2017, the announcement of the 2019 general election came as no surprise. For months Boris Johnson had been signalling his wish for an election to break the hold of a 'zombie parliament', but had been thwarted by the Fixed-term Parliament Act as well as by the Opposition. Securing an election took four attempts—and the acceptance of a negotiated EU Withdrawal Agreement—all of which had already stimulated intense media speculation (see Chapter 1, pp. 1–27). That said, press reporting of the campaign's formal beginning conveyed far more uncertainty about the outcome than it had in 2017. This in large part reflected the painful lessons of the previous election, where media commentators failed to anticipate the Conservatives losing a polling lead that exceeded Johnson's advantage in 2019.

In a guarded welcome, *The Sun*'s leader column stated 'The PM has no choice but to roll the dice ... An election is a massive gamble for the nation and for Boris' (30 October 2019). Similarly, the *Daily Mail*'s editorial declared it 'The Most Crucial Vote since the War ... and We Cannot Let it Be the Nightmare before Christmas' (30 October 2019). This was also reflected in the same edition's front-page headline: 'At Last Boris Wins Election Date—and He's Leading the Polls. But with Lib Dems and Brexit Party Threatening Tory Vote in Key Seats, the Stark Warning ... DON'T LET THE GRINCH STEAL YOUR

CHRISTMAS' (*Daily Mail*, 30 October 2019). *The Times*, *The I* paper and the *Financial Times* similarly emphasised the unpredictability of the outcome, albeit in less polemical terms. Only two national titles exuded greater confidence, with the *Daily Express* proclaiming: 'December 12—When Britain Will Vote... Once and for All ... to Deliver Brexit' (30 October 2019). In contrast, the *Daily Mirror* declared: 'IT'S TIME TO STUFF THE TURKEY. MPs Back Christmas Showdown and Give Voters Chance to Get Rid of Johnson' (30 October 2019).

In one important respect, however, there was a newspaper consensus—a presumption that the campaign in prospect would be dominated and defined by Brexit. Yet for all that Boris Johnson may have wanted to fight a single-issue media campaign in 2019 and, despite the intensifying crisis over Brexit, there were no guarantees he would have more success than his predecessor. His opponents were equally intent on shifting the media and public agenda on to different issues, including the NHS, austerity, the future of the Union, social inequalities, public ownership and climate change.

THE LAST HURRAH OF THE PARTISAN PRESS?

If the political terrain had changed considerably since 2017, then so had the partisan and economic landscape of the national press. In 2018, Reach (formerly the Trinity Mirror group) acquired Northern & Shell's publishing assets, which included the *Daily Express*, the *Sunday Express*, the *Daily Star* and the *Star on Sunday*. This ended the influence of their previous proprietor, Richard Desmond, a convinced Eurosceptic who had steered the *Express* to back UKIP in the 2015 election. In September 2018, Geordie Greig was appointed editor of the *Daily Mail*, leading to speculation that this might shift the editorial tone of a paper whose disdain for left-wingers, the EU and multiculturalism had been personified by Greig's predecessor Paul Dacre. In October 2019, it was announced that the *Daily Telegraph* and the *Sunday Telegraph* were being put up for sale by their owners the Barclay brothers for a fraction of the £660 million purchase price paid for them in 2004. During the campaign itself and after months of speculation, it was confirmed that *The i* paper—which retained editorial but not proprietorial links with the online-only *The Independent* newspaper—had finally been acquired by the Daily Mail Group.

There was a further major decline in the circulation of print editions of all national titles between the two elections (see Tables 10.1 and

10.2), continuing a long-running trend.[1] In November 2019, daily and Sunday newspaper circulations were down 25% on the equivalent figures for May 2017. The financial state of the papers was more mixed, with some national titles recording considerable losses while others had clambered back towards financial viability. *The Sun* and the *Sun on Sunday*'s £68 million deficit in 2018 was largely due to ongoing compensation payouts for the phone hacking scandal. The *Daily* and *Sunday Telegraph*'s 90% fall in profits over the same period was blamed on a vertiginous decline in readership and printed advertising revenue. In contrast, *The Times*, the *Sunday Times*, the *Financial Times*, the *Daily Mail* and the *Mail on Sunday* all recorded stable profits. In mid-2019, *The Guardian* announced its first operating profit since 1998. These titles had managed to offset financial losses created by circulation and print advertising declines by a range of means, such as changes in production formats, increased digital subscription revenues, online advertising, expanded online readerships and significant job losses. Whether continued substantial circulation declines would ameliorate or accentuate titles' partisan tendencies was also an open question. Would titles seek to shore up existing readership bases by hardening their party and political allegiances or adopt less strident positions in the search for new readers outside of their traditional core groups? (Tables 10.1 and 10.2).

Table 10.1   Daily newspapers' 2019 partisanship with circulations

Title Owner (Chair) Editor	Partisanship 2019 (2017)	Circulation 2019 (2017)	Circulation loss 2017–2019 (%)
Daily Mirror Reach (Nick Prettejohn) Alison Phillips	Strong Labour (Strong Labour)	455,000 (687,000)	−34
Daily Express Reach (Nick Prettejohn) Gary Jones	Very Strong Conservative (Very Strong Conservative)	298,000 (386,000)	−23
Daily Star Reach (Nick Prettejohn) Jon Clark	None (None)	289,000 (438,000)	−34

(continued)

Title Owner (Chair) Editor	Partisanship 2019 (2017)	Circulation 2019 (2017)	Circulation loss 2017–2019 (%)
The Sun News UK (Rupert Murdoch) Tony Gallagher	Very Strong Conservative (Very Strong Conservative)	1,217,000 (1,617,000)	−25
Daily Mail Daily Mail & General Trust (Viscount Rothermere) Geordie Greig	Very Strong Conservative (Very Strong Conservative)	1,133,000 (1,454,000)	−22
Daily Telegraph Telegraph Media Group (Barclay Brothers) Chris Evans	Very Strong Conservative (Strong Conservative)	309,000 (467,000)	−34
The Guardian Guardian Media Group (Neil Berkett) Katharine Viner	Weak Labour (Moderate Labour)	129,000 (154,000)	−16
The Times News UK (Rupert Murdoch) John Witherow	Strong Conservative (Moderate Conservative)	365,000 (446,000)	−18
The i Daily Mail & General Trust (Viscount Rothermere) Oliver Duff	None (None)	220,000 (263,000)	−16
Financial Times Nikkei (Tsunea Kita) Lionel Barber	Very Weak Liberal Democrat (Weak Conservative)	163,000 (197,000)	−17
Totals	Share of endorse- ments by circulation C 73% Lab 13% LD 4% None 11%	4,578,000 (6,109,000)	−25

Source Audit Bureau of Circulations for November 2019 (April 2017)

Table 10.2 Sunday newspapers' 2019 partisanship with circulations

Title Owner (Chair) Editor	Partisanship 2019 (2017)	Circulation 2019 (2017)	Circulation loss 2017–2019
Sunday Mirror Reach (Nick Prettejohn) Peter Willis	Very Strong Labour (Moderate Labour)	372,000 (585,000)	−36%
Sunday Express Reach (Nick Prettejohn) Michael Booker	Very Strong Conservative (Very Strong Conservative)	259,000 (335,000)	−23%
Star on Sunday Reach (Nick Prettejohn) Denis Mann	None (None)	172,000 (252,000)	−32%
Sun on Sunday News UK (Rupert Murdoch) Victoria Newton	Very Strong Conservative (Strong Conservative)	1,033,000 (1,358,000)	−24%
Mail on Sunday Daily Mail & General Trust (Viscount Rothermere) Ted Verity	Very Strong Conservative (Strong Conservative)	966,000 (1,239,000)	−22%
Sunday Telegraph Telegraph Media Group (Barclay Brothers) Allister Heath	Very Strong Conservative (Strong Conservative)	247,000 (355,000)	−30%
The Observer Guardian Media Group (Neil Berkett) Paul Webster	Strong Anti-Conservative (Strong Anti-Conservative)	160,000 (181,000)	−12%
Sunday Times News UK (Rupert Murdoch) Tony Gallagher	Strong Conservative (Moderate Conservative)	653,000 (780,000)	−16%
Sunday People Reach (Nick Prettejohn) Peter Willis	Very Strong Labour (Strong Anti-Conservative)	144,000 (228,000)	−37%
Totals	Share of endorsements by circulation C 79% Lab 13% LD 0% None 4% Other 4%	4,006,000 (5,313,000)	−25%

Source Audit Bureau of Circulations for November 2019 (April 2017)

LEGACY LONGEVITY

Financial considerations aside, in the lead-up to the campaign, there were many who were ready to claim that the major decline in the circulation of newspapers demonstrated their decreasing relevance in general elections.[2] Indeed, following the surge in Labour support during the 2017 campaign, there was much speculation that social media platforms and start-up digital media outlets now represented the new kingmakers in UK politics.[3] However, if the press are conceived less as news*papers* and more as news *brands* existing both in print and online (including as mobile apps), then reports of the death of the industry have been greatly exaggerated once again. Approximately half of the British public still use national newspapers one way or another to acquire news.[4] While this represents a smaller reach than that of TV news—used by three-quarters of the public[5]—newspapers have long provided a vociferous and distinctively partisan set of perspectives on current affairs compared with their broadcast counterparts, whose coverage must observe strict due impartiality rules, especially during elections. The impact of the press on public debate is, then, different in qualitative and quantitative terms from that of broadcasting, and it would be naïve to equate the decline of the printed newspaper with the decline of the broader 'partisan press' product.

There is also evidence of the enduring longevity of 'legacy' media institutions—the press, television, radio and magazines. For example, three-quarters of the top 20 most-used news sources in the UK are either TV channels (six), newspapers in print or online (five), radio stations (three) or legacy media websites (one).[6] BBC sources alone occupy seven spots in this top 20 chart, with BBC One used by well over half of news consumers. Across multiple attributes of importance, accuracy, trustworthiness and diversity of opinion, TV and newspapers are rated very highly, whereas users give social media relatively low scores, particularly for trustworthiness and accuracy.[7]

The digital news environment itself is also structured and dominated by legacy news media outlets. The BBC looms as large here as it does offline, with by far the largest online reach of any news outlet in the UK.[8] Meanwhile, the digital equivalents of the major national weekday newspapers reach many millions of people every day.[9] *The Sun*'s daily reach via mobile, tablet and desktop, for instance, is estimated at 8.6 million individual users, *The Guardian*'s at 8.3 million and the *Daily Mail*'s at 7.4 million. The next most popular are the *Daily Mirror*'s with 5 million, the *Daily Express* with 4 million and the *Daily Telegraph* reaching 3.5 million.[10] *The Independent*, which ceased its print operation in 2016, continues to reach 5.3 million people per day. Newspapers have proved well able to preserve their agenda-setting powers by shifting the focus of their influence from print to online, while the longstanding broadcast dominance of the BBC has been replicated in the online environment.

Legacy news institutions continued to have a substantial direct impact during the short campaign. This is enhanced in the contemporary 'hybrid media' environment[11] by the way in which news content produced by legacy media outlets sets the political agenda on social media platforms, where it is the most widely circulated political content. The parties themselves recognise this enduring influence, as shown by a willingness to accommodate favourable or, alternatively, exclude hostile journalists from the press corps allowed to attend their official campaign events (for example, see below for more on the Conservatives' banning the *Daily Mirror*). Across each of the major social media platforms—Facebook, Twitter, Instagram and Snapchat—the largest source for news use is legacy media news organisations, considerably more than the next category of 'friends and family'.[12] And while a relatively small minority 'actively follow' specific news programmes, online-only news organisations or individual journalists (who often break news on social media *before* they file a report via their news organisation), almost one-third of those who use Facebook or Twitter for news actively follow legacy media news organisations.[13] More passive consumption of news on social media comes from users seeing news stories that are trending (ranging between 47% of news users on Instagram and 57% of news users on Twitter), and to a certain extent from users seeing links to or comments on news stories posted by others.[14] This last activity highlights the largely reactive nature of even the most active forms of news engagement online, contrary to early hopes of a turn to so-called 'produser' creative activity in which citizens (i.e. the producer-users) would take a more active role in driving news production and dissemination. In some ways, print media outlets—which traditionally had their greatest inter-media agenda setting impact on the morning broadcast news—have now colonised spaces online that provide them with a recurring influence throughout the daily news cycle. Even in a news environment of 24/7 hyper-immediacy and low barriers to entry, professional news organisations have, so far at least, largely preserved their influence.

DIGITAL NATIVES

The recent emergence of various online-only political news sites has been cited as a factor in the political decline of the national press, and interest has grown in their influence, reach and approach. Among these are mainstream outlets which have become highly professionalised organisations (e.g. *HuffPost* and *BuzzFeed*), alongside so-called 'alternative news' outlets (e.g. *Breitbart*, *The Canary* and *Novara Media*) which offer more stridently partisan fare. Table 10.3 illustrates the reach of the ten largest internet-only news sites, amongst those of legacy news organisations.[15] Several of the former outlets are clustered together at approximately 4–6% of news audiences, the largest of which is *HuffPost*. Even the most popular of the explicitly partisan digital outfits (i.e. *Breitbart*, *The Canary* and *Another Angry Voice*) attracted only 1% of audiences per week, casting doubt over their allegedly growing influence beyond their existing and highly engaged activist readerships (Table 10.3).

Table 10.3 Top 20 online news brands among UK news users (Adapted from Fletcher et al., *A Mile Wide, an Inch Deep*)

News brand	Type	Weekly use (%)
BBC News	Legacy	45
The Guardian	Legacy	18
MailOnline	Legacy	15
Sky News	Legacy	10
Other local/regional newspaper website	Legacy	9
The Telegraph	Legacy	7
HuffPost	Digital	6
The Independent/i100	Digital	6
BuzzFeed News	Digital	6
The Sun	Legacy	6
Yahoo! News	Digital	6
MSN News	Digital	6
The Metro	Legacy	5
The Mirror	Legacy	4
LADbible News	Digital	4
The Times	Legacy	4
Breitbart	Digital	1
The Canary	Digital	1
Russia Today	Digital	1
Another Angry Voice	Digital	1

In contrast, 71% of the news audience went to national news sites like the BBC and 40% to local news sites like the *Birmingham Mail* and the *Liverpool Echo*. This pattern skews even further when considering *time spent* on news sites, which indicates regular and loyal consumption: here, partisan, satire and blog pages received only 1% of time spent on news sites, while the BBC (28%) and *MailOnline* (21%) collectively garnered 49% of the time people spent reading online news during the campaign.[16]

One way in which online-only news sites and bloggers attempt to maximise their impact is via social media sharing, through which individual posts are sometimes viewed hundreds of thousands or even millions of times.[17] For partisan online news outlets in particular, small budgets mean their very existence relies in large part on the mechanisms that sites like Facebook and Twitter offer for the 'viral' spread of content. In the 2017 campaign, this activity was credited by some with providing crucial impetus to Jeremy Corbyn's Labour Party, particularly as many of these sites skew to the left and attempted to act as a bulwark against the right-wing press and what they see as a right-leaning BBC.[18]

By 2019, the impact of alternative news sites, and left-wing variants in particular, on the election debate seemed to have waned considerably. In 2017, *The Guardian* had described such sites as a 'new force shaping the election debate',[19] while *Buzzfeed* published an article headlined 'This was the Election Where the Newspapers Lost Their Monopoly on the Political News Agenda'.[20] Labour's post-mortem into its 2019 defeat turned only briefly to the sites' role in the party's online campaign, attributing their limited impact to an echo chamber effect.[21] Furthermore, the potential influence of these newcomers had been inhibited by changes to Facebook's news-sharing algorithm in 2018 which deprioritised posts from 'businesses, brands and the media' in favour of more posts from 'friends, family and groups'[22] and newsroom cuts in 2019 at *The Canary* (the most successful of these sites in the 2017 campaign) following challenges, including a blacklisting campaign by the Stop Funding Fake News initiative and a corresponding fall in advertising revenue.[23] Nevertheless, despite the wider perception, left-wing alternative news sites actually *increased* their reach on Twitter overall between the two campaigns.[24] There is of course the possibility that the supposed significance of these platforms in 2017 was based on post hoc rationalisation, as may also be true of the dismissal of their contribution to the 2019 campaign.

STATED POSITIONS: EDITORIAL RESPONSES

The Conservatives once again enjoyed a handsome advantage in support from the major national and Sunday newspapers (Tables 10.1 and 10.2). Although half the dailies did not align themselves with the incumbent, the ones that did were very enthusiastic and collectively dominated the traditional print market with nearly three-quarters of circulation. The fervently pro-Conservative *The Sun* and the *Daily Mail* alone accounted for more sales than every other daily combined. Many more would, of course, have seen this content because readerships always exceed circulations and, as we have seen, millions more now habitually access online versions of these publications. A similar pattern was evident across the Sunday newspapers.

From the start of the election campaign, the *Daily Mail* demonstrated its staunchly Conservative credentials with its front-page editorial likening Jeremy Corbyn as 'the Grinch' who threatened to 'steal your Christmas' (30 October 2019). This set the tone for a campaign featuring a series of hard-hitting attacks on Labour and its leader. The paper's coverage culminated in a front-page paean, without image, to the Prime Minister and headlined with one word: 'Boris' (12 December 2019). The *Mail on Sunday* was similarly passionate in its Conservative partisanship, offering a stark front-page warning 'Save Us from a Friday 13th Horror' in an edition which included a denunciation of Corbyn by the Prime Minister, alongside the paper's 'Vote Boris' endorsement (8 December 2019).

The Sun vied with the *Daily Mail* to be the most consistently loyal Tory newspaper. Having welcomed the election, the paper called it the 'Biggest vote of our lives' (30 October 2019). Much editorialising about Labour ensued, including polemics about the party's 'Mad manifesto' (21 November 2019), 'Racist Left' (27 November 2019) and 'Lies on NHS' (4 December 2019). This culminated in the best-selling daily revisiting its (in)famous 1992 polling day edition headline to state that had Neil Kinnock won that election, the outcome would have been 'a picnic' compared with a 'Corbyn regime' (12 December 2019). The endorsement 'Save Brexit Save Britain' was complemented by an editorial accompanied by a mock-up of a classic First World War propaganda poster with the updated slogan 'What Did You Do on December 12th, Daddy?' (12 December 2019).

The *Daily Express* and *Sunday Express*, too, were both staunchly behind the Conservatives and Boris Johnson. Consciously or not, the editorial line of the papers revisited positions originally popularised by the titles' distinctive crusader branding. That motif had first been adopted during the inter-war years to promote stronger trading ties within the Empire. Since 2010, Express newspapers had formally campaigned for the UK to leave the EU, so it was apposite that the company's titles would now couch their endorsements with reference to this issue. Whereas the *Sunday* title implored readers to 'Vote Tory if you really want to get Brexit done' (8 December 2019), the sister *Daily* added a personal touch with a front-page photograph of the Prime Minister emblazoned with a sterling reminder 'Brexit and Britain in your hands' (12 December 2019).

Whereas the aforementioned pro-Conservative 'popular' titles were stalwarts of the 'Tory press', their enthusiasm was shared by their 'quality' counterparts *The Times* and especially the *Daily Telegraph*. The latter was as determinedly anti-Labour as any other paper, with editorials warning of its 'assault on the middle-class' (23 November 2019), framing Labour as 'anti-semitic from top to bottom' (6 December 2019) and warning of plans to install a 'Marxist' government (11 December 2019). *The Times* was more emollient in terms of its partisanship, expressing dismay about 'Irresponsible Populists' with 'fantasy economics' leading both the major parties (4 November 2019). Critical of Brexit, the paper nonetheless saw Labour as a greater threat to business (19 November 2019) with its 'economically ruinous' manifesto (22 November 2019). There was also belated praise for the Conservatives' 'Moderate Manifesto' (25 November 2019), followed by a firm endorsement of the incumbent government (11 December 2019). The *Sunday Times* was more discernibly enthusiastic for Boris Johnson than its sister daily, adopting language similar to its *Telegraph* rivals in warning of the possibility of 'a hard left government' (3 November 2019) before extolling the merits of the incumbent one (8 December 2019).

The *Mirror* newspapers continued to offer a staunch defence of Labour and stinging criticism of the Conservatives. Highly critical editorialising earned the title the rare distinction of being, as it claimed, 'Banned for telling the truth' after its journalists were denied access to the Prime Minister's battle bus (21 November 2019). A campaign heavily promoting Labour stories culminated in the formal endorsement which harked back to the party's 1945 campaign messaging in declaring 'For Them: Vote Labour' (12 December 2019). The Sunday sister newspaper and their *People* stablemate followed suit with similarly enthusiastic endorsements of Corbyn and his ambitious plans (8 December 2019). *The Guardian*, the other newspaper with traditional Labour sympathies, was decidedly less committed, having previously been critical of the leadership. The paper scolded Corbyn over his handling of the anti-semitism controversy before offering the lukewarm conclusion that a government led by him would be 'not perfect but progressive' (11 December 2019). However, the paper's Sunday sister *The Observer* failed to muster even a tepid Labour endorsement. Instead, it urged readers to vote against the Conservatives for what it called 'progressives' of all parties (8 December 2019).

The *Financial Times* had endorsed the Conservatives and Labour in recent decades, but Brexit had soured its opinion of both. The two main leaders were a 'dispiriting choice' according to the paper's first election editorial, which also denounced Boris Johnson and his 'populist messages' (30 October 2019) in terminology resembling the initial scepticism of *The Times*. The closest it came to an endorsement was a reiteration of its negative opinion of both main 'populist' alternatives (6 December 2019). The editorial offered highly qualified support to the anti-Brexit Liberal Democrats, despite their 'poor campaign' and deficient leadership.

Although the *Daily Star* and *The i* newspapers are very different in style, they share a common attachment to an independent line during election campaigns. This did not change following both titles' acquisition by companies responsible for the staunchly partisan *Mirror* and *Mail* respectively. While the papers enabled partisan guest columnists to comment on developments, they also made a virtue of their impartiality, with *The i* declaring 'The Media Won't Decide This Election' (3 December 2019). Having re-introduced an editorial column, the *Daily Star* was resolutely blunt when it came to its electoral preference. The title's polling day front-page 'Clowning Street' (12 December 2019), complete with pictures of the two main leaders as circus performers, reflected the paper's dismay over the choice before the country. Adapting the words of the Stealers Wheel classic, the editorial lamented the situation: 'Clowns to the left of us, jokers to the right'.

HEADLINE ACTS: 'BORIS' VERSUS 'CORBYN'

The supposed advent of multi-polar politics vaunted in the 2015 general election seemed a distant memory four years on—or at least in press terms. Candidates and activists from the two main parties dominated newspaper reporting of the 2019 campaign. According to Loughborough University's figures, Tory and Labour sources accounted for 86% of featured politicians in weekday press coverage, up 1% on levels found in 2017 and 16% higher than in 2015.[25] Overall, Labour sources gained slightly more news presence than the incumbent party (Labour: 46% of all party-political sources; the Conservatives: 44%). Elsewhere, the Liberal Democrats competed with the Brexit Party for a distant third place (6% versus 5% respectively). The SNP, the Green Party, Plaid Cymru and all other parties accounted for the scant remaining 3%.[26] This meagre percentage included coverage of the DUP, who had been significant power brokers in the previous Parliament, but who were relegated to the margins of the national press.

Election news reporting in the UK has long displayed 'presidentialised' tendencies, with party leaders being the main focus of press coverage.[27] This remained the case in 2019, but with some nuances. Reporting of the Conservatives was even more leader-focused than before, with Boris Johnson accounting for 59% of all direct quotation of Conservative sources, up from 51% for Theresa May in the 2017 campaign. This increase is particularly notable when one recalls that a central plank of the Conservatives' initial election strategy in 2017 was a focus on May's 'strong and stable' leadership and, even after that backfired, her missteps ensured she remained the centre of attention. In contrast, reporting of Jeremy Corbyn and Labour charted a different trajectory. Corbyn's share of all Labour Party quotations fell from 53% in 2017 to 40% in 2019, while Corbyn himself accounted for 35% of all Labour sources reported, down from 45% in 2017. The 2017 campaign had seen both his reputation and confidence grow perceptibly; however, 2019 was very different. The shift reflects higher prominence given to other senior Labour figures such as John McDonnell, the Shadow Chancellor, who was chairing the party's election campaign. Across the campaign, McDonnell gained more than twice the coverage given to the then Chancellor Sajid Javid and even the Liberal Democrat leader Jo Swinson (5% of all party political appearances, compared with 2% and 2%, respectively).

Leaders and key frontbench figures didn't always monopolise the headlines. Both main parties entered the campaign in some internal disarray. A parliamentary rebellion over Brexit in October had seen the Prime Minister withdraw the whip from 21 Conservative MPs, including some senior party figures (see Chapter 1, pp. 1–27). Several of these recalcitrants contested the election as independents, including David Gauke, Anne Milton and Dominic Grieve. The Labour leadership also faced criticism from former MPs who had resigned the whip, including

Frank Field, John Woodcock and Ian Austin (see also Chapter 6, pp. 193–241). In the first week of the formal campaign, Austin wrote an opinion piece for the *Daily Mail* in which he attacked his former leader's fitness for high office, stating his 'patriotic duty … means supporting Boris Johnson and not Jeremy Corbyn in this election' (Don't Stop Brexit, Nigel … Stand Your Troops Down', *Daily Mail*, 7 November 2019). These sentiments were echoed on the same day by Woodcock ('Second Ex-Labour MP Urges People to Vote for Boris Johnson to Stop Jeremy Corbyn', *The Independent*, 7 November 2019). These interventions gained substantial follow-on press coverage, to the point that Austin became the sixth most prominently reported figure in the first week of the formal campaign, ahead of Nicola Sturgeon and Jo Swinson. Although such Labour renegades faded from view as the campaign intensified, they attracted far more coverage than dissident ex-Conservatives.

Austin and Woodcock's attacks on Jeremy Corbyn illustrate how politicians are frequently the *subject* rather than the *source* of press coverage. In 2019, the focus, intensity and character of such personalisation differed greatly, depending on the partisanship and market orientation of different papers. Table 10.4 provides a summary of all the main daily and Sunday headlines across the formal campaign. A cursory examination of these headlines shows how frequently they frame policy around the parties' leaders ('Boris Boost as Economy Bounces Back', *Daily Express*, 11 November 2019; 'Corbyn's £83BN Tax Robbery', *Daily Mail*, 22 November 2019). Figure 10.1 develops this point by presenting 'word clouds' of campaign headlines from the dailies—the more frequently a word featured in headlines, the larger it appears. The two main party leaders are always prominent, though the names applied to them vary. The mononym 'Boris' resonated across all popular newspapers regardless of partisan declarations. Even the hostile *Daily Mirror* couldn't deny the popular coinage of the 'Boris brand' in British public life. Equivalent informal terms of reference for the opposition leader ('Jez'/ 'Jezza'/ 'Jeremy') gained no meaningful traction. The Labour leader was consistently referred to by his surname in the pro-Tory popular press. In contrast, the quality press—regardless of political orientation—more frequently used surnames and full names when referring to the two main party leaders. In the pro-Tory qualities, 'Corbyn' hit the headlines more often than 'Johnson', with the reverse the case in the Labour-supporting *The Guardian*.

Table 10.4 Front-page lead stories, 30 October–12 December

	Daily/Sunday Mirror	Daily/Sunday Express	The Sun/Sun on Sunday	Daily/Sunday Mail	Daily Star/Daily Star on Sunday	Daily/Sunday Telegraph	The Guardian/The Observer	The Times/Sunday Times	The i	Financial Times
30 October	It's time to stuff the turkey	December 12 when Britain will vote … once and for all … to deliver Brexit	New Year's leave	Don't let the grinch steal your Christmas	(Roy: I'm Chubby Browned off)	Christmas election	Parliament breaks deadlock with December 12 election	December 12 poll will get Brexit done, says Johnson	Countdown begins for Christmas election	MP's back December 12 vote as Johnson recalls rebels from exile
31 October	Boris & Trump plot NHS sell-off	(So many lives could have been saved)	(Will: my Strictly tears)	Poll: Boris more trusted than Corbyn on NHS	(Fadi's sick blast at George)	Brexit Party could aid Tories by not fighting hundreds of seats	Corbyn: the Tories don't represent the people, we do	Morgan in exodus of moderate Tory MPs	(Resign now: Grenfell families' challenge to fire chief)	(Fed unveils quarter-point rate cut but tempers hope of more easing)
1 November	(Bercow: I want £1 M to be in I'm a Celebrity)	Trump: PM and Farage need to strike pact	(Kyle bile even more vile)	Trump tells Farage: do deal with Boris	(Hat's racist!)	Trump urges Farage to do a deal with Johnson	(BAT faces landmark legal case over Malawian families' poverty wages)	Trump tells Johnson to join forces with Farage	Corbyn vows to transform UK by tackling wealthy elite	(Trump impeachment hearings to be held in open after key vote)
2 November	NHS car park vultures' £46 M extra	Boris: vote Tory or you'll get Corbyn	(Shirley: never have boob implants, girls)	Boris: we don't need you, Nigel	(Flakes make me millions)	Tories promise election tax cut	Fracking banned in UK after government U-turn	Johnson to ban fracking	Fracking to be banned after U-turn by Tories	Earthquake fears spark UK fracking ban
Sunday 3 November	(Sick pictures of Amelia's dead body posted on Facebook)	Boris: I'll get Brexit all wrapped up	(City ace fury as champ flirts with wife)	(Charles hit by 'fake art')	(Strictly terrifying)	'Jews will leave if Corbyn wins'	Tories act to prevent NHS crisis hitting poll hopes	Double trouble for Boris after Corbyn bounce	N/A	N/A

(continued)

	Daily/Sunday Mirror	Daily/Sunday Express	The Sun/Sun on Sunday	Daily/Sunday Mail	Daily Star/Daily Star on Sunday	Daily/Sunday Telegraph	The Guardian/The Observer	The Times/Sunday Times	The i	Financial Times
4 November	Labour: we'll save free TV licences	Boris: I'll cut taxes for every worker	(Midlife crisis)	(Hospitals deluged by 5,000 diabetics every day)	(Britain in the freezer)	Farage 'could ruin UK's hope of Brexit'	Obey me on Brexit, Corbyn warns Cabinet dissenters	(Gangs use top schools to traffic Asian girls)	(NHS feels the strain as heart failure cases soar)	(Saudi Aramco finally launches IPO with goals of raising $60bn)
5 November	(The end of smear testing)	PM tells Corbyn: 'come clean' on Brexit	(Don't try this at home!)	(Is this the end of smear tests?)	(We have ways of making you laugh)	Post union 'plotting to wreck election'	PM accused of cover-up over report on Russian meddling in UK politics	Labour's four-day week 'to cost taxpayers £17bn'	(The woman who defied Alzheimer's)	(SoftBank to loosen grip of start-up founders after WeWork debacle)
6 November	(Birth test revolution)	(DNA test at birth to save lives)	(God save fur Queen!)	Rail union's Xmas misery for millions	Grinches ruin Xmas	'The tragedy of the modern Labour Party under Jeremy Corbyn is that they detest the profit motive so viscerally… they point their fingers at individuals with a relish and a vindictiveness not seen since Stalin persecuted the kulaks'	Rees-Mogg condemned over remarks on Grenfell	(China tries to gag UK universities)	Rees-Mogg grounded by Tories	Javid furious as top civil servant blocks pricing of Labour pledges

(continued)

	Daily/Sunday Mirror	Daily/Sunday Express	The Sun/Sun on Sunday	Daily/Sunday Mail	Daily Star/Daily Star on Sunday	Daily/Sunday Telegraph	The Guardian/The Observer	The Times/Sunday Times	The i	Financial Times
7 November	Power to the North	Boris: Come with us or get horror show	(Knifemen ... 0 Gunners ... 1)	Labour's election calamity as deputy walks out	(Unbelievable Jeff!)	Watson quits Commons	Watson quits as deputy as Corbyn strengthens grip	Watson quits as deputy leader of Labour Party	Labour stunned as Watson quits	Labour's vow to take borrowing to £400bn fires spending battle
8 November	Shameful	Vote Boris!	(Cop on Prem ace murder charge)	The Labour veterans who plead: vote Tory	(Booby bling terror)	Vote Conservative, say Corbyn rebels	Labour and Tories launch bidding war on spending	Corbyn bid to launch 1970s-style cash spree	Spend, spend, spend	(Merkel locks horns with Macron after he attacks 'brain dead' NATO)
9 November	(Palace fury as Kate's pic used to flog facelifts)	Labour vote collapses in heartlands	(Sugar baddie)	Stand down Nigel!	(The killer monsoon)	Blunkett: I despair at hard-Left Labour	Private surgery for NHS patients soars under Tories	(Scandal of scammers on Google)	Roads turned into rivers	(Woodford protégé hit by downgrades)
Sunday 10 November	(ITV show on my Becky's murder has ruined my life)	Farage gives Tories final ultimatum	(Strictly Alex: I want Kevin)	£1.2 trillion: that'll cost every UK household £43,000	(Ant & Dec snubbed me on cruelty)	Scale of Labour's 'reckless' spending revealed	Fury as decision on police probe into PM shelved until after poll	£1 trillion Labour splurge 'to bankrupt UK'	N/A	N/A
11 November	£845 M for the forgotten children	Boris boost as economy bounces back	(My mini miracles)	The end of veterans' witch-hunt	(Phoenix rises)	Tories to end 'unfair' trials of Troubles veterans	Nearly half of rape victims decline to go ahead with prosecutions	Parties clash over claim Corbyn will spend £1trn	Tory Russian connection: Johnson fears fallout	(Lagarde's ECB team pushes for bigger say on decisions)

(continued)

	Daily/Sunday Mirror	Daily/Sunday Express	The Sun/Sun on Sunday	Daily/Sunday Mail	Daily Star/Daily Star on Sunday	Daily/Sunday Telegraph	The Guardian/The Observer	The Times/Sunday Times	The i	Financial Times
12 November	Sold down the river	Farage's election gift for Boris	Cheers Nige!	Nice one, Nigel … but it's still not enough	(Bring back Grange Hill to save Britain)	Farage retreats from every Tory seat	Farage urged to give Tories free run at Labour seats	HS2 will boost north despite soaring costs	Farage's retreat	Farage hints at broader retreat as party ditches fight for Tory seats (Top 6 auditors tested on resilience as ministers eye industry break-up)
13 November	Labour's 10-point plan to save the NHS	Thanks Nigel! Tories surge to 14-point lead	(Harry's no-ho-ho to Queen)	(The hero who died without justice)	(Dreaming of a woke Christmas)	Brexit will start green revolution, pledges PM	Labour vows to outspend Tories with £26bn 'rescue' plan for NHS	Tories lead by 14 points after Farage climbdown	Battle for the NHS	(Health websites share personal medical data with ad groups)
14 November	Give me a world I can grow up in	PM: Brexit deal will unleash Britain's potential	(Huntley meltdown)	Fury over Corbyn ISIS chief gaffe	(Sugar chump Claude)	Tories offer Farage eleventh-hour deal	Backlash as union chief calls for Labour to curb free movement	Labour split over 4-day week for NHS staff	Tory wife's revenge	
15 November	Betrayed	Tax cuts to put heart back into Britain	(Who dared won)	Condemned by his own candidates	(Albert scare)	Farage accuses No 10 of dirty tricks	Councils call for huge funding rise to tackle flood devastation	Labour vows billions to nationalise broadband	Labour pledges free broadband for everyone	(Google plan to lock down user data draws fire from advertisers)
16 November	(Andrew: I let the side down)	(TV grilling for Prince at palace)	(Andy: I've let the side down)	(Andrew: I let Queen down)	(On me bed, son)	(Andrew: I let the side down)	Business backlash over Labour broadband plan	(Duke: I let the side down)	(Prince: I've let him down my family)	Labour's BT nationalisation vow sparks fears of investment freeze

(continued)

	Daily/Sunday Mirror	Daily/Sunday Express	The Sun/Sun on Sunday	Daily/Sunday Mail	Daily Star/Daily Star on Sunday	Daily/Sunday Telegraph	The Guardian/The Observer	The Times/Sunday Times	The i	Financial Times
Sunday 17 November	(No sweat ... and no regret)	Millions face threat to their pension	(No sweat ... I was at Pizza Express)	(Not one single word of remorse)	(Christmas flood chaos)	Every Tory candidate signs Brexit deal pledge	(I didn't have sex with teen, I was at home after pizza party: Prince)	(Army 'covered up torture and child murder')	N/A	N/A
18 November	(Cop: Andrew's sex alibi beggars belief)	Boris to trigger a Brexit boom	(It was a great success, Ma'am)	(Andrew: my regret over TV interview)	(Flakes told: Choose your own race)	(Andrew under fire from the Palace)	(Apologise to Epstein's victims now, Prince told)	(Defiant duke stands by 'car crash' TV interview)	(Prince is pressured to meet FBI)	(Aramco pares back fundraising goal to $25bn in latest IPO hitch)
19 November	(Andrew's accuser films BBC interview)	(Queen backs Prince Andrew despite backlash)	(Net closes on Andy)	(Andrew out in the cold)	(Bantz RIP)	(Businesses and charities abandon Duke)	Staffing crisis putting safety of patients at risk, warn NHS chiefs	(City backers abandon Andrew)	Election ignites	Johnson shelves corporation tax cut
20 November	(Andrew cop's notebook holds key evidence)	Corbyn dodges Brexit question nine times	(Poison Prince)	Laughable, Mr Corbyn	(Fan-Dabi Dozy)	Corbyn jeered over Brexit	Leaders stake their ground: Johnson Brexit, Corbyn NHS	Neck and neck after TV clash	Insults fly at leaders' TV debate	Labour vows to 'rewrite' corporate rule book with workers on boards
21 November	[I'm sorry mummy]	(Andrew shamed into stepping down)	(Prince Endy)	(Outcast)	(Scrooge ban on Xmas crackers)	(Duke departs from public life)	Labour in £75bn pledge to tackle UK housing crisis	(Duke stands down after crisis talks with Queen)	(Crisis at the palace)	(Sondland 'followed' orders from Trump on Ukraine quid pro quo)

(continued)

	Daily/Sunday Mirror	Daily/Sunday Express	The Sun/Sun on Sunday	Daily/Sunday Mail	Daily Star/Daily Star on Sunday	Daily/Sunday Telegraph	The Guardian/The Observer	The Times/Sunday Times	The i	Financial Times
22 November	On your side	£80BN raid on your wallets	(The grin reaper)	Corbyn's £83BN tax robbery	(Flare thugs destroyed my boobs)	(UK starts bringing back ISIL children)	Corbyn unveils Labour's most radical manifesto for decades	Corbyn hails £83bn dream spending plan	Corbyn's blueprint for power	Corbyn's tax and spend manifesto stirs spectre of 1970s for business
23 November	(Sleazy rider)	Cure for dementia closer with £1.6BN cash boost	(Go Nads!)	(End of GP home visit)	(This time next year he'll be a millionaire)	Corbyn would refuse to back his own deal in Brexit vote	Corbyn 'neutral' on Brexit as PM attacked on trust	Corbyn 'neutral' on Brexit	(Duke of nothing)	Ministers risk NHS tax breach in bid to head off pre-poll crisis
Sunday 24 November	Payouts for 3.8 M women denied pensions	PM: My big Christmas gift to Britain	(Andy paedo's pal at palace)	MI6 chief: Corbyn is security danger	(Corrie Kym maimed by her chihuahua)	Tories to axe hospital car parking fees for millions	Labour pledges £58bn to help women caught in pension trap	Boris: I pledge not to raise your taxes	N/A	N/A
25 November	(Andrew's accuser will talk to FBI)	Boris pledges 50,000 extra nurses	Merry Brexmas ad Happy Blue Year!	Good sense v nonsense	(Car nut Jezza: I'm now a crusty)	'The stakes have never been higher'	Johnson stakes just £2.9bn in public spending gamble	Johnson places NHS at heart of 'critical' election	Johnson sets out health and safety manifesto	Johnson presents post-Brexit vision in low-risk pitch to voters
26 November	Labour's care revolution for pensioners	(Why are we still failing Britain's women?)	Swing then you're winning	Chief Rabbi: the soul of our nation is at stake	(Strictly's rumba rompers)	Labour denies plot to sacrifice Corbyn	Child poverty 'will surge to 60-year high under Tories'	Corbyn not fit for high office, says Chief Rabbi	Corbyn's pension promise: I will borrow to pay WASPI women	(Uber loses London licence again as driver fraud raises safety fears)

(continued)

	Daily/Sunday Mirror	Daily/Sunday Express	The Sun/Sun on Sunday	Daily/Sunday Mail	Daily Star/Daily Star on Sunday	Daily/Sunday Telegraph	The Guardian/The Observer	The Times/Sunday Times	The i	Financial Times
27 November	Tory minister's trade talks with US drug firm boss	Has Corbyn's horror show gifted Boris keys to No 10?	(Worth a few bob the builder)	Torn apart	(£105 M lotto win nearly killed me)	Corbyn refuses to apologise to Jews	Corbyn struggles to rebuff anti-semitism accusations	Corbyn refuses to apologise	Corbyn refuses to say sorry	(Man City's $500 m stake sale breaks sports valuation record)
28 November	The proof	Boris: Why austerity was wrong for Britain	(Prem boss wanted to score with me)	Revealed: Labour's triple tax whammy on millions	(You're a Wright bully!)	Election is too close to call, warns Cummings	Secret papers prove Tories want to sell NHS—Corbyn	Johnson heads for big majority	Johnson on course to break deadlock	(Lagarde bid to put climate change at centre of ECB monetary policy)
29 November	Boris: working class men are drunk, criminal & feckless	Outcry over Labour Brexit 'lies'	(Still no justice)	(Yard pays £900 k to MP accused by abuse liar)	(Cheek to cheeky)	Tories threaten 'biased' Channel 4	(So who was to blame? Fury of the Hillsborough families)	Tories and Labour in battle for the north	PM's climate meltdown	(Ex-Nissan chief says Japanese nationalists hurt carmaker)
30 November	(The heroes of London Bridge)	(The heroes who stood up to terror)	(Heroes of the Bridge)	(Bravery on the Bridge)	(Heroes)	(Terror returns to London Bridge)	(Two killed in London Bridge terror attack)	(The terrorist wearing a tag)	(The heroes of London Bridge)	(Two killed and three injured in London Bridge terror attack)
Sunday 1 December	Freed., and plotting carnage	Soft justice plays Russian roulette with our lives	(Killed by beast he tried to help)	(Exposed: Andrew's deals with tax haven tycoons)	(Jack, 25: slain by a Jihadi nut they let go free)	PM's fury over 70 freed terrorists	PM thrusts terror attack into centre of election battle	Boris vows to lock terrorists up and throw away the key	N/A	N/A

(continued)

	Daily/Sunday Mirror	Daily/Sunday Express	The Sun/Sun on Sunday	Daily/Sunday Mail	Daily Star/Daily Star on Sunday	Daily/Sunday Telegraph	The Guardian/The Observer	The Times/Sunday Times	The i	Financial Times
2 December	Betrayed	Boris blitz on freed Jihadis begins	(The angels stolen by pure evil)	New blitz on freed Jihadis	(−14 Arctic bubble will sweep in from Norway)	Terrorists freed early to be sent back to jail	PM accused of exploiting deaths in terror attack	(Spy chiefs on alert for London Bridge copycats)	'They always saw the best in people'	(Merkel's grand coalition at risk after SPD elects new leadership)
3 December	(Murder at the school gates)	('Extinguish hatred with his kindness')	Corbyn is security risk	(Andrew's new TV humiliation)	Snowflakes: Mr Clever is a sexist	Corbyn's dossier 'points to Russians'	'Jack would be livid his death has been used to further an agenda of hate'	Two hundred extremists face curbs on movement	The media won't decide this election i You Decide	Deregulation would threaten City's access to market, Brussels warns
4 December	Labour to put £6,716 in your pocket	Trump: I wouldn't want NHS on silver platter	Trump thumps chump over NHS lies	(Deadly gamble on our health)	(McNuggets)	We have no interest in the NHS, says Trump	Corbyn ups pressure over NHS as Trump rows back	We'll force tech giants to pay more tax, says PM	Corbyn casts doubt on Trump's NHS pledge	Johnson defies Trump threats with pledge on digital sales tax
5 December	Boris is Mr Greedy	Speechless! Corbyn caught out pretending he watches the Queen's speech in the morning	Boris: my 10 Commandments	Corbyn caught out over Queen	(Psycho eagle snatches Jack Russell)	Tax cuts for millions within days of Brexit	(Trump leaves NATO talks after ridicule from allies)	Johnson to offer tax cut after Brexit	NHS cuts killed my mother	(M&G halts trading in £2.5bn fund as high outflows spark sell-off fears)

(continued)

	Daily/Sunday Mirror	Daily/Sunday Express	The Sun/Sun on Sunday	Daily/Sunday Mail	Daily Star/Daily Star on Sunday	Daily/Sunday Telegraph	The Guardian/The Observer	The Times/Sunday Times	The i	Financial Times
6 December	How can anyone trust him?	Boris fury over new plot to 'fiddle' Brexit	(Hero on parole)	Brexit Party bigwigs urge: vote Boris	('Harassed by Vicar of Dibley's girl')	'Corbyn has made Labour a welcoming refuge for anti-semites. The party is cast in his image'	(The rising toll of measles: nearly 10 m cases and 142,000 deaths)	Brexit Party defectors urge Farage to withdraw	Crunch time for Corbyn	(Saudi Aramco's $25.6bn breaks IPO record despite valuation blow)
7 December	(Shock new Andrew sex claim)	TV clash puts Boris out in front	(£105 M wad carrier)	Boris: we must fight for every single vote	(80MPH)	Don't lecture me on Ireland, Mr Corbyn	(Serial rapist had been freed from jail in error)	TV channels accused of 'hysterical' election bias	UK diplomat quits with tirade over 'half-truths'	(Global football league idea 'insane')
Sunday 8 December	(Jungle Cliff jailed for bank robbery)	Boris: Brexit is now up to you	(ITV axe Dan and Jac reunion)	Save us from a Friday 13th horror	(Holly's jungle snub)	Tories unveil strict limits on unskilled migrants	Calls grow to stop Johnson with tactical voting as race tightens	Exposed: the secret Labour files of shame	N/A	N/A
9 December	Desperate	Boris: the last chance to save Brexit and Britain	Waking up to Corbyn as PM on Friday 13th would just be the start of a ... NIGHTMARE	PM blasts Labour Brexit betrayal	(A major incident)	Corbyn will betray Brexit, says Johnson as he takes fight to Labour's heartlands	Corbyn in last-ditch drive to focus on voters' finances	Johnson to blitz seats in Labour heartlands	NHS waiting times ordeal for patients 'covered up'	(Beijing orders removal of foreign PCs and software)
10 December	Here's another picture you won't want to look at, Mr Johnson	Boris threat to axe BBC TV licence	You're fired Corbyn	Boris: I might axe TV licence	(Scourge of the Xmas dognappers)	Corbyn could win without gaining a seat	Tories accused of lying to distract from image of boy on hospital floor	(British tourists injured after volcano erupts)	(No sign of life)	(Oil boom star Tullow plunges 70% after cut to output forecast)

(continued)

	Daily/Sunday Mirror	Daily/Sunday Express	The Sun/Sun on Sunday	Daily/Sunday Mail	Daily Star/Daily Star on Sunday	Daily/Sunday Telegraph	The Guardian/The Observer	The Times/Sunday Times	The i	Financial Times
11 December	Johnson saw my son's death not as a tragedy but as an opportunity	Demolition job on Corbyn … by his own man!	'Labour's probably doing well among middle-class graduates. Remainy people. If you are in smalltown Midlands and the North, it's abysmal out there. They can't stand Corbyn. And they think…LABOUR HAS BLOCKED BREXIT'	Britain's future down to the wire	(We miss hugs and kisses with Maddie)	PM pledges to get tough on serious criminals	Final scramble for votes in 'most important election in a generation'	Tory lead narrows ahead of final election rallies	Corbyn closes on Johnson as race tightens	Johnson ready to shake up overseas aid if he wins vote
12 December	For them … vote Labour	Brexit and Britain in your hands	Save Brexit save Britain	Your vote has never been more vital. Today, you MUST brave the deluge to go to your local polling station and back … Boris	Clowning Street	Election on knife edge as Tory lead narrows	Corbyn urges voters to deliver 'shock to the establishment'	Tories face last-minute threat from Brexit Party	Britain's future: you decide	Polls cast doubt on Tory hopes of securing a decisive majority

The prevalence of references to 'Labour' across most of the press groupings is also striking (with the *Daily Star* being the sole exception). This prominence relative to the other main party is partly explained by the greater variety of terms used to label the Conservatives which dissipates their visual prominence in these diagrams (e.g. 'Tory', 'government' and 'Tories'). But it also confirms how the Prime Minister colonised a far higher proportion of his party's headline coverage than Corbyn did with Labour-focused reports. Overall, Johnson accounted for 60% of Conservative Party references in headlines, whereas Corbyn was included in 49% of equivalent references to the Labour Party.[28]

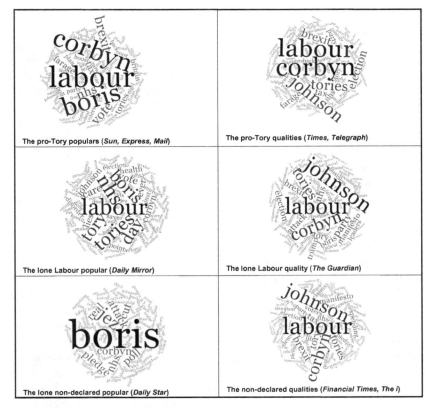

Fig. 10.1 Word clouds of weekday election news headlines

The leaders and their parties were distinctly presented in the headline coverage of different sections of the press throughout the campaign. In the pro-Conservative titles, Corbyn and Labour were more commonly reported as the subject of comments from other sources rather than active sources of political action and opinion (e.g. 'MI6 Chief: Corbyn is Security Danger', *Mail on Sunday*, 24 November 2019; '£1 Trillion Labour Splurge "to Bankrupt UK"', *Sunday Times*, 10 November 2019). A total of 70% of Labour-focused headlines presented the party and its representatives in this more passive context. Furthermore, these headlines consistently accentuated the negative, particularly when reporting on Corbyn; 86% of all headline references to the Labour leader in these titles were negative in tone and/or implication, and the charge sheet was a long one. These included accusations that Corbyn was a threat to national security ('The Terrorist's Friend', *The Sun*, 14 November; 'Corbyn is Security Risk', *The Sun*, 3 December 2019; 'Corbyn as PM Would Be Putin's Useful Idiot', *Daily Telegraph*, 11 December 2019), a delusional economist ('I've No Axe to Grind But I'm Staggered by Corbyn's Economic Illiteracy', *Daily Mail*, 27 November 2019), a political extremist ('Jez Driving Marxist Labour to Total Ruin', *The Sun*, 25 November 2019; 'Corbyn's Class War against Capitalism Will Ruin the Many, Not Just the Few', *Daily Telegraph*, 21 November 2019) and anathema to the electorate ('A Win for Corbyn? No Chance, Says Shadow Minister', *The Times*, 11 December 2019).

However, the most persistent personal criticism of Corbyn related to antisemitism. Some of this coverage attacked the leader for inaction, with the *Mail on Sunday* quoting actor and former Labour supporter Tracey-Ann Oberman saying 'Corbyn's Trolls Drove Me to Quit the Party My Jewish Family Thought Would Always Protect Them' (17 November 2019). The *Sunday Telegraph* columnist Zoe Strimpel went further, accusing the Labour hierarchy of sanctioning racism: 'Jews are horrified by the prospect of a Corbyn win—as everyone should be … in seeing Corbynism as an existential insult' (10 November 2019). But the most significant intervention of this kind came from Britain's Chief Rabbi Ephraim Mirvis. Writing in *The Times*, he revisited various aspects of the controversy and indicated 130 cases involving party members were still unresolved; all this was evidence that meant 'the very soul of our nation is at stake' (26 November 2019). Like others, Mirvis held Corbyn personally culpable for 'a new poison'. The Chief Rabbi's intervention came the day before Corbyn's dedicated leader's interview with the BBC's

Andrew Neil and his perceived failure to effectively respond was widely criticised, with even the sympathetic *Daily Mirror* reporting 'Jez Dodges Jewish Apology Four Times' (27 November 2019). Commenting on the encounter, *The Sun* used its cover story to condemn 'Corb's 4 Refusals on Jews Apology' (27 November 2019). Inside the same edition, Tanya Gold excoriated the party: 'Labour's been over-run by racists who do not know they're racists. It begins with Corbyn. It ends with a frightened child.'

In stark contrast to press treatment of Corbyn, the Conservatives—and Johnson in particular—were far more frequently presented as dynamic and decisive ('Boris to Trigger a Brexit Boom', *Daily Express*, 18 November 2019; 'Boris's 100 Day Plan', *Daily Mail*, 4 December 2019; 'PM Comes out Fighting as He Fires Poll Starting Gun with Trump-Style Rally', *Daily Express*, 7 November 2019). Where they were the subject of comment, it was overwhelmingly positive in nature ('Shopkeepers Hail Boris Package as Sure-Fire Boost for Business', *Daily Express*, 15 November 2019).

These patterns reversed in the headlines of the two Labour-supporting titles. Johnson was portrayed negatively in 87% of headline mentions, with recurrent criticisms raised directly or by third parties about his judgement, honesty and suitability for high office ('Johnson's Deceit and His Bad Brexit Deal Combine to Put the NHS in Danger', *The Guardian*, 28 November 2019; 'Johnson's Print Rants Reveal His Prejudices', *Daily Mirror*, 2 December 2019; 'Dunblane Dad: Boris is Not Fit to Be PM', *Daily Mirror*, 9 December 2019). The Labour leader and his party were more frequently presented in an assertive way ('Labour Vows to Outspend Tories with £26bn "Rescue" Plan for NHS', *The Guardian*, 12 November 2019; 'Corbyn: I'm Confident on Election Tactics', *The Guardian*, 10 December 2019; 'Corbyn Will Give Rights & Security to Renters', *Daily Mirror*, 25 November 2019).

PRESS ENGAGEMENT

The preceding analysis already gives some idea of the issues that dominated press reporting of the 2019 campaign. Here we address these matters more directly, considering in particular whether the Prime Minister was successful in making 2019 'the Brexit election'. A core element of this strategy was the need to maintain the interest and engagement of his supporters in the popular press throughout the campaign—something that can never be assumed. During the campaign, two other major events competed for news space with the election. The first was a prime-time television interview with Prince Andrew in which he unsuccessfully sought to counter serious allegations about his links to the notorious American convicted paedophile Jeffrey Epstein. The second was a serious terrorist incident in London's Fishmongers' Hall on 29 November in which three people, including the terrorist himself, were killed.

Conscious of the prominent contemporaneous non-electoral stories vying for public attention, the most obvious measure for interpreting press engagement in the campaign is to assess the content and frequency of election front-page news. The content of the front-page coverage signals editorial positions, while coverage frequency indicates interest in the election and the desire for partisan intervention. A campaign marked by public disaffection, few major policy disagreements and the expectation of a landslide tends to see less enthusiastic activism from partisan outlets. In this context, Table 10.5 shows the number of front-page lead stories about the election in each of the daily newspapers for the most recent four campaigns.

The 2019 campaign was covered extensively across the press, with six of the ten newspapers carrying election coverage in two-thirds of their front-page leads during the final few weeks. All newspapers bar the *Financial Times* increased their front-page coverage compared with 2017, particularly the *Daily Mirror*, the *Daily Express* and *The Times*. In

Table 10.5   Front-page items about the election, 2010–2019[29]

	2010	2015	2017	2019
Daily Mirror	11	11	6	13
Daily Express	9	6	9	16
The Sun	15	8	6	9
Daily Mail	12	10	10	14
Daily Star	1	3	1	2
Daily Telegraph	18	18	15	17
The Guardian	18	15	12	16
The Times	18	18	9	16
The Independent/ The i	17	10	13	17
Financial Times	9	9	9	9

Note Data show number of front pages per title for the final 21 days of campaigning (weekdays and Saturdays)

2017, only the *Daily Telegraph* gave the campaign this degree of prominence, and indeed 2019 saw more front pages about the election across the press than in both the 2015 and 2017 campaigns. The increase since 2017 can be attributed primarily to two terrorist attacks during the 2017 campaign in Manchester and London, both of which dominated front pages for several days and produced temporary suspensions in campaigning. In contrast, none of the titles—particularly those supporting the Johnson administration—afforded top billing to other such events in 2019 to the same extent, despite further tragedy at Fishmongers' Hall and the Prince Andrew story. The terrorist attack resulted in a single day of solemn pause before front-page coverage returned to 'business as usual'. The Prince Andrew story, which appeared earlier on in the campaign, actually had a greater suppressive effect on election news, with only one-third of front-page coverage in the week following the royal interview centring on the election.

Manifesto Launches and Issues

Turning to events that traditionally help define elections, the launch of the party manifestos offer one of the best opportunities in a campaign for deeper press engagement with policy. These set-piece events, which are typically rather dull, attracted more attention than usual in 2017 when the main parties' launches did not go to plan.[30] In 2019, in contrast, the Conservative manifesto focused overwhelmingly on the 'get Brexit done' mantra, while Labour's manifesto was more expansive in its commitments even than the radical 2017 offering (see Chapter 6, pp. 193–241).

Labour's manifesto, launched a few days before their opponents' on 21 November, was preceded by an ambitious announcement on 15 November to provide universal free broadband by 2030 by part-nationalising BT. The negative reception to this announcement in much of the press foreshadowed the derisive response to the manifesto itself a week later. The proposal was variously labelled a 'blueprint to bankrupt Britain' (*Daily Mail*), an 'attack on aspiration' (*Daily Express*), a 'manifesto for economic disaster' (*Daily Telegraph*), a 'recipe for decline' (*Financial Times*), 'Labour pains' (*The Times*) and a 'road to ruin' (*The Sun*). Some credit was forthcoming for the party's 'strikingly ambitious radicalism' (*The Guardian*), attempts to address 'areas that genuinely need fixing' (*Financial Times*) and for responding to a public 'hungry for change' (*The Times*). Only in the *Daily Mirror* did the party obtain full-throated support ('Desperate times call for bold measures and Labour's manifesto is offering that'). The extent of Labour's spending plans received the harshest criticism, with *The Times* warning that 'these figures are just not credible', the *FT* criticising 'misguided' plans which would 'exponentially increase the risks to the economy', and *The i* paper opining that the manifesto commitments, without accompanying tax rises, 'damages credibility'. The *Daily Mail* put it rather more bluntly: 'Jeremy Corbyn would spray your money around like a drunk at the races.'

If scrutiny of the Labour manifesto launch centred on the party's expensive ambitions, coverage of the Conservative launch a few days later highlighted its relative caution. Leader writers hailed 'sense with Boris' (*Daily Mail*), a chance to 'move on' (*Daily Express*) and a 'proper dose of reality politics' (*The Sun*) in the popular dailies. On Brexit, Johnson was praised for clarity in *The Times* ('he cannot be accused of obfuscating. He has a deal and he wants a mandate to get it signed and ratified'), the *Daily Mail* (his 'sensible programme for Brexit Britain is rooted in the real world') and *The Sun* ('he has given us ... a firm promise to deliver Brexit in two months'), but in truth scrutiny of the details was lacking in most editorial responses except the *Financial Times*. Most dwelt on the contrast between the two parties: for the *Daily Telegraph*, the Conservatives were 'having to make the argument against [Labour's] fiscal incontinence while at the same time making spending pledges of their own', while the *Daily Mail* labelled it the 'diametric opposite' to Labour's 'destructive socialism' and the *Daily Express* admitted that while some voters may not be 'the biggest fans of Boris', they 'must be in no doubt that all of us would be much worse off if Jeremy Corbyn gets the keys to Downing Street'. The Prime Minister's biggest fans could perhaps be found at *The Sun*, which saved its highest praise for Johnson himself: 'with his infectious optimism, sunny disposition and unshakable patriotism, we believe he can deliver'. On the contrary, the *Daily Mirror* and *The Guardian* rebuked Johnson and his party for their 'lies' and 'dishonesty'. For *The Guardian*, Johnson's biggest indiscretion was the 'big lie' of the 'get Brexit done' mantra, which 'bears no relation to reality'. The newspaper summarised the problem with a metaphor: 'Manifestos are supposed to show what's on offer, but this is not a proper menu and the hefty bill for the inedible meal you never ordered may be arriving soon.' All told, coverage of the manifesto launches offered lashings of invective, but only a few morsels of policy detail.

Table 10.6 compares issue prominence in weekday press coverage of the 2019 election with the preceding two campaigns. While leader commentaries lacked policy detail, this did not translate into a wider lack of policy emphasis in coverage. Daily press reporting of the 2019 campaign contained similarly low levels of so-called 'electoral process' coverage to 2017—that is, coverage of the evolving dynamics of the campaign, the electoral prospects and conduct of the major contenders, vox pops, etc. Overall, there was far less of the 'coalitionology' that featured so prominently in 2015 coverage, even though a hung parliament was still deemed a credible outcome until it was finally skewered with the publication of the exit poll prediction. But to what extent did the press agenda reflect the preferred policy agendas of the competing parties? As previously noted, the Conservatives desired a campaign dominated by Brexit (as, indeed, did the Liberal Democrats and the Brexit Party). Labour wanted the opposite: a multi-issue campaign concerning a much broader range of issues, most notably healthcare, anti-austerity, the renationalisation of key industries, and the environment.

The prominence of the categories 'Standards/scandals' and 'Minorities/religion' in the top 10 signals the extensive coverage about internal Labour conflicts and allegations of anti-semitism. This was also the first general election campaign since 2010 where immigration did not

Table 10.6   The key issues in the 2019 general election (weekday press coverage 7 November–12 December inclusive)

	2019 %	2017 (rank) %	2015 (rank)
Electoral process	32	34 (1)	44.5 (1)
Brexit/EU	11	10 (2)	3 (8)
Business/economy/trade	9	5 (7)	13 (2)
Health/healthcare	7	7 (3)	4 (6)
Standards/scandals	8	4 (9)	4 (4)
Taxation	6	6 (5)	6.5 (3)
Minorities/religion	5	–	–
Defence/military/security/terrorism	4	7 (4)	–
Public services	3	–	–
Environment	2	–	–

Note Percentages = (number of appearance of an issue/all issues * 100). Up to three issues could be coded per news item

feature among the top issues in the press. Environmental coverage also scraped into the list for the first time, in part because of the floods and also the campaign focus of some opposition parties (e.g. Labour's 'Green New Deal'). Elsewhere, coverage centred on issue domains that have proven predictably newsworthy: the economy and business, taxation, and health and healthcare provision. As Table 10.6 shows, the issue agenda in national press coverage of the 2019 campaign was similarly multi-polar to that of the preceding election. 'Brexit/EU' was once again the most prominent issue in press coverage. Although the topic only dominated the first and last weeks of the formal campaign, these were the key periods that Conservative strategists would likely have wanted the subject to come to the fore.

BREXIT: A DONE DEAL?

Despite its variable newsworthiness, the Tory press, in particular, promoted Brexit as *the* campaign issue, with the *Daily Mail* and *The Sun* regularly using the running header 'the Brexmas Election'. *The Sun* published analysis by the think-tank Onward that reinforced this framing: 'In post-Brexit Britain the typical voter is "Workington Man"—a white man over 45 who did not go to university and voted Leave' (30 October 2019). *The Sun* and the *Daily Mail* both also pointedly referred to 'Brexmas', linking the approaching holiday season to the Conservatives' core objective, while also ridiculing the threat from 'Kamikaze Nigel' Farage (the *Daily Mail*, 2 November 2019). While *The Sun* had previously warned of the risk to the Tories posed by Farage, notably during the 2015 election when his then party UKIP was surging in the polls, the tone of the *Daily Mail* marked a hardening of its attitude towards him compared to four years before, when columnist Stephen Glover was expressing sympathy if not support for his campaign.[31] Following the Brexit Party decision to stand down its candidates in marginal Tory seats, press interest—favourable or not—waned as attention turned to ridiculing Labour's nuanced position on the EU as 'Corbyn's Brexit Cop-out' (*Daily Mail*, 18 November 2019). But the dominance of Brexit faded as the campaign progressed. By the fourth week, this very familiar issue had fallen behind others such as health and the economy, where there were new policy debates to be had. Boris Johnson lamented this at the time: 'people have slightly lost their focus on the political crisis that we face. Unless we get this thing done, unless we get Brexit done, this country cannot move forward' (*The Sun*, 2 December 2019). The final week witnessed a marked reversion, with Brexit reasserting itself as the dominant policy issue in press reporting to the extent that Dominic Lawson felt able to applaud 'get Brexit done' as the 2019 equivalent of 2016's all-pervasive 'take back control' formula (*Daily Mail*, 9 December 2019). Even the Remain-supporting *The Guardian* felt obliged to join in the press recycling of Johnson's core slogan when it appeared on the bulldozer he was driving in his closing photo opportunity of the campaign (11 December 2019). The message was reinforced by sympathisers like Allister Heath of the *Daily Telegraph* who wrote 'Today is our final chance to save Brexit—and even democracy itself' (12 December 2019), a sentiment echoed by *The Sun* in its front-page exhortation to 'Save Brexit Save Britain' (12 December 2019).

'Get Brexit done' was, of course, a soundbite that obscured as much as it conveyed. What the bald statistics do not capture is the extent to which coverage of all issues was affected and inflected by Brexit. For example, much coverage of health and healthcare during the midpoint of the campaign revolved around the implications of a post-Brexit US/ UK trade deal that might expose the NHS to commercial exploitation by US pharmaceutical interests ('Corbyn Calls for NHS to Be off Table as Trump Flies into UK', *The i paper*, 3 December 2019; 'Trump: I wouldn't Want NHS on Silver Platter', *Daily Express*, 4 December 2019). Only stories with a manifest and substantial reference to the UK's withdrawal from the EU were coded as Brexit-related, but on many occasions such links were implicit yet obvious to readers. What this shows is how Brexit became more of an omnipresent contextual factor than a focal point during the midsection of the campaign, to the extent that it 'was at once everywhere, yet nowhere'.[32] This reflected the lack of substantive discussion of the 'oven-ready deal' promised repeatedly by Johnson as his vehicle to 'get Brexit done' and eagerly supported by press sympathisers such as the *Daily Telegraph* (12 December 2019). Less attention was paid to possible alternative deals or the prospect of another referendum. But even these outcomes attracted more coverage than the risk of 'no deal', which had dominated political discussions of Brexit for much of the year and which the Prime Minister was now seemingly keen to downplay. Subsequent debate would reveal his 'oven-ready' alternative to be something of an over-simplification, as Andrew Rawnsley of *The Observer* warned when commenting that there was 'no more deceptive slogan' than 'get Brexit done' (24 November 2019).

The anti-Brexit commentary that did appear in the press was con-centrated in non-Conservative newspapers. The criticisms were varied, with the *Daily Mirror* warning 'Don't Let it Be a Brexit Election' (30 October 2019), while Aditya Chakrabortty of *The Guardian* conceded that the issue had become 'a proxy for anger' about other matters (12 December 2019). In the *Financial Times*, Martin Wolf accused Johnson of promoting 'demagogic nationalism' (1 November 2019) and worried about future UK–EU relations. The *Financial Times* argued that Brexit would 'scupper' the Tories' plans for governing (25 November 2019), while Martin Kettle questioned whether and how withdrawal could be delivered (*The Guardian*, 12 December 2019). Discussion of the other parties' approaches was dismissive if not downright critical. The contro-versial Liberal Democrat plans to revoke Article 50 without a further referendum were denounced as 'extreme' by Kate Maltby (*The i* paper, 7 December 2019) and 'outrageous' by centre-left commentator Philip Collins (*The Times*, 1 November 2019). For Labour, as noted above, the party's second referendum pledge and Corbyn's pledge to remain neutral if a second vote occurred offered his press opponents further grounds for attack, with *The Sun* dismissing his policy as 'Brexcuses' (25 November 2019). This was also a sore point for *Daily Mirror* columnist Fiona Phillips, a Remain supporter who expressed frustration over the party's ambivalence (23 November 2019).

CONCLUSION: PRESS MATTERS

The parlous condition of the national press was starkly evident in the lead-up to the 2019 campaign, with some titles still struggling to sustain financial viability in the increasingly digital news ecosystem and several with 'for sale' signs in their front yard. Nevertheless, although the days of the *printed* press may be numbered, the news brands created from print media look more likely to endure. These brands retain substantial public reach through digital platforms, and by 2019 some had found ways to use this reach to clamber back into profitability—although such green shoots were soon to be flattened by the COVID-19 pandemic.

Certainly, there was no sign that financial precarity bred political timid-ity. The partisanship of the pro-Conservative press in particular was stri-dent and insistent in its enthusiasm for Boris Johnson and its detestation

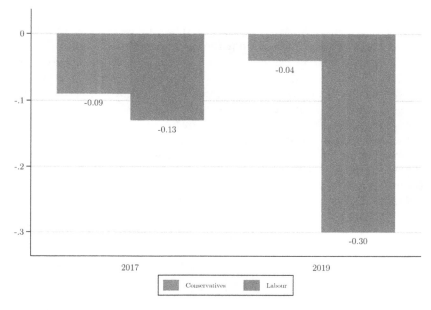

Fig. 10.2   Press evaluations of Conservative and Labour policies and candidates

of Jeremy Corbyn. While this repeats long-established patterns, there is evidence that the intensity of pro-Conservative partisanship in this campaign significantly exceeded previous levels. Figure 10.2 compares the ratio of negative to positive news stories related to each party in the 2017 and 2019 general elections,[33] and finds a significant ratcheting-up of negative Labour coverage in 2019.[34] There was none of the complacency evident in 2017 and Corbyn was taken much more seriously as a political threat. Moreover, pro-Conservative campaign press coverage in 2019 was for many outlets the culmination of a long anti-Labour campaign whose principal lines of attack were trialled and trailed repeatedly over the preceding years. This was very different from the lead-up to 2017— an unexpected snap election preceded by a lengthy period with the 'Tory press' divided between Leave and Remain stances at a time when Corbyn's Labour Party was widely deemed an unelectable irrelevance.

Boris Johnson was ultimately successful in ensuring that Brexit dominated press coverage at key moments of the campaign, in particular the opening and closing days.[35] Yet despite this prominence, press debate rarely engaged with the continuing complexities and uncertainties of the UK's withdrawal from the EU. Johnson's self-styled 'oven-ready' Withdrawal Agreement got the largest and most positive share of the coverage during the campaign, although it wasn't the only item on the menu. Significantly, the prospect of a 'no deal' Brexit was the least-reported outcome, even though it remained a distinct post-election possibility. This shows how the distinction between two different negotiations—formal withdrawal from the EU and agreement on a future relationship post-Brexit—tended to be ignored in coverage. Amid all the soundbites and photo opportunities about 'getting Brexit done', Boris Johnson's greatest success was in presenting his 'oven-ready deal' as a done deal rather than a deal with lots still to be done.

NOTES

1. See, for example, Dominic Wring and David Deacon, 'A Bad Press: Newspapers', in Philip Cowley and Dennis Kavanagh, *The British General Election of 2017*. Palgrave Macmillan, 2018; David Deacon and Dominic Wring, 'Still Life in the Old Attack Dogs: The Press' in Philip Cowley and Dennis Kavanagh, *The British General Election of 2015*. Palgrave Macmillan.

2. Peter Preston, 'This Election Proves That Media Bias No Longer Matters', *The Guardian*, 11 June 2017, https://www.theguardian.com/media/2017/jun/11/media-bias-no-longer-matters-general-election-2017.

3. Jim Waterson, 'This was the Election Where Newspapers Lost Their Monopoly on the Political News Agenda', *BuzzFeed*, 18 June 2017, https://www.buzzfeed.com/jimwaterson/how-newspapers-lost-their-monopoly-on-the-political-agenda.

4. Ofcom, 'News Consumption in the UK: 2020', 2020, p. 13, https://www.ofcom.org.uk/__data/assets/pdf_file/0013/201316/news-consumption-2020-report.pdf.

5. Ibid, p. 12.

6. Ibid, p. 19.

7. Ibid, p. 72.

8. Richard Fletcher, Nic Newman and Anne Schulz, *A Mile Wide, an Inch Deep: Online News and Media Use in the 2019 UK General Election*. Reuters Institute for the Study of Journalism, 2020, https://reutersinstitute.politics.ox.ac.uk/mile-wide-inch-deep-online-news-and-media-use-2019-uk-general-election.

9. See https://pamco.co.uk/pamco-data/latest-results.

10. In an average month, the reach in millions of these outlets is estimated to be 37.7 (*The Sun*), 35.2 (*The Guardian*), 33.6 (*MailOnline*), 33.8 (*The Independent*) 30.3 (*Daily Mirror*), 29.1 (*Daily Express*) and 28.2 (*Daily Telegraph*).
11. Andrew Chadwick, *The Hybrid Media System: Politics and Power*, 2nd edn. Oxford University Press, 2017.
12. Ofcom, 'News Consumption in the UK: 2020', p. 45.
13. Ibid, p. 44.
14. Ibid.
15. Adapted from Fletcher et al., *A Mile Wide, an Inch Deep*.
16. Fletcher et al., *A Mile Wide, an Inch Deep*.
17. Jim Waterson, 'How a Small Group of Pro-Corbyn Websites Built Enormous Audiences on Facebook', *BuzzFeed*, 6 May 2017, https://www.buzzfeed.com/jimwaterson/the-rise-of-the-alt-left.
18. Declan McDowell-Naylor and Richard Thomas, 'An Uncertain Future for Alternative Online Media?' in Daniel Jackson, Einar Thorsen, Darren Lilleker and Nathalie Weidhase (eds), *UK Election Analysis 2019: Media, Voters and the Campaign*. Centre for Comparative Politics and Media Research, 2019, http://www.electionanalysis.uk/uk-election-analysis-2019/section-7-news-and-journalism/an-uncertain-future-for-alternative-online-media; Richard Thomas and Declan McDowell-Naylor, 'UK Election 2019: How the Growing Reach of Alt-media is Shaping the Campaign', *The Conversation*, 13 November 2019, http://theconversation.com/uk-election-2019-how-the-growing-reach-of-alt-media-is-shaping-the-campaign-126947.
19. Robert Booth, 'DIY Political Websites: New Force Shaping the General Election Debate', *The Guardian*, 1 June 2017, https://www.theguardian.com/politics/2017/jun/01/diy-political-websites-new-force-shaping-general-election-debate-canary.
20. Waterson, 'This Was the Election Where the Newspapers Lost Their Monopoly on the Political News Agenda'.
21. Declan McDowell-Naylor, 'Are Alternative Media Still Relevant to the Labour Party? What Labour's Election Review Says and What it Doesn't', *Media@LSE*, 1 July 2020, https://blogs.lse.ac.uk/medialse/2020/07/01/are-alternative-media-still-relevant-to-the-labour-party-what-labours-election-review-says-and-what-it-doesnt.
22. Rowland Manthorpe, 'The UK's Left is Scrambling to Adapt to Facebook's Algorithm Change', *Wired UK*, 20 March 2018, https://www.wired.co.uk/article/facebook-algorithm-changes-engagement-labour; Mark Zuckerberg, 'One of Our Big Focus Areas for 2018 is Making Sure the Time We All Spend on Facebook is Time Well Spent',

Facebook (status update), 11 January 2018, https://www.facebook.com/zuck/posts/10104413015393571.

23. Chris York, 'Pro-Corbyn Website *The Canary* Blames "Political Zionists" after it's Forced to Downsize', *HuffPost*, 2 August 2019, https://www.huffingtonpost.co.uk/entry/the-canary-anti-semitism_uk_5d445ceee4b0acb57fcbcab4?guccounter=2.

24. McDowell-Naylor and Thomas, 'An Uncertain Future for Alternative Online Media?'.

25. David Deacon, Jackie Goode, David Smith, Dominic Wring, John Downey and Cristian Vaccari, 'Media Reporting of the 2019 General Election, Report 5', Centre for Research in Communication and Culture, Loughborough University, 2019, https://www.lboro.ac.uk/news-events/general-election/report-5.

26. It should be noted that these figures relate to the England print versions of national titles only; distributions would be different for versions produced in other nations.

27. Anthony Mughan, *Media and the Presidentialization of Parliamentary Elections*. Palgrave Macmillan, 2000.

28. One party reference was coded per headline. Where more than reference occurred, the first named reference and/or the party actor with the most active status in the headline was selected.

29. Adapted from Margaret Scammell and Charlie Beckett, 'Labour No More: The Press' in Dennis Kavanagh and Philip Cowley, *The British General Election of 2010*. Palgrave Macmillan, 2010; Deacon and Wring, 'Still Life in the Old Attack Dogs'; Wring and Deacon, 'A Bad Press'.

30. For detailed accounts of both parties' 2017 manifesto dramas, see Cowley and Kavanagh, *The British General Election of 2017*, Chapter 8.

31. Deacon and Wring, 'Still Life in the Old Attack Dogs'.

32. Deacon et al., 'Media Reporting of the 2019 General Election'.

33. Summarising analysis by Loughborough University presented at greater length in Deacon et al., 'Media Reporting of the 2019 General Election'.

34. Each party was rated separately in each election item published in the two study samples (i.e. the most prominent coverage in weekday editions during the formal campaign). If an item mainly or solely focused on positive matters for a party, it was given a value of +1. If it mainly/ solely focused on negative matters for a party, it was assigned a value of −1. Items where there was (a) no clear evaluation, (b) contained positive and negative issues in broadly equal measure or (c) no mention of the party was made were coded as zero. Items where no reference was made to the party were excluded from the calculation. To standardise these measures, the unweighted number of positive minus negative items were divided

by the total number of newspaper items in each campaign. This produced a decimal number between -1 and $+1$, where -1 = complete negativity, $+1$ = complete positivity and 0 = complete balance of negativity/positivity.

35. Deacon et al., 'Media Reporting of the 2019 General Election'.

CHAPTER 11

Political Recruitment Under Pressure, Again: MPs and Candidates in the 2019 General Election

Chris Butler, Rosie Campbell, and Jennifer Hudson

All the major UK parties have well-established formal candidate selection procedures, governed by party constitutions and with clearly demarcated roles for central offices, parliamentary assessment boards (the Conservatives), trade unions (Labour), approved lists and local party associations. These rules and procedures operated, with some adjustments throughout the entire period following the October 1974 election until 2017. This period of stability was disrupted by the snap elections called in 2017 and 2019. Snap elections strain party selection processes, forcing the parties to shortcut the usual procedures. The limited timeframe provides both constraints and opportunities for competing elements within parties. Central party candidate selection teams have diminished capacity to vet candidates, risking some poor choices, but the potential to reduce the involvement of local party associations can also give the centre the opportunity to shape the selection process to serve national leadership goals and promote favoured candidates. Tensions have certainly arisen because of the accelerated candidate selection processes, but rather than disruption, one of the most striking findings of this chapter is how well-established trends in the backgrounds of MPs and candidates evident over a prolonged period have continued, and sometimes accelerated, in the more fraught selection environment of the last two elections.

R. Ford et al., *The British General Election of 2019*,
https://doi.org/10.1007/978-3-030-74254-6_11

A total of 3,327 candidates stood in the 2019 general election, marginally up from the 3,304 who stood in 2017, but substantially down from 3,971 in 2015 and far short of the record 4,150 who stood in 2010. An average of 5.1 candidates stood per constituency in 2019; they represented 69 parties along with 224 independent candidates and the Speaker. Of these, 1,274 (over a third) lost their £500 deposit by failing to meet the 5% minimum vote share threshold, contributing £637,000 to the Treasury's lost deposit fund.[1]

The Conservatives contested 635 seats (including 4 in Northern Ireland), Labour 631 (all the seats in Great Britain save the Speaker's seat in Chorley) and the Liberal Democrats stood in 611 constituencies in Great Britain. The SNP contested all 59 seats in Scotland and Plaid Cymru 36 of the 40 in Wales. UKIP contested 44 seats, a fraction of the 378 they contested in 2017, the 624 they fought in 2015 or the 558 they contested in 2010. The Brexit Party, which was only registered with the Electoral Commission in February 2019, filled a sizeable portion of the gap left by UKIP, contesting 275 seats. The Green Party stood candidates in 497 seats, slightly up from the 467 seats it contested in 2017, but substantially down on the record 573 candidates stood in 2015.

In the run-up to the 2019 election, there was a repeat of the 2017 pattern with speculation, and media coverage, about the potential impact of pacts between the parties (see Chapter 5, pp. 154–192). Although these came to much greater fruition than in 2017, they had little effect on outcomes outside of Northern Ireland (see Chapter 13). An electoral pact between Leave parties in mainland UK failed to materialise. Nigel Farage, leader of the Brexit Party, called on the Conservatives to enter an agreement whereby the party would not contest Conservative-held and target seats should the Conservatives agree not to field candidates in more than 80 Leave-voting seats named by the Brexit Party.[2] While Boris Johnson declined, Farage, bowing to considerable pressure from Brexit-supporting political allies and grassroots activists,[3] announced that Brexit Party candidates would not stand against Conservative incumbents, but would continue to contest opposition-held seats (see Chapter 6, pp. 193–241). However, no formal electoral pact was agreed.

On the anti-Brexit side, there were again calls for pro-Remain parties to form electoral pacts.[4] The Labour Party and the SNP ruled out joining any electoral pacts, but the Liberal Democrats, Plaid Cymru and the Greens came together under the banner 'Unite to Remain', an agreement covering 60 seats across England and Wales (see Chapter 5, pp. 154–192).[5] The Greens stood aside for the Liberal Democrats in Penistone & Stockbridge despite incumbent Lib Dem MP Angela Smith, who had been elected as a Labour MP, having abandoned the constituency for supposedly greener pastures. However, the Greens did not stand aside in Carshalton & Wallington, where the Liberal Democrats' longest-serving MP Tom Brake lost by fewer votes than the Greens polled. Some Lib Dems involved in persuading candidates to step aside expressed their frustration with the autonomy of local Green parties, which made it impossible to develop a single nationwide agreement. Of the 60 constituencies covered by the arrangement, Unite to Remain candidates won nine, although all bar Richmond Park were already being defended by Unite to Remain parties. The Liberal Democrats lost North Norfolk despite the Greens having stood down to support them. Elsewhere the Liberal Democrats stood aside for Dominic Grieve in Beaconsfield, but not for David Gauke in South West Hertfordshire. Similarly, they did not challenge Change UK candidates Anna Soubry in Broxtowe nor Gavin Shuker in Luton South, but did stand against Mike Gapes in Ilford South and Chris Leslie in Nottingham East. According to party officials, one of the principal reasons Liberal Democrat Party HQ resisted calls by some activists not to stand down in more seats was because the party's permitted spending on the national campaign depended on the number of seats it was contesting.

In Northern Ireland, considerable new ground was broken with electoral pacts (see Chapter 12, pp. 421–459). In the 2017–2019 Parliament, 10 of the 11 Northern Irish MPs who took up their seats had been members of the strongly pro-Brexit DUP, who subsequently supported the Conservative government. The desire to remove DUP MPs prompted the SDLP to stand aside for Sinn Féin in marginal constituencies, something they had resisted in 2017 given Sinn Féin's refusal to take up their seats in Westminster.[6] Significantly, the cross-community Green Party also stood aside for the successful SDLP candidate in Belfast South.[7] The Ulster Unionist leader Steve Aiken initially declared that his party would not stand aside for the DUP given their Brexit stance, but later relented following pressure from party members.[8] However, the UUP decision not to stand in Belfast North failed to save DUP Westminster Leader Nigel Dodds, who lost to Sinn Féin in a seat where the SDLP stood down. The lack of a UUP candidate in Fermanagh & South Tyrone also failed to produce a DUP gain in a highly marginal seat. The Alliance Party won its first parliamentary seat since 2010 in

North Down, where the veteran Independent Lady Sylvia Hermon had stood down. The Alliance Party had refused to participate in an electoral pact with Sinn Féin and the SDLP given their non-sectarian tradition,[9] but in North Down it benefited from both main Republican parties standing down for it.

In total, 74 MPs did not seek re-election in 2019,[10] including 32 Conservative MPs, 20 Labour, three Liberal Democrats and 16 Independents (two seats had already been vacated by John Bercow, the former Speaker, and John Mann, who took up a life peerage). The number of MPs retiring from Parliament in 2019, whilst lower than the average of 86 between 1979 and 2015, was considerably higher than the 31 in 2017. This relatively high number of retirements after a Parliament which only lasted 30 months reflected the conflicts over Brexit, which had led to an astonishingly large number of MPs leaving their party during the Parliament, with many of these exiles subsequently opting to retire rather than fight under new colours. There were 19 retiring defectors who had supported Remain in the referendum, including Liberal Democrat Heidi Allen (elected as a Conservative MP); Change UK MPs Ann Coffey and Joan Ryan (formerly Labour MPs) and 15 independent MPs (6 of whom were previously Labour MPs and 9 of whom were former Conservative MPs).[11] The retiring independents included three particularly high-profile former Conservatives: the former Chancellor Phillip Hammond, the former Home Secretary Amber Rudd and Kenneth Clarke, the 'Father of the House' who had held many Cabinet-level posts in his long Commons tenure. In addition to the defectors, the retirees included other high-profile rebels, such as five Conservative MPs who had temporarily lost the party whip during the Parliament for rebelling against the government by supporting a motion to pass a bill to prohibit a 'no deal' Brexit without parliamentary approval (see Chapter 3, pp. 69–105). Other notable retirements include the former Liberal Democrat Party leader Sir Vince Cable and Tom Watson, Deputy Leader of the Labour Party.

Also among the retirees departing the Commons in 2019 were a crop of younger, talented MPs with plenty of ministerial experience, but relatively short parliamentary careers. The average age of the retiring MPs was 60 and the average number of years they had spent in the Commons was 18, but these figures hide variation by party and sex. Overall, 19 women MPs stood down, which is roughly proportionate to the representation of women in the House, but the nine Conservative

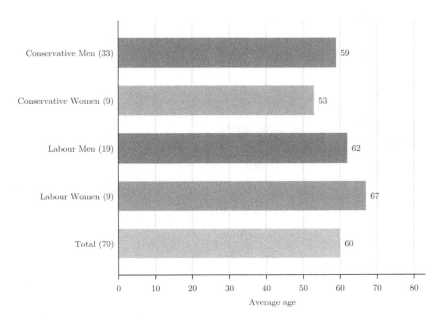

Fig. 11.1 Retiring Labour and Conservative MPs' average ages by gender. *Note* This figure includes all retiring MPs elected in 2017 as Labour or Conservative candidates, including those who left their parties during the Parliament

(or former Conservative) women MPs who retired were noticeably younger and had spent less time on average in the House than either retiring Conservative men or retiring Labour MPs. The average age of Conservative (and former Conservative) women MPs was 53 and they had spent on average only 10 years in the Commons (Figs. 11.1 and 11.2). These women could have been prominent in politics for another decade or so. Heidi Allen, Nicky Morgan and Caroline Spelman, three prominent members of this group, raised the issue of the harassment and intimidation of politicians, and the increasing polarisation and hostility in British politics among their reasons for exiting the Commons.[12]

Of the 574 sitting MPs who stood again (two seats were vacant at the time of the election), 79 lost their seats and 495 were re-elected, while 15 MPs who had been MPs prior to 2017 were returned to Parliament.[13] The 79 incumbent MPs defeated in the election comprised

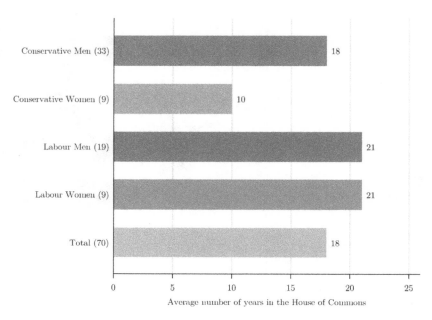

Fig. 11.2 Average years in the House for retiring Labour and Conservative MPs by gender. *Note* This figure includes all retiring MPs elected in 2017 as Labour or Conservative candidates, including those who left their parties during the Parliament

46 Labour MPs (including Dennis Skinner, also know as the Beast of Bolsover, unseated after 49 years), 7 Conservative MPs (including Zac Goldsmith—see below), 7 independents, 11 Liberal Democrats, 3 Change UK, 2 DUP, 1 Sinn Féin, 1 SNP MP and Frank Field of the Birkenhead Social Justice Party, formerly a Labour MP.

The election saw a number of former MPs return to Parliament including eight Conservatives, five SNP MPs and one Liberal Democrat.[14] Alongside the eight Conservative MPs who returned to the Commons after a break, there was also the unusual case of Mims Davies MP for Mid Sussex (and MP for Eastleigh from 2015 to 2019). She announced she was standing down due to the impact of a political career on her family life as a single parent, then reversed course and stood in Mid Sussex when the previous MP Nicholas Soames announced he was retiring, provoking some controversy over the local selection process.[15]

The SNP had lost 21 seats in the 2017 election, remaining the largest Scottish party, but falling back from the 2015 landslide where they took 56 of the 59 seats. In 2019, five of the 21 defeated SNP MPs returned to the House as the SNP recovered. The SNP MPs who sat from 2015 to 2017 and returned in 2019 were: Margaret Ferrier (Rutherglen),[16] John MacKenzie Nicolson (East Dunbartonshire 2015–2017; Ochil & South Perthshire after 2019),[17] Anne McLaughlin (Glasgow North East), Kirsten Oswald (East Renfrewshire) and George Thompson (Midlothian). A handful of Liberal Democrats MPs who had lost their seats in 2015 and failed to regain them in 2017 stood again without success in 2019.[18] Two former Liberal Democrat MPs who had lost their seats in 2017 also stood again: Sarah Olney romped home with a majority of nearly 8,000 in her third electoral battle with Zac Goldsmith in Richmond Park, but Mark Williams fell to third in his attempt to win back Ceredigion.

Familial ties have long been a mainstay of the Commons and the 2019 election was no different.[19] The House has a long history of married couples, with current examples including Andrea Jenkyns and Jack Lopresti (both Conservative), Esther McVey and Philip Davies (both Conservative) and Harriet Harman and Jack Dromey (both Labour), as well as siblings such as Maria Eagle and Angela Eagle (both Labour) and Rachael Reeves and Ellie Reeves (both Labour).[20] In two constituencies, spouses took over seats previously held by their partners. Conservative Natalie Elphicke won the Dover constituency, taking over from her husband Charlie Elphicke who represented Dover from 2010 to 2019 (see below). Likewise, Andrew Griffiths represented Burton from 2010 to 2019, with the seat won by Kate Griffiths in 2019. The Commons is a family affair in other ways, with several sitting MPs whose parents or grandparents also once sat in the House. Hilary Benn (Labour), first elected in 1999, is the fourth generation of Benns to sit in the House, following in the footsteps of Tony Benn (Labour 1950–1983, 1984–2001), William Wedgewood Benn (Liberal 1906–1927; Labour 1929–1931, 1937–1942) and Sir John Benn (Liberal 1891–1895, 1904–1910). Another family for whom Commons service is a tradition is the Cryers: Labour MP John Cryer is the son of Ann Cryer (1997–2010) and Bob Cryer (first elected in 1974, died in office in 1994). The Speaker of the House, Lindsay Hoyle, is the son of Doug Hoyle (Labour) who served in the Commons for more than 20 years.[21] Perhaps the most striking event for those with an interest in political dynasties was the departure of Nicolas Soames (Mid Sussex), who had served in Parliament since 1983. Soames' retirement means Parliament is without a member of the Churchill clan for the first time in over 350 years.[22]

CANDIDATE SELECTION IN THE 2019 GENERAL ELECTION

The Conservatives

The 2017 snap election gave the parties experience in selecting candidates under pressure and the hung parliament outcome meant the possibility of another snap election was ever present, with speculation of a coming poll intensifying throughout 2019.[23] Thus, the parties had fast-track processes in place and had already begun selecting candidates and endorsing incumbent MPs' candidatures when the election eventually came. Nonetheless, the divides opened up by Brexit and other party conflicts meant that there were still many key selections to complete in newly vacated retirement seats and seats where the incumbent had resigned from the party. With an election once again called early, the parties had just over seven weeks to fill these various planned and unplanned vacancies, while also organising their election campaigns.

The accelerated selection process utilised by the Conservative Party in 2017 had produced a backlash from some local associations, members and candidates. In 2017, the central party made use of Part IV, Clause 17 of the party's Constitution, which allows the party board 'to do anything' it sees fit in the interests of the party, to put in place special selection rules to allow the Conservative Party Board to select over 300 candidates within three weeks. The traditional day-long parliamentary assessment boards were replaced by a 45-min interview with a pass/fail outcome and candidates were not able to apply directly to retirement or target seats. Instead, local parties were offered a choice of three candidates chosen by the central party candidates' team, in consultation with the officers of the local association. In some cases, this consultation was somewhat minimal and many local associations felt their role had been diminished. Many candidates also complained that they found the process difficult to navigate. The *ConservativeHome* website evidenced widespread dissatisfaction among aspirant candidates and local party members about the procedures employed in 2017.[24] In the aftermath of the election, Theresa May commissioned Sir Eric Pickles to conduct a review of the party's campaign and candidate selection was a significant aspect of his remit (see Chapter 3, pp. 69–105). Among his recommendations was that: 'Parliamentary candidates should be in place in battleground seats by June 2018 to ensure they are well-established within the seat before the next scheduled General Election on 5th May 2022.' The early selections were intended to avoid many of the problems encountered by local associations and aspirant candidates in 2017.[25] Yet despite Pickles' recommendations, there were still many selections outstanding when the election was announced in 2019.

The large number of MP resignations in Conservative-held seats and the transformation of the electoral battleground, with the Conservatives newly competitive in seats long held by Labour, meant that there were simply more key seats to fill than had previously been typical. Thus, the special rules deployed in 2017 were needed again to manage selections within a constrained time period. There were again complaints from local associations regarding the transparency of the process and allegations of pressure from CCHQ to select their preferred candidates.[26] In some cases, candidates on the party's approved list were not given the opportunity to apply to all competitive seats. The expedited process gave CCHQ a pivotal role in drawing up shortlists.[27] Centralisation may have helped the party to secure a greater diversity of candidates selected in winnable seats than had been the case with the traditional association-led procedures. Candidate shortlists were kept secret until shortly before the selection, but the *ConservativeHome* website collated the lists where possible and published them, arguing that public vetting would lead to a more rigorous process.[28]

ConservativeHome's Editor (and former Tory MP) Paul Goodman observed there was less evidence of local associations being bypassed than in 2017.[29] Nevertheless, there were still some controversial individual selections. Natalie Elphicke's selection to stand in Dover raised some eyebrows. Her predecessor was her husband Charlie Elphicke (the couple are no longer together), who was suspended from the party after being charged with sexually assaulting two women. Sources claimed that she was announced as the local candidate without the local association being given a choice among any other potential candidates.[30] In a mirror of these strange events, Kate Griffiths, estranged wife of Andrew Griffiths, stood in his constituency of Burton after he stood down following the emergence of allegations that he may have violated the party code of conduct by sending sexually explicit messages to two women.[31] Kate Griffiths did, however, face competition on a shortlist for the seat.

In the aftermath of the 2019 election, CCHQ announced a further overhaul of the selection process. A new competency framework is to be employed and a pilot reassessment of candidates on the approved list will be undertaken.[32]

Labour

In the 2019 election, Labour stood candidates in all 631 seats outside of Northern Ireland, rejecting the option for alliances with other parties in target constituencies. The party's approach to candidate selection was heavily influenced by context, both in the run-up to the 2019 general election and by the internal politics that had heavily influenced the party's approach to selection in the previous two elections. Having been caught on the back foot in 2017 and in anticipation of another early general election, Labour had completed 117 selections—targeting key marginals first—by the time the 2019 general election had been called.[33] In non-priority seats, a central process governed 2019 selections. Applications were submitted to a single office, with all names going on a spreadsheet, and candidates could apply for a small number of constituencies. Names were divided up and sent to regional and Constituency Labour Party (CLP) panels, and candidates were selected by the imposition of a joint panel. In some constituencies, candidates were selected from a list, whereas in others there were interviews prior to selection.

However, by the time of the Labour Party conference in Brighton in late September 2019, it was clear that an election was now not far away, and the party would need to move much more quickly. Key selections included 20 retirement seats (e.g. Kate Hoey (Vauxhall), Kevin Barron (Rother Valley) and Roberta Blackman-Woods (City of Durham)) and 14 defections stemming from both Labour's position on Brexit and the ongoing crisis within the party on anti-semitism (e.g. Frank Field (Birkenhead), Ann Coffey (Stockport), Chuka Umunna (Streatham) and Luciana Berger (Liverpool Wavertree)). In Bassetlaw, John Mann, stood down to take up a peerage before the election, and the local party selected Sally Gimson. However, she was deselected just a few weeks later by the National Executive Committee (NEC), which cited allegations made against her by her local party in Camden.[34] Gimson was one of three candidates to be deselected by the NEC, moves seen by some as an effort to remove anti-Corbyn candidates. Kier Morrison was ultimately selected for the seat, which Labour went on to lose.

Recognising the need for a truncated selection process for remaining constituencies, the party leadership had begun outlining options in the late summer, but the process was not without confusion. By early October, the NEC had agreed a new, fast-tracked selection process for priority seats—targets, retirements and deselections—a longlist of candidates was to be drawn up exclusively by the NEC, while mixed panels of NEC, regional board and local party reps would create shortlists. Final decisions would be taken by CLPs and the process was meant to be completed in seven days.[35] There were then two groups of candidates, one where candidates were immediately selected following an interview by a panel made up of the NEC, regional board and local party representatives. The other group were interviewed, but then in some constituencies, hustings were held and the candidate was selected by the CLP. According to the *LabourList* website, Labour-held seats that had held hustings by 3 November could progress to local votes; local votes would be prohibited for others not as far along.[36]

Rule changes were seen by some as an opportunity to exert more influence over the selection of candidates, particularly those from the left wing of the party. However, there is not a lot of evidence to suggest that pro-Corbyn/Momentum candidates were more likely to be selected overall. Candidates in retirement seats suffered particularly because the trade unions—which frequently get first choice on candidate nominations—were divided in their support for left-wing candidates, consequently diluting the power of the left and resulting in greater losses than might have been expected, particularly when the more left-favouring trade unions and Momentum preferred different candidates. This was true in London in particular, where Momentum-backed left-wing candidates performed poorly against more moderate candidates with strong union backing.

Another challenge for Labour was the quality of the candidate pool. In 2017, there had been a lot of 'retreads' from 2010 and 2015, but after 2017, there were a lot of new entrants, some of whom were not long-term Labour Party members and had not come up through various party institutions. As a result, there was a greater lack of discipline on message and a number of disciplinary issues, resulting in candidates being removed and replaced, with allegations of anti-semitism sometimes an issue (for example, Gideon Bull in Clacton[37] and Safia Ali in Falkirk).[38]

A key issue for Labour was whether trigger ballots—a vote of the CLP to determine whether an MP can stand again unopposed or whether they should face a full reselection process with other candidates vying for the Labour-held seat—would be used. Labour opted not to use them in 2017 (lacking time due to the snap election), with all sitting MPs automatically selected. This was a change on the party's previous approach in previous elections. In 2018, Labour changed its rules for trigger ballots, making it easier to deselect an MP by lowering the threshold to have a full/open selection process from 50 to 33% of local party or affiliated trade union branches (see Chapter 4, pp. 107–157).[39]

Trigger ballots typically happen at the midpoint of a sitting Parliament, but the leadership was fearful of calling for the use of triggers too early; if they went too early and there were a lot of defections, this could potentially generate a big split in the PLP. However, it is not clear that the Labour leadership ever intended to use trigger ballots extensively. By February 2019, some MPs who Labour's membership or leadership may have wanted to trigger had already left the party anyway, along with others who departed as a consequence of wider internal conflicts and defections around Brexit. In the end, triggers were left until the last minute. Diana Johnson (Kingston upon Hull North) was the first MP triggered (the trigger failed and she was reselected without competition), followed by Margaret Hodge (Barking), who failed her trigger ballot. Hodge was thought to have been targeted by some in her CLP in part for her high-profile criticism of Jeremy Corbyn's record on race and anti-semitism.[40] Triggers were eventually used against a small and politically mixed set of six incumbent Labour MPs—Roger Godsiff, Diana Johnson, Margaret Hodge, Emma Lewell-Buck, Kate Osamor and Virendra Sharma—before being paused due to time constraints with all other incumbent MPs automatically reselected.[41]

The Liberal Democrats

The majority of Liberal Democrat selections for the 2019 election took place under emergency procedures which were invoked to speed up the selection process due to the occurrence of another snap election. Outside a top tier of around 80 constituencies, candidates were simply appointed by regional or, in the case of Scotland and Wales, state parties in agreement with local party chairs. Although regional parties were encouraged to bear diversity in mind when appointing, they were not bound by any quotas relating to under-represented groups.

Under the emergency procedures, local party members in target seats selected candidates at a hustings following a short campaign. One small change in the procedures compared to 2017 was that shortlisted candidates had to undergo an enhanced approvals process, similar to the procedure for parliamentary by-elections, which involved an additional interview to ensure they had the skills to stand in a winnable constituency. In England, there was provision for target seats to use all-women or all-disabled shortlists. The Scottish party adopted a rule that there had to be 50/50 gender representation across its top 10 seats. In Wales, however, procedures to increase the representation of women could not be invoked due to the party's only elected politician above council level being Kirsty Williams AM.

In two English seats where incumbent MPs were standing down (North Norfolk and Twickenham), all-women shortlists were adopted. In 2017, an all-disabled shortlist had been used to select the Liberal Democrat candidate for Eastbourne, the former MP Stephen Lloyd, but no all-disabled shortlists were used this time around. In other seats undergoing a selection procedure, the shortlist had to include at least two candidates with 'protected characteristics', which covered female, BAME, LGBT and disabled candidates. Local parties in target seats which selected candidates under normal, non-emergency procedures had to complete a diversity monitoring form to demonstrate evidence to party HQ that they had reached out to encourage potential candidates from under-represented groups before they were allowed to start their selection procedure.

The party has a long-term project to support female candidates, known as the Campaign for Gender Balance. This engages senior volunteers to encourage female candidates to come forward and mentor them through the assessment and selection process. In 2018, the party established the Campaign for Racial Equality as a similar body to encourage BAME candidates, but it was not fully operational in time for selections for the 2019 election.

The biggest challenge for the Liberal Democrats in terms of candidates was how to manage the string of defectors to their parliamentary party between June and October 2019 (see Chapter 5). Once defectors had been accepted by the parliamentary party, as sitting Liberal Democrat MPs they automatically became the de facto 2019 candidate for that constituency, usurping any previously selected candidate. However, in most cases the defectors felt they did not have a good chance of holding their current seats under their new party banner and sought different constituencies to stand in. The party knew that the high profiles of many defectors would offer them an electoral boost in winnable seats, but almost all of the top target seats had already selected candidates by summer 2019. In some cases, the movement of defectors was handled fairly smoothly. The existing candidate for Finchley & Golders Green amicably made way for Luciana Berger to stand in the constituency with the highest Jewish population in the country. Chuka Umunna caused some upset, having reportedly indicated an intention to stay and fight Streatham before moving to Cities of London & Westminster in early September. More controversy came with Sam Gyimah, who was unveiled as the party's twentieth MP at the party's conference in September 2020, by which time only around 25 constituencies had yet to select candidates. Gyimah was originally earmarked by the leader's office to stand in Putney, but the previously selected candidate refused to stand aside. He was eventually granted a chance in Kensington after the existing Liberal Democrat candidate was helpfully offered a position as Communities Adviser to the party's leader in the House of Lords.[42]

BACKGROUND OF MPs

Gender

A record number of 220 women MPs were elected to the House of Commons in 2019, taking the percentage of women up from 32% in 2017 to 34%. This was further incremental progress towards gender parity, though women still remain in a minority in Parliament and their proportion is far short of women in the electorate, where they make up more than half of eligible voters (Fig. 11.3). The headline figures mask considerable party differences: all of the major parties have increased the number of women in their parliamentary parties over time, but the Labour Party and the Liberal Democrats are well ahead of the rest. After a disastrous election for the party in 2015, the Liberal Democrats returned to Parliament with no women MPs and eight men. As described previously, the party set targets and initiatives to improve the representation of women in the parliamentary party and after the 2019 election, 64% of Liberal Democrat MPs were women. Using all-women

Table 11.1 Number (and percentage) of women elected by party 2015–2019

	2015	2017	2019
Conservative	68 (21)	67 (21)	87 (24)
Labour	99 (43)	119 (45)	104 (51)
SNP	20 (36)	12 (34)	16 (33)
Liberal Democrat	0	4 (33)	7 (64)
Plaid Cymru	1 (33)	1 (25)	1 (33)

shortlists (AWS), the Labour Party has increased the representation of women on its benches over a sustained period. Labour returned 104 women MPs to their benches in 2019 or 51% of all Labour MPs. Thus, Labour and the Liberal Democrats were far ahead of the Conservatives (24%) and the SNP (33%) (Table 11.1).

These figures demonstrate the success of the sometimes controversial AWS policy, first employed by the Labour Party in the run-up to the 1997 election where local associations were required to select from a shortlist of only women candidates in half of all winnable seats. The fact that AWS have been deployed in retirement and target seats is key to their success; prior to their use, women candidates were more likely to be selected in seats the party did not expect to win. The continued use of AWS by the Labour Party has repeatedly been challenged by both men who felt discriminated against[43] and factions within the party trying to secure key seats for their favoured candidates.[44] Yet regardless of such controversies, the policy is still in place. Despite this historic resistance, there has been a contagion effect, with other parties following Labour's example. After years of internal battles, the Liberal Democrats adopted new rules in 2016 which permit the use of AWS[45] and the SNP have also introduced an AWS policy.[46] Labour and the Liberal Democrats, the two parties who used AWS in the 2019 general election, now represent women proportionally, or in excess in the case of the Liberal Democrats, to their share of the electorate; due to this fact, neither party will be permitted by the Equality Act 2010 to use AWS in the next general election, unless the representation of women dips below the proportion of women in the electorate.[47] Historically candidate data has simply recorded whether candidates identify as men or women, while in recent years the category of non-binary has been added. In 2019, five candidates stood for election who identify as non-binary—one Labour, one Liberal Democrat and three Greens—though none was elected (Table 11.2).

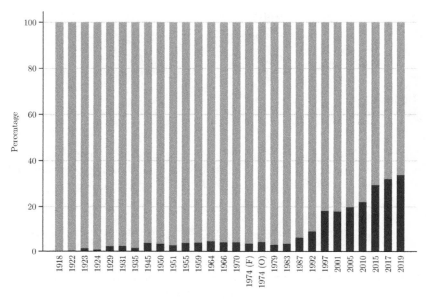

Fig. 11.3 Percentage of women (purple) and men (grey) elected to the House of Commons 1918–2019

Table 11.2 Women and non-binary candidates by party, numbers (and percentages) 2019

	Women	Non-binary
Conservative	193 (30)	
Labour	335 (53)	1 (0.2)
SNP	20 (34)	
Liberal Democrat	187 (31)	1 (0.2)
Plaid Cymru	9 (25)	
Green Party	191 (41)	3 (0.6)
Brexit	56 (20)	
UKIP	8 (18)	
English Democrats	1 (20)	

LGBT+

A record 51 MPs who identified as lesbian, gay, bisexual or trans (LGBT+) were elected to the House of Commons in 2019, up four on 2017. Two further MPs have 'come out' since the election, including Liberal Democrat Layla Moran as the first openly pansexual MP. The SNP remains the party with the greatest LGBT representation, with 21% of their parliamentary party self-identifying as LGBT. There are now 24 LGBT Conservative MPs, up from 19 in 2017, and 18 Labour LGBT MPs.

Black, Asian and Minority Ethnic (BAME) MPs

The 2019 general election also returned a record number of BAME MPs, with 65 (10%) describing themselves as BAME, up from just 4 in 1987; 37 of these BAME MPs are women (57%) (Fig. 11.4). This historic

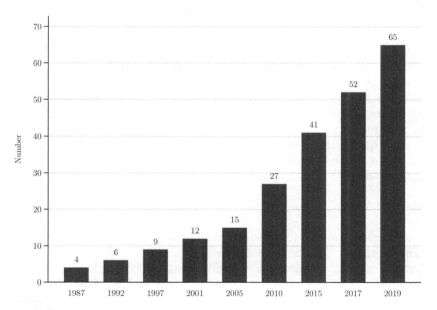

Fig. 11.4 BAME MPs elected to the House of Commons 1987–2019 (*Source* House of Commons Library Briefing Paper CBP01156, 22 October 2020, 'Ethnic Diversity in Politics and Public Life')

high is still somewhat below the proportion of BAME individuals in the British population, though closer to the proportion of BAME adults, as many of Britain's ethnic minority communities have much younger age profiles than the white population. The overall progress towards ethnic minority representation also masks big differences between the parties and by ethnic group. There are currently 41 Labour (20% of the parliamentary party), 22 Conservative (6% of the parliamentary party), 2 Liberal Democrat (18% of the parliamentary party) and no SNP BAME MPs.[48] The pool of Labour and Liberal Democrat MPs returned to the Commons was more ethnically diverse than the pool of candidates that each party stood; 12% of all Labour and 8% of all Liberal Democrat candidates were from a BAME background. The reverse was true for the Conservative Party—11% of Conservative candidates were BAME, nearly twice the share among elected Conservative MPs. In total, 12% of Brexit Party candidates, 6% of Green Party candidates and 3% of Plaid Cymru candidates were from BAME communities. The SNP fielded no BAME candidates in 2019.[49] The retirement of Keith Vaz, one of the first four BAME MPs elected in 1987, provided an interesting case study in the complexity of ethnic minority representation. Vaz was replaced as Labour MP for Leicester East by Claudia Webbe, a close ally of Jeremy Corbyn and also a BAME candidate, but from a different minority community and with no background in Leicester politics (though born in Leicester, she had left at the age of 18 and was an Islington councillor at the time of selection). The seat saw by far the largest swing from Labour to the Conservatives in an ethnically diverse seat, with Leicester East's large Indian community abandoning Labour in large numbers for the Conservatives' Indian candidate Bhupendra Dave, who reportedly emphasised both his local roots and his ethnic origins.[50]

Age

The average age of MPs elected in 2019 is 49.7, which is not significantly different from average age in 2017 (50.5) or in 2015 (50.6). In fact, average age has not changed much since 1979: the highest average age was 51.2 in 2005 and the lowest was 48.8 in 1983. The stability in the average age of MPs elected to the House of Commons involves significant changes in the generational profile of the Commons, with older cohorts fading out and younger cohorts taking their place in the legislature for the first time.

The 'Baby of the House' after the 2019 election is Nadia Whittome (Nottingham East) who was 23 when she was elected. She succeeds Mhairi Black (Paisley & Renfrewshire South) who was just 20 when first elected in 2015 (and is now, aged 24, already the veteran of three successful general election campaigns in her seat). The 'Father of the House' is Sir Peter Bottomley, who was first elected in 1975 and has represented three constituencies—Woolwich West, Eltham and now Worthing West. As the longest-serving male MP, he and Barry Sheerman (Huddersfield) now form part of a rapidly shrinking cohort of MPs elected in the 1970s. Two other grandees elected even earlier left Parliament in 2019: Ken Clarke retired before the election after 49 years as the MP for Rushcliffe, while Dennis Skinner was defeated after 49 years as the MP for Bolsover. The other remaining member of the 1970s cohort is Margaret Beckett, who was first elected in 1974. Beckett is not 'Mother of the House' as she lost her first seat in the 1979 election, before returning in 1983 as MP for Derby South, the seat she has represented ever since. The 'Mother of the House' is instead Harriet Harman (Camberwell & Peckham). First elected in 1982, she holds the record for the longest continuous service by a female MP.[51] She and Diane Abbott (Hackney North & Stoke Newington) are the only other female MPs elected in the 1980s. They were joined in 2019 by a cohort of 12 male MPs first elected in that decade, the last Commons witnesses of the Thatcher era.

Three turbulent general elections in five years, and some large waves of retirements, have resulted in a rapid turnover in the Commons and a reduction in parliamentarians' experience. Just under a quarter of MPs (23%) now sitting in the Commons were first elected in 2019, 9% were first elected in 2017 (or thereafter via by-elections) and 22% were first elected in 2015 (or thereafter). A majority of MPs in the 2019 Commons therefore have five years of parliamentary experience or less. A further 23% were first elected in the 2010 general election (or thereafter), with another 12% elected since 2001. Just 11% of MPs were first elected before 2001.

As shown in Table 11.3, for all MPs elected in 2019, 33% are aged 45–54, 25% are 55–64 and 23% are 35–44. A total of 9% of MPs are 25–34 or 65+; just 1% of MPs are 18–24. It's clear that the distribution of age in Parliament skews to the older groups, but how representative in terms of age are elected MPs compared to the population? The Commons under-represents both ends of the age distribution and over-represents the middle: just 1% of MPs come from the 18–24

Table 11.3   2019 MPs' age distributions by party[52]

	18–24	25–34	35–44	45–54	55–64	65+	Total
Conservative	2 (1)	34 (9)	87 (24)	135 (37)	76 (21)	27 (8)	361 (100)
Green Party	0 (0)	0 (0)	0 (0)	0 (0)	1 (100)	0 (0)	1 (100)
Labour	1 (1)	14 (7)	45 (22)	57 (28)	59 (29)	26 (13)	202 (100)
Liberal Democrat	0 (0)	0 (0)	5 (46)	3 (27)	2 (18)	1 (9)	11 (100)
Plaid Cymru	0 (0)	1 (25)	1 (25)	1 (25)	0 (0)	1 (25)	4 (100)
SNP	0 (0)	8 (17)	8 (17)	13 (27)	17 (35)	2 (4)	48 (100)
Total MPs	3 (1)	57 (9)	146 (23)	209 (33)	155 (25)	57 (9)	627 (100)
Adult population share (%)	(11)	(16)	(16)	(17)	(16)	(24)	(100)

Note Age is not available for a small number of MPs. Numbers in parenthesis are percentages

group, compared to 11% of the adult population, while 9% of MPs come from the 65+ group, compared to 24% of British adults. MPs are much more likely than the general population to be in the 35–64 age range— 81% of MPs fall into this middle range, compared to 49% of the adult population.

There are differences between the parties as well. The SNP has the highest percentage of MPs in the 55–64 age group (35%), compared to 29% for Labour and 21% for the Conservatives. Comparatively, Labour MPs are older on average, with 42% of MPs aged 55+ compared to 29% for the Conservatives. Efforts to 'renew the left' during Corbyn's tenure as Leader of the Opposition met with mixed success. While the Socialist Campaign Group (SCG), the main 'hard left' group, now has a lot more younger MPs in the 25–34 age group than the Commons overall (18% for the SCG vs 9% for MPs overall), it also had more MPs of pensionable age (15% of SCG members are 65+ compared to 9% of all MPs), How long veterans of the left such as Diane Abbott, Jeremy Corbyn, John McDonnell and Jon Trickett will remain in Parliament is unknown, but Labour's left will need to continue recruiting more young MPs like Nadia Whittome and Zarah Sultana in order for the SCG to maintain its Commons presence in future.[53]

MPs' Educational Background

There was no further broadening of the educational background of MPs in 2019: 48% of MPs attended comprehensive schools, down from

Table 11.4   MPs' school background in 2019 (change from 2017)

	Comprehensive	Selective	Fee-paying
Conservative	38% (+4)	17% (−4)	44% (±0)
Labour	64% (−1)	17% (−5)	19% (+6)
SNP	83% (−5)	8% (+2)	8% (+2)
Liberal Democrat	50% (−10)	13% (+3)	38% (+8)

a high point of 52% in 2017.[54] The proportion of MPs who attended a fee-paying school rose among all the main parties apart from the Conservatives. A record 38% of Conservative MPs were educated at comprehensive schools. The Liberal Democrats remained the parliamentary party with the second-highest proportion of privately educated MPs at 38%, with just 8% of SNP MPs having attended fee-paying schools. Eton College is still the most commonly attended school by MPs, with 11 alumni, although this represents a record low for the school. However, 6% of all MPs were educated at just 10 fee-paying schools[55] (Table 11.4).

The proportion of MPs with degrees continues to rise, with 87% of MPs elected in 2019 having attended university.[56] Over a third of MPs for whom we have data also hold a postgraduate degree. Table 11.5 sets out these figures by party.[57] A total of 24% of SNP MPs for whom we have information do not hold degrees, which is significantly higher than the proportions for other parties. The educational background of MPs from the three Britain-wide parties is now strikingly similar; only 10% of Labour MPs do not have a degree, down from 23% as recently as 2015. Meanwhile, the proportion of MPs who attended Oxbridge continues to slowly decline, with 22% of MPs having attended Oxbridge compared to 24% in 2017. However, over 300 MPs graduated from a select group of 14 universities, of which only Aberystwyth and Hull are not members of the Russell Group.[58] There is little difference in the proportion of Oxbridge graduates between Britain-wide parties, with 29% of Conservative MPs having attended Oxbridge, a fall from 34% in 2017. Elected MPs are much more likely to have attended Oxbridge than unsuccessful candidates.

Table 11.5 also shows the highest educational qualification of candidates by party.[59] There is a considerable range in the proportion of

Table 11.5 Highest educational qualification of MPs and candidates by party (percentage)

	MPs				Candidates			
	No Degree	Undergrad	Postgrad	Attended Oxbridge[a]	No Degree	Undergrad	Postgrad	Attended Oxbridge
Conservative	14	51	35	29	11	47	42	13
Labour	10	53	37	21	12	39	49	13
SNP	24	51	24	0				
Liberal Democrat	0	55	45	18	8	44	48	15
Plaid Cymru					17	25	58	9
Green Party					2	55	43	13
Brexit Party					21	37	41	17

[a]Includes those who attended Oxbridge for either undergraduate or postgraduate qualifications

Note The individual figures in the table have all been rounded up/down to the nearest whole number

Table 11.6   Undergraduate fields of study of MPs by party (percentage)

	Conservative	Labour	SNP	Lib Dem	Other
Agriculture	3	1	0	0	0
Business/Management	9	6	18	0	7
Economics	6	5	0	10	0
Education/Literature/Humanities	18	21	9	50	21
Law, Politics	37	38	42	30	64
Maths	1	2	0	0	0
Medicine/Health	3	2	6	0	0
Music	0	0	0	0	0
Other	5	4	6	0	0
Other Social Sciences	6	9	3	10	7
PPE	4	6	0	0	0
Science, Engineering, Tech	7	6	15	0	0

candidates without a degree, ranging from just 2% of Green Party candidates to 21% of Brexit Party candidates. However, 89% of unsuccessful candidates had a university degree, a higher proportion than ever before, and 46% had a postgraduate degree.

MPs were most likely to have studied law or politics for their first degrees. There are some patterns between different parties and their MPs' fields of study. Liberal Democrat MPs were more likely to have studied humanities, while SNP MPs were more likely to have studied business or management degrees, as well as science, engineering or technology degrees. A total of 22 MPs studied PPE (Politics, Philosophy and Economics) at Oxford (Table 11.6).

Occupation

In terms of MPs' previous occupations, we see a continuation of previous trends. The decline in the representation of MPs from traditional 'brokerage' occupations such as the law, education and medicine continues. These professions were once considered a fertile recruitment pool for potential politicians. They afforded parliamentary aspirants plenty of personal flexibility in terms of control over their time and sufficient financial resource to support selection and campaigning activities. In addition, candidates from such professions benefited from a respectable profile in their constituencies and an arena to practise many of the skills required of an MP. However, this route into politics has declined as politics itself has professionalised. In 2019, just 9% of Conservative MPs and nearly 12% of Labour MPs were drawn from a brokerage profession, nearly half the proportion found in 2017. MPs whose previous occupation was closely related to formal politics (instrumental occupations) now make up the majority of both Labour and Conservative MPs. Nearly 75% of Labour MPs were drawn from instrumental occupations and over 55% of Conservative MPs were also previously employed in a field closely related to politics, both figures substantially higher than those for 2017. The nature of the Conservative backbenches has changed substantially between 2017 and 2019. Overall, 25% of Conservative MPs are identified as having been employed in business or commerce immediately prior to their first election, down from 41% in 2017. The Conservative Party's success in former Labour Red Wall seats has led to an intake of very different Conservative MPs, many of whom were local politicians rather than working in commerce or the City before their first election. On the Labour benches, there are 23 MPs who were employed as trade union officials immediately prior to their first election, up five on the figure for 2017. This trend reflects the increased significance of the trade unions during Jeremy Corbyn's time as Labour leader. Finally, and perhaps astonishingly, according to our data, there are currently no MPs who were employed in a manual occupation immediately prior to entering Parliament. The exit of Dennis Skinner, Ronnie Campbell and Kevin Baron also means that there are no former miners on the Labour benches for the first time ever. Perhaps the most telling symbol of the transformation of traditional class politics is that the only former miner we have identified in the Commons is the newly elected Conservative MP for Ashfield, Lee Anderson, who was a Labour councillor and office manager for the Ashfield Labour MP Gloria De Piero before defecting to the Conservatives in 2018 and defeating his former boss in the 2019 contest[60] (Table 11.7).

Table 11.7 Occupation for MPs immediately prior to their first election to the Commons

	Conservative		Labour		SNP		Liberal Democrat	
	MPs	Candidates	MPs	Candidates	MPs	Candidates	MPs	Candidates
Brokerage	33 (9.0%)	19 (7.5%)	23 (11.6%)	50 (12.7%)	4 (8.3%)	0	2 (18.2%)	70 (12.4%)
Legal profession	29 (7.9%)	12 (4.8%)	15 (7.5%)	12 (3.0%)	2 (4.2%)	0	1 (9.1%)	25 (4.4%)
Education	4 (1.1%)	7 (2.8%)	8 (4.0%)	38 (9.6%)	2 (4.2%)	0	1 (9.1%)	45 (8.0%)
Physicians/dentists	4 (1.1%)	2 (1.0%)	0	3 (<1%)	1 (2.1%)	0	0	8 (1.4%)
Architects/surveyors/engineers	8 (2.2%)	5 (2.0%)	0	7 (1.8%)	0	0	0	13 (2.3%)
Instrumental	201 (55.1%)	153 (60.7%)	148 (74.4%)	222 (56.3%)	31 (64.6%)	6 (54.5%)	7 (63.6%)	282 (50.1%)
Councillor/other elected office	157 (43%)	126 (50%)	103 (51.8%)	169 (42.9%)	25 (52.1%)	1 (9.1%)	4 (36.4%)	243 (43.2%)
Political/social/policy research	34 (9.3%)	21 (8.3%)	19 (9.5%)	24 (6.1%)	3 (6.3%)	4 (36.4%)	2 (18.2%)	36 (6.4%)
Party official	0	0	1 (<1%)	0	0	0	0	0
Journalism/broadcasting/media	10 (2.7%)	6 (2.4%)	2 (<1%)	5 (1.3%)	3 (6.3%)	1 (9.1%)	0	3 (<1%)
Trade union official	0	0	23 (11.6%)	24 (6.1%)	0	0	0	0
Lobbyist	0	0	0	0	0	0	1 (9.1%)	0

(continued)

Table 11.7 (continued)

	Conservative		Labour		SNP		Liberal Democrat	
	MPs	Candidates	MPs	Candidates	MPs	Candidates	MPs	Candidates
Business/commerce	92 (25.0%)	50 (19.8%)	10 (5.0%)	39 (9.9%)	8 (16.7%)	4 (36.4%)	2 (18.2%)	108 (19.2%)
Other	39 (10.7%)	30 (11.9%)	18 (9%)	71 (18%)	5 (10.4%)	1 (9.1%)	0	101 (17.9%)
Agriculture/farmers	1 (<1%)	0	0	0	0	0	0	0
Armed services	7 (1.9%)	3 (1.2%)	2 (1%)	2 (<1%)	0	0	0	4 (<1%)
Civil service and local authority administration	4 (1.1%)	2 (<1%)	2 (1%)	7 (1.8%)	0	1 (9.2%)	0	4 (<1%)
Clergy	0	0	0	0	0	0	0	0
NHS	3 (<1%)	6 (2.4%)	2 (1.0%)	13 (3.3%)	1 (2.1%)	0	0	16 (2.8%)
Other	4 (1.1%)	4 (1.6%)	0	9 (2.3%)	0	0	0	11 (2.0%)
Other white collar	1 (<1%)	1 (<1%)	2 (1.0%)	4 (1.0%)	0	0	0	14 (2.5%)
Retired	0	2 (<1%)	0	2 (<1%)	0	0	0	3 (<1%)
Social worker	0	0	2 (1.0%)	7 (1.8%)	0	0	0	1 (<1%)
Voluntary sector	5 (1.4%)	4 (1.6%)	6 (3.0%)	12 (3.0%)	2 (4.2%)	0	0	19 (3.4%)
Clerical/secretarial	1 (<1%)	0	0	0	0	0	0	1 (<1%)
Writer/literary/artist	1 (<1%)	1 (<1%)	2 (1.0%)	5 (1.3%)	1 (2.1%)	0	0	7 (1.2%)
Manual worker	0	0	0	12 (3.0%)	0	0	0	2 (<1%)

Conclusion

The 2019 election saw the continuation of trends identified in previous chapters on political recruitment in this series. A barely perceptible increase in the representation of women in the Commons that was apparent prior to 1997 was replaced by the rapid increase of women MPs on the Labour benches, more gradual but steady improvement on the Conservative benches and among SNP MPs, and considerable variation in the gender balance of Liberal Democrat MPs that is currently tipped in favour of women. Likewise, there has been considerable improvement in the proportional representation of BAME MPs at Westminster. However, there is still a gap between the proportion of women and members of BAME communities in the electorate and their representation in the Commons.

The transformation of the educational and occupational backgrounds of MPs continues. The Commons is now entirely dominated by university graduates and increasingly dominated by those who have already made politics their main profession prior to being elected. The revolution in class politics that is now evident among voters was preceded by a class dealignment in the social backgrounds of MPs, something brought into sharp relief by the fact that there are now no MPs that we have been able to identify whose paid employment immediately prior to election was in a manual occupation and, for the first time in electoral history, no former miners sit on the Labour benches.

Notes

1. Carl Baker, Elise Uberoi and Richard Cracknell, 'General Election 2019: Full Results and Analysis', House of Commons Library, 28 January 2020, https://commonslibrary.parliament.uk/research-briefings/cbp-8749/#fullreport.

2. 'Brexit: Nigel Farage Election Pact Proposal Rejected by No 10', *BBC News*, 11 September 2019, https://www.bbc.co.uk/news/uk-politics-49665789.

3. 'General Election 2019: Nigel Farage Defends Decision Not to Contest Tory Seats', *BBC News*, 5 December 2019, https://www.bbc.co.uk/news/election-2019-50676921.

4. Ashley Kirk and Patrick Scott, 'Jeremy Corbyn Should Consider a "Remain Alliance": He'd Be Prime Minister if it Had Happened in 2017', *Daily Telegraph*, 12 November 2019,

https://www.telegraph.co.uk/politics/2019/11/12/corbyn-should-think-twice-remain-alliance-prime-minister-had.

5. 'General Election 2019: Liberal Democrats, Greens and Plaid Cymru Agree Pact', *BBC News*, 7 November 2019, https://www.bbc.co.uk/news/election-2019-50327937.

6. 'General Election 2017: SDLP Rejects Sinn Féin Call', *BBC News*, 8 May 2017, https://www.bbc.co.uk/news/uk-northern-ireland-39837972.

7. Suzanne Breen, 'Greens to Back SDLP in South Belfast as UUP Urged to Stand Aside in More Seats', *Belfast Telegraph*, 5 November 2019, https://www.belfasttelegraph.co.uk/news/politics/general-election-2019/greens-to-back-sdlp-in-south-belfast-as-uup-urged-to-stand-aside-in-more-seats-38661517.html.

8. John Manley, 'Pressure Mounts on Steve Aiken to Abandon Plan to Challenge Nigel Dodds in North Belfast', *Irish News*, 1 November 2019, https://www.irishnews.com/news/northernirelandnews/2019/11/01/news/pressure-mounts-on-steve-aiken-to-abandon-plan-to-challenge-nigel-dodds-in-north-belfast-1753578.

9. Andrew Madden, 'Naomi Long Defends Stance on "Divisive and Sectarian" Electoral Pacts', *Belfast Telegraph*, 8 November 2019, https://www.belfasttelegraph.co.uk/news/politics/general-election-2019/alliance-leader-naomi-long-defends-stance-on-divisive-and-sectarian-electoral-pacts-38673118.html.

10. Carl Baker, Elise Uberoi and Richard Cracknell, 'General Election 2019: Full Results and Analysis', House of Commons Library, 28 January 2020, https://commonslibrary.parliament.uk/research-briefings/cbp-8749.

11. Alongside these, the independent former Ulster Unionist, Lady Sylvia Hermon, also retired in 2019. Lady Hermon is the only retiring independent in this election to have been returned as an independent at previous elections. She defected from the Ulster Unionists ahead of the 2010 election and was the only independent MP elected at the 2010, 2015 and 2017 general elections.

12. 'Women MPs Say Abuse Forcing Them from Politics', *BBC News*, 31 October 2019, https://www.bbc.co.uk/news/election-2019-50246969.

13. House of Commons Library Briefing Paper, Number CBP 8749, 'General Election 2019: Results and Analysis', 19 December 2019, https://commonslibrary.parliament.uk/research-briefings/cbp-8749.

14. The eight Conservative MPs who returned to the Commons after a break were: Caroline Ansell, MP for Eastbourne (and 2015–2017); James Davies, MP for Vale of Clwyd (and 2015–2017); Flick Drummond, MP for Meon Valley (and MP for Portsmouth South 2015–2017); Richard Fuller, MP for North East Bedfordshire (and MP for Bedford 2010–2017); Jason McCartney, MP for Colne Valley (and 2010–2017);

Karl McCartney, MP for Lincoln (and 2010–2017); Amanda Solloway, MP for Derby North (and 2015–2017); and Anthony Timpson, MP for Eddisbury in Cheshire (and MP for Crewe & Nantwich 2008–2017).

15. Patrick Maguire, 'MP Anger Grows over Conservative Candidate Selections', *New Statesman*, 10 November 2019, https://www.newstatesman.com/politics/uk/2019/11/mp-anger-grows-over-conservative-candidate-selections.

16. Ferrier subsequently lost the SNP whip in 2020 for using public transport whilst suffering from COVID-19.

17. Nicholson had defeated 2019 Liberal Democrat leader Jo Swinson in 2015, then was defeated by Swinson in turn when she returned to Parliament in 2017. In 2019, he switched to a different seat.

18. These were Gordon Birtwistle in Burnley, Andrew George in St Ives, John Leech in Manchester Withington, Tessa Munt in Wells, and Alan Reid in Argyll & Bute.

19. Sarah Priddy, 'MPs Related to Other Current or Former Members in the 2019 Parliament', House of Commons Library, 21 September 2020, https://commonslibrary.parliament.uk/research-briefings/sn04809.

20. Ellie Reeves has a particularly dense web of familial Commons connections: as well as a Commons sibling (Rachel), she has a Commons spouse, John Cryer, who is himself the son of two former MPs—Ann Cryer (Labour, Keighley 1997–2010) and Bob Cryer (Labour, Keighley 1974–1983; Bradford South 1987–1994).

21. Other current MPs whose parents also served in the Commons include Labour MP Stephen Kinnock (son of former Labour leader Neil Kinnock), DUP MP Ian Paisley Jr. (son of former DUP leader Ian Paisley Sr.) and incoming Conservative MP Laura Farris (daughter of Conservative MP Michael McNair-Wilson).

22. Churchill family members who served in the House of Commons include: George Spencer-Churchill (1790–1796, 1802–1806); George Spencer-Churchill (1818–1820, 1826–1831, 1832–1835, 1838–1840); John Spencer-Churchill (1844–1845, 1847–1857); Randolph Churchill (1874–1895); Winston Churchill (1901–1964); Randolph Churchill (1940–1945); Christopher Soames (1950–1966); Winston Churchill (1970–1997); and Nicholas Soames (1983–2019). In the 145 years from 1874 to 2019, the Commons had no Churchill only twice—the six years between the death of Randolph Churchill (the elder) in 1895 and the arrival of Winston Churchill (the elder) in 1901, and the four years between the departure of Christopher Soames in 1966 and the arrival of Winston Churchill (the younger) in 1970. However, there was always a Churchill in Parliament even if one did not sit in the Commons, as members of the wider Churchill dynasty also sat in the House of Lords

as Dukes of Marlborough continuously from 1650 until the removal of most hereditary peers in 1999.

23. Emilio Casalicchio, 'Tory MPs "Preparing for Another Snap Election" amid Brexit Splits', *PoliticsHome*, 20 May 2018, https://www.politicshome.com/news/article/tory-mps-preparing-for-another-snap-election-amid-brexit-splits.

24. Mark Wallace, 'Centralisation and Chaos – Inside the Rush to Select Conservative Candidates in Time for the Election', *ConservativeHome*, 9 May 2017, https://www.conservativehome.com/thetorydiary/2017/05/centralisation-and-chaos-inside-the-rush-to-select-conservative-candidates-in-time-for-the-election.html.

25. Eric Pickles, 'Eric Pickles General Election Review 2017', https://esrcpartymembersprojectorg.files.wordpress.com/2016/07/tory2017_ge-review-document.pdf, p. 10.

26. Mark Wallace, 'Introducing the Six Candidates Shortlisted for Devizes', *ConservativeHome*, 28 October 2019, https://www.conservativehome.com/parliament/2019/10/introducing-the-six-candidates-shortlisted-for-devizes.html.

27. Mark Wallace, 'The Hertford and Stortford Candidate Selection: A Shortlist, a Controversy and a Cautionary Tale', *ConservativeHome*, 24 October 2019, https://www.conservativehome.com/parliament/2019/10/the-hertford-and-stortford-candidate-selection-a-shortlist-a-controversy-and-a-cautionary-tale.html.

28. Mark Wallace, 'Meet the Candidates Hoping to Form the 2019 Conservative Parliamentary Intake', *ConservativeHome*, 15 November 2019, https://www.conservativehome.com/parliament/2019/11/meet-the-candidates-hoping-to-form-the-2019-conservative-parliamentary-intake.html.

29. Paul Goodman, 'Selections: How Activists Find Themselves Crushed by the Attritional, Grinding Juggernaut of the Party Machine', *ConservativeHome* 20 November 2019, https://www.conservativehome.com/thetorydiary/2019/11/147932.html.

30. Rosie Kinchen, 'Mystery Deepens over How Natalie Elphicke Bagged Her Dover Seat', *The Times*, 9 August 2019, https://www.thetimes.co.uk/article/mystery-deepens-over-how-natalie-elphicke-bagged-her-dover-seat-zzdk8h36g Keith Single, Chairman of the Dover Conservative Association, defended the selection, saying Natalie Elphicke was 'of course strongly endorsed by both our members and the wider public locally'. See Caroline Wheeler, Gabriel Pogrund and Henry Dyer, 'Wife of Disgraced Tory Charlie Elphicke Inherited Dover Seat in "Coup"', *Sunday Times*, 2 August 2020, https://www.thetimes.co.uk/article/wife-of-disgraced-tory-charlie-elphicke-inherited-dover-seat-in-coup-xjbrtz35s.

31. 'General Election 2019: Kate Griffiths Selected as Burton Tory Candidate', *BBC News*, 13 November 2019 https://www.bbc.co.uk/news/election-2019-50398957.

32. Paul Goodman, '"The First Real Overhaul of the Candidate Selection Process since 2002"', *ConservativeHome*, 27 October 2020, https://www.conservativehome.com/parliament/2020/10/the-first-real-overhaul-of-the-candidate-selection-process-since-2002.html.

33. Sienna Rodgers, 'Exclusive: New Selection Process Agreed by Labour's Ruling Body', *LabourList*, 8 October 2019, https://labourlist.org/2019/10/exclusive-new-selection-process-agreed-by-labours-ruling.

34. 'Sally Gimson: Bassetlaw Labour Candidate Deselected by NEC', *BBC News*, 6 November 2019, https://www.bbc.co.uk/news/uk-england-nottinghamshire-50322652.

35. Jeremy Corbyn and Tom Watson argued for an all-members selection process, but were voted down. Among members, this was seen to bias those in Labour without a senior position (e.g. councillor). The NEC approach maximised speed and participation.

36. Sienna Rodgers, 'Labour Candidate Selections in Retirement, Defection and Suspension Seats', *LabourList*, 31 October 2019, https://labourlist.org/2019/10/labour-candidate-selections-in-retirement-defection-and-suspension-seats.

37. Bull quit the race following the allegation, and was subsequently found not to have violated party rules by the Labour NEC. See James Dwan, 'Labour's Clacton Candidate Quits Election Race over Accusation He Made Antisemitic Comment to Jewish Colleague', *Clacton and Frinton Gazette*, 8 November 2019, https://www.clactonandfrintongazette.co.uk/news/north_essex_news/18023675.labours-clacton-candidate-quits-election-race-accusation-made-antisemitic-comment-jewish-colleague.

38. 'General Election 2019: Labour Candidate Removed over Anti-semitism Claims', *BBC News*, 28 November 2019, https://www.bbc.co.uk/news/election-2019-50585278.

39. Sienna Rodgers, 'Labour's NEC Agrees Reformed Trigger Ballot and Tougher Leader Nomination Threshold', *LabourList*, 22 September 2018, https://labourlist.org/2018/09/labours-nec-agrees-reformed-trigger-ballot-and-tougher-leader-nomination-threshold.

40. Sienna Rodgers, 'Margaret Hodge Becomes Second "Triggered" Labour MP', *LabourList*, 28 September 2019, https://labourlist.org/2019/09/margaret-hodge-becomes-second-triggered-labour-mp.

41. The 'triggered' half-dozen were a politically diverse group, including both Corbyn loyalists and critics of the Labour leader. Some concerns were expressed that five of the six were either female, BAME or both.

Johnson and Hodge comfortably secured reselection, while the other four had local selection processes suspended by the early general election. All were reselected except Godsiff, who was subsequently deselected by Labour's NEC. The impact of 'trigger ballots' was in the end even more limited than in 1983, when an earlier wave of member activism and internal reform spearheaded by Tony Benn and a young Jon Lansman resulted in eight deselections of sitting MPs, while for many others the threat of deselection prompted defection to the SDP. One of those who defected in response to deselection pressure from local left-wing activists was Michael O'Halloran. His replacement as Labour candidate and then MP for Islington North was a young Bennite named Jeremy Corbyn. See Byron Criddle, 'Candidates' in David Butler and Dennis Kavanagh, *The British General Election of 1983*. Palgrave Macmillan.

42. Joe Murphy, 'Former Tory Minister Sam Gyimah: I Can Take Kensington for the Lib Dems', *Evening Standard*, 29 October 2019, https://www.standard.co.uk/news/politics/former-tory-minister-sam-gyimah-i-can-take-kensington-for-the-lib-dems-a4273231.html.

43. Richard Berry, 'Resistance to All Women Shortlist in South Wales Has a Complex Set of Causes Beyond Gender Politics But That Doesn't Make it Right', *Democratic Audit*, 7 July 2014, https://www.democraticaudit.com/2014/07/07/resistance-to-all-women-shortlists-in-south-wales-has-a-complex-set-of-causes-beyond-gender-politics-but-that-doesnt-make-it-right.

44. Jessica Elgot, 'Labour Accused of Trading All Women Seats for its Favourite Sons', *The Guardian*, 15 August 2019, https://www.theguardian.com/politics/2019/aug/15/labour-accused-of-trading-all-women-seats-for-its-favourite-sons.

45. Richard Morris, 'How The Lib Dems Learned to Love All Women Shortlists', *New Statesman*, 25 April 2017, https://www.newstatesman.com/politics/staggers/2017/04/how-lib-dems-learned-love-all-women-shortlists.

46. Kathleen Nutt, 'SNP Plan to Have All Female Shortlists in 2021', *The National*, 16 October 2019, https://www.thenational.scot/news/17970826.snp-plan-all-female-shortlists-2021.

47. Eliot Chappell, '51% of Labour MPs are Women. What Now for All Women Shortlists?', *LabourList*, 31 December 2019, https://labourlist.org/2019/12/51-of-labour-mps-are-women-what-now-for-all-women-shortlists.

48. The dismal history of the representation of BAME communities in politics in Scotland has been the subject of debate; see Hannah Rodger, 'MSP Calls for Greater Diversity in Politics as Scots Elect Just Five BAME

People to Parliament', *The Herald*, 8 June 2020, https://www.scotland-scensus.gov.uk/census-results/at-a-glance/ethnicity. The 2011 census puts the BAME population of Scotland at 4%; see https://www.scotland-scensus.gov.uk/census-results/at-a-glance/ethnicity.

49. Rhiannon Davies, 'SNP "Must Face up to" Lack of Ethnic Minority Parliamentary Candidates', *The Source*, 4 December 2019, https://sourcenews.scot/snp-must-face-up-to-lack-of-ethnic-minority-parliamentary-candidates.

50. Indian-origin Labour councillors in Leicester gave voice to similar discontent, with a group of six of them publicly accusing the Labour leadership of being 'anti-Indian' and 'anti-Hindu' during the election campaign. The councillors accused Labour of 'pro-active policy of keeping British Hindu candidates out of parliamentary seats including Leicester East'. See Dan Martin, 'Labour Leicester East Councillors Accuse Jeremy Corbyn of Being "Anti-Indian" and "Anti-Hindu"', *Leicester Mercury*, 11 December 2019, https://www.leicestermercury.co.uk/news/leicester-news/labour-leicester-east-councillors-accuse-3632626.

51. Beckett has the record for the longest cumulative service by a female MP.

52. Percentages of the population are derived from https://www.ons.gov.uk/peoplepopulationandcommunity/populationandmigration/populationprojections/datasets/tablei21lowpopulationvariantukpopulationinagegroups.

53. Labour's electoral retreat in 2019 also hampered LOTO efforts to renew the parliamentary left. While 17 new Labour MPs elected in 2019 joined the SCG, this was offset by the loss of 8 existing members: 6 members were defeated Labour candidates in 2019 (Emma Dent Coad, Karen Lee, Laura Pidcock, Danielle Rowley, Dennis Skinner and Laura Smith) and another 2 members departed (Ronnie Campbell retired and Chris Williamson was blocked from standing). Five of those defeated were first elected in Corbyn's first campaign in 2017, so only three of the new SCG MPs from that election still held their seats in 2019 (Dan Carden, Marsha de Cordova and Lloyd Russell-Moyle.

54. Note: The data for schooling is based on 527 MPs.

55. Eton College (11), Harrow School (4), Winchester College (4), Manchester Grammar School (3), Marlborough College (3), Millfield (3), Radley College (3), Robert Gordon's College (3), Shrewsbury School (3) and St Paul's Girls' School (3).

56. Based on data for 574 out of 650 MPs.

57. We do not provide percentages for Plaid Cymru or Green Party MPs, nor for SNP candidates due to low numbers.

58. The most common places of undergraduate study for MPs are: Oxford (84), Cambridge (48), LSE (19), Glasgow (15), Manchester (15), Durham (14), Edinburgh (14), Birmingham (12), Exeter (12), Aberystwyth (11), Bristol (10), Hull (10), Newcastle (10) and Nottingham (10).
59. Data for university education of 1,085 unsuccessful candidates.
60. Nicholas Meirs, 'Labour Frontbencher Gloria De Piero's Former Office Manager to Stand Against Her for the Tories', *PoliticsHome*, 3 July 2019, https://www.politicshome.com/news/article/labour-frontbencher-glo-ria-de-pieros-former-office-manager-to-stand-against-her-for-the-tories.

CHAPTER 12

The Devolved Nations

Ailsa Henderson, Roger Awan-Scully, and Jonathan Tonge

SCOTLAND (AILSA HENDERSON)

None of the larger parties contesting seats in Scotland had the same leadership teams in 2019 as in 2017 and several of the leadership changes came close to the 2019 election itself. This churn in the cast of political characters owed much to the ongoing Brexit chain reaction and the challenges facing the parties attempting to confront it. First to go was the SNP's Westminster leader Angus Robertson, who lost his Moray seat in the 2017 general election. While all local authorities in Scotland voted Remain in 2016, Moray offered the narrowest margin—50.1% Remain to 49.9% Leave. In a five-way contest, Robertson fell victim to the re-alignment of Leave voters behind the Conservatives, the only Leave-supporting major party in Scotland. He was replaced in Westminster by Ian Blackford, who in 2015 had won the seat once held by Liberal Democrat leader Charles Kennedy. Blackford spent much of the 2017–2019 period complaining that the UK government was failing to consult Scotland on the preparation of the EU Withdrawal Bill. This frustration extended to a lack of parliamentary time to discuss the impact of Brexit on Scotland and on Scottish devolution. In a particularly heated

R. Ford et al., *The British General Election of 2019*, https://doi.org/10.1007/978-3-030-74254-6_12

exchange at PMQs in June 2018—sparked by devolved issues being given just 15 min of the three hours allotted to debate on Lords amendments to the Withdrawal Bill the previous day—Blackford was ordered from the chamber by Speaker John Bercow after his behaviour was deemed unparliamentary, prompting most of the SNP's MPs to walk out in solidarity. Critics attacked the incident as a stunt designed to heighten constitutional tensions and satisfy party supporters, while Blackford himself defended his behaviour as reflecting frustration over the treatment of the Scottish Parliament and a 'power grab' of devolved powers by the Westminster government. These are not mutually exclusive interpretations: the party reported signing up 1,100 new members within a day of the walkout.[1]

Two months after the 2017 election, the first since the 2014 independence referendum in which Scottish Labour had gained ground, Kezia Dugdale resigned as leader, arguing that the next leader needed time to turn around Scottish Labour's fortunes before the 2021 devolved elections.[2] In the resulting leadership election, Richard Leonard defeated Anas Sarwar, gaining 56% of the vote.[3] One of his first acts as leader was to reject calls to suspend his predecessor Dugdale for heading to Australia while Parliament was in session so that she could take part in *I'm a Celebrity Get Me out of Here*. Leonard's 2018 conference speech revealed he had voted for Corbyn in the UK Labour leadership ballot, and the party adopted the 'for the many not the few' tagline employed by UK Labour, thus underlining that Scottish Labour would not, unlike Welsh Labour, pursue a markedly different line from their Westminster counterparts. However, while Leonard's economic policies owed more to Corbynism, his approach to independence was less sanguine than the UK leader; Leonard repeatedly declared his opposition to a second independence referendum. This, and the decision to support Jeremy Corbyn's ambivalent/nuanced line on Brexit, continued to hurt Scottish Labour's polling throughout 2018 and 2019.

The pursuit of a hard Brexit at Westminster posed difficulties for the Scottish Conservatives. Most of the Scottish political class supported Remain, but while Scottish Conservatives had included vocal Remain advocates in 2016 and 2017 (with Ruth Davidson appearing on the Remain side in one high-profile 2016 debate), the 2017–2019 government's efforts to make progress on withdrawal saw the near-total re-alignment of the Scottish party behind a hard Brexit line. This is best exemplified in the 17 parliamentary votes in 2019 on different formulations of exit terms. In the three 'meaningful' votes, SNP, Scottish Labour and Scottish Liberal Democrat MPs consistently opposed the government. In the first meaningful vote, only 2 (Ross and Thomson) of the 12 Scottish Conservative MPs were among the 118 Conservatives voting against the government. By the second meaningful vote, this was reduced to one (Thomson). By the third, none of the Scottish Conservatives at Westminster opposed the government. If in 2014 the SNP was isolated from all other parties, the sole large party campaigning for independence, by 2019 the Scottish Conservatives, erstwhile supporters of Remain and a soft Brexit, had divorced themselves from all other Scottish parties on a different constitutional issue.

Boris Johnson's replacement of Theresa May in 2019 immediately placed the Scottish Conservatives in a difficult position given his poor personal polling north of the border, including among Scottish Conservative members. Their MPs had, after all, allegedly attempted to prevent him from becoming leader in a plan dubbed 'Operation Arse'.[4] Half of Scottish voters who backed the Conservatives in 2017 claimed they would abandon the party if he became leader. The same poll suggested 20% of 2014 No voters would switch to vote Yes in an independence referendum if Johnson was Prime Minister; hypothetical, and therefore worth treating with caution, but indicative of the extent to which Johnson was problematic, even among Scottish voters who shared his view of the union.[5] When people say that the argument for independence is being made in London, Johnson's toxicity is one of the factors they have in mind.[6] By December 2019, almost half of all Scottish voters polled were giving Johnson the lowest possible performance rating available.[7]

Boris Johnson and Scottish Conservative leader Ruth Davidson embrace after the BBC One 'Great Debate' on the EU referendum, 22 June 2016 (© PA Images/Alamy Stock Photo)

However important the arrival of a new Prime Minister, the August 2019 departure of Scottish Conservative leader Ruth Davidson was perhaps the more consequential change for Scottish Conservatives. Theresa May had not been particularly beloved by Scottish voters. Her replacement by an even less popular UK leader was, in a way, another pea in the soup. Davidson, however, had significantly improved the electoral performance of the Scottish party, had gone some way to detoxifying the Conservatives' image in Scotland and had successfully positioned the Scottish Conservatives as the party best able to hold the SNP to account in Holyrood. Davidson and her Holyrood colleagues were part of a well-orchestrated 2016 campaign to stop the SNP's proposed 'named persons' scheme, in which each child would have an appointed adult monitor their wellbeing until they reached 18, kicking it into the long grass until 2017 when it was declared unworkable. They had also continually highlighted the dismal international test results of Scottish school students, calling for a reset in Scotland's beleaguered Curriculum for Excellence. Reflecting her influence and achievements, Davidson's image prominently adorned Scottish Conservative election literature for the 2017 Westminster elections. She was a high-profile advocate of a form of Brexit that minimised risks to the union. Both she and Secretary of State for Scotland David Mundell threatened to quit in October 2018 if the Brexit deal undermined the integrity of the union by providing different rules for Northern Ireland. Having taken maternity leave in the autumn of 2018, Davidson attributed her 2019 departure to her opposition to Brexit and a wish to spend more time with her son and partner. Her relations with Johnson, although not cited in the resignation letter, could not have been easy. The ditching of Davidson's close friend Mundell as Secretary of State, against the wishes of the Holyrood party, had apparently made her livid. Her departure meant that the Scottish Conservatives were led at the 2019 election by acting leader Jackson Carlaw, reprising the role he had held during Davidson's maternity leave, a man whose personal polling was, like that of Scottish Labour leader Richard Leonard, mediocre.

This was not the only time the Mundell family had a role in the departure of a politician. Lamenting the performance of MSP Oliver Mundell at the 2017 Conservative Party conference, England-based pro-independence blogger Stuart Campbell suggested in his March 2017 *Wings over Scotland* blog that Mundell *fils* was the type of politician 'that makes you wish his dad had embraced his homosexuality sooner'. In response, Dugdale, then leader of Scottish Labour, labelled the blogger homophobic in her *Daily Record* column. He in turn sued her for defamation and £25,000 damages. Having initially covered her legal costs, Scottish Labour withdrew financial support from Dugdale, now a rank-and-file MSP, in 2018 supposedly at the behest of Labour HQ. The *Daily Record* stepped in, but only to assist with costs for separate stages of the legal fight. The move by UK Labour HQ was deeply unpopular with Dugdale (who reportedly contacted Corbyn but received no reply), with MPs, including Ian Murray, Scotland's sole Labour MP in 2015 (and 2019), and with Scottish party members, with activists taking to social media to report they were resigning from the party as a result of Dugdale's treatment and Leonard's complicity in it. Campbell eventually lost the case in April 2019, though he was held not to have been homophobic. Less than two weeks later, Dugdale announced she was leaving Holyrood before the summer recess.

Probably the least influential leadership change for Scottish politics was the replacement of Vince Cable as Liberal Democrat leader by Jo Swinson in July 2019. Once the 'baby of the house', the East Dunbartonshire MP had served as Deputy Leader throughout Cable's leadership. Following Cable's departure, she beat Ed Davey with 62% of the vote, becoming the youngest and first female leader of the party. Perhaps seeing parallels to the Scottish Conservatives, Swinson's image and personal brand dominated the 2019 campaign literature. But Davidson's popularity—with her own party and the wider electorate—far outstripped Swinson's and her prominence in campaign material had followed an extended period repositioning the party, whereas Swinson had been in post for mere months as leader. Unfortunately for Swinson, the proportion of Scottish voters who professed to have no opinion of her leadership was two or three times that for other party leaders.[8]

Throughout all of this, Nicola Sturgeon remained at the helm of the SNP, with her personal polling figures far outstripping any rivals. In government since 2007, the SNP's popularity was seemingly impervious to the individual policy failings identified by their opponents. While it has become typical to point out that the SNP are perceived by voters to be best at standing up for Scotland, they are also seen as the best party to manage every policy area put to respondents in surveys. Sturgeon's personal popularity is credited with boosting support for both her party and the independence cause it champions. Throughout 2018 and 2019, however, what began as an internal party matter led to multiple inquiries and a criminal trial with potentially far-reaching consequences (Fig. 12.1).

In August 2018, Sturgeon's predecessor as First Minister, Alex Salmond, resigned from the party following a series of sexual misconduct allegations stemming from his time as First Minister. Dissatisfied with how the Scottish government had handled its investigation of the

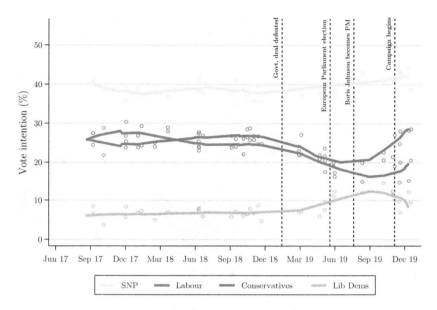

Fig. 12.1 Scottish voting intentions in Westminster elections 2017–2019

allegations, he called for an inquiry, crowdsourcing financial support for his case. Four events in January 2019 influenced the further trajectory of the story. First, the Court of Session ruled that the government's investigation had been 'unlawful', not least by appointing an investigator who had prior knowledge of the accusations. Admitting fault, the Scottish government paid Salmond's legal fees. This was not the end of the matter. Second, the Scottish Parliament announced it would hold its own investigation into the former First Minister's allegations. Third, Salmond was arrested on 14 charges, including various counts of attempted rape, sexual assault and indecent assault. Fourth, Sturgeon's personal involvement in the original Scottish government investigation prompted a self-referral to the independent ministerial ethics body. The panel decided to put its investigation on hold until the conclusion of Salmond's trial. The calendar of events would have made a spring 2020 UK election less appealing to the SNP than one in late 2019. The issue was not cited by voters as an important factor in their vote in 2019, it had no deleterious effect on SNP polling and it surfaced rarely in the campaign, but these various dealings are noteworthy in this particular context because they provided the first significant political risk to Sturgeon *personally*.[9]

Graeme Keyes cartoon 'Sturgeon Reignites Independence Debate (Graeme Keyes, 10 October 2018 © Graeme Keyes)

The comings and goings of party leaders, however interesting in themselves, exist within the wider context of Scottish political culture. Scottish politics has long been dominated by two axes of party competition: a left–right axis on economic issues and a constitutional axis focused on the status quo vs more powers (up to and including independence). Since 2016, however, that constitutional axis has incorporated two issues: independence (No–Yes) and Brexit (Remain-Leave). One might expect a Remain-supporting Scottish electorate to express frustration at being taken out of the EU against its will and therefore show greater support for independence, not least since both sides of the campaign in the 2014 referendum had made it clear that continued EU membership was a priority, but there was no immediate shift in independence preferences after 2016. Those moving from No to

Yes were roughly cancelled out by voters switching the other way, and while this churn changed the coalitions for and against independence, there was little net shift in overall support.[10] This in itself is important, because support for independence and support for the SNP are not always in lockstep. However steady support for independence, support for the SNP rises and falls based on factors other than the constitution, including the appeal of alternative parties and their perceived handling of policy issues. The SNP's best result came in 2015, an election that highlighted Scotland's place in the union. They faced a tougher fight in 2017, when a broader range of issues was on the agenda.

By 2019, a few things had changed with critical effect. Corbyn and Labour's lack of clarity on Brexit led to declining support for the Labour Party and particularly for its leader, both of whom were perceived to be out of step with Remain-supporting Scotland (see Chapter 4). At the same time, the UK government's failure to secure a withdrawal agreement made a 'hard' Brexit more likely (see Chapter 2, pp. 50–52). As a result, neither of the two main rivals to form a UK government was particularly popular in Scotland. Yet the Liberal Democrats' avowedly pro-Remain stance also failed to gain traction in Scotland, suggesting even a clear position on an issue of high importance to voters is insufficient if no one believes those advocating it will ever manage to put it into practice. Lib Dem involvement in the 2010 Coalition government and particularly the high-profile U-turn on tuition fees also cast a long shadow in Scotland. Facing three rival parties hamstrung by unpopular leaders and past policy choices, the SNP largely had to navigate the 2019 election quietly and let the other parties turn off Scottish voters in their own inimitable ways.

On Brexit, the Conservatives were clear, but their choices were unpopular. By contrast, Labour were unclear and their refusal to choose was unpopular. On an independence referendum, both parties seemed equally murky, but broadly unsupportive. At times, the Conservatives' Scottish representatives seemed *less* hostile than their Westminster counterparts: in July 2019, the then Secretary of State for Scotland David Mundell repeatedly claimed that if the SNP won a majority at Holyrood, it would be hard to deny the mandate for an independence referendum, a view that chimed with earlier statements made by Ruth Davidson. That November, Boris Johnson asserted he would not support an independence referendum while Prime Minister. A fortnight later, his new Secretary of State for Scotland, Alister Jack, claimed once again that an SNP majority would provide a sufficient democratic mandate for a referendum. Labour's mixed messaging ran the other way: the party's Scottish representatives often seemed *more* hostile than their UK counterparts. In September 2019, Scottish Labour leader Richard Leonard said that the SNP winning a devolved election would not be enough to justify an independence referendum, contradicting Shadow Chancellor John McDonnell, who had said the previous month that if MSPs voted for a referendum, Labour shouldn't block it. Leonard later clarified that independence was not a priority (October) and that a referendum would not be supported in the formative years of a UK Labour government (10 November), meaning not until 2021 (17 November). When coupled with the party's shifting position on Brexit, this highlights Labour's struggles to communicate a coherent or consistent position on either of the two dominant constitutional issues facing the Scottish electorate.

The Conservatives' pursuit of a hard Brexit continued to alienate the Scottish electorate, with polling showing exceptionally low levels of Scottish support for this approach, and opposition to hard Brexit helped to keep independence on the political agenda. As a result, Scottish voters had by 2019 become divided into four 'tribes': Yes Remainers, Yes Leavers, No Remainers and No Leavers. The SNP's hunt for votes was mostly confined to the two Yes tribes, and the transformation of the Scottish Conservatives from a Remain-supporting to a hard Brexit party meant that it was likely to fare best with 'No Leavers'. That left two parties—Labour and the Liberal Democrats—with no obvious tribe as their sole preserve, fighting for votes primarily within the 'No Remain' camp.

If Scottish voters, while unwilling to support a party that deviated on two constitutional issues, could countenance backing a party with different preferences on one, then the Conservatives and the SNP were also in with a chance of winning support among 'No Remainers'. There is, however, a degree of asymmetry here. The SNP had something of a lock on the Yes side and Conservatives a lock on the Leave side, and so, for advocates of change on either of the two constitutional issues, the choice of who to support was relatively simple. Labour and the Liberal Democrats were therefore unlikely to reap similar rewards among 'Yes Remainers'. Because 'No Remainers' formed the largest single group in Scotland, any effort to understand what might happen in Scottish elections requires us to disaggregate the electorate by its constitutional tribes, with particular attention to how each of the parties has courted, and then fared, among 'No Remainers'. Facing a Scottish government that wanted independence and a UK government pursuing Brexit, it is perhaps not surprising that one-quarter of 'No Remainers' reported feeling politically homeless.

The last contextual feature of recent Scottish voting is its volatility. The SNP near-clean sweep of seats in 2015 was not just a case of the party winning all those constituencies where it had placed second in 2010. The party's huge surge won it seats where it had placed third or even fourth in the previous election. The level of constituency-level change required to win it 56 seats saw more movement in the SNP numbers alone than the total volatility across all four main parties in the 2017 elections.[11] If that suggests that by 2017 the Scottish electorate had become more predictable, it is worth noting there were still swings of more than 20 points in five constituencies in 2017[12] and swings of over 15 points across a further 49 constituencies. 'No Remainers', who represented more than half the Scottish electorate, were a significant driver of that volatility.

The Campaign in Scotland

The 2019 Scottish Election Study suggests that campaigns have an uneven impact. More than one in three voters (36%) decide before the campaign has begun. For the remainder, campaigns, including high-profile events like debates, can help to focus minds, and this continues until polling day itself. We know, for example, that just under one in five (17%) voters say they make up their minds in the final days of the campaign, and just over one in five (22%) say they decide very, very late, including only after arriving at the polling station.

There were 15 leaders' debates over the course of the 2019 campaign, but only five in Scotland and only two, on 3 and 10 December, featuring the Scottish leaders of the four largest parties in Scotland. The remainder had a variety of stand-ins, including MSPs not standing for election to Westminster. Post-debate online polling of readers of *The Herald* suggested that more than seven out of ten believed Sturgeon had won the first debate. Interim Scottish Conservative party leader Jackson Carlaw came out best of the other leaders in the first debate, but was still a distant second to Sturgeon; indeed, the fact that he claimed second place with only 7% of respondents rating him best speaks to how poorly the others had done. Scottish Labour leader Richard Leonard fared slightly better in the second debate.[13]

It is not possible to write about Scottish elections without referring to the notion of first and second order electoral contests. Westminster elections are typically viewed as more important, and therefore feature higher turnout and greater levels of voter interest. The SNP traditionally did worse in Westminster than Holyrood before 2015, as voters recognised that a party standing only in Scotland had little chance of forming (or influencing the formation of) the UK-wide government. The independence referendum, and the efforts of the Conservative Party in 2015 to portray the SNP as potential kingmakers, helped to change this perspective, with lasting consequences. Scottish voting preferences across Holyrood and Westminster have converged, and campaigning on devolved and reserved issues has blurred together. The 2017 election saw opposition parties seek, in a UK election, to mobilise voter dissatisfaction with the SNP's record on devolved Holyrood issues. In 2019, all Scottish parties focused instead on policies *outside* Holyrood's purview, Brexit being chief among them. Labour, the Liberal Democrats and the SNP each campaigned on the view that a Conservative government led by Johnson would result in a chaotic hard/no deal Brexit and would pose risks to the NHS and jobs. The Conservatives in Scotland focused on a different constitutional issue. Rather than emphasising, as they had in England, the need to 'get Brexit done' or the dangers of a Corbyn government or a hung parliament, they framed the Scottish choice around a different constitutional issue, arguing that a Conservative vote was a vote to 'take on the SNP' and stop independence. Different parties shifted the area and territorial frame of their focus depending on which they felt would best work to their advantage.

For its part, the SNP largely continued their longstanding campaign message of 'standing up for Scotland', but with a minor adaptation. If the 2014 Yes Scotland messaging began by talking optimistically of the potential of a young nation and ended by emphasising the risks of union, then the 2019 campaign SNP messaging had more of a 'late referendum campaign' feel to it. The SNP framed the 2019 choice as 'stand up for Scotland or disaster awaits', with campaign posters featuring the top of Boris Johnson's blond head leaving Scottish voters in no doubt as to who the author of the disaster would be. Yet there are two caveats to this advantage. The SNP's advantage—also found on every other issue—is less a reflection of the party's own strengths than the weaknesses of its opponents. And standing up for Scotland matters more in some elections than others. In 2017, for some voters, stopping Brexit pulled many away from the SNP (back) to Labour. But by 2019, a divided and weak Labour Party was no longer seen as a credible option to stop the Conservatives.

SNP campaign poster 'Its Time To Decide' (© Scottish National Party)

The Result in Scotland

On the face of things, the 2019 Scottish electoral results have much in common with the 2015 general election. The SNP regained 13 of the seats lost in 2017, though falling shy of their 56-seat landslide in 2015. This occurred chiefly at the expense of the Labour Party, which lost six seats and again found itself reduced to one Edinburgh South MP who claimed Scotland had been let down by his party and its leader.[14] An analysis of Labour switchers suggest that Corbyn, the party's economic positioning and Labour hostility to independence were all significant sources of defections away from Labour, something which suggests that the party's more 'muscular unionism' will continue to cause problems until it finds a way to accommodate the policy mood in Scotland.[15]

The Conservative vote held up relatively well overall in 2019, but was too evenly spread in an electoral system which rewards concentrated support, so the party lost more than half of its 13 seats, all to the SNP. However, the Scottish Conservatives did hold on to six seats and 25% of the vote, despite having recently lost their popular Scottish leader, having gained an unpopular Westminster leader and having campaigned for a hard Brexit opposed by most Scots. The Scottish Conservatives remained competitive in many seats, including plenty beyond the borders seats to which they had previously retreated in lean times and narrowly retained Moray, the site of Angus Robertson's unseating. The result reinforced the message that the Scottish Conservatives were the only party capable of taking on the SNP—an important claim to stake ahead of the 2021 devolved elections.

Despite the fact that their new leader represented a Scottish constit-uency, the Liberal Democrats made only a small advance in votes (up 2.5 points) and no net change in seats. They lost 12 deposits, and while they managed to win the ultra-marginal North East Fife, the only defeat of an SNP incumbent, that contest bucked the trend. In a particularly bruising 149-vote defeat, UK party leader Jo Swinson lost her East Dunbartonshire seat to the SNP (Table 12.1).

If we look at vote retention, the SNP fared best, keeping 88% of their 2017 voters. The Conservatives held on to 78% of theirs. The Liberal Democrats kept more than 6 in 10, with 15% voting SNP and 10% each switching to Labour and the Conservatives. Labour lost half their existing support, of which half moved to the SNP. These patterns are best understood in terms of Scotland's four constitutional tribes. 'Yes Remainers' overwhelmingly backed the SNP (88%), leaving the party even more dominant among this group than in 2017. By contrast, two-thirds of 'No Leavers' voted Conservative, roughly the same as in 2017. Both parties were able to win large majorities among the tribe who shared both of their constitutional preferences. The SNP remained ahead among 'Yes Leavers' (50%), with half as many of this group

Table 12.1 The 2019 general election result in Scotland

	Votes	% Vote (change on 2017)	Seats (change on 2017)
SNP	1,242,000 (+264)	45.0 (+8.1)	48 (+13)
Conservative	693,000 (−65)	25.1 (−3.5)	6 (−7)
Labour	512,000 (−205)	18.6 (−8.5)	1 (−6)
Liberal Democrat	263,000 (+84)	9.5 (+2.8)	4 (0)
Scottish Green	28,000 (+22)	1.0 (+0.8)	0 (0)
Others	20,000 (+13)	0.7 (+0.5))	0 (0)
Turnout	*2,759,000 (+110)*	*68.1 (+1.7)*	

voting Conservative. But this reflected a change of fortunes for each. The Conservatives more than doubled the proportion of 'Yes Leavers' they had attracted in 2017, while the SNP and Labour each lost supporters in this tribe. 'No Remainers', the largest tribe, were also the most fragmented, with Labour winning a narrow plurality (29%) over the SNP (25%). While this might seem to provide the bright spot for Labour, this is also where it saw its greatest drop in support, having captured more than 40% of this group in 2017. The SNP proved better able to pick up the support of Unionist Remainers than the Liberal Democrats, whose positions were closer to the preferences of this group (Table 12.2).

There are two oddities to Scottish Labour's fortunes in 2019. First, they managed to hold on to more of their Yes supporters than their No supporters, albeit from a lower 2017 base. Second, when they lost their No supporters, they lost them largely to a Yes-supporting party, the SNP. This reflects an asymmetry in Scottish voters' constitutional priorities. The SNP enjoys greater support among Yes voters, even among those who disagree with its stance on Brexit, in a way that the Conservative Party does not dominate the support of Leave voters. While this remained true in 2019—with the SNP increasing its support by 11 points among 'Yes Remainers'—the Conservative Party lost ground with its natural constituency of 'No Leavers', though its Brexit campaigning attracted the support of 'Yes Leavers'. Yet when forced to choose, most 'Yes Leavers' still prioritised independence, and hence the SNP, over Brexit and the Conservatives.

All of this sets the stage for the devolved elections in 2021, where the economic effects of Brexit, the recent pandemic and the continued

Table 12.2 Scotland's four tribes, 2019 (change from 2017)

	Yes Remainers	Yes Leavers	No Remainers	No Leavers
SNP	88 (+11)	50 (−8)	25 (+12)	9 (+4)
Conservative	1 (−2)	27 (+12)	23 (−9)	67 (−2)
Labour	9 (−8)	16 (−8)	29 (−13)	14 (−5)
Liberal Democrat	2 (0)	3 (0)	20 (+7)	7 (+2)
Column sample size	*550*	*250*	*636*	*362*

Source Scottish Election Study 2017, 2019. Results are column percentages for 2019, with change from 2017 in parentheses

leadership of Boris Johnson will continue, if current trends hold, to deliver an electoral win for the SNP. Independence is consistently polling near or above 50%, Sturgeon's perceived handling of the COVID-19 pandemic remains popular and the SNP is perceived by the electorate to offer greater competence across a number of policy fields than any of the possible rivals. As in other domains, the party/government benefits from the comparisons it invites. And yet the SNP are not invulnerable. Salmond's launch of a new pro-independence party hot on the heels of a Scottish Parliament committee inquiry into the government's handling of sexual misconduct allegations against him guarantees that the issue, and Sturgeon's role in it, will not quietly slip away. For keen observers of polling, parties and voting, Scottish politics again promises not to disappoint.

WALES (ROGER AWAN-SCULLY)

Wales voted (narrowly) for Brexit in June 2016. That fact, along with the UK-wide majority that it contributed to, dominated the political landscape for the next few years. The Welsh voted against the advice of nearly all Wales' political class and against Wales' apparent economic self-interest—Wales was a major recipient of EU structural funds and farm subsidies, and had the ports which handled most trade with Ireland. Yet Leave was the verdict, with many struggling communities in Wales voting along strikingly similar lines to similar places in England.

Three years of growing Brexit gridlock changed few Welsh minds, despite the regular airing of Brexit anxieties by the Welsh Labour government. Regular Welsh polls tracking Brexit opinions between 2016 and 2019 found no more than a tiny overall shift towards remaining in the EU.[16] For a while, it appeared as if Brexit might drive an historic shift in Welsh voting behaviour in the 2017 snap election. But the stumbling Conservative campaign, and a strong Labour resurgence, in fact saw Welsh Labour gain three seats from the Conservatives.

However, the dramatic changes in fortune of the 2017 campaign were relatively modest compared to the extraordinary fluctuations in party support during 2019. Labour's poll rating, which had been trending gently downwards after their 2017 campaign surge, collapsed in the early months of 2019. The decline in Conservative fortunes was even more dramatic as the first and then second Brexit deadlines were missed. The failure of Theresa May's government to deliver saw much of their Leave-supporting vote move towards the Brexit Party. On the other side of the great Brexit divide, Remain voters defected en masse from Welsh Labour to Plaid Cymru and the Liberal Democrats, both of whom saw clear electoral dividends: Plaid finished second in the European election—the first time they had ever beaten Labour in a Wales-wide vote, while the Welsh Liberal Democrats re-established their parliamentary presence by winning the August 2019 by-election in Brecon & Radnorshire.[17]

By mid-summer, a truly chaotic multi-party contest appeared possible in Wales. The late July Welsh Political Barometer poll had support for the five leading parties within a nine percentage-point range (from 24 to 15%); it also put Welsh support for Labour at an all-time low. Figure 12.2 shows changes in party support in all published Welsh polls between the 2017 general election and the start of the 2019 campaign.

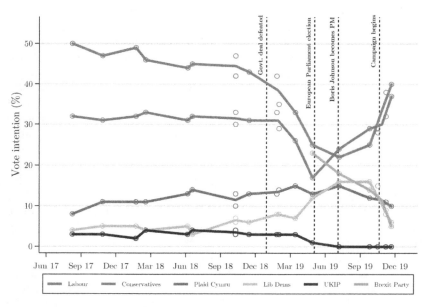

Fig. 12.2 Welsh voting intentions in Westminster elections 2017–2019

The Campaign in Wales

Welsh Labour entered the 2019 election campaign defending nearly three-quarters of the seats in Wales and with few realistic prospects for gains. The Welsh Labour campaign was also missing one of its greatest assets in 2017, Carwyn Jones, who had stood down as First Minster and Welsh Labour leader in late 2018 following heavy criticism from some quarters of his handling of events surrounding the sacking, and subsequent suicide, of Welsh government Cabinet member Carl Sargeant in December 2017.[18]

Jones' successor was Mark Drakeford, a man admired across the political spectrum for his intellect and command of policy detail, but lacking Jones' popular touch and relish for the campaign trail. Polling suggested Drakeford was invisible to many Welsh voters and unpopular with most of the rest. Recognising that their new leader was unlikely to be an electoral asset, Welsh Labour took a very different approach to the campaign in 2019. In 2017, Jones had been front and centre of a campaign which did everything possible to emphasise the distinctiveness of the Welsh party: he featured prominently in all Welsh Labour's electoral broadcasts, whereas Jeremy Corbyn was never seen or mentioned.[19] In 2019, Wales was tied in much more closely to the London-based campaign. The Welsh manifesto was only modestly different in content and presentation, another departure from 2017. And Drakeford himself played only a limited part in the campaign; for instance, the two major televised debates, hosted by ITV Wales and BBC Wales, saw Labour represented by other figures,[20] whereas in 2017 it had been First Minister Jones who had (very effectively) put forward Labour's case.

After an ultimately disappointing 2017 general election, the Welsh Conservatives had gone through their own internal turmoil. The party had no clear Welsh leader and relations between Assembly leader Andrew RT Davies and Welsh Secretary Alun Cairns were poor. Neither man was still in post for the 2019 election campaign. Davies resigned in June 2018, amidst rumoured discontent with his leadership from many Assembly colleagues, to be replaced by his former deputy, Paul Davies. The circumstances surrounding Cairns' departure were far more serious and potentially damaging for the Welsh Conservatives. It emerged in the autumn of 2019 that Cairns' former constituency agent Ross England had been blamed by a judge for deliberately collapsing a rape trial where the alleged victim was another employee of the local party (though

England claimed otherwise); it was further alleged that Cairns had been fully aware of this, yet had failed to take action.[21] Cairns denied this, but on the first official day of the 2019 campaign, he resigned as Welsh Secretary (although he remained Tory candidate in Vale of Glamorgan).[22]

Cairns' resignation was one of several early stumbles for the Welsh Conservative campaign; there were also controversies about other candidates, including in target seats.[23] Perhaps unsurprisingly, therefore, the party's 2019 campaign had little Welsh-specific content, concentrating instead on Britain-wide themes: the pledge to 'get Brexit done' and the choice between Boris Johnson and Jeremy Corbyn for Prime Minister. After the disappointments of 2017, the Welsh Tories had only eight seats to defend, but a number of attractive targets. In particular, there was a clutch of five seats in Leave-supporting north-east Wales that were all winnable on modest swings.

Plaid Cymru also fought the 2019 general election under new leadership. After some electoral success in 2016,[24] Plaid equalled their best-ever total of four parliamentary seats in 2017 by unexpectedly capturing Ceredigion from the Liberal Democrats. Yet there was an awareness within Plaid that they had had a narrow escape in 2017: both Ceredigion and Arfon, which had been held despite a strong Labour challenge, were won by around 100 votes. By the summer of 2018, an increasing sense of drift under the leadership of Leanne Wood within much of the party led to her being challenged by two Assembly colleagues, former MP Adam Price and Rhun ap Iorwerth, with Price winning the subsequent leadership contest decisively.

Price brought a naturally combative style to leadership, which was evident in his effective performances in the 2019 televised debates. He was also willing to take political risks. Plaid stood aside for their fellow pro-Remain party the Liberal Democrats in the August 2019 Brecon & Radnorshire by-election, presaging their involvement in the broader 'United to Remain' pact, also involving the Greens, in the general election. The alliance arranged electoral pacts, aiming to maximise the number of MPs elected who would oppose Brexit. Such pacts covered 49 of the 533 seats in England (roughly 9%), but 11 of the 40 constituencies in Wales (27.5%), with Plaid standing aside in four of them. Plaid initially had high hopes (based in part on private polling) that this alliance would prove popular with voters and would prevent them being marginalised from the debate as in past UK-wide elections. These hopes were to prove fruitless.

The Liberal Democrats' contribution to the 'United to Remain' pact was to stand aside in eight seats; as such, their modest rise in overall vote share from 2017 disguises a somewhat stronger improvement in the places they actually stood. However, it was a measure of their long-run decline that the party which in 2010 had secured a fifth of the Welsh vote and saved its deposit in every seat now had only two realistic targets: Ceredigion and the Brecon & Radnorshire seat won by their Welsh leader Jane Dodds a few months earlier. The Brexit Party stood in all but the eight Welsh seats won by the Conservatives in 2017. While the party was squeezed in Wales as elsewhere, with pro-Leave voters moving towards the Conservatives, Wales still produced the Brexit Party's third-highest vote share of any UK region, with Blaenau Gwent one of only three seats anywhere where the party finished second.[25] This reflected both Welsh pro-Leave sentiment and a higher percentage of Brexit Party candidates in Welsh seats than in most of England.

The limited number of Welsh polls during the campaign told a very similar story to that seen in the Britain-wide polls (see Chapter 8). The Conservatives squeezed the Brexit Party vote among Leave supporters, and the problems of their Welsh campaign had little impact on voters. Meanwhile, the Liberal Democrats faded after their summer resurgence, as 'Unite to Remain' failed to gain any significant traction with voters.

The Result in Wales

The six seats that changed hands in Wales all went directly from Labour to the Conservatives: Bridgend in South Wales (Carwyn Jones' seat in the Senedd), Ynys Mon, plus four of the five seats Labour had previously

Table 12.3 The 2019 general election result in Wales

Party	Votes	% Vote (change on 2017)	Seats (change on 2017)
Labour	632,035	40.9% (−8.0)	22 (−6)
Conservative	557,234	36.1% (+2.5)	14 (+6)
Plaid Cymru	153,265	9.9% (−0.5)	4 (−)
Liberal Democrats	92,171	6.0% (+1.5)	0 (−)
Brexit Party	83,908	5.4% (+5.4)	0 (−)
Others	25,744	1.6% (−0.9)	0 (−)

held in north-east Wales. The Conservatives' gains were all in places that had voted for Brexit, and across Wales their vote share advanced most in places that had been more pro-Leave in 2016.[26] Other evidence supports the impact of Brexit on Welsh choices in 2019. Brexit was consistently the top issue cited as driving votes during the campaign, with 55% of respondents in the final pre-election poll naming it as a top concern. Evidence from the British Election Study also suggests that Brexit preferences translated strongly into final vote choices for many people. Table 12.4 shows the vote choices of Welsh Leave and Remain supporters. The Conservatives did very well in dominating the vote amongst Leave supporters in Wales, pushing the Brexit Party down to little more than 10% support.[27]At the same time, however, Labour did almost as well among Welsh Remain voters, despite the efforts of the 'Unite to Remain' parties (Table 12.4).

Leadership proved much less of an advantage for Labour in Wales in 2019 than in the previous general election. By the end of the 2017 campaign, Labour had the two most popular politicians in Wales in Carwyn Jones and Jeremy Corbyn. In 2019, by contrast, the final Welsh poll suggested that Jeremy Corbyn was substantially less popular than in 2017, averaging only 3.7 on a 0–10 scale, compared with an average of 4.9 by the end of the 2017 campaign. Corbyn's end-of-campaign average rating was, in fact, marginally behind that of Boris Johnson (who averaged 3.8). Moreover, while Johnson's ratings overall were hardly fantastic, he polled very strongly with Conservative and Leave supporters. The voters' verdict on Mark Drakeford, meanwhile, was dismal. By the final poll of the campaign, 48% of Welsh respondents were still offering a 'Don't Know', while among the half of Welsh voters who had an opinion, Drakeford had slumped to a truly dreadful average rating of 3.2.[28] The messages

Table 12.4   2019 General election vote choice by EU referendum vote intention, Wales

Party	Remain (%)	Leave (%)
Labour	66	12
Conservative	9	68
Plaid Cymru	13	4
Liberal Democrat	11	1
Brexit Party	0	13
Others	2	2

Welsh Labour were trying to sell in 2019 may well have been flawed, but there were also problems with the key messengers.

27 Out of 27 Ain't Bad?

In one sense, the 2019 general election result in Wales was wholly predictable. For the twenty-seventh general election in a row, Labour came first in terms of both votes and seats. David Lloyd George, in December 1918, remains the last political leader to defeat Welsh Labour in a general election. But rarely can 'victory' have meant so little. Labour's seat total slumped by six—matching their worst post-war result in 1983. Welsh Labour came within a whisker of being wiped out north of the South Wales valleys and saw many majorities slashed elsewhere.[29]

For the Welsh Conservatives, by contrast, 2019 saw a momentous advance: the most parliamentary seats won since the Thatcher landslide of 1983 and the highest Welsh vote share since 1900. And in at least one other respect, the general election in Wales was particularly notable. Wales was the part of Britain where the 'Unite to Remain' pact, involving the Greens, the Liberal Democrats and Plaid Cymru, was most prominent. Wales also thereby provided the clearest evidence of the abject failure of that pact.

The prospects for the next Welsh devolved election also looked uncertain. The general election—indeed, the politics of 2019 as a whole—had demonstrated that even in its ultimate Welsh bastion, loyalties to Labour were now weakening. It was also clear that Mark Drakeford was unlikely to provide Welsh Labour with inspiring campaign leadership. For the Conservatives, Wales punched above its weight in contributing to Johnson's substantial parliamentary majority. The Tories emerged from the general election very much on the front foot and eyeing further Senedd gains in 2021. But their new seats mostly had slim majorities, and voters who had swung to the Conservatives over Brexit might easily defect again if that policy started to go wrong; meanwhile, fundamental problems of leadership within the Welsh Conservatives had not gone away. Plaid Cymru's strategy for the election, the Remain Alliance, was a clear failure. The comparison between Plaid's 2019 general election performance and that of their Scottish sister party was once again a painful one. Yet their new leader had performed well in the campaign and they could look forward to 2021 with at least some reasons for hope.

Northern Ireland (Jonathan Tonge)

The 2019 election in Northern Ireland had two major influences, in addition to the routine sectarian head-counting: Brexit and the absence of devolved government since January 2017. The contest brought an end to the controversial tenure of the Democratic Unionist Party (DUP) in the Westminster spotlight as suppliers of the Conservative government's majority. That uneasy arrangement had, however, already run its course when Prime Minster Johnson agreed a renegotiated Brexit deal which ignored the objections of his erstwhile allies.

Cut adrift, the DUP had a tough election, its representation in the Commons reduced from ten to eight MPs as the South and North Belfast constituencies were lost to the Social Democratic and Labour Party (SDLP) and Sinn Féin respectively. The latter reverse was particularly grievous, resulting in the departure of Deputy Leader Nigel Dodds, who had led the DUP's Westminster team. Sinn Féin won seven seats (no net change from 2017), but, as ever, its MPs, in refusing an oath of allegiance to a British monarch, would not take their places in the Commons. Sinn Féin's gain of North Belfast was balanced by defeat in Foyle to the nationalist SDLP on a huge swing. With South Belfast also won from the DUP, the SDLP, wiped out in 2017, returned to the Commons with two seats.

The contest was marked by substantial falls in the total votes cast for the main parties of unionism and nationalism, with the DUP and Sinn Féin down more than 100,000 votes in total, reflecting voter frustration at the prolonged hiatus of devolved government. This aided the Alliance Party, neither unionist nor nationalist and blameless in the collapse of the Stormont Executive and Assembly. It won one seat, capturing North Down with an extraordinary 36% increase in vote share. With the SDLP and Alliance joining the DUP in the Commons, Northern Ireland's Westminster representation was more varied than in the previous Parliament, in which only the DUP sat, but the region's MPs were marginalised, given the large Conservative majority. Table 12.5 summarises the results. The remainder of this section draws upon data from the 2019 Northern Ireland General Election Study.[30] Data are from the study unless indicated otherwise.

The outline of the result had been foreshadowed in the (few) polls that took place between the 2017 and 2019 general elections (Fig. 12.3).

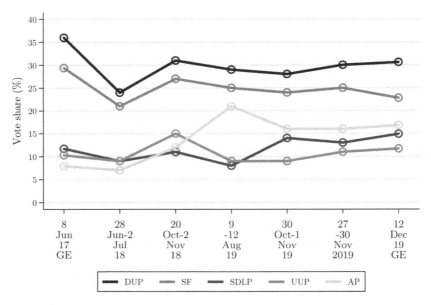

Fig. 12.3 Northern Irish voting intentions in Westminster elections 2017–2019

Each of the four inter-election surveys indicated that the DUP and Sinn Féin were performing substantially below their 2017 high-water marks, as public frustration grew over their inability to restore devolved government. The polls did not suggest that the Ulster Unionist Party (UUP) and the SDLP, as the smaller unionist and nationalist parties respectively, were likely to be major beneficiaries of the disenchantment, but did indicate the growth of Alliance from Northern Ireland's fifth-largest to third-largest party, a trend that was confirmed at the election.

THE CAMPAIGN IN NORTHERN IRELAND: BELFAST, BREXIT, BORIS AND 'BETRAYAL'

The election campaign was marked by rows over Brexit, the absence of devolved government and its local impact upon the NHS, and, as ever, the constitutional question of Northern Ireland's future status. Brexit was listed by voters as the most important issue, followed by the NHS, amid an acute (pre-COVID-19) health crisis linked to the absence of local decision-making. The old question of Northern Ireland's place in the UK versus Irish unity was listed third in terms of voter concerns. Brexit exacerbated pre-existing constitutional divisions.

At times, the campaign appeared as the DUP versus the rest, as the other parties lambasted Arlene Foster's party as the author of Brexit mismanagement. The arguments thrown at the DUP were, first, that its backing of Brexit in 2016 had been unthinking, offered in the expectation that 'Remain' would win; second, that the DUP had mishandled its position when holding the balance of power at Westminster, outflanked on Brexit and predictably cast aside by Boris Johnson; third, that it had contributed to the demise of devolved power-sharing through incompetence in government and had done little to facilitate restoration; and, fourth, that it had been out of touch on social issues such as same-sex marriage and abortion, to the extent that Westminster had intervened to legislate. On all counts, the DUP remained unrepentant.

Whilst these divisions were deep enough, the legacy of the Troubles was also evident. The campaign was at its most bitter in North Belfast, the constituency where the most lives were lost during the conflict. Here, John Finucane stood for Sinn Féin against Nigel Dodds. Finucane's solicitor father, Pat, was murdered by loyalist paramilitaries, acting in collusion with the British security services,[31] with the Finucane family continuing to press for a full public inquiry into the killing. During the election campaign, loyalists displayed a lurid poster in the constituency, headlined 'The Real Finucane Family', dripping with blood and highlighting the IRA connections of other members of the Finucane family. Dodds disavowed the poster as 'nothing to do with our campaign', whilst insisting that Sinn Féin repudiate all past IRA violence:

> They can't be selective. We condemn every act of violence from every paramilitary organisation. Do they do that? Will they do that? Will they condemn the IRA, who went into a hospital 20 years ago and shot a police officer guarding me? Do they condemn it? No they don't.[32]

Although the constituency arithmetic looked difficult for the DUP from the moment the SDLP declined to split the nationalist vote in not fielding a candidate, the DUP hoped residual antipathy towards Sinn Féin might allow Dodds to prevail. The SDLP's 2,058 votes in 2017 almost matched Dodds' 2,081 majority. DUP optimism grew to the extent that one party official, in an organisation not known for its gambling tendencies, placed a medium-sized wager on Dodds' victory on election day. With so much effort made to defend the constituency, 73% of DUP voters reported being canvassed by their party in North Belfast, compared to 64% across Northern Ireland. A senior figure within the DUP insisted:

> We left everything on the field. We'd never had so many volunteers to canvass. We tried canvassing the nationalist middle-class to no effect. Our majority walked off to the Alliance. We increased our working-class vote. I kept saying, though, that our middle-class voters were too quiet and some of them deserted us.[33]

The DUP hoped to escape punishment for their Brexit stance. With 88% of nationalists voting to remain in the EU, compared to only 34% of unionists, the issue exacerbated divisions.[34] Yet, as the UK prepared to depart the EU, it was not only anti-Brexit nationalists who were unhappy. The pro-Brexit DUP rejected a 'Boris Brexit' which uniquely aligned Northern Ireland to the EU's Single Market and customs rules, fearing this would introduce trade barriers with Great Britain. In 2018, Boris Johnson, a backbencher after resigning as Foreign Secretary, told the DUP annual conference that Theresa May's Brexit deal, which threatened similar unique EU alignment for Northern Ireland, was one 'no British Conservative government could or should sign up to'.[35] May's plan kept the politically sensitive border on the island of Ireland unchanged, but, Johnson told his 'fellow unionists', marginalised Northern Ireland's place in the UK. Having launched his Conservative Party leadership bid at another party's conference, Prime Minister Boris Johnson then concluded an EU deal which betrayed his promise to the DUP and placed trade between Great Britain and Northern Ireland within EU rules.

Martyn Turner—'Can I phone a friend?', *Irish Times*, 18 October 2019
© Martyn Turner

Given the DUP acted as midwife to Brexit, the derision heaped upon the party by Remainers during the election campaign was unsurprising. Even some DUP supporters had cooled on Brexit, with backing for departure from the EU falling from 75% in 2016 to 56% at the 2019 election.[36] Support for Brexit among the broader electorate fell from 44% at the referendum to 32% in 2019.

The DUP's main vote losses were to the pro-Remain Alliance Party, with defectors drawn predominantly from the middle-class, anti-Brexit section of the DUP's support. Only 22% of DUP voters accepted the checks on goods transported between Great Britain and Northern Ireland as part of Johnson's deal, fearing this represented a shift to closer economic integration with the Irish Republic—a shift with longer-term constitutional implications.

The election was marked by 'Remain pacts' as other parties sought to capitalise on disaffection with the DUP, whose support for a pro-Brexit UK government ended in a Brexit they now disowned. In addition to the SDLP standing aside to help Sinn Féin gain North Belfast, neither nationalist party contested the infertile terrain of East Belfast and North Down, a modest contribution towards the anti-Brexit Alliance's spectacular victory in the latter. Unionists complained that 'Remain' pacts were 'pan-nationalist' agreements, whilst themselves engaging in pan-unionist deals. The UUP, which had been pro-Remain in the 2016 referendum and then accepting of Brexit but not the Johnson version, stood aside for the DUP in North Belfast. The DUP reciprocated for the UUP in an equally unsuccessful pact in Fermanagh & South Tyrone. The new divides of 'Remain' versus 'Leave' were thus mapped onto the much older 'Orange versus Green' politics of unionism and nationalism.

Party Fortunes

For the DUP, the election was necessarily defensive: it was seeking to defend an overall majority of Northern Ireland's seats and hoped for another mathematical miracle to retain Westminster influence. Only 4% of DUP voters had opposed the confidence-and-supply deal with the Conservatives[37] and DUP members favoured the Conservatives over Labour by seven to one.[38] The DUP deal had netted £1 billion of extra funding, and the party's election manifesto trumpeted the resulting benefits for health, education and employment.[39]

Table 12.5   The 2019 general election result in Northern Ireland

	Votes	% Vote	% Change from 2017	Seats	Seat change from 2017
DUP	244,127	30.6	−5.4	8	−2
Sinn Féin	181,853	22.8	−6.7	7	–
Alliance	134,115	16.8	+8.8	1	+1
SDLP	118,737	14.9	+3.1	2	+2
UUP	93,123	11.7	+1.4	0	0
Others	31,412	3.2	−1.5	0	−1

Turnout: 61.8% (−3.6%)

The DUP's main electoral losses were among its middle-class supporters, a fact evident in the party's failure to take North Down, Northern Ireland's most affluent seat, previously held by the retiring Independent Unionist Lady Sylvia Hermon and now captured by the Alliance. It was not only Brexit that was problematic for the DUP. There was also a 'raging debate within the party' over how much attention to give to

Assembly restoration.[40] Some feared the DUP would take much of the blame for the three-year Assembly hiatus, given that the party had presided over the Renewable Heating Incentive (RHI) debacle, an expensive subsidies fiasco overseen by DUP ministers and special advisers.[41] Others argued that Sinn Féin would be seen as the culprits, given that they had collapsed the devolved institutions when their Deputy First Minister, Martin McGuinness, resigned in January 2017.

Sinn Féin approached the election conscious that the party's absence from the Assembly might be viewed unfavourably, but hoping that support for its strong anti-Brexit position would balance this out. The election in the North and the one in the Republic of Ireland three months later were important tests for the post-conflict, 'new guard' leadership of Mary Lou McDonald, party President, and Michelle O'Neill, Northern leader and Vice President. McDonald succeeded Gerry Adams, who had been President for 35 years, in 2018, and O'Neill, Deputy First Minister in the restored Executive, replaced Martin McGuinness, who died shortly after quitting the power-sharing institutions.

Sinn Féin's notable triumph over Dodds could not conceal electoral punishment elsewhere, with a larger overall decline (6.7 points) than any other party. This was Sinn Féin's first significant loss of support at a Northern Ireland general election since 1992. The loss of Foyle to SDLP leader Colum Eastwood, on an 18.4% swing, was particularly troubling. Whilst Sinn Féin had only captured the seat for the first time in 2017, and by a mere 169 votes, the party held its ard fheis (annual conference) in the constituency in the month prior to the election and used the occasion for a canvassing drive, and did not expect a reverse on anything like that scale. The result offered evidence that nationalists wanted the Assembly back. No one blamed the SDLP for its collapse.

The reversal was temporary. Less than two months after the UK general election, Sinn Féin topped the poll in its Irish equivalent, obtaining 24.5% of first-preference votes, an increase of almost 11 points. Sinn Féin fielded only 42 candidates, of whom 37 were elected. Had more candidates stood, the party would have been in lead position to form a government. For decades, Sinn Féin was seen predominantly as a northern party with a northern leadership, grounded in northern conflict. Now, with a strong southern leadership team, Sinn Féin polled an even higher percentage vote share south of the border than it did in the North, having become the majority choice of nationalists in both jurisdictions. The new (tough) test for Sinn Féin will be to capitalise on this popularity to increase pressure for referendums in each entity on a united Ireland.

The most striking development in 2019 was the rise in vote share from fifth to third place of the Alliance Party. Naomi Long's party has always rejected unionism and nationalism and claims neutrality on Northern Ireland's constitutional future. More than half (51%) of Alliance voters say they are 'neither unionist nor nationalist'; however, the party also attracted support beyond this category in 2019, with 23% of the party's voters identifying as unionist and 17% as nationalist. Stephen Farry captured North Down for the Alliance with 45% of the vote, a remarkable increase from the 9% obtained in 2017. The Alliance's vote rose 11 points overall, and the party improved its vote share in 17 of the 18 constituencies, its new supporters drawn particularly from 2017 DUP and Sinn Féin voters. The Alliance garnered the support of a quarter of all non-voters from two years earlier. The party has the youngest voter base, half being aged 45 or under. It attracts voters from across the religious divide: 49% Protestant, 39% Catholic, 1% other religions and 11% no religion. Alliance voters also straddle three main identities: 31% British; 33% Irish and 26% Northern Irish, with 10% holding other identities.

Whilst Northern Ireland's political system is built upon the unionist versus nationalist fault line, those identifying as 'neither unionist nor nationalist' amounted to 40% of the 2019 electorate, compared to only 28% declaring as unionist and 25% as nationalist. Alliance has a large and growing electoral pool to fish. If the party can attract mass support from those eschewing traditional ideological labels, it could pose a serious challenge to the traditional order. But this remains an 'if'. Only half of electors stating they are neither unionist nor nationalist bothered voting in 2019, compared to 78% of unionists and 84% of nationalists. Northern Irish elections remain contests primarily of traditional true believers.

Election Ramifications: Devolution and the Perennial Constitutional Question

The fall in vote shares for the DUP and Sinn Féin and the marginalisation of Northern Ireland's MPs made the rapid post-election restoration of the devolved power-sharing Executive and Assembly inevitable. Its acrimonious collapse in 2017 came when Sinn Féin walked out, claiming mistreatment by the DUP. By the 2019 election, voters were angry over the unaddressed local health crisis, with no minister to take decisions over, for example, long hospital waiting lists. There was overwhelming support for the return of the devolved institutions among electors: only

2% opposed their return. This was despite chronic instability and regular collapses, with the Executive and Assembly suspended for 45% of the time between January 1999 and January 2020.

The Secretary of State threatened new Assembly elections if the parties did not return to government in Northern Ireland. Some of the most contentious issues, on which the Assembly was too divided to resolve, had been dealt with at Westminster, with same-sex marriage and abortion being legalised. The RHI inquiry report, released after the election, proved a damp squib, and no heads rolled.

Devolved government returned one month after the election under the *New Decade, New Approach* deal.[42] Its framework had been worked out privately and multilaterally prior to the election.[43] The agreement introduced the Irish-language provision demanded by nationalists and established an Office of Identity and Cultural Expression. Provision for an official opposition was bolstered, but all the main parties chose to enter the Executive. The Secretary of State, Julian Smith, resurrected the 2014 Stormont House Agreement on conflict legacy, with provision for continuing prosecutions of anyone who had perpetrated crimes during the Troubles, regardless of the organisation. This alarmed some Conservatives, who were not keen on seeing British soldiers on trial. This, combined with Smith's anti-Brexit sympathies, may have ensured that one of the first impacts of *New Decade, New Approach* was his sacking and replacement by Brandon Lewis.

Some issues rumbled on. In June 2020, a DUP Assembly motion challenging the liberalisation of abortion was passed, but had no legal effect. Only 8% of DUP voters believed there should be an Irish Language Act, which the new deal had in effect introduced, but only a mere 3% of Sinn Féin voters believed there should *not* be such provision. All parties complained that *New Decade, New Approach* offered little fresh cash, but none had much appetite to again collapse devolution.

The stability of the revived devolved government remained uncertain as the parties simultaneously attempted to advance their divergent constitutional positions. Irish nationalists, whilst strongly opposed to Brexit, hoped that enforced departure from the EU might bolster support for a united Ireland, or at least weaken opposition to the prospect amongst non-nationalists. The 1998 Good Friday Agreement permits the Secretary of State for Northern Ireland to call a border poll if public opinion within Northern Ireland appears to support a united Ireland. Yet the evidence from polls and election results suggests that there is still much distance to travel. Table 12.6 shows support for Irish unification by party and overall.

Table 12.6 Long-term constitutional preference for Northern Ireland, by party voted for (percentage)

Party voted for	Northern Ireland to remain in the UK	United Ireland	Other	Don't know
DUP	96.6	2.0	0.4	1.0
UUP	94.9	0.7	2.2	2.2
Alliance	58.8	25.7	3.7	11.8
Sinn Féin	10.4	83.9	3.0	2.7
SDLP	20.4	70.6	0.0	9.0
All voters	56.0	35.1	1.9	7.0
All electors, including non-voters	54.2	28.7	1.7	15.4

Note 1,977
Source Northern Ireland General Election Survey (2019)

The pro-unity figure of almost 29% among all 2019 respondents is modest, albeit the highest yet from a non-online, interview-based survey. Online surveys, containing more politically engaged samples, have produced much higher levels of support for unification.[44] At the general election, combined support for nationalist parties favouring a united Ireland totalled 39%. This is below the peak of 43% recorded in 2001, the first general election after the 1998 Good Friday Agreement. The combined unionist vote has ebbed further, from 52% in 2001 to only 42% in 2019. The balance of identities has also shifted. In 1998, British identifiers (41%) comfortably exceeded those identifying as Irish (27%).[45] By 2019, Irish identifiers, at 35%, were slightly more numerous than British (34%), while Northern Irish identification remained unchanged across two decades at 23%.

Although 81% of voters backed unionist or nationalist parties at the general election, almost 40% of the electorate profess to be 'neither unionist nor nationalist'. That grouping breaks almost three to one in favour of the constitutional status quo, despite Brexit. Nationalists need to convert some to Irish unity if they are to achieve their aims. The contentious Brexit process unfolded in a context of growing Irish identity and fading attachment to unionism. Nonetheless, although support for Brexit was always a minority taste in Northern Ireland and fell further as both sides of its constitutional divide turned against the eventual Johnson deal, the face-to-face interview survey evidence suggests little momentum for a united Ireland—thus far at least.[46]

Still Polls Apart?

Despite the strong Alliance performance, there are reasons to be sceptical about the prospects for a thaw in Northern Ireland's sectarian divide. The correlation between religious community and vote alignment, while weaker than before, remains very strong.[47] In the 2019 Northern Ireland election survey, the percentage of Catholics who admitted voting for either the DUP or the UUP was an emphatic zero. Only 1% of Protestants voted for Sinn Féin, rising to 5% backing the SDLP. Table 12.7 provides the religious support bases of each party at the election.

Table 12.7   Religion of each party's voters, 2019 general election in Northern Ireland (percentage)

	Catholic	Protestant	No religion
DUP	0	97	3
UUP	0	95	5
Alliance	39	49	11
Sinn Féin	98	1	1
SDLP	87	5	6

Note 1,981
Source Northern Ireland General Election Survey, 2019

More than two decades after the Good Friday Agreement, there is very little decoupling of the link between religion and voting. There is virtually no willingness to vote for parties from the 'other side', any thawing being confined mainly to an increased willingness of both Catholics and Protestants to vote for the Alliance.

Polarisation is also evident in party leader ratings. Almost one-third of DUP voters ranked their soon to be deposed leader, Arlene Foster, at ten out of ten and more than two-thirds at eight or above. In contrast, a majority (56%) of Sinn Féin voters gave Foster the minimum rating of zero and only 2% rated her at six or above. Reciprocating the antipathy, 43% of DUP voters ranked Michelle O'Neill at zero and 75% at two or below. Meanwhile the majority (55%) of Sinn Féin voters ranked their leader at eight or above, whereas only 1% of unionist voters gave O'Neill a positive rating.

Although it has been suggested that British or Irish political parties might stand in Northern Ireland (local Conservatives do; the Labour Party does not) to help tackle the sectarian logjam, this idea also divides voters on sectarian lines. Only 9% of DUP voters want Irish political parties to contest elections in Northern Ireland and only 8% of Sinn Féin voters want British political parties to take part.

Conclusion

The main 2019 election concerns in Northern Ireland were constitutional: Brexit and the future of devolution. Growing voter demands for the return of devolved government fuelled a surge in support for the Alliance, whose voters were most likely to list the absence of the decision-making Executive as a key election issue. Yet the duly resurrected Executive and Assembly are still shaped by the old sectarian fault line that the Alliance attempts to challenge. The DUP and Sinn Féin dominate, providing the First Minister and Deputy First Minister respectively, along with seven of the ten Executive ministers. The next Assembly election, scheduled for 2022, seemed set to be a close contest between the two parties, despite their relatively weak performance in the 2019 Westminster election.

Movement towards greater Irish economic unity under a bespoke Brexit for Northern Ireland, involving EU Single Market alignment, means that calls for a border poll on a united Ireland will remain vocal. The fallout from Brexit has increased their volume, although evidence of a major attitudinal shift is limited so far. As with the constitutional question itself, prospects for change divide unionists and nationalists deeply. Whilst 65% of nationalists think unification with the rest of Ireland has become more likely, only 18% of unionists concur. A border poll is in any event unlikely anytime soon. A united Ireland is still some way off, but, as unionists enjoyed Northern Ireland's centenary in 2021, prospects for a bicentennial celebration also seem cloudy.

NOTES

1. Pippa Crerar, Peter Walker and Libby Brooks, 'SNP MPs Walk out of Commons in Protest over Brexit Debate', *The Guardian*, 14 June 2018, https://www.theguardian.com/politics/2018/jun/13/snp-mps-walk-out-of-commons-in-protest-over-brexit-debate.
2. As it turned out, Scottish Labour members were able to participate in a second leadership contest before the devolved elections, as Richard Leonard resigned in January 2021, six months before they were due to be held. His defeated rival from 2017, Anas Sarwar, won the new contest, thus becoming in February 2021 the first Muslim leader of a political party in the UK.
3. Jackie Baillie served as interim leader, a role she would later reprise in 2021.

4. As reported by the *Daily Record* in October 2018, the Scottish Conservative plan was to discredit Boris Johnson as a possible party leader. For the most part the operation involved making clear to colleagues and constituency members that polling figures suggested a Johnson-led party would perform poorly in Scotland, returning it to levels of support before the gains under Davidson. See Torcuil Crichton, 'Scots Tories Launch Operation Ars* to Stop Boris Johnson Becoming Party Leader', *Daily Record*, 2 October 2018, https://www.dailyrecord.co.uk/news/politics/scots-tories-launch-operation-ars-13343163.

5. Panelbase, 18–20 June 2019, https://www.drg.global/wp-content/uploads/ST-Tables-for-publication-200619.pdf.

6. Johnson's toxicity in Scotland sets him apart, a fact dramatically illustrated by a poll invoking one of Scotland's great recent fictional creations, Harry Potter. Polling in July 2019, before he became leader, YouGov found that 46% of the Scottish electorate thought Johnson would have been placed in Slytherin House had he attended Hogwarts. For those unfamiliar with the *Harry Potter* oeuvre, students at Hogwarts, the Potter books' boarding school for wizards, are assigned into different houses by a 'sorting hat' which assesses their personalities. Slytherin, whose symbol is a snake, is a house associated with (in the words of the sorting hat) 'cunning folk [who] use any means to achieve their ends'. See https://d25d2506s-fb94s.cloudfront.net/cumulus_uploads/document/idf34h3ini/InternalResults_190722_Boris_w.pdf.

7. Equivalent 'very bad' scores were 27% for Sturgeon, 24% for Swinson and 35% for Corbyn. Panelbase, 3–6 December 2019. See the link in Footnote 5 above.

8. Panelbase, 3–6 December 2019, https://www.drg.global/wp-content/uploads/W1781w24-Tables-for-publication-061219.pdf.

9. Midway through the March 2020 trial, Salmond's lawyer Gordon Jackson QC was overheard on a crowded train carriage not only identifying two of the complainants in the case and discussing tactics to discredit witnesses, but also describing Salmond as a bully and a 'sex pest'. Jackson later referred himself to the Scottish Legal Complaints Commission (SLCC) over the remarks and stood down from his role as Dean of the Faculty of Advocates. The criminal trial concluded later that month. One charge having been dropped by the Crown, Salmond was found not guilty of 12, with one charge 'not proven', the uniquely Scottish verdict option that lies between guilty and not guilty. The ministerial conduct investigation and the parliamentary inquiry were still ongoing at the time of writing. Jackson's case was referred for investigation by the Faculty of Advocates in August 2020; that investigation had yet to report at the time of writing.

10. The impact was asymmetrical, with 'No Remainers' most likely to switch to Yes. Brexit played a smaller role in converting previous Yes supporters to No.

11. The scale of change was comparable only to the swing to Sinn Féin in Ireland in 1918, a swing which heralded independence for the Irish Free State soon after.

12. Gordon, Inverness, Ross, Skye & Lochaber, West Aberdeenshire and Banff & Buchan.

13. 3 December debate: https://www.heraldscotland.com/news/18079032. nicola-sturgeon-voted-winner-stv-leaders-debate-online-poll; 10 December debate: https://www.heraldscotland.com/news/18092733. online-poll-think-won-bbc-scotland-leaders-debate.

14. The once dominant force of Scottish politics also lost its deposit in six seats, after failing to poll above 5% of the vote.

15. On Labour switchers, see Ailsa Henderson, Rob Johns, Jac Larner and Chris Carman, 'Scottish Labour as a Case Study in Party Failure: Evidence from the 2019 UK General Election in Scotland', *Scottish Affairs*, 29(2) (2020): 127–40. On the risks of 'muscular unionism', see Ailsa Henderson 'Labour Must Be Careful in Chasing the Unionist Vote', *The Times*, 26 June 2020, https://www.thetimes.co.uk/article/labour-must-be-careful-in-chasing-the-unionist-vote-523t6gjgv.

16. Wales voted for Brexit by a margin of 52.5% to 47.5% in June 2016. Between July 2016 and the December 2019 general election, there were 22 published polls in Wales which asked how respondents would vote in a second Brexit referendum; findings ranged between an eight point advantage to Remain and a three point lead for Leave, with the mean average being a 3.45 point Remain lead. Findings from all polling in Wales since 2012 can be found at https://blogs.cardiff.ac.uk/electionsinwales/opinion-polls.

17. A by-election was forced in Brecon & Radnorshire by a recall petition, after Conservative MP Chris Davies was convicted of expenses fraud. A notable feature of the by-election was that Plaid Cymru and the Green Party both decided not to stand candidates, urging their supporters to vote for their fellow pro-Remain party, the Liberal Democrats.

18. After the death of Sargeant, Jones faced sustained and repeated criticism from some opposition figures as well as a small number of current and former Labour Senedd members. During the inquest, Jones was also criticised by counsel for the Sargeant family for his handling of the case and for alleged inconsistencies in his evidence, which Jones refuted. The coroner recorded a verdict of death by suicide at the conclusion of the inquest in July 2019.

19. The highly Welsh-focused Labour approach to the 2017 campaign is discussed in Laura McAllister and Roger Awan-Scully, 'For Wales, Do Not

See England? An Analysis of the 2017 General Election', *Parliamentary Affairs* (2019), https://doi.org/10.1093/pa/gsz041.

20. In the ITV Wales debate, Labour was represented by Shadow Solicitor-General Nick Thomas-Symonds and in the BBC Wales debate by Shadow Defence Secretary Nia Griffith.

21. Alun Cairns' alleged involvement in the Ross England case is discussed further in 'Alun Cairns Resigns in Ross England Rape Trial "Sabotage" Row', *BBC News*, 6 November 2019, https://www.bbc.co.uk/news/uk-wales-politics-50302173.

22. Despite his difficulties, Cairns retained the competitive marginal seat he first won from Labour in 2010 with an increased majority.

23. The Conservative candidate in Ynys Mon was intended to be Chris Davies, who had been unseated as MP for Brecon & Radnorshire only months earlier. After complaints locally, Davies stood aside the day before nominations closed, only for last-minute substitute Virginia Crosbie, who had little previous association with the constituency, to win the seat in the subsequent election.

24. In the 2016 devolved election, Plaid overtook the Conservatives to regain their status as the second-largest party in the Welsh Assembly. On the same day, the party also won two of the four Welsh Police and Crime Commissioner elections.

25. The Brexit Party's highest regional vote share in 2019 was recorded in North East England (8.1%), with its second highest coming in the Yorkshire and Humber region (at 5.9%).

26. There is a strong positive correlation between the estimated Leave percentage vote in the 2016 Brexit referendum and the change in Conservative vote share in each Welsh constituency between 2017–19 (Pearson's $r = .53$, $p < .001$). The correlation between the estimated Leave share and the change in Tory vote share between 2015 and 2019 (thus allowing for the impact of the 2016 referendum result across both the 2017 and 2019 elections) is even stronger ($r = .60$, $p < .001$). Constituency estimates for the 2016 Brexit vote are those generated by Chris Hanretty and are available at https://docs.google.com/spreadsheets/d/1b71SD-KPFbk-ktmUTXmDpUP5PT299qq24orEA0_TOpmw/edit?usp=sharing.

27. *Source*: British Election Study Internet Panel, Wave 19; number of respondents $= 1,170$.

28. The final pre-election Welsh poll in 2017 had given Carwyn Jones an average popularity rating of 5.0 on the 0–10 scale.

29. Labour clung on in Alyn & Deeside, its one remaining seat outside the South Wales valleys, by just 213 votes.

30. The Northern Ireland general election survey was conducted between 28 December 2019 and 11 February 2020. The Principal Investigator was Professor Jon Tonge (University of Liverpool) with co-investigators Professor Peter Shirlow (Liverpool), Professor Bernadette Hayes (Aberdeen), Professor Jocelyn Evans (Leeds) and Dr Paul Mitchell (LSE). It involved interviews with a representative sample of 2,003 respondents in 90 electoral wards across Northern Ireland's 18 constituencies. It was funded by the Economic and Social Research Council and the University of Liverpool Heseltine Institute.

31. Peter Cory, *Cory Collusion Inquiry Report: Patrick Finucane.* HMSO, 2004, HC 470.

32. Quoted in 'Posters Attacking Finucane Family "Nothing to Do" with DUP – Nigel Dodds', *Irish Times*, 20 November 2019, https://www.irishtimes.com/news/ireland/irish-news/posters-attacking-finucane-family-nothing-to-do-with-dup-nigel-dodds-1.4088701. Finucane criticised the banners as 'not representative of unionism', saying: 'It's not a style of campaigning or politics that I would be comfortable with … I don't wish to refight old battles, or use politics as a way of inflicting hurt on somebody else – no matter what the circumstances.'

33. Interview with senior DUP official, 20 May 2020.

34. John Garry, 'The EU Referendum Vote in Northern Ireland: Implications for Our Understanding of Citizens' Political Views and Behaviour', Northern Ireland Assembly Knowledge Exchange Seminar Series 2016–2017, http://www.niassembly.gov.uk/globalassets/documents/raise/knowledge_exchange/briefing_papers/series6/garry121016.pdf, p. 2.

35. Speech to the DUP annual conference, Belfast, 24 November 2018, https://www.youtube.com/watch?v=FRGBU2TNc_k.

36. Garry, 'The EU Referendum Vote in Northern Ireland', p. 6.

37. Jonathan Tonge and Jocelyn Evans, 'Northern Ireland; Double Triumph for the Democratic Unionist Party', *Parliamentary Affairs*, 71(1) (2018): 139–54.

38. Jonathan Tonge, Máire Braniff, Thomas Hennessey, James McAuley and Sophie Whiting, *The Democratic Unionist Party: From Protest to Power.* Oxford University Press, 2014.

39. DUP, *Let's Get the UK Moving Again.* Westminster Election manifesto, 2019.

40. Interview with senior DUP official, 20 May 2020.

41. For an excellent account, see Sam McBride, *Burned: The Inside Story of the 'Cash-for-Ash' Scandal and Northern Ireland's Secretive New Elite.* Merrion, 2019.

42. HM Government, *New Decade, New Approach*, January 2020, https://assets.publishing.service.gov.uk/government/uploads/system/uploads/

attachment_data/file/856998/2020-01-08_a_new_decade__a_new_ approach.pdf.

43. The British and Irish governments worked together on the deal, with informal input from the main Northern Irish parties that would once again have to work together in a restored power-sharing administration.

44. Lucid Talk runs a regular series of online panel surveys. Its first after the general election (February 2020) reported 46.8% support for Northern Ireland staying in the UK, with 45.4% backing a united Ireland. The two most recent face-to-face surveys before the election both found support for a united Ireland at only 21%: John Garry, Kevin McNicholl, Brendan O'Leary and James Pow, *Northern Ireland and the UK's Exit from the EU*. QUB, 2018, https://www.qub.ac.uk/sites/brexitni/ BrexitandtheBorder/Report/Filetoupload,820734,en.pdf.

    See also the Northern Ireland Life and Times Survey, 'Political Attitudes', ARK, 2018, https://www.ark.ac.uk/nilt/2018/Political_ Attitudes/NIRELND2.html.

45. Northern Ireland Life and Times Survey, 'Community Relations', ARK, 2018, https://www.ark.ac.uk/nilt/1998/Community_Relations/NINATID.html.

46. Even among electors saying they are pro-Remain, there is a very slight majority for Northern Ireland remaining in the UK, although excluding 'Don't knows', it could hardly be closer, at 50.5% for the constitutional status quo and 49.5% wanting a united Ireland.

47. The correlation between Protestant religious community background and unionist bloc vote was 0.93, while on the Catholic nationalist side, the figure was 0.95 (both significant at $p < 0.001$).

CHAPTER 13

The Geography of a Brexit Election: How Constituency Context and the Electoral System Shaped the Outcome

John Curtice, Stephen Fisher, and Patrick English

The 2019 election was called to end the stalemate over Brexit that had dominated the 2017–2019 Parliament. Voters were invited to express their judgement on whether or not Brexit should proceed on the basis of the revised Withdrawal Agreement the Prime Minister had negotiated with the EU. However, the level of support for Remain and Leave in the EU referendum varied across the country in a way that cut across the existing geography of party support. Both Conservative and Labour seats were divided between those where a majority had backed Leave and those where most had voted Remain. Consequently, if voters did decide how to vote in the 2019 election on the basis of their views about Brexit (see Chapter 14), the parties in favour of Brexit would be expected to have advanced most strongly in constituencies with most Leave voters, while the parties that were supportive of a second referendum prospered most in constituencies with most Remain supporters. The first question addressed by this chapter is whether indeed this proved to be the case.

Meanwhile, any such pattern would potentially have consequences for the character of the constituencies represented by the parties in the House of Commons. It may have enabled parties to win constituencies in which they were not usually successful, while losing ones they had hitherto

462 THE BRITISH GENERAL ELECTION OF 2019

normally won. At the same time, any change in the geography of party support may also have had implications for the total number of seats won by each party. After all, one striking feature of the election was that, at 47%, the share of the vote won by those parties that were arguing in favour of implementing Brexit was less than the combined tally of 52% secured by those parties that were willing to put the issue to a second referendum.[1] Perhaps the Conservatives' ability to win an overall majority of 80 (their best result since 1987) did not simply rest on how many votes they secured? Maybe it also rested on their being more successful at winning seats—and especially a set of longstanding (but Leave-voting) Labour seats that supposedly formed a northern 'Red Wall'—than their national share of the vote might have led us to anticipate?

Although the principal question put before voters was the binary one of whether or not to proceed with Brexit, they had to express their views by voting for one of a multiplicity of parties. This meant that the verdict delivered by the election could depend not just on how many votes were cast for each option, but also how those votes were distributed across the parties. If, say, support for pro-second referendum parties was scattered across multiple parties while backing for Brexit nearly all went to just one party, pro-Brexit candidates would have a better chance of being elected even when this was not the majority view in their constituency.

However, a potential way of counteracting this risk would be for parties who shared the same view on Brexit to agree an electoral pact in which only one of them fought each constituency. This tactic was adopted in England and Wales by some of the parties opposed to Brexit, namely the Liberal Democrats, the Green Party and Plaid Cymru, who, as part of a 'Unite to Remain' alliance, agreed to nominate only one candidate in each of 60 constituencies. This represented the most substantial electoral pact in a British general election since the Liberal Party and the Social Democratic Party (SDP) formed an electoral alliance at the 1983 and 1987 contests. Meanwhile, an alternative tactic was for a party to decide unilaterally to stand down in certain constituencies. This was the step taken by the Brexit Party, which did not contest any of the constituencies being defended by the Conservative Party. This chapter also addresses what impact these actions had on the outcome.

Our evidence comes from two sources. First, we analyse the constituency election results themselves, though unless otherwise stated, our analysis is confined to Great Britain, and excludes Northern Ireland (on which see Chapter 12). Our principal focus is on how the rises and falls in party support since the previous election in 2017 varied according to the geographical location and the social or political character of constituencies. Second, we use the wave of interviews conducted for the British Election Study internet panel (BESIP) immediately after the 2019 election.[2] Because the BESIP interviewed as many as 30,000 respondents, the sample is big enough to enable us to compare and contrast the behaviour of individual voters in different kinds of constituencies, and thereby help us understand why parties prospered more in some kinds of seats than in others. Note that further details of some of our analyses, including a summary of the overall result, are to be found in the statistical Appendix to this book.

For the third election in a row, the outcome in Scotland was very different from that in England and Wales, with the SNP by far the most popular party. Consequently, we analyse the outcome there separately. We begin our analysis by looking at the relationship in England and Wales between the performance of the principal parties and how a constituency voted in the 2016 EU referendum. This leads us into a discussion, first, of the battle for votes among Leave voters and constituencies, followed by a similar analysis of Remain people and places. Thereafter we assess the impact on their support of the stance on Brexit taken by individual MPs. Subsequently we turn our attention, first, to Scotland and, then, to the pattern of turnout, before finally assessing how the electoral system translated votes into seats.

THE IMPACT OF BREXIT IN ENGLAND AND WALES

The geography of Brexit was sharply reflected in the performance of the parties. As Table 13.1 shows, the pro-Brexit Conservatives' share of the vote increased by nearly six points on 2017 in seats that are estimated to have backed Leave most heavily in 2016, while the party's vote fell by a couple of points in constituencies where most had voted Remain. At the same time, in those seats that it contested, the Brexit Party's share of the vote was nearly three times higher on average in seats that had backed Leave than it was in those places where Remain had secured a majority.

The reverse pattern is evident, albeit less strongly, in the geography of Labour and Liberal Democrat performance, both of which parties were willing to put Brexit to a second referendum. While Labour's vote fell by six points where most voters had backed Remain, it dropped by nearly nine points where a majority had supported Leave. However, even in

Table 13.1 Party performance by estimated outcome of the 2016 EU referendum, England and Wales

2016 EU referendum result	Mean 2017–2019	Mean change in % vote 2017–2019			Mean % vote 2019	
	Swing	Conservative	Labour	Liberal Democrat	Brexit Party	Seats
Remain over 60%	+1.4	−2.8	−5.6	+6.6	2.0	64
Remain 50–60%	+2.5	−1.4	−6.5	+6.5	3.4	107
All Remain Seats	+2.1	−2.0	−6.2	+6.5	2.7	171
Leave 50–60%	+4.7	+2.0	−7.5	+3.9	5.6	240
Leave over 60%	+8.3	+5.9	−10.6	+2.6	10.3	160
All Leave seats	+6.2	+3.6	−8.7	+3.4	7.6	400
All seats	+4.9	+1.9	−8.0	+4.3	5.7	571

Note Constituencies contested by the Speaker in 2017 (Buckingham) and 2019 (Chorley) are excluded. Seats represent the total number of constituencies in that category. The Liberal Democrats contested only 550 seats in both 2017 and 2019, while the Brexit Party fought only 259 in 2019, and the means for these parties are based only on these seats. Swing is the change in the Conservative share of the vote less the change in the Labour share divided by two; a positive sign thus indicates a net swing to the Conservatives and a negative one a swing to Labour. 2016 referendum results are estimates for each constituency by Chris Hanretty (see Chris Hanretty, 'Areal Interpolation and the UK's Referendum on EU Membership', *Journal of Elections, Public Opinion, and Parties*, 27(4) (2017): 466–483)

the most pro-Remain constituencies, Labour's support still typically fell more heavily than that of the Conservatives. Consequently, Labour profited little from their relative success at retaining the support of Remain voters (see Chapter 14), capturing just one pro-Remain seat from the Conservatives (Putney). Meanwhile, the rise in Liberal Democrat support was nearly twice as high in Remain seats than in Leave ones, though it was much the same in the most pro-Remain seats as it was in those where Remain scored between 50 and 60%. In contrast, there was a much more marked increase in Conservative support and fall in Labour's tally in the most heavily pro-Leave seats than there was in those that voted less strongly for Leave. It would seem that the most pro-Leave parts of England and Wales were more determined than those in the most pro-Remain parts to reflect their views about Brexit in how they voted.

In practice, however, the pattern of party performance reflected more than just how a constituency had voted in 2016. This becomes apparent in Table 13.2, in which we conduct the analysis in Table 13.1 separately for those constituencies won by the Conservatives in 2017 and those won by Labour—which between them account for all but 13 of the seats contested in England and Wales. This brings to light two further striking points. The first is that the Liberal Democrats performed particularly well in Conservative Remain seats (that is, seats that voted Remain in 2016 and returned a Conservative MP in 2017)—on average, the party's vote was up by 10 points in such constituencies and by as much as 16 points in those where over 60% had voted Remain. However, they were unable to replicate this performance in Labour Remain seats. This suggests the Liberal Democrats were better able to win over Remain voters where a vote for the party might help avoid the election of a pro-Brexit Conservative MP than they were when a more sympathetic Labour MP was already in place. However, we should note that it was the Conservatives themselves, not Labour, who found it most difficult to maintain their support in Conservative Remain seats, raising questions about the origin of the increased Liberal Democrat support in these constituencies (see Chapter 14).

The second striking pattern is that Labour performed especially badly in seats they were defending that had voted heavily for Leave. On average, the party's share of the vote fell by nearly 14 points in such constituencies, well above the loss of eight points it suffered in England and Wales as a whole. As a result, at just over nine points, the swing from Labour to the Conservatives in the most heavily pro-Leave seats the party was attempting to defend was also well above what it was elsewhere. In contrast, at a little over eight points, the fall in Labour's vote in Conservative-held seats where over 60% voted Leave was little different from the average drop in the party's support across England and Wales as a whole. So, in a mirror image of what happened in Remain seats, voters seem to have been more likely to swing behind a pro-Brexit candidate in those Leave seats where the locally incumbent party had views on Brexit that were at odds with those of most voters. However, given that one of the key differences between the most pro-Leave Labour seats and the most pro-Leave Conservative ones was the presence of a relatively successful Brexit Party candidate, we may also wonder

Table 13.2 Party performance by estimated outcome of the 2016 EU referendum and the winning party in 2017, England and Wales

Winning party 2017: 2016 EU referendum result:	Mean 2017–2019 Swing		Mean change in % share of vote 2017–2019						Mean % vote 2019 Brexit Party	Seats	
			Conservatives		Labour		Liberal Democrats				
	Con	Lab	Con	Lab	Con	Lab	Con	Lab	Lab	Con	Lab
Remain over 60%	+2.3	+1.3	−5.0	−2.3	−9.6	−4.9	+16.1	+4.3	2.0	11	48
Remain 50–60%	+1.8	+3.4	−2.8	−0.1	−6.3	−6.9	+9.1	+3.9	3.4	55	48
All Remain seats	+1.9	+2.4	−3.2	−1.2	−6.9	−5.9	+10.3	+4.1	2.7	66	96
Leave 50–60%	+4.1	+5.6	+1.6	+2.3	−6.6	−9.0	+5.1	+2.3	5.6	147	89
Leave over 60%	+7.5	+9.3	+6.9	+4.7	−8.2	−13.9	+3.2	+1.7	10.3	91	69
All Leave seats	+5.4	+7.2	+3.6	+3.3	−7.2	−11.1	+4.4	+2.1	7.7	238	158
All seats	+4.7	+5.4	+2.2	+1.6	−7.1	−9.2	+5.7	+2.8	5.9	304	254

Note See note to Table 13.1. In the case of the Liberal Democrats and the Brexit Party, figures are based only on the seats they contested

whether the presence of Brexit Party candidates may have contributed to Labour's difficulties in its Leave seats.

There was, then, a clear relationship between how a constituency voted on Brexit in 2016 and how the parties fared in the 2019 election. The pro-Brexit Conservatives advanced in Leave seats, while they lost ground in Remain constituencies. The Brexit Party also fared better in Leave seats. Meanwhile, the increase in support for the anti-Brexit Liberal Democrats was more marked in Remain constituencies, while the 'Brexit-sceptic' Labour Party lost less ground in such seats than it did in Leave seats. At the same time, it appears that many of these patterns were particularly marked in constituencies that had hitherto been represented by a party whose stance on Brexit was at odds with the views of most voters in the seat.

As we anticipated earlier, this Brexit-related pattern of party performance did indeed prove disruptive of much of the existing geography of party support. Labour suffered their heaviest losses in the North East and in Yorkshire & the Humber (see Table A2.4, pp. 610–12 in the Appendix), both regions where hitherto the party was relatively strong. No less than 41% and 35% respectively of the constituencies in these two regions were Labour-held seats where over 60% had voted Leave in 2016. This pattern also helps explain why the Brexit Party performed best of all in these two regions. Meanwhile, apart from London, where over three-quarters of seats had voted Remain, the only region outside the capital in which support for the Conservatives fell was the South East—hitherto one of the party's strongest regions, but one where as many as 35% of the seats were Conservative Remain constituencies. Conversely, the Conservatives profited in the North East from the large proportion of Labour Leave seats, though the party advanced most of all in the East and West Midlands where, at just over 50%, there were proportionately more strongly Leave seats than anywhere else in England and Wales (albeit most of them already Conservative-held). The Liberal Democrats, meanwhile, not only made particular progress in the South East, with its high proportion of Conservative Remain seats, but also in London, which accounted for over half of the Conservative seats where the Remain tally had been over 60% in 2016. This success in and around the metropolis stood in stark contrast to the days in the 1950s, 1960s and 1970s, when the Liberal Party looked to the Celtic fringe for its best performances. In short, all of Britain's parties often recorded some of their best performances in relatively unfamiliar territory.

THE BATTLE FOR LEAVE VOTERS

While there was a clear link between the outcome of the EU referendum locally and change in party support between 2017 and 2019, we have seen that the strength of this pattern depended on the previous political character of a seat. So, how can we account for the particularly sharp movements towards the Liberal Democrats (and away from the Conservatives) in Conservative Remain seats and the swing away from Labour (to the apparent advantage of the Brexit Party) in Labour Leave seats? One possibility, as we have already suggested, is that the prospect of being represented by a party whose views did not match their own gave Remain voters in Conservative Remain seats and Leave voters in Labour Leave constituencies a particular incentive to vote differently from how they did in 2017. However, voters with a similar disposition do not necessarily have to behave differently in different places in order for constituencies to swing differently. It may be that the explanation lies in differences between constituencies in the character of the support that the parties had secured in 2017. It is to these possibilities that we now turn.

We analyse first of all what happened in Labour Leave seats—not that this is a straightforward issue to address. We might anticipate that a constituency that elected a Labour MP in 2017 after having voted Leave in 2016 is one where most Labour voters voted Leave—and given that Labour were losing ground among Leave voters, that their heavy losses in such seats were inevitable. However, Labour might have won a plurality of the vote in Labour Leave constituencies by marshalling the vast majority of the minority Remain vote there. Indeed, data from the BESIP show that it was neither true that a majority of those who voted Labour in 2017 in Labour Leave seats backed Leave, nor was it the case that most Leave supporters in such seats supported Labour in 2017.

That said, although they still only represented a minority of Labour's vote, a higher proportion of the party's support came from Leave voters in Labour Leave seats (38%) than it did in Labour Remain constituencies (19%)—indeed, in seats where more than 60% had voted Leave, the proportion was as high as 43%. In addition, a higher proportion of Leave voters (36%) backed Labour in Labour Leave seats than did so in Conservative Leave constituencies (19%). Consequently, Labour were more vulnerable in their Leave-inclined seats to any outgoing tide among their Leave voters.

The BESIP suggests that among Leave voters as a whole, only half (50%) of those who voted Labour in 2017 and who participated in the 2019 election backed the party again in 2019 (see also Chapter 14). Crucially this proportion differed little between Labour Leave (52%) and Conservative Leave seats (47%).[3] In short, the rate at which Labour lost support among their Leave supporters was not particularly high in Labour Leave seats. However, whereas losing around half of their Leave voters meant that Labour's share of the Leave vote fell in Conservative Leave seats from 19 to 11%, a drop of eight points, in Labour Leave constituencies the consequence was a fall from 36 to 19%—a drop of as much as 17 points. Labour lost ground so heavily in Labour Leave seats because they were more reliant on Leave voters in such seats—and not because Leave supporters in Labour Leave seats were especially likely to have defected from the party.

This finding has implications for the post-election debate since the election about the causes of the relatively heavy loss of support—and, in consequence, of seats—that Labour suffered in so-called 'Red Wall' constituencies. This debate often seems to have rested on the assumption that voters in the North of England and the Midlands were particularly strongly motivated to switch away from Labour. Our analysis suggests that Leave voters in Labour Leave seats in the North and the Midlands were no more likely to defect from Labour than Leave supporters elsewhere; it was just that such voters were particularly numerous in 'Red Wall' seats.

That said, at −6.2 points, Labour's vote fell on average much less in Labour Leave seats in the South of England (where there were only 16 such seats) than it did elsewhere (−11.7), while the increase in Conservative support (+1.1) was more muted in these seats than elsewhere (+3.6) too.[4] Indeed, Labour's performance was also a little better in Conservative Leave seats in the South of England—though not to the same extent. So, perhaps Labour were a little more successful in retaining support among Leave voters in the South. However, there are too few Labour Leave voters in South of England Labour Leave seats in the BESIP sample for us to be able to identify the presence or absence of any such pattern with confidence.[5] What can be said is Labour did not perform better in Remain seats in the South of England (average fall −6.6) than elsewhere (−5.3), suggesting that Labour were not *generally* more successful at stemming their losses in the South.

However, even if Leave voters defected from Labour at much the same rate irrespective of where they lived, it might still be the case that

Labour may not have lost as much ground in Labour Leave seats but for the presence—and relatively strong performance—of the Brexit Party. After all, the BESIP suggests that Leave voters were more likely to vote for the Brexit Party in seats where Leave voters were more numerous.[6] This pattern was especially strong in heavily pro-Leave constituencies in the North East, Yorkshire & the Humber, and Wales—the three regions where the Brexit party performed best (see Table A2.4, pp. 610–12). Perhaps this pattern helps explain why Labour lost ground so heavily in Leave seats?

The Brexit Party's decision to contest only constituencies that had been won by one of the opposition parties in 2017 appeared to be motivated by a combination of fear and belief. The party feared that if it stood in Conservative-held seats, it might split the pro-Leave vote, thereby putting some of these seats at risk of being captured by a pro-second referendum party. However, at the same time, the party apparently believed that in opposition-held seats it could attract Labour Leave voters who would be unwilling to support the Conservatives, and thereby help deny Labour victory.

But was this presumption correct? At first glance, the answer is obvious. According to the BESIP, 40% of those who voted for the Brexit Party in England and Wales in 2019 voted for the Conservatives in 2017, while only 30% backed Labour (another 22% had supported UKIP). Consequently, the absence of Brexit Party candidates in Conservative-held seats must have been helpful to the Conservatives, while the decision to contest opposition-held ones was unhelpful. In fact, however, the difference between these two proportions was much smaller in seats that voted Leave in 2016 and where, as we have seen, the Brexit Party performed best: here, 36% of the Brexit Party's vote came from the Conservatives, only slightly above the 32% that came from Labour.[7] So, perhaps the Brexit Party's decision to stand in opposition seats was at least not harmful to the Conservatives?

In reality, the impact of the Brexit Party cannot be discerned by simply looking at how those who voted for it in 2019 behaved in 2017. What matters is who they *would* have supported in 2019 had they not been able to vote for Nigel Farage's party—which would not necessarily have been the party they backed in 2017. This counterfactual, though, is inevitably more difficult to discern.

One possible approach is to compare the swing from Labour to the Conservatives in seats where the Brexit Party stood with the swing in those where it did not. Table 13.2 shows that, apart from the most pro-Remain seats, the swing to the Conservatives was rather higher in seats that Labour were defending (which in almost all instances were seats the Brexit Party was contesting) than it was in those that the Conservatives were defending. Moreover, the swing to the Conservatives was higher the better the Brexit Party performed.[8] This suggests that the Brexit Party won more votes from those who would otherwise have backed Labour than it did from those who would have voted Conservative.

Yet if this were the case, we would expect Labour to have lost more support among their Leave voters where the Brexit Party stood than where it did not. However, Table 13.3 reveals that where the Brexit Party stood, rather more Labour Leave voters (57%) voted Labour again than did so where the Brexit Party was absent from the ballot (48%). The picture is much the same if we look at only those seats in which a majority voted Leave—underlining our earlier point that Leave voters in Labour Leave seats were not particularly likely to have stopped voting for the party in 2019. What was different in seats where the Brexit Party stood

Table 13.3   2019 Vote by 2017 vote among Leave voters by whether or not Brexit Party stood

All seats	*Brexit Party stood*			*Brexit Party did not stand*		
	2017 Vote					
2019 Vote	*Conservative* %	*Labour* %	*UKIP* %	*Conservative* %	*Labour* %	*UKIP* %
Conservative	87	26	46	95	40	84
Labour	2	57	7	2	48	2
Brexit Party	8	11	39	-	-	-
	(1,990)	(1,094)	(223)	(4,418)	(1,114)	(307)
Leave seats	*Brexit Party stood*			*Brexit Party did not stand*		
	2017 Vote					
2019 Vote	*Conservative* %	*Labour* %	*UKIP* %	*Conservative* %	*Labour* %	*UKIP* %
Conservative	87	29	44	95	40	83
Labour	2	52	7	2	48	2
Brexit Party	9	13	45	-	-	-
	(1,319)	(778)	(168)	(3,633)	(932)	(261)

Source BESIP wave 19. Movements to other parties not shown and those who did not vote in 2019 are excluded from the denominator. Figures in brackets represent the weighted Ns on which the figures are based.

was that some (albeit still only a minority of) former Labour Leave voters switched to the Brexit Party, whereas elsewhere (seemingly) nearly all who were minded to defect from Labour because of Brexit voted Conservative. At the same time, where the Brexit Party stood, the Conservatives were less successful at winning over those who had voted UKIP in 2017, while some of the Conservatives' own supporters switched to the Brexit Party. All of this suggests that where it stood, the Brexit Party cost the Conservatives potentially significant levels of support.

Still, this conclusion rests quite heavily on the inference that, given what happened in seats where the Brexit Party did not stand, those who switched from Labour to the Brexit Party would, in the absence of a Brexit Party candidate, have voted Conservative. One way of assessing whether this appears likely is to compare the evaluations of the parties and leaders held by those who switched from Labour to the Brexit Party with the equivalent evaluations among those who moved from Labour to the Conservatives. If those Leave voters who switched to the Brexit Party would have voted Conservative in the absence of a Brexit Party candidate, we would anticipate that their attitude to Labour, the Conservatives and the Brexit Party should have been similar to the views of those who did swing to the Conservatives.

The BESIP suggests this was not the case. Asked to give the parties a score out of ten, those Leave voters who switched from Labour to the Brexit Party gave the Conservatives a mean score of 3.8, little different from the mean score for Labour (3.6) (while the Brexit Party scored 6.8).[9] In contrast, those who switched to the Conservatives gave their new party a mean score of 6.2, somewhat ahead of the Brexit Party at 5.2 and well ahead of Labour at 3.3.[10] Meanwhile, although Boris Johnson (5.3) was more popular than Jeremy Corbyn (1.4) among those who switched from Labour to the Brexit Party, the Prime Minister was significantly less popular among this group than among those who switched to the Conservatives (7.1).[11] In short, while this evidence does not suggest that those who switched from Labour to the Brexit Party would, in the absence of a Brexit Party candidate, have all reverted back to Labour, it seems they were less enamoured of the Conservatives than were those who did switch in that direction, and that therefore some of them might not have voted Conservative in the absence of a Brexit Party candidate.

Given this evidence, we have estimated how Labour Leave voters in opposition-held seats would have behaved in the absence of a Brexit Party candidate by modelling the behaviour of Labour Leave voters in

Conservative-held seats and applying the resulting equation to their counterparts elsewhere.[12] This suggests that around 70% would have voted for the Conservatives, while 30% would have stuck with Labour. In addition, we assume that nearly all those who switched from the Conservatives to the Brexit Party would otherwise have voted for the Conservatives,[13] as would those who switched from UKIP to the Brexit Party. On the basis of these assumptions, it appears that the net effect of the Brexit Party's intervention was typically to reduce the swing from Labour to the Conservatives by just over two-thirds of the vote that the Brexit Party won locally. As a result, the Brexit Party may have cost the Conservatives around 25 of the seats that Labour managed to retain—most of them Leave-voting seats in the North of England and the Midlands—and thereby enabled Labour to avoid an even heavier loss of seats.

But what of the Brexit Party's decision not to contest Conservative-held seats? If the party was mostly taking votes from the Conservatives, this decision must have helped put those seats out of the grasp of the Conservatives' opponents, especially so given that (unsurprisingly) Leave voters in such constituencies were more likely than Leave voters in Labour seats to have voted Conservative in 2017, some of whom might have been attracted to the Brexit Party.[14] However, given there was a swing to the Conservatives in most seats anyway, there are few constituencies that the Conservatives were defending where they won in 2019 by a narrow margin, while all of them were seats where most voters had backed Remain in 2016 and thus were places where the Brexit Party would have been unlikely to have performed well. To estimate just how well they might have done, we have modelled the geographical variation in Brexit Party support where the party did stand and applied the resulting equation to those seats where it did not.[15] We also assume that most of the votes it is estimated the Brexit Party would have won in practice went to the Conservatives. This analysis suggests there was just a handful of seats where the decision of the Brexit Party to stand down might have helped avoid a Conservative defeat, though they include the seats of two prominent Brexiteers, Iain Duncan Smith (Chingford & Wood Green) and Dominic Raab (Esher & Walton).[16]

For the most part, Nigel Farage's nomination strategy proved a hindrance rather than a benefit to the Conservatives. Standing down in Conservative-held seats made only a marginal difference to the outcome. Meanwhile, where it did stand, the party was not especially successful at garnering the support of those who would otherwise have voted Labour, and as a result may have denied Boris Johnson what might otherwise have been an overall majority of around 130. More limited though it was than on the pro-second referendum side of the Brexit debate, the division of support for pro-Brexit parties that did occur still significantly reduced the scale of the Conservatives' election success.

SEEKING THE REMAIN VOTE

But how do we account for the relative success of the Liberal Democrats—and the decline in Conservative support—in Conservative Remain seats? And what impact did the formal electoral pact between the Liberal Democrats, the Greens and Plaid Cymru have on the outcome of the election? Moreover, is there any evidence that, faced with more than one pro-second referendum party from which to choose, Remain voters took matters into their own hands and voted tactically for whichever party was best placed to win an overall majority?

In many respects, the position in which the Conservatives found themselves in the Remain seats they were defending was very similar to the one in which Labour found themselves in their Leave fiefdoms. Again, the description 'Conservative Remain' is potentially misleading—most Conservative voters in these seats backed Leave, not Remain, in 2016. However, it was still the case that, according to the BESIP, rather more of the Conservative vote in these seats (32%) consisted in 2017 of those who had voted Remain than was the case in Conservative Leave constituencies (25%). At the same time, the level of support for the Conservatives in 2017 among Remain voters was much higher in Conservative Remain seats (29%) than in Labour Remain constituencies (12%). Consequently, just as Labour were more vulnerable to an outflow of their Leave voters in Labour Leave seats, the Conservatives were more vulnerable in Conservative Remain seats to any departure of Remain voters from the party's ranks.

However, Remain voters who had backed the party in 2017 proved rather more loyal to the Conservatives in Remain seats than Leave-supporting Labour voters were to their choice in Leave constituencies. Just over three in five (62%) voted for the party again, compared with the equivalent figure of 50% among Labour Leave voters. However, it was still the case that whereas in Labour Remain seats this loss of support among Remain voters resulted in only a three-point drop in the Conservatives' share of the Remain vote (from 12 to 9%), in Conservative Remain seats it generated as much as an eight-point drop (from 29 to 21%). Meanwhile, when Remain voters defected from the Conservatives, they did so primarily not to Labour, but to the Liberal Democrats—and especially so in Conservative Remain seats.[17] In short, the Liberal Democrats proved particularly able to exploit the Conservatives' vulnerability to a loss of Remain supporters in the party's Remain seats (see Chapter 5).

Yet the Liberal Democrats were also particularly successful at winning over Labour voters in Conservative Remain seats. According to the BESIP, as many as 22% of 2017 Labour Remain voters in these seats switched to the Liberal Democrats, more than twice the figure (10%) across England and Wales as a whole. As a result, despite Labour's relative strength in general among Remain voters (see Chapter 14, pp. 497–499), the party's vote fell almost as heavily in Conservative Remain constituencies (−6.9) as it did in Conservative Leave seats (−7.2). So here there is some evidence that the local political context did make a difference to how voters behaved.

One circumstance that might have encouraged some Labour voters to switch to the Liberal Democrats was residence in a seat where Labour trailed in third place. This might have motivated Labour supporters to vote tactically in such seats for the Liberal Democrats. However, there were only half-a-dozen Conservative Remain seats where the Liberal Democrats secured second place in 2017 and were less than 20% behind—and where there might therefore seem to be some chance of tactical voting (beyond whatever may already have taken place in 2017) making a difference. Meanwhile, at +8.6 points, the average increase in the Liberal Democrat vote in these seats was less than that recorded in Conservative Remain seats where the Liberal Democrats started off in third place (+9.9 points).[18] The Conservative Remain seats where the Liberal Democrats advanced most strongly were in fact among the five seats where the party started in second place but more than 20% behind. However, even the +12.7 point increase in support the party enjoyed in these seats was too small for any of them to be taken from the Conservatives.

As the further analysis in the Appendix shows (p. 580), not the least of the reasons for this pattern was that in most of the constituencies that represented the Liberal Democrats' best prospects there was only a small Labour vote left to be squeezed. Meanwhile, there is also little evidence that Liberal Democrat supporters cast a tactical vote for Labour in seats where their party began in third place. In short, tactical switching between the two anti-Brexit parties, Labour and the Liberal Democrats, did little to counteract the overall fragmentation of the Remain vote between the two parties in England and Wales.

Under the terms of the electoral pact agreed by the Liberal Democrats, the Greens and Plaid Cymru, the Liberal Democrats did not face opposition from their partners in 43 seats.[19] Most of these (32) were being defended by the Conservatives, including 21 Remain seats in England where the Greens stood down. In six of these, the Greens had in fact not contested the seat in 2017, and thus the benefit of the pact was confined to avoiding votes being lost afresh to the Greens this time around. In the remaining 15, the Greens had won 2.0% of the vote on average in 2017, while in those Conservative Remain seats that the party did fight again in 2019, its vote increased on average by +1.1 points. Thus, if the pact had been fully effective, it should have boosted the Liberal Democrat performance by three points. In practice, the Liberal Democrat vote increased on average in these seats by +16.5 points, six points above the +10.3 point increase the party enjoyed in Conservative Remain seats in general. These seats also witnessed an above average fall of −10.4 points in Labour's vote, suggesting that rather than simply enabling the Liberal Democrats to secure support from potential Green supporters, the pact also had the effect of increasing the credibility of the Liberal Democrat challenge locally.[20] In contrast, while in the six Conservative Leave seats in England where the Greens stood down the Liberal Democrats appear to have garnered much of the support that might otherwise have gone to the Greens, there is no sign of the pact having had a spillover effect on potential Labour supporters.[21] Meanwhile, nowhere is it clear that the pact enabled the Liberal Democrats to win a seat they would not otherwise have won.[22]

The Liberal Democrats themselves stood down in 20 seats,[23] in half of them in favour of the Greens. One of these was the seat held by the Greens' only MP, Caroline Lucas, who had not faced Liberal Democrat opposition in 2017 either. In the eight seats in England where the Liberal Democrats stood down afresh for the Greens (evenly divided between Remain and Leave seats), the party had won just 4.5% of the vote in 2017, a figure that, given the party's performance elsewhere, would probably have at least been doubled if the party had stood again.[24] Support for the Greens in these eight seats increased by +7.3 points, around six points above the +1.4 point increase in support for the party elsewhere. Thus, the apparent boost of six points to the Greens' tally still only represented at most two-thirds of the vote the

Liberal Democrats would have been expected to garner. Meanwhile, it is possible that the apparent shortfall in the Greens' ability to garner potential Liberal Democrat support benefited the Conservatives more than Labour in these seats. Certainly, once we take into account the Brexit character of the seats in question, the Conservatives performed nearly three points better than we might have anticipated, whereas Labour only did half a point better—a difference that in the highly marginal seat of Stroud might have been crucial in enabling the Conservatives to make what was one of only two gains in a Labour Remain seat.

The Liberal Democrats' decision to stand down in Plaid Cymru's favour in seven seats was never likely to deliver more than a small reward. On average, the Liberal Democrats only won 2.4% of the vote in these seats in 2017, and given their vote only increased on average by +2.2 points across Wales as a whole, the party is unlikely to have won much more than 5% in these seats if it had stood again. After taking into account the outcome of the EU referendum locally in 2016, on average Plaid Cymru's performance was around two points better in these seven seats, suggesting that at most only half of those who would otherwise have voted Liberal Democrat switched to Plaid Cymru.[25] The pact did not deliver Plaid any benefit in terms of seats. While it covered the highly marginal seat of Arfon, where the party was only 0.3 of a point ahead of Labour in 2017, the general decline in Labour support means that Plaid Cymru would likely have won the seat anyway.

Many—but not all—voters do appear to have been willing to switch their support to whichever party was representing the Unite to Remain pact in their constituency. It may in some instances have even attracted support away from Labour. However, potential Liberal Democrat voters were seemingly somewhat less willing to switch to the Greens or Plaid Cymru than vice versa—a reluctance that in some instances may have seen them back the Conservatives instead—while nowhere does the pact appear to have enabled any of the participants to win a seat because they were attracting the support of too few Remain supporters in the first place. Much like the Liberal/SDP Alliance of 1983 and 1987, the exercise demonstrated how difficult it can be for an electoral pact to overcome the barriers to third-party electoral success posed by the single-member plurality electoral system.

BREXIT AND CANDIDATES

Between 2017 and 2019, Brexit exposed some significant rifts within both the Conservatives and Labour. As a result, some MPs stood for a different party than in 2017, while others attempted to defend their seat as an independent (see Chapter 11). Yet others had at some point rebelled against their party's line on Brexit, but still represented their party at the 2019 election. None of these courses of action proved to have a significant impact at the election.

No less than eight former pro-Remain Conservative MPs stood under a different banner in 2019. Many of them performed relatively well. Four who stood for the Liberal Democrats all registered an above-average increase (+14.9 points) in their new party's support. Two out of the three who stood as independents won over a quarter of the vote. However, a third who sought re-election as an independent won only 7%, while one former Conservative who stood under the banner of Change UK won just 8%. Crucially, none of these eight rebels succeeded in being elected or, indeed, in denying their former party victory locally. Further analysis on this topic can be found in the Appendix.

One reason why an MP might rebel against their party—while still being a candidate for it at the next election—is in the belief that their rebellious stance is popular with their local electorate and will help them retain their seat at the next election. Yet the decision by some Labour MPs in Leave seats to vote in favour of the revised EU Withdrawal Agreement negotiated by Boris Johnson (see p. 128) brought them little apparent reward. On average, the 15 such rebels saw their support fall on average by −14.6 points, well above the −10.3 point drop suffered on average by other MPs standing for re-election in Labour Leave seats. Only half that difference arose because some of the seats represented by the 15 rebels had a particularly high Leave vote in 2016.

On the other side of the Commons, three of the 21 Conservative MPs who voted in September 2019 in favour of a motion that paved the way for legislation that prevented the government from leaving the EU without a deal (see pp. 58–59) went on to represent their party again in their pro-Remain seat. Their rebellion did not reap any obvious reward either. At −4.5 points, the average fall in their vote was above the −2.6 point fall in the Conservative vote registered in other Conservative Remain seats where the incumbent MP stood again. On this evidence of the fate of party rebels, it seems that few Labour Leave or Conservative Remain voters paid any regard to the particular stance of their local MP.[26]

On the other hand, the rift that opened up between the Conservative Party and some of its pro-Remain MPs in the weeks leading up to the election does seem to have damaged the party's performance in some Conservative Remain seats. There were four such seats where the former pro-Remain (and in each case relatively high-profile) MP had either left the party over Brexit or, after voting against the government in September 2019, had not had the whip restored by the time of the election.[27] On average, the party's support in these seats dropped by −6.1 points. This is well above the average drop of −2.2 points in six Conservative Remain constituencies where the local MP never lost the Conservative whip over Brexit but, nevertheless, still opted to stand down.[28] At the same time, the party also seems to have lost support where a Remain seat was represented by a strongly pro-Brexit MP. Five who were clearly in that position on average saw their vote fall by −5.1 points, compared with −2.4 points in other Tory Remain seats.[29] It seems that the Conservatives did suffer somewhat where Conservative Remain voters had particular reason locally to be aware of the gap between their view of Brexit and that of their party.

However, what mattered most about candidates was not so much their personal views about Brexit as the personal reputation they had acquired in their local constituency. Previous elections have established that MPs defending their seat for the first time tend to outperform their party colleagues.[30] This, it seems, is because MPs can develop a personal vote on the basis of the local constituency service they provide, which helps insulate them from defeat when they first attempt to defend their seat. Table 13.4 shows that first-term incumbents who were defending a seat their party had gained at the last election on average performed better than other candidates standing in seats that their party was defending. The pattern is evident for both parties within both Remain and Leave seats, and even though Conservative first-term incumbents were disproportionately contesting Leave seats and Labour first-term incumbents Remain ones. Table 13.4 also shows that both the Conservatives and Labour performed less well in seats where the incumbent MP stood down, and thereby put at risk whatever personal vote they may have accumulated over the years, a pattern that in particular might have accounted for Labour's first loss on election night, Blyth Valley, where the longstanding MP, Ronnie Campbell, had stood down.[31]

Table 13.4 Mean change in Conservative and Labour share of the vote 2017–2019 by incumbency status of candidate, England and Wales

	Mean change in % Conservative vote 2017–2019 in Conservative-held seats	Seats	Mean change in % Labour vote 2017–2019 in Labour-held seats	Seats
First-term incumbent in seat gained in 2017	+11.0	8	−3.9	28
Incumbent standing in seat held by their party before 2017	+2.3	246	−9.5	187
Incumbent not standing in seat held by their party before 2017	−0.2	49	−11.4	37
All seats	+2.2	303	−9.2	252

Note This table excludes Brecon & Radnor, which changed hands from Conservative to Liberal Democrat in a by-election during the 2017–2019 Parliament, and two seats gained by Labour in 2017 where the new incumbent did not defend the seat in 2019

Although both Conservative and Labour first-term incumbents profited from this pattern, it mattered much more to those fighting under the Labour banner—both because there were many more first-time incumbents in Labour's ranks and because their above-average performance was a potential bulwark against an outgoing electoral tide. Indeed, all 11 seats that Labour held against the overall swing to the Conservatives in England and Wales were seats where Labour had a first-term incumbent standing for re-election.[32] However, some of those were saved for Labour primarily because they were also strongly Remain-voting. Once we take into account the variation in party performance by 2017 winning party and the strength of the 2016 Leave vote (see Table 13.2), the number of seats which look to have been saved for Labour by the incumbency effect seems to have been around five, though the precise number and the actual identities of those seats depends on statistical assumptions as to the exact nature of the pattern of performance by 2017 winning party and the strength of the 2016 Leave vote.

SCOTLAND

The outcome of the EU referendum was very different in Scotland to that in England and Wales, with no less than 62% voting in favour of staying in the EU. It might therefore be anticipated that a Conservative campaign based on getting 'Brexit done' would prove less successful north of the border. However, because the SNP were among the parties advocating a second EU referendum, the Conservatives' principal opponents south of the border, Labour and the Liberal Democrats, faced more intense competition for the support of Remain voters.

Both considerations mattered. In sharp contrast to the +1.7 point increase in the Conservatives' overall share of the vote in England and Wales, the party's support north of the border fell back by −3.5 points. At the same time, however, Labour's support fell somewhat more heavily (−8.5 points) than in England and Wales (−7.7 points), while at +2.8 points, the increase in Liberal Democrat support fell short of what the party achieved elsewhere (+4.3 points). Meanwhile, in a partial reversal of the decline in support the party suffered in 2017,[33] the SNP performed strongly, with a +8.1 point increase in support.

Yet while the contrast between the performances of the parties north and south of the border reflects the different politics of Brexit in Scotland, within Scotland itself there was only a modest association between party performance and how a constituency voted in the 2016 referendum. True, as Table 13.5 shows, the Conservative vote did fall back rather more in constituencies where the Leave vote had been lowest in 2016. Even so, the difference between the two-and-a-half point drop in seats where more than 38% voted Leave and the five point

Table 13.5 Party performance by estimated outcome of the 2016 EU referendum, Scotland

| % Leave 2016 | Mean change in % share vote 2017–2019 | | | | |
	Conservative	Labour	Liberal Democrat	SNP	Seats
0–33	−4.9	−8.6	+3.4	+8.5	13
33–38	−4.1	−7.6	+3.8	+8.2	11
38–43	−2.4	−8.9	+1.5	+8.3	20
43+	−2.5	−8.0	+2.9	+6.9	15
All seats	−3.3	−8.4	+2.7	+8.0	59

fall where less than one in three did so is smaller than was evident in England and Wales. The SNP advanced a little less in those seats where the Leave vote had been particularly high in 2016, but otherwise there is no clear pattern. The Liberal Democrats performed a little better in seats where Remain had been strongest, but the picture is far from consistent. Meanwhile, there is no evidence at all of Labour losing less ground in more pro-Remain areas. All in all, this is a rather different picture from the Brexit-dominated tapestry that, as we have seen, pertained south of the border (see Table 13.1).[34]

Scotland's electoral politics is, of course, also shaped by the distinctive issue of the country's constitutional status. Given that the SNP were also seeking—in no small part because of Brexit—to hold another referendum on independence, perhaps the division on that subject intensified and had an impact on the geography of the parties' performances? Of that, however, there is little sign. At +7.5 points, the average increase in SNP support in those constituencies lying in local authority areas where a majority voted in favour of independence in 2014 is little different from the +7.1 point increase in those areas where less than 40% voted Yes.

But perhaps the question of independence made a difference to voters' choice of pro-union party? Maybe some switched to whichever party appeared best placed locally to defeat the SNP? However, as detailed in the Appendix, only a small number of voters appear to have behaved in that way, and furthermore their behaviour affected the outcome in just one or two seats. The Conservatives did a little better—and Labour worse—where the Conservatives appeared best placed to win (either by retaining an existing seat or taking an SNP one). There are also some signs that a small number of Conservative supporters may have switched to Labour where Labour was running a close second to the SNP, though an above-average performance by Labour in those seats they were defending seems to have been occasioned by personal voting for a first-time incumbent rather than tactical switching. Meanwhile, although Conservative supporters seem to have switched to the Liberal Democrats in some of the seats where the latter were in contention, elsewhere—including in the East Dunbartonshire seat lost by the Liberal Democrats' UK leader, Jo Swinson—they appear to have withdrawn their former tactical support for the local Liberal Democrat candidate.

In any event, the most striking pattern of the results is not the inter-relationship between the performances of the pro-union parties, but rather a clear relationship between Labour and SNP performance. On average, the SNP vote increased by +10.7 points where Labour's vote fell by more than 10 points, but by only +6.0 points where Labour support fell by less than six points. That many voters switched between Labour and the SNP is confirmed by the BESIP, which shows that over a quarter (26%) of those who voted Labour in 2017 switched to the SNP in 2019, a pattern that was especially—though far from exclusively—evident among those who had voted Remain (see Chapter 14).

Turnout

Despite the intensity of the political developments that had led up to the election (see Chapter 1) and even though the election was fought on a newly compiled electoral register (see Appendix, p. 593), compared with 2017 turnout fell on average across Britain as a whole by −1.4 points. As Table 13.6 shows, in England and Wales this drop was somewhat higher in seats that voted Leave than it was among those that backed Remain, though this pattern was more apparent in seats that the Conservatives were defending than it was in Labour-held seats.[35] Indeed, turnout was

Table 13.6   Mean change in % turnout 2017–2019 by estimated outcome of the 2016 EU referendum and winning party 2017, England and Wales

| | Mean change in % turnout 2017–2019 | | | | | |
| | Seat won in 2017 by | | | Seats | | |
2016 EU referendum result	Conservative	Labour	All seats	Conservative	Labour	All seats
Remain over 60%	+1.3	−1.9	−1.3	11	48	64
Remain 50–60%	−0.3	−2.8	−1.5	55	48	107
All Remain seats	−0.1	−2.3	−1.4	66	96	171
Leave 50–60%	−0.9	−2.8	−1.6	147	89	240
Leave over 60%	−1.8	−2.9	−2.2	91	69	160
All Leave seats	−1.2	−2.8	−1.9	238	158	400
All seats	−1.0	−2.6	−1.7	304	254	571

slightly up in the most pro-Remain Conservative-held seats, a pattern that appears to have been occasioned by the strength of the Liberal Democrat performance in many of these seats (see Appendix, pp. 594–95). However, irrespective of the outcome of the 2016 EU referendum locally, turnout fell more sharply in Labour-held seats than Conservative ones. This might be thought an indication that Labour had difficulty in mobilising some of their support and, indeed, analysis of the BESIP suggests that those who voted Labour in 2017 and Leave in 2016 were particularly likely to have abstained in 2019. However, in 2017, turnout increased more in Labour seats than it did in Conservative ones[36] and if the turnout in 2019 is compared with what happened in 2015, the change in Labour seats (+1.4) is virtually identical to that in Conservative constituencies (+1.3). The higher fall in turnout in Labour seats at this election may be an indication that voters were mobilised to an unusual degree in some of Labour's strongholds in 2017 rather than reflecting particular disenchantment with the party (not least among Leave voters) in 2019.

Yet, the pattern of falling turnout was bucked entirely in the most pro-Remain part of the country, Scotland, where there was a +1.8 point increase in participation. As a result, for only the second time ever, at 68.2% overall, turnout there was higher than in both England (67.4%) and Wales (66.6%). However, as the Appendix shows (see p. 595), rather than simply reflecting the predominance of Remain voters, the increase in turnout north of the border was also stimulated by the dramatic increase in the number of marginal seats in Scotland following the 2017 election.

VOTES AND SEATS

We have seen that Brexit produced a substantial change in the geography of party support at the 2019 election. But what impact did this changed geography have on the outcome of the election in terms of seats? To what extent did it result in a change in the geography of the seats that are represented by Conservative and Labour MPs? And, above all, how significant a role did it play in the Conservatives' success in securing an overall majority of 80?

One way of addressing these questions is to compare the number of seats each party won with what the tally would have been if every party's vote had risen and fallen in every constituency in line with the change in its overall share of the vote—what we call a 'uniform swing' projection.

Given the very different pattern of party competition in Scotland from that in England and Wales, we undertake this calculation separately for the two parts of Britain.[37] For constituencies in England and Wales, we assume that each party's vote rises or falls in line with the overall change in its support across England and Wales, while in Scotland, we assume that each party's share of the vote changes in line with its Scotland-wide tally. The result of applying this procedure and how it compares with the actual result is shown in Table 13.7.

The calculation reveals that even if there had been a uniform swing, the Conservatives would still have won an overall majority—and thus been able to deliver Brexit. This is hardly surprising. After all, there was as much as a +4.6% swing from Labour to the Conservatives,[38] enough to put the Conservatives 11.7 points ahead of Labour. This was by far the biggest lead in votes to be enjoyed by any party since Labour's landslide victory in 1997 and is certainly of a size that we would expect the single-member plurality electoral system to turn into an overall majority. To that extent, the geographical variation in party performance was not decisive in determining the outcome. Rather, what was crucial, given the electoral system, was the fact that the Conservatives were so far ahead of their principal rivals—primarily because they were more successful at corralling the Leave vote than their rivals were at gathering together the pro-Remain vote (see Chapter 14, pp. 495–551).

Table 13.7   How the outcome of the election in seats differed from a uniform swing projection

| | Seats (UK) | | |
	Uniform Swing	Actual	Difference
Conservative	351	365	+14
Labour	209	203	−6
Liberal Democrat	17	11	−6
Green	1	1	0
Nationalist	54	52	−2
Other	18	18	0
Overall Conservative majority	52	80	+28

Note 'Uniform Swing' shows the outcome in seats if the changes in party support since 2017 in each constituency had been the same as the changes in the overall level of support across England and Wales/Scotland as a whole

That said, we might ask what would have happened had the election been a binary ballot in which voters were simply presented with the choice of voting for a pro-Brexit candidate or a pro-second referendum one—and that these two blocks had secured the same share of the vote in every constituency as the parties that represented those options achieved in 2019. Given that more voters voted for parties that backed a second referendum than backed one of the pro-Brexit parties, we might anticipate that a block that represented that option would have won a majority of seats. This, however, is not the case. The pro-Brexit parties won a larger share of the vote in 328 constituencies, while the pro-second referendum parties were ahead collectively in just 304. The pro-Brexit block were at an advantage because the size of the electorate and the level of turnout were both lower in seats where the pro-Brexit parties were strongest, while less of their support would have been 'wasted' in pilling up large majorities in safe seats.[39] Thus, even if the election had been structured as a binary choice on Brexit, there is no guarantee that the electoral system would have produced a House of Commons that reflected the outcome in terms of votes.

But while a Conservative majority was not a surprise, given the lead the party enjoyed in votes, Table 13.7 reveals that the party did win 14 more seats than it would have done if the swing had been uniform. As a result, the government is left with a bigger cushion against the threat of backbench rebellion than it would otherwise have enjoyed. The party that most obviously lost out as a result of the geographical variation in party performance was the Liberal Democrats, who, despite a four-point increase in their share of the vote, emerged with one seat fewer than they had won in 2017—well short of the gain of five seats they might have hoped to secure. At the same time, both Labour's representation and that of the nationalist parties was also somewhat less than it would have been under a uniform swing. In short, the geographical variation in party support resulted in the pro-second referendum parties winning fewer seats than they might have hoped.

However, what is also striking is the character of those seats that were 'won' and 'lost' against the uniform national tide. Overall, as many as 45 seats fell into this category—and almost all are consistent with (if not necessarily always simply occasioned by) the variation in party performance that we have seen was associated with Brexit. The Conservatives won 20 seats that, under our uniform projection, Labour would have been expected to retain—all were Leave constituencies (albeit in some

instances won on swings that were even higher than might have anticipated even when we take into account the strength of support for Leave
in 2016).[40] The Conservatives also won four seats that, although they
were Leave seats, the Liberal Democrats would have been expected to
win[41] together with three that were successfully defended against a
challenge from the SNP—these last three all seats that had (by Scottish
standards) a relatively high pro-Leave vote.[42] Conversely, Labour held
11 seats that the party would on our uniform projection have lost and
also made one gain from the Conservatives. Nine of these 12 seats voted
Remain (albeit in some instances with a result that was exceptionally
good for Labour, even taking into account the character of the seat),[43]
while the other three were constituencies where a new incumbent Labour
MP was defending a seat for the first time (see pp. 479–80).[44] Meanwhile,
the Liberal Democrats gained just one very pro-Remain seat from the
Conservatives,[45] while the party lost out in a net tally of two seats where
the local battle was with other pro-second referendum parties.[46]

This variation had a marked impact on the geography of Conservative
and Labour representation. All but one of the 20 Leave seats that
the Conservatives gained from Labour with an above-average swing
were located in or north of Birmingham, with the one exception
(Bridgend) being in South Wales. This was a reflection of the fact that
the Conservatives' best prospects for making such gains were located
in the Midlands and the North of England. Fifteen of the 20 seats the
Conservatives gained on an above-average swing had Labour majorities in 2017 of between 10 and 16%—and there were only three such
seats in the South of England. Moreover, all but one of the 20 seats that
the Conservatives secured from Labour via an above-average swing had an
above-average proportion of people engaged in routine and semi-routine
occupations, while every one of the 20 seats had a below-average proportion
who had reported in the 2011 Census as being in good health. In short,
these Brexit-induced Labour losses occurred in just the kind of constituency
that would once have been regarded as heartland territory for the party.

In contrast, all but one of the dozen seats that the Conservatives
would have won under a uniform swing but which ended up in Labour's
grasp were located to the south of England's second city (including two in South Wales); this reflected the fact that nearly two-thirds
of Conservative Remain constituencies were in the South of England
or Wales. These seats that Labour won against tide were often a world
apart, socially, from those that the party lost on an above-average

swing—most had an above-average proportion of people with degrees and in professional and managerial occupations. Meanwhile, between them, these patterns of gains and losses against the national tide ensured that as many as 35% of Conservative MPs now represent constituencies in the North of England, the West Midlands or Wales, whereas otherwise the figure would have been 32%. The proportion is also noticeably higher than the equivalent proportion (28%) in 1987, that is, the last time the Conservatives enjoyed a similarly sized majority.

Just over four out of five Conservative MPs in England and Wales now represent Leave constituencies, while all seven Liberal Democrat MPs represent Remain ones. However, despite its losses in terms of Leave seats, the Labour Party still finds itself divided between the 47% of its MPs who represent Remain seats and the 53% who represent Leave ones—a pattern that still leaves it with a disjuncture between the predominantly Pro-Remain character of the party's voters and the character of the constituencies the party represents.

CONCLUSION

The choices voters made in response to the principal question put before them in the 2019 election—should Brexit be done—had a significant impact on the geography of party performance. Leave constituencies swung strongly to the Conservatives, while the party lost support in Remain seats. Labour struggled above all in the most pro-Leave parts of the country, while the Liberal Democrats' otherwise limited advance was strongest in Remain seats. Indeed, so strong were these patterns that even when the views of individual candidates on Brexit were at odds with those of their party, this made little difference to their electoral fate.

For the most part, however, this pattern did not arise because voters behaved differently in different kinds of constituency; it occurred because the prevalence of those voters who were more likely to swing from one party to another varied geographically. The Conservatives did not lose ground most heavily in Remain seats because Remain voters in such seats were more likely to defect from the party; rather, it was because there were more Remain voters in such seats who had voted Conservative in 2017. Equally, Labour's difficulties in defending their Leave seats, including those widely dubbed as 'Red Wall' seats, simply reflected the fact that more of their supporters in these seats had voted

Leave in 2017, and not that Leave voters in such seats were especially likely to swing away from Labour.

However, the geographical variation in party performance still had implications for the outcome in seats. It enabled the Conservatives to secure a substantially larger majority than would otherwise have been the case, while the party's parliamentary representation was tilted rather more towards less affluent England north of Birmingham. The geography of nominations mattered too. The Conservatives' appeal to Leave voters was strengthened by the decision of the Brexit Party to stand down in seats the Conservatives were defending, but the Conservative majority might well have been even bigger—perhaps as much as 130 seats—if the Brexit Party had not contested those seats that were being defended by the opposition parties.

Geography mattered too because the single-member plurality system places a premium on unity. True, the geography of Remain support was potentially unfavourable to those on the pro-second referendum side of the Brexit debate even before a vote had been cast. But this was compounded by a fragmentation of Remain support across different parties.[47] That risk could only be overcome if the pro-second referendum parties entered into an electoral pact or if Remain voters voted tactically for whichever of those parties was best placed to defeat the Conservatives locally. While the limited electoral pact forged between the Liberal Democrats, the Greens and Plaid Cymru did have a beneficial impact on their respective performances, the partners to the pact were not sufficiently popular in the first place to turn what was often little more than a modicum of extra support into seat gains. Meanwhile, there was relatively little evidence of Remain voters switching tactically between Labour and the Liberal Democrats, and especially so in seats where such switching might have had a realistic chance of securing a Conservative defeat.

The decision to hold a multi-party election to resolve what had become a binary choice did not stop most voters from expressing their views on their ballot paper. However, resolving the issue via such an election meant that the outcome was determined not simply by which was the most popular view, but also by the geographical distribution of the vote. On the one hand, the number of Leave MPs elected was reduced by the decision of the Brexit Party to stand. On the other hand, the greater fragmentation of Remain support and a less favourable electoral geography cost the pro-second referendum parties dear—and may well have played a decisive role in determining the choice the country eventually made.

NOTES

1. The 47% is the combined tally of support for the Conservatives, the Brexit Party and UKIP in Great Britain. The 52% is the total share of the vote won by Labour, the Liberal Democrats, the SNP, Plaid Cymru and the Green Party. None of the Northern Irish parties was in favour of the Brexit deal that had been negotiated, though the DUP was in favour of Brexit in principle and the UUP was willing to accept Brexit so long as it was executed in a way that did not undermine the Union.

2. Details of this survey are to be found at https://www.britishelectionstudy. com/data-object/wave-19-of-the-2014-2023-british-election-study-in-ternet-panel.

3. Though the figure is somewhat lower than the 63% who were loyal to Labour in Remain seats.

4. The South is defined here as the Eastern, London, South East and South West regions.

5. At 52%, the proportion of all Labour Leave voters in the South who voted Labour again was little different from the equivalent proportions in the Midlands (50%) or the North (54%).

6. A total of 18% of Leave voters voted for the Brexit Party in constituencies where more than 60% voted Leave, compared with 9% in seats where less than 60% did so.

7. Moreover, the two proportions are virtually identical in those seats where the Brexit Party won more than 8% of the vote—here 35% of the Brexit Party vote came from the Conservatives and 34% from Labour. These were often seats with a high proportion of Labour Leave voters.

8. In seats where the Brexit Party won less than 4% of the vote, the average swing from Labour to Conservative was +3.0. In those where the Brexit Party secured more than 8%, it was +8.7.

9. At the same time, in response to a separate question, voters who supported the Brexit Party in 2019 after voting Labour in 2017 were not significantly more likely to report that they would ever vote for the Conservatives than they were Labour.

10. Confining this comparison to those living in constituencies where the Brexit Party stood makes no material difference to this comparison, other than that those who switched from Labour to the Conservatives in these seats scored the Brexit Party somewhat lower at 4.8.

11. Chapter 14 contains further analysis of Boris Johnson's relative popularity with switchers from Labour to the Conservatives.

12. We fitted a multinomial model based on characteristics such as age, gender, education, views on the Brexit, Conservative and Labour parties, and on their leaders. The model accurately predicted the voting behaviour of 91% of the Labour Leave voters who switched to the Conservatives in Conservative-held seats and 90% of those who stayed loyal to Labour.

13. The mean score given to the Conservative Party among those who switched from the Conservatives to the Brexit Party was 7.2, only a little below the 7.9 registered by those who stayed loyal to the Conservatives.
14. Where the Brexit Party did not stand, 69% of Leave supporters voted Conservative in 2017; 54% did so in seats where the Brexit Party stood.
15. Included in the model are terms for the Leave share of the vote in 2016, UKIP's share of the vote in 2015, a number of regional dummies, the percentage white, the percentage born in the UK, the percentage in good health, the prevalence of fast food restaurants, and the level of Conservative spending locally.
16. Two more marginal cases are Winchester and the Scottish seat of Moray.
17. Across all seats in England and Wales, 21% of Conservative Remain voters switched to the Liberal Democrats, while only 8% transferred to Labour. In Conservative Remain seats, these proportions were 29% and 5% respectively.
18. Though the party's performance in these seats ranged from a drop of −12.9 points in the party's vote in Southport to an increase of +28.9 points in Surrey South West.
19. One of these was the Buckingham seat of the former Speaker, John Bercow.
20. In those Conservative Remain seats in England that the Greens did contest, the Conservative vote fell by only −2.5 points, while support for Labour dropped by −5.9 points. Although these seats were on average not as pro-Remain as those where the Greens did stand down, the relative weakness of the Labour performance and the relative strength of that of the Liberal Democrats in the seats the Greens did not contest is still evident even if we control for the strength of the Remain vote locally in 2016.
21. The Liberal Democrat vote increased by +8.7 points in these seats, nearly four points more than in all Conservative Leave seats. This is commensurate with the 1.8% of the vote the Greens enjoyed in these seats in 2017 and the +1.6 point increase in support in Conservative Leave seats where the Greens did fight again. At −7.6 points, the fall in Labour support is little different from the −7.2 point figure in Conservative Leave seats as a whole.
22. There were three seats where Plaid Cymru stood down for the Liberal Democrats. Plaid won 3.7% of the vote in these seats in 2017, in two of which the Greens also stood down (having won 1.3% of the vote in 2017). However, the average increase in the Liberal Democrat vote in these seats was unremarkable at +2.1 points, suggesting that the pact had little impact.

23. Three—Beaconsfield, Broxtowe, and Luton South—were seats where the local pro-Remain MP was attempting to defend their seat as an Independent (see p. 587). Like Labour, the party also did not contest the Chorley seat of the new Speaker.

24. The Greens also seem not to have garnered all of the potential Liberal Democrat and Plaid Cymru vote in the one Welsh seat, Vale of Glamorgan, in which they were given a clear run. At +5.2 points, the increase in the Green vote was no more than four points above what it might otherwise have been, and was less than the combined Plaid and Liberal Democrat tally in 2017 of 6.2 points.

25. In the three of the seven seats that voted Remain, Plaid Cymru's vote increased by +3.3 points, compared with +1.5 points elsewhere. In the four of the seven seats that voted Leave, Plaid's support increased by +0.6 of a point, whereas elsewhere it fell by −1.4 points. This calculation is little affected by the additional withdrawal of the Greens in Caerphilly, where the party won just 1.1% of the vote in 2017.

26. Chris Hanretty, Jonathan Mellon and Patrick English, 'Members of Parliament are Minimally Accountable for Their Issue Stances (and They Know it)', *American Political Science Review* (early view).

27. These were South Cambridgeshire (former MP, Heidi Allen), Putney (Justine Greening), Runnymede & Weybridge (Philip Hammond), and Rushcliffe (Ken Clarke).

28. Arundel, Cities of London & Westminster, Hertford & Stortford, Milton Keynes North, Ruislip & Northwood, and Truro & Falmouth.

29. There were five Conservative MPs representing Remain seats who voted against the Brexit deal negotiated by Theresa May on all three occasions when it was put before the Commons. They were Adam Afriyie (Windsor, −5.8), Steve Baker (Wycombe, −4.8), Ranil Jayawardena (Hampshire North East, −6.0), John Redwood (Wokingham, −7.1; and Theresa Villiers (Chipping Barnet, −1.6).

30. See, for example, John Curtice, Stephen Fisher and Robert Ford, 'Appendix 1: The Results Analysed' in Philip Cowley and Dennis Kavanagh, *The British General Election of 2015*. Palgrave Macmillan, 2015, pp. 397–399; John Curtice, Stephen Fisher, Robert Ford and Patrick English, 'Appendix 1: The Results Analysed' in Philip Cowley and Dennis Kavanagh, *The British General Election of 2017*. Palgrave Macmillan, 2018, pp. 459–460.

31. In addition, Ivan Lewis' decision to stand down in Bury South, won by the Conservatives with a majority of just 0.8%, may well have cost Labour that seat. Ronnie Campbell's retirement in Blyth Valley (majority 1.7%) certainly made Labour vulnerable in what was the Conservatives' first gain on election night, though whether it was decisive in costing Labour the strongly pro-Leave seat is more debatable.

32. These were, in order of their marginality in 2017: Canterbury, Bedford, Warwick & Leamington, Portsmouth South, Battersea, Reading East, Gower, Weaver Vale, Cardiff North, Bristol North West, and Enfield Southgate.

33. Curtice et al., 'The Results Analysed', 2017, p. 467.

34. This is also reflected in a more modest relationship than in England and Wales between how individuals voted in the EU referendum in 2016 and the change in party support between 2017 and 2019. For example, according to the BESIP, there was only a one-point increase in Conservative support among Leave voters in Scotland compared with an 11 point rise south of the border. Meanwhile, support for Labour in Scotland fell by just as much among Remain voters as Leave supporters, whereas in England and Wales, the party's vote fell more heavily among Leave voters.

35. This pattern comes on top of a tendency in 2017 for turnout to increase more in Remain seats than Leave ones. See Curtice et al., 'The Results Analysed', 2017, p. 480. As a result, on average, turnout was +3.3 points higher than in 2015 in the most pro-Remain seats, while it was slightly down (−0.1) in the most pro-Leave ones.

36. Ibid., p. 483.

37. Curtice et al., 'The Results Analysed', 2015, pp. 416–417.

38. 4.8 points in England and Wales.

39. The average electorate in seats where the pro-Brexit parties were ahead was 71,555, while it was 74,762 where pro-second referendum parties were ahead. The average turnout in the two sets of seats was 66.5% and 68.1% respectively. On average, the total share of the vote won by pro-Brexit parties in seats where they were ahead was 58.5%, whereas the pro-second referendum parties won as much as 65.8% of the vote where they were ahead.

40. They are: Birmingham Northfield, Blyth Valley, Bolsover, Bridgend, Burnley, Bury South, Clwyd South, Delyn, Don Valley, Durham North West, Heywood & Middleton, Hyndburn, Leigh, Redcar, Sedgefield, Stoke Central, West Bromwich East, West Bromwich West, Wolverhampton North East, and Ynys Môn.

41. The Liberal Democrats lost Carshalton & Wallington, Eastbourne, and Norfolk North, while they failed to gain St Ives.

42. Banff & Buchan, Dumfries & Galloway, and Moray.

43. These comprised: Battersea, Bristol North West, Canterbury, Cardiff North, Enfield Southgate, Gower, Reading East, and Warwick & Leamington, all which were held by Labour, together with Putney, which was gained from the Conservatives.

44. Bedford, Portsmouth South, and Weaver Vale. In addition, the result in Canterbury reflected both its status as a Remain seat and one with a new incumbent Labour MP.

45. St Albans.
46. The Liberal Democrats gained Fife North East from the SNP, but failed to gain Ceredigion from Plaid Cymru and both Leeds North West and Sheffield Hallam from Labour.
47. The Conservatives won 51 constituencies where most voters backed pro-second referendum parties, whereas there were only 14 seats where a pro-second referendum candidate was elected even though more voters backed pro-Brexit parties.

CHAPTER 14

The British Voter in 2019

THE BREXIT ELECTION?

While Brexit dominated the short campaign and the Parliament preceding it, vote choices in 2019 also reflected deeper changes. Labour have become increasingly reliant on the votes of younger generations, university graduates and ethnic minorities, while the Conservatives have attracted growing support from older people and those with lower levels of educational attainment. Such trends have unfolded over decades, driven by the decline of traditional industries, educational expansion and rising ethnic diversity, not to mention the shifting policy positions and electoral appeals of both main parties over many elections.[1] All of these transformations have contributed to the long-term decline of class as the dominant fault line in British electoral politics: with both parties now winning similar levels of support from working-class and middle-class voters, it no longer makes much sense to talk of Labour as a working-class party or the Conservatives as a middle-class party in terms of voting patterns.

Brexit has catalysed this process, accelerating long-running changes already underway and mobilising a longstanding but formerly latent values divide in the electorate. Brexit has also helped break down traditional but often already frayed party loyalties, particularly among older, white socially conservative voters who in 2016 voted to leave the EU and who once made up a substantial part of Labour's core vote. Indeed, it was

R. Ford et al., *The British General Election of 2019*, https://doi.org/10.1007/978-3-030-74254-6_14

the geographical concentration of such voters in many former industrial towns in the North, the Midlands and Wales that had voted heavily for Leave that enabled the Tories to break through Labour's 'Red Wall' in 2019 (see Chapter 13). Labour was well aware of its problems in such seats during the Parliament and the campaign, and indeed well before this, but never found an effective response.

While Brexit was the defining issue of the campaign, the election was also a choice between two potential Prime Ministers—Boris Johnson and Jeremy Corbyn. In the end, Johnson's pledge to 'get Brexit done' proved a winning message with Leave voters unimpressed by Labour's ambivalence on Brexit—voters Corbyn proved unable to attract with a radical domestic policy offer. The cards available for the two leaders to play on Brexit in turn partly reflected their parties' circumstances. The Conservative membership and leadership were relatively unified in their support for Brexit, while most of the party's minority of Remain-leaning voters prioritised stopping Corbyn over stopping Brexit. Labour was more divided: the party's strongly Remain activist base and many of its MPs were attracted to a second referendum as a means to overturn Brexit, an outcome which by the time of the election was also openly supported by many of Corbyn's frontbench team. But this policy was anathema to many of Labour's Leave supporters, who regarded the first referendum mandate as sacrosanct. The party's efforts to balance these polarised demands ended up undermining its credibility with both sides. Labour's campaign was also hobbled by wider distrust of its leader Jeremy Corbyn, whose ratings had declined steadily since 2017 (see Chapter 8, pp. 285–286) and who was particularly toxic with Conservative-leaning Remain voters.

Labour had a bad salesman with a bad product to sell. This made Johnson's task easier, but the Conservatives still had to convince voters that, despite three years of deadlock, they really could 'get Brexit done' and deliver an 'oven-ready deal', thus providing the resolution a frustrated electorate craved. One under-appreciated aspect of the 2019 election was that the leader who won the Conservative Party its first large majority in a generation, Boris Johnson, was actually no better liked by voters than his predecessor, Theresa May, who lost the party its majority in 2017. Another was that Johnson won his majority in part thanks to reaping the harvest May had sown two years earlier, when the Conservatives made major advances in Leave-voting Labour seats. Johnson had the good fortune to be facing a diminished opponent defending a weakened position, and one saddled with the near-impossible task of trying to keep both Labour's Leave and Remain wings satisfied.

A Tale of Two Tribes in England and Wales

Two years of parliamentary wrangling over Brexit strained both main parties' coalitions. The most dramatic demonstration of this came in the European Parliament elections in May 2019, when both parties' support collapsed. Although voters have long treated European Parliament elections as a low-stakes opportunity to punish incumbents and flirt with smaller parties, these dramatic results revealed just how dissatisfied and volatile the electorate had become. Both parties suffered mass defections—by Leavers to the Brexit Party and by Remainers to the Liberal Democrats and the Greens, with the Conservatives and Labour securing just 8.8% and 13.6% of the national vote respectively.[2] Indeed, at that moment, it seemed possible that the Leave and Remain tribes might abandon one or both of the grand old parties of British politics altogether, triggering an unprecedented political re-alignment (see Chapter 8, pp. 283–284).

However, the Conservatives' replacement of Theresa May with Boris Johnson started to reverse this trend, with Johnson's relentless hard Brexit messaging steadily winning back Leave voters. Remain support was slower to return to Labour and much uncertainty still remained about where 'cross-pressured' voters—those with views on Brexit that were at odds with their favoured party's position—would go. By election day, though, the Leave vote had well and truly consolidated behind the Conservatives in England and Wales. According to data from the British Election Study (BES) post-election survey (see Fig. 14.1), 74% of people who had voted to leave the EU in the 2016 referendum voted Conservative in 2019, an increase of 13 percentage points on 2017.[3] Just 16% of Leavers voted for Labour (a drop of 11 points) and fewer still backed the Brexit Party (5%).[4] The Remain vote, in contrast, was splintered. Although Labour won the largest share, they could only secure 49% (a fall of three points), followed by the Conservatives who won 25% (down eight points), despite campaigning on a promise to 'get Brexit done' at all costs. The Liberal Democrats trailed in third among Remain voters on 20%, with a rise of seven points on 2017 bitterly disappointing those in the party who had hoped for a major breakthrough after the summer of 2019. Remain fragmentation meant that even though Remainers appear to have turned out at a slightly higher rate, the Conservatives emerged with a commanding overall vote and seat lead.[5] This reflected both the Conservatives' success in unifying Leave support, but also their success in holding on to a crucial slice of the Remain vote.

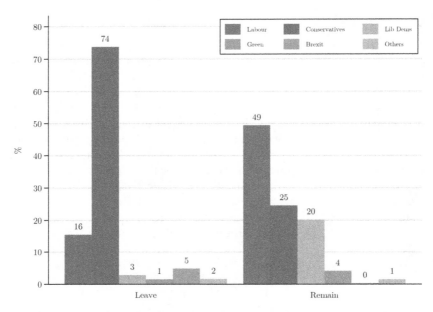

Fig. 14.1 2019 general election vote by Leave and Remain vote in the 2016 referendum, England and Wales[6]

The Conservatives retained 86% of their 2017 supporters, well ahead of Labour's 79%. Labour suffered defections on both sides of the Brexit divide. Over 1 in 10 people who voted Labour in 2017 (11%) voted Conservative in 2019—these were, overwhelmingly, Labour Leave voters. In contrast, only 1 in 20 of those who voted Tory in 2017 (5%) switched their vote to Labour. Labour also lost a strongly Remain chunk of their 2017 support (6%) to the Liberal Democrats, which confirmed that the party had been squeezed on both sides of the Brexit divide. The Liberal Democrats themselves managed to retain 60% of their 2017 vote, losing 18% of it to Labour and 16% to the Conservatives, a lower retention rate than their larger opponents, but eight percentage points higher than in 2017 (and some 28 points higher than in 2015).

Liberal Democrat losses were larger among voters with strongly negative views of the larger parties' leaders. Hostility to Boris Johnson predicted switching from the Liberal Democrats to Labour, while hostility to Jeremy Corbyn predicted switching from the Liberal Democrats to the Conservatives. It seems many voters bought into the brutal logic of first-past-the-post, despite the Lib Dems' efforts to market their own leader as a potential Prime Minister, and were less willing to stick with the smaller party if doing so risked letting a leader they intensely opposed into Downing Street. Brexit also changed the Liberal Democrats' coalition just as it did the larger parties' support bases. Some 63% of those who switched from the Liberal Democrats to the Conservatives had voted Leave in the EU referendum (see Fig. 14.2), and such voters gave much lower marks to the party's strongly pro-EU leader Jo Swinson. The Liberal Democrats' focus on opposition to Brexit in 2019 came with some costs for a party, whose traditional strongholds still included some relatively Leave-leaning areas.

The sharpest demographic divide in 2019 voting was again by age. Labour led among under-35s by 56–28%, but trailed the Conservatives by 21–61% among those aged 65 and over. Given that the younger group turned out at a rate of 53% and the older group at 77%, and the greying population meant there were almost twice as many over-65s as under-35s in the electorate, this age divide handed a sizeable electoral advantage to the Conservatives. It also marked a slight retreat for Labour on their so-called 'youthquake' in 2017,[7] when the party won under-35s by a margin of 61% Labour to 27% Conservative.[8] By contrast, the educational divide in the electorate grew in 2019. The Conservatives enjoyed a large lead among those with intermediate or no qualifications (51% Conservative to 29% Labour), a group that had heavily voted Leave in 2016, but were marginally behind among university graduates (36% Conservative to 38% Labour) who had voted heavily for Remain in 2016. This 22 point advantage among the least qualified represented a big increase from 2017, when the party had only a 6 point lead in this group.

Labour support fell by 14 percentage points, to 36%, among the occupational groups usually defined as working class (C2DEs), putting the party 7 points behind the Conservatives, on 43% (up 4). This represents a 9 point swing from Labour to the Conservatives among working-class voters. Both main parties lost support among middle-class (ABC1) voters. The Conservatives, down 2 on 45%, remained substantially ahead of Labour, down 4 on 32%.[9] While the 2019 election did not upend class politics altogether, the much larger swing to the Conservatives among working-class voters continued the long decline of the class divide in party support. Traditional measures of social class no

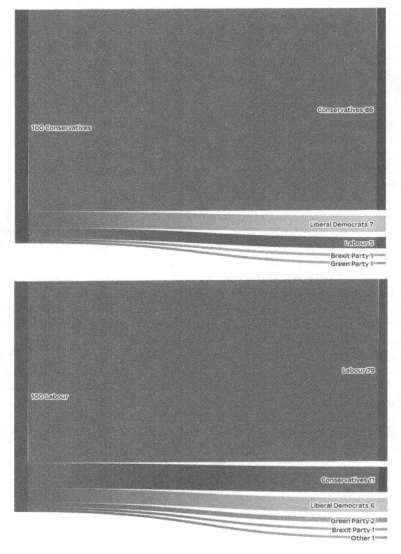

Fig. 14.2 Flowchart of 2017 Conservative and Labour voters to 2019 general election vote in England and Wales (BES, face-to-face survey)

longer work well as predictors of support for either party. This was also true for the Liberal Democrats, who made gains among all classes.

Consistent with historical voting patterns, ethnic minorities heavily favoured Labour over the Conservatives (54% Labour to 24% Conservative), but this lead was substantially down on 2017.[10] This was driven more by a drop in ethnic minority support for Labour (down 18 points on 2017) than any increase in ethnic minority voting for the Conservatives (up 5 points), with the Liberal Democrats being the main beneficiary (doubling their support from 7 to 14%). White voters favoured the Conservatives by a larger margin in 2019 than in 2017, though again this was driven more by Labour decline than Conservative advance. Lastly, there was a considerable gender gap in the vote, with the Conservatives holding an 18 point lead among men (47% Conservative to 29% Labour), but were just 5 points ahead among women (42% Conservative to 37% Labour). This was twice the size of the gender gap in 2017 and was consistent with pre-election speculation that Boris Johnson could have a 'women problem'.[11]

Both the Liberal Democrats and the Greens did considerably better with graduates, while the Brexit Party did best among those with no educational qualifications. This reflected the educational divide in support for Brexit as well as the longer-term tendency for the Lib Dems and Green party to do better with university graduates, who are more socially liberal. The age profile of the Lib Dem and Green vote was relatively flat, though the former appear to have done slightly better among those aged 35–44. Much like their predecessor party UKIP, Nigel Farage's Brexit Party did better among white voters and the over-55s and of course those who had voted most heavily in favour of Leave in 2016 (Table 14.1).

YEARS IN THE MAKING: THE BATTLE FOR LEAVERS, REMAINERS AND THE 'RED WALL'

Two general elections have been fought since the EU referendum of 2016. With Brexit playing a prominent part in both campaigns, it is worth looking at the cumulative patterns of change in voter behaviour across both elections together. To explore this, we draw upon the British Election Study Internet Panel (BESIP), a recurring online survey that interviewed around 30,000 people 14 times between May 2015 and December 2019. The large size of the sample makes measurement of the voting intentions of specific parts of the electorate less susceptible to random noise than most conventional polls.[13]

Table 14.1 Demographics of the 2019 vote in England and Wales (BES post-election survey)[12]

	Con	Lab	Lib Dem	Brexit Party (vs UKIP 2017)	Green	Other	Con-Lab lead	Turnout (all)
				2019 (change vs 2017)				
	%	%	%	%	%	%	±%	%
All	47 (+2)	35 (−7)	12 (+4)	2 (−)	3 (+1)	1 (−)	+12	66 (−3)
Gender								
Male	49 (+4)	31 (−9)	13 (+4)	3 (+1)	3 (+1)	1 (−)	+18	70 (+1)
Female	44 (−1)	38 (−5)	11 (+4)	2 (−)	3 (+1)	2 (−)	+6	63 (−6)
Age								
18–24	29 (+6)	55 (−13)	11 (+7)	2 (+2)	3 (−2)	0 (−1)	−26	53 (+3)
25–34	26 (−4)	57 (+1)	11 (−)	2 (+1)	4 (+3)	1 (−)	−31	53 (+2)
35–44	35 (+5)	43 (−9)	15 (+2)	1 (−)	4 (+1)	3 (−1)	−8	59 (−2)
45–54	48 (−)	34 (−6)	12 (+3)	1 (−)	3 (+1)	2 (−1)	+14	71 (−)
55–64	54 (+11)	26 (−16)	12 (+4)	3 (−1)	4 (+3)	2 (+1)	+28	72 (−9)
65+	61 (−2)	21 (−5)	12 (+7)	3 (−)	2 (−1)	1 (−1)	+40	77 (−7)
Ethnic group								
White	50 (+1)	31 (−7)	12 (+4)	3 (+1)	3 (+1)	2 (−)	+19	67 (−5)
Ethnic minorities	24 (+5)	59 (−13)	14 (+7)	0 (−1)	2 (+1)	1 (+1)	−25	59 (+7)
Household income[a]								
Under £15,600	46 (+12)	39 (−16)	6 (+4)	5 (+2)	3 (−1)	2 (−)	+7	49 (+8)
£15,600–46,799	51 (+5)	34 (−5)	10 (+2)	1 (−3)	3 (+2)	1 (−1)	+17	65 (−1)
£46,800 or more	43 (−7)	34 (−3)	17 (+6)	2 (−)	3 (+1)	1 (−)	+9	75 (−8)
Social class[b]								
ABC1	45 (−2)	32 (−4)	14 (+4)	1 (−)	3 (+2)	5 (−)	+13	73 (−3)
C2DE	43 (+4)	36 (−14)	9 (+6)	3 (−)	2 (+1)	7 (+4)	+7	56 (+2)

(continued)

Table 14.1 (continued)

| | Con | Lab | Lib Dem | Brexit Party (vs UKIP 2017) | Green | Other | Con-Lab lead | Turnout (all) |
	2019 (change vs 2017)							
	%	%	%	%	%	%	± %	%
Qualifications								
No qualifications	55 (+4)	33 (−5)	6 (+2)	4 (−2)	1 (+1)	1 (−)	+22	52 (−8)
Other qualifications	52 (+5)	30 (−13)	10 (+5)	3 (+1)	3 (+1)	1 (−)	+22	62 (−1)
Degree or higher	38 (−3)	39 (−4)	16 (+4)	1 (−)	4 (+2)	1 (−1)	−1	78 (−3)
2016 EU referendum vote								
Remain	25 (−8)	49 (−3)	20 (+7)	0 (−)	4 (+3)	1 (−)	−24	83 (−3)
Leave	74 (+13)	16 (−11)	3 (−)	5 (−)	1 (−1)	2 (−)	+58	75 (−4)
2017 vote								
Con	86 (−)	5 (−3)	7 (+3)	1 (−)	1 (−)	1 (−)	+81	82 (−7)
Lab	11 (+4)	79 (−9)	6 (+3)	1 (+1)	2 (+1)	0 (−1)	−68	83 (−2)
Lib Dem	15 (−3)	19 (−8)	60 (+8)	0 (−)	4 (+1)	1 (+1)	−4	91 (−3)

Base: 2,643 adults aged 18+, interviewed by multiple modes (1,420 interviews by computer-assisted personal interview (CAPI), 877 online and 346 postal), 12 December 2019 to 13 July 2020. Weighted to actual results by self-reported vote

[a] In the 2017 BES, the income bands are: under £15,600; £15,600–44,999; and £45,000 or more

[b] The National Statistics Socio-economic classification (NS-SEC) is recoded to approximate to the National Readership Survey (NRS) measures of social grade: where 'Large employers and higher managerial and administrative occupations' (1.1), 'Higher professional occupations' (1.2), 'Lower managerial, administrative and professional occupations' (2), 'Intermediate occupations' (3) and 'Small employers and own account workers' (4) are coded as ABC1 (upper, middle and lower middle class), and 'Semi-routine occupations' (6), 'Routine occupations' (7) and 'Never worked and long-term unemployed' (8) are coded as C2DE (working class and non-working)

Conservative support increased dramatically among Brexit backers across the two elections.[14] Much of this gain came soon after the referendum: Conservative support among Leavers had already risen from under 40% just before the EU referendum to nearly 70% at the 2017 general election. Support among Leavers then faded as the Brexit plans of Theresa May's government floundered, before collapsing in the spring and summer of 2019 in the wake of the failure of May's Withdrawal Agreement and the emergence of the Brexit Party. The Conservatives' fortunes with Leave voters then rebounded under Boris Johnson, and the party rose to a new peak of around 80% by the time of the 2019 election. On the other side of the Brexit divide, the Conservative vote share among Remainers declined steadily throughout the post-Brexit period (Fig. 14.3). The cumulative loss was substantial—around a third of the voters who then backed remaining in the EU supported David Cameron's Conservatives in 2015, but four years later, only 11% of current Remain supporters still backed the party under Boris Johnson.[15]

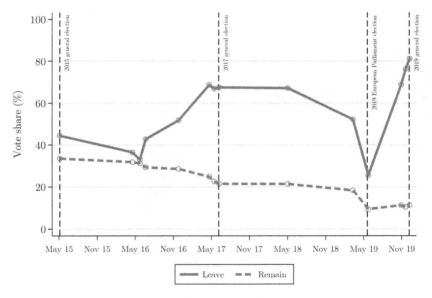

Fig. 14.3 Conservative share of the vote among Leavers and Remainers, BESIP England and Wales, 2015–2019

Labour support skewed towards those who favoured remaining in the EU even before the referendum was held, and the balance of the party's support did not shift much in the immediate aftermath (see Fig. 14.4). Labour made gains across the Brexit divide in the 2017 election, albeit slightly larger gains among Remainers. Labour then started leaking Leave *and* Remain supporters at fairly similar rates during the course of 2017–2018, but the party's Remain support then collapsed to a greater extent than its Leave support around the time of the European Parliament elections in May 2019. Labour recovered more Remainers than Leavers in the second half of 2019, suggesting that the party's strengthened commitment to a second referendum had tipped the balance of its appeal towards Remain.

The Liberal Democrats steadily gained support among Remainers following the 2016 referendum, only to lose them during the 2017 election campaign. The party then recovered Remain supporters between June 2017 and March 2019, before surging to new heights in May 2019

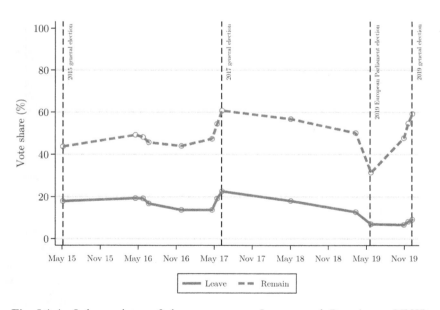

Fig. 14.4 Labour share of the vote among Leavers and Remainers, BESIP England and Wales, 2015–2019

(see Fig. 14.5). In this context, it is understandable that the Liberal Democrats came to believe they were on the cusp of an electoral breakthrough. However, just as in 2017, the party was unable to hold on to its new support in the general election campaign. Liberal Democrat support among Remainers fell around ten points during the 2019 campaign, with these voters mostly switching (back) to Labour. Although Leave voters represented only a small part of the Lib Dems' support base, the steady decline in the party's popularity among Leavers left it needing even larger advances with Remainers to stay competitive in most of its target seats.

Accounts of the geography of the 2019 election have highlighted the critical importance of Conservative breakthroughs in the 'Red Wall' in delivering the new government's large majority (see Chapter 13). But were the voters in these Labour seats in the Midlands and North of England any different from the rest of the electorate, or were these just the seats where the voters most prone to swing to the

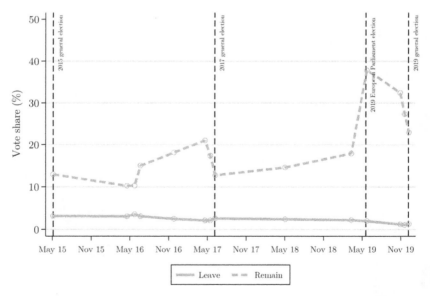

Fig. 14.5 Liberal Democrat share of the vote among Leavers and Remainers, BESIP England and Wales, 2015–2019

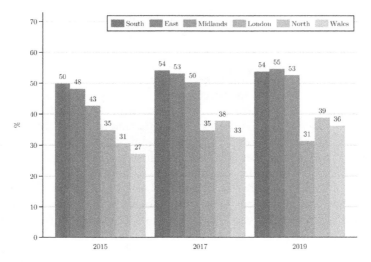

Fig. 14.6 Conservative vote share by region in the 2015, 2017 and 2019 elections, BESIP England and Wales

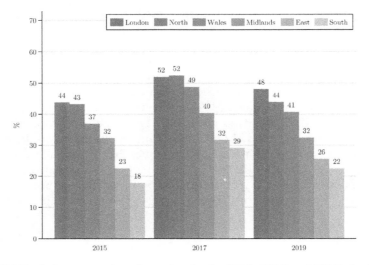

Fig. 14.7 Labour vote share by region in the 2015, 2017 and 2019 elections, BESIP England and Wales

Conservatives happened to be most concentrated or most influential? Looking first at regional variations in Conservative and Labour support across the 2015, 2017 and 2019 elections, we find a number of notable changes (see Figs. 14.6 and 14.7). There is a significant shift in the regional balance of Conservative support between 2015 and 2019, with the party's support rising more in the Midlands (up 10 points) and North (up 8) than the South (up 4). The Midlands are now as strong for the Conservatives as its traditional South and East heartlands, while London has fallen behind Wales and the North to become the Conservatives' weakest region outside of Scotland.[16] There is less change in the regional balance of Labour's vote over the three elections—Labour support rises and falls across all regions in concert. This suggests that any change in the geography of party competition in England and Wales was driven by a shift in the regional basis of Conservative rather than Labour support.

At what point did the seats in the 'Red Wall' in particular start to come under threat from the Conservatives? A comparison of the preferences of voters residing in the 40 constituencies identified as the 'Red Wall' by electoral strategist James Kanagasooriam (see Chapter 8) with those of voters in the other constituencies in England and Wales reveals an interesting trend (see Fig. 14.8). At the 2015 election, the Conservative vote was 10 points lower in the Red Wall seats than the average in all other constituencies. This gap narrowed steadily in the wake of the EU referendum, and by December 2019 had nearly vanished. By comparison, Labour started some 12 points higher on average in Red Wall seats than other seats in 2015, and largely retained this advantage until June 2017—with a similar campaign surge that year in the Red Wall seats as elsewhere (see Fig. 14.9). It is only after the 2017 election that Labour's advantage in the Red Wall began to decline, falling to just 6 points by December 2019. The fall of the Red Wall was the product of a pincer movement—a Conservative advance from 2016 onwards, which combined with relative Labour decline after 2017 to put many of these once-safe Labour seats in jeopardy.

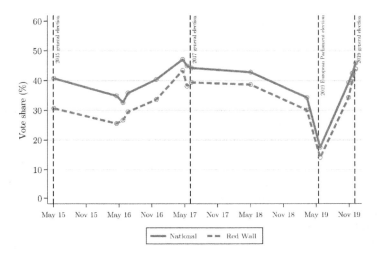

Fig. 14.8 Conservative vote share in 'Red Wall' constituencies and other England and Wales constituencies, BESIP, 2015–2019

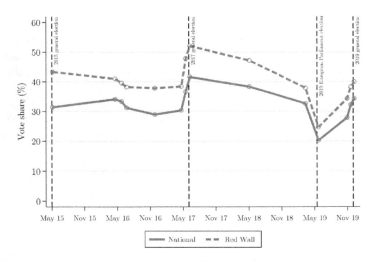

Fig. 14.9 Labour vote share in 'Red Wall' constituencies and other England and Wales constituencies, BESIP, 2015–2019

LABOUR'S LOST VOTERS

In October 2019, the Conservative think-tank Onward identified 'Workington man' as the crucial swing voter that either party had to attract to secure a majority:

> 'Workington Man' is … likely to be over 45 years old, white, does not have a degree and has lived in his home for over 10 years. He voted to Leave the EU in 2016 and thinks the country is moving away from his views both economically and culturally.[17]

This characterisation proved prescient. The Conservatives' 2019 victory was built on leads among the over-45s, male voters, white voters, Leave supporters, those with lower educational attainment and homeowners. The relative concentration of many of these groups in former industrial areas in the North, the Midlands and Wales was at the root of Labour's struggles in the 'Red Wall'.

Whilst Conservative gains were concentrated, Labour's eight point overall fall in vote share scattered in several directions. The voters that Labour lost directly to the Conservatives—a large group by historical standards—were quite different from those lost to the bloc of parties taking a firmer Remain stance, namely the Liberal Democrats, the Greens and Plaid Cymru.[18] Labour's efforts to bridge the Brexit divide ended up costing them votes from both Brexit tribes. We can use the BESIP to pinpoint the characteristics and attitudes which predicted defection among 2017 Labour voters in England and Wales to the Conservatives on the one hand, and to the Remain bloc of parties on the other. Of the 3,061 BESIP respondents who reported a Labour vote in 2017, the party lost 320 Leave voters to the Conservatives and 328 Remain voters to the Remain parties. Yet while Labour lost equally on the Leave and Remain flanks in *absolute* terms, this represented a much larger *proportional* loss of Leavers, who were already a minority of Labour's coalition in 2017. Over 40% of Leavers who voted Labour in 2017 defected to the Conservatives, while 15% of the 2017 Labour Remainers switched to another Remain party in 2019.[19]

A small but important minority of Labour voters in the BESIP switched directly to the Conservatives (around 12% of 2017 Labour voters). If we look only at these voters' demographic characteristics, we can see the 'Workington Man' pattern quite clearly—the probability of switching from Labour to the Conservatives was substantially higher for non-graduates (15 vs 7% for graduates), for those aged 45–64 (12%)

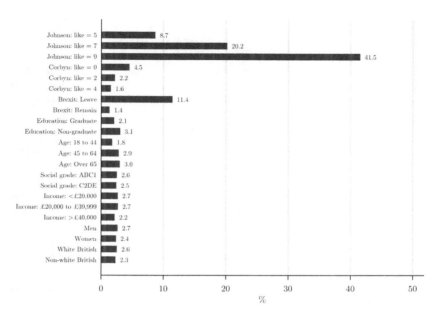

Fig. 14.10 Probability of switching from Labour (2017) to Conservative (2019) in England and Wales, BESIP

and over 65 (13 vs 6% for those under 45), and working-class voters (14 vs. 9% for middle-class voters). However, most of the demographic differences disappear once we add voters' Brexit preferences and views of the leaders into our model, as Fig. 14.10 illustrates. This chart depicts the probability of individuals with particular characteristics switching their vote directly from Labour in 2017 to the Conservatives in 2019.[20] Once we control for Brexit preferences and attitudes to the leaders, there are not large demographic differences in rates of switching to the Conservatives.[21] The effects of such underlying demographic factors tend to work *through* differences in voters' Brexit preferences and evaluations of the leaders. In other words, it was stronger support for Brexit and more positive views of Johnson which led older voters, non-graduates and so on to switch to the Conservatives at higher rates.

The highest rate of Labour to Conservative switching is found among those with positive views of Boris Johnson. Over 4 in 10 of otherwise average 2017 Labour voters who rated Johnson at 9 out of 10 are predicted to switch to the Conservatives, as are a fifth of those who rated the Conservative leader at 7 out of 10, and nearly 1 in 10 of those who rated Johnson at 5 out of 10. Leave support is also associated with switching to the Conservatives, on top of views of Johnson—roughly one in ten 2017 Labour Leavers with otherwise average characteristics are expected to switch. Strongly disliking Jeremy Corbyn (0 out of 10 likeability) was also associated with a higher probability of switching to the Conservatives, but negative views of Corbyn were weaker predictors of switching to the Conservatives than positive ratings of Johnson in a model including views of both leaders. This data, at least, suggests that Labour's 2019 losses to the Conservatives were driven more by the attraction of Johnson than the toxicity of Corbyn.

But there is more to it than that. Judgements of the leaders are themselves influenced by other considerations—for example, Leave supporters were unsurprisingly more positively disposed towards a leader campaigning to 'get Brexit done'. Likewise, particular demographic groups (e.g. older and working-class voters) were more likely to favour Brexit. In practice, it therefore seems likely that Johnson's appeal to some parts of the Labour electorate was itself driven by his strong personal association with the cause of Brexit—and support for Brexit was in turn strongest among particular groups of voters. The appeal of Johnson was inextricably linked to the desire for Brexit among frustrated Leave voters.

Labour also suffered substantial losses to the 'Unite to Remain' parties—the Liberal Democrats, Plaid Cymru and the Greens. In a model looking only at demographic factors (Fig. 14.11), Labour suffered the highest rates of defection to the Remain alliance among graduates, high-income voters and the middle class (ABC1 voters). Once we include views of Brexit and leader evaluations, the latter again emerge as critical, but in this case it is views of the Labour leader which have the biggest effect. Negative evaluations of Jeremy Corbyn ('0', strongly dislike on an 11-point scale) are the strongest predictor of switching away from Labour among this group, with 25% of otherwise average 2017 Labour voters who gave Corbyn the lowest ratings predicted to switch to the Remain alliance instead. Positive views of Swinson are also associated with higher defection—a fifth of otherwise average 2017 Labour voters who gave Liberal Democrat leader Jo Swinson the highest marks are predicted to switch. Unsurprisingly, Remain support also predicts defection to the Remain alliance—around 1 in 10 otherwise average 2017 Labour Remainers are predicted to switch to another Remain party in 2019.

However, as we saw in the discussion of Labour to Conservative defections, the strong effects of leader assessments reflect how

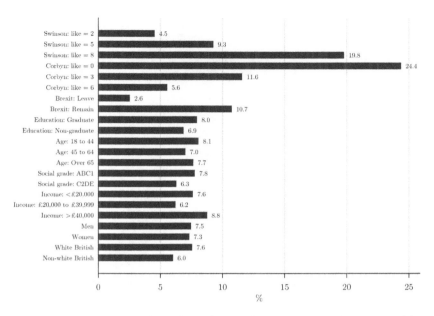

Fig. 14.11 Probability of switching from Labour (2017) to the Remain bloc (2019) in England and Wales, BESIP

judgements of leaders themselves encapsulate a wider set of attitudes, which are then structured in turn by demographic factors. If evaluations of party leaders are removed from the model, then having voted Remain becomes the strongest predictor of defection from Labour to the other Remain parties. On the Remain side of the divide, as on the Leave side, perceptions of party leaders were bound up with Brexit attachments—Leave partisanship was associated with more positive views of Johnson among Labour voters, while Remain partisanship was associated with more negative views of Corbyn. Labour's balancing act on Brexit was in this respect a failure—it tarnished Corbyn in the eyes of Remainers, while failing to blunt the appeal of Johnson to Leave voters.

We can also look at the 2019 election through a different lens by setting aside views of leaders and Brexit, and focusing instead on underlying value divides in the electorate. In Figs. 14.12 and 14.13, we look at how voters' positions on two value dimensions—the traditional economic value divide over free markets and the role of the state, and the 'liberal-authoritarian' divide between individual rights and liberties, and

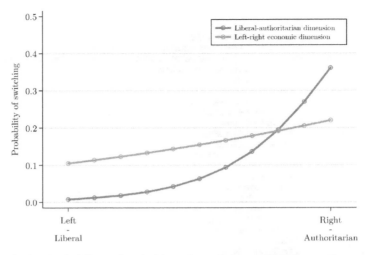

Fig. 14.12 Probability of switching from Labour (2017) to Conservative (2019) in England & Wales by left–right & liberal-authoritarian values, BESIP

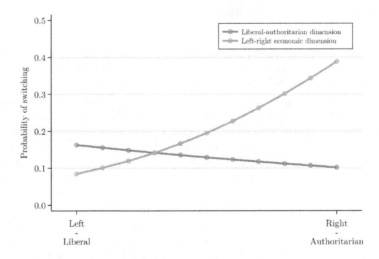

Fig. 14.13 Probability of switching from Labour (2017) to the Remain bloc (2019) in England & Wales by left–right & liberal-authoritarian values, BESIP

respect for authority and tradition—predicted switching from Labour to the Conservatives and to the other Remain parties.[22] Traditional economic values still play a role in switching to the Conservatives, with more economically right-wing 2017 Labour voters switching at higher rates than very left-wing voters. But liberal-authoritarian values have a larger effect at both ends of the spectrum—the most socially liberal 2017 Labour voters were more loyal to the party than the most economically left-wing voters, while the most authoritarian 2017 Labour voters were far more likely to switch to the Conservatives than the most economically right-wing 2017 Labour voters. Over a third of Labour's most authoritarian 2017 supporters backed the Conservatives in 2019.

Yet while authoritarian values most strongly predict switching from Labour to the Conservatives, it is right-wing economic values which most strongly predicted switching from Labour to the Remain bloc—almost 40% of the most economically right-wing 2017 Labour voters predicted a switch to other Remain parties. By contrast, the probability of switching to the Liberal Democrats, the Greens and Plaid Cymru is highest among the most socially liberal Labour voters, and declines as we move to more authoritarian views. One possible interpretation of these results is that Labour faced distinct problems on different ideological dimensions with Leave and Remain voters—Corbyn's Labour were perhaps seen as too socially liberal by the authoritarian Leave voters it lost, while also being seen as too economically left wing by voters defecting to other Remain parties, and perhaps also by the Remainers Labour were unable to attract from the Conservatives.

THE FOUR TRIBES OF SCOTTISH ELECTORAL POLITICS

As was discussed further in Chapter 12, the election in Scotland involved the collision of two questions of sovereignty, Brexit and Scottish independence, which have divided voters into four 'tribes': 'Yes Remainers', 'Yes Leavers', 'No Remainers' and 'No Leavers'.[23] The balance of the election in Scotland was ultimately shaped by the size of these groups and who they voted for. These distinct blocs of the electorate are partly evident in the demographic and political breakdown of the vote presented in Table 14.2.[24]

While constitutional questions dominate Scottish politics, there are also demographic patterns worth noting. The first is the steep age gradient, with the SNP strongest among younger voters (much like Labour

Table 14.2 Demographics of the vote in Scotland, BESIP, wave 19 (post-election wave)

	SNP	Con	Lab	Lib Dem	Other	SNP-Con lead
	%	%	%	%	%	±%
All	45	25	18	10	2	+20
Gender						
Male	43	27	18	9	3	+16
Female	46	22	19	11	2	+24
Age						
18–24	54	18	19	6	3	+36
25–34	56	11	22	10	1	+45
35–44	48	16	23	10	4	+32
45–54	46	24	20	8	2	+22
55–64	46	24	18	9	2	+22
65+	33	39	13	13	2	−6
Housing tenure						
Owned	36	35	14	13	2	+1
Mortgage	43	20	23	11	3	+23
Social renter	56	16	20	5	3	+40
Private renter	56	12	22	8	2	+44
Qualifications						
No qualifications	43	30	18	8	1	+13
Other qualifications	44	28	17	8	2	+16
Degree or higher	46	20	18	13	2	+26
EU referendum voting intention (current)						
Remain	58	6	21	13	2	+52
Leave	17	63	11	4	4	−46
Scottish independence voting intention (current)						
Yes	80	2	13	3	2	+78
No	9	50	23	16	3	−41
2017 vote						
SNP	89	4	4	1	1	+85
Con	3	77	7	11	2	−74
Lab	26	9	55	7	2	+17
Lib Dem	15	14	7	61	2	+1

Base: 2,969 adults aged 18+, interviewed online 13–23 December 2019. Weighted to actual results by self-reported vote

south of the border) and older voters favouring the Conservatives in Scotland as they do in England and Wales. Scottish Labour did best among people between their mid-twenties and mid-forties. The SNP also had a large lead among those living in rented properties, whereas Scottish Conservatives were more likely to own their homes. Unlike England and Wales, there was no large educational divide. Both SNP and Labour support was drawn fairly evenly from university graduates and those with no qualifications. The Conservative vote was slightly more likely to have no educational qualifications, while the Liberal Democrat voter was slightly higher among graduates.

Turning to the four constitutional 'tribes', Yes Remainers made up the largest group in December 2019 (36% of the electorate), No Leavers the next-largest group (25%), followed by No Remainers (20%) (see Fig. 14.14). People not aligned to any tribe, due to their not expressing

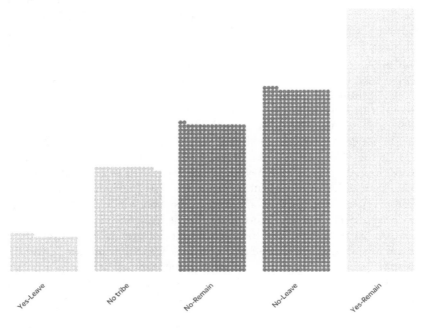

Fig. 14.14 The size of Scotland's constitutional tribes in December 2019, BESIP

a view on Scottish independence or Brexit (or both), made up 14% of the electorate, while Yes Leavers made up just a small fraction (5%). Using the BESIP, we can examine how the vote choices of each constitutional tribe have evolved from 2015 to 2019. Yes Remainers (Fig. 14.15) strongly align with the SNP, though with some variations: SNP support in this group peaked at the 2015 election, which was held soon after the independence referendum, and was somewhat lower at both the 2017 and 2019 general elections. Labour made some inroads in relation to this group in 2018, but lost most of these gains by the 2019 general election. The SNP has also lost some ground since 2015 in the smallest tribe of Yes Leavers, with the Conservatives in particular making gains in 2019, probably by recruiting members of this group who prioritise Brexit over independence.

The No Remainers were the tribe most up for grabs: all four large Scottish parties polled above 20% with this group at some point, and three out of the four held the lead (see Fig. 14.16). Labour secured over 40% of this group in 2015, fell to under 30% around the time of the EU referendum, then recovered by the time of the 2017 election. Labour's support among No Remainers declined steadily thereafter, with the Liberal Democrats the main beneficiaries. Labour then recovered some ground again in the 2019 election campaign, pushing the Lib Dems back into second place. But both the SNP and the Conservatives won substantial slices of the vote in this group as well, suggesting that the internal tensions in No Remain voters' constitutional preferences left them at least somewhat open to multiple parties' appeals.

The biggest political re-alignment among the four Scottish tribes was in the 'No Leave' bloc. In May 2015, the Scottish Conservatives won close to 40% of these voters (see Fig. 14.17). This rose to over 50% by the EU referendum, and by the 2017 election, the Scottish Conservatives won 70% of the No Leave vote—a lead of more than 50 points over Scottish Labour. As Brexit became hardwired into the Scottish party system, the long-moribund Scottish Conservatives have found a new political purpose as the natural home for unionist Brexiteers. Despite Johnson's very poor ratings among Scottish voters overall (see Chapter 12), the Scottish Conservatives were able to rally support from the No Leave vote, nearly 80% of whom voted Conservative in 2019.

Together, these trends reveal how Scottish politics has been re-aligned by two divisive constitutional questions: whether Scotland should remain part of the UK and whether the UK should leave the EU. The growing alignment of No Leave support with the Conservative vote and

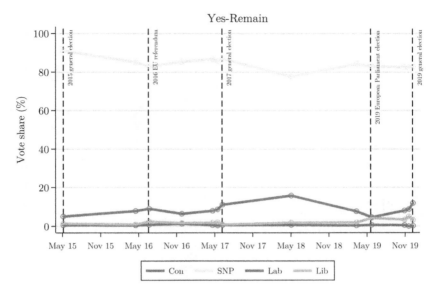

Fig. 14.15   Party share of the Yes Remain vote, Scotland BESIP, 2015–2019

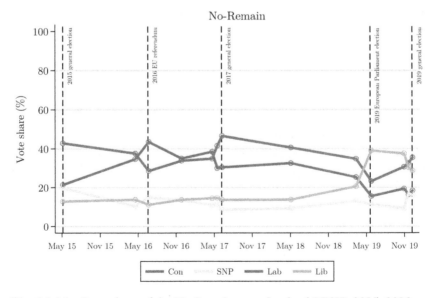

Fig. 14.16   Party share of the No Remain vote, Scotland BESIP, 2015–2019

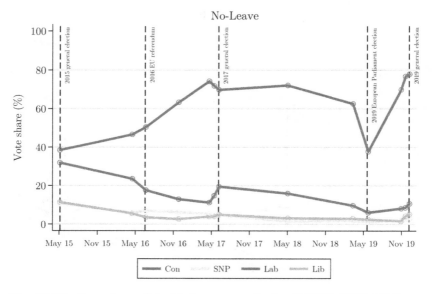

Fig. 14.17   Party share of the No Leave vote, Scotland BESIP, 2015–2019

Yes Remain behind the SNP has squeezed out Labour and the Liberal Democrats with these groups. It is perhaps only the persistence of a large, cross-pressured No Remain electorate that has kept what are now the third parties of Scottish politics alive in an era of polarised constitutional conflict.

A SURPRISINGLY STABLE CAMPAIGN?

After the dramatic upheavals of 2017, what surprised many about the 2019 contest was how little public opinion moved. In 2017, Jeremy Corbyn and Labour had advanced dramatically over the short campaign, and almost closed what seemed like an unassailable lead for Theresa May and the Conservatives by election day. By contrast, 2019 delivered the election many had expected in 2017. The Conservatives once again entered the contest with a big poll lead and a more popular leader, and once again sought an electoral mandate to deliver Brexit. But this time, the campaign changed little.

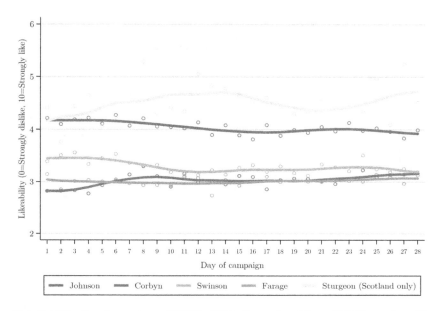

Fig. 14.18 Leader ratings, BESIP, 2019 Campaign Wave (13 November–11 December)[26]

Using the rolling campaign survey run by the BES, we can see how voters' views of all the main party leaders evolved day by day from 13 November through to polling day itself (see Fig. 14.18). Voters' assessments of all the leaders barely budged over these four weeks.[25] The overall mood was 'none of the above', with every party leader on average more disliked than liked (on an 11 point scale from 0 for 'Strongly dislike' to 10 for 'Strongly like'). During the campaign, 40% of respondents gave Boris Johnson a positive rating (greater than 5 on the 11 point scale), followed by Nigel Farage on 26%, Jeremy Corbyn on 23% and Jo Swinson on 20%. In Scotland, 44% of voters gave Nicola Sturgeon a positive score. Johnson's and Swinson's scores declined a little over the short campaign, and Corbyn's rose a little, but the movements were pretty minor. Voters seemed fairly settled in their views of all the party leaders.

This stability was in stark contrast to the 2017 campaign, as Fig. 14.19 illustrates. In that election Corbyn had started off well behind the incumbent Prime Minister, Theresa May, whose ratings were well

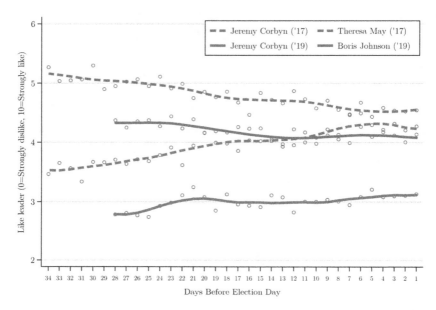

Fig. 14.19 Conservative and Labour leader ratings, BESIP, 2017 and 2019 Campaign Waves (*Note* 2017 BES campaign wave 5 May–7 June; 2019 BES campaign wave 13 November–11 December)

above her successor Boris Johnson's at the same point in 2019. This large initial gap in leader ratings was almost entirely wiped out over the 2017 campaign, as May's ratings slumped and Corbyn's popularity surged. One irony of 2019 was that Johnson triumphed where May failed despite starting and ending the campaign with significantly poorer ratings than his predecessor. Indeed, Johnson's ratings for most of the 2019 campaign were below Corbyn's ratings in 2017. Yet this still left Johnson well ahead of a much-diminished Labour leader, who began the campaign with much worse ratings than in 2017 and made little progress in the campaign. The controversies of the previous two years—such as the Salisbury poisoning, anti-semitism and Brexit—had left an indelible impression on the public. Johnson was thus able to deliver victory despite being less well liked than May, in part because their common opponent had in the interim become toxic in the eyes of many voters.

Insights from the Focus Groups

Focus groups, structured discussions led by a professional facilitator between a small group of people selected to reflect a particular demographic or political profile, are very popular with political parties as a way to better understand voters' thinking. They can cast light on the perceptions and motivations of voter groups in a more nuanced and granular way than polling data allows. Focus groups conducted by parties are seldom made public, as these are often used to understand the values and concerns of target voters and to test key messages for the campaign (see Chapter 8). As noted in earlier chapters, the slogan that came to define the 2019 election, 'Get Brexit done', itself emerged (in part) from focus group research, though both Johnson and May had used versions of it even before electric reactions in a focus group in Bury confirmed its appeal (see Chapter 1).

We here draw on insights from the unusually large number of focus groups conducted either during the campaign or in the immediate aftermath of the election whose results have been made public (see Table 14.3). Because the election was defined by the issue of Brexit, most of the focus groups were conducted in target seats selected based on their Brexit leanings. The most common locations were Labour-held constituencies in the Midlands, the North and Wales that had voted heavily for Leave in 2016. Some of these exercises were carried out for media clients, with James Johnson of JL Partners running groups covered on Channel 4 and James Morris of Edelman running groups reported by *HuffPost*. Others were commissioned by party grandees. Former Deputy Chair of the Conservative Party and sometime pollster Lord Ashcroft commissioned a series of 15 campaign focus groups in battleground seats. After the election, in January 2020, he ran a further 18 groups in former Labour constituencies as part of his report *Diagnosis of Defeat: Labour's Turn to Smell the Coffee*[27] (similarly, the Tony Blair Institute commissioned Deltapoll to conduct six focus groups in the last week of the campaign in three Labour heartland areas where the party's support had declined—Bishop Auckland, Walsall and Worksop (in the Bassetlaw constituency)).[28]

Consistent with the survey analysis above, two motives emerged clearly in focus groups of Labour-to-Conservative switchers or potential switchers: Brexit and the party leaders. These two concerns were very

Table 14.3 List of focus groups in England, Wales and Scotland during or soon after the 2019 election campaign

Organised by... (number of groups)	Date	Location	Sample
Lord Ashcroft (3)	Campaign, week of 8 November	Cambridge (Lab) Finchley & Golders Green (Lab) Richmond Park (Con)	Remain-voting Lib Dem targets
Lord Ashcroft (3)	Campaign, week of 15 November	Stoke-on-Trent North (Lab) Bolton North East (Lab) West Bromwich East (Lab)	Leave-voting Conservative targets
Lord Ashcroft (3)	Campaign, week of 22 November	Alyn and Deeside (Lab) Wrexham (Lab) Newport West (Lab)	Leave-voting Conservative targets in Wales
Lord Ashcroft (3)	Campaign, week of 29 November	Aberdeen South (Con) East Renfrewshire (Con) Glasgow North East (Lab)	SNP targets lost by the party in 2017
Lord Ashcroft (3)	Campaign, week of 6 December	Bishop Auckland (Lab) Warwick & Leamington (Lab) Wimbledon (Con)	Bellwether constituencies for the Conservative vote: a Leave-voting seat in the North, a 'middle England' seat won surprisingly by Labour in 2017; and a Remain-voting seat in London held by a re-instated rebel
Deltapoll (for the Tony Blair Institute) (6)	Final week of the campaign	Bishop Auckland Walsall Worksop (part of the Bassetlaw constituency)	Traditional Labour voters, some of whom had decided to not vote Labour in this election and others who were still considering whether to vote Labour

(continued)

Table 14.3   (continued)

Organised by... (number of groups)	Date	Location	Sample
JL Partners for Channel 4 (1)	Week commencing 25 November	A marginal constituency 'on the edge of Birmingham'	Leave-voting former Labour voters (2017)
Edelman (James Morris) (1)	14 November	Watford	Undecided voters
Edelman (James Morris) (1)	9 December	Peterborough	Undecided women voters
Lord Ashcroft (18)	January 2020	Bolsover Bridgend Burnley Don Valley Scunthorpe Sedgefield Stoke-on-Trent North West Bromwich East Wrexham	People who voted Labour in 2017, who did not vote or voted for other parties in 2019, or who voted Labour in 2015 but voted for other parties in 2017 and 2019

often rolled together in voters' minds. Corbyn was perceived as fence-sitting and indecisive on the central issue of the election, whereas Johnson was seen as offering the promise of resolution:

> The Labour Party, their stance on Brexit was just wishy-washy for ages and I still think it is now. The message that they send over, are they for Brexit or are they against Brexit? Jeremy Corbyn still hasn't said. (Male, Worksop, *Northern Discomfort*)

> You need somebody who's got direction, and he hasn't got any at all. (Male, Bishop Auckland, *Northern Discomfort*)

> I knew people were going to vote Tory because they were fed up with "are we or aren't we?" (Former Labour voter, *Diagnosis of Defeat*)

> It was easy because I wanted Brexit, and that alone told me I had to vote Conservative because Labour weren't going to go through with it. (Former Labour voter, *Diagnosis of Defeat*)

Some former Labour voters saw their vote as being a 'one-off', lent to elect a Conservative government with a mandate to deliver what people wanted and end an impasse which many voters found intensely frustrating.

> It was a vote to say "we're sick and tired of all the faff". People thought he [Johnson] had the balls to take control of Brexit. (Former Labour voter, *Diagnosis of Defeat*)

> Get Brexit done, because Brexit will be forever, but a government is just going to run its term and then we can vote again. (Labour held, Leave-voting constituency in Wales, Ashcroft)[29]

Focus group participants saw Johnson as a strong leader who had what it took to break the Brexit deadlock. This was contrasted with Corbyn's 'dithering' and evasion, highlighting how Labour's compromise approach to Brexit could negatively impact perceptions of the party's leader. Reservations remained about Johnson's personal character flaws ('If he'll lie to the Queen he'll lie to anybody'), but were set ultimately set aside:

> It feels like we've actually got a leader of the country. He comes across as passionate about the country and the people. If it's all a front, he does it very well. (Former Labour voter, *Diagnosis of Defeat*)

Corbyn was viewed as weak, with criticism of his lack of patriotism and distrust of his credentials on defence and national security recurring themes. Corbyn's meetings with terrorist organisations like the IRA and Hezbollah were frequently cited by voters as a cause for concern. Older stories like his refusal to sing the national anthem at a Battle of Britain memorial service in 2015 were joined by more recent events such as his equivocation over Russia's involvement in the Salisbury poisonings, which came together in voters' minds as evidence of a fundamental problem with the Labour leader:

> I like the Labour Party, I just don't like Jeremy Corbyn. (Female, Worksop, *Northern Discomfort*)

That's the extreme link he has, it's the link with the terrorists and his Israel views. His policies, I just think they're a flash in the pan, just quick "Free Wi-Fi for everybody, come on, get some votes in". (Male, Walsall, *Northern Discomfort*)

He is not patriotic. He meets all those terrorist parties. You want someone with good old values. (Former Labour voter, *Diagnosis of Defeat*)

He's anti-Royal as well. He refused to sing the national anthem. (Former Labour voter, *Diagnosis of Defeat*)

Distrust of Corbyn was not driven only by concerns on Brexit and national security. Focus group participants were also concerned was that he and Labour were too left-wing ('extreme', 'hard left', 'radical'), and that Labour's manifesto policies were unrealistic, incoherent and unaffordable. Voters also felt they were being bought off ('Free broadband – it was like someone in South America throwing money off the back of a lorry')[30]:

It was pie in the sky. People are not daft. (Former Labour voter, *Diagnosis of Defeat*)

There are just too many things free. I think you should be able to work for things and gain them. (Female, Walsall, *Northern Discomfort*)

I should vote for Corbyn's Labour because my youngest boy, he'd get at £6,000 year increase straight away. My wife who should have retired at 60, she'd be getting a back-dated pension. Where the hell is the money coming from? It's all very well saying "We'll do that". (Male, Bishop Auckland, *Northern Discomfort*)

There was a broader sense among these voters that Labour had moved away from the things they valued, while the Conservatives under Johnson had changed and now better represented the priorities of working people and for people who wanted to get on in life:

Labour: It's for young people and students, and the unemployed. It used to be for normal working people, who pay for their house, pay for their car. (Former Labour voter, *Diagnosis of Defeat*)

Conservatives: I think they've changed. They're more for the people, all the country, not just one class. It used to be that the Conservatives were for the rich, but I don't think that's true anymore. (Former Labour voter, *Diagnosis of Defeat*)

Anyone who's worked all their life, has bought a house, wants to keep hold of that, and that means the Conservatives. (Former Labour voter, *Diagnosis of Defeat*)

The decision to vote Conservative was still hard for some participants. Several of the groups highlighted that this wrenching break with past loyalties meant their voting might be more unpredictable in the future, with decisions made on a case-by-case basis rather than driven by long-standing party attachments:

There's no loyalty now. I'll take each case as it comes. (Former Labour voter, *Diagnosis of Defeat*)

It was easy for me, the simple fact that I couldn't possibly have voted for Corbyn, although I've been a Labour voter all my life. He was too far to the left. (Former Labour voter, *Diagnosis of Defeat*)

I'm not saying I would never go back to Labour. I'm voting Conservative on Thursday and it's the first I've ever voted Conservative.' (Male, Bishop Auckland, *Northern Discomfort*)

I think the working-class people; a lot of people are Labour, and they wanted to see the old Labour back that was going towards more the centre ground ... I think they can bring it back because I think most people, a lot of people from round here, they aren't Conservative so we're all struggling to know who to vote for. (Female, Walsall, *Northern Discomfort*)

Former Labour voters in Leave areas flirting with the Conservatives were not the only ones put in the focus group spotlight. At the beginning of the campaign, Lord Ashcroft conducted focus groups in three Remain-voting constituencies—Cambridge, Finchley & Golders Green[31] and Richmond Park[32]—which the Liberal Democrats were hoping to take, in part by winning over Conservative Remainers. There was much unease in these focus groups about the party's policy of revoking Article 50 (see Chapter 5), with participants worried that it would lead to social unrest:

'We'd have riots in the streets. It would be dangerous. To resolve it we need to put it to a vote.' Despite the feeling that unilaterally reversing Brexit went against democratic principles, it was the risk of a Corbyn government that most put off Conservative voters considering the Lib Dems:

> The only thing that would sway my vote is if I felt it was safe to vote for Luciana [Berger]. The thing stopping me voting for her is the fear of Jeremy Corbyn getting in. If I was feeling confident that he's so far behind in the polls that there's no chance he could get into power, I'd go with my hope rather than my head. My head is telling me, vote Conservative, my heart is telling me, actually, I'm going to vote for someone I believe in. (Former Conservative voter, Finchley & Golders Green)

> You could have the best Labour MP in the world standing and I would never vote Labour with Corbyn as leader because he's an anti-semite. A vote for him is a vote for extremism. (Former Conservative voter, Finchley & Golders Green)

This chimes with the survey evidence on Conservative Remainers' hostility to Corbyn and belief that a Corbyn-led government presented greater risks to the country than Brexit. Voters were taking a much harder, more critical look at the Labour leader than they had in 2017.

In Labour-held, Leave-voting seats in the 'Red Wall' targeted by the Conservatives, Lord Ashcroft's focus groups were asked what Jeremy Corbyn would do if he found himself unexpectedly free on a Friday night[33]:

> He'd go outside in the garden and sit on the fence all night.
> A nice sit-down dinner with someone who doesn't like Britain.

These impressions highlighted how far Corbyn had gone backwards since 2017, and was now seen as indecisive on Brexit and a sympathiser to Britain's enemies. What about Boris Johnson? Voters had no illusions about the Conservative leader.

> You know he's going to get up to something.
> A bit of a messy night out. It wouldn't be civilised. I think there would be apologies the next morning.

THE NEW POLITICAL DIVIDES IN LONG-TERM PERSPECTIVE

BES researchers have conducted surveys of the British electorate after every general election for many decades. We can use the resulting trove of data to examine how the demographic and attitudinal foundations of the parties' electoral coalitions have shifted over the four turbulent decades from Margaret Thatcher's first election win in 1979 to Boris Johnson's Brexit-busting majority in 2019. In the discussion and charts that follow, we focus on long-term changes in the support for the main governing parties, Labour and the Conservatives, to identify some of the longer-term trends which helped to shape the 2019 election outcome.

Education is a growing electoral fault line in many advanced democracies, and the expansion of higher education since the 1990s has increased the disruptive potential of political conflicts which divide graduates and non-graduates. In 1970, only around one in ten people attended university, limiting the impact of education divides. By 2019, around half of each cohort of 18-year-olds went on to university and over 40% of working-age voters now hold a degree.[34] Educational divides matter more now.[35]

Between 1979 and 2015, levels of Conservative support among university graduates and people with no qualifications tracked each other relatively closely. The 2017 general election provided the first hints of an educational divide, as the Conservatives' recruitment of support from the collapsing UKIP drove a sharp rise among the share of the party's voters with no qualifications, while at the same time the party's support declined among graduates (see Fig. 14.20a).[36] This trend accelerated in 2019, ballooning the education gap in Conservative support to 20 points, by far the largest seen in the past 40 years.

Labour traditionally did better amongst the least qualified than the most qualified, a reflection of the overlap between education divides and traditional class divisions. But declines in Labour support amongst the least qualified steadily narrowed this gap during the 2000s and 2010s (see Fig. 14.20b). In the first post-Brexit election of 2017, the education divide reversed, as Labour surged among graduates while support among those with no qualifications barely budged. In 2019, this new education divide grew further, to over ten points, as Labour's support among those with no qualifications dropped at a faster rate than it did among graduates.

Voters are also more divided by age than they used to be. There were claims—later contested—after the 2017 election that unprecedented

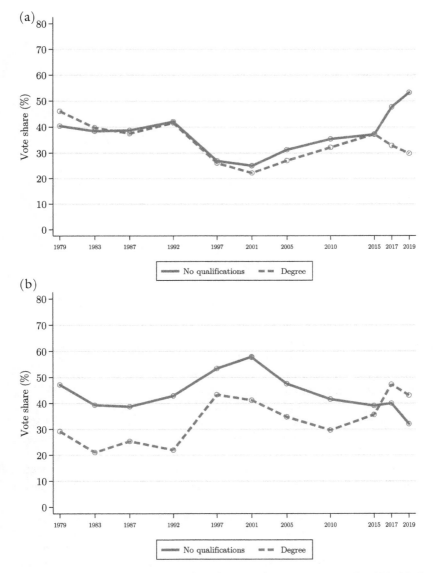

Fig. 14.20 a Conservative vote by educational attainment, BES 1979–2019. **b** Labour vote by educational attainment, BES 1979–2019

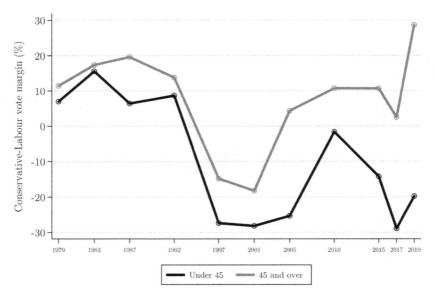

Fig. 14.21   Conservative-Labour vote margin by age, BES 1979–2019

mobilisation of young voters in a 'youthquake' had driven Labour's surprisingly strong performance.[37] The long-term trends do indeed suggest
a growing age divide in voting behaviour, but this first appears in the
2015 election, before Corbyn's 'youthquake' (Fig. 14.21). Big shifts in
behaviour have occurred at both ends of the age spectrum in the last
three elections. The Conservatives have made large and sustained gains
among older voters, while Labour similarly advanced with younger
groups in 2015 and 2017, then held on to more support among the
young in 2019. British party competition in the late 2010s has been a
conflict between the generations to a greater extent than in any other
period in the last 40 years.

As education and age divides have become more prominent, the political influence of social class has faded. Class differences in vote choice
between the routine and semi-routine occupations typically thought
of as 'working class' and the professional and non-manual occupations
thought of as 'middle class' have been declining since the early 1990s
(see Fig. 14.22a, b).[38] The class gap in Conservative support declined

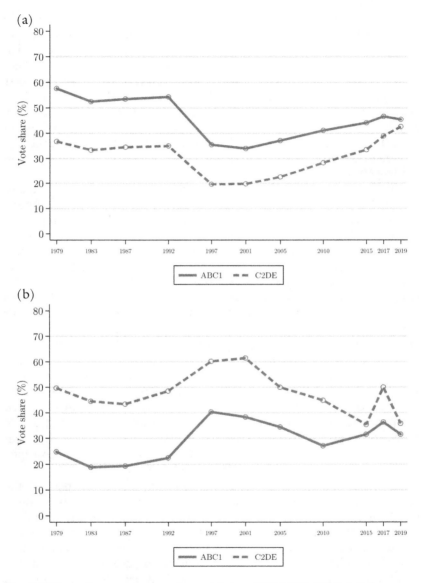

Fig. 14.22 **a** Conservative vote by social class, BES 1979–2019. **b** Labour vote by social class, BES 1979–2019

from around 20 points in 1979 to less than 5 points in 2019, driven in particular by steady increases in working-class Conservative voting from the 1990s onwards. The trend for Labour has been even more pronounced in the opposite direction (Fig. 14.22b), with sharper declines in working-class than middle-class support in every election from 2001 through to 2015, reducing the class divide in Labour voting from around 20 points in 1997 (and 25 points in 1979) to just a few percentage points in 2015. There was a small rebound in class voting in the 2017 election, but this largely reversed itself in 2019, when the link between class and Labour vote choice was weaker than at any point in the last 40 years.

These demographic shifts in the parties' electoral coalitions are also reflected in shifts in the issues and values which divide their supporters. We start with Europe, the focal point of the 2019 contest.[39] In 1979, pro-European voters leaned heavily towards the Conservatives (see Fig. 14.23a), with nearly two-thirds of pro-European Economic Community (EEC) voters backing the party. This reflected Margaret Thatcher's strong support for the EEC in the 1975 referendum, and a strong and vocal Eurosceptic tradition on the Labour left. By 2019, this situation had completely reversed. The Conservatives' embrace of Brexit have made them the party of choice for Eurosceptics, winning the support of four out of five Leavers (nearly double the share of Eurosceptics who had voted Tory just four years before).

In 1979, Labour secured around half the Eurosceptic vote (see Fig. 14.23b), a share which has been shrinking ever since. In 2019, just 12% of Leavers voted for Labour, while half of Remainers backed the party. The partisan divide in attitudes to Europe was turned upside down between the two referendums of 1975 and 2016, with Brexit itself accelerating the polarisation of voters between a now-Eurosceptic Conservative Party and a now more Europhile Labour Party.

The re-alignment of party competition stretches well beyond the issue of Europe. We see a similar trend on socially conservative values, which we can measure using attitudes to the death penalty, a stable indicator of such values available across 40 years of election studies.[40] The Conservatives have always done somewhat better among voters holding more 'authoritarian' views such as favouring the death penalty, but the party slowly lost ground among this group between 1979 and 1997—in part due to the Labour Party burnishing its law-and-order credentials.[41] This trend reversed after the Conservatives went into opposition in 1997

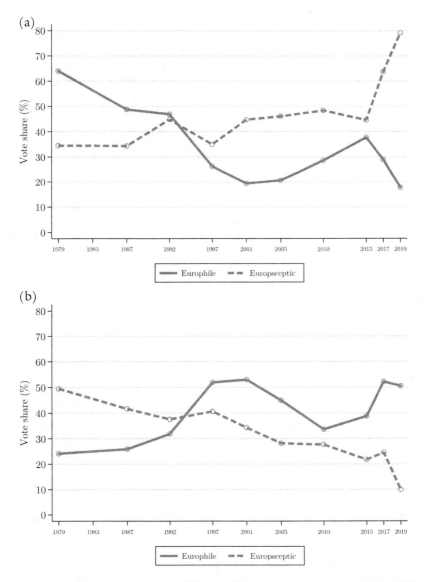

Fig. 14.23 a Conservative vote by attitudes to Europe, BES 1979–2019.
b Labour vote by attitudes to Europe, BES 1979–2019

and the party has been gaining ground with authoritarians ever since (Fig. 14.24a). The gap in Conservative support between death penalty supporters and opponents has grown dramatically in the last three elections, from under 15 points to over 30 points. A large majority of people who support the death penalty now back the Conservatives, while a large majority of death penalty opponents now reject the party. A similar values gap has opened up in Labour support. Labour have long done somewhat better among the socially liberal opponents of the death penalty (Fig. 14.24b), but support for the party on both sides of this values divide tended to rise and fall in parallel, until 2019, when Labour support fell much more sharply among death penalty supporters than opponents.

Using survey questions fielded in the BES (and in the British Social Attitudes Survey in years where data is not available in the BES), we can map how the average position of each party's supporters and voters overall on two dimensions—liberal-authoritarian values, and traditional economic values—over successive elections from 1992 to 2019.[42] Figure 14.25a plots the average position of the electorate as a whole, including non-voters, with relative left–right economic values (capturing preferences on redistribution, trade unions, public vs private ownership, and concern about income inequality) plotted on the x-axis, and liberal-authoritarian cultural values (capturing preferences on tradition, moral standards, tolerance and the right to protest) on the y-axis. The figure reveals that the average voter has steadily moved leftwards on the economic values scale since 1992. The biggest leftward shift occurred between 1992 and 1997, with another sizeable leftward shift between 2010 and 2015. By comparison, the leftward move of the electorate in 2019 was small, but still meant the average voter was more left-leaning on economic issues than at any point over the past three decades. The electorate has also steadily become more liberal in terms of its social values over this period, with the biggest shift occurring between 2010 and 2015. Once again, the most recent move in a liberal direction between 2017 and 2019 was modest, but left the electorate at its most liberal on cultural issues in 30 years. The Conservatives' electoral resurgence should not be taken as evidence of a broader shift to the right in the electorate; in fact, the opposite is the case on both economic and social value dimensions—Britain is slowly becoming a more left-liberal country.

When we break down the average positions of party supporters (Fig. 14.25b), we can see the two parties have followed very different

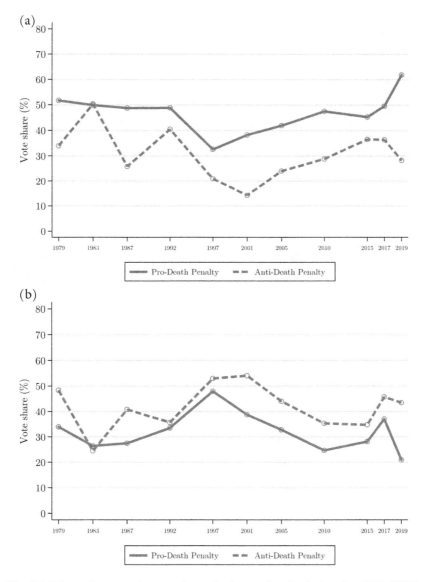

Fig. 14.24   **a** Conservative vote by attitudes to the death penalty, BES 1979–2019. **b** Labour vote by attitudes to the death penalty, BES 1979–2019

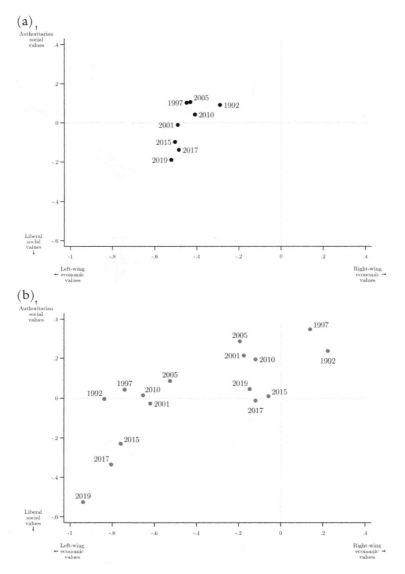

Fig. 14.25   a The values positions of voters, BES 1992–2019. **b** The values positions of voters by party, BES 1992–2019

paths. The Conservatives have remained relatively close to the average values of the electorate, while Labour voters have become steadily more distinctive on both dimensions. The average Conservative made a size-able leftward shift on economic values since the 1990s and, with some fluctuations, has moved steadily in a more socially liberal direction too. Though the Conservatives became a little more authoritarian in 2019, the shift was minor and did not reverse the longer-term liberal shift. Today's average Conservative voter is very different from their 1990s predecessor—both more economically left wing and more socially lib-eral. The average Labour voter has moved even more, but in two distinct phases. The party's support became more economically right wing in the 1990s and 2000s, then since 2010, the average Labour voter has made a pronounced shift to the left on both cultural and economic values, with each successive election moving the average Labour voter further away from the average British voter, even though the whole electorate is slowly moving in the same direction. It is primarily Labour's large shift to the left on both dimensions over the past decade that has left the two parties' supporters further apart in 2019 than any previous election in the past 30 years.

THE BRITISH VOTER AFTER 2019

The result of the British general election of 2019 reflected both the dis-ruptions caused by the 2016 referendum and longer-term changes in the foundations of the parties' electoral coalitions. Without question, Brexit was a defining issue for many voters as they marked their ballot papers. The Leave vote coalesced behind the Conservatives, who won around three-quarters of it, with Brexit attachments helping the party retain the lion's share of their 2017 vote. Remain support was more frag-mented, with Labour winning just half and the Conservatives a substan-tial minority despite their clear commitment to getting Brexit done. For Conservative Remainers, disagreement with the party on Brexit was not sufficient cause to risk a Corbyn premiership. Labour's 2017 coalition crumbled, losing Leave and Remain supporters in equal measure, though in relative terms this meant losing a larger share of the Leave voters that the party had won in 2017. Labour's promise of a new Brexit deal was not enough to head off Boris Johnson's appeal to Leave voters, and the party's promise of a second referendum did not prevent substantial losses to the Liberal Democrats and other Remain parties. Labour had little choice but to try and bridge the Brexit divide, given how the party's vote was distributed socially and geographically. But, in the end, the divide could not be bridged.

The 2019 election also demonstrated how the demographic profile of the parties has changed. The Conservatives secured a nine point swing from Labour among 'C2DEs', one traditional definition of the working class, a much larger swing than the party achieved among the middle-class 'ABC1s'. The large age divide in voting which opened up in 2017 was present once again, while the educational divide in the electorate continued to grow—the Conservatives held a sizeable lead among voters with no qualifications, but were marginally behind Labour among university graduates. Some of these headline figures can distort the picture of electoral change, especially where key social and economic trends are inter-linked. For example, due to educational expansion and changes in the economy, the share of working-class voters is shrinking among the pro-Labour young and growing amongst Conservative-leaning older cohorts, including the over 65s, a group mainly out of the labour market. Thus, while Labour trailed among C2DEs by seven points overall, it led by five points among working-age working-class voters (those under 65 in the same social class). While class is no longer a strong predictor of voting behaviour in Britain, it is a little premature to start calling the Conservative Party the party of the workers.

Views on the party leaders were closely related to patterns of vote switching in 2019. More positive assessments of Boris Johnson were a strong predictor of switching to the Conservatives among 2017 Labour voters, even more so than support for leaving the EU. However, the two are closely intertwined—views about Brexit shaped views of the leaders in an election where the question of who voters trusted to resolve Brexit loomed very large. And while Boris Johnson was less well-liked by voters in general than Theresa May had been two years previously, Jeremy Corbyn was considerably more unpopular too, giving the Conservatives a considerable leadership advantage. Dislike of Corbyn was a strong predictor of switching from Labour to the Unite to Remain parties, though this too was bound up with Brexit partisanship. Corbyn's ambivalence over Brexit increased his toxicity with strongly Remain voters, and cost Labour votes on this side of the Brexit divide too.

Labour's efforts to balance their message on Brexit were successful in one regard—the party lost Leave and Remain supporters in around equal numbers, suggesting that the compromise stance was equally unappealing to both camps. But this in fact meant that defection rates were much higher in relative terms among Labour Leave supporters, given that they represented a much smaller but important part of the 2017 Labour coalition. In a sense, both sides of the argument within the party over its strategy were right: those in LOTO who favoured focusing on Remainers were right that minimising the rate of loss from the much larger group of Remain supporters was vital, but their colleagues who wanted to prioritise Leavers proved correct in thinking that Leave-voting Labour supporters would be alienated by the party's embrace of a second referendum. If Labour had lost Remainers at an equivalent rate as Leavers, the result would have been electoral catastrophe. If they had lost Leavers in even greater numbers, the party's seat losses in traditional strongholds would have been even greater. The compromise agreed pleased neither side, but it is not obvious that the party would have done much better by embracing either side of the argument more fully. There were no easy answers.

Though Brexit loomed large in this election, the shifts in voter behaviour also reflected longer-term trends, including the disappearance of the traditional class divide within the electorate, with Britain no longer a 'two-class, two-party' system. In its place, educational and generational divides have emerged, making Labour the party of younger voters who are also more likely to have a university degree, while the Conservatives dominate among older voters with lower levels of educational attainment. These new divides do not map simply onto affluence or poverty, as higher levels of homeownership and a lack of exposure to the labour market put much of the growing grey vote in Britain in a quite different economic position, on average, than their younger counterparts. Such generational tensions are already influential and may become more so in future elections. More broadly, these long-term changes reflect the growing importance of value divides in the electorate, with evidence from the BES revealing how voters expressing socially conservative views have swung behind the Conservatives, even as the nation as a whole becomes more socially liberal. In 2019, the loyalties of voters on the liberal side of the value divide were scattered across a number of parties—Labour, the Lib Dems, the Greens, the SNP and Plaid Cymru—with this fragmentation giving a clear electoral advantage to the Conservatives, who managed to use Brexit to unite the other side of the value divide.

Notes

1. Maria Sobolewska and Robert Ford, *Brexitland*. Cambridge University Press, 2020.
2. The previous lowest combined Conservative and Labour vote share in European Parliament elections was 42.4% in 2009 (compared to the total of 24.4% in May 2019).
3. In recent elections (2015, 2017 and 2019), the BES has conducted both an online and a face-to-face survey of British voters after the general election. The online survey typically takes place over the few weeks immediately following the election and is designed to be nationally representative (with respondents drawn from the YouGov panel). The face-to-face survey, using random probability sampling, is fielded over a longer time period to allow for in-person interviewing. While both the surveys ask people who they voted for, differences in method, timing and random error can lead estimates of voting behaviour to differ somewhat. We draw on both data sources, as the online survey offers a much larger sample (around 30,000 respondents) and is fielded at a greater number of time points, while the face-to-face survey allows comparison over a more extended time period (back to 1979 for the purposes of this analysis) and the 'gold standard' random probability design is argued to be less susceptible to the over-representation of politically engaged respondents (see Patrick Sturgis, Nick Baker, Mario Callegaro, Stephen Fisher, Jane Green, Will Jennings, Jouni Kuha, Ben Lauderdale and Patten Smith, *Report of the Inquiry into the 2015 British General Election Opinion Polls.* National Centre for Research Methods, British Polling Council and Market Research Society, 2016). All survey data used in this analysis can be downloaded from the BES website (https://www.britishelection-study.com/data) via the *cross-sectional data* and *panel study data* pages (see Ed Fieldhouse, Jane Green, Geoffrey Evans, Jonathan Mellon and Christopher Prosser, *British Election Study Internet Panel Waves 1–19*, 2019; Ed Fieldhouse, Jane Green, Geoffrey Evans, Herman Schmitt, Cees van der Eijk, Jonathan Mellon and Christopher Prosser, *British Election Study, 2015: Face-to-Face Post-Election Survey. UK Data Service. SN: 7972*, 2016; Ed Fieldhouse, Jane Green, Geoffrey Evans, Herman Schmitt, Cees van der Eijk, Jonathan Mellon and Christopher Prosser, *British Election Study, 2017: Face-to-Face Post-Election Survey*, 2018; Ed Fieldhouse, Jane Green, Geoffrey Evans, Jonathan Mellon, Christopher Prosser, Roosmarijn de Geus and Jack Bailey, *2019 BES Post-Election Random Probability Survey v.1.1.1*, 2021.

4. The Brexit Party had not stood candidates in the 317 seats that the Conservative Party was defending—with voters only able to vote for it in 275 constituencies, which considerably depressed its overall vote share.

5. The BES face-to-face survey found that the Brexit balance of the electorate in England and Wales was 53% Remain to 47% Leave (in the 2017 general election, the balance had been 53–47% in the other direction). In 2019, the BES put the turnout gap between the two groups at 8% (see Table 14.1).

6. *Source*: BES face-to-face survey (for further methodological details, see Table 14.1). Note that using reported Leave/Remain vote (10,678 respondents) in Wave 9 (June/July 2016) of the BESIP (weighted to the 2019 result) gives a very similar vote breakdown: Leave=Conservative 75%, Labour 13%, Brexit Party 5%, Liberal Democrats 3%, Greens 2%, Other 2%; Remain=Labour 50%, Liberal Democrats 22%, Conservatives 21%; Greens 4%, Brexit Party 0%, Others 3%. (Using *earliest recorded* referendum vote in the BESIP gives the vote breakdown: Leave=Conservative 74%, Labour 14%, Brexit Party 5%, Liberal Democrats 3%, Greens 2%, Other 2%; Remain=Labour 53%, Liberal Democrats 22%, Conservatives 19%; Greens 4%, Brexit Party 0%, Others 2%.)

7. Will Jennings and Patrick Sturgis, 'Was There a "Youthquake" in the 2017 General Election?', *Electoral Studies* 64(102065) (2020), https://doi.org/10.1016/j.electstud.2019.102065a; Philip Cowley and Dennis Kavanagh, 'The Election in Retrospect' in *The British General Election of 2017*. Palgrave Macmillan, p. 419.

8. For purposes of comparison, these figures are based on weighting to self-reported vote. The validated vote weighting available for 2017 puts them at 63–27% (with the difference not statistically significant due to the small sample size of the under-35s subgroup, $N=192$).

9. These aggregations of occupational groups to the National Readership Survey (NRS) categories of middle and working class conceal some notable patterns in specific subgroups. Among voters in the skilled working class ('intermediate occupations', 'small employers and own account workers' and 'lower supervisory and technical occupations'), the Conservatives led Labour by 21 points (52–31%). Among the highest professional classes ('large employers and higher managerial and administrative occupations' and 'higher professional occupations'), Labour was marginally ahead (37–35%).

10. See Anthony Heath, Stephen Fisher, Gemma Rosenblatt, David Sanders and Maria Sobolewska, *The Political Integration of Ethnic Minorities in Britain*. Oxford University Press, 2013.

11. James Morris, 'Voters Haven't Forgotten That Boris Johnson Has a Problem with Women', *HuffPost*, 10 December 2019, https://

www.huffingtonpost.co.uk/entry/general-election-2019-boris-johnson_uk_5defb0d2e4b07f6835b9a59c.

12. The BES is traditionally conducted face-to-face, designed as a random probability sample. The exceptional circumstances of the COVID-19 pandemic led face-to-face fieldwork to be stopped on 18 March 2020. After a short pause in data collection, the remaining fieldwork was conducted online (using a 'push-to-web' design) and via a mail-in survey.

13. Differences in the timing and the survey methodology of the BES online panel and the face-to-face survey (as noted previously) can lead to slightly different headline figures.

14. In our analysis of trends in party support, we use current voting intentions for leaving or remaining in the EU (measured in the corresponding wave of the BESIP). This is because using the recorded vote at the time of the EU referendum in June 2016 (Wave 9) would reduce the sample size considerably. It would also exclude voters who have joined the electorate since and would not capture the sorting of partisans into Leave and Remain camps over time (in response to elite cues).

15. The Conservatives received a vote share of just 11% with respondents in the BESIP who backed remaining in the EU in December 2019 (Wave 19). This number was much lower than the 21% vote share among those who originally reported having voted Remain in June 2016 (Wave 9). This shrinkage of the Remain portion of the party's vote suggests that perhaps one in ten 2019 Conservative voters were one-time Remainers who switched their support to Leave over the course of this period.

16. The Conservatives also advanced in Scotland after 2015, though for rather different reasons. London was therefore the only region in Britain in which the Conservatives' vote share among BES panellists was no higher in 2019 than in 2015.

17. Will Tanner and James O'Shaughnessy, *The Politics of Belonging.* Onward, 2019, p. 19, https://www.ukonward.com/wp-content/uploads/2019/10/Politics-of-Belonging-FINAL.pdf.

18. And in Scotland, the SNP, but our analysis focuses here on England and Wales.

19. These figures suggest both sides in Labour's long-running Brexit campaign strategy debate (see Chapter 6) had a point—the pro-second referendum advocates were right that stemming Remain losses was more important in *absolute* terms, but the Leave-focused strategists were correct to claim that Labour had greater *relative* problems with its Leave voters, who were also more concentrated in marginal target seats (see Chapter 13). This distinction between absolute and relative losses was also highlighted by researchers during the 2019 campaign as a reason why the Brexit Party was very likely to pose a greater threat to the

Conservatives even if it succeeded in appealing more to Labour Leave than Conservative Leave voters, because there were simply a lot more Conservative Leave voters available to win. See Chris Prosser, 'The Brexit Party is a Threat to Boris Johnson, Not Jeremy Corbyn. Here's Why', UK in a Changing Europe, 6 November 2019, https://ukandeu.ac.uk/the-brexit-party-is-a-threat-to-boris-johnson-not-jeremy-corbyn-heres-why.

20. The figure plots the predicted probabilities from a multivariate logistic regression of a selection of independent variables (leader likeability, support for Leave or Remain, educational attainment, age, social grade, household income, gender and ethnicity) on the dichotomous outcome of whether individuals switched their vote from Labour to the Conservatives or not. The predicted probabilities hold all other variables at their means to allow direct comparisons of relative effects. The leader likeability scores are set at their mean value as well as one standard deviation below and above the mean *for those voters who switched* (because a large number of the voters are reliable partisans, there is clustering around the extreme values of the scale, which makes this more informative in seeking to understand what drove those voters who defected).

21. Because the variables for leader likeability and Brexit preferences are such strong predictors of vote switching for 2017 Labour voters, the baseline demographic predictors indicate a fairly low propensity of individuals to change their vote (once the former are held at their means). These demographic predictors indicate the lowest probability of switching in the Labour-to-Conservative model, where attitudes towards Boris Johnson and support for Leave dominate in terms of size of effect. The baseline propensity of these voters to switch to Remain-supporting parties is somewhat higher, as the effects of dislike of Corbyn and like of Swinson and support for Remain are relatively weaker.

22. Anthony Heath, Geoffrey Evans and Jean Martin, 'The Measurement of Core Beliefs and Values: The Development of Balanced Socialist/Laissez-Faire and Libertarian/Authoritarian Scales', *British Journal of Political Science*, 24 (1994): 115–58. These are composite scales each based on five survey items (using a five-point scale: 'strongly agree', 'agree', 'neither agree nor disagree', 'disagree', 'strongly disagree' and 'don't know'), as listed below:

> *Authoritarianism-liberalism:* 'Young people today don't have enough respect for traditional British values'; 'For some crimes, the death penalty is the most appropriate sentence'; 'Schools should teach children to obey authority'; 'Censorship of films and magazines is necessary to uphold moral standards'; 'People who break the law should be given stiffer sentences'.

Left–right: 'Government should redistribute income from the better off to those who are less well off'; 'Big business takes advantage of ordinary people'; 'Ordinary working people do not get their fair share of the nation's wealth'; 'There is one law for the rich and one for the poor'; 'Management will always try to get the better of employees if it gets the chance'.

23. James Mitchell and Ailsa Henderson, 'Tribes and Turbulence: The 2019 UK General Election in Scotland', *Parliamentary Affairs*, 73(1) (2020): 142–56, https://doi.org/10.1093/pa/gsaa027.
24. Analysis in this section uses the 3,223 Scottish voters from the post-election wave of the BESIP.
25. Over 90% of voters asked daily could express a view on Johnson, Corbyn and Farage, while the figure for the Liberal Democrats' less well-known leader Jo Swinson was typically closer to 80%. Less than half of voters could offer a view on the joint Green Party leaders Jonathan Bartley and Siân Berry, though they were well regarded by the minority of voters who were aware of them.
26. The line-of-best-fit for the figure is calculated with 'lowess' (locally weighed scatterplot smoothing).
27. Ashcroft had famously undertaken a study in 2005 on the Conservatives' electoral troubles, *Smell the Coffee: A Wake-up Call for the Conservative Party*. Both reports can be found on his website. See Lord Ashcroft, *Diagnosis of Defeat: Labour's Turn to Smell the Coffee*, February 2020, https://lordashcroftpolls.com/wp-content/uploads/2020/02/DIAGNOSIS-OF-DEFEAT-LORD-ASHCROFT-POLLS-1.pdf; and for the earlier report, see: https://lordashcroftpolls.com/wp-content/uploads/2011/12/smell-the-coffee.pdf.
28. Peter Kellner, Patrick Lougran and Deltapoll UK, *Northern Discomfort: Why Labour Lost the General Election*. Tony Blair Institute for Global Change, 2019. https://institute.global/sites/default/files/articles/Northern-Discomfort-Why-Labour-lost-the-General-Election.pdf.
29. Lord Ashcroft, 'My Latest Focus Groups from Three Leave-Voting, Labour-Held Tory Targets in Wales', *ConservativeHome*, 22 November 2019, https://www.conservativehome.com/platform/2019/11/lord-ashcroft-my-latest-focus-groups-from-three-leave-voting-labour-held-tory-targets-in-wales.html.
30. Ashcroft, *Diagnosis of Defeat*.
31. Where Luciana Berger was standing for the Liberal Democrats, having defected from Labour via Change UK (see Chapter 5).
32. Lord Ashcroft, 'My Focus Groups in Heavily Remain-Voting Liberal Democrat Targets', *ConservativeHome*, 8 November 2019, https://

www.conservativehome.com/platform/2019/11/lord-ashcroft-my-focus-groups-in-three-heavily-remain-voting-liberal-democrat-targets.html.

33. Lord Ashcroft, 'My Next Three Focus Groups in Labour-Held, Leave-Voting Constituencies', *ConservativeHome*, 15 November 2019, https://www.conservativehome.com/platform/2019/11/lord-ashcroft-my-next-three-focus-groups-in-labour-held-leave-voting-constituencies.html.

34. The share of graduates in the working-age population (21–64) rose from 24 to 40% between 2002 and 2017: https://www.ons.gov.uk/employmentandlabourmarket/peopleinwork/employmentandemployeetypes/articles/graduatesintheuklabourmarket/2017.

35. University education is also a strong predictor of turnout, magnifying the electoral power of graduates.

36. In earlier periods, there were substantial education gaps in support for the Liberal Democrats (who did best among graduates) and for UKIP and the BNP (who both did best among voters with no qualifications).

37. Sturgis and Jennings, 'Was There a "Youthquake" in the 2017 General Election?'; John Curtice and Ian Simpson, *Why Turnout Increased in the 2017 General Election and the Increase Did Not Help Labour*. NatCen Social Research, 2018; Christopher Prosser, Edward Fieldhouse, Jane Green, Jonathan Mellon and Geoffrey Evans, 'Tremors But No Youthquake: Measuring Changes in the Age and Turnout Gradients at the 2015 and 2017 British General Elections', *Electoral Studies*, 64 (2020): 102129, https://doi.org/10.1016/j.electstud.2020.102129.

38. Measures of social class in the BES differ slightly between some elections. We recode these into the broad categories of ABC1s (middle classes—including higher managerial, lower managerial, skilled non-manual and lower non-manual) and C2DEs (working classes—including skilled manual, unskilled or semi-skilled manual, and unemployed):

    1979: National Readership Survey social grade (A, B, C1A, C1B, C2, D categories), with respondents' assigned a social class using their father's social grade if no information was available.
    1983: Goldthorpe-Llewellyn class (ABC1: high-grade professional and managerial, low-grade professional and managerial, routine non-manual and petty bourgeoisie; C2DE: manual foreman and technicians, skilled manual, semi- and unskilled manual), using respondents' father's social class if no information was available.
    1987–1997: Registrar General's social class scheme (ABC1: professional, managerial/technical, skilled non-manual; C2DE: skilled manual, partly skilled, unskilled), using respondents' father's social class if no information was available.

2001: National Readership Survey social grade (A, B, C1, D2, D, E categories).

2005: Registrar General's social class scheme (ABC1: professional, managerial/technical, skilled non-manual; C2DE: skilled manual, partly skilled, unskilled), using respondents' father's social class if no information was available.

2010: Occupational class (ABC1: professional or higher technical work, manager or senior administrator, clerical, sales or services, small business owner; C2DE: foreman or supervisor of other workers, skilled manual work, semi-skilled or unskilled manual work), using parent/partner's social grade if no information was available or had never had a job.

2015–2019: National Statistics socio-economic classification (ABC1: large employers and higher managerial and administrative occupations, higher professional occupations, lower managerial, administrative and professional occupations, intermediate occupations, small employers and own account workers; C2DE: lower supervisory and technical occupations, semi-routine occupations, routine occupations), using parent's social grade if no information was available or never had a job.

39. Different questions have been asked about Britain's relationship with Europe (the EC, the EEC and the EU) in the BES. We code responses into Eurosceptic or pro-European categories, excluding respondents who are unsure or who favour neither side:

1979: Will staying in the Common Market make Britain better off or worse off, or will things stay about the same?/Will leaving the Common Market make Britain better off, worse off, or will stay the same? ('Better off', 'stay the same', 'worse off').

1987: Do you think Britain should continue to be a member of the EEC—the Common Market—or should it withdraw? ('Continue', 'withdraw').

1992–1997: Do you think Britain should continue to be a member of European Community or should it withdraw? ('Continue', 'withdraw').

2001–2010: Overall, do you approve or disapprove of Britain's membership in the European Union? ('Strongly approve', 'approve', 'neither', 'disapprove', 'strongly disapprove').

2015: If there was a referendum on Britain's membership of the European Union, how do you think you would vote? Would you vote to leave the EU or to stay in? ('Leave the EU', 'Stay in the EU', 'I would not vote').

2017–2019: If there was another referendum on Britain's membership of the European Union, how do you think you would vote? Would you vote to leave the EU or to stay in? ('Leave the EU', 'Stay in the EU', 'I would not vote').

40. Different questions have been asked about the death penalty in the BES over this period (with a missing value in 2015 replaced with a question from the British Social Attitudes Survey). We code responses into those in favour or against the death penalty, excluding respondents who are unsure or do not favour either side:

> 1979: I am going to read out a list of things that some people believe a government should do {Bringing back the death penalty}. For each one you can say whether you feel it is: 'Very important that it should be done'; 'Fairly important that it should be done'; 'It doesn't matter either way'; 'Fairly important that it should not be done'; 'Very important that it should not be done'; 'Don't know'.
> 1983: Britain should bring back the death penalty ('Agree', 'Not sure', 'Disagree').
> 1987: For some crimes the death penalty is the most appropriate sentence. ('Agree strongly', 'Agree', 'Neutral', 'Disagree', 'Disagree strongly', 'Don't know').
> 1992–1997: Britain should bring back the death penalty ('Strongly agree', 'Agree', 'Neutral', 'Disagree', 'Strongly disagree', 'Don't know').
> 2001–2010: The death penalty, even for very serious crimes, is never justified ('Strongly agree', 'Agree', 'Neutral', 'Disagree', 'Strongly disagree', 'Don't know').
> 2015 (British Social Attitudes Survey): For some crimes, the death penalty is the most appropriate sentence ('Strongly agree', 'Agree', 'Neither agree nor disagree', 'Disagree', 'Strongly disagree', 'Don't know').
> 2017–2019: For some crimes, the death penalty is the most appropriate sentence ('Strongly agree', 'Agree', 'Neither agree nor disagree', 'Disagree', 'Strongly disagree', 'Don't know').

41. Will Jennings, Stephen Farrall, Emily Gray and Colin Hay, 'Penal Populism and the Public Thermostat: Crime, Public Punitiveness, and Public Policy', *Governance*, 30(3) (2017): 463–81; Will Jennings, Stephen Farrall, Emily Gray and Colin Hay, 'Moral Panics and Punctuated Equilibrium in Public Policy: An Analysis of the Criminal Justice Policy Agenda in Britain', *Policy Studies Journal*, 48(1) (2020): 207–34.

42. These two scales were not consistently included in the same form before 1992, so we shorten the time horizon of our analysis. Further, in order to construct scales which are comparable across all election years, we have restricted the scales to four items in each dimension:

> *Authoritarianism-liberalism*: 'Young people today don't have enough respect for traditional British values'; 'Censorship of films and magazines is necessary to uphold moral standards'; 'People in Britain should be more tolerant of those who lead unconventional lives'; 'People should be allowed to organise public protests against the government'.
>
> *Left–right*: 'Ordinary working people do not get their fair share of the nation's wealth'; 'There is one law for the rich and one for the poor'; 'There is no need for strong trade unions to protect working conditions and wages'; 'Private enterprise is the best way to solve Britain's economic problems'.
>
> These scales differ in their absolute values from those used on the BESIP or British Social Attitudes surveys, so it is important to use them to judge relative positions rather than as a definite measure of the proportion of the electorate in particular positions.

CHAPTER 15

The Election in Retrospect

The 2019 general election delivered the first substantial Conservative majority since 1987. Boris Johnson joins the select group of half a dozen post-war Prime Ministers to have secured majorities of 75 seats or more at general elections.[1] Only Tony Blair and Margaret Thatcher in their pomp have won larger majorities in the last 50 years. A lot was at stake in the 2019 election, making this decisive outcome historically significant. The contest concluded three years of fraught argument over Britain's withdrawal from the EU and provided a final opportunity for the British public to confirm or reject the referendum mandate delivered three years earlier. By returning the first sizeable parliamentary majority for the Conservative Party in a generation, Britain's voters ensured that their Prime Minister would indeed 'get Brexit done' and thus set the country on a new path. But the election's implications stretched beyond the high politics of Brexit negotiations. The Conservatives' new majority was the culmination of an unprecedented two-decade advance, one which had reshaped the party's electoral coalition. This should be start of a new paragraph. The Conservative Party has increased its vote in every election since 1997, including three elections in a row as the incumbent government, a feat unmatched in modern political history.

The Conservative coalition has changed as it has grown, with revival in Scotland in 2017 followed in 2019 with gains in the Midlands and

© The Author(s), under exclusive license to Springer Nature Switzerland AG 2021
R. Ford et al., *The British General Election of 2019*,
https://doi.org/10.1007/978-3-030-74254-6_15

North of England, and in North Wales. While it may be going a bit too far to claim that the Conservatives are a 'one nation' party once again, the party's revival has been built on a broadening base. As the Conservatives' base has expanded, Labour's has narrowed, with the latter party retreating to big-city and university seats where graduates, young people and ethnic minorities congregate. Geographical disadvantage magnified the scale of Labour's defeat, reducing the party to its smallest Commons cohort in over 80 years. Labour's 2019 electoral collapse called an end to the party's four-year experiment with radicalism under veteran socialist Jeremy Corbyn—an experiment which, for a brief moment in 2017, looked capable, against all the odds, of delivering the UK's most left-wing government since the Second World War.

After the fireworks of 2017 and two years of volatile and polarised politics, the most exceptional feature of the 2019 campaign was its sheer ordinariness. The Conservatives went into the campaign with a comfortable poll lead, which they held through to polling day, and which proved broadly accurate when the results were announced. The campaign changed little, and the party led by the person voters saw as the better candidate for Prime Minister, and seen as more competent economic stewards, emerged victorious. The Conservatives' manifesto offered enough generosity to attract voters tired of austerity, but not so much as to appear reckless with public money. The main controversies involved the party's ruthless approach to message control, in particular limiting Boris Johnson's availability to the media, including controversially reneging on campaign broadcast commitments. Voters did not seem troubled by these evasions, which incensed Westminster insiders and parts of the media. Yet the precedent set is nonetheless troubling. Already fraught negotiations between parties and broadcasters will become even harder with all concerned worried that the frontrunners will not feel bound by agreements. While some of the set-piece debate and interview events of recent campaigns have been underwhelming, they are surely preferable to a situation in which leaders, particularly popular frontrunners, seek only to engage the media on their own terms.[2]

Jeremy Corbyn's second bid for Downing Street was, like his first, an all-in bet on radical change. In 2017, that wager nearly paid off. In

2019, the same leader and the same team lost their shirts. Some of this may reflect the vagaries of fortune, in whose hands every gambler places their fate. Corbyn was lucky in 2017 to face a weak opponent in Theresa May and luckier still when her campaign repeatedly misfired. He was lucky when campaign events, including terror attacks and a potentially catastrophic leak of his party's manifesto, ended up playing in his favour. He was even lucky with the summer weather, which swelled the crowds and increased the visual impact of his mass rallies. Nothing seemed to break Corbyn's way this time round. His opponent, though no more popular, offered a more appealing message sold with more discipline, and proved better able to shrug off mistakes. Meanwhile, leaks from Labour's campaign and elsewhere were even more frequent and did nothing but harm. Damp and freezing weather thinned the crowds at Labour's campaign rallies and sapped the mood of the candidate. Labour's only stroke of good fortune came in the unlikely form of Nigel Farage, whose Brexit Party interventions may have saved the party from even worse calamity, as John Curtice and colleagues explain in Chapter 13.

Luck certainly plays a role in campaigns, a larger role perhaps than those running them would like to admit. But there was more to Labour's collapse than just a change in fortunes. The 2019 defeat was also the product of long-evident weaknesses in strategy, communications and management in Corbyn's LOTO, which the 2017 success disguised but did not resolve. The most obvious of these was Brexit—an issue Labour successfully ducked in the 2017 campaign, but could no longer ignore in its sequel. The party never addressed the fundamental dilemma the issue posed: Brexit demanded a choice, yet Labour could not afford the electoral costs of choosing. Corbyn should not be judged too harshly for his struggles to solve a problem which would have taxed any leader. Yet his focus on party unity at all costs in the end lumbered his party with a Frankenstein policy which, in attempting to please everyone, pleased nobody. The failure to build a coherent Brexit policy then fed into a broader failure to build a coherent electoral strategy, with an endless argument over whether to focus on Leave or Remain voters crippling the Labour campaign and undermining its ability to speak persuasively to either. This dispute, in turn, stemmed from the most fundamental failure of all—the failure of Corbyn to lead. A leader unable to decide spawned a fractured court, as senior aides fought for primacy, all claiming to speak in Corbyn's name. The battles over Brexit policy, campaign strategy and much else besides were also proxy wars over power and influence, feuds which the man nominally in charge seemed unable or unwilling to resolve. Faction and ideology fed into this conflict, which was worsened by the toxic disputes over anti-semitism. The result was one of the most fragmented, conflicted and chaotic major party election campaigns in modern British political history. It was not an enjoyable experience for those who worked on it. In marked contrast to the Conservatives we talked to, almost no one we spoke to on the Labour side had positive memories of their 2019 experience, and many likened the interviews discussing it to counselling sessions. While elections do not turn on such things, a divided and unhappy workforce added one more burden to a struggling Labour campaign.

Boris Johnson's biography is not atypical for Prime Ministers. He is the twentieth holder of his office to attend Eton and the twenty-eighth to attend Oxford University. Yet in other respects, the Commons elected in 2019 was different from its predecessors, as long-running trends towards increased representation of women and ethnic minorities continued. A record 220 women MPs were returned in 2019, with women forming a majority of the MPs elected by both Labour and the Liberal Democrats, though at 34% of all MPs, women are still well short of fair representation in the Commons overall. The 2019 Commons features a record 65 MPs from Britain's black, Asian and minority (BAME) communities (10% of the total). More BAME MPs sat in Boris Johnson's first Cabinets than sat in the whole Commons when Margaret Thatcher achieved a similar majority in 1987.[3] The election brought other changes to the Commons. Unprecedented internal strife over Brexit prompted a record wave of defections and retirements, with many well-known veterans departing. Partly as a result, but also as a consequence of the Conservatives' big win, nearly a quarter of the 2019 Commons cohort were new arrivals, and more than half had spent less than five years in Parliament. The Commons suffered an unusually large loss of political experience and institutional memory in 2019, one which may impact on the behaviour of MPs in years to come.

* * *

Both main parties' campaigns were reactions to the previous contest. The Conservatives, though returned to government for a third successive term in 2017, behaved like someone determined to change their ways after a brush with death. Everything the party could change, it did. The Conservative leadership overhauled party organisation and communications under Theresa May and worked to ensure that candidates were selected and installed early. When Johnson took over, a new campaign chief, Isaac Levido, was installed early and given clear and uncontested authority, ensuring no repeat of the bitter infighting which marred the 2017 campaign. Whereas May's powerful senior aides Nick Timothy and Fiona Hill had sought to steer her campaign, Johnson's own Rasputin, the powerful and controversial advisor Dominic Cummings, stepped back to allow others to manage things in CCHQ. And this time, a far more thorough and inclusive manifesto process produced a radically different manifesto, offering more spending but less controversial reform. A disciplined Prime Minister stuck to his script and avoided hostages to fortune, yet managed to do so without sounding anything like as robotic and lifeless as his predecessor.[4] The greater urgency of the Brexit crisis helped make Johnson's relentlessly repeated 'get Brexit done' slogan more resonant, successfully convincing sufficient Leave voters to see the election through the lens of their 2016 referendum choices.

While the Conservatives' 2017 defeat was an orphan, credit for the 2019 triumph was widely shared: Isaac Levido was universally praised for calm and disciplined campaign management; those recruited to help the party research and execute its targeting strategy were praised for its accuracy; the social media team was praised for its willingness to take creative risks and court controversy; the manifesto team was lauded for producing a document which avoided the pratfalls of 2017; CCHQ was commended for overhauling organisation and fundraising and for better supporting local candidates and campaigns; and Johnson won plaudits for his signature mix of message discipline and showmanship. Johnson's campaign also managed to present the Conservatives' new leader as the candidate of 'change', even though his party had been in office for nearly a decade. This was not wholly implausible—Johnson was the first committed Brexiteer to take office, and his vision of Brexit, though often vague, clearly involved radical changes. One indirect benefit of Johnson's disruptive fights with Parliament was to make credible the idea that he was an opponent of the status quo, an idea which helped the Prime Minister not only to mobilise disaffected Leave voters, but also to shrug off responsibility for the unpopular policies of his predecessors.

The outcome of a campaign colours judgements of the choices made. Winning campaigns are thought wise, while losing campaigns are dissected for blunders. The Conservatives benefited from a favourable context, thanks in part to the outcome of the supposedly failed 2017 campaign. Theresa May achieved a larger increase in vote share in 2017 than Boris Johnson did in 2019, and that increase was concentrated in the Leave-voting parts of England and Wales where Johnson made most of his seat gains. May's consolidation of Leave support provided the platform for the larger victory which followed. The immense labours of Johnson's predecessor over the course of the 2017–19 Parliament also delivered much of the Withdrawal Agreement Johnson campaigned and won on, as well as pushing through Parliament much of the legislation needed to make Brexit a reality (see Chapter 2).[5] Johnson succeeded where May failed by unifying his party behind a deal, but without May's long struggles, Johnson's questionable claim to have an 'oven-ready' Brexit deal would have been even less credible.[6] Johnson was the beneficiary of May's failures as well as her successes. The extended parliamentary turmoil of 2019 intensified Leave voters' frustration, making a campaign focused on pledges to resolve Brexit more effective. And May's collapse in 2017 had made the prospect of a Corbyn government more plausible, resulting in greater critical scrutiny of Corbyn and intensified hostility to Labour from the right-wing press (as discussed in Chapter 10). Greater and more entrenched hostility to Corbyn gave Johnson a relative advantage over May, despite his own poor approval ratings. The toxification of Corbyn may have been particularly important in helping the Conservatives retain the support of a critical minority of Remain voters with deep reservations about Johnson's approach to Brexit. Though the election was seen as a triumph for the 'get Brexit done' campaign, Johnson's victory was also facilitated by the appeal of 'keep Corbyn out' among some of the voters who didn't want Brexit to happen at all.[7]

The 2017 election was not treated as a defeat by Corbyn's supporters in the Labour grassroots and allies in the party leadership, who saw the large increase in Labour's vote as electoral vindication of their radical politics. While some aides paid lip service to the need to build on advances and address weaknesses, little of substance was done, and a widely shared assumption that 'one last heave' would put Corbyn into Downing Street went unchallenged for too long. Labour went into the 2019 campaign with the same leader, a nearly identical senior campaign team, the same approach to their manifesto, the same (chaotic) approach to comms and campaigning, and with the same strategic goal—to change the subject away from Brexit and towards a radical domestic policy offer which Corbyn's aides believed would mobilise voters hungry for change. But, as Labour soon found, you cannot step into the same river twice.

One of Labour's successes in 2017 was challenging the premise of the election. A contest called over Brexit was reframed as a referendum on the Conservatives' domestic policy record. Voters did not at this point see the resolution of Brexit as urgent and so went along with Labour's vague promise of a different deal, while the party's proposals for public spending struck a chord with an austerity-weary electorate. The atmosphere was different in 2019. Brexit was more urgent, the nation was more divided, and voter frustration at a deadlocked political process was more intense. Brexit compromises which looked unifying in 2017 now looked weak and indecisive, while efforts to shift the discussion to other issues risked alienating both sides of the polarised Brexit divide. While Labour did enjoy some success in encouraging voters to focus on the NHS, particularly early in the campaign, the bold, attention-grabbing gestures which had worked so well in 2017 now backfired, as a lengthening list of expensive pledges intensified voter concerns that Labour promises were neither credible nor deliverable.

Labour also found to their cost in 2019 how much their previous success had relied on a weak opponent. Theresa May's misfiring manifesto and stilted campaign appearances made her the perfect foil to Corbyn's relaxed radicalism. Johnson was a very different competitor. Labour found their most popular policy initiatives neutralised by big spending Conservative counter-offers in the areas voters cared about most, such as health, education and policing. On the other hand, the Johnson campaign offered no equivalent to May's dementia tax fiasco. And Labour found they could not pin the unpopular legacy of a decade of austerity Conservative government on a Conservative Prime Minister who presented himself as a fellow opponent of austerity.

Jeremy Corbyn had become the unexpected star of the 2017 campaign. His approval ratings surged as he mobilised restive younger voters tired of spending cuts and stagnant wages. Footage of large youthful crowds chanting Corbyn's name at mass rally events became a staple of

2017 campaign coverage. This magic deserted Labour's leader in 2019. Two years of critical coverage focusing on his dubious past associations, his ambivalent response to the Salisbury terror attacks and Labour's long, toxic rows over anti-semitism had taken their toll. Though Corbyn's ratings at the start of the 2019 campaign were little worse than at the start of the previous contest, negative views of the Labour leader were now more entrenched and the campaign could not turn them around. Corbyn and Brexit generated a vicious circle for Labour—indecision and doublespeak on Brexit had tarnished Corbyn's image as a principled, plain-spoken leader, while pervasive distrust of Corbyn made it harder to sell Labour's compromise policy to either Remain or Leave voters.

Meanwhile, although Labour's 2019 campaign was led by pretty much the same people as in 2017, two long years of perpetual infighting had transformed relations among them. A once tight-knit team of advisors was now fractured, and deep divisions crippled decision making, and encouraged senior managers to work with their teams in silos. A flat organisational structure which had just about worked when everyone was pulling in the same direction now proved to be a recipe for chaos. No one had the authority necessary to settle disputes and set the overall direction, so arguments never ended and the campaign went round in circles. Poor organisation at the top also weakened the potential advantage Labour had from a much larger activist base. The Conservatives learned in 2017 how corrosive distrust and disunity can be in a campaign. In 2019, it was Labour who paid this price, ending up with a campaign so dysfunctional that members of the senior leadership team sought to minimise communication with each other rather than grind out decisions collectively.

Labour's result was immediately judged a major failure. It was a historically terrible result in terms of seats won, though less awful in terms of votes cast. Labour's share had fallen lower than the 32.2% achieved in 2019 on four occasions in the previous 30 years—including 2010 and 2015, the two elections held immediately before Corbyn took over. Corbyn's vote share was just three points less than the 35.2% achieved by Tony Blair in 2005 when Labour were returned for a historic third term. Labour remained well above their post-war low ebb in 1983, when they fell to 27.6% of the vote, yet Corbyn ended up with even fewer seats than Michael Foot achieved in that contest. Several factors combined to turn a bad vote outcome into an awful seat outcome. Labour's mediocre vote has to be weighed against a historically outstanding Conservative vote share of 43.6%, the highest achieved by any party in 40 years,[8] meaning the Conservatives had a very large 11.4 point vote lead over Labour.[9] The two largest parties dominated the vote for the second election running, despite Labour's slump. The Conservatives and Labour took nearly 76% of all votes cast and over 80% of those cast in England—a higher combined share than in every election from 1997 to 2015. While this 'ersatz two-party politics' lacks the class and partisan foundations of the earlier era of two-party dominance, it has nonetheless endured for a second election running and is becoming rooted in new social divisions focused on age, education and social values (see Chapter 14).

The dividing lines of this new two party-competition disadvantage Labour in several ways. The party has become more reliant on support from social groups who cluster together in the same seats—young people, university graduates and ethnic minority voters who all congregate in and around big cities and university towns. The geography of the Brexit vote was similarly unhelpful—the Remain vote was concentrated, while Leave votes were spread more evenly. This complicated Labour's strategy—the party could not win without a strong appeal to voters in the majority of Leave-leaning seats, yet too much focus on Leave voters risked alienating the Remain voters who provided the bulk of their support. The party tried to offer something for both, which pleased neither. But it is not obvious that any alternative approach would have done better. Labour also face a continuing problem with Scotland, where the party still has little to offer voters polarised over independence. The path to a majority is long indeed while the SNP continue to dominate this one-time Labour stronghold. Yet Labour's position also looks less bad when one considers that the SNP and nearly all of the other third parties returning a total of 82 MPs to the Commons are more likely to support Labour than the Conservatives in any future hung parliament.[10] Labour may be weaker, but they have more potential allies. While a Labour majority government looks further off than ever, a Labour minority government remains a credible prospect.

One paradox of the 2019 election is that the two parties that took the most strident positions on the defining issue of the day both failed make a mark. The Liberal Democrats and the Brexit Party both staked their campaigns on radical positions at opposite poles of the Brexit debate. The Liberal Democrats sought to end Brexit immediately and unilaterally, while the Brexit Party (as its name suggested) wanted to enact it immediately and unilaterally, without even agreeing an exit deal with the EU. Both parties had breakthrough results in the European Parliament elections of June 2019, then sank in the polls relentlessly thereafter.

The Liberal Democrats' proposal to 'revoke Article 50' and halt the Brexit process completely via Parliament proved unexpectedly divisive. The party had thought that the six million signatures an online petition proposing the same policy had attracted in summer 2019 showed that this idea had a big market. Yet the broader electorate proved hostile to a policy held to violate a widely held folk democratic norm that only a second referendum mandate could over-ride the first. Even strongly Remain voters attacked it as elitist and undemocratic, while for Leave voters—still an important constituency for the party in some of its traditional strongholds—unilateral reversal of Brexit was anathema.

Yet while the revoke Article 50 pledge was problematic, it was in fact the Liberal Democrats' traditional enemies—geography and the electoral system—that did them the most harm. In vote share terms, the 2019 election was a relative success—the 4.3 percentage point increase in vote share was the largest achieved since the merged party formed in 1988. But this still left the Liberal Democrats at just 11.6%, well below the shares routinely achieved pre-Coalition.[11] Their advance was particularly dramatic in Conservative-held, but strongly Remain, parts of southern England, where double-digit increases were common. Yet the Liberal Democrats' starting position was so weak in most of these seats that even very substantial vote share gains were not sufficient to win. Meanwhile, the party underperformed in traditional areas of strength—often less strongly Remain areas where the party's Brexit stance did not go down well. While opposition to Brexit brought in new voters, it could not undo the electoral damage done by the Coalition.

The Liberal Democrats' leader Jo Swinson was automatically removed after the election, having lost her seat. Her 144-day tenure was the shortest in the party's history. Yet the 2019 outcome was not wholly negative. The election reorganised the geography of Liberal Democrat support in a way which may create a platform for future success. Two of the biggest strategic problems for the party in 2019—deciding where it was strong and convincing voters it was credible locally—will be easier to solve at the next election. There is now a very clear battleground for the Liberal Democrats to fight on, with a swathe of target seats where the party starts in a strong second place. Perhaps Swinson will be to her successor, Ed Davey, as May was to Johnson—the leader who fails to deliver on their ambitions, yet bequeaths an electoral map which can drive a breakthrough performance in the following campaign. Or perhaps not.

What of the Brexit Party? The latest vehicle for British politics' arch-disruptor Nigel Farage turned out to be even less successful than his previous outfit UKIP when it came to winning Westminster seats and much less effective when it came to vote share.[12] Yet despite these limitations, the Brexit Party was in historical terms a remarkably successful innovation, winning over 600,000 votes despite standing candidates in less than half of the country and ignoring much of the most naturally favourable terrain for its politics. Its indirect electoral impact was substantial—as Curtice et al. show in Chapter 13, by splitting the Leave vote in Labour seats, the Brexit Party may have cost the Conservatives as many as 25 gains from Labour. Farage's decision to stand down candidates in Conservative seats was one of the most consequential campaign decisions taken by any politician in 2019. And without the Brexit Party's continued intervention in Labour seats, Johnson's majority could have been a landslide.

If Brexit has been reshaping electoral coalitions in England and Wales since at least 2016, the forces reshaping Scottish politics go back further still. Scottish politics has been in constant flux since 2014. The constitutional re-alignment unleashed by the independence referendum in 2014 carried all before it the following spring, producing a historic landslide for the SNP in 2015 on a scale similar to the total victory of Sinn Féin in the 1918 election, which heralded the Irish Republic's separation from the UK. Brexit unsettled this re-alignment, as while the SNP's support for EU membership attracted new votes from Remainers, it alienated Brexiteers, helping fuel a Scottish Conservative renaissance in 2017. Corbyn's Labour flopped in Scotland in 2017 even as they surged elsewhere, though thanks to a general fallback in SNP support, Labour were able to regain some Scottish seats.

The 2019 election in Scotland was all of these trends redux. The dual appeal of independence and Remain drove another landslide for the SNP, powered by a sharp increase in support for independence among formerly unionist Remainers, many of whom now saw exit from the UK as Scotland's only route back into the EU. Conversely, the dual appeal of union and Brexit cemented the Conservatives as the second party in much of Scotland, helping them hold on to six seats, and remain competitive in many others, despite Boris Johnson's toxic personal ratings in Scotland. Labour's efforts to bridge both constitutional divides again fell flat, the party fell to its lowest Scottish vote share since 1918, and it lost all the seats regained in 2017. If the road back for Labour in England and Wales looks long, the route to recovery in Scotland, where it once again holds just one seat, is even more daunting.

The SNP's fresh landslide mandate has made renewed constitutional conflict all but certain in Scotland. Sturgeon asserted that the Scottish result represented a demand for independence from a nation opposed to both Brexit and the Westminster Conservative government. Johnson retorted that Scotland's people had already had their say on independence and had rejected it. The battle of wills between the Scottish First Minister and the UK Prime Minister over a second Scottish independence referendum may become one of the defining conflicts of the next Parliament. If the SNP prevail, securing and then winning a second vote on independence, then the constitutional wrangling which so frustrated voters in the 2017–19 Parliament may yet return to dominate the agenda of its successor. On the other hand, if the Conservative government stands firm in its refusal to grant a second referendum, this could lead to an intensifying legal, political and constitutional crisis without any obvious path towards resolution.

There is also a third possibility. If the SNP secure another vote on independence and once again lose it, the fallout from a second failure for a party already showing considerable internal strains could be substantial. Factional conflict within the SNP could intensify, and with the independence issue settled, Scottish voters may start to look elsewhere. The SNP have looked unbeatable in recent years, but then so too did Scottish Labour for many decades before 2007. And a change in the Scottish electoral landscape would have major consequences for the next UK electoral contest.

It is not only in Scotland that the current constitutional settlement looks unstable. In Northern Ireland, the 2019 election revealed a volatile electorate dissatisfied with the main governing parties' failure to make devolved government work. The new institutional arrangements after Brexit threaten to bring new political disruption, as unionists are unhappy with arrangements which introduce new barriers with the rest of the UK, while nationalists wish to minimise the barriers between the North and the Irish Republic. With Sinn Féin doing well on both sides of the Irish border, the possibility of "border poll" on Northern

Ireland's future status may rise up the political agenda, yet another divisive referendum in a region where the risks of constitutional conflict are all too obvious. Growing upheaval in the other UK nations may also encourage separatist sentiment in Wales too, where a century and a half of relative Conservative under-performance continued once again in 2019, despite the party's capture of several marginal seats, and where Brexit threatens to bring considerable economic upheaval. The winds of change may even start blowing in England, where city-region devolution is becoming embedded and introducing confident new voices on the national political stage, with strong incentives to fight their regions' corners against Westminster. The constitutional upheavals which began with devolution in the late 1990s and which Brexit intensified may yet have some way to run.

* * *

The 2019 Conservative victory resolved, for the moment, two issues which had framed British politics for much of the previous four years: Brexit and Corbynism. The British public had mandated an end to the UK 43-year association with the EU in 2016, kicking off one of the most complex negotiations in British political history, conducted from March 2017 to the impossibly tight two-year timetable set out in Article 50 of the EU's Lisbon Treaty.[13] By the time Johnson entered Downing Street, Brexit had already ended the political careers of two Prime Ministers. Defeat in the 2016 referendum was the end of David Cameron, who tried and failed to reform and renew the status quo. The process of finding the exit overwhelmed Cameron's successor, Theresa May, who first failed to secure the large Commons majority she deemed necessary to complete the Brexit process, then failed to adapt to the resulting more constrained political context. May showed remarkable resilience, persevering despite repeated rejections of her attempts to reconcile incompatible demands on an impossible timetable, but she could never overcome the damage done by the failed election campaign of June 2017. Installed by Conservative Brexiteers after two years of frustrating deadlock, Johnson staked his premiership on massive gambles to complete the process and emerged victorious. He tore up constitutional norms, expelled veteran MPs from his party and sought at every turn to dramatise the opposition he faced, before asking British voters once again to give a Conservative Prime Minister the mandate needed to 'get Brexit done'.

Brexit put immense pressure on all of Britain's political institutions. A majoritarian governing model built around perpetual competition between government and opposition struggled to accommodate complex negotiations that cut across party lines in unpredictable ways. As the Brexit process approached its climax, resignations, defections, rebellions, government defeats, opposition chaos and legislative turmoil became almost daily occurrences. Brexit left no governing institution or political process untouched. Cabinet government was destabilised as achieving the unity necessary for collective responsibility proved close to impossible. There were 37 ministerial resignations from the May government, far more than in any recent predecessor.[14] Nearly all were over Brexit, and the resignation of senior Cabinet Brexiteers twice unravelled May's strategy at critical points—after the 'Chequers summit' in July 2018 and after the negotiation of the 'all UK backstop' in November 2018. Brexit also put the country's political parties under unprecedented pressure, with record levels of defections and the launch of two new parties in the spring of 2019 to represent opposite poles of the Brexit divide—one a collection of pro-European parliamentary refugees from Labour and the Conservatives, the other a reunited band of Brexiteer campaigners railing against Westminster. The toll this had taken by the end of the 2017–19 Parliament was remarkable. The Conservatives had 19 fewer MPs at dissolution than at the start of the Parliament, having at one point been 30 MPs down. The Parliamentary Labour Party, buffeted by the twin forces of Brexit and Corbyn, had 20 fewer MPs at dissolution. The Liberal Democrat parliamentary contingent nearly doubled to 20, while a dozen pro-EU MPs broke away to form a new party, Change UK, which itself soon disintegrated into several fragments. The Parliament began with one independent MP (Northern Ireland's Lady Sylvia Hermon); it ended with at least 21.[15]

Brexit also eroded the discipline of those who stuck with their parties. Rebellions were constant, building to the record-breaking serial rejections of May's Withdrawal Agreement, and MPs began to organise themselves around Brexit preferences ahead of party affiliations. Cross-party groups of like-minded MPs emerged, with their own whipping operations. The behaviour of MPs became ever harder to predict from one vote to the next, forcing party leaders to live from day to day. Despite the disintegration of party organisation, the Commons as a whole achieved unprecedented influence over the executive through the combination of a hung parliament, party fragmentation and a sympathetic speaker willing to rule creatively. The Fixed-term Parliaments Act meant that the government could not use confidence votes to impose discipline and lowered the stakes of Commons defeats. Backbench MPs used the opportunity presented by this unique confluence of events to seize control of the agenda via a range of arcane parliamentary manoeuvres. Yet MPs' newfound power proved almost entirely negative—while they found many ways to block the government's will on Brexit, they could not advance an alternative agenda. In the end, with a little help from a Prime Minister seemingly unafraid of sowing division between 'the people' and Parliament, this just intensified voter frustration at what they saw as Westminster's fruitless theatrics.

The Brexit crisis also sucked in other British institutions. The courts were brought into the argument via legal challenges launched by Remain campaigners against the government, forcing it to give a role to Parliament in invoking Article 50 and overturning Boris Johnson's effort to prorogue Parliament for five weeks. Brexit also destabilised the politics of devolution and relations among the constituent nations of the UK. The SNP-run devolved Scottish government at Holyrood repeatedly protested its exclusion from the Brexit process, which it framed as dragging Scotland out of the EU against the will of its a majority of its citizens. The Brexit negotiation was also bound up with the Northern Ireland peace process. The status of Northern Ireland as a territory, and in particular where and how any borders between a post-Brexit Britain and the EU would operate in Ireland, proved to be the most intractable question in the whole process. The influence exercised by the strongly unionist DUP on the May government alienated the nationalist community, while the imposition of border checks in the Irish Sea eventually agreed by Boris Johnson infuriated the unionist community. Post-Brexit disruptions are likely to be most keenly felt in the UK's most politically divided territory, with repercussions which may reverberate for many years to come.

Ben Jennings—Angel of the North Cartoon (Ben Jennings, *The Guardian*, 15 December 2019 © Ben Jennings)

The consolidation of support from Leave voters in England and Wales was widely seen as the key to Johnson's success in 2019. Overwhelming support from Leave voters powered many of the Conservative victories in the 'Red Wall' which grabbed the most attention in the immediate aftermath of the election. These were indeed striking successes, with Conservative MPs returned from seats which had rejected the party for two generations or more.[16] Yet there was more here than met the eye. The Conservatives' 2019 vote gains were relatively modest in many of these seats, and the party's breakthroughs often owed much to larger advances made by Theresa May in 2017 and to Labour's general 2019 retreat. Labour's decline in the 'Red Wall,' a story running back over multiple elections, was in some cases overstated. While Labour's losses in, for example, parts of the North East were unprecedented, in other seats the party had plumbed lower depths in the 1970s or 1980s and then recovered.[17] Even the worst Red Wall defeats involved much more than Labour-to-Conservative switching—the Conservatives often benefited from the consolidation of a longstanding, but previously fragmented, non-Labour vote and may also have gained from differential turnout, with disaffected but still anti-Conservative former Labour voters staying home on polling day.[18]

The focus on Conservative breakthroughs in the Leave-voting, historically Labour 'Red Wall' also risked distorting understanding of an election win which also depended on swings to the Conservatives in more traditional marginals, and on limiting the swings against the party in the blue parts of the country less enamoured of Johnson or Brexit. Conservative wins in perennial battlegrounds such as Ipswich and Bury may not have the historic resonance of a win in Bolsover or Blyth Valley, but contributed just the same to the party's Commons majority. The focus on Conservative advances in the North of England regions risked overlooking the decisive Conservative advance in the marginal rich regions of the Midlands, where the overall Conservative vote share is now as high as in its traditional heartlands in the South of England (see Chapter 14). While some Conservative gains came in declining, post-industrial towns, others did not fit this template, and the story of economic change even in post-industrial areas is more complex than narratives of decline allow. The Conservative gains in 'Barratt Home Britain' often came from voters who felt they were doing well and who expected to do even better in future.[19] Meanwhile, in many of England's wealthier and more Remain-leaning seats, the Conservatives benefited from the same forces which until 2019 cushioned Labour's decline in the 'Red Wall'—strong starting positions and large initial majorities. The Conservative vote declined in most of the seats in Berkshire, Buckinghamshire, Cambridgeshire, Oxfordshire and Surrey, yet large initial majorities and a split opposition vote typically left the party comfortably ahead still, helped by intense opposition to Corbyn which may have prevented larger losses. The Home Counties may not be so easy to defend against less polarising opposition in future.

The disruptions of Brexit, an unprecedented political shock which upended the political agenda and divided the electorate in new ways, took most of the headlines in the 2019 election and the Parliament preceding it.[20] The referendum campaign had forged new political identities—'Leaver' and 'Remainer'—whose power over voters intensified as the political conflict over Brexit polarised. By the time of the 2019 election, large swathes of the British electorate saw not just their choices, but their political identities, primarily through the lens of Brexit. Few had felt this strongly about the EU, in either direction, four years earlier when David Cameron's unexpected majority had set the Brexit ball rolling. The gruelling process of Brexit negotiations since 2017 had seen both sides of the Brexit divide increasingly disillusioned with the state of

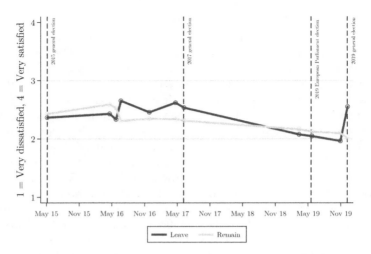

Fig. 15.1   Satisfaction with UK democracy (Leavers and Remainers), BESIP, 2015–19

UK democracy (see Fig. 15.1). The outcome of the 2019 election gave a boost to the democratic confidence of Leavers, restoring their satisfaction with democracy to levels last seen immediately after the referendum, while Remainers were left more pessimistic than ever.

Yet while the policy agenda imposed in 2016 was almost entirely new, the electoral story of Brexit is more complicated. Brexit was as much a catalyst as a shock—accelerating long-term changes in the parties' electoral coalitions that had already been underway for many years and which were driven in turn by long-term changes in British society.[21] The Leave voters and Leave-leaning seats that Corbyn's Labour struggled with in 2019 were similar kinds of people and places to those whose flirtations with UKIP caused Ed Miliband difficulties in 2015, and whose growing concerns about immigration were already causing Tony Blair difficulties in 2005. Labour's troubles with disaffected, socially conservative white voters in England and Wales can be traced back a generation or more. Similar feelings of disaffection and marginalisation also helped to trigger the collapse of the Labour Party in Scotland after the 2014 independence referendum, a collapse the Scottish party has yet to even begin recovering from.

Initially, Labour were cushioned from the impact of retreat among these sections of the electorate by the concentration of such voters in safe seats where local Labour majorities could withstand a lot of erosion and where there was no viable challenge able to unify local opposition.[22] Before Brexit, such voters either backed protest parties of the radical right, whose appeal was too narrow to win seats, or stayed at home. After Brexit, they turned to the Conservative Party, which had the reach and organisation to combine them into winning coalitions. The influx of Leave voters powered increases in the Conservatives' national vote share in both 2017 and 2019—a remarkable achievement for an incumbent government. But this re-alignment may be hard to sustain with the issues that drove it—first immigration and then Brexit—no longer at the top of the political agenda.

Heavy defeat in the 2019 election also ended Labour's four-year experiment with radical politics under Jeremy Corbyn. Corbyn faced fierce opposition within and without from the moment he took the helm in 2015. His chaotic leadership and dismal poll ratings encouraged Theresa May to call the early election of 2017, anticipating a Conservative landslide. Corbyn's internal critics believed much the same thing, expecting the Labour membership's flirtation with radicalism to end in electoral disaster. Several were rumoured to be ready to launch their challenges to Corbyn the day after the polls closed.[23] Instead, the 2017 campaign turned everything upside down. Corbyn's personal ratings surged, May's collapsed and Labour closed a 20 point gap in the polls. Corbyn won the largest increase in Labour's vote share since 1945, securing his ascendency within the Labour Party, and leading his aides and allies to believe they were one step away from power.

After the hubris of 2017 came the nemesis of 2019. Labour lost four-fifths of the vote share gained in the previous election and slumped to its lowest seat total since 1935. After a decade in opposition, Labour was still slipping further away from power, gaining support where it was already winning and losing ground where it needed to compete. As Chapter 13 reveals, Labour now needs a 12 point swing to achieve to return to power with a majority of two, a swing larger even than the party achieved in its historic victories of 1997 or 1945. That challenge may get harder yet if, as expected, overdue boundary changes are implemented in the coming Parliament and increase Labour's disadvantage vis-à-vis the electoral system.

No one in Labour doubted that the 2019 campaign was a disaster and, like the Conservatives after 2017, the need for change was obvious. But there was no consensus about how to recover. A battle over how to interpret Corbyn's legacy began the moment the exit poll was announced and looks likely to run for some time. The Labour left saw 2019 as a freak result produced by the unbridgeable divisions of Brexit. With Brexit 'done', they argue Labour should revive the approach of 2017, when the party came within a whisker of power with a radical leader offering an unapologetically radical programme. The Labour right believe the freak result was 2017, when a shambolic, misfiring Conservative campaign masked the underlying weaknesses of a Corbyn project which was, in their view, doomed from the outset. For Corbyn's internal critics, the lesson of 2017 was that even when given an open goal to shoot at, he could not deliver a win. For the Labour right, it is instead the 2019 result which needs to set the tone, demonstrating the catastrophic unpopularity of left radicalism when set against an even moderately disciplined and competent Conservative party. While the factional battle to interpret Labour's four-year experiment with 'a new kind of politics' will doubtless rage on in the opinion pages and among the grassroots, the leadership succession contest was swiftly won by the moderates. Keir Starmer, Labour's Brexit Secretary under Corbyn, became the party's new leader in April 2020. While he emphasised continued commitment to the radical Corbyn domestic policy legacy in his leadership campaign, Starmer is seen by Corbynites and Corbynsceptics alike as a candidate of the party's right wing.

Like his left predecessor Michael Foot in 1983, Corbyn bequeaths a party even more divided and even further from power than when he took office. Indeed, a review of the 1983 volume in this series reveals some striking parallels between the 2019 campaign and the earlier left led Labour campaign—a Labour leader 'at his happiest pressing the flesh and addressing rallies of the party faithful'; a Conservative campaign 'less about the Conservatives' record in government or its plans than about the credibility of Labour'; an 'inept' campaign that 'lack[ed] central direction and control', featured 'last-minute ad-hoc decision making' and was openly criticised by internal opponents as it was unfolding; a party which in the words of one Labour candidate had spent 'so long arguing amongst ourselves that we have grown away from ordinary Labour voters'; and voters who 'either did not believe [Labour's] promises or doubted its ability to carry them out'.[24]

The same themes of factionalism, disorganisation, introversion, internal feuding and low credibility with voters all recurred in 2019. But some positive legacies remain from the Corbyn project. Corbyn's ascendency revitalised the Labour membership to an extraordinary extent, making Labour the largest mass membership political party in Western Europe. Some of this grassroots energy was focused on Corbyn rather than his party and may fade now he has departed, but Labour is unlikely to return to the status quo ante. As long as not everyone who joined the party to elect and then protect Corbyn as leader quits its ranks, a revitalised membership may be one of his lasting legacies.[25]

It is less clear whether the organisational changes of the Corbyn era will endure. The democratisation reforms he enacted were surprisingly modest for a founding member of the Campaign for Labour Party Democracy and, while their very modesty may help them survive, they have not fundamentally changed the party's internal power structures. Corbyn's experiment with community organisers was criticised as an expensive flop and was closely associated with some of the more divisive figures from his leadership, so is unlikely to survive in the same form. The balance of power in Labour's organisational structures looks likely to swing back to the right more quickly than it swung to the left under Corbyn, as the same denser organisational and professional networks that helped the Labour right dig in under Corbyn now help them recover control. Another long spell in the wilderness looks likely for the Labour left—unless, of course, Keir Starmer is seen to fail sooner rather than later.

Yet while they look set to lose their grip on the levers of internal power, Corbyn's two landslide internal victories and major vote gains in 2017 have given the Labour left renewed belief that the radical politics they believe in can be popular within and beyond Labour. When combined with left-wing trade union support, renewed membership and the growth of allied activist structures such as Momentum, the result is likely to be a louder and more confident left voice within Labour, and hence a continuation of more volatile and polarised internal politics in the years to come. A return to something like the Blair-era 'supremacy' of the party's right looks unlikely.[26] A revitalised left will be sure to seize upon every policy misstep and electoral mishap of the new leadership, and to press hard for Corbyn's policy legacy to be protected and built upon.

But will the left stay inside Labour if it thinks it can no longer control the party? Radical left politics in contemporary Britain is as fissiparous as elsewhere. Many of those who joined Labour under Corbyn have a greater loyalty to the leader than to the party. Many may lack the patience for another long stretch as internal opposition to the moderates running the party. With Green politics increasingly the vehicle of choice for economic and social radicals across Europe, the Greens may provide an attractive alternative home for disaffected younger progressive and cosmopolitan voters attracted under Corbyn. A resurgent Green Party could further split the progressive electorate, adding to Labour's electoral challenges against a unified right.

This assumes that the right can stay unified. The Conservatives' current advantages depend on holding together an electoral coalition which is now unusually broad. It is not clear what binds the new and old wings of the Conservative party in Parliament or the country beyond support for Brexit and hostility to Corbyn. Neither rallying point will be available at the next election. Johnson's interventionist economic approach will—unless it is to involve vast borrowing—mean taking money from richer, traditionally Tory places and showering it on poorer, formerly Labour places. Voters already looked restive in 2019 in parts of the southern suburban heartlands, with large swings to the Liberal Democrats making some long safe seats newly marginal. But a reversion to the small state/austerity politics still favoured by many Conservative MPs and a fair few of its activists would involve a flow of money the other way, antagonising Leave-voting recruits with lingering suspicions of Johnson's Conservatives in the party's new 'Red Wall' seats. Whatever the new government does economically thus comes with substantial political risks, not all of which can be easily compensated for by stoking a culture war against the supposed excesses of the left's 'identity politics'. Those risks should provide opportunities for the opposition, which is unlikely to fight the next election with a leader as polarising as Corbyn. As a result, 2019 may prove to be a high-water mark, though also one which has left the incumbent with a large Commons majority to cushion its fall.

While the 2019 campaign did not deliver the dramatic shifts seen in other recent British elections, the outcome certainly did. The Liberal Democrats lost their leader Jo Swinson on election night and Northern Ireland's DUP paid for their grudging support of a minority Conservative government with the loss of their Westminster leader Nigel Dodds. Labour's leader did not resign that night, eager to avoid the chaotic interregnum triggered by his predecessor's election night departure, but made clear that his departure was imminent, thus firing the starting gun on his party's succession contest, which proceeded through the spring. Both the Liberal Democrats and Labour launched wide-ranging public reviews of their disappointing 2019 performances. Change was in the air for the victorious Conservatives too. Johnson had campaigned as a different kind of Conservative and, in the days after his victory, reiterated his desire to govern as one. There were repeated, if vague, pledges to 'level up' the country through large-scale public investment, and within two months Johnson had replaced his fiscally Conservative chancellor Sajid Javid with Rishi Sunak, who, while not necessarily any more comfortable with the Prime Minister's big spending approach, appeared more willing nonetheless to do his bidding. Johnson's radical senior advisor Dominic Cummings, who kept his powder dry during the campaign, was soon back on the scene, albeit, it turned out, rather more temporarily than many had imagined in the immediate aftermath of Johnson's triumph.

While no election turns on a slogan alone, there is no doubting the magnetic appeal of 'get Brexit done', the three-word message which defined a contest, as 'take back control' had done in the 2016 referendum. The Conservatives' slogan struck a chord with Leave voters wearied and frustrated by two years of political deadlock, and by mobilising and unifying them helped to secure the decisive victory necessary to turn the slogan into reality. Johnson duly passed his 'oven-ready' deal as promised—his Withdrawal Agreement sailed through the Commons with a majority of 99 on 9 January 2020, less than a month after polling day. Like many TV dinners, Johnson's deal looked less appetising on close inspection and may yet bring on indigestion. Nevertheless, and as promised, Johnson took Britain out of the EU on 31 January 2020, meeting the Article 50 deadline at the fourth attempt. Hopes for a respite from the storms of the past three years did not last long. On the very same day that Britain's exit from the EU became official, Public Health England announced the first UK case of COVID-19. Within three months, the nation would be in an unprecedented peacetime lockdown, with its Prime Minister fighting for life in a London intensive care unit. Johnson overcame many political and electoral challenges to secure his 2019 majority. The challenges ahead were sterner still.

NOTES

1. The previous large majorities were in 1945, 1959, 1966, 1983, 1987, 1997 and 2001. Only two of these victories (1959 and 1964) were followed by wins for the opposition, and, as Appendix 1 shows, both of

these occurred at a time when there were many more marginal seats in play than is typical today. Partly for this reason, the conventional wisdom just a few years ago was that big governing majorities were a thing of the past (see, for example, Dennis Kavanagh and Philip Cowley, *The British General Election of 2010.* Palgrave Macmillan, 2010, pp. 347–49).

2. Though in fairness, avoidance of televised debates in particular was the standard approach for popular leaders before 2010. And parties with less popular leaders are both less likely to pursue such evasions—they need opportunities to change public perceptions—and less likely to get away unscathed if they do, as illustrated by the widespread criticism of Theresa May's avoidance of debates in 2017.

3. Four ethnic minority MPs were elected in 1987—the first four ethnic minority MPs of the post-war era. Six ethnic minority MPs attended Johnson's first post-election Cabinets—Sajid Javid (Chancellor), Priti Patel (Home Secretary), Alok Sharma (International Development Secretary), Rishi Sunak (Chief Secretary to the Treasury), James Cleverley (Party Chair) and Kwasi Kwarteng (Business, Energy and Industrial Strategy). Johnson's early appointments include Britain's first Home Secretary of Indian heritage (Priti Patel) and the first Chancellors of Pakistani and Indian heritage (Sajid Javid and then Rishi Sunak). Only five ethnic minority MPs have served in all previous Cabinets (two of them appointments by Johnson's predecessor Theresa May who then also served in Johnson's Cabinet). At Johnson's post-election reshuffle in February 2020, Javid departed and was replaced by Sunak, and Suella Braverman attended Cabinet having been appointed as Britain's second ethnic minority Attorney General.

4. Johnson's predecessor, Theresa May, also took a disciplined approach to campaigning, but her endless repetition of 'strong and stable' in 2017 led her to be characterised as a dull, unresponsive 'Maybot' (see Philip Cowley and Dennis Kavanagh, *The British General Election of 2017.* Palgrave Macmillan, 2018, pp. 433–35). Communications strategies stand or fall, at least in part, on the qualities of the leaders charged with executing them.

5. See, for example, the assessments of progress from the Institute for Government: Joe Owen, Lewis Lloyd, Tim Durrant and Jill Rutter, 'Brexit: Six Months to Go', September 2018, https://www.institutefor-government.org.uk/sites/default/files/publications/brexit-six-months-to-go-final-WEB.pdf; Joe Owen and Tim Durrant, 'Brexit: Two Months to Go', January 2019, https://www.instituteforgovernment.org.uk/sites/default/files/publications/brexit-two-months-to-go-final-web.pdf.

6. Johnson's Withdrawal Agreement did not resolve the issue of Britain's future relationship with the EU, which remained to be negotiated after it was passed into law. Johnson's deal also left a number of highly

contentious questions open, such as how to manage the implementation of customs checks between Northern Ireland and the rest of the UK.

7. Lord Ashcroft's post-election polling, for example, features multiple examples of how Conservative Remainers, though opposed to Brexit, saw Corbyn in Downing Street as a bigger danger to the country: https://lordashcroftpolls.com/2019/09/state-of-the-nation-my-new-polling-on-the-political-landscape-and-the-battle-lines-for-the-next-election.

8. The only higher vote share achieved by either party since 1970 was the 43.6% achieved by the Conservatives under Margaret Thatcher in 1979.

9. The Conservatives' vote lead was the fourth largest recorded in the post-war era, exceeded only by the 14.8 point lead for the Conservatives in 1983, the 12.5 point lead for Labour in 1997 and the 11.5 point lead achieved by the Conservatives in 1987.

10. The large number of third-party MPs returned to the Commons despite Labour and Conservative dominance of the overall vote reflects the more efficient distribution of the vote for these parties, which is in most cases highly concentrated in particular regions, facilitating the conversion of votes to seats. The SNP, for example, win over 7% of the seats in Parliament with less than 4% of the UK-wide vote, as their vote is concentrated entirely in Scotland.

11. The figure refers to the increase in vote share in Great Britain, as the Liberal Democrats do not stand in Northern Ireland. Even after the rebound in 2019, the Liberal Democrat vote share was, at 11.6%, barely over half the share achieved in the last pre-Coalition election of 2010 (23.0%).

12. Even accounting for seats it did not contest.

13. The Article 50 process was originally designed to reassure the poorer, post-communist countries entering the EU that they could exit the union if it pursued policy changes they found undesirable, but were unable to veto. While British Eurosceptics supported the article, it was never envisaged that Britain would be the country invoking a procedure which, in the words of the British diplomat Lord Kerr, who helped craft it, was 'a procedure for storming out' dictatorial intended to provide a mechanism for undemocratic Member States sanctioned by the EU could use to depart the union. See Andrew Gray, 'Article 50 Lord Kerr: I Didn't Have the UK in Mind', *Politico*, 28 March 2017, https://www.politico.eu/article/brexit-article-50-lord-kerr-john-kerr. See also Martijn Huysmans, 'Enlargement and Exit: The Origins of Article 50', *European Union Politics*, 20(2) (2019): 155–75.

14. Theresa May lost more ministers outside reshuffles in less than three years of government than Margaret Thatcher or Tony Blair lost in over ten. See https://www.instituteforgovernment.org.uk/publication/whitehall-monitor-2020/ministers.

15. https://members.parliament.uk/parties/Commons?fordate=2019-11-05.

16. Rother Valley and its predecessor seats had only returned Labour MPs since 1918 (101 years); Durham North West, Don Valley, Leigh, and Newcastle-under-Lyne had all returned Labour MPs in every election since 1922 (97 years), while the early declaring Conservative gain of Blyth Valley was one of 11 seats which had returned Labour MPs in every election since 1935 (84 years) (though in the case of Blyth Valley, this includes a single victory for the deselected MP Eddie Milne, who won the February 1974 election as an independent Labour candidate).

17. Philip Cowley and Matthew Bailey, 'Labour's History of Highs and Lows – and What it Reveals', *The Times*, 12 February 2020, https://www.thetimes.co.uk/article/labours-history-of-highs-and-lows-and-what-it-reveals-qbbh2twgz.

18. For example, the 32.7% share of the vote won by defeated Labour incumbent Melanie Onn in Great Grimsby is exactly the same share her predecessor Austin Mitchell won in his final victory of 2010. Mitchell prevailed because the two-thirds of Grimsby voters who backed someone else divided between five parties and an independent candidate. Onn similarly prevailed in 2015 with less than 40% of the vote because local opposition split evenly between the Conservatives and UKIP. Turnout in Great Grimsby also fell by nearly four points in 2019, a fall well above the national average.

19. See, for example, Duncan Weldon, 'The Truth Behind the Tories' Northern Strongholds', *The Economist*, 31 March 2021, https://www.economist.com/britain/2021/04/03/the-truth-behind-the-tories-northern-strongholds.

20. Edward Fieldhouse, Jane Green, Geoffrey Evans, Jonathan Mellon, Christopher Prosser, Hermann Schmitt and Cees van der Eijk, *Electoral Shocks: The Volatile Voter in a Turbulent World*. Oxford University Press, 2020.

21. Maria Sobolewska and Robert Ford, *Brexitland*. Cambridge University Press, 2020.

22. Labour also received an influx of voters from the Liberal Democrats after the latter party's collapse in 2015, helping to offset the loss of socially conservative school leavers to UKIP (ibid., Chapter 7).

23. Cowley and Kavanagh, *The British General Election of 2017*, pp. 94–95.

24. All quotes from Chapter 12 of David Butler and Dennis Kavanagh, *The British General Election of 1983*. Palgrave Macmillan, 1983.

25. See, for example, Tim Bale, 'Ploughed under? Labour's Grassroots Post-Corbyn', *Political Quarterly*, 92(2) (2021): 220–28.

26. Lewis Minkin, *The Blair Supremacy: A Study in the Politics of Labour's Party Management*. Manchester University Press, 2014.

Appendix 1: Further Analysis of the Results

John Curtice, Stephen Fisher, and Patrick English

This appendix provides additional analysis of the constituency results further to the material contained in Chapter 13.

Measuring Party Performance

When the election campaign was called, it was widely suggested that the outcome was particularly unpredictable.[1] One reason was the expectation that, thanks to the impact of Brexit on how people voted, there would be substantial variation between constituencies in the pattern of movement since 2017, variation that in turn could have an impact on how votes translated into seats.

Table A1.1 presents various measures of the change in support across constituencies recorded by the four parties that contested at least three-quarters of the seats at the election, together with the change in turnout. It shows for each party not only the change in its share of the overall votes cast across Britain as a whole, but also (i) the average (mean) change in its support in those seats that it fought in both 2017 and 2019, and (ii) the change in the median constituency, that is, the figure that divides constituencies into one half where the party's performance was better than average and one half where it was worse. The table also shows the equivalent statistics for two summary measures of the net change in support or swing between the Conservatives and Labour.

© The Editor(s) (if applicable) and The Author(s), under exclusive license
to Springer Nature Switzerland AG 2021
R. Ford et al., *The British General Election of 2019*,
https://doi.org/10.1007/978-3-030-74254-6

Table A1.1   Measures of change in support since 2017

	Overall	Mean	Median	Standard deviation
Change in Con vote	+1.2	+1.4	+1.4	4.6
Change in Lab vote	−8.0	−8.0	−7.6	4.3
Change in Lib Dem vote	+4.3	+4.1	+3.4	4.5
Change in Green vote	+1.1	+1.4	+1.3	1.4
Total-vote swing	+4.6	+4.7	+4.4	3.4
Two-party swing	+6.1	+6.1	+6.2	4.4
Change in turnout	−1.4	−1.4	−1.4	2.3

Note Buckingham (no Labour or Liberal Democrat candidate in 2017) and Chorley (no Conservative or Liberal Democrat candidate in 2019) are excluded from the calculation of all statistics apart from turnout. These two seats are also excluded from all analysis of party performance in Chapter 13 and this appendix. The Liberal Democrats only fought 611 seats, two of which the party did not contest in 2017. Excluding Chorley, the Greens fought 494 seats, 406 of which they also contested in 2017

Total vote swing is the average of the change in the Conservative share of the vote and the Labour share of the vote. Two-party swing is the change in the Conservative share of the votes cast for Conservative and Labour only (that is, the two-party vote). In both cases, a plus sign indicates a swing to the Conservatives and a minus sign a swing to Labour

If there is significant variation in party performance, the overall, mean and median changes can diverge from each other. If a party advances more strongly in constituencies in which fewer people voted, the mean increase in its share of the vote will be higher than the increase in its overall share—a pattern that might mean that it gains more seats than would otherwise be the case. However, there is little sign of that having happened. For the most part, the mean and overall changes are much the same. The biggest difference (of 0.3 points) arises in the case of the Greens, but here the comparison is affected by the fact that the party did not contest 137 seats.[2] Still, the mean increase in the Conservative share of the vote was slightly above the increase in the party's overall vote share, suggesting that the party advanced a little more strongly in seats where fewer people voted.

Meanwhile, the mean and the median will differ if a party does especially well or especially badly in a minority of seats. If a party does especially well in some seats, this will increase the mean change in its vote share, but will have relatively little impact on the median. If a party does very badly in a minority of constituencies, the median is likely to be higher than the mean. At +3.4, the median increase in the Liberal Democrat vote is well below the mean of +4.1. The party evidently did exceptionally well in some seats. The median fall in Labour support is somewhat less than the mean, indicating that the party lost support especially heavily in some seats. As a result, the median total vote swing between Conservative and Labour was also somewhat less than the mean.

These differences between the mean and the median change in party support indicate that there were some notable variations between constituencies in the parties' performances. However, a broader summary measure of the extent of this variation is given in the final column of Table A1.1, which shows the standard deviation of the change in each party's support across constituencies. The bigger the standard deviation, the more a party's performance varied from seat to seat.

In truth, marked variation in party performance from one constituency to another has been a feature of every British election since 1979, and for the most part, the standard deviation figures in the final column of Table A1.1 are little different from those recorded at other elections during the last 40 years.[3] While party performance did vary considerably from one constituency to another, the scale of the variation was far from exceptional. That said, as in 2017, it was the Conservatives whose performance varied the most. This stands in sharp contrast to the picture at every other election before 2017. This suggests that, at the last two elections, Brexit has had a particularly marked impact on the geography of Conservative support.[4]

TACTICAL VOTING BETWEEN PRO-SECOND REFERENDUM PARTIES

As noted in Chapter 13, there was relatively little sign of voters switching tactically from Liberal Democrat to Labour. That is true both of Remain seats the Conservatives were defending and those where Labour were the incumbents, but where the seat might be thought to have been at risk of being lost to the Conservatives.[5]

At +9.9 points, the average increase in the Liberal Democrat vote in Conservative Remain seats where the Liberal Democrats were starting in third place was only slightly less than the +10.5 point increase registered where the party began in second place, while, at −6.7, the fall in Labour's vote was only a little less where Labour started second than where it started third (−7.8). That said, the increase in the Liberal Democrat vote in the more marginal Conservative Remain seats where Labour were the main challenger (that is, where the Conservatives were less than 10 points ahead of Labour in 2017) was rather less (+6.3), while Labour's vote fell by a more modest −4.5 points in such seats. However, the Conservatives also performed relatively well in these seats, their vote falling on average by only −0.8 of a point, and this served to negate whatever tactical switching from the Liberal Democrats to Labour may have occurred.[6] Meanwhile, at +4.0 points, the increase in the Liberal Democrat vote in those Labour Remain seats where the Labour lead over the Conservatives had been less than 12 points in 2017 was only a little less than the +4.7 point increase in other Labour Remain seats. That said, an unusual −2.4 point drop in the Liberal Democrat vote in Canterbury appears to have benefited Labour (whose vote increased by +3.3 points) much more than the Conservatives (+0.5), and this could have been decisive in enabling Labour to retain what had been an unexpected and highly marginal gain in 2017.[7] Aside from this, tactical switching from the Liberal Democrats to Labour had no discernible impact on the outcome in seats.[8]

Chapter 13 also indicates that in Conservative Remain seats where the Liberal Democrats started off in a relatively close second place, they performed less well than they did in those seats where they were a more distant second. In most of these seats, there were relatively few Labour votes left to squeeze—on average, Labour had won just 13.7% of the vote in these seats in 2017. There was one exception—St Albans, where the Liberal Democrats had moved from third to second place in 2017, but Labour still had 23% of the vote. Here there was a −14.4 point drop in Labour's vote and a +17.7 point increase in Liberal Democrat support. This apparent fresh tactical switching from Labour to the Liberal Democrats—worth perhaps as much as 7.5 points of the total vote—is likely to have been decisive in enabling the Liberal Democrats to win the seat. But as in the case of tactical switching from the Liberal Democrats to Labour, it seems that switching from Labour to the Liberal Democrats only cost the Conservatives one seat.

Still, there were some remarkable Liberal Democrat advances in Conservative Remain seats, including a few where the party started off in third place.[9] These occurred in the south-eastern corner of England (that is, London, the South East and East Anglia), where the party's vote increased on average by +12.3 points, compared with +4.9 points elsewhere. The party's performance was also particularly strong in Conservative Remain seats with more graduates.[10] This repeats a pattern that was in evidence in the 2017 election and suggests that the Liberal

Democrats' strongly anti-Brexit stance had a particular appeal for a core group of Remain supporters living in or near the capital who were represented by a Conservative (and thus pro-Brexit) local MP. However, this success cannot simply be ascribed to tactical voting between Labour and the Liberal Democrats, for it came at the expense of the Conservatives as well as Labour.[11] However, absent a local Conservative MP, the tendency for the Liberal Democrats to do better in seats in the south-east of England and those with more graduates was much more muted, and insofar as they did advance, they seem to have done so primarily at the Conservatives' expense.[12]

TACTICAL VOTING IN SCOTLAND

In Scotland, the debate about the country's constitutional status sits alongside the debate about Brexit.[13] But whereas one party, the SNP, is dominant among the parties who advocate independence, support for those parties who wish to maintain the Union is divided between the Conservatives, Labour and the Liberal Democrats. In a mirror image of the position of the pro-second referendum parties in England and Wales, this fragmentation potentially put the unionist parties at a disadvantage unless voters backed whichever unionist party appeared best able to win locally.

Of this, however, there were only limited signs. Consider, for example, the picture in those seats where the Conservatives came first or second in 2017. Here the Conservative vote (an average drop of −2.8 points) held up only a little better than elsewhere (−3.6 points), while, conversely, at −9.4 points, the fall in the Labour vote was just a little higher than in other seats (−7.8 points). These figures imply that maybe around 1% or so of voters switched from Labour to the Conservatives, but no more. The picture is little different if we confine our attention to those seats, 14 in all, where the Conservatives were third in 2015 but moved into first or second place in 2017, and where, consequently, there was a new incentive for the supporters of the other unionist parties that had slipped into third place or below to switch to the Conservatives. At −2.7 points, the drop in the Conservative vote was again only a little less than elsewhere. Similarly, if we focus on the dozen seats that the Conservatives gained in 2017, we find that the party's share of the vote fell on average by −2.8 points, only a little below the −3.4 point fall elsewhere,[14] while, at −9.2 points, the fall in Labour's vote was just under a point worse than the party's performance elsewhere (−8.3). The ability of the Conservatives to profit from a squeeze on the Labour vote in some of these newly acquired seats was constrained by the fact that Labour was already weak locally. Only in one instance (Dumfries & Galloway, where the Conservative vote was up by +0.8 of a point and Labour's down by −11.7) does it look plausible to suggest that tactical voting might have saved the incumbent Conservative MP. The picture is much the same in those seats that in 2017 had been successfully defended by the SNP, but where the Conservatives now found themselves less than five points behind the nationalists. Even though this position might have been thought to have created an incentive for unionist voters to switch to the Conservatives in these seats, again the evidence—an average fall in the Conservative vote of −2.4 points and a drop in Labour support of −9.4 points—suggests at most only limited tactical voting.[15]

The position in seats where Labour started off in first or second place varied from constituency to constituency, but again not in a way that is suggestive of widespread anti-SNP tactical voting. Labour's vote fell on average by −8.1 points in such seats, only a little below the −8.7 point fall the party experienced where it was starting off in third place. However, the party did perform relatively well in the subset of these seats that it won in 2017. Here, Labour's vote fell on average by just −5.5 points. This, though, was not accompanied by any equivalent marked weakness in either the Conservative or the Liberal Democrat performance, but rather by a weaker SNP advance of +4.9 points—more than three points below what the nationalists were achieving elsewhere. This suggests that Labour's relative success in these seats is better accounted for by the ability of the local Labour MP, who in all but one case was first elected in 2017, to secure personal support for their recent service to the constituency, rather than because of anti-SNP tactical voting.[16] However, nowhere was this sufficient to enable Labour to defend the seat against the national tide.

That said, there are some signs that Labour may have profited from tactical switching by unionist voters in seats where the party had been a close second to the SNP in 2017. In the nine seats where the SNP majority over Labour was less than five points in 2017, Labour's vote fell on average by −6.5 points, whereas in less marginal seats where Labour finished second, the party's vote fell by as much as −10.1 points. Meanwhile, at −5.1 points, the fall in Conservative support was nearly twice as large in marginal SNP/Labour contests than in less marginal ones. However, given that support for Labour was in decline, this apparent tactical movement proved too little to enable Labour to gain any seats.

The willingness—or otherwise—of Conservative supporters to switch tactically also mattered in the handful of seats, just five in total, where the Liberal Democrats shared first and second place with the SNP. The Liberal Democrat performance varied very substantially in these seats. In Fife North East, where the party lost out very narrowly to the SNP in 2017, the party registered what was by far its best performance anywhere in Scotland, an increase of +10.2 points. On the other hand, in both Orkney & Shetland, a seat held by the Liberals or the Liberal Democrats ever since 1950, and East Dunbartonshire, the seat that the party's UK leader, Jo Swinson, recaptured in 2017, the party's vote actually fell back, in both cases by as much as −3.8 points.

Much of this variation seems to be accounted for by the behaviour of Conservative supporters. The Liberal Democrat advance in Fife North East was accompanied by the heaviest fall anywhere in Conservative support (−11.1 points), making the constituency one clear instance where apparent tactical voting cost the SNP a seat. In contrast, support for the Conservatives actually increased in Orkney & Shetland (by +1.2 points) and fell by only half a point in East Dunbartonshire. Both of these seats are ones where the Conservative vote has previously appeared to have been squeezed to the advantage of the Liberal Democrats, and it appears that some former Liberal Democrat voters now decided to switch back to the Conservatives—perhaps in the Northern Isles because the local MP (Alistair Carmichael) now appeared to be safe, while in East Dunbartonshire some erstwhile Conservatives may have been reluctant to vote tactically for someone (Jo Swinson) who was no longer just their local MP but also her party's UK leader. In any event, in withdrawing their support, they appear to have been instrumental in ensuring that Ms Swinson became the first party leader to lose his or her seat since Sir Archibald Sinclair of the Liberal Party in 1945.[17]

THE GREEN PARTY

The Greens recorded their second-best performance in a general election. On average, the party (together with the autonomous Scottish Greens) won 3.4% of the vote in the 494 seats that it contested in Great Britain, well up on the 2.1% that it won in 2017 (when it fought 460 seats), but still below the record 4.2% that it secured in 2015 (568 seats). In those seats that the party fought both times, its vote was up on average by +1.4 points on 2017, but down by −0.9 of a point on 2015.[18]

The party's performance reflected the outcome of the EU referendum locally in 2016, but less strongly than in the case of the larger parties (see Table A1.2).[19] The party's share of the vote was twice as high (5.6%) in seats in England and Wales where over 60% voted Remain than it was in those seats where more than 60% had voted Leave (2.8 points). In addition, the party's share of the vote increased between 2017 and 2019 by one point more in the most pro-Remain seats that it fought both times than it did in the most pro-Leave seats. But beyond the most pro-Remain seats, there was little relationship between the party's performance and the strength of the Remain vote in 2016. Moreover, the party was furthest adrift from its performance in 2015 in the most pro-Remain seats that it fought, while it did not perform particularly well in pro-Remain Scotland.[20]

Table A1.2 Green Performance 2015–2019 by Estimated EU Referendum Vote in England and Wales

Brexit vote 2016	Mean % vote			Mean change in % vote	
	2015	2017	2019	2015–2019	2017–2019
Remain over 60%	7.7	3.3	5.6	−2.7	+2.2
	(63)	(57)	(51)	(51)	(48)
Remain 50–60%	4.7	2.0	3.3	−1.4	+1.4
	(104)	(91)	(85)	(83)	(78)
All Remain seats	*5.8*	*2.5*	*4.2*	*−1.9*	*+1.7*
	(167)	*(148)*	*136)*	*(134)*	*(126)*
Leave 50–60%	3.9	2.0	3.3	−0.7	+1.4
	(228)	(191)	(205)	(196)	(175)
Leave over 60%	3.0	1.7	2.8	−0.1	+1.2
	(140)	(116)	(130)	(117)	(102)
All Leave seats	*3.5*	*1.9*	*3.1*	*−0.5*	*+1.4*
	(368)	*(307)*	*(335)*	*(313)*	*(277)*
All seats	4.3	2.1	3.4	−0.5	1.4
	(535)	(455)	(471)	(447)	(403)

Note Each entry in the table is confined to seats contested by the Greens. Figures in brackets represent the number of seats on which the mean is based. Buckingham and Chorley are excluded

Plaid Cymru

Plaid Cymru's support has long been concentrated in those constituencies with the most Welsh speakers. However, this relationship became even stronger in 2019. The party suffered sharp declines in three South Wales constituencies (Blaenau Gwent (−15.6), Cynon Valley (−8.6), and Rhondda (−5.3)) where it had hitherto performed relatively well, despite the fact that they contain relatively few Welsh speakers, while the three largest increases in the party's vote were in three of the four most Welsh-speaking constituencies, all seats that the party already held (Arfon (+4.3), Ceredigion (+8.7), and Dwyfor Merionnydd (+3.2)). So far as Westminster elections at least are concerned, the party's hopes of gaining significant ground in less Welsh-speaking parts of the country appear to be as remote as ever.

The three seats where the party's support fell back especially heavily all voted relatively strongly for Leave, while the three in which it advanced most strongly all voted for Remain. However, once we put these seats to one side, there is no relationship between the outcome of the referendum locally in 2016 and Plaid's performance at this election. The average increase in the party's vote in the 15 seats where more than 55% voted Leave was, at +0.2, almost exactly the same as that in the 15 seats where less than 55% did so (+0.1). It seems that for the most part, voters' reactions to Brexit were not central to the party's fortunes.

The Brexit Party and UKIP

With an average share of 5.5% where it stood, the Brexit Party performed rather more strongly than UKIP had done in 2017 (when its average tally was 3.3%). But Nigel Farage's new party was generally still well short of what his old party had achieved at the height of its general election popularity in 2015 (an average vote share of 13.5%). Even in seats where over 60% had voted Leave in 2016, the Brexit Party's average 10.3% share of the vote represented little more than half of what UKIP had secured in the same seats in 2015 (19.9%). True, the party did come somewhat closer to emulating UKIP's 2015 vote in the North East, Yorkshire and Wales, where on average the party's vote was 'only' 7.3 points lower than UKIP's vote in 2015. But elsewhere, its vote was as much as 13.5 points lower.[21] In short, Farage was unable to make the same impact on voters across the country that he had managed to achieve four years earlier.

UKIP, of course, had not entirely given up the ghost; however, it was a shadow of its former self, fighting just 35 seats in England and Wales—well down on the 368 it contested in 2017, although 11 of those that it contested were seats it had chosen not to contest in 2017.[22] On average, the party managed just 1.1% of the vote, down −2.3 points in the two dozen seats that it had also contested in 2017. Even in those seats where more than 60% had voted Leave in 2016, the party won only 1.6% of the vote. In contrast to the Brexit Party, UKIP did contest some seats held by the Conservatives. However, the resulting absence of a Brexit Party candidate profited UKIP little: on average, it won just 0.4% more of the vote in such seats, and was down on its 2017 vote by just a point less than elsewhere. In short, UKIP had relatively little success in winning over those who perhaps might have voted for the Brexit Party had the latter been standing locally, and thus did little to negate the impact of Mr Farage's decision not to contest seats the Conservatives were defending. Meanwhile, in seats that were contested by both UKIP and the Brexit Party, the extra competition for the Eurosceptic vote had little discernible impact on the Brexit Party's performance.[23]

Candidates

New and Old Liberal Democrats

A record number of seven former Conservative and Labour MPs stood at this election for the Liberal Democrats. All bar one[24] registered an above-average performance as compared with that of other Liberal Democrats contesting similar kinds of seat, on average securing a +15.4 point increase in support. This was despite the fact that only two of them stood in the constituency they had hitherto represented and where they might thus have been able to bring a personal vote with them to their new party.[25] However, none did well enough to secure election. The most striking performance was achieved by Luciana Berger in Finchley & Golders Green (+25.2); Ms Berger left the Labour Party over its failure to handle anti-semitism and was contesting the constituency with the largest Jewish population in Britain. She managed to push Labour into third place, as did her former Labour colleague, Chuka Umunna, in the heavily pro-Remain Cities of London & Westminster seat (+19.6).

Also of particular note was the performance of former Conservative MP Phillip Lee in the Remain seat of Wokingham (+21.8), which was represented by the prominent pro-Brexit MP John Redwood. Despite these relatively strong performances, the fate of the Liberal Democrat defectors in 2019 will have done little to encourage others to make a similar move in future.

Three other former MPs, two Labour and one Conservative, fought under the banner of Change UK, which had been formed in February 2019 as a new centrist pro-Remain party, but which subsequently lost many of its parliamentary recruits to the Liberal Democrats (see Chapter 5). They fared even less well than their former colleagues. On average, the three candidates won just 6.5% of the vote. The most successful was the former high-profile Conservative MP Anna Soubry, who secured 8.5% of the vote; although her Broxtowe seat had voted Leave, unlike her two colleagues, she had the advantage that the Liberal Democrats did not stand against her. Even so, at +4.4%, the increase in her support on what the Liberal Democrats had achieved locally in 2017 was not more than would have been anticipated if a Liberal Democrat candidate had contested the seat instead.

The individual popularity of the party's local standard bearers has long been of particular importance for the Liberal Democrats. This was again apparent in 2019. In the two seats where the local Liberal Democrat MP stood down (Norman Lamb in North Norfolk and Sir Vince Cable in Twickenham), the party's performance was down on what would have been expected given the balance of Remain and Leave support locally.[26] But what has also mattered for the Liberal Democrats at recent elections has not only been the popularity of their current MPs, but also that of the party's former MPs who have stood again in seats that they formerly represented. These candidates often appear to have retained some of their personal popularity despite no longer being the local MP.[27] However, there is a risk that this proves to be a diminishing asset over time. There were four seats in England where the former Liberal Democrat MP tried for a second time to regain their seat, but on average, their vote fell by −2.0 points.[28] But even in the one seat that was only lost in 2017 and where the former MP stood again, Ceredigion, support for the party fell by −11.6 points in what uniquely was a contest between the Liberal Democrats and Plaid Cymru. That said, the party's chances of recapturing two seats, Cheltenham and Cheadle, may well have been diminished by the fact that the former MP who had stood again in 2017 did not do so in 2019; at +4.8 points, the average increase in the party's vote in these seats was well below what would have been expected for a Conservative Remain seat (see p. 466, Table 13.2) and in both cases left the party narrowly trailing the Conservative winner. Equally, the party certainly seems to have suffered in two Labour Remain seats, Sheffield Hallam (−1.3) and Leeds North West (−15.9), by the fact that the Liberal Democrat MP who lost in 2017 opted not to rejoin the fray.

CANDIDATE ETHNICITY AND GENDER

A record number of ethnic minority MPs (65) were elected in 2019 (see Chapter 11).[29] Indeed, both the Conservatives (67) and Labour (75) fielded a record number of ethnic minority candidates in England and Wales, though those nominated by Labour were more likely than were those nominated by the Conservatives to be standing in a winnable seat.[30] Meanwhile, as at other recent elections, fielding such a candidate appears to have made a difference to the vote secured by Conservative candidates, but not by their Labour counterparts.[31] Where the Conservatives fielded an ethnic minority candidate in 2019 after not having done so in 2017, their vote fell on average by −1.2 points. In contrast, Conservative support increased by +2.1 points where either a white candidate or an ethnic minority candidate was fielded on both occasions. This discrepancy cannot be accounted for by the incumbency status of the candidate (see pp. 479–480) or the ethnic composition of the constituency, while it is apparent in both Leave and Remain seats. What is more, where the Conservative candidate in 2019 was white but the previous candidate was from a minority background in 2017, the average rise in the Conservative vote was, at +2.8 points, a little higher than elsewhere. The relatively socially conservative character of Conservative support still appears to be reflected in a reluctance by a few of the party's potential voters to back a more ethnically diverse parliamentary party.

In contrast, no such reluctance is evident in Labour's support. At −8.1 points, the average drop in support for the party in seats where it nominated a white candidate in 2017 but a minority candidate in 2019 was exactly the same as it was in seats where either a white candidate stood both times or an ethnic minority candidate did so. True, support for the party fell rather less—by −5.6 points—where an ethnic minority candidate in 2017 was replaced by a white candidate in 2019. However, this seems largely to reflect the fact that nearly all such changes occurred in Conservative-held seats where for the most part support for Labour was falling somewhat less anyway.

In Scotland, where most constituencies only have a small ethnic minority population, there were relatively few ethnic minority candidates. Three stood for the Conservatives; on average, their share of the vote fell by −3.1 points, little different from the Scotland-wide average for the party. Meanwhile, four ethnic minority candidates stood for Labour. In two instances—Aberdeen North (−16.8) and Falkirk (−18.6)—there were especially heavy falls in the Labour vote; however, in Falkirk, the Labour candidate was disowned by the party following claims of anti-semitic social media posts. The two other Labour ethnic minority candidates—in Glasgow Central (a seat where one in four identified as ethnic minority at the last census and where the Labour vote fell by only −5.3 points) and in Angus (where it fell by −8.3 points)—did not fare especially badly.

For the first time, the proportion of female MPs in the Commons exceeded one in three (220 or 34%). Indeed, slightly over half (51%) of successful Labour candidates were women, the first time that either of the two largest parliamentary parties has comprised more female than male MPs. This reflected the fact that Labour female candidates were just as likely as men to be nominated in a winnable seat—in England and Wales, the share of the vote won by Labour in 2017 in seats that were contested by a woman in 2019 was, at 44.0%, slightly above the 43.7% achieved two years previously in seats where Labour nominated a man. The outcome had nothing to do with any particular propensity—or reluctance—to vote for female Labour candidates—at −8.0 points, the average drop in Labour support in seats fought by a man in 2017 and a woman in 2019 was exactly the same as the average drop in seats that were fought by a candidate of the same gender both times.

In contrast, at +0.6 of a point, the increase in Conservative support in seats where the party's nominee had been a man in 2017 but was a woman in 2019 was rather less than the +2.3 point rise registered in seats where the gender of the candidate was unchanged. However, much of this difference disappears once we take into account the level of support for Leave locally.[32] The fact that a lower proportion of Conservative female candidates (51%) were elected than were their male counterparts (68%) was a consequence of the fact that female Conservative candidates were less likely to be standing in a winnable seat. On average, the

Table A1.3   Change in Conservative, Labour and Liberal Democrat support, 2005–2015 and 2015–2019 by EU Referendum Vote

	Mean Change in % vote						Seats
	Conservative		Labour		Liberal Democrat		
2016 EU referendum result	2005–15	2015–19	2005–15	2015–19	2005–15	2015–19	
Remain over 60%	+4.5	−5.5	+5.1	+6.3	−16.4	+8.0	64
Remain 50–60%	+5.3	−0.1	−0.5	+4.4	−15.6	+6.7	107
All Remain seats	*+5.0*	*−2.1*	*+1.6*	*+5.1*	*−15.9*	*+7.1*	*171*
Leave 50–60%	+6.0	+7.7	−4.9	+3.0	−14.9	+3.0	240
Leave over 60%	+4.7	+16.1	−9.0	−2.0	−12.2	+1.6	160
All Leave seats	*+5.5*	*+11.0*	*−6.5*	*+1.0*	*−13.8*	*+2.4*	*400*
All seats	+5.3	+7.1	−4.1	+2.2	−14.4	+3.9	571

Conservatives won 40.7% of the vote in 2017 in seats where the party was represented by a woman in 2019, whereas the figure was 45.5% where the candidate was a man. Meanwhile, just over 40% of the candidates nominated by one of the four largest parties in Scotland were women, while women comprised only around one in three (32%) of those elected. However, there is no systematic evidence that women performed any worse (or better) than men.[33]

THE LONG-TERM IMPACT OF BREXIT

This was the second election in a row at which there was a relationship between party performance and the outcome of the EU referendum locally. As a result, as Table A1.3 shows, the cumulative impact of this relationship since 2015 has been substantial. Support for the Conservatives has fallen over this period in Remain constituencies, whereas the party is now much stronger in Leave seats. Support for Labour, meanwhile, has risen most among the most pro-Remain seats, but has fallen back in the most pro-Leave seats. At the same time, the recovery in Liberal Democrat support since 2015 has been much more marked in Remain seats than Leave ones.

However, the UK's relationship with the EU—and thus its potential to influence how people voted—was already the subject of political debate before 2015. That election saw UKIP win as much as 13% of the vote across Britain as a whole and displace the Liberal Democrats as the third most popular party in England. Meanwhile, concern about immigration—a concern that eventually played a key role in the EU referendum[34]—also manifested itself in a relatively high level of support for the British National Party (BNP) in 2010, an election at which UKIP also achieved what then also was a record level of support.[35] So perhaps there were already signs of a significant shift in the geography of party support before 2015?

There were some. True, the increase in support for the Conservatives between 2005 and 2015 varied little between Remain and Leave constituencies—in stark contrast to the position since.[36] However, the same was not true of support for Labour. During this period, the Labour vote increased in those seats that went on to give more than 60% of their support to Remain, while it fell back markedly in seats that backed Leave. In part, Labour may have gained disproportionately in some Remain seats from the particularly marked decline in Liberal Democrat support that occurred in some such constituencies.[37] At the same time, however, Leave seats voted most heavily for the BNP in 2010 and for UKIP in 2015, and analyses at the time suggested that these increases may have hurt Labour more than the Conservatives.[38] In any event, it is clear that the relative decline in Labour support in more pro-Leave parts of Britain pre-dates the EU referendum and its aftermath.

As a result of all these changes, Britain's electoral geography looks very different from a decade and a half ago. Back in 2005, support for Labour was highest in the most pro-Leave constituencies, but by 2015, this was already no longer the case (see Table A1.4). Now the party is weakest in these seats, while it is strongest in the most pro-Remain seats in the country. Meanwhile, although in 2005 the Conservatives were somewhat weaker in the most pro-Remain seats, otherwise the level of support for the party bore little relationship to the outcome of the EU referendum. Now the party is far stronger in Leave Britain than it is in Remain Britain. And although the Liberal Democrats have long since fared relatively well in the most pro-Remain parts of the country, the concentration of the party's support in those places is now much more marked.

Table A1.4 Average Conservative, Labour and Liberal Democrat Share of the Vote, 2005, 2015 and 2019, by EU Referendum Vote

2016 EU referendum result	Conservative	Labour	Liberal Democrat	Seats
	%	%	%	
Remain over 60%				64
2005	25.4	38.8	27.6	
2015	29.9	43.8	11.2	
2019	24.4	50.1	19.3	
Remain 50–60%				107
2005	36.2	32.6	24.8	
2015	41.5	32.1	9.3	
2019	41.4	36.6	16.1	
Leave 50–60%				240
2005	35.6	34.7	23.3	
2015	41.6	29.9	8.4	
2019	49.2	32.9	11.5	
Leave over 60%				160
2005	32.1	43.5	16.9	
2015	36.8	34.5	4.8	
2019	52.9	32.5	6.3	

These patterns have had important implications for what was until recently regarded as a staple feature of post-war British electoral geography—that predominantly middle-class constituencies vote heavily for the Conservatives, while working-class ones tend to be bastions of Labour support. Seats that voted Leave typically have a relatively large proportion of working-class voters and fewer in professional and managerial occupations, while the opposite is true of the most pro-Remain constituencies.[39] The fact that the former group of seats has swung strongly to the Conservatives while the latter has moved in Labour's direction means that, as Table A1.5 shows, the Conservatives have gained ground heavily since 2005 in strongly working-class seats, while Labour's position has strengthened in middle-class seats.[40] Labour's support is still somewhat higher in the most working-class constituencies, but the Conservatives are no longer particularly weak in such seats. Indeed, of all the parties, it is now the Liberal Democrats, supposedly Britain's cross-class party, whose level of support differs most between the most and least working-class constituencies. Chapter 14 shows how the social class of

Table A1.5 Conservative, Labour and Liberal Democrat support, 2019, and change in support 2005–2019, by % Working Class

% working class	Conservative		Labour		Liberal Democrat		Seats
	% vote 2019	Change in % vote 2005–19	% vote 2019	Change in % vote 2005–19	% vote 2019	Change in % vote 2005–19	
Less than 21%	41.8	+3.1	33.2	+4.5	19.8	−6.8	137
21–25%	49.5	+10.8	32.4	+0.9	13.2	−10.9	138
25–30%	49.9	+15.6	34.2	−2.6	9.7	−12.1	145
More than 30%	43.0	+19.3	41.2	−9.5	5.0	−12.2	151

Note Working class: percentage of working-age population in routine or semi-routine occupations, 2011 Census

individual voters made little difference to how people voted in 2019, and it is clear that this is reflected in a changed geography of party support too.[41] Brexit and its associated issues such as immigration have truly had a profound impact on the pattern of voting behaviour in Britain.

REGISTRATION AND TURNOUT

The 2019 election was fought on a new electoral register introduced less than a fortnight earlier (at the beginning of December 2019). This was the newest register to be used at any election since February 1974, at which election the register had also only come into force just a fortnight before. Meanwhile, in contrast to 1974, the comprehensiveness of the register was potentially enhanced by the fact that those eligible to vote but missing from the register when it was originally compiled could apply online to be added to the list of voters until just over a fortnight before polling day.

As at previous elections since its introduction in 2014, the availability of online rolling registration produced a flood of applications—around 3.85 million were filed between the day the election was called on 29 October and the cut-off date of 26 November.[42] But as in 2015 and 2017,[43] the number of names that were ultimately added represented a small proportion of the applications: there were just over 350,000 more names on the register on election day than there had been when the register was originally compiled. With voters unable to check online whether or not they were already registered, most of those who applied in the run-up to the election were in fact already on the register.

Online registration applications are most likely to be filed by younger people. However, this is not necessarily evidence of a particular enthusiasm among younger voters to participate—after all, they are more likely to be missed by the regular registration procedure in the first place.[44] In any event, at 818, the average names added to the register in constituencies where at the time of the 2011 Census more than 10% were aged 18–24 proved to be much the same as the Figure (830) for seats where less than 7% belonged to that age group. Meanwhile, suggestions that the procedure was of more benefit to Labour than the Conservatives[45] were not confirmed by the fact that on average, 689 names were added in Conservative-held seats compared with 362 in Labour ones.

All other things being equal, the newness of the register should have served to increase the officially recorded level of turnout—the register should have contained fewer people who had died since its compilation. Yet, at 67.5%, overall official turnout was −1.4 points down on 2017. Participation was still higher than at any election between 2001 and 2015, but still lower than at any between 1945 and 1997. It seems that the strength of voters' inclination to cast a ballot remains lower than it was for much of the post-war period.

Voting theory and past experience suggests that people should be more likely to cast a ballot when the contest appears close.[46] That expectation was fulfilled at this election. In seats in England and Wales where the winning party had a majority of less than five points in 2017, turnout fell by just −0.8 of a point. In contrast, in those where the majority had been more than 10 points, the drop was −1.9 points. Even bigger was the difference between those seats where the winner's majority had been more than 10 points in 2015 but less than five points in 2017 (a −0.1 drop) and those which had been marginal in 2015 but were no longer so in 2017 (a −2.9 point drop).

Turnout held up relatively well in seats where the Liberal Democrats were mounting a challenge to the Conservatives. Not only did turnout on average slip by just −0.1 of a point in seats where the Liberal Democrats had been second to the Conservatives in 2017, but the same was true of those Conservative-held seats where the Liberal Democrats gained second place from Labour in 2019. Moreover, in those Conservative/Liberal Democrat battles where the Liberal Democrat vote rose by more than 10 points, turnout actually edged up on average by +0.3 of a point. The Liberal Democrats' campaigning efforts were concentrated in these seats—on average, the party spent 70% of the permitted spending limit in seats where it ended up second to the Conservatives, compared with 32% across England and Wales as a whole—and it may well be that the resulting local campaign activity motivated some voters to go to the polls.

In Scotland, where turnout increased by +1.8 points, the 2017 election left a legacy of 22 seats where the winning margin had been less than five points—compared with none in 2015—and another 24 where the majority was less than 10 points (five in 2015). This marked change in the country's electoral geography partly explains much of the increased turnout north of the border. In seats where the majority in 2017 was less than five points, turnout increased on average by +2.1 points, while in those where it was between 5 and 10 (and had been more than 10 in 2015) by +1.5 points. Elsewhere, the rise was a more modest +1.0 point. Even in Scotland's safer constituencies, turnout often increased—at a time when, as noted earlier, Brexit had breathed new life into the debate about independence. The potential of the latter to draw voters to the polls had previously been demonstrated at the 2014 referendum and the 2015 general election.[47]

BIAS AND EXAGGERATION IN THE ELECTORAL SYSTEM

The single-member plurality electoral system is often defended on the grounds that it enables voters to choose between alternative governments.[48] This implies that although it might give the largest party a bonus in terms of seats, it should still be even-handed in its treatment of the two largest parties—for example, if the positions of the parties had been reversed at this election, Labour would have profited from its operation to the same extent as the Conservatives did. If this is not the case, the system may be said to be treating the Conservatives more favourably than Labour. To address this issue, we examine what would happen were another election to be held on the current constituency boundaries, with the same turnout, levels of third-party support and electoral geography, but with different levels of support for Labour and the Conservatives. In other words, we examine what would be the impact on the outcome in seats of a uniform swing between the two largest parties, given the electoral geography of party support in 2019.

Table A1.6 Relationship between votes and seats following the 2019 general election

Swing to Con from 2019 result	% vote (GB)			Seats (UK)			
	Con	Lab	Con lead	Con	Lab	Others	Majority
0.0	44.7	33.0	11.7	365	203	82	Con 80
−3.5	41.2	36.5	4.7	325	238	88	None
−5.85	38.85	38.85	0.0	290	267	93	None
−7.0	37.7	40.0	−2.3	278	280	92	None
−11.7	33.0	44.7	−11.7	232	324	94	None
−12.0	32.7	45.0	−12.3	229	326	95	Lab 2
−15.5	29.2	48.5	−19.3	194	366	90	Lab 82

Table A1.6 reveals that the electoral system is not currently even-handed in its treatment of the Conservatives and Labour. If Labour had enjoyed as large a lead over the Conservatives as the Conservatives secured in 2019 (11.7 points), rather than winning a majority of 80, the party would have narrowly missed out on obtaining an overall majority at all. To replicate the scale of the Conservatives' success, Labour would have had to have been 19 points ahead of the Conservatives—a bigger lead than any party has achieved at any post-war election. Meanwhile, if the two parties had exactly the same share of the vote, the Conservatives would still be ahead by 23 seats—Labour would have to be just over two points ahead of the Conservatives before they secured more seats than their principal rivals.

The Conservatives were rewarded more richly than Labour would have been because their vote was more efficiently distributed across constituencies. Even though Labour were well behind the Conservatives in terms of the overall popular vote, the party's average percentage majority in those seats that it did manage to win was, at 25.3%, only a little below the 26.7% lead the Conservatives enjoyed in the seats they won. At 20%, the proportion of seats Labour won with a majority of more than 40% almost matched the proportion that the Conservatives won by that same margin (23%). Meanwhile, if, as a result of a uniform swing, the two parties were to win the same share of the overall vote nationally, the average majority in seats Labour would win would be 28.9%, compared with just 21.8% in seats won by the Conservatives.

But the system does not work entirely in the Conservatives' favour. Although in October 2018 the parliamentary boundary commissions (there is one in each part of the UK) published proposals for new constituency boundaries based on the registered electorate in December 2015, their proposals were never put before Parliament. As a result, the election was fought on boundaries that were almost two decades old and thus failed to reflect the pattern of population movement since then—a pattern that for a long time had seen the electorate grow more rapidly in rural and suburban areas (and much of the south-eastern corner of England) represented by Conservative MPs than it had in more urban areas where Labour were stronger.[49]

Consequently, those seats that elected a Conservative MP in 2019 on average contained 2,470 more registered voters (74,679) than did seats won by Labour (72,209). However, this gap was not as large as it had been in 2015 and 2017. In 2017, the average constituency won by the Conservatives contained 3,922 more registered voters, while in 2015 this figure stood at 3,829. In fact, the difference between Conservative and Labour constituencies in their rate of growth in the electorate has come to a halt, as the movement of voters out of the inner city has slowed and in some instances (such as London) been reversed.[50] Between 2017 and 2019, the electorate grew by 1,134 in seats won by Labour in 2017, a figure that matched the equivalent increase of 1,101 in seats won by the Conservatives. Meanwhile, constituencies with more Leave voters— in which the Conservatives advanced most strongly and made nearly all of their gains—typically have a smaller electorate than those that backed Remain. Consequently, at 69,210, the average electorate in seats gained by the Conservatives at this election was well below that in the average constituency won by Labour (72,209), thereby reducing the difference in the size of the average Conservative and Labour constituency. In short, the change in the electoral geography of party support brought about by Brexit served to reduce the extent to which differences in the registered electorate worked to the Conservatives' disadvantage. This means that the new parliamentary constituencies that should be implemented before the next election are now likely to have less of a partisan impact than they would have had previously.[51]

That said, two other potential sources of bias worked more to the Conservatives' disadvantage than in 2017. As noted in Chapter 13, turnout fell rather more in Labour than in Conservative seats. As a result, at 63.8%, the average turnout in seats won by Labour at this election was over five points below the equivalent figure among Conservative seats (69.0%). On average, as many as 5,498 fewer votes were cast in the average Labour seat than in the typical Conservative one—far bigger than the difference of 2,470 between them in the size of the registered electorate. Meanwhile, the Conservatives 'waste' rather more votes than Labour in losing in constituencies won by third parties. On average, the party won 23.9% of the vote in seats won by parties other than the Conservatives or Labour, while Labour won only 18.8%, whereas in 2017, these proportions were, at 25.7% and 25.9% respectively, almost identical. The difference is wholly accounted for by the fact that the Conservatives were far stronger (average vote share 29.0%) than Labour (7.5%) in the 11 seats won at this election by the Liberal Democrats.

In delivering a substantial overall majority for one party, the outcome of the 2019 election stood in marked contrast to that of the three preceding contests, which produced two hung parliaments and one very narrow majority. These outcomes had raised question marks about the continued ability of the single-member plurality electoral system to produce the safe overall majorities that are a crucial underpinning to the claim that the system facilitates a choice between alternative governments. Does the substantial majority achieved by the Conservatives in 2019 mean that these doubts can now be put to rest?

Not necessarily. Another key feature of Table A1.6 is the wide range of outcomes—from a Conservative majority of just under five points to a Labour one of 12—that under our assumptions would result in no overall majority. Meanwhile, even the majority of 80 obtained by the Conservatives was relatively small by historical standards, given the party's 11.7 point lead. Almost exactly the same Conservative lead in 1987 (11.8 points) resulted in an overall majority of 102, while the only slightly larger lead secured by Labour in 1997 (12.8 points) resulted in a landslide majority of 179.

Substantial though they were, the changes in the electoral geography of party support at the 2019 election did nothing to increase the likelihood that the single-member plurality electoral system will produce safe overall majorities in future. That likelihood depends on two conditions.[52] First, relatively few seats are won by 'third' parties. Yet, thanks to the geographical concentration of some of these parties' support, as many as 82 such MPs were elected in 2019 (including 18 from Northern Ireland), up 12 on 2017 and well above the figure recorded at any election before 1997. Second, a significant proportion of seats should be closely contested between the Conservatives and Labour, so that relatively small swings in votes produce a high turnover of seats. However, at 88, the number of such seats remains almost the same as it was in 2017 (89) and is little more than half what it was in the 1950s and 1960s.[53] The Conservatives may have won a safe overall majority at this election, but there is no guarantee that they—or Labour—will be able to do so again.

NOTES

1. See, for example, Matthew Goodwin, 'Why Britain's 2019 Election Is Its Most Unpredictable in Recent History', 7 November 2019, https://www.chathamhouse.org/2019/11/why-britains-2019-election-its-most-unpredictable-recent-history; and Chris Hanretty, 'Why UK Election Outcome Is Impossible to Predict', *Politico*, 29 October 2019, https://www.politico.eu/article/why-uk-election-outcome-is-impossible-to-predict-boris-johnson-brexit-labour-conservative-party.

2. The increase in the Greens' share of the overall vote in those seats that the party fought in both 2017 and 2019 was +1.5 points, little different from the mean figure in our table.

3. See John Curtice, Stephen Fisher, Robert Ford and Patrick English, 'Appendix 1: The Results Analysed' in Philip Cowley and Dennis Kavanagh, *The British General Election of 2017*. Palgrave Macmillan, p. 451 and the relevant tables in previous appendices to books in *The British General Election of* ... series.

4. On the relationship between the geography of Brexit and party performance in 2017, see ibid., pp. 453–454.

5. Given the strength of the Conservative performance in Leave constituencies, there was little prospect that tactical switching between Labour and the Liberal Democrats would make a difference to the outcome in any such seat. In the event, at −6.8, the average fall in Labour's vote in Leave seats where the party was within 10 points of the Conservatives in 2019 was little different from the −7.2 drop that the party suffered in Conservative Leave seats as a whole, while a slightly below-average increase in the Liberal Democrat vote (+2.7 points) was accompanied by an above-average increase in Conservative support (+5.6). Meanwhile, the Liberal Democrat vote fell in the two Leave seats where the party started off within 10 points of the Conservatives—as indeed it did in two of the three Leave seats the Liberal Democrats were attempting to defend against a Conservative challenge (while in the third the increase was only +0.1 of a point). As in many a Remain seat, there was little of a Labour vote (average 12.7% in 2017) left to squeeze in these seats.

6. The one seat in this group that Labour did gain from the Conservatives, Putney, was one instance where there was a sharp decline in Conservative support (−8.4 points) and it is this rather than anti-Conservative tactical voting that primarily seems to have accounted for the party's loss of the seat.

7. The outcome in Canterbury may well have been influenced by the decision of the original Liberal Democrat candidate to stand down and indicate his support for the local Labour MP.

8. For a contrary view from one of the organisations that promoted anti-Conservative tactical voting during the election campaign, see Best for Britain, *Impact Report: General Election 2019*, Best for Britain, 2020, available at: https://www.bestforbritain.org/2019electionimpact. The analysis in this report is based on a comparison of the outcome with a forecast of the outcome in each constituency provided by polling at the beginning of the campaign rather than, as here, a comparison of the change in party support since 2017 in different kinds of constituency.

9. The standard deviation in the change in the Liberal Democrat vote in Conservative Remain seats was as much as 7.4, far higher than for any other combination of 2017 winning party and EU referendum outcome. The party's performances ranged from a drop of −12.9 points in Southport to an increase of +28.9 points in Surrey South West.

10. The Liberal Democrat vote increased by +12.5 points in seats where 34% or more have a degree, compared with +5.6 points elsewhere. The two patterns are independent of each other. Thus, the Liberal Democrats' best performances were in Conservative Remain seats in the south-eastern corner of England that had a high proportion of graduates (+14.2 points) and their least impressive ones in seats elsewhere with fewer graduates (+2.5).

11. Support for the Conservatives fell by −5.0 points in Conservative Remain seats in the south-east of England with more graduates, compared with −1.1 points in other Conservative Remain seats. The equivalent figures for Labour are −9.0 and −4.5 points respectively.

12. The Liberal Democrat vote rose by +6.2 points in Labour Remain seats in the south-east with most graduates compared with +3.0 points in other such seats. The Conservative vote fell in the former group by −3.1 points, compared with −0.3 of a point in the latter. The equivalent drops for Labour were −5.6 and −6.0 points respectively. It has been argued that the particularly strong Liberal Democrat performance in Kensington (which was fought by the defecting Conservative MP, Sam Gyimah, and where the party's vote increased by +9.1 points) was responsible for Labour's failure to defend what had been their most marginal seat in 2017. However, in line with the general pattern in Labour Remain seats, the above-average

Liberal Democrat performance in a London seat with a very high proportion of graduates appears to have come at the expense of the Conservatives, who, nonetheless, still enjoyed a small but decisive +0.2 point swing from Labour.

13. John Curtice and Ian Montagu, *Is Brexit Fuelling Support for Independence?* NatCen Social Research, 2020, available at https://whatscotlandthinks.org/wp-content/uploads/2020/11/SSA-2019-Scotland-paper-v5.pdf; John Curtice, 'High Noon for the Union?', *IPPR Progressive Review*, 27(3) (2020): 223–34.

14. In two of these seats the incumbent Conservative did not stand again, and thus any personal vote that they may have garnered as the local MP might have been lost. Indeed, in one instance, Aberdeen South, the Conservative vote fell quite heavily after the local MP was debarred from standing. If we exclude the two seats where the incumbent did not stand again, the fall in Conservative support averages −2.5 points.

15. In practice, it looks as though tactical switching might have occurred in some of these highly marginal SNP/Conservative seats, but not in others. In three (Argyll & Bute, Ayrshire Central, and Lanark & Hamilton East), the Conservative share of the vote actually increased, whereas in two others (Edinburgh South West (−8.7) and Perth & North Perthshire (−5.6)), it fell back quite heavily. Meanwhile, in two of the three seats where the Conservative vote increased, the Labour vote dropped by more than average, while in the third it was the Liberal Democrat vote that fell back.

16. It is also the case that campaign spending data suggest that Labour fought a better-resourced campaign in most of the seats they were defending than was the case in 2017. On average, the party spent 24% more of the allowable maximum than it had done at the previous election. However, just as big an increase in spending was registered in those seats where the party came second to the SNP, without it bringing any discernible benefit.

17. It is also notable that, according to the returns of constituency spending, the Conservatives fought East Dunbartonshire much more intently than in 2017, while the opposite was the case in Fife North East. In 2017, the party only spent 6% of the permitted maximum on campaigning in East Dunbartonshire, whereas in 2019 it spent 73%. In Fife North East the proportion fell from 50 to 19%.

18. The figures quoted in this paragraph exclude not only Scotland but also Buckingham and Chorley.

19. This is consistent with the evidence of the BESIP, which suggests that 68% of Green voters backed Remain in 2016, compared with 87% of Liberal Democrat voters and 78% of Labour supporters.

20. In 12 seats that the party fought in 2015 and 2019, the party's vote was down on average by −0.8 points, similar to the equivalent figure in England and Wales (see Table A1.2).

21. There were just three seats where the Brexit Party outpolled UKIP's 2015 tally by more than a point. These were the two Barnsley seats previously mentioned together with Blaenau Gwent.

22. With an average Leave vote of 51.3%, the seats that UKIP opted to contest were not necessarily ones where the party might have been expected to do particularly well, suggesting that the decision as to which seats to contest was not part of a coordinated strategy. The party also fought seven seats in Scotland (10 in 2017). If we include these in our tally, UKIP's share of the vote averaged 1.0%, and was down −1.9 points in those seats it also contested in 2017.

23. At 5.4%, the Brexit Party's share of the vote in the 13 seats in England and Wales that were also contested by UKIP was just 0.3 points less than elsewhere, while the difference between its vote and that secured by UKIP in 2015 was −7.4 points, a little less than the figure elsewhere (−7.7 points).

24. The former Labour MP, Angela Smith, in Altrincham & Sale West.

25. In the event, the two that did, Antoinette Sandbach in Eddisbury (+12.6) and Sarah Wollaston in Totnes (+15.9), both former Conservative MPs, proved to be no more successful than those defectors who fought elsewhere.

26. The Liberal Democrat vote fell in Norfolk North by as much as −18.1 points. In Twickenham, the decline was just −0.7 of a point, but this was still a relatively poor performance in what was a strongly pro-Remain seat.

27. Curtice et al., 'The Results Analysed', 2017, pp. 463–64.

28. The four were Gordon Birtwhistle (Burnley, −6.0), Andrew George (St Ives, −1.6), John Leech (Manchester Withington, −0.8), and Tessa Munt (Wells, +0.3). A similar fate befell the one former MP in Scotland who stood again, Alan Reid in Argyll. His share of the vote fell by −4.0 points. See also fn. 15.

29. Elise Uberoi and Rebecca Lees, *Ethnic Diversity in Politics and Public Life*. House of Commons Library Briefing Paper CBP01156, House of Commons, 2020, available at https://researchbriefings.files.parliament.uk/documents/SN01156/SN01156.pdf.

30. The average Labour vote in 2017 in seats where an ethnic minority candidate stood in England and Wales was 49.9%, well above the equivalent figure of 42.4% for white candidates. The equivalent figures for the Conservatives were 37.1% and 45.0% respectively. See also Patrick English, 'High Rejection, Low Selection: How "Punitive Parties" Shape Ethnic Minority Representation', *Party Politics* (early view).

31. Curtice et al., 'The Results Analysed', 2017, pp. 460–61 and previous appendices in *The British General Election of* … series; Stephen Fisher, 'Racism at the Ballot Box: Ethnic Minority Candidates' in Philip Cowley and Robert Ford (eds), *More Sex, Lies and the Ballot Box*. Biteback, 2016.

32. Moreover, the average increase in Conservative support in seats where a man replaced a woman was, at +0.7 of a point, also lower than in seats where the gender of the candidate was unchanged.

33. It should also be noted that we did not find any evidence of ballot box discrimination against Conservative, Labour or Liberal Democrat candidates for whom we were able to find an online record of LGBT+ self-identification. Modelling suggests that this recorded LGBT+ identity was not correlated with a worse performance in terms of change in share of the vote than that of candidates for whom we did not find such a public expression.

34. John Curtice, 'Why Leave Won the UK's EU Referendum', *Journal of Common Market Studies*, 55(S1) (2017): 19–37; Harold Clarke, Matthew Goodwin and Paul Whiteley, *Brexit: Why Britain Voted to Leave the European Union*. Cambridge University Press, 2017; Maria Sobolewska and Robert Ford, *Brexitland: Identity, Diversity and the Reshaping of British Politics*. Cambridge University Press.

35. Sean Carey and Andrew Geddes, 'Less Is More: Immigration and European Integration at the 2010 General Election', *Parliamentary Affairs*, 63(4) (2010): 849–65; Robert Ford and Matthew Goodwin, 'Angry White Men: Individual and Contextual Predictors of Support for the British National Party', *Political Studies*, 58(1) (2010): 1–25; Dennis Kavanagh and Philip Cowley, *The British General Election of 2010*. Palgrave Macmillan, 2010.

36. In this section, we use for the 2005 election the estimates by Rallings and Thrasher of what the outcome in each constituency would have been if the election had been fought on the boundaries that were introduced in 2010. See Colin Rallings and Michael Thrasher, *Media Guide to the New Parliamentary Constituencies*. Local Government Chronicle Elections Centre, 2007.

37. John Curtice, Stephen Fisher and Robert Ford, 'Appendix 1: The Results Analysed' in Philip Cowley and Dennis Kavanagh, *The British General Election of 2015*. Palgrave Macmillan, 2015, pp. 392–93.

38. John Curtice, Stephen Fisher and Robert Ford, 'Appendix 2: The Results Analysed', in Kavanagh and Cowley, *The British General Election of 2010*, pp. 407–8; Curtice et al., 'The Results Analysed', 2015, pp. 405–8.

39. According to the 2011 Census, on average, 28% are or were previously engaged in a semi-routine or routine occupation in Leave seats, but only 19% in Remain constituencies.

40. That the more recent decline in Labour support in working-class seats is a consequence of the party's loss of support among Leave voters is underlined by further analysis of the change in support between 2017 and 2019. According to the BESIP, support for Labour among working-class Leave voters almost halved from 32% in 2017 to 17% in 2019—but the same near-halving (from 20 to 11%) was also apparent among Leave voters in professional and managerial occupations. Labour's support fell more in working-class seats not because the party was losing the support of working-class voters in general, but rather because the more working class a seat, the greater the proportion of Labour voters who were Leave supporters, and the greater the proportion too of Leave voters who backed Labour in 2017.

41. We should note that although it may have weakened, the link between the class composition of a constituency and the level of support for the Conservatives and Labour has not, in contrast to the individual-level relationship, disappeared entirely. This is particularly clear if we look at the proportion of people in a constituency in a professional or managerial occupation (which has long had the strongest relationship with Conservative and Labour support—see William Miller, *Electoral Dynamics in Britain since 1918*. Macmillan, 1977). For example, in seats where more than 35% are employed in such occupations, the average level of support for Labour is just 27.8%, while in those where less than 25% are employed in that way, support for the party stands at 48.4%. The equivalent figures for the Conservatives are 47.3% and 35.7% respectively.

42. Electoral Commission, *The UK Parliamentary Election 2019*. Electoral Commission, 2020, available at https://www.electoralcommission.org. uk/sites/default/files/2020-04/UKPGE%20election%20report%20 2020.pdf.

43. Cowley and Kavanagh, *The British General Election of 2015*, pp. 22–23 and 40; Curtice et al., 'The Results Analysed', 2017, pp. 478–79.

44. Electoral Commission, *2019 Report: Accuracy and Completeness of the 2018 Electoral Registers in Great Britain*. Electoral Commission, 2019, available at https://www.electoralcommission.org.uk/who-we-are-and-what-we-do/our-views-and-research/our-research/ accuracy-and-completeness-electoral-registers/2019-report-accuracy-and-completeness-2018-electoral-registers-great-britain.

45. Ben Quinn, 'More Than 100,000 Apply to Register to Vote in UK in 48 Hours', *The Guardian*, 4 September 2019, https://www.theguardian.com/politics/2019/sep/04/ more-than-100000-people-apply-register-vote-youth-uk-general-election.

46. David Denver, Gordon Hands and Iain MacAllister, 'Constituency Marginality and Turnout in Britain Revisited', *British Elections and Parties Review*, 13 (2003): 174–94.

47. Curtice et al., 'The Results Analysed', 2015, p. 416.
48. G. Bingham Powell, Jr., *Elections as Instruments of Democracy: Majoritarian and Proportional Visions.* Yale University Press, 2000; Philip Norton, 'The Case for First Past the Post', *Representation*, 34(2) (1997): 84–88; Alan Renwick, *A Citizens' Guide to Electoral Reform.* Biteback, 2011.
49. Anthony Champion, 'Population Movement within the UK' in Roma Chappell (ed.), *Focus on People and Migration.* Palgrave Macmillan, 2005, pp. 91–114.
50. Anthony Champion, 'Internal Migration and the Spatial Distribution of the Population' in Anthony Champion and Jane Falkingham (eds), *Population Change in the United Kingdom.* Rowman & Littlefield, 2016, pp. 125–41.
51. One source of disparity that the new review will still tackle is the over-representation of Wales, a part of Britain that is still predominantly Labour. However, within England, the average Labour-held constituency now contains only 1,671 fewer registered voters than the average Conservative-held one.
52. John Curtice and Michael Steed, 'Electoral Choice and the Production of Government: The Changing Operation of the Electoral System in the United Kingdom since 1955', *British Journal of Political Science*, 12(3) (1982): 249–98; Graham Gudgin and Peter Taylor, *Seats, Votes and the Spatial Organisation of Elections.* Pion, 1979.
53. John Curtice, 'A Return to "Normality" at Last? How the Electoral System Worked in 2019', *Parliamentary Affairs*, 73(S1) (2020): 29–47.

Appendix 2: The Voting Statistics

Table A2.1 Votes and seats, 1945–2019

	Turnout/electorate	Seats/votes	Conservative[a]	Labour	Liberal (Democrats)[b]	Scottish and Welsh Nationalists	Other
1945[c]	73.3%	640	39.8%–213	48.3%–393	9.1%–12	0.2%	2.5%–22
	32,836,419	24,082,612	9,577,667	11,632,191	2,197,191	46,612	628,251
1950	84.0%	625	43.5%–299	46.1%–315	9.1%–9	0.1%	1.2%–2
	34,269,770	28,772,671	12,502,567	13,266,592	2,621,548	27,288	354,676
1951	82.5%	625	48.%–321	48.8%–295	2.5%–6	0.1%	0.6%–3
	34,645,573	28,595,668	13,717,538	13,948,605	730,556	18,219	180,750
1955	76.8%	630	49.7%–345	46.4%–277	2.7%–6	0.2%	0.9%–2
	34,858,263	26,760,493	13,311,936	12,404,970	722,405	57,231	263,951
1959	78.7%	630	49.4%–365	43.8%–258	5.9%–6	0.4%	0.6%–1
	35,397,080	27,859,241	13,749,830	12,215,538	1,638,571	99,309	175,987
1964	77.1%	630	43.4%–304	44.1%–317	11.2%–9	0.5%	0.8%–0
	35,892,572	27,655,374	12,001,396	12,205,814	3,092,878	133,551	215,363
1966	75.8%	630	41.9%–253	47.9%–363	8.5%–12	0.7%	0.9%–2
	35,964,684	27,263,606	11,418,433	13,064,951	2,327,533	189,545	263,144
1970	72.0%	630	46.4%–330	43.%–288	7.5%–6	1.3%–1	1.8%–5
	39,342,013	28,344,798	13,145,123	12,178,295	2,117,033	381,819	524,527
February 1974	78.1%	635	37.8%–297	37.1%–301	19.3%–14	2.6%–9	3.2%–14
	39,770,724	31,340,162	11,872,180	11,646,391	6,058,744	804,554	991,036
October 1974	72.8%	635	35.8%–277	39.2%–319	18.3%–13	3.5%–14	3.2%–12
	40,072,971	29,189,178	10,464,817	11,457,079	5,346,754	1,005,938	914,590
1979	76.0%	635	43.9%–339	37.0%–269	13.8%–11	2.0%–4	3.3%–12
	41,093,264	31,221,361	13,697,923	11,532,218	4,313,804	636,890	1,039,563
1983	72.7%	650	42.4%–397	27.6%–209	25.4%–23	1.5%–4	3.1%–17
	42,197,344	30,671,136	13,012,315	8,456,934	7,780,949	457,676	144,723

Year	Turnout	Electorate	Votes	Seats					
1987	75.3%	43,181,321	32,536,137	650	42.3%–376 / 13,763,066	30.8%–229 / 10,029,778	22.6%–22 / 7,341,290	1.7%–6 / 543,559	2.6%–17 / 852,368
1992	77.7%	43,249,721	33,612,693	651	41.9%–336 / 14,092,891	34.4%–271 / 11,559,735	17.8%–20 / 5,999,384	2.3%–7 / 783,991	3.5%–17 / 1,176,692
1997	71.5%	43,757,478	31,286,597	659	30.7%–165 / 9,602,857	43.2%–418 / 13,516,632	16.8%–46 / 5,242,894	2.5%–10 / 782,570	6.8%–20 / 2,141,644
2001	59.4%	44,403,238	26,368,798	659	31.7%–166 / 8,357,622	40.7%–412 / 10,724,895	18.3%–52 / 4,812,833	2.5%–9 / 660,197	6.8%–20 / 1,813,251
2005	61.2%	44,261,545	27,123,652	646	32.4%–198 / 8,772,473	35.2%–356 / 9,547,944	22.0%–62 / 5,981,874	2.2%–9 / 567,105	8.2%–22 / 2,234,267
2010	65.1%	45,610,369	29,687,409	650	36.1%–307 / 10,726,555	29.0%–258 / 8,606,518	23.0%–57 / 6,836,188	2.2%–9 / 656,780	9.6%–19 / 2,861,368
2015	66.2%	46,354,197	30,697,279	650	36.9%–331 / 11,334,226	30.4%–232 / 9,347,033	7.9%–8 / 2,415,916	5.3%–59 / 1,636,140	19.4%–20 / 5,963,964
2017	68.8%	46,835,836	32,204,124	650	42.5%–318 / 13,670,983	40.0%–262 / 12,877,858	7.4%–12 / 2,371,861	3.5%–39 / 1,142,034	6.8%–19 / 2,175,687
2019	67.3%	47,562,702	32,014,110	650	43.6%–365 / 13,966,454	32.2%–203 / 10,295,882	11.5%–11 / 3,696,419	4.4%–52 / 1,395,645	8.3%–19 / 2,659,710

Notes

[a] Includes Ulster Unionists 1945–1970

[b] Liberals 1945–1979; Liberal–SDP Alliance 1983–1987; Liberal Democrats 1992–

[c] The 1945 figures exclude university seats and are adjusted for double counting in the 15 two-member seats

Table A2.2 Party performance (UK)

Party	Votes	% share (change)	Average % share	Seats (change)	Candidates	Lost deposits
Conservative	13,966,454	43.6 (+1.2)	43.8	365 (+47)	635	4
Labour	10,295,882	32.2 (−7.8)	33.9	203 (−59)	632	12
Liberal Democrat	3,696,419	11.5 (+4.2)	11.5	11 (−1)	611	136
Scottish National Party (SNP)	1,242,380	3.9 (+0.8)	45.1	48 (+13)	59	0
Green	865,715	2.7 (+1.1)	3.4	1 (0)	497	465
Brexit Party	644,257	2.0 (+2.0)	5.5	–	275	164
Democratic Unionist Party (DUP)	244,128	0.8 (−0.1)	33.0	8 (−2)	17	0
Sinn Féin	181,853	0.6 (−0.2)	26.5	7 (0)	15	2
Plaid Cymru	153,265	0.5 (−0.0)	11.7	4 (0)	36	10
Alliance Party of Northern Ireland (APNI)	134,115	0.4 (+0.2)	17.4	1 (+1)	18	2
Social Democratic and Labour Party (SDLP)	118,737	0.4 (+0.1)	17.1	2 (+2)	15	2
Ulster Unionist Party (UUP)	93,123	0.3 (+0.0)	12.9	–	16	2
Yorkshire Party	29,201	0.1 (+0.0)	2.1	–	28	28
United Kingdom Independence Party (UKIP)	22,817	0.1 (−1.8)	1.0	–	44	44
Ashfield Independents	13,498	0.0	27.6	–	1	0
Liberal Party	10,876	0.0	1.2	–	19	19
Change UK	10,006	0.0	6.4	–	3	1
Aontú	9,814	0.0	3.2	–	7	7
Monster Raving Loony Party	9,739	0.0	0.8	–	24	24
People Before Profit	7,526	0.0	9.4	–	2	1
Birkenhead Social Justice Party	7,285	0.0	17.2	–	1	0
Christian People's Alliance	6,486	0.0	0.5	–	29	29
Heavy Woolen District Independents	6,432	0.0	12.2	–	1	0

Note The cut-off for inclusion was 5,000 votes. Below that line are a variety of other parties, including the Social Democratic Party, the Animal Welfare Party, the North East Party, the English Democrats, the Libertarian Party and Mebyon Kernow. Also excluded are any non-party candidates, including sitting MPs such as Dominic Grieve and David Gauke who had lost their party whip and unsuccessfully sought re-election as independents

Table A2.3 Party performance (Northern Ireland)

Party	Votes	% share (change)	Average % share	Seats (change)	Candidates	Lost deposits
Democratic Unionist Party (DUP)	244,128	30.6 (−5.4)	33.0	8 (−2)	17	0
Sinn Féin	181,853	22.8 (−6.7)	26.5	7 (0)	15	2
Alliance Party of Northern Ireland (APNI)	134,115	16.8 (+8.8)	17.4	1 (+1)	18	2
Social Democratic and Labour Party (SDLP)	118,737	14.9 (+3.1)	17.1	2 (+2)	15	2
Ulster Unionist Party (UUP)	93,123	11.7 (+1.4)	12.9	–	16	2
Aontú	9,814	1.2 (+1.2)	3.2	–	7	7
People Before Profit	7,526	0.9 (+0.3)	9.4	–	2	1
Conservative	5,433	0.7 (+0.2)	3.4	–	4	4
Green	1,996	0.2 (−0.7)	1.7	–	3	3

Table A2.4 National and regional results

UK

| Seats won in 2019 (change since 2017) | | | | | Turnout | Share of votes cast in 2019 (change since 2017) | | | | | | |
Con	Lab	Lib Dem	Nat & Other			Con	Lab	Lib Dem	Nat	Brexit	Green	Other
345 (+48)	180 (−48)	7 (−1)	1 (0)	England	67.4 (−1.7)	47.2 (+1.7)	34 (−7.9)	12.4 (+4.6)	0 (0)	2.0	3.0 (+1.2)	1.3 (−1.6)
68 (+28)	89 (−28)	1 (0)	0 (0)	North	64.9 (−2.1)	39.6 (+2.2)	43.5 (−9.4)	7.8 (+2.7)	0 (0)	5.3	2.4 (+1.2)	1.5 (−2.0)
82 (+16)	23 (−16)	0 (0)	0 (0)	Midlands	65.8 (−2.1)	54.1 (+4.2)	32.9 (−8.7)	7.9 (+3.5)	0 (0)	1.4	2.8 (+1.2)	1 (−1.6)
195 (+4)	68 (−3)	6 (−1)	1 (0)	South	69.4 (−1.3)	48.7 (+0.4)	29.6 (−6.8)	16.3 (+5.9)	0 (0)	0.6	3.5 (+1.2)	1.2 (−1.3)
14 (+6)	22 (−6)	0 (0)	4 (0)	Wales	66.6 (−2.0)	36.1 (+2.5)	40.9 (−8.0)	6 (+1.5)	9.9 (−0.5)	5.4	1 (+0.7)	0.6 (−1.6)
6 (−7)	1 (−6)	4 (0)	48 (+13)	Scotland	68.1 (+1.6)	25.1 (−3.5)	18.6 (−8.5)	9.5 (+2.8)	45 (+8.1)	0.5	1 (+0.8)	0.3 (−0.2)
365 (+47)	203 (−59)	11 (−1)	53 (+13)	Great Britain	67.5 (−1.4)	44.7 (+1.2)	33 (−8.0)	11.8 (+4.3)	4.5 (+0.8)	2.1	2.8 (+1.1)	1.1 (−1.4)
0 (0)	0	0	18 (0)	Northern Ireland	61.8 (−3.6)	0.7 (+0.2)	0 (0)	0 (0)	0 (0)	0 (0)	0.2 (−0.7)	99.1 (0.5)
365 (+47)	203 (−59)	11 (−1)	71 (+13)	United Kingdom	67.3 (−1.5)	43.6 (+1.2)	32.2 (−7.8)	11.5 (+4.2)	4.4 (+0.8)	2.0 (0)	2.7 (+1.1)	3.6 (−1.4)

Regions

| Seats won in 2019 (change since 2017) | | | | | Turnout | Share of votes cast in 2019 (change since 2017) | | | | | | |
Con	Lab	Lib Dem	Nat & Other			Con	Lab	Lib Dem	Nat	Brexit	Green	Other
126 (0)	60 (0)	5 (0)	1 (0)	South East	68.8 (−1.7)	46.6 (−0.2)	32.1 (−6.8)	16.1 (+6.8)	0 (0)	0.7 (+0.7)	3.4 (+1.0)	1.2 (−1.5)
21 (0)	49 (0)	3 (0)	0 (0)	Greater London*	67.5 (−2.7)	32 (−1.1)	48.1 (−6.4)	14.9 (+6.1)	0 (0)	1.4 (+1.4)	3.1 (+1.3)	0.5 (−1.3)
3 (0)	25 (0)	0 (0)	0 (0)	Inner London	67.2 (−2.0)	20.2 (−2.5)	58.8 (−6.0)	14.9 (+6.3)	0 (0)	1.4 (+1.4)	4.3 (+2.0)	0.4 (−1.3)
18 (0)	24 (0)	3 (0)	0 (0)	Outer London	67.7 (−3.1)	39.9 (0)	41 (−6.9)	15 (+6.0)	0 (0)	1.3 (+1.3)	2.3 (+0.8)	0.6 (−1.3)
105 (0)	11 (0)	2 (0)	0 (0)	Rest of South East	69.6 (−1.2)	55.1 (0.3)	22.7 (−6.9)	16.7 (+7.2)	0 (0)	0.3 (+0.3)	3.5 (+0.8)	1.6 (−1.6)
57 (−1)	4 (0)	1 (+1)	0 (0)	Outer Met. Area	69.6 (−1.2)	55.7 (−0.4)	21.8 (−8.0)	17.3 (+8.7)	0 (0)	0.2 (+0.2)	2.7 (+0.7)	2.3 (−1.2)
48 (+1)	7 (0)	1 (−1)	1 (0)	Other S.E	69.7 (−1.1)	54.5 (1.0)	23.6 (−5.8)	16.1 (+5.6)	0 (0)	0.4 (+0.4)	4.4 (+0.9)	0.9 (−2.1)
48 (+1)	6 (−1)	1 (0)	0 (0)	South West*	72 (0.2)	52.8 (+1.4)	23.4 (−5.8)	18.2 (+3.2)	0 (0)	0.4 (+0.4)	3.8 (+1.5)	1.6 (−0.7)
16 (0)	2 (0)	0 (0)	0 (0)	Devon & Cornwall	72.3 (0.0)	53.8 (+3.6)	22.9 (−5.4)	16.2 (+0.1)	0 (0)	0.4 (+0.4)	3.0 (+1.3)	3.7 (−0.1)
32 (+1)	4 (−1)	1 (0)	0 (0)	Rest of S.W	71.8 (0.2)	52.3 (+0.4)	23.6 (−6.0)	19.1 (+4.7)	0 (0)	0.3 (+0.4)	4.1 (+1.6)	0.5 (−1.0)
21 (+3)	2 (−2)	0 (−1)	0 (0)	East Anglia*	68.3 (−1.5)	55.9 (+2.8)	24.8 (−8.5)	14.1 (+4.9)	0 (0)	0.6 (+0.6)	3.7 (+1.7)	0.9 (−1.4)
38 (+7)	8 (−7)	0 (0)	0 (0)	East Midlands*	67.1 (−1.9)	54.8 (+4.0)	31.7 (−8.8)	7.8 (+3.5)	0 (0)	1.5 (+1.5)	2.6 (+1.1)	1.7 (−1.4)
44 (+9)	15 (−9)	0 (0)	0 (0)	West Midlands*	64.7 (−2.3)	53.4 (+4.4)	33.9 (−8.6)	7.9 (+3.5)	0 (0)	1.4 (+1.4)	3 (+1.3)	0.5 (−1.9)
14 (+6)	14 (−6)	0 (0)	0 (0)	W. Mids. Met. Co	60.6 (−3.2)	44.4 (+4.5)	44.1 (−8.3)	6.1 (+2.4)	0 (0)	2.5 (+2.5)	2.3 (+1.1)	0.6 (−2.1)
30 (+3)	1 (−3)	0 (0)	0 (0)	Rest of W. Mids	68.2 (−1.5)	60.5 (+4.1)	25.8 (−8.6)	9.3 (+4.3)	0 (0)	0.4 (+0.4)	3.5 (+1.5)	0.4 (−1.7)

				Region								
26 (+9)	28 (−9)	0 (0)	0 (0)	Yorks & Humber*	64.3 (−2.0)	43.1 (+2.6)	38.9 (−10.1)	8.1 (+3.1)	0 (0)	5.9 (+5.9)	2.3 (+1.0)	1.8 (−2.5)
3 (+3)	11 (−3)	0 (0)	0 (0)	S. Yorks Met. Co	68.8 (−1.7)	46.6 (−0.2)	42.3 (−14.7)	7.8 (+1.9)	0 (0)	13.6 (+13.6)	2.3 (+1.1)	1.7 (−4.4)
9 (+4)	13 (−4)	0 (0)	0 (0)	W. Yorks Met. Co	67.5 (−2.7)	32 (−1.1)	46 (−7.3)	6.1 (+2.1)	0 (0)	4.2 (+4.2)	2 (+0.9)	1.9 (−2.0)
14 (+2)	4 (−2)	0 (0)	0 (0)	Rest of Y&H	67.2 (−2.0)	20.2 (−2.5)	27.4 (−10.6)	10.6 (+5.1)	0 (0)	2.6 (+2.6)	2.5 (+1.0)	1.8 (−1.7)
27 (+10)	42 (−10)	0 (0)	0 (0)	North West	65.3 (−2.3)	36.2 (+1.1)	48.8 (−7.6)	7.3 (+2.5)	0 (0)	4.1 (+4.1)	2.5 (+1.4)	1 (−1.4)
9 (+5)	18 (−5)	0 (0)	0 (0)	Gtr. Manc. Met. Co	62.5 (−1.7)	34.9 (+2.4)	47.9 (−9.0)	8.8 (+2.5)	0 (0)	5.5 (+5.5)	2.4 (+1.4)	0.5 (−3.0)
1 (0)	14 (0)	0 (0)	0 (0)	Merseyside Met. Co	68 (−1.8)	20.2 (−1.2)	65.2 (−6.0)	5.6 (+1.3)	0 (0)	4.7 (+4.7)	2.7 (+1.2)	1.6 (0.0)
17 (+5)	10 (−5)	0 (0)	0 (0)	Rest of N.W	66.7 (−3.2)	46.3 (+1.2)	40.6 (−7.3)	6.9 (+3.0)	0 (0)	2.4 (+2.4)	2.6 (+1.5)	1.2 (−0.7)
15 (+9)	19 (−9)	0 (0)	0 (0)	North	65.1 (−1.8)	40.8 (+3.9)	40.1 (−11.9)	8.2 (+2.3)	0 (0)	6.9 (+6.9)	2.2 (+1.1)	1.8 (−2.3)
0 (0)	12 (0)	0 (0)	0 (0)	Tyne & Wear	63.6 (−2.7)	30.9 (+2.4)	47.8 (−13.0)	7 (+3.0)	0 (0)	9.1 (+9.1)	3.1 (+1.5)	2 (−3.0)
15 (+9)	7 (−9)	1 (0)	0 (0)	Rest of North	65.9 (−1.2)	45.9 (+4.5)	36.2 (−11.2)	8.8 (+2.0)	0 (0)	5.7 (+5.7)	1.8 (+0.9)	1.6 (−1.9)
14 (+6)	22 (−6)	0 (0)	0 (0)	Wales*	66.6 (−2.0)	36.1 (+2.5)	40.9 (−8.0)	6 (+1.5)	0 (0)	5.4 (+5.4)	1 (+0.7)	0.6 (−1.6)
3 (+1)	21 (−1)	0 (0)	0 (0)	Industrial S. Wales	64.7 (−2.5)	32 (+1.5)	47.2 (−8.5)	4.8 (+2.0)	6.6 (−1.2)	6.9 (+6.9)	1.6 (+1.1)	0.9 (−1.8)
11 (+5)	1 (−5)	0 (0)	4 (0)	Rural Wales	69.8 (−1.1)	42.6 (+4.0)	30.9 (−7.1)	7.8 (+0.6)	15.2 (+0.6)	3.1 (+3.1)	0.2 (0)	0.2 (−1.2)
6 (−7)	4 (0)	4 (0)	48 (+13)	Scotland*	68.1 (+1.6)	25.1 (−3.5)	18.6 (−8.5)	9.5 (+2.8)	45 (+8.1)	0.5 (+0.5)	1 (+0.8)	0.3 (−0.2)
3 (−1)	0 (0)	0 (0)	4 (+1)	Ayrshire & Borders	67.6 (+0.2)	38.4 (−1.8)	11.7 (−9.8)	5.8 (+3.0)	43.7 (+8.4)	0	0.3 (+0.3)	0.1 (0)
0 (−1)	0 (−3)	0 (−1)	20 (+5)	Clydeside	65.8 (+1.8)	17.4 (−3.7)	27.2 (−7.4)	7.3 (+2.3)	46.6 (+8.2)	0.2 (+0.2)	0.9 (+0.6)	0.3 (−0.3)
0 (−1)	1 (−2)	1 (0)	9 (+3)	Rest of Central Belt	70.6 (+1.6)	22.4 (−4.3)	21.3 (−10.3)	10.6 (+4.2)	42.8 (+8.3)	0.4 (+0.4)	2.2 (+1.8)	0.2 (0)
3 (−4)	0 (−1)	1 (0)	11 (+4)	NE & Fife	68.6 (+2.3)	31.2 (−3.7)	11.7 (−8.7)	9.8 (+3.2)	45.9 (+8.0)	0.7 (+0.7)	0.5 (+0.5)	0.2 (−0.1)
0 (0)	0 (0)	2 (0)	4 (0)	Highlands & Islands	70.4 (+0.9)	23.8 (−1.7)	8.2 (−6.6)	21.3 (−0.7)	43.6 (+7.4)	1.8 (+1.8)	0.8 (+0.5)	0.4 (1.0)
0 (0)	0 (0)	0 (0)	18 (0)	N Ireland	61.8 (−3.6)	0.7 (+0.2)	0 (0)	0 (0)	0 (0)	0 (0)	0.2 (−0.7)	99.1 (+0.5)

Notes

The English Regions are the eight *Standard Regions*, which are now obsolete but were used by the OPCS until the 1990s

The *Outer Metropolitan Area* compromises those seats wholly or mostly in the Outer Metropolitan Area as defined by the OPCS. It includes the whole of Surrey and Hertfordshire, the whole of Berkshire except Newbury, and the constituencies of: Bedfordshire South West; Luton North; Luton South (Bedfordshire); Beaconsfield; Chesham & Amersham; Wycombe (Buckinghamshire); Basildon & Billericay; Basildon South & East Thurrock; Brentwood & Ongar; Castle Point; Chelmsford; Epping Forest; Harlow; Rayleigh & Wickford; Rochford & Southend West; Southend West; Thurrock (Essex); Hampshire North East (Hampshire); Chatham & Aylesford; Dartford; Faversham & Kent Mid; Gillingham & Rainham; Gravesham; Maidstone & The Weald; Rochester & Strood; Sevenoaks; Tonbridge & Malling; Tunbridge Wells (Kent); Arundel & South Downs; Crawley; Horsham; and Sussex Mid (West Sussex)

Industrial Wales (a description no longer entirely accurate but used for continuity with previous volumes) includes Gwent, the whole of Glamorgan, and the Llanelli constituency in Dyfed

Ayrshire & Borders comprises: Ayr, Carrick & Cumnock; Ayrshire Central; Ayrshire North & Arran; Berwickshire, Roxburgh & Selkirk; Dumfries & Galloway; Dumfriesshire, Clydesdale & Tweeddale; and Kilmarnock & Loudoun

Clydeside includes all Glasgow seats, both Dunbartonshire seats, both Paisley & Renfrewshire seats, plus Airdrie & Shotts; Coatbridge, Chryston & Bellshill; Cumbernauld, Kilsyth & Kirkintilloch East; East Kilbride, Strathaven & Lesmahagow; Inverclyde; Lanark & Hamilton East; Motherwell & Wishaw; Renfrewshire East; and Rutherglen & Hamilton West

Rest of Central Belt includes all Edinburgh seats, plus East Lothian; Falkirk; Linlithgow & East Falkirk; Livingston; Midlothian; and Stirling

NE & Fife includes both Aberdeen seats, both Dundee seats, plus Aberdeenshire West & Kincardine; Angus; Banff & Buchan; Dunfermline & West Fife; Fife North East; Glenrothes; Gordon; Kirkcaldy & Cowdenbeath; Moray; Ochil & South Perthshire; and Perth & North Perthshire

Highlands & Islands includes Argyll & Bute; Caithness, Sutherland & Easter Ross; Inverness, Nairn, Badenoch & Strathspey; Na H-Eileanan An Iar; Orkney & Shetland; and Ross, Skye & Lochaber

In all but four cases, the Government Statistical Service (GSS) regions are covered in the table above. These regions are indicated with an asterisk (*). The results for the four other GSS regions are:

	Seats won in 2019 (change since 2017)					Share of votes cast in 2019 (change since 2017)							
	Con	Lab	Lib Dem	Nat & Other		Turnout	Con	Lab	Lib Dem	Nat	Brexit	Green	Other
Eastern	52 (+2)	5 (−2)	1 (0)	0 (0)		68.2 (−1.6)	57.2 (+1.5)	24.4 (−8.3)	13.4 (+5.5)	0 (0)	0.4 (+0.4)	3.0 (+1.1)	1.7 (−1.2)
North East	10 (+7)	19 (−7)	0 (0)	0 (0)		64.2 (−1.8)	38.3 (+3.8)	42.6 (−12.9)	6.8 (+2.3)	0 (0)	8.1 (+8.1)	2.4 (+1.1)	1.9 (−2.4)
North West	32 (+12)	42 (−12)	1 (0)	0 (0)		65.6 (−2.2)	37.5 (+1.3)	47.3 (−7.6)	7.9 (+2.5)	0 (0)	3.9 (+3.9)	2.5 (+1.4)	1.1 (−1.4)
South East	74 (+1)	8 (0)	1 (−1)	1 (0)		70.2 (−1.0)	54 (−0.6)	22.1 (−6.5)	18.2 (+7.7)	0 (0)	0.3 (+0.3)	3.9 (+0.8)	1.4 (−1.8)

Table A2.5 Constituency results

These tables list the votes in each constituency in percentage terms.

In England and Wales, the constituencies are listed alphabetically within counties, as defined in 1974. The figure in the 'Other' column is the total percentage received by all other candidates than the parties listed in the table.

* denotes a seat won by different parties in 2017 and 2019.
† denotes a seat that changed hands in a by-election between 2017 and 2019.
‡ denotes a seat held by the Speaker in 2017 or 2019.

The table provides a figure for the change in the share of the vote only where candidates from a party stood in *both* 2017 and 2019.

Swing is given in the conventional (total vote or 'Butler') form—the average of the Conservative % gain (or loss) and the Labour % loss (or gain) (measured as % of the total poll). It is only reported for seats where those parties occupied the top two places in 2017 and 2019. This is the practice followed by previous books in this series since 1955.

ENGLAND	Turnout %	Turnout ±	Con %	Con ±	Lab %	Lab ±	LD %	LD ±	Brexit %	Grn %	Grn ±	Other No & %	Swing
Avon, Bath	76.9	+2.6	30.9	-4.9	12.7	-1.9	54.5	+7.2	1.2			0.7 (1)	2.8
Bristol East	70.6	+0.5	32.4	-1.9	53.1	-7.6	6.8	+4.0	3.6	4.0	+1.9		-0.7
Bristol North West	73.3	+1.6	38.7	-3.1	48.9	-1.7	8.8	+3.6		3.5	+1.2		5.8
Bristol South	65.6	+0.1	32.7	+2.0	50.5	-9.5	7.7	+4.3	4.2	4.9	+2.3		0.8
Bristol West	76.1	-0.9	11.7	-2.1	62.3	-3.7	7.7		1.2	24.9	+12.0		1.1
Filton & Bradley Stoke	72.6	+2.7	48.9	-1.1	38.4	-3.3	9.3	+3.3		2.9	+0.6	0.5 (1)	3.7
Kingswood	71.5	+1.2	56.2	+1.3	33.4	-6.1	6.9	+3.3		2.4	+0.4	1.0 (1)	3.7
Somerset North	77.4	+0.4	52.9	-1.3	24.6	-2.0	17.8	+8.2		4.7	+1.5		0.3
Somerset North East	76.4	+0.7	50.4	-3.3	24.2	-10.5	22.1	+13.8		2.5	+0.2	0.8 (1)	3.6
Thornbury & Yate	75.2	+0.5	57.8	+2.6	8.1	-4.0	34.1	+2.7					
Weston-Super-Mare	67.4	-1.3	57.5	+4.4	26.7	-6.0	12.5	+3.3	1.9	3.3	+1.7		5.2
Bedfordshire, Bedford	66.1	-1.4	43.0	-2.2	43.3	-3.5	9.7	+3.9		2.0	+0.0	2.1 (2)	0.7
Bedfordshire Mid	73.7	-1.3	59.8	-1.9	21.7	-6.8	12.6	+6.6		3.8	+1.0	3.9 (1)	2.4
Bedfordshire North East	71.7	-1.7	59.1	-1.8	21.8	-6.7	12.3	+6.6		2.9	+1.0		2.4
Bedfordshire South West	66.7	-3.1	60.4	+1.2	25.6	-8.2	10.2	+5.5		3.8	+2.1	1.9 (2)	4.7
Luton North	62.5	-7.3	33.5	+0.4	55.2	-8.7	4.8	+3.1	2.9	1.8	+0.4	11.1 (3)	4.5
Luton South	60.7	-8.0	31.0	-1.3	51.8	-10.6			3.8	2.4	+1.4		4.7
Berkshire, Bracknell	68.8	-1.8	58.7	-0.1	22.2	-8.0	14.3	+6.8		3.8		1.0 (1)	3.9
Maidenhead	73.7	-2.9	57.7	-7.0	14.0	-5.4	24.4	+13.2		3.9	+2.4		-0.8
Newbury	71.9	-1.5	57.4	-4.1	7.3	-6.8	30.6	+9.2		4.1	+1.6		
Reading East	72.5	-0.6	37.9	-4.4	48.5	-0.6	9.0	+2.9	1.5	2.8	+0.8	0.5 (1)	-1.9
Reading West	68.0	-1.5	48.4	-0.5	40.2	-3.1	8.9	+3.0		2.5	+0.6	0.4 (1)	1.3
Slough	58.8	-6.4	30.9	-0.7	57.6	-5.3	6.6	+4.2	2.8	2.1			2.3
Windsor	71.6	-1.6	58.6	-5.8	15.2	-7.7	21.3	+11.2		3.3	+0.7	1.6 (2)	1.0
Wokingham	73.8	-1.6	49.6	-7.1	10.4	-14.7	37.7	+21.7		2.2	-0.1	0.1 (1)	3.8

Constituency													
Buckinghamshire, Aylesbury	69.9	−1.3	54.0	−0.9	25.4	−4.7	16.6	+7.0		4.0	+1.8		1.9
Beaconsfield	74.5	+2.2	56.1	−9.1	9.9	−11.5	26.2	+13.3		3.5	+1.0	30.4 (2)	1.2
Buckingham‡	76.3	+10.2	58.4	−6.7	12.0	−7.7			2.0			1.4 (2)	
Chesham & Amersham	76.8	−0.3	55.4	−5.3	12.9	−4.9	26.3	+4.1		5.5	+2.5		1.2
Milton Keynes North	68.3	−3.3	49.5	+2.0	39.5	−5.7	8.0	+4.4		3.1	+1.4	1.2 (2)	3.5
Milton Keynes South	66.4	−3.4	50.0	+2.5	39.2	−0.2	7.3	+4.2		2.3	+0.5	2.6 (3)	4.1
Wycombe	70.1	+0.7	45.2	−4.8	37.5	−3.9	11.9	+0.8	1.9	2.7	+0.4	0.5 (3)	−2.3
Cambridgeshire, Cambridge	67.2	−4.0	15.5	−0.8	48.0	−8.6	30.0	+3.6		4.0	+1.8		8.4
Cambridgeshire North East	63.3	+0.2	72.5	+8.1	15.9	−8.3	8.1	+5.7		3.4	+1.5		6.1
Cambridgeshire North West	68.0	−0.6	62.5	+3.8	22.2	−15.6	10.7	+23.4		4.7	+2.7		5.1
Cambridgeshire South	76.7	0.5	46.3	−5.5	11.7	−11.4	42.0	+13.2					4.0
Cambridgeshire South East	74.2	+1.0	50.0	−3.3	16.3	−8.9	32.1	+7.4		3.8	+1.9		4.3
Huntingdon	69.9	−1.0	54.8	−0.4	22.0	−6.7	15.9	+1.5	4.4	1.5	−0.3	1.6 (1)	3.3
Peterborough*	65.9	−0.9	46.7	−0.1	41.3	−7.1	4.9	+4.1	2.5	2.6	+1.0	3.5 (2)	2.5
Cheshire, Chester, City of	71.7	−5.7	38.3	−2.2	49.6	−7.6	6.8	+5.4		2.8	+1.0	1.1 (3)	5.0
Congleton	70.7	−2.6	59.0	+2.4	26.5	−9.7	10.5	+2.4		1.8			7.9
Crewe & Nantwich*	67.3	−2.5	53.1	+6.1	37.4	−11.6	4.8	+12.6	2.6	2.2		1.1 (1)	5.8
Eddisbury	71.9	−1.2	56.8	−0.1	22.0	−5.8	18.1	+3.2		2.0	+0.7	0.3 (1)	2.2
Ellesmere Port & Neston	69.3	−4.9	35.4	−1.4	53.3	−9.4	4.9	+2.1	4.4	2.1	+1.3	0.9 (1)	5.1
Halton	64.2	−3.2	22.4	+0.8	63.5	−4.2	3.9	+4.4	8.1	2.0			5.1
Macclesfield	70.7	−1.5	52.5	−0.1	32.6	−6.2	10.6	+6.7		4.3	+2.1		2.0
Tatton	70.9	−1.4	57.7	−0.8	22.2	−12.2	15.7	+4.1		4.3	+2.2		2.7
Warrington North	64.6	−2.9	40.9	+4.3	44.2	−6.1	6.6	+3.9	5.6	2.7	+1.4		8.3
Warrington South*	72.0	−0.4	45.5	+1.3	42.3	−6.6	9.3	+3.3	2.6				3.7
Weaver Vale	71.9	−1.5	43.8	+0.1	44.9	−14.8	6.5	+2.3	2.7	2.1	+0.5	0.3 (1)	3.3
Cleveland, Hartlepool	57.9	−1.2	28.9	−5.3	37.7	−15.2	4.1	+1.4	25.8	2.1		3.4 (2)	4.8
Middlesbrough	56.1	−2.3	25.8	−0.9	50.5	−13.0	2.4	+1.2	6.4	1.6	+0.9	13.3 (1)	7.2
Middlesbrough South & Cleveland East	66.1	+0.3	58.8	+9.2	34.5		4.1	−1.8	7.1	2.6			11.1
Redcar*	62.0	−1.7	46.1	+12.8	37.4	−18.1	4.9			1.2		3.2 (1)	15.5

ENGLAND	Turnout %	Turnout ±	Con %	Con ±	Lab %	Lab ±	LD %	LD ±	Brexit %	Grn %	Grn ±	Other No & %	Swing
Stockton North	61.8	−2.7	40.6	+4.1	43.1	−13.8	4.0	+2.5	9.5			2.9 (1)	8.9
Stockton South*	71.3	+0.1	50.7	+3.8	41.1	−7.4	4.3	+2.5	4.0				5.6
Cornwall, Camborne & Redruth	71.7	+0.9	53.1	+5.7	35.9	−8.3	7.0	+0.8		2.7	+0.5	1.3 (1)	7.0
Cornwall North	73.9	−0.1	59.4	+8.6	8.7	−3.3	30.8	−5.8				1.1 (1)	
Cornwall South East	74.7	+0.7	59.3	+3.9	20.2	−2.4	16.1	−3.3		2.8	+0.3	1.6 (1)	3.2
St Austell & Newquay	69.8	+0.8	56.1	+6.5	26.4	−2.5	10.5	−11.0		2.9		4.1 (2)	4.5
St Ives	74.7	−1.6	49.3	+6.2	6.9	−7.3	41.0	−1.6		1.9		0.9 (2)	
Truro & Falmouth	77.2	+1.3	46.0	+1.7	38.3	+0.7	12.1	−2.9		2.9	+1.4	0.7 (1)	0.5
Cambria, Barrow & Furness	65.6	−2.9	51.9	+4.8	39.3	−8.2	4.4	+1.7	2.9	1.5	+0.7		6.5
Carlisle	65.9	−3.3	55.2	+5.3	35.8	−8.1	6.6	+3.7				2.4 (1)	6.7
Copeland	68.9	−0.6	53.7	+4.7	40.0	−5.1	4.4	+1.2		1.8			4.9
Penrith & The Border	70.8	−0.5	60.4	+0.0	21.7	−4.5	11.2	+3.4		4.5	+2.3	2.2 (1)	2.2
Westmorland & Lonsdale	77.8	−0.1	45.3	+0.9	4.4	−4.9	48.9	+3.1	1.4				
Derbyshire, Amber Valley	67.8	−1.4	49.3	+7.5	39.2	−11.9	3.7	+0.9	4.2	1.4		2.2 (1)	9.7
Bolsover*	65.1	−2.2	63.9	+7.3	26.8	−11.6	6.3	+3.9		3.0	+1.6		9.5
Chesterfield	61.8	−1.5	47.4	+6.9	35.9	−16.0	3.8	+0.9	9.0	1.7		2.1 (2)	11.5
Derby North*	63.6	−2.9	37.0	+2.2	40.2	−14.6	8.8	+3.4	10.6	2.5	+0.9	0.9 (1)	8.4
Derby South	64.2	−5.4	45.2	+0.8	39.8	−8.7	7.3	+2.7	4.1	2.2		1.4 (1)	4.8
Derbyshire Dales	58.1	−6.7	36.9	+3.4	51.1	−7.3	6.2	+3.5	5.8				5.3
Derbyshire Mid	76.9	−0.1	58.7	−1.3	23.9	−7.2	13.2	+6.9		4.1	+2.1		2.9
Derbyshire North East	73.2	−1.5	58.8	+0.2	27.6	−7.9	9.6	+6.1		3.9	+1.6		4.1
Derbyshire South	68.0	−1.8	58.7	+9.5	32.6	−11.0	6.1	+3.4		2.6	+1.2		10.2
Erewash	67.3	−1.6	62.8	+4.0	26.5	−9.4	7.4	+3.8		3.3	+1.6		6.7
High Peak*	67.3	−0.9	56.5	+4.4	34.7	−8.3	5.1	+2.6		2.3	+0.9	1.4 (3)	6.3
Devon, Devon Central	72.9	−0.6	45.9	+0.5	44.8	−4.9	5.1	+0.1		2.1			2.7
Devon East	78.2	+0.4	55.3	+1.2	24.8	−2.2	15.1	+3.4		4.9	+2.2		1.7
Devon North	73.5	+0.2	50.8	+2.3	4.5	−6.9	2.8	+0.3	2.2	1.1		40.8 (2)	
Devon South West	73.3	−0.2	56.6	+10.8	9.2	−3.5	30.0	−8.0		3.2	+1.8	1.0 (1)	
Devon West & Torridge	73.6	−0.6	62.4	+2.5	22.2	−7.7	11.6	+6.5		3.8	+1.6		5.1
Exeter	74.3	+0.4	60.1	+3.6	17.2	−4.5	18.3	+0.6		3.5	+0.8	0.9 (1)	4.1
	68.5	−3.2	34.7	+1.8	53.2	−8.8			2.5	8.6	+6.8	1.0 (2)	5.3

Constituency													
Newton Abbot	72.5	+0.5	55.5	+0.1	17.8	-4.5	22.2	+1.7		2.9	+1.1	1.6(1)	2.3
Plymouth Moor View	63.7	-1.8	60.7	+8.8	31.5	-9.3	5.2	+3.2		2.7	+1.5		9.1
Plymouth Sutton & Devonport	68.3	+1.4	38.9	-1.1	47.9	-5.4	4.8	+2.4	5.5	2.9	+1.7		2.2
Tiverton & Honiton	71.9	+0.2	60.2	-1.1	19.5	-7.6	14.8	+6.7		3.8	+0.3	1.6(1)	3.2
Torbay	67.2	-0.2	59.2	+6.2	13.0	-5.2	24.0	-1.1		2.5	+1.2	1.3(1)	1.7
Totnes	78.2	+0.4	55.3	+1.2	24.8	-2.2	15.1	+3.4		4.9	+2.2	1.0(1)	
Dorset, Bournemouth East	66.5	+1.3	50.6	-1.3	32.7	-2.8	11.0	+4.5		4.2	+1.6	1.5(2)	0.8
Bournemouth West	62.0	+1.2	53.4	-0.1	31.3	-4.9	10.7	+4.1		4.6	+1.8		2.4
Christchurch	72.6	+0.6	65.2	-4.3	12.6	-7.2	17.9	+9.9		4.3	+1.6		1.4
Dorset Mid & Poole North	74.8	+0.6	60.4	+1.1	7.0	-6.4	29.9	+2.5		2.7			
Dorset North	73.1	+0.1	63.6	-1.3	12.0	-6.6	20.3	+6.8		4.0	+1.1		2.7
Dorset South	69.2	-2.6	58.8	+2.7	25.2	-8.4	10.6	+4.8		4.4	+0.0	0.9(1)	5.5
Dorset West	74.4	+2.0	55.1	-0.4	9.4	-8.9	32.0	+8.5		3.5	+0.7		
Poole	68.2	+0.6	58.7	+0.7	20.8	-8.7	15.5	+6.6		3.4	+0.8	1.7(1)	4.7
Durham, Bishop Auckland*	65.7	+1.8	53.7	+6.8	35.9	-12.1	4.8	+2.0	5.6	2.4	+1.3		9.5
Darlington*	65.5	-2.0	48.1	+4.8	40.5	-10.1	4.8	+2.5	3.5	3.3	+1.7	0.7(1)	7.4
Durham, City of	68.6	+0.6	31.7	+1.9	42.0	-13.4	16.2	+6.3	6.7	2.7	+1.4		7.7
Durham North	63.2	-1.5	32.9	+3.0	44.2	-15.7	6.8	+2.2	11.1	2.5	+0.7	2.3(1)	9.3
Durham North West*	66.0	-0.6	41.9	+7.5	39.5	-13.3	5.9	-1.2	6.7	2.4	+2.1	3.4(2)	10.4
Easington	56.5	-1.8	26.4	+3.7	45.5	-18.2	4.4	+3.1	19.5	4.6		4.2(1)	11.0
Sedgefield*	64.6	-0.5	47.2	+8.4	36.3	-17.1	4.7	+2.8	8.5	4.6		0.9(1)	12.7
East Sussex, Bexhill & Battle	72.1	-1.0	63.6	+1.6	19.5	-5.2	12.3	+4.8					3.4
Brighton Kemptown	69.5	-3.0	35.0	-3.3	51.6	-6.8	6.1	+3.1	2.7				1.7
Brighton Pavilion	73.4	-3.1	17.5	-1.7	22.8	-4.0			1.3	57.2	+4.9	1.2(3)	
Eastbourne*	69.5	-3.4	48.9	+4.8	7.0	-1.2	41.0	-5.9	2.8	4.4		0.3(1)	
Hastings & Rye	67.4	-2.5	49.6	+2.7	42.1	-4.1	7.3	+3.9				1.0(1)	3.4
Hove	75.9	-1.7	28.1	-3.5	58.3	-5.8	6.6	+4.3	2.0	2.6	+2.7	0.6(2)	1.2
Lewes	76.7	+0.3	47.9	-1.6	5.8	-5.3	43.4	+4.1				0.2(1)	
Wealden	73.4	-0.9	60.8	-0.4	15.4	-6.8	18.7	+8.3		5.1	+1.8		3.2

ENGLAND	Turnout %	Turnout ±	Con %	Con ±	Lab %	Lab ±	LD %	LD ±	Brexit %	Grn %	Grn ±	Other No & %	Swing
Essex; Basildon & Billericay	63.1	−1.8	67.1	+6.1	20.8	−10.3	8.5	+5.0		3.2		0.5 (1)	8.2
Basildon South & Thurrock East	60.8	−3.2	66.2	+9.3	22.2	−10.3	4.3	+2.8				7.3 (1)	9.8
Braintree	67.1	−2.3	67.5	+4.7	18.7	−8.9	9.5	+5.2				4.3 (3)	6.8
Brentwood & Ongar	70.4	−0.1	68.6	+2.8	13.7	−6.7	13.6	+5.2		3.2	+1.4	1.0 (1)	4.8
Castle Point	63.6	−0.7	76.7	+9.5	16.6	−8.5	6.7	+4.4					9.0
Chelmsford	71.1	+0.9	55.9	+2.2	18.0	−11.8	25.1	+12.9				1.0 (1)	7.0
Clacton	61.3	−3.0	72.3	+11.0	15.5	−9.9	5.8	+3.8		2.8	+1.2	3.6 (3)	10.5
Colchester	64.6	−2.3	50.4	+4.6	32.8	−2.5	13.9	−3.0		2.9	+1.3		3.5
Epping Forest	67.7	−0.3	64.4	+2.4	20.3	−5.8	10.7	+5.0		3.9	+1.5	0.7 (2)	4.1
Harlow	63.7	−2.6	63.5	+9.4	31.0	−7.3	5.5	+3.4					8.4
Harwich & Essex North	70.1	−1.7	61.3	+2.7	22.4	−8.0	11.3	+5.8		3.7	+1.7	1.3 (2)	5.4
Maldon	69.6	−0.7	72.0	+4.1	12.4	−8.9	11.9	+7.5		3.7	+1.5		6.5
Rayleigh & Wickford	69.6	−0.9	72.6	+5.9	16.1	−8.2	7.6	+4.8		3.6	+1.7		7.0
Rochford & Southend East	61.0	−3.3	58.7	+10.0	32.0	−4.9	6.1	+3.4				3.2 (2)	7.4
Saffron Walden	72.5	−0.8	63.0	+1.2	13.2	−7.6	19.2	+5.2		4.7			4.4
Southend West	67.4	−2.3	59.2	+4.0	28.1	−5.9	11.4	+6.9				1.2 (1)	4.9
Thurrock	59.6	−4.8	58.6	+19.1	34.4	−4.5	3.2	+1.6		1.7		2.2 (1)	11.8
Witham	70.1	−1.1	66.6	+2.3	17.8	−8.6	9.3	+3.8		6.3	+2.5		5.5
Gloucestershire, Cheltenham	73.2	+1.0	48.0	+1.3	4.9	−4.6	46.3	+4.2				0.7 (1)	
Cotswolds, The	74.7	+0.4	58.0	−2.6	11.6	−6.3	25.0	+8.6		5.4	+2.5		1.8
Forest Of Dean	72.1	−1.0	59.6	+5.3	28.8	−7.1				9.1	+6.7	2.5 (1)	6.2
Gloucester	66.1	+0.9	54.2	+3.9	35.1	−5.0	8.1	+3.0		2.6	+1.2		4.5
Stroud*	78.0	+1.0	47.9	+2.0	42.1	−4.9			1.6	7.5	+5.3	0.9 (1)	3.5
Tewkesbury	72.8	+0.3	58.4	−1.6	15.2	−6.6	21.8	+8.3		4.6	+1.9		2.5
Greater London, Barking	57.1	−4.8	26.5	+4.0	61.2	−6.6	3.3	+2.1		1.8	+0.3		
Battersea	75.6	+4.6	36.1	−5.5	45.5	−0.4	15.3	+7.3	7.2	2.5	+1.0		5.3
Beckenham	73.6	−2.4	54.0	−5.4	25.8	−4.3	16.2	+8.3	0.6	4.1	+1.4		−2.5
Bermondsey & Old Southwark	62.9	−4.2	16.5	+3.6	54.1	+0.9	26.6	−4.5	2.8				−0.5

Constituency													
Bethnal Green & Bow	68.6	-0.9	10.8	-1.9	72.7	+0.9	9.7	+4.7	1.8	4.2	+1.7	0.7 (1)	-1.4
Bexleyheath & Crayford	66.1	-3.1	59.8	+4.2	29.5	-6.0	6.5	+3.9		3.0	+1.7	1.2 (1)	5.1
Brent Central	58.5	-6.5	22.2	+2.7	64.7	-8.4	9.9	+5.0		3.3	+1.7		5.5
Brent North	61.9	-6.4	36.3	+3.6	51.9	-11.0	7.8	+5.0	1.8	1.6	+0.5	0.5 (2)	7.3
Brentford & Isleworth	68.0	-4.4	32.2	-5.5	50.2	-7.2	12.5	+7.5	2.0	3.1			0.9
Bromley & Chislehurst	68.3	-3.3	52.6	-1.4	28.7	-4.7	14.5	+7.3		3.4	+0.9	0.8 (2)	1.7
Camberwell & Peckham	63.5	-3.6	11.5	-1.3	71.3	-6.5	9.0	+3.1	1.8	6.2	+3.4	0.2 (1)	2.6
Carshalton & Wallington*	67.3	-4.3	42.4	+4.1	12.4	-6.1	41.1	+0.1	2.1	1.5	+0.6	0.4 (1)	
Chelsea & Fulham	69.8	+3.7	49.9	-2.8	23.2	-10.0	25.9	+14.9					3.6
Chingford & Woodford Green	74.1	+2.9	48.5	-0.7	45.9	+1.9	5.7	+1.3	2.1			1.1 (1)	-1.3
Chipping Barnet	72.0	+0.2	44.7	-1.6	42.6	-3.1	10.3	+4.9		2.2	-0.3	0.1 (1)	0.7
Cities of London & Westminster	67.1	+4.3	39.9	-6.7	27.2	-11.2	30.7	+19.6		1.7	-0.4	0.5 (2)	
Croydon Central	66.4	-4.9	39.2	-3.2	50.2	-2.1	6.5	+4.6	1.8	2.2	+1.2		-0.6
Croydon North	62.9	-5.3	21.3	+1.4	65.6	-8.5	8.0	+5.3	1.5	2.9	+1.3	0.6 (1)	5.0
Croydon South	70.7	-2.7	52.2	-2.2	31.4	-4.4	12.6	+6.9		3.0	+1.2	0.7 (1)	1.1
Dagenham & Rainham	61.6	-3.4	43.8	+3.9	44.5	-5.6	2.7	+1.7	6.6	1.4	+0.2	1.0 (2)	4.7
Dulwich & West Norwood	69.4	-2.5	16.4	-3.1	65.5	-4.2			1.0	16.5	+14.0	0.6 (2)	0.5
Ealing Central & Acton	72.6	-2.0	27.1	-7.7	51.3	-8.4	17.2	+11.7	1.2	3.2			0.3
Ealing North	66.6	-3.6	31.8	+3.3	56.5	-9.5	8.8	+6.4		2.9	+1.5		6.4
Ealing Southall	65.4	-3.9	22.7	+1.4	60.8	-9.4	9.3	+5.1	2.1	4.0	+1.7	1.1 (2)	5.4
East Ham	61.9	-5.6	15.6	+2.8	76.3	-6.9	4.0	+2.8	2.0	1.6	+0.8	0.5 (1)	4.8
Edmonton	61.4	-5.0	25.3	+2.2	65.0	-6.5	5.3	+3.4	2.1	2.1	+0.7	0.2 (1)	4.3
Eltham	68.2	-3.4	39.7	-1.1	47.0	-7.4	6.7	+3.6	3.5	3.0			3.2
Enfield North	66.0	-5.4	37.4	+0.5	51.8	-6.2	6.5	+4.4	1.8	2.5	+1.3		3.3
Enfield Southgate*	72.1	-2.0	39.1	-3.6	48.5	-3.2	9.2	+5.2	1.0	2.2	+0.6		-0.2
Erith & Thamesmead	63.3	-0.5	39.0	+3.9	48.0	-9.5	4.8	+3.1	5.4	2.1	+1.0	0.7 (1)	6.7
Feltham & Heston	59.1	-5.8	35.6	+3.8	52.0	-9.2	6.5	+3.9	3.5	2.4	+0.8		6.5
Finchley & Golders Green	71.0	-0.4	43.8	-3.1	24.2	-19.6	31.9	+25.3					
Greenwich & Woolwich	66.4	-2.4	22.1	-3.4	56.8	-7.6	13.7	+6.5	2.3	4.4	+1.4	0.7 (2)	2.1

ENGLAND	Turnout %	Turnout ±	Con %	Con ±	Lab %	Lab ±	LD %	LD ±	Brexit %	Grn %	Grn ±	Other No & %	Swing
Hackney North & Stoke Newington	61.5	-4.7	11.9	-0.7	70.3	-4.8	7.5	+0.8	1.1	8.8	+4.1	0.4 (2)	2.0
Hackney South & Shoreditch	60.9	-5.7	10.8	-0.1	73.3	-6.2	8.9	+3.2	1.4	5.4	+2.7	0.2 (1)	3.0
Hammersmith	69.5	-2.3	23.5	-4.6	57.9	-6.0	13.4	+8.0	1.9	3.4	+1.8		0.7
Hampstead & Kilburn	66.3	-4.1	24.2	-8.2	48.9	-10.1	22.9	+15.8	1.2	2.8	+1.5		1.0
Harrow East	68.6	-2.2	54.4	+5.0	37.9	-8.1	7.7	+4.6		2.3	+1.0		6.5
Harrow West	66.1	-6.0	34.3	-0.1	52.4	-8.4	9.0	+6.5	1.9	1.7	+0.5	0.4 (1)	4.2
Hayes & Harlington	60.8	-4.4	34.7	+6.1	55.8	-10.7	4.4	+3.2	2.9	1.7	+0.6		8.4
Hendon	66.6	-1.6	48.8	+0.8	41.1	-4.9	8.4	+4.6				0.3 (2)	2.8
Holborn & St Pancras	66.0	-1.0	15.6	-2.7	64.5	-5.6	12.9	+6.1	1.8	4.8	+1.5	0.9 (1)	1.4
Hornchurch & Upminster	66.8	-2.5	65.8	+5.5	22.6	-6.0	7.2	+4.7		3.6	+1.6	0.5 (2)	5.8
Hornsey & Wood Green	74.7	-3.2	11.2	-3.7	57.5	-7.9	26.0	+9.9	1.8	3.6	+1.7	0.4 (1)	3.9
Ilford North	68.7	-6.1	40.1	+0.5	50.5	-7.2	5.3	+3.4	1.2	1.7	+0.4		4.9
Ilford South	62.9	-7.0	20.5	-0.4	65.6	-10.2	3.4	+2.0	1.9	1.3		7.3 (1)	3.2
Islington North	71.6	-1.8	10.2	-2.3	64.3	-8.7	15.6	+6.6	1.9	8.0	+4.0	0.4 (1)	1.4
Islington South & Finsbury	67.8	-1.3	16.8	-3.8	56.3	-6.6	20.0	+7.9	1.4	4.2	+1.7	0.4 (1)	0.2
Kensington*	67.7	+3.9	38.3	-3.9	38.0	-4.3	21.3	+9.1	2.4	1.2	-0.8	0.3 (3)	1.9
Kingston & Surbiton	74.2	-2.0	33.9	-4.2	10.7	-4.1	51.1	+6.4	0.9	1.7	+0.8	1.3 (3)	
Lewisham Deptford	68.7	-1.6	11.4	-2.3	70.8	-6.2	10.4	+5.1	1.3	5.6	+2.6	0.4 (2)	3.5
Lewisham East	66.0	-3.2	21.5	-1.5	59.5	-8.5	11.2	+6.8	1.4	3.8	+2.1	1.2 (4)	1.1
Lewisham West & Penge	69.8	-3.1	19.8	-3.2	61.2	-5.4	12.0	+5.8	2.8	4.6	+2.4	0.4 (1)	1.1
Leyton & Wanstead	68.7	-2.2	18.0	-2.8	64.7	-5.1	10.5	+4.1	2.0	4.1	+1.1	1.0 (1)	4.2
Mitcham & Morden	65.3	-4.7	25.1	+0.9	61.1	-7.5	8.1	+5.0	1.8	2.5	+1.2	0.5 (1)	4.4
Old Bexley & Sidcup	69.8	-3.0	64.5	+3.1	23.5	-5.8	8.3	+5.0		3.2	+1.5	0.5 (1)	3.7
Orpington	70.7	-3.6	63.4	+0.4	17.5	-6.9	15.5	+8.9		3.7	+1.6		0.0
Poplar & Limehouse	66.7	-0.6	15.9	-4.2	63.1	-4.2	14.4	+7.7	2.6	3.5	+1.8	0.6 (1)	
Putney*	77.0	+4.9	35.7	-8.4	45.1	+4.4	16.9	+5.3	2.4	2.2	-0.1		-6.4
Richmond Park*	78.7	-0.5	41.2	-4.0	5.2	-3.9	53.1	+8.0				0.5 (2)	
Romford	65.3	-2.7	64.6	+5.2	26.7	-5.1	5.7	+3.3		3.0	+1.4		5.1
Ruislip, Northwood & Pinner	72.7	+0.0	55.6	-1.7	24.6	-6.5	15.1	+8.0		3.1	+0.7	1.7 (3)	2.4
Streatham	66.7	-4.3	16.0	-5.3	54.8	-13.7	23.5	+17.0	1.1	4.5	+1.5		4.2
Sutton & Cheam	70.3	-3.5	50.0	-1.1	14.3	-6.3	33.4	+6.8		2.3	+0.6	0.1 (1)	
Tooting	76.0	+1.4	28.2	-4.8	52.7	-6.9	14.2	+8.9	0.8	4.0	+2.5		1.1

Constituency													
Tottenham	61.9	−5.8	11.6	+0.1	76.0	−5.6	6.8	+3.3	1.1	4.0	+1.4	0.5 (3)	2.8
Twickenham	76.0	−3.6	34.2	−3.8	8.5	−0.7	56.1	+3.3	1.3		+0.4	1.2 (8)	2.1
Uxbridge & South Ruislip	68.5	+1.7	52.6	+1.8	37.6	−2.4	6.3	+2.3		2.3	+2.4	0.2 (1)	
Vauxhall	63.5	−3.5	16.7	−1.9	56.1	−1.2	21.3	+0.7	1.1	4.5			1.3
Walthamstow	68.8	−2.1	12.3	−1.8	76.1	−4.5	5.9	+3.1	1.6	3.6	+1.1	0.5 (1)	1.3
West Ham	61.5	−4.2	16.3	+0.1	70.1	−6.7	6.9	+3.9	2.8	3.0	+1.4	1.0 (2)	3.4
Westminster North	65.5	−2.3	29.1	−4.2	54.2	−5.7	13.0	+7.8	1.0	2.5	+1.1	0.3 (1)	0.8
Wimbledon	77.7	+0.5	38.4	−8.1	23.7	−11.9	37.2	+22.7				0.7 (1)	
Greater Manchester, Altrincham & Sale West	74.9	+2.8	48.0	−3.0	36.8	−2.0	11.0	+3.3		2.9	+1.0	1.2 (2)	−0.5
Ashton-under-Lyne	56.8	−3.7	37.0	+5.1	48.1	−12.3	3.6	+2.0	8.2	3.1	+1.8		8.7
Blackley & Broughton	52.6	−3.4	24.6	+3.0	61.9	−8.6	4.1	+2.3	7.1	2.4	+1.2		5.8
Bolton North East*	64.5	−2.7	45.4	+3.2	44.5	−6.1	4.2	+1.3	4.3	1.6	+0.8		4.6
Bolton South East	58.7	−2.7	34.3	+4.6	53.0	−7.7	3.5	+1.6	7.3	1.9	+0.7		6.2
Bolton West	67.4	−2.8	55.3	+7.4	37.3	−8.8	5.5	+2.6		1.9			8.1
Bury North*	68.1	−2.8	46.2	+1.8	46.0	−7.6	3.4	+1.5	2.6	1.7			4.7
Bury South*	66.9	−2.3	43.8	+2.3	43.0	−10.2	4.6	+2.5	3.3	1.7		3.5 (3)	6.2
Cheadle	75.0	+0.6	46.0	+1.4	12.3	−6.8	41.8	+5.5					9.8
Denton & Reddish	58.3	−0.3	34.1	+6.1	50.1	−13.5	4.3	+2.1	7.9	2.9	+1.7	0.8 (1)	
Hazel Grove	69.9	+0.0	48.8	+3.3	12.4	−8.0	38.8	+5.9					8.3
Heywood & Middleton*	59.2	−3.2	43.1	+5.0	41.7	−11.6	4.4	+2.2	8.3	2.6			12.3
Leigh*	60.7	−0.8	45.3	+9.4	41.1	−15.1	4.8	+2.8	6.7			2.1 (2)	9.1
Makerfield	59.7	−3.5	34.4	+3.0	45.1	−15.1	4.8	+1.9	13.1	2.6			
Manchester Central	56.7	+1.6	14.8	+0.6	70.4	−7.0	6.5	+3.2	4.5	3.6	+1.9		3.8
Manchester Gorton	58.3	−2.7	9.5	+2.2	77.6	+1.3	5.5	−0.2	3.5	3.8	+1.6	0.2 (1)	0.5
Manchester Withington	69.2	−2.6	11.0	+0.7	67.7	−3.9	15.1	−0.9	2.5	3.7	+2.1		
Oldham East & Saddleworth	64.0	−1.2	40.3	+3.2	43.5	−11.0	5.2	+1.7	6.5	1.7		2.8 (2)	7.1
Oldham West & Royton	60.9	−2.4	30.3	+2.7	55.3	−9.9	3.3	+1.3	7.5	1.5	+0.6	2.1 (2)	6.3

ENGLAND	Turnout %	Turnout ±	Con %	Con ±	Lab %	Lab ±	LD %	LD ±	Brexit %	Grn %	Grn ±	Other No & %	Swing
Rochdale	60.1	−4.0	31.2	+2.8	51.6	−6.4	7.0	−1.1	8.2	2.1			4.6
Salford & Eccles	61.6	+0.6	24.5	−0.7	56.8	−8.7	6.1	+3.4	8.5	4.1	+2.4		4.0
Stalybridge & Hyde	58.0	−1.5	38.0	−0.2	44.9	−12.3	4.3	+2.0	8.5	3.3	+1.0	1.0 (1)	6.0
Stockport	63.8	−0.9	27.9	−0.5	52.0	−11.3	12.1	+7.8	4.6	3.4	+1.9		5.4
Stretford & Urmston	69.2	−0.7	27.5	+0.0	60.3	−6.5	5.9	+3.9	3.5	2.7	+1.4		3.2
Wigan	59.5	−3.6	31.8	+3.3	46.7	−15.5	5.4	+3.5	13.2	2.9	+1.3		9.4
Worsley & Eccles South	59.4	−2.5	38.5	−0.2	45.7	−11.3	5.6	+3.2	7.2	2.9	+1.1		5.6
Wythenshawe & Sale East	58.7	−1.4	30.1	+0.4	53.3	−8.9	7.0	+3.7	6.1	3.5	+2.2	0.1 (1)	4.7
Hampshire, Aldershot	66.0	+1.8	58.4	+3.3	23.5	−8.1	14.4	+7.0		3.7	+1.4		5.7
Basingstoke	66.0	−2.4	54.1	+1.4	28.1	−7.7	12.5	+6.4		3.9	+1.9	1.4 (1)	4.5
Eastleigh	70.3	−0.2	55.4	+5.0	12.8	−7.2	29.0	+3.3		2.8	+1.5		
Fareham	73.1	+0.8	63.7	+0.7	18.1	−7.1	14.0	+7.2		4.2	+1.9		3.9
Gosport	65.9	−0.8	66.5	+4.6	18.5	−8.7	11.3	+6.6		3.7	+1.7		6.6
Hampshire East	74.4	−0.3	58.8	−4.9	11.1	−5.9	24.2	+9.0		4.6	+1.4	1.4 (2)	0.5
Hampshire North East	75.1	−2.2	59.5	−6.0	9.7	−7.6	25.4	+13.3		3.0	+0.4	2.4 (2)	0.8
Hampshire North West	70.9	−1.3	62.1	+0.0	15.8	−7.6	17.5	+7.7		4.6	+2.3		3.8
Havant	63.7	−0.2	65.4	+5.6	18.0	−7.3	12.4	+6.4		3.5	+1.1	0.7 (1)	6.5
Meon Valley	72.4	−0.6	63.5	−2.2	10.3	−8.0	21.1	+10.2		4.0	+1.6	1.1 (1)	3.0
New Forest East	69.1	−1.7	64.5	+1.9	14.8	−5.0	14.6	−0.6		4.8	+2.4	1.3 (1)	3.5
New Forest West	71.0	−1.2	63.8	−3.0	13.1	−6.5	15.3	+5.7		7.7	+4.8		1.8
Portsmouth North	64.4	−1.8	61.4	+6.6	27.0	−6.7	7.4	+1.9		2.8	+1.2	1.4 (1)	6.6
Portsmouth South	63.9	+0.1	37.3	−0.2	48.6	+7.6	11.4	−5.9				0.5 (1)	−3.9
Romsey & Southampton North	75.3	+0.7	54.2	−3.0	11.5	−7.7	33.1	+11.9	2.1			1.2 (1)	
Southampton Itchen	65.6	+0.4	50.5	+4.0	41.0	−5.5	5.3	+2.2		2.2	+0.6	1.0 (1)	4.7
Southampton Test	64.2	−2.6	35.7	+1.5	49.5	−9.2	7.7	+3.6	3.5	3.2		0.5 (1)	5.4
Winchester	77.9	−0.9	48.3	−3.7	4.6	−5.9	46.6	+12.1				0.5 (1)	
Hereford and Worcester, Bromsgrove	72.3	−1.2	63.4	+1.4	20.8	−10.5	12.5	+7.9		3.3	+1.2		6.0
Hereford & Herefordshire South	68.9	−2.1	61.2	+7.7	21.6	−2.2	12.5	+5.4		4.8	+2.4		5.0
Herefordshire North	72.6	−1.4	63.0	+1.0	13.3	−5.6	14.3	+2.6		9.3	+3.8	1.0 (1)	3.3
Redditch	67.4	−2.8	63.3	+11.0	26.9	−9.1	6.6	+4.0		3.1	+2.3	0.5 (1)	10.1
Worcester	69.3	−0.3	50.8	+2.7	37.5	−5.7	7.2	+3.8		3.3	+1.0	1.1 (1)	4.2

Constituency													
Worcestershire Mid	71.8	−0.7	66.7	+1.4	16.8	−6.2	11.5	+5.3		3.9	+1.4	1.1 (1)	3.8
Worcestershire West	75.5	−0.5	60.7	−0.8	16.5	−7.2	18.1	+8.7		4.7	+1.9		8.1
Wyre Forest	64.8	−1.0	65.2	+6.8	22.8	−9.5	8.1	+4.3		3.9	+1.9		4.6
Hertfordshire, Broxbourne	63.8	−0.8	65.6	+3.4	23.2	−5.7	8.5	+5.4		2.7	+1.0		5.2
Hemel Hempstead	69.3	−1.0	56.5	+1.5	28.1	−8.8	12.3	+6.1		3.1	+1.1		0.5
Hertford & Stortford	73.5	+0.6	56.1	−4.2	23.4	−5.1	14.3	+6.2		4.5	+1.5	1.6 (2)	1.3
Hertfordshire North East	72.7	−0.5	56.6	−2.1	23.7	−4.7	15.5	+7.8		4.3	−1.1		
Hertfordshire South West	76.0	+1.2	49.6	−8.4	11.8	−13.9	10.2	−1.5		2.4	−0.2	26.0 (1)	4.2
Hertsmere	70.6	−0.5	62.5	+1.4	21.7	−6.9	12.6	+7.2		3.2	+1.3		
Hitchin & Harpenden	77.1	−0.3	47.1	−6.0	16.9	−15.7	35.4	+24.8		1.7	+0.3	0.6 (2)	
St Albans*	78.1	−0.2	39.2	−3.9	8.7	−14.4	50.1	+17.7		3.1	+0.9	0.3 (1)	5.5
Stevenage	66.6	−3.1	53.1	+2.8	35.2	−8.2	8.7	+4.5					2.0
Watford	69.7	+1.9	45.5	−0.1	37.9	−4.2	16.1	+7.0		3.1	+1.5	0.6 (1)	3.4
Welwyn Hatfield	69.5	−1.4	52.6	+1.6	31.6	−5.2	12.7	+5.3		2.6	+1.3		6.5
Humberside, Beverley & Holderness	67.2	−1.8	62.1	+3.7	23.9	−9.3	8.7	+3.7		3.1	+1.7	2.7 (1)	
Brigg & Goole	65.8	−2.4	71.3	+10.9	20.7	−12.2	5.0	+3.2		3.0	+1.8		11.6
Cleethorpes	62.9	−2.9	69.0	+11.9	22.8	−12.6	5.5	+3.2		2.8	+2.2		12.2
Great Grimsby*	53.9	−3.7	54.9	+12.7	32.7	−16.7	3.2	+0.5	7.2	1.6	+1.1	0.5 (1)	14.7
Haltemprice & Howden	70.0	−1.9	62.4	+1.4	21.5	−9.5	10.5	+5.7		3.5	+0.9	2.1 (1)	5.4
Hull East	49.3	−6.2	35.4	+5.5	39.2	−19.1	5.3	+1.8	17.8	2.4	−0.8		12.3
Hull North	52.2	−5.2	27.6	+2.4	49.8	−14.0	6.1	+1.1	13.9	2.6			8.2
Hull West & Hessle	52.1	−5.3	33.6	+3.7	42.7	−10.4	5.6	−0.8	18.0	0.2			7.1
Scunthorpe*	60.9	−4.4	53.8	+10.3	36.7	−15.3	2.3	+0.9	5.4	1.8			12.8
Yorkshire East	65.2	−1.4	64.4	+6.1	21.2	−9.2	8.0	+4.0		3.2	+1.4	3.2 (1)	7.7
Isle of Wight, Isle of Wight	65.9	−1.4	56.2	+4.9	24.3	+1.3				15.2	−2.1	4.3 (3)	1.8
Kent, Ashford	67.1	−1.5	56.2	+3.1	22.0	−7.7	10.1	+4.9		4.4	+2.1	1.4 (1)	5.4
Canterbury	75.0	+2.3	45.2	+0.5	48.3	+3.3	5.7	−2.4				0.8 (1)	−1.4
Chatham & Aylesford	60.5	−3.3	66.6	+9.6	23.8	−9.9	6.6	+4.1		2.5	+1.2	0.5 (1)	9.7

ENGLAND	Turnout %	Turnout ±	Con %	Con ±	Lab %	Lab ±	LD %	LD ±	Brexit %	Grn %	Grn ±	Other No & %	Swing
Dartford	65.7	−3.4	62.9	+5.4	27.5	−5.8	6.9	+4.3		2.7	+1.2		5.6
Dover	66.4	−3.3	56.9	+4.5	32.6	−7.3	5.7	+3.1		2.7	+0.9	2.1 (2)	5.9
Faversham & Mid Kent	68.7	−6.2	63.2	+2.1	19.6	−6.5	12.2	+5.7		4.2	+1.3	0.7 (1)	4.3
Folkestone & Hythe	66.8	−1.4	60.1	+5.4	24.0	−4.5	9.8	+2.6		4.6	+0.3	1.6 (4)	5.0
Gillingham & Rainham	62.5	−4.5	61.3	+5.9	28.4	−7.7	5.4	+2.6		2.3	+1.2	2.6 (3)	6.8
Gravesham	64.9	−2.2	62.2	+6.6	29.4	−7.1	5.4	+3.0		2.9	+1.5		6.8
Maidstone & The Weald	67.9	−0.7	60.4	+4.0	18.3	−3.8	16.4	+0.1		4.2	+2.5	0.7 (1)	3.9
Rochester & Strood	63.3	−1.7	60.0	+5.6	27.1	−8.9	7.2	+4.9		2.5	+1.1	3.2 (2)	7.3
Sevenoaks	71.0	−0.6	60.7	−3.0	13.6	−7.3	19.8	+11.5		3.9	+0.6	1.9 (2)	
Sittingbourne & Sheppey	61.2	−1.6	67.6	+7.4	20.0	−10.6	6.3	+3.5		2.3	+1.2	3.9 (3)	9.0
Thanet North	66.2	−0.3	62.4	+6.2	26.7	−7.3	7.1	+3.9		3.7	+2.0		6.7
Thanet South	65.9	−2.9	56.1	+5.3	34.2	−3.8	5.7	+2.6		4.0	+2.4		4.6
Tonbridge & Malling	71.9	−1.6	62.8	−0.9	14.5	−7.8	15.5	+8.9		7.2	+3.1		
Tunbridge Wells	73.0	+0.5	55.1	−1.8	14.8	−11.7	28.3	+18.4				1.8 (2)	
Lancashire, Blackburn	62.8	−4.4	24.0	−2.9	64.9	−4.8	2.5	+1.0		1.7		0.7 (1)	1.0
Blackpool North & Cleveleys	60.9	−3.2	57.6	+8.2	35.5	−9.0	3.9	+2.0	6.2	1.9	+1.0	1.1 (1)	8.6
Blackpool South*	56.8	−3.0	49.6	+6.5	38.3	−12.0	3.1	+1.3	6.1	1.7	+0.7	1.1 (1)	9.2
Burnley*	60.6	−1.7	40.3	+9.4	36.9	−9.9	9.0	−6.0	8.6	1.9	+0.8	3.3 (2)	9.6
Chorley‡	51.7	−21.1			67.3	+12.0				9.0	+8.1	23.7 (1)	
Fylde	69.8	−0.7	60.9	+2.1	25.3	−8.1	8.0	+3.0		3.7	+1.0	2.0 (1)	5.1
Hyndburn*	59.9	−3.3	48.5	+8.0	41.5	−11.8	2.9	+1.1	5.1	2.0			9.9
Lancashire West	71.8	−2.4	36.3	−1.1	52.1	−6.8	4.9	+2.9	4.3	2.4	+1.1		2.8
Lancaster & Fleetwood	64.5	−3.9	41.6	+1.0	46.8	−8.3	4.5	+1.9	4.0	3.1	+1.4		4.6
Morecambe & Lunesdale	67.2	−1.1	52.8	+5.1	38.8	−5.8	5.1	+1.4		2.1	+1.0	1.2 (1)	5.5
Pendle	68.1	−1.0	54.2	+5.1	40.2	−5.9	3.5	+1.4		1.5	+0.4	0.6 (1)	5.5
Preston	56.6	−5.0	25.8	+2.0	61.8	−6.2	5.1	+1.8	5.3	2.0	+1.0		4.1
Ribble Valley	69.8	−1.0	60.3	+2.5	27.0	−6.9	8.6	+2.8		3.1	+0.7	1.0 (1)	4.7
Rossendale & Darwen	67.1	−2.1	56.5	+5.6	37.0	−7.5	4.1	+1.0		2.4	+0.8		6.5
South Ribble	71.4	−1.0	55.8	+3.0	35.0	−4.3	6.9	+3.1		2.2	+1.3		3.6
Wyre & Preston North	70.8	−2.0	59.7	+1.4	28.0	−7.0	8.4	+3.6		3.3	+1.4	0.6 (1)	4.2
Leicestershire, Bosworth	69.2	+0.4	63.9	+7.2	17.3	−6.7	16.1	−1.2		2.7	+0.8		6.9

Constituency													
Charnwood	69.6	−1.1	63.4	+3.1	23.0	−7.8	8.8	+5.1		4.8	+2.9		5.4
Harborough	71.5	−1.6	55.3	+3.0	25.2	−5.6	15.9	+3.2		3.0	+1.1	0.7 (1)	4.3
Leicester East	63.0	−4.4	38.6	+14.4	50.8	−16.2	5.7	+3.1		1.8	−0.2	0.7 (1)	15.3
Leicester South	64.5	−2.3	21.8	+0.2	67.0	−6.5	5.5	+2.9	2.5	3.3	+1.0		3.4
Leicester West	53.5	−4.3	37.6	+6.3	49.7	−11.1	5.2	+3.1	2.4	2.8	+1.2		8.7
Leicestershire North West	68.2	−2.9	62.8	+4.6	24.9	−8.5	6.7	+0.3	4.7	4.6	+2.5	0.9 (2)	6.5
Leicestershire South	71.4	−0.4	64.0	+2.6	22.3	−6.3	9.5	+5.2		4.2	+2.3		4.5
Loughborough	68.5	+0.5	51.2	+1.3	38.0	−4.0	7.6	+4.0		2.8	+1.0	0.4 (1)	2.6
Rutland & Melton	70.5	−2.9	62.6	−0.2	16.4	−6.3	13.7	+5.5		4.9	+1.9	2.4 (2)	3.0
Lincolnshire, Boston & Skegness	60.1	−2.6	76.7	+13.1	15.2	−9.7	4.7	+2.9				3.4 (1)	11.4
Gainsborough	66.9	−0.9	66.4	+4.6	21.4	−7.3	10.1	+3.0		4.0	+2.7	2.1 (1)	5.9
Grantham & Stamford	68.7	−0.5	65.7	+3.7	19.3	−7.2	11.0	+5.5					5.5
Lincoln*	67.6	+0.9	47.9	+3.2	41.0	−6.9	4.8	+2.1	2.1	2.4	+1.2	1.8 (2)	5.0
Louth & Horncastle	65.7	−1.1	72.7	+8.7	17.5	−9.2	7.9	+4.1		2.6	+1.1	2.0 (1)	9.0
Sleaford & North Hykeham	70.2	−2.1	67.1	+2.9	18.2	−7.6	8.0	+3.9		3.3	+1.5	4.0 (2)	5.3
South Holland & The Deepings	64.7	−1.1	75.9	+6.0	13.2	−7.2	6.6	+3.7		3.3	+1.5	1.0 (1)	6.6
Merseyside, Birkenhead	66.4	−1.3	13.1	−5.3	59.0	−17.8	3.8	+1.3	3.5	3.3	+1.2	17.2 (1)	
Bootle	65.7	−3.3	9.2	−2.9	79.4	−4.6	3.7	+2.0	5.3	2.4	+1.0		0.9
Garston & Halewood	70.1	−1.1	13.0	−4.6	72.3	−5.4	6.2	+3.0	5.5	2.2	+0.8	0.6 (1)	0.4
Knowsley	65.3	−2.5	8.1	−1.2	80.8	−4.6	2.0	−0.1	6.1	2.3	+1.4	0.7 (1)	1.7
Liverpool Riverside	65.7	+2.8	7.8	−1.9	78.0	−6.6	5.1	+2.6	3.4	5.7	+2.4		2.3
Liverpool Walton	65.1	−2.1	9.9	+1.3	84.7	−1.0	1.9	+0.3		2.0	+0.8	1.6 (1)	1.2
Liverpool Wavertree	68.4	−1.6	9.7	−2.3	72.2	−7.4	9.3	+2.8	4.4	3.1	+1.8	1.2 (1)	2.5
Liverpool West Derby	67.0	−2.3	9.4	−0.5	77.6	−5.2	2.9	+1.7	4.6	1.4	+0.6	4.2 (1)	2.4
St Helens North	62.9	−3.1	26.6	−0.5	52.3	−11.5	5.6	+3.0	11.3	4.1	+1.7		5.5
St Helens South & Whiston	63.6	−3.3	20.5	−1.3	58.5	−9.3	5.7	+1.8	10.6	4.5	+1.9		4.0
Sefton Central	72.9	−2.5	27.8	−5.3	57.5	−5.5	6.7	+4.0	4.8	2.5	+1.2	0.8 (2)	0.1
Southport	68.0	−1.1	47.6	+8.9	39.0	+6.4	13.5	−12.9					1.3
Wallasey	70.1	−1.6	24.9	+1.7	64.3	−7.1	4.0	+2.4	4.4	2.4	+1.1		4.4

ENGLAND	Turnout %	Turnout ±	Con %	Con ±	Lab %	Lab ±	LD %	LD ±	Brexit %	Grn %	Grn ±	Other No & %	Swing
Wirral South	76.0	-2.3	37.2	-1.7	51.2	-6.1	6.7	+3.8	2.8	2.2	+1.2		2.2
Wirral West	77.3	-1.2	41.2	-0.9	48.2	-6.1	6.3	+3.7	2.0	2.2	+1.3		2.6
Norfolk, Broadland	72.9	+0.5	59.8	+1.7	21.2	-8.5	16.1	+8.2		2.5	+0.8	0.6 (1)	5.1
Great Yarmouth	60.4	-1.4	65.8	+11.6	25.1	-10.9	3.8	+1.6		2.4	+1.2	2.8 (3)	11.3
Norfolk Mid	68.4	-1.2	62.4	+3.4	22.2	-7.9	13.8	+8.7					5.7
Norfolk North*	71.9	-3.5	58.6	+16.9	7.7	-2.3	30.3	-18.1	3.4			1.7 (1)	
Norfolk North West	64.7	-3.1	65.7	+5.5	23.0	-9.0	7.8	+4.9		3.5	+1.8		7.3
Norfolk South	72.5	-1.1	58.0	-0.2	24.0	-7.0	14.0	+5.7		4.0	+1.5		3.4
Norfolk South West	65.6	-1.7	69.0	+6.2	18.1	-9.7	8.1	+3.6		3.2		1.6 (1)	8.0
Norwich North	68.9	+0.3	50.5	+2.8	40.3	-6.3	5.8	+2.5		2.3	+0.6	1.1 (1)	4.6
Norwich South	66.4	-2.9	29.0	-1.6	53.7	-7.2	9.2	+3.7	3.2	4.8	+1.9		2.8
North Yorkshire, Harrogate & Knaresborough	73.1	-0.4	52.6	-2.9	9.6	-10.5	35.6	+12.2				2.1 (1)	
Richmond [Yorks]	69.9	-0.6	63.6	-0.4	16.4	-7.0	12.1	+6.2		4.3	+1.3	3.5 (2)	3.3
Scarborough & Whitby	66.8	-1.7	55.5	+7.1	34.8	-6.7	6.1	+3.4				3.6 (1)	6.9
Selby & Ainsty	72.0	-1.9	60.3	+1.5	24.6	-9.6	8.6	+4.5		3.2		3.4 (1)	5.6
Skipton & Ripon	75.0	+0.5	59.5	-3.2	19.1	-9.2	14.8			4.7	-1.7	1.9 (1)	3.0
Thirsk & Malton	69.9	-1.2	63.0	+2.9	18.5	-7.5	12.0	+5.1		4.0	+2.0	2.5 (4)	5.2
York Central	66.1	-2.6	27.8	-2.4	55.2	-10.0	8.4	+3.7	3.0	4.3		1.4 (2)	3.8
York Outer	74.1	-1.6	49.4	-1.8	31.3	-5.4	18.1	+7.8				1.3 (1)	1.8
Northamptonshire, Corby	70.2	-2.1	55.2	+6.0	38.3	-6.5	6.5	+3.9					6.2
Daventry	74.1	+0.2	64.6	+0.8	19.1	-5.5	12.3	+5.0		4.1	+2.4		3.2
Kettering	67.5	-1.7	60.3	+2.4	26.4	-10.2	6.8	+3.5		3.1	+0.9	3.3 (1)	6.3
Northampton North	67.3	-1.3	53.2	+6.0	39.3	-6.0	5.1	+2.6		2.4	+0.8		6.0
Northampton South	65.7	-0.7	51.2	+4.3	39.7	-4.3	6.1	+2.7		3.0	+1.3		4.3
Northamptonshire South	73.7	-2.1	62.4	-0.1	20.9	-6.4	11.8	+6.2		3.9	+1.8	0.9 (2)	3.2
Wellingborough	64.3	-2.9	62.2	+4.7	26.5	-7.6	7.9	+4.5		3.5	+1.7		6.2
Northumberland, Berwick-upon-Tweed	70.3	-1.5	56.9	+4.4	21.6	-2.9	18.2	-2.9		3.3	+1.4		
Blyth Valley*	63.4	-3.6	42.7	+5.4	40.9	-15.0	5.3	+0.7	8.3	2.8	+0.6		10.2
Hexham	75.3	-0.5	54.5	+0.4	31.6	-2.5	10.1	+3.0		3.7	+1.0		1.4

Wansbeck	64.0	−4.4	40.3	+7.5	42.3	−15.1	6.3	+1.5	7.8	3.0	+1.3	0.4 (1)	11.3
Nottinghamshire, Ashfield*	62.6	−1.4	39.3	−2.4	24.4	−18.1	2.3	+0.3	5.1	1.4	+0.6	27.6 (1)	18.4
Bassetlaw*	63.5	−3.0	55.2	+11.9	27.7	−24.9	6.6	+4.3	10.6				
Broxtowe	75.7	+0.7	48.1	+1.3	38.5	−6.8				3.3	+2.0	10.1 (4)	4.0
Gedling*	70.0	−2.5	45.5	+2.6	44.1	−7.8	4.6	+2.5	3.6	2.2	+1.2		5.2
Mansfield	63.9	−0.6	63.9	+17.3	30.8	−13.7	3.3	+1.9				2.0 (2)	15.5
Newark	72.2	−0.7	63.3	+0.6	23.5	−6.2	9.7	+4.6		3.6			3.4
Nottingham East	60.4	−3.3	20.9	−0.8	64.3	−7.1	4.9	+2.3	3.4	3.0	+1.2	3.6 (1)	3.2
Nottingham North	53.1	−4.2	36.4	+5.3	49.1	−11.1	4.5	+2.7	7.6	2.5	+1.1		8.2
Nottingham South	60.6	−7.1	29.1	−1.7	55.2	−7.1	8.2	+4.9	4.2	3.3	+2.0		2.7
Rushcliffe	78.5	+0.5	47.5	−4.3	34.9	−3.2	15.9	+11.1				1.7 (2)	−0.6
Sherwood	67.7	−2.4	60.8	+9.3	30.1	−11.7	5.5	+3.4		2.3	+1.1	1.3 (1)	10.5
Oxfordshire, Banbury	69.8	−3.6	54.3	+0.0	27.6	−6.5	14.0	+8.4		4.1	+2.2		3.3
Henley	76.7	+0.5	54.8	−4.3	9.7	−10.4	30.9	+16.0		4.7	+1.4	1.0 (3)	
Oxford East	63.0	−5.8	20.9	−1.1	57.0	−8.2	13.9	+4.8	2.3	4.8	+1.5		3.5
Oxford West & Abingdon	76.4	−3.0	38.1	−4.3	7.2	−5.4	53.3	+9.5	1.4				
Wantage	73.9	−0.2	50.7	−3.4	15.2	−11.7	31.9	+17.4				2.2 (1)	
Witney	73.1	−0.5	55.2	−0.3	14.3	−6.4	30.5	+10.0					
Shropshire, Ludlow	72.3	−1.1	64.1	+1.2	15.1	−9.2	17.0	+6.3		3.8	+1.7		5.2
Shrewsbury & Atcham	71.8	−1.8	52.5	+2.6	33.5	−5.0	10.0	+2.7		3.0	+1.1	1.0 (1)	3.8
Shropshire North	67.9	−1.2	62.7	+2.2	22.1	−9.0	10.0	+4.7		3.2	+0.1	2.0 (1)	5.6
Telford	62.1	−3.5	59.7	+10.9	34.1	−13.0	6.2	+4.1					12.0
Wrekin, The	69.2	−3.0	63.5	+8.0	25.2	−11.0	8.3	+5.6		3.0	+1.4	1.3 (1)	9.5
Somerset, Bridgwater & West Somerset	67.6	+2.3	62.1	+7.0	19.8	−8.8	13.5	+2.7		3.3	+1.4		7.9
Somerton & Frome	75.6	−0.1	55.8	−0.9	12.9	−4.3	26.2	+5.4		5.1	+1.4		
Taunton Deane	71.9	−1.9	53.6	+0.7	7.4	−8.0	35.2	+7.6				3.8 (1)	
Wells	75.2	+1.4	54.1	+4.0	7.0	−4.7	37.9	+0.3				0.9 (2)	

ENGLAND	Turnout %	Turnout ±	Con %	Con ±	Lab %	Lab ±	LD %	LD ±	Brexit %	Grn %	Grn ±	Other No & %	Swing
Yeovil	71.9	+0.2	58.4	+3.9	6.3	−6.1	31.1	+1.4		2.7	+1.0	1.5 (2)	
South Yorkshire, Barnsley Central	56.5	−4.3	21.4	−2.8	40.1	−23.8	3.2	+1.8	30.4	2.4	+1.0	2.4 (2)	
Barnsley East	54.8	−4.1	27.3	+0.3	37.6	−21.9	3.5	+1.7	29.2	2.4			9.6
Don Valley*	60.3	−1.9	43.2	+1.4	35.2	−17.8	4.2	+2.3	13.7	1.9		1.8 (1)	9.0
Doncaster Central	58.2	−1.7	34.5	+0.2	40.0	−17.9	4.2	+1.9	16.5	2.4		2.4 (1)	9.0
Doncaster North	56.2	−2.2	32.9	+5.2	38.7	−22.1	3.6	+2.0	20.4			4.5 (5)	13.7
Penistone & Stocksbridge*	69.8	+0.0	47.8	+4.7	33.3	−12.5	10.2	+6.1	8.7				8.6
Rother Valley*	65.1	−0.7	45.1	+4.8	32.1	−16.0	5.2	+2.9	12.9	2.5	+0.7	2.1 (1)	10.4
Rotherham	57.8	−2.2	32.6	+6.2	41.3	−15.1	5.9	+1.2	17.2	3.0		3.0 (1)	10.6
Sheffield Brightside & Hillsborough	57.1	−2.4	25.5	+3.9	56.5	−10.8	3.8	+1.3	9.7	3.0	+1.2	1.5 (1)	7.4
Sheffield Central	56.7	−5.1	13.1	+0.2	66.7	−4.2	6.4	+1.2	3.9	9.0	+0.9	0.9 (3)	2.2
Sheffield Hallam	78.2	+0.6	25.8	+2.1	34.6	−3.7	33.4	−1.3	2.7	2.9	+1.4	0.5 (2)	
Sheffield Heeley	63.8	−1.2	30.3	+1.6	50.3	−9.7	6.8	+2.3	8.3	4.2	+2.1		5.7
Sheffield South East	61.9	−1.3	35.9	+4.4	46.1	−12.4	5.1	+1.8	10.7			2.3 (1)	8.4
Wentworth & Dearne	55.8	−2.9	35.1	+3.8	40.3	−24.7	4.1	+0.3	16.9			3.6 (2)	14.2
Staffordshire, Burton	65.0	−2.5	60.7	+2.7	30.9	−6.9	5.5	+3.0		2.9	+1.3		4.8
Cannock Chase	61.9	−2.3	68.3	+13.3	25.4	−12.1				6.3	+4.6		12.7
Lichfield	70.5	−1.4	64.5	+1.0	20.8	−8.1	10.4	+5.5		3.2	+0.6	1.1 (1)	4.5
Newcastle-under-Lyme*	65.6	−1.2	52.5	+4.4	35.9	−12.3	5.3	+1.6	4.3	2.1			8.4
Stafford	70.5	−5.4	58.6	+3.9	30.5	−9.3	6.2	+3.2		4.6	+2.2		6.6
Staffordshire Moorlands	66.7	−3.9	64.6	+6.4	26.9	−6.9	5.7	+2.3		2.8	+1.6		6.7
Staffordshire South	67.9	−1.7	73.0	+3.3	16.5	−8.7	6.6	+3.9		3.9	+1.6		6.0
Stoke-on-Trent Central*	57.9	−0.4	45.4	+5.6	43.3	−8.2	3.5	+1.4	5.3	2.6	+1.4		6.9
Stoke-on-Trent North*	58.8	+0.4	52.3	+7.0	36.6	−14.3	3.2	+1.0	5.9	1.3	−0.4	0.8 (1)	10.7
Stoke-on-Trent South	61.4	−1.7	62.2	+13.1	33.7	−13.7	4.1	+2.1					13.4
Stone	71.8	−1.9	63.6	+0.4	23.6	−4.7	8.9	+4.4		4.0	+2.6		2.5
Tamworth	64.3	−1.7	66.3	+5.3	23.7	−11.1	5.3	+1.1		2.0		2.7 (2)	8.2
Suffolk, Bury St Edmunds	69.1	−3.1	61.0	+1.8	20.6	−8.9				15.7	+11.5	2.7 (1)	
Ipswich*	65.6	−1.9	50.3	+4.6	39.3	−8.1	4.9	+2.6	2.9	2.6	+0.9		6.3
Suffolk Central & Ipswich North	70.3	−2.1	62.7	+2.5	21.1	−8.6	11.5	+7.2		4.7	+1.8		5.6

Constituency													
Suffolk Coastal	71.2	−2.0	56.5	−1.5	21.3	−9.2	15.0	+8.0		4.7	+1.5	2.6 (1)	3.8
Suffolk South	70.2	−1.7	62.2	+1.7	19.4	−8.4	12.5	+6.7		5.9	+2.7		5.0
Suffolk West	64.1	−2.8	65.8	+4.6	20.7	−7.5	9.1	+4.9		4.4	+2.6		6.1
Waveney	61.8	−3.5	62.2	+7.8	26.9	−9.9	5.1	+3.2		5.3	+2.8		8.9
Surrey, Epsom & Ewell	73.3	−0.8	53.5	−6.1	17.2	−7.8	23.5	+11.0		3.4	+0.6	0.5 (1)	
Esher & Walton	77.7	+3.8	49.4	−9.3	4.5	−15.2	45.0	+27.7				2.4 (1)	0.9
Guildford	75.5	+1.7	44.9	−9.7	7.7	−11.3	39.2	+15.3		3.3	+0.7	1.1 (3)	−0.3
Mole Valley	76.5	+0.4	55.4	−6.4	5.2	−8.7	34.3	+15.0		6.0	+1.8	8.3 (2)	5.2
Reigate	71.6	−0.5	53.9	−3.5	19.5	−5.2	19.4	+8.5		3.5	+0.9	1.8 (2)	
Runnymede & Weybridge	69.0	+0.1	54.9	−6.0	20.6	−5.3	17.3	+10.0		4.3	+2.1	1.2 (1)	
Spelthorne	69.8	+0.8	58.9	+1.6	21.7	−8.8	15.1	+9.6		3.9	+2.1	3.6 (3)	
Surrey East	71.8	−0.4	59.7	+0.0	13.8	−5.4	19.4	+8.9		3.8	−0.1		
Surrey Heath	72.1	+0.5	58.6	−5.6	9.2	−11.8	27.3	+16.4		2.8	+0.8	3.2 (2)	
Surrey South West	76.3	−1.1	53.3	−2.4	7.9	−4.7	38.7	+28.9		2.8	+1.6	1.1 (1)	
Woking	71.5	−1.0	48.9	−5.2	16.4	−7.5	30.8	+13.3		4.3	+2.9		
Tyne and Wear, Blaydon	67.3	−2.9	31.2	+3.1	43.3	−12.8	8.1	−1.0	12.8	2.8	+1.1	1.1 (1)	8.0
Gateshead	59.2	−5.4	34.7	+10.8	53.6	−11.5	7.3	+3.3				1.8 (3)	11.2
Houghton & Sunderland South	57.8	−3.1	32.9	+3.2	40.7	−18.7	5.8	+3.6	15.5			2.3 (1)	11.0
Jarrow	62.6	−3.8	27.6	+2.6	45.1	−20.0	5.8	+3.1	10.1	2.0	+0.3		11.3
Newcastle Upon Tyne Central	64.8	−2.2	24.8	+0.2	57.6	−7.3	7.2	+2.3	6.8	3.6	+2.0	9.4 (3)	3.8
Newcastle Upon Tyne East	68.0	+0.8	24.4	+3.1	60.1	−7.5	10.5	+4.3		5.1	+3.2		5.3
Newcastle Upon Tyne North	68.6	−4.5	33.2	−0.8	45.4	−9.9	9.3	+4.0	9.2	2.9	+1.8		4.6
South Shields	60.3	−3.9	20.3	−5.6	45.6	−15.9	4.0	+2.3	17.0	3.4	−0.1		5.1
Sunderland Central	59.8	−2.2	35.4	+2.0	42.2	−13.4	7.0	+3.0	11.6	2.8	+1.2	9.7 (1)	7.7
Tynemouth	72.5	−0.9	39.4	+2.9	48.1	−8.9	6.8	+3.7	3.5	2.3	+1.2	1.1 (1)	5.9
Tyneside North	63.9	−1.8	30.7	+3.4	49.7	−14.8	6.4	+3.5	10.4	2.8	+1.5		9.1
Washington & Sunderland West	56.6	−3.7	32.6	+3.7	42.5	−18.2	5.5	+3.2	14.5	2.7	+1.4	2.2 (1)	11.0
Warwickshire, Kenilworth & Southam	77.2	−0.2	57.7	−3.1	17.9	−7.6	19.0	+9.4		4.5	+2.3	0.9 (1)	2.3

ENGLAND	Turnout %	Turnout ±	Con %	Con ±	Lab %	Lab ±	LD %	LD ±	Brexit %	Grn %	Grn ±	Other No & %	Swing
Nuneaton	64.3	-2.2	60.6	+9.0	31.5	-9.8	4.1	+2.1		3.7	+2.1		9.4
Rugby	70.3	-0.8	57.6	+3.3	31.1	-7.2	8.3	+2.7		3.0	+1.2		5.2
Stratford-on-Avon	74.4	+0.6	60.6	-2.3	11.3	-10.6	24.3	+12.4		3.8	+1.3		4.2
Warwick & Leamington	71.0	-1.8	42.3	-2.1	43.8	-2.9	9.2	+4.0	1.5	2.8	+0.6	0.4 (2)	0.4
Warwickshire North	65.3	+0.1	65.9	+8.9	26.8	-12.1	4.5	+2.3		2.8	+0.8		10.5
West Midlands,													
Aldridge-Brownhills	65.4	-1.2	70.8	+5.4	20.4	-9.5	6.0	+2.7		2.0	+0.8	0.9 (1)	7.4
Birmingham Edgbaston	61.5	-2.6	36.9	-2.6	50.1	-5.2	7.9	+4.3	2.5	2.6	+1.3		1.3
Birmingham Erdington	53.3	-3.9	40.1	+1.7	50.3	-7.7	3.7	+1.7	4.1	1.8	+0.2		4.7
Birmingham Hall Green	65.9	-3.5	13.9	-1.1	67.8	-9.8	6.9	+1.2	1.7	1.5	+0.0	8.1 (1)	4.3
Birmingham Hodge Hill	57.5	-3.8	15.0	+0.8	78.7	-2.4	1.7	+0.0	3.4	0.7	-0.1	0.6 (1)	1.6
Birmingham Ladywood	56.2	-2.8	11.3	-1.9	79.2	-3.5	5.3	+2.5	2.0	2.2	+0.9		0.8
Birmingham Northfield*	58.5	-2.8	46.3	+3.6	42.5	-10.7	4.6	+2.4	3.8	2.2	+0.3	0.6 (1)	7.2
Birmingham Perry Barr	58.5	-4.5	26.8	+0.2	63.1	-5.0	4.5	+2.1	3.3	2.0	+0.7	0.4 (1)	2.6
Birmingham Selly Oak	59.8	-6.0	30.9	-1.0	56.0	-6.9	6.4	+3.1	2.9	3.7	+1.9		3.0
Birmingham Yardley	57.1	-4.2	29.8	+10.0	54.8	-2.3	8.8	-9.1	5.3	1.4	+0.7		6.1
Coventry North East	58.5	-2.9	35.4	+5.4	52.7	-10.8	4.6	+2.1	4.7	2.6	+1.5		8.1
Coventry North West	63.4	-2.8	43.4	+6.6	43.8	-10.1	5.7	+3.1	4.1	3.0	+1.7		8.4
Coventry South	63.5	-3.0	42.5	+4.4	43.4	-11.7	7.5	+4.7	3.2	2.4	+1.1	1.0 (1)	8.0
Dudley North*	59.2	-3.5	63.1	+16.6	31.6	-14.9	3.3	+2.4		2.0	+1.4		15.7
Dudley South	60.2	-2.1	67.9	+11.5	25.3	-10.9	4.4	+2.8		2.4	+1.4		11.2
Halesowen & Rowley Regis	62.0	-2.5	60.5	+8.6	32.0	-8.1	4.1	+2.2		2.2	+1.2	1.3 (3)	8.3
Meriden	63.4	-3.6	63.4	+1.4	21.3	-5.6	10.4	+5.5		4.9	+2.3		3.5
Solihull	70.3	-2.7	58.4	+0.3	19.9	-1.9	18.0	+2.3		3.7	+1.6		1.1
Stourbridge	65.4	-1.8	60.3	+5.7	30.6	-7.7	5.5	+3.2		2.3	+1.2	1.4 (1)	6.7
Sutton Coldfield	69.2	-0.7	60.4	-0.6	23.6	-8.4	12.2	+7.8		3.9	+2.1		3.9
Walsall North	54.4	-2.2	63.8	+14.2	31.1	-11.7	3.4	+1.8		1.7			13.0
Walsall South	62.4	-2.9	41.0	+3.8	49.1	-8.2	3.8	+2.4	3.9	1.5	+1.0	0.7 (1)	6.0
Warley	59.7	-3.4	27.9	+1.7	58.8	-8.4	4.3	+2.3	6.6	2.4	+1.0		5.0
West Bromwich East*	58.0	-3.3	46.7	+8.5	42.3	-15.7	3.6	+2.1	4.1	1.7	+0.4	1.5 (2)	12.1
West Bromwich West*	53.4	-1.3	50.5	+10.9	39.5	-12.5	2.7	+1.7	5.3	1.9	+1.0		11.7
Wolverhampton North East*	55.6	-4.5	51.7	+11.4	39.8	-13.0	2.8	+1.2	3.9	1.8	+0.4		12.2

Wolverhampton South East	53.2	−7.0	42.7	+8.0	46.4	−11.8	3.0	+1.8	6.3	1.6	+0.4		9.9
Wolverhampton South West*	68.0	−2.7	48.3	+4.1	44.3	−5.1	5.0	+3.1	2.5		−0.1		4.6
West Sussex, Arundel & South Downs	75.1	−0.7	57.9	−4.4	15.8	−6.9	21.2	+13.3		4.1		0.9 (1)	
Bognor Regis & Littlehampton	66.1	−1.6	63.5	+4.5	19.6	−5.3	11.0	+4.5		3.6	+1.6	2.4 (2)	4.9
Chichester	71.6	+1.1	57.8	−2.3	14.8	−7.6	22.7	+11.5		4.1	+0.8	0.5 (2)	
Crawley	67.2	−1.2	54.2	+3.6	37.4	−8.3	5.5	+1.7		2.9			5.9
Horsham	72.9	−2.0	56.8	−2.8	14.9	−6.8	23.4	+11.0		4.2	+1.2	0.8 (1)	
Sussex Mid	73.7	+0.5	53.3	−3.6	17.9	−7.1	24.3	+11.6		3.6	+1.0	1.0 (2)	
Worthing East & Shoreham	70.7	+0.3	51.0	+2.1	37.0	−2.4	7.8	+3.0		3.8	+1.4	0.5 (1)	2.2
Worthing West	69.5	−0.6	55.8	+0.4	28.6	−4.6	11.0	+5.6		3.7	+0.7	0.9 (1)	2.5
West Yorkshire, Batley & Spen	66.5	−0.6	36.0	−2.8	42.7	−12.8	4.7	+2.4	3.2	1.3	+0.0	12.2 (1)	5.0
Bradford East	60.4	−4.5	21.9	+1.5	63.0	−2.4	7.5	+5.7	6.1	1.5	+0.9		2.0
Bradford South	57.6	−3.0	40.4	+2.2	46.3	−8.2	3.8	+2.5	7.1	2.5	+1.6		5.2
Bradford West	62.6	−4.8	15.2	−1.4	76.2	11.5	3.0	+1.5	3.5	1.8	+0.8	0.2 (1)	−6.5
Calder Valley	72.9	−0.6	51.9	+5.7	41.9	−3.2	5.0	+1.6		1.8		1.2 (1)	4.5
Colne Valley*	72.3	+0.7	48.4	+2.2	40.0	−7.7	6.3	+2.1	2.1	1.9	+0.3	1.4 (3)	4.9
Dewsbury*	69.4	−0.1	46.4	+1.3	43.7	−7.3	4.3	+2.1	3.3	3.0	+0.1	0.4 (1)	4.3
Elmet & Rothwell	71.9	−2.2	57.9	+3.6	28.1	−9.7	8.9	+4.5		2.0	+1.4	2.1 (1)	6.7
Halifax	64.6	−3.2	40.7	−1.0	46.3	−6.6	4.9	+2.7	6.1	2.1			2.8
Hemsworth	59.6	−4.4	34.8	+0.9	37.5	−18.5	3.9	+2.0	13.5	4.2		8.2 (3)	9.7
Huddersfield	63.9	−1.5	37.2	+4.2	49.0	−11.4	5.7	+3.0	4.0	4.3	+1.0		7.8
Keighley*	72.3	−0.1	48.1	+2.0	43.9	−2.6	4.9	+2.5	1.6	2.2		1.5 (2)	2.3
Leeds Central	54.2	+0.9	22.6	+2.1	61.7	−8.5	4.8	+2.5	6.1	3.8	+1.8	0.6 (1)	5.3
Leeds East	58.0	−4.8	35.7	+5.1	49.8	−11.5	4.6	+2.8	7.6	2.8	+1.2		8.3
Leeds North East	71.6	−4.0	23.6	−7.4	57.5	−5.6	11.2	+7.5	3.5	3.2	+2.5	0.3 (1)	−0.9
Leeds North West	72.8	+4.8	26.8	+7.2	48.6	+4.5	19.1	−15.9	2.6		+1.6	1.8 (3)	
Leeds West	59.5	−2.7	28.9	+2.7	55.1	−8.9	4.4	+2.3	6.7	3.2	+0.7		5.8

ENGLAND

	Turnout %	Turnout ±	Con %	Con ±	Lab %	Lab ±	LD %	LD ±	Brexit %	Grn %	Grn ±	Other No & %	Swing
Morley & Outwood	65.9	−2.5	56.7	+6.0	35.0	−11.7	4.4	+1.8		2.1		1.8 (1)	8.8
Normanton, Pontefract & Castleford	57.1	−3.2	35.3	+5.2	37.9	−21.6	6.5	+5.1	16.6			3.7 (1)	13.4
Pudsey	74.1	−0.2	48.8	+1.4	42.3	−4.4	5.7	+2.4		1.6		1.6 (1)	2.9
Shipley	72.9	−0.1	50.8	−0.5	39.2	−3.3	5.9	+1.8		2.4		1.6 (1)	1.4
Wakefield*	64.1	−1.7	47.3	+2.3	39.8	−9.9	3.9	+1.9	6.1			2.9 (2)	6.1
Wiltshire, Chippenham	73.9	−0.8	54.3	−0.4	11.2	−8.5	34.5	+8.9					
Devizes	69.4	−0.6	63.1	+0.4	15.4	−5.6	16.0	+6.7		5.5	+2.3		
Salisbury	72.1	−1.1	56.4	−1.7	18.0	−7.5	19.6	+8.4		4.6	+2.5	1.4 (1)	2.9
Swindon North	66.9	−1.6	59.1	+5.5	29.8	−8.6	8.0	+4.4		3.1	+1.5		7.1
Swindon South	69.4	−1.4	52.3	+3.9	39.2	−4.3	8.5	+4.4					4.1
Wiltshire North	74.7	−0.5	59.1	−1.2	10.4	−7.1	26.9	+9.2		3.5	+1.4		
Wiltshire South West	70.4	−0.8	60.2	+0.2	20.8	−5.7	14.6	+4.8		4.4	+1.8		3.0

WALES

	Turnout %	Turnout ±	Con %	Con ±	Lab %	Lab ±	LD %	LD ±	Plaid %	Plaid ±	Brexit %	Grn %	Grn ±	Others No & %	Swing
Clwyd, Aberconwy	71.3	+0.2	46.1	+1.5	39.7	−2.9	5.7	+2.8	8.5	−1.4					2.2
Alyn & Deeside	68.5	−2.5	42.0	+1.6	42.5	−9.6	5.9	+3.5	3.4	+0.8	6.2				5.6
Clwyd South*	67.3	−2.4	44.7	+5.6	41.3	−9.4	4.1	+2.2	5.9	−0.2	4.0				7.5
Clwyd West	69.7	−0.1	50.7	+2.7	34.0	−5.6	5.6	+2.9	9.7	+0.1					4.2
Delyn*	70.3	−2.5	43.7	+2.2	41.4	−10.8	6.1	+3.5	3.7	−0.1	5.1				6.5
Vale Of Clwyd*	65.7	−2.3	46.4	+2.3	41.5	−8.7	4.0	+2.2	4.2	+0.2	4.0				5.5
Wrexham*	67.4	−2.9	45.3	+1.7	39.0	−9.9	4.3	+1.9	6.4	+1.4	3.6	1.3			5.8
Dyfed, Carmarthen East & Dinefwr	71.4	−1.9	34.5	+8.2	21.0	−8.8			38.9	−0.4	5.6				
Carmarthen West & Pembrokeshire South	71.2	−0.9	52.7	+5.9	34.3	−5.2	4.4	+2.2	8.6	−0.7					5.5
Ceredigion	71.1	−2.2	22.1	+3.8	15.8	−4.4	17.4	−11.6	37.9	+8.7	5.1	1.7	+0.3		
Llanelli	63.2	−4.7	30.0	+6.3	42.2	−11.3			18.4	+0.2	9.4				8.8

Preseli Pembrokeshire	71.2	−0.9	50.4	+7.0	38.5	−4.2	4.6	+2.0	6.5	+0.1	20.6	1.3			5.6
Gwent, Blaenau Gwent	59.6	−3.7	19.0	+4.3	49.2	−8.8	4.3	+3.3	5.7	−15.5	14.1	1.9			7.9
Islwyn	62.0	−2.2	28.8	+1.6	44.7	−14.1	3.8	+1.9	6.7	−0.9		2.7	+0.8	0.9 (1)	1.7
Monmouth	74.8	−1.8	52.1	−1.0	32.2	−4.4	9.8	+5.6	2.4	−0.3	6.8	1.6			8.1
Newport East	62.0	−2.4	39.0	+4.2	44.4	−12.1	5.8	+3.2	2.4	0.0	4.0	2.1			5.5
Newport West	65.2	−2.3	41.6	+2.3	43.7	−8.6	5.9	+3.7	2.7	+0.3	15.4	2.2	+0.9		8.3
Torfaen	59.6	−2.5	31.8	+0.8	41.8	−15.8	4.9	+2.7	3.9	−1.5	4.0				
Gwynedd, Arfon	68.9	+0.7	15.2	−1.1	35.6	−4.9			45.2	+4.3	5.9				9.7
Dwyfor Meirionnydd	67.5	−0.4	32.4	+3.3	13.4	−7.3			48.3	+3.2	6.0				6.8
Ynys Môn*	70.4	−0.2	35.5	+7.7	30.1	−11.8			28.5	+1.1	4.3	1.9			6.1
Mid-Glamorgan, Bridgend*	66.7	−2.8	43.1	+3.3	40.3	−10.3	5.6	+3.5	4.8	+0.6	11.2			4.7 (2)	6.2
Caerphilly	63.5	−0.6	27.9	+2.7	44.9	−9.5			16.0	+1.6	10.1			5.8 (1)	7.9
Cynon Valley	59.1	−2.8	22.2	+2.8	51.4	−9.6	3.1	+1.3	8.5	−5.3	11.2				7.6
Merthyr Tydfil & Rhymney	57.3	−3.2	19.6	+1.5	52.4	−14.3	3.5	+1.0	7.6	−0.6	11.2			5.8 (1)	6.8
Ogmore	61.5	−3.7	27.7	+2.5	49.7	−12.7	4.1	+2.5	8.2	+0.7	8.5	1.8			7.6
Pontypridd	64.7	−1.1	29.4	+2.7	44.5	−10.9			12.8	+2.5	7.5			5.8 (3)	6.8
Rhondda	59.0	−6.2	15.8	+5.7	54.4	−9.7	2.1	+1.2	13.7	−8.6	12.6	1.5			
Powys, Brecon & Radnorshire†	74.5	+0.7	53.1	+4.6	9.5	−8.2	35.9	+6.7						1.4 (2)	0.8
Montgomeryshire	69.8	1.1	58.5	+6.7	16.3	+0.4	23.0	−2.2						2.1 (1)	
South Glamorgan, Cardiff Central	65.3	−2.8	20.1	+0.3	61.2	−1.2	15.1	+1.6			2.4			1.2 (3)	
Cardiff North	77.0	−0.4	36.2	−5.9	49.5	−0.6	6.8	+3.5	3.0	−0.3	2.5	1.6		0.4 (1)	−2.6
Cardiff South & Penarth	64.2	−2.2	29.0	−1.2	54.1	−5.4	5.9	+3.1	4.7	+0.5	4.0	2.3	+1.3		2.1
Cardiff West	67.4	−2.4	28.0	−1.8	51.8	−4.9	5.9	+3.3	8.4	−1.1	3.5	2.5			1.6
Vale Of Glamorgan	71.6	−1.0	49.8	+2.3	43.3	−0.1	3.4	+1.6				5.9	+5.2	0.9 (1)	1.2
West Glamorgan, Aberavon	62.3	−4.4	20.6	+2.9	53.8	−14.3			8.6	+0.3	9.8	1.4		2.3 (1)	8.6
Gower	72.0	−1.3	41.3	−1.4	45.4	−4.4	5.0	+3.0	5.1	+1.5	3.1				1.5

WALES	Turnout %	Turnout ±	Con %	Con ±	Lab %	Lab ±	LD %	LD ±	Plaid %	Plaid ±	Brexit %	Grn %	Grn ±	Others No & %	Swing
Neath	65.1	-3.4	28.0	+4.3	43.3	-13.4	4.0	+2.1	12.2	-1.7	8.7	2.0		1.8 (2)	8.8
Swansea East	57.4	-2.6	28.1	+2.1	51.8	-11.6	4.2	+2.4	5.7	+0.9	8.5	1.7	+0.7		6.9
Swansea West	62.8	-2.8	29.0	-2.4	51.6	-8.1	8.4	+4.9	5.5	+1.4	5.5				2.9

SCOTLAND	Turnout %	Turnout ±	Con %	Con ±	Lab %	Lab ±	LD %	LD ±	SNP %	SNP ±	Brexit %	Grn %	Grn ±	Others No & %	Swing
*Ayrshire & Borders, Ayr, Carrick & Cumnock**	64.7	-0.1	38.5	-1.6	13.3	-10.5	4.6	+2.7	43.5	+9.4					
Ayrshire Central	66.7	+1.4	34.8	+0.4	14.1	-11.9	4.9	+2.6	46.2	+9.0					
Ayrshire North & Arran	65.5	+0.7	30.8	-0.4	13.9	-13.6	4.4	+2.0	48.5	+9.6		2.3			
Berwickshire, Roxburgh & Selkirk	71.3	-0.2	48.4	-5.4	4.7	-3.9	8.1	+3.3	38.8	+6.0					
Dumfries & Galloway	69.0	-0.6	44.1	+0.8	9.2	-11.7	6.1	+3.7	40.6	+8.2					
Dumfriesshire, Clydesdale & Tweeddale	71.9	-0.4	46.0	-3.4	8.5	-8.1	7.2	+3.2	38.3	+8.2					
Kilmarnock & Loudoun	63.9	+0.5	24.3	-2.4	18.9	-9.9	5.1	+3.0	50.8	+8.5				0.9 (1)	
Clydeside, Airdrie & Shotts	62.1	+2.9	17.6	-5.6	32.0	-5.1	3.6	+1.5	45.1	+7.5		1.7			
Coatbridge, Chryston & Bellshill*	66.1	+2.8	12.7	-3.6	35.4	-7.2	3.2	+1.2	47.0	+7.9		1.7			
Cumbernauld, Kilsyth & Kirkintilloch East	69.1	+3.3	16.2	-2.1	24.5	-9.4	6.5	+3.7	52.9	+9.3					
Dunbartonshire East*	80.3	+2.1	14.1	-0.5	9.1	-5.4	36.8	-3.8	37.1	+6.8		1.7		1.2 (3)	
Dunbartonshire West	67.9	+2.7	14.3	-2.9	28.5	-9.2	4.2	+1.9	49.6	+6.8		1.9		1.6 (1)	
East Kilbride, Strathaven & Lesmahagow	69.4	+2.1	21.2	-4.1	22.7	-9.0	6.7	+3.7	46.4	+7.5		2.0		1 (1)	
Glasgow Central	57.9	+2.0	9.2	-4.7	33.1	-5.3	4.9	+2.0	49.2	+4.5		3.6			
Glasgow East	57.1	+2.5	14.8	-4.0	33.2	-5.3	4.2	+2.7	47.7	+8.9					

Constituency														
Glasgow North	63.3	+1.2	10.5	-4.2	31.4	-3.0	6.6	+3.2	46.9	+9.3	0.9	3.6	-6.1	
Glasgow North East*	55.5	+2.5	10.5	-2.4	39.4	-3.5	3.2	+1.2	46.9	+4.7				
Glasgow North West	62.7	+1.8	15.2	-2.9	28.5	-7.4	6.8	+3.3	49.5	+7.0				
Glasgow South	66.9	+2.5	13.1	-5.9	29.1	-7.4	5.9	+2.6	48.1	+7.0	1.1	2.6		
Glasgow South West	57.1	+0.9	11.5	-4.2	34.6	-5.9	3.9	+2.0	47.9	+7.2	2.2			
Inverclyde	65.8	-0.6	15.7	-5.8	29.5	-8.0	6.4	+3.9	48.4	+9.9				
Lanark & Hamilton East	68.3	+3.1	32.1	+0.1	20.2	-11.6	5.7	+3.3	41.9	+9.3				
Motherwell & Wishaw	64.5	+3.0	16.1	-4.2	32.3	-5.4	3.8	+1.6	46.4	+7.9				1.4 (1)
Paisley & Renfrewshire North	69.0	-0.1	22.6	-5.0	23.0	-8.8	7.4	+4.2	47.0	+9.6				
Paisley & Renfrewshire South	66.9	-1.1	17.6	-1.9	25.4	-9.1	6.8	+3.6	50.2	+9.6				
Renfrewshire East*	76.6	-0.1	35.1	-4.9	12.4	-14.3	7.5	+5.5	44.9	+13.7				
Rutherglen & Hamilton West*	66.5	+3.0	15.0	-4.6	34.5	-3.1	5.2	+0.9	44.2	+7.2				1.2 (1)
Rest of Central Belt, East	71.7	+1.1	26.5	-3.1	29.5	-6.6	7.0	+3.8	36.2	+5.6				0.8 (1)
Lothian														
Edinburgh East	68.9	+2.8	13.7	-4.9	26.7	-8.0	6.9	+2.6	48.4	+5.9		4.3		
Edinburgh North & Leith	73.0	+1.8	18.5	-8.7	22.1	-9.1	11.2	+6.6	43.7	+9.7	0.9	3.3	+0.3	0.2 (1)
Edinburgh South	75.1	+1.0	16.4	-3.3	47.7	-7.2	7.7	+4.8	25.4	+3.0		2.7		
Edinburgh South West	70.9	+1.5	24.6	-8.7	14.3	-12.4	9.5	+5.2	47.6	+12.0	1.2	2.4		0.2 (1)
Edinburgh West	75.2	+1.4	17.0	-4.9	8.2	-6.7	39.9	+5.6	33.0	+4.4		1.9		
Falkirk	66.1	+0.7	25.8	-0.4	11.2	-18.6	7.1	+5.1	52.5	+13.6		3.4	+1.7	
Linlithgow & Falkirk East	66.4	+1.3	24.7	-4.4	18.2	-12.9	7.6	+4.2	44.2	+7.9		2.0		1.0 (1)
Livingston	66.3	+1.7	22.3	-2.1	21.8	-10.9	6.3	+3.5	46.9	+6.9		2.6		
Midlothian*	68.4	+2.1	21.7	-3.7	29.7	-6.6	7.0	+3.2	41.5	+7.1				
Stirling*	76.8	+2.5	33.5	-3.5	8.1	-14.0	5.4	+2.0	51.1	+14.4		1.8		
North East and Fife, Aberdeen North	59.9	+0.7	20.1	-2.6	13.2	-16.8	7.6	+3.0	54.0	+12.7	2.7	2.4		
Aberdeen South*	69.4	+1.0	35.9	-6.2	8.4	-12.1	11.0	+5.1	44.7	+13.2				
Aberdeenshire West & Kincardine	73.4	+2.2	42.7	-5.2	4.6	-6.5	11.7	+3.1	41.1	+8.6				
Angus*	67.5	+4.5	40.4	-4.8	4.8	-8.3	5.7	+2.5	49.1	+10.6				
Banff & Buchan	63.4	+1.8	50.1	+2.2	4.1	-5.3	5.4	+1.9	40.4	+1.3				
Dundee East	68.4	+3.2	24.3	-3.1	13.4	-12.7	7.9	+4.1	53.8	+11.0				0.7 (1)
Dundee West	64.5	+2.8	12.4	-3.8	24.3	-8.8	5.9	+2.9	53.8	+7.1				0.6 (1)
Dunfermline & West Fife	69.8	+2.4	21.0	-3.7	24.4	-9.5	8.0	+2.1	44.4	+8.8	3.1	2.4		
Fife North East*	75.3	+4.1	13.0	-11.1	3.7	-5.9	43.1	+10.2	40.2	+7.3				

SCOTLAND

	Turnout %	Turnout ±	Con %	Con ±	Lab %	Lab ±	LD %	LD ±	SNP %	SNP ±	Brexit %	Grn %	Grn ±	Others No & %	Swing %
Glenrothes	63.3	+2.4	16.7	-2.8	22.8	-11.9	6.4	+3.4	51.1	+8.3	3.1				
Gordon*	70.2	+1.9	41.3	+0.5	5.5	-6.4	10.6	-1.0	42.7	+6.9					
Kirkaldy & Cowdenbeath*	64.5	+1.0	20.1	-3.2	32.6	-4.2	6.2	+3.8	35.2	-1.0	2.4	3.5			
Moray	68.7	+1.4	45.3	-2.3	5.0	-6.0	4.6	+2.4	44.2	+5.4					
Ochil & South Perthshire*	73.4	+2.8	38.7	-2.8	8.6	-11.4	5.5	+2.3	46.5	+11.2				0.8 (1)	
Perth & Perthshire North	74.5	+2.7	36.6	-5.6	4.6	-5.8	7.0	+2.0	50.6	+8.3				0.7 (1)	
Highlands and Islands, Argyll & Bute	72.2	+0.7	35.2	+2.0	6.8	-5.8	14.2	-4.0	43.8	+7.8	1.2				
Caithness, Sutherland & Easter Ross	67.0	+1.1	16.5	-6.2	6.2	-6.2	37.2	+1.4	36.6	+7.4	3.6				
Inverness, Nairn, Badenoch & Strathspey	70.2	+1.5	28.8	-1.7	7.5	-8.7	10.7	-1.6	47.9	+8.0	2.0	3.1			
Na H-Eileanan An Iar [Western Isles]	68.6	-1.0	22.2	+5.7	28.3	-5.5	4.4	+2.7	45.1	+4.5					
Orkney & Shetland	67.7	-0.4	9.9	+1.2	6.7	-4.8	44.8	-3.8	34.0	+5.0	3.9			0.7 (1)	
Ross, Skye & Lochaber	73.5	+1.8	17.3	-7.6	6.1	-6.1	24.6	+3.7	48.3	+8.1	1.8			1.8 (2)	

NORTHERN IRELAND

	Turnout %	Turnout ±	UUP %	UUP ±	DUP %	DUP ±	APNI %	APNI ±	SF %	SF ±	SDLP %	SDLP ±	Other %
East Antrim	57.5	-3.2	14.7	+2.8	45.3	-12.1	27.3	+11.7	5.7	-3.6	2.4	-0.9	4.6
North Antrim	57.1	-6.9	18.5	+11.3	47.4	-11.5	14.1	+8.5	12.8	-3.5	6.7	+1.4	0.6
South Antrim	59.9	-3.3	29.0	-1.8	35.3	-3.0	19.1	+11.6	11.4	-6.7	5.3	-0.1	0.0
Belfast East	64.1	-3.5	5.9	+2.6	49.2	-6.6	44.9	+8.9					
Belfast North*	67.9	+0.6			43.1	-3.1	9.8	+4.4	47.1	+5.4			
Belfast South*	67.7	+1.5	2.7	-0.8	24.7	-5.8	14.3	-3.9			57.2	+31.3	1.2
Belfast West*	59.1	-6.0			13.5	0.0	4.9	+3.1	53.8	-12.9	7.7	+0.7	20.2
North Down*	60.6	-0.3	12.1		37.9	-0.3	45.2	+35.9					4.8
South Down	62.9	-4.4	6.6	+2.7	15.3	-2.1	13.9	+10.3	32.4	-7.5	29.2	-6.0	2.5

NORTHERN IRELAND	Turnout %	Turnout ±	UUP %	UUP ±	DUP %	DUP ±	APNI %	APNI ±	SF %	SF ±	SDLP %	SDLP ±	Other %
Fermanagh & South Tyrone	69.7	-6.1	43.2	-2.3			5.2	+3.6	43.3	-3.9	6.8	+2.0	1.5
Foyle*	63.4	-2.0	2.3		10.1	-6.0	2.7	+0.8	20.7	-19.0	57.0	+17.7	7.1
Lagan Valley	60.0	-2.1	19.0	+2.2	43.1	-16.4	28.8	+17.7	2.4	-1.1	3.9	-3.7	2.8
East Londonderry	56.8	-4.4	9.2	+1.5	40.1	-8.0	15.1	+8.9	15.6	-10.9	15.7	+4.9	4.4
Newry & Armagh	62.5	-5.9	8.3	0.0	21.7	-2.9	8.3	+5.9	40.0	-8.0	18.6	+1.7	3.2
Strangford	56.0	-4.2	10.7	-0.7	47.2	-14.8	28.4	+13.7	1.5	-1.3	5.3	-0.9	6.9
West Tyrone	62.2	-5.8	6.7	+1.6	22.0	-4.9	9.7	+7.4	40.2	-10.6	17.8	+4.8	3.6
Mid Ulster	63.3	-4.8	5.9	-0.6	24.5	-2.4	7.9	+5.6	45.9	-8.6	14.3	+4.5	3.6
Upper Bann	60.4	-3.6	12.4	-3.0	41.0	-2.6	12.9	+8.3	24.6	-3.4	9.2	+0.7	1.5

Notes:
UUP: Ulster Unionist Party
DUP: Democratic Unionist Party
APNI: Alliance Party of Northern Ireland
SF: Sinn Féin
SDLP: Social Democratic and Labour Party

Table A2.6   Seats changing hands

Conservative Gains from Labour
Ashfield
Barrow & Furness
Bassetlaw
Birmingham Northfield
Bishop Auckland
Blackpool South
Blyth Valley
Bolsover
Bolton North East
Bridgend
Burnley
Bury North
Bury South
Clwyd South
Colne Valley
Crewe & Nantwich
Darlington
Delyn
Derby North
Dewsbury
Don Valley
Dudley North
Durham North West
Gedling
Great Grimsby
Heywood & Middleton
High Peak
Hyndburn
Ipswich
Keighley
Kensington
Leigh
Lincoln
Newcastle-under-Lyme
Penistone & Stocksbridge
Peterborough
Redcar
Rother Valley
Scunthorpe
Sedgefield
Stockton South
Stoke-on-Trent Central
Stoke-on-Trent North

Stroud
Vale of Clwyd
Wakefield
Warrington South
West Bromwich East
West Bromwich West
Wolverhampton North East
Wolverhampton South West
Workington
Wrexham
Ynys Môn

Conservative Gains from Liberal Democrats
Carshalton & Wallington
Eastbourne
Norfolk North

Labour Gains from Conservatives
Putney

Liberal Democrat Gains from Conservative
Richmond Park
St Albans

Liberal Democrat Gains from SNP
Fife North East

SNP Gains from Conservative
Aberdeen South
Angus
Ayr, Carrick & Cumnock
Gordon
Ochil & South Perthshire
Renfrewshire East
Stirling

SNP Gains from Labour
Coatbridge, Chryston & Bellshill
East Lothian
Glasgow North East
Kirkcaldy & Cowdenbeath
Midlothian
Rutherglen & Hamilton West

SNP Gains from Lib Dems
Dunbartonshire East

Other Gains
Belfast North (Sinn Féin gain from DUP)
Belfast South (SDLP gain from DUP)
Foyle (SDLP gain from Sinn Féin)
North Down (Alliance gain from
Independent)

Table A2.7   Exceptional results

TURNOUT

12 largest and smallest % turnout

Dunbartonshire East	80.3
Richmond Park	78.7
Rushcliffe	78.5
Sheffield Hallam	78.2
Devon Central	78.2
St Albans	78.1
Stroud	78.0
Winchester	77.9
Westmorland & Lunesdale	77.8
Wimbledon	77.7
Esher & Walton	77.7
Somerset North	77.4
[...]	
Leeds Central	54.2
Great Grimsby	53.9
Leicester West	53.5
West Bromwich West	53.4
Birmingham Erdington	53.3
Wolverhampton South East	53.2
Nottingham North	53.1
Blackley & Broughton	52.6
Hull North	52.2
Hull West & Hessle	52.1
Chorley	51.7
Hull East	49.3

12 largest increases and decreases in % turnout

Buckingham	+10.2
Putney	+4.9
Leeds North West	+4.8
Battersea	+4.6
Angus	+4.5
Cities of London & Westminster	+4.3
Fife North East	+4.1
Kensington	+3.9
Esher & Walton	+3.8
Chelsea & Fulham	+3.7
Cumbernauld, Kilsyth & Kirkintilloch East	+3.3
Dundee East	+3.2
[...]	
Faversham & Mid Kent	−6.2
Slough	−6.4
Brent North	−6.4
Brent Central	−6.5
Derby South	−6.7
North Antrim	−6.9
Ilford South	−7.0
Wolverhampton South East	−7.0
Nottingham South	−7.1
Luton North	−7.3
Luton South	−8.0
Chorley	−21.1

MARGINALITY

12 largest and smallest % majorities

Liverpool Walton	Lab	74.8
Knowsley	Lab	72.7
Bootle	Lab	70.3
Liverpool Riverside	Lab	70.2
Liverpool West Derby	Lab	68.2
Manchester Gorton	Lab	68.1
Birmingham Ladywood	Lab	67.9
Tottenham	Lab	64.4
Walthamstow	Lab	63.9
Birmingham Hodge Hill	Lab	63.7
South Holland & The Deepings	Con	62.7
Liverpool Wavertree	Lab	62.4

		N	
[...]			
Coventry South	Lab	401	0.9
Bolton North East	Con	378	0.9
Bury South	Con	402	0.8
Dagenham & Rainham	Lab	293	0.7
Caithness, Sutherland & Easter Ross	LD	204	0.6
Alyn & Deeside	Lab	213	0.5
Coventry North West	Lab	208	0.4
Kensington	Con	150	0.3
Bedford	Lab	145	0.3
Dunbartonshire East	SNP	149	0.3
Bury North	Con	105	0.2
Fermanagh & South Tyrone	SF	57	0.1

CONSERVATIVE

12 largest rises and falls in % vote share

Thurrock	+19.1
Mansfield	+17.3
Norfolk North	+16.9
Dudley North	+16.6
Leicester East	+14.4

Walsall North	+16.6
Cannock Chase	+14.4
Walsall North	+14.2
Cannock Chase	+13.3
Stoke-on-Trent South	+13.1
Boston & Skegness	+13.1
Redcar	+12.8
Great Grimsby	+12.7
Bassetlaw	+11.9
[...]	
Ross, Skye & Lochaber	−7.6
Ealing Central & Acton	−7.7
Wimbledon	−8.1
Hampstead & Kilburn	−8.2
Herefordshire South West	−8.4
Putney	−8.4
Edinburgh North & Leith	−8.7
Edinburgh South West	−8.7
Beaconsfield	−9.1
Esher & Walton	−9.3
Guildford	−9.7
Fife North East	−11.1

12 highest and lowest % vote share (GB)

Castle Point	76.7
Boston & Skegness	76.7
South Holland & the Deepings	75.9
Staffordshire South	73.0
Louth & Horncastle	72.7
Rayleigh & Wickford	72.6
Cambridgeshire North East	72.5
Clacton	72.3
Maldon	72.0
Brigg & Goole	71.3
Aldridge-Brownhills	70.8
Norfolk South West	69.0
[...]	
Glasgow North	10.5
Glasgow North East	10.5

Islington North	10.2
Orkney & Shetland	9.9
Liverpool Walton	9.9
Liverpool Wavertree	9.7
Manchester Gorton	9.5
Liverpool West Derby	9.4
Glasgow Central	9.2
Bootle	9.2
Knowsley	8.1
Liverpool Riverside	7.8

Note This list excludes Northern Ireland, where all four of the worst Conservative performances occurred. They polled lower than in any seat in Great Britain in all of the four constituencies in which they stood, losing their deposit in all. Their best performance came in North Down, where they polled 4.8%, and their worst in Lagan Valley (2.1%)

LABOUR

12 largest rises and falls in % vote share

Bradford West	+11.5
Portsmouth South	+7.6
Southport	+6.4
Leeds North West	+4.5
Putney	+4.4
Canterbury	+3.3
Chingford & Woodford Green	+1.9
Isle of Wight	+1.3
Manchester Gorton	+1.3
Bethnal Green & Bow	+0.9
Bermondsey & Old Southwark	+0.9
Truro & Falmouth	+0.7
[...]	
Hemsworth	−18.5
Falkirk	−18.6
Houghton & Sunderland South	−18.7
Hull East	−19.1
Finchley & Golders Green	−19.6
Jarrow	−20.0

Normanton, Pontefract & Castleford	−21.6
Barnsley East	−21.9
Doncaster North	−22.1
Barnsley Central	−23.8
Wentworth & Dearne	−24.7
Bassetlaw	−24.9

12 highest and lowest % vote share

Liverpool Walton	84.7
Knowsley	80.8
Bootle	79.4
Birmingham Ladywood	79.2
Birmingham Hodge Hill	78.7
Liverpool Riverside	78.0
Manchester Gorton	77.6
Liverpool West Derby	77.6
East Ham	76.3
Bradford West	76.2
Walthamstow	76.1
Tottenham	76.0
[...]	
Moray	5.0
Cheltenham	4.9
Angus	4.8
Berwickshire, Roxburgh & Selkirk	4.7
Winchester	4.6
Perth & Perthshire North	4.6
Aberdeenshire West & Kincardine	4.6
Esher & Walton	4.5
Devon East	4.5
Westmorland & Lonsdale	4.4
Banff & Buchan	4.1
Fife North East	3.7

LIBERAL DEMOCRATS

12 largest rises and falls in % vote share

Surrey South West	+28.9
Esher & Walton	+27.7
Finchley & Golders Green	+25.3
Hitchin & Harpenden	+24.8

Cambridgeshire South	+23.4	Esher & Walton	45.0
Wimbledon	+22.7	Orkney & Shetland	44.8
Wokingham	+21.7	Lewes	43.4
Cities of London &	+19.6	[...]	
Westminster		Wolverhampton North East	2.8
Tunbridge Wells	+18.4	Devon East	2.8
St Albans	+17.7	Dagenham & Rainham	2.7
Wantage	+17.4	West Bromwich West	2.7
Streatham	+17.0	Blackburn	2.5
[...]		Middlesbrough	2.4
Bermondsey & Old Southwark	−4.5	Scunthorpe	2.3
Cornwall North	−5.8	Ashfield	2.3
Portsmouth South	−5.9	Rhondda	2.1
Eastbourne	−5.9	Knowsley	2.0
Burnley	−6.0	Liverpool Walton	1.9
Devon North	−8.0	Birmingham Hodge Hill	1.7
Birmingham Yardley	−9.1		
St Austell & Newquay	−11.0	BREXIT PARTY	
Ceredigion	−11.6		
Southport	−12.9	**12 highest and lowest % vote share**	
Leeds North West	−15.9		
Norfolk North	−18.1	Barnsley Central	30.4

Note The table lists constituencies in which Liberal Democrat candidates stood in *both* 2019 and 2017. There were 20 seats where the Liberal Democrats stood in 2017 but not in 2019, often relating to candidates stood down as part of the 'Unite to Remain' electoral pact. In the following seats without a Liberal Democrat candidate in 2019, the Liberal Democrats' 2017 share was sufficient that they would make the list of largest falls if included: Dulwich & West Norwood (8.0%), Beaconsfield (7.9%), Bristol West (7.3%), Bury St Edmunds (5.7%) and Pontypridd (4.9%)

Barnsley East	29.2
Hartlepool	25.8
Blaenau Gwent	20.6
Doncaster North	20.4
Easington	19.5
Hull West & Hessle	18.0
Hull East	17.8
Rotherham	17.2
South Shields	17.0
Wentworth & Dearne	16.9
Normanton, Pontefract &	16.6
Castleford	
[...]	
Tottenham	1.1
Streatham	1.1
Glasgow South	1.1
Hackney North & Stoke Newington	1.1

12 highest and lowest % vote share

Twickenham	56.1
Bath	54.5
Oxford West & Abingdon	53.3
Richmond Park	53.1
Kingston & Surbiton	51.1
St Albans	50.1
Westmorland & Lonsdale	48.9
Winchester	46.6
Cheltenham	46.3

Enfield Southgate	1.0
Dulwich & West Norwood	1.0
Westminster North	1.0
Edinburgh North & Leith	0.9
Glasgow North	0.9
Kensington	0.9
Tooting	0.8
Battersea	0.6

Note The Brexit Party was founded in November 2018 and so did not stand candidates in the 2017 general election. UKIP, the party long associated with Brexit Party leader Nigel Farage (who led UKIP from 2006 to 2009 and 2011 to 2016), stood just 44 candidates in 2019 and only secured more than 2% of the vote in four seats: Carlisle (2.4%), Houghton & Sunderland South (2.3), Washington & Sunderland West (2.2%) and Rochester & Strood (2.1%)

Saffron Walden (4.7%), Brighton Kemptown (4.6%), Edinburgh East (4.3%) and York Central (4.3%). There were also a number of seats where the Greens stood no candidate in 2019, having stood in 2017, often standing candidates down as part of the 'Unite to Remain' pact. There were 17 seats where the Greens stood no candidate in 2019, having won more than 2% of the vote in 2017—the strongest five 2017 performances among these were: Buckingham (16.3%), North Down (6.5%), Belfast South (5.1%), Totnes (4.2%) and Rushcliffe (2.8%)

GREEN PARTY

Largest rises and falls in % vote share

Dulwich & West Norwood	14.0
Bristol West	12.0
Bury St Edmunds	11.5
Exeter	6.8
Forest of Dean	6.7
Stroud	5.3
Vale of Glamorgan	5.2
Brighton Pavilion	4.9
New Forest West	4.8
Cannock Chase	4.6
Hackney North & Stoke Newington	4.1
Islington North	4.0
[…]	
Herefordshire South West	−0.2
Leicester East	−0.2
Peterborough	−0.3
Chipping Barnet	−0.3
Stoke on Trent North	−0.4
Cities of London & Westminster	−0.4
Kensington	−0.8
Hull West & Hessle	−0.8
Herefordshire North East	−1.1
Skipton & Ripon	−1.7
Isle of Wight	−2.1
Glasgow North	−6.1

Note The table lists constituencies in which Green candidates stood in *both* 2017 and 2019. There are four seats where the Greens stood in 2019, having not stood in 2017, where the increase in their vote would make the above list:

12 highest and lowest % vote share

Brighton Pavilion	57.2
Bristol West	24.9
Dulwich & West Norwood	16.5
Bury St Edmunds	15.7
Isle of Wight	15.2
Herefordshire North	9.3
Forest of Dean	9.1
Sheffield Central	9.0
Hackney North & Stoke Newington	8.8
Exeter	8.6
Islington North	8.0
New Forest West	7.7
[…]	
Liverpool West Derby	1.4
Birmingham Yardley	1.4
Ilford South	1.3
Wrexham	1.3
Batley & Spen	1.3
Blaenau Gwent	1.3
Stoke-on-Trent North	1.3
Kensington	1.2
Redcar	1.2
Devon East	1.1
Birmingham Hodge Hill	0.7
Hull West & Hessle	0.2

SNP

Largest and smallest rises in % vote share

Stirling	+14.4
Renfrewshire East	+13.7

Falkirk	+13.6
Aberdeen South	+13.2
Aberdeen North	+12.7
Edinburgh South West	+12.0
Ochil & South Perthshire	+11.2
Dundee East	+11.0
Angus	+10.6
Inverclyde	+9.9
Edinburgh North & Leith	+9.7
Ayrshire North & Arran	+9.6
[...]	
Berwickshire, Roxburgh & Selkirk	+6.0
Edinburgh East	+5.9
East Lothian	+5.6
Moray	+5.4
Orkney & Shetland	+5.0
Glasgow North East	+4.7
Na H-Eileanan An Iar (Western Isles)	+4.5
Glasgow Central	+4.5
Edinburgh West	+4.4
Edinburgh South	+3.0
Banff & Buchan	+1.3
Kirkaldy & Cowdenbeath	−1.0

Note The SNP gained vote share in every seat but one in Scotland, having lost vote share in the previous election in every single Scottish seat.

12 highest and lowest % vote share

Aberdeen North	54.0
Dundee East	53.8
Dundee West	53.8
Cumbernauld, Kilsyth & Kirkintilloch East	52.9
Falkirk	52.5
Stirling	51.1
Glenrothes	51.1
Kilmarnock & Loudon	50.8
Perth & Perthshire North	50.6
Paisley & Renfrewshire South	50.2
Dunbartonshire West	49.6
Glasgow North West	49.5
[...]	
Dumfries & Galloway	40.6

Banff & Buchan	40.4
Fife North East	40.2
Berwickshire, Roxburgh & Selkirk	38.8
Dumfriesshire, Clydesdale & Tweeddale	38.3
Dunbartonshire East	37.1
Caithness, Sutherland & Easter Ross	36.6
East Lothian	36.2
Kirkaldy & Cowdenbeath	35.2
Orkney & Shetland	34.0
Edinburgh West	33.0
Edinburgh South	25.4

PLAID CYMRU

Largest rises and falls in % vote share

Ceredigion	+8.7
Arfon	+4.3
Dwyfor Meirionnydd	+3.2
Pontypridd	+2.5
Caerphilly	+1.6
Gower	+1.5
Swansea West	+1.4
Wrexham	+1.4
Ynys Môn	+1.3
Swansea East	+0.9
Alyn & Deeside	+0.8
Ogmore	+0.7
[...]	
Monmouth	−0.3
Carmarthen East & Dinefwr	−0.4
Merthyr Tydfil & Rhymney	−0.6
Carmarthen West & Pembrokeshire South	−0.7
Islwyn	−0.9
Cardiff West	−1.1
Aberconwy	−1.4
Torfaen	−1.5
Neath	−1.7
Cynon Valley	−5.3
Rhondda	−8.6
Blaenau Gwent	−15.5

Note Plaid Cymru stood candidates down in four seats as part of the 'Unite to Remain' electoral pact. In none of these had the party secured more than 6% of the vote in 2017. The seats were as follows (2017 performance in brackets): Montgomeryshire (5.6%), Vale of Glamorgan (4.3%), Brecon & Radnorshire (3.1%) and Cardiff Central (2.5%)

10 highest and lowest % vote share

Dwyfor Meirionnydd	48.3
Arfon	45.2
Carmarthen East & Dinefwr	38.9
Ceredigion	37.9
Ynys Môn	28.5
Llanelli	18.4
Caerphilly	16.0
Rhondda	13.7
Pontypridd	12.8
Neath	12.2
Clwyd West	9.7
Carmarthen West &	8.6
Pembrokeshire South	
[...]	
Swansea West	5.5
Gower	5.1

Bridgend	4.8
Cardiff South & Penarth	4.7
Vale of Clwyd	4.2
Torfaen	3.9
Delyn	3.7
Alyn & Deeside	3.4
Cardiff North	3.0
Newport West	2.7
Newport East	2.4
Monmouth	2.4

INDEPENDENT

12 best Independent results

Devon East	40.4
Beaconsfield	29.0
Herefordshire South West	26.0
Chorley	23.7
Middlesbrough	13.3
South Shields	9.7
Luton South	9.3
Birmingham Hall Green	8.1
Guildford	7.4
Jarrow	7.3
Basildon South & Thurrock East	7.3
Merthyr Tydfil & Rhymney	5.8

Table A2.8 By-election results, 2017–2019

	Date	Con	Lab	Lib Dem	Best other	Other candidates (N)	Turnout
West Tyrone	3.5.2018	N/A	N/A	N/A	**Sinn Féin 46.7**; DUP 23.9	3	55.1
Lewisham East	14.6.2018	14.4	**50.2**	24.6	Green 3.6	10	33.3
Newport West	4.4.2019	31.3	**39.6**	4.6	UKIP 8.6	8	37.1
Peterborough	6.6.2019	21.4	**30.9**	12.3	Brexit Party 28.9	12	48.4
Brecon & Radnorshire *Liberal Democrat gain; Conservatives regain at general election*	1.8.2019	39.0	5.3	**43.5**	Brexit Party 10.5	3	59.7

Note Winning party at the by-election in bold. All held by the incumbent party, in both the by-election and then the 2019 general election, unless indicated otherwise

INDEX

647